Serial PIC'n

PIC MICROCONTROLLER
SERIAL COMMUNICATIONS

FROM

SQUARE 1

ROGER L. STEVENS

VERSION 1.0

NOTICE

The material presented in this book is for the education and amusement of students, hobbyists, technicians and engineers. Every effort has been made to assure the accuracy of this information and its suitability for this purpose. Square 1 Electronics and the author assume no responsibility for the suitability of this information for any application nor do we assume any liability resulting from use of this information. No patent liability is assumed for use of the information contained herein.

TRADEMARKS

PIC is a registered trademark of Microchip Technology Inc. in the U.S.A.
Registered trademarks:

PICmicro	Microchip Technology Inc.
I²C	Philips Semiconductors
SPI	Motorola, Inc.
Microwire	National Semiconductor
1-Wire	Dallas Semiconductor
MicroLAN	Dallas Semiconductor
IBM	International Business Machines
PC/AT	International Business Machines
TRI-STATE	National Semiconductor Corporation
Terminal	Microsoft Corporation
HyperTerminal	Microsoft Corporation
Windows	Microsoft Corporation
DEC	Digital Equipment Corporation

ISBN 0-9654162-2-4

PUBLISHER

Square 1 Electronics
P.O. Box 501
Kelseyville,CA 95451 U.S.A.

Voice   (707)279-8881
FAX   (707)279-8883
EMAIL   sqone@pacific.net
http://www.sq-1.com

Serial PIC'n

PIC MICROCONTROLLER
SERIAL COMMUNICATIONS
FROM

SQUARE 1

Tool Box Modules and Applications

On-Chip UART Tools and Applications   (Chapter 6)

Serial Peripheral Interface (SPI) Tools and Applications (Chapter 9)

Introduction

Welcome to the world of serial communications - specifically serial data communications using the PICmicro! The Microchip PICmicro series of microcontrollers has enjoyed tremendous growth in the embedded control arena in recent years. PICmicro embeded applications are prime targets for serial communications, especially on-board device-to-device communications.

This book introduces serial communications, including asynchronous and synchronous communications. It shows you how to communicate serially with the PICmicro family of microcontrollers and provides you with a large set of serial communications functions and subprograms. These source code modules make up the PICmicro Serial Communications Toolbox and implement most of the serial operations you will need for your embeded PICmicro applications.

Chapter 1 introduces serial communications and the PICmicro resources necessary to implement serial communications. A description of the PICmicro Serial Communications Toolbox and notes on programming style are included in the chapter.

Chapters 2, 3, and 4 cover asynchronous serial communications, protocols and flow control, the RS232 Standard interface and the ASCII character set.

Chapter 5 covers PICmicro software driven asynchronous serial communications. Several half-duplex and full-duplex methods are described. Polled, timed-out and interrupt driven reception schemes are covered along with bit rate detection and flow control. Several application programs demonstrate the methods introduced in the chapter.

Chapter 6 describes the PICmicro on-chip UART and includes several application programs using the UART. Block and packet data transfer techniques are demonstrated.

Chapter 7 introduces synchronous serial communications techniques and their application to embedded systems. The I^{2}C, SPI and Microwire standards are included.

Chapter 8 covers the I^{2}C Bus. The I^{2}C bus is described in detail and several PICmicro implementations of the I^{2}C bus functions are included. Interfacing the PICmicro to I^{2}C peripherals including EEPROMs, serial analog-to-digital converters and PICmicro based slave devices is discussed and interface software modules are included for each device. Application examples using the I^{2}C peripheral devices are included. Implementation of the PICmicro as an I^{2}C peripheral slave device is covered. Several applications using the PICmicro as a slave device are provided.

Chapter 9 covers the SPI Bus. The SPI Bus is described in detail and PICmicro software and hardware implementations of the SPI Bus functions are included. Interfacing the PICmicro to SPI peripherals including EEPROMs, serial analog-to-digital converters and display drivers is discussed and interface software modules are included for each device. Application examples using the SPI peripheral devices are provided. The on-chip SPI hardware is discussed and several applications of the on-chip hardware are included. Implementation of the PICmicro as an SPI slave device is covered and several slave applications are included.

Chapter 10 covers the Microwire Interface. The Microwire Interface is described in detail and PICmicro software implementations of the interface are included. Applications interfacing the PICmicro to Microwire peripherals including EEPROMs, serial analog-to-digital converters and display drivers are included. An application configuring a PICmicro as a Microwire slave is also included.

Chapter 11 covers the Dallas 1-Wire (tm) Bus. The 1-Wire Bus is described in detail and PICmicro software implementations of the bus are included. Applications interfacing the PICmicro to 1-Wire peripherals including a digital thermometer and a serial input port expander are included. An application configuring a PICmicro as a 1-Wire slave is also included.

Serial Communications Software Toolbox

Program source modules to implement specific serial communications subprograms and functions are provided. These modules address common serial communications tasks. The modules are not specific to a particular PICmicro and may be used unchanged for most serial communications applications. Sample application programs using the Toolbox Modules are also provided. The Toolbox includes 150 serial-communications-specific modules, 28 application programs and several other handy subprograms.

Applications Hardware

Most of the demonstration applications are implemented with an 18 pin PICmicro. These 18 pin applications all use the same circuitry. The on-chip UART and SPI applications are implemented with a 28 pin PICmicro requiring a second circuit. All asynchronous and all synchronous master demonstration applications use one or the other of these two hardware circuits. The PICmicro slave applications require an additional circuit. The circuits are configured to accept most variants of the 18 and 28 pin PICmicro devices. Where hardware slave functions are used, circuits appropriate to the specific slave device are necessary.

Demonstration Application Hardware Configurations:

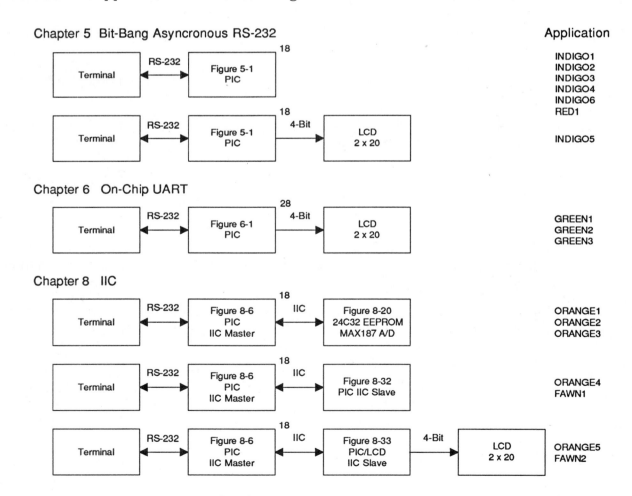

2

Application

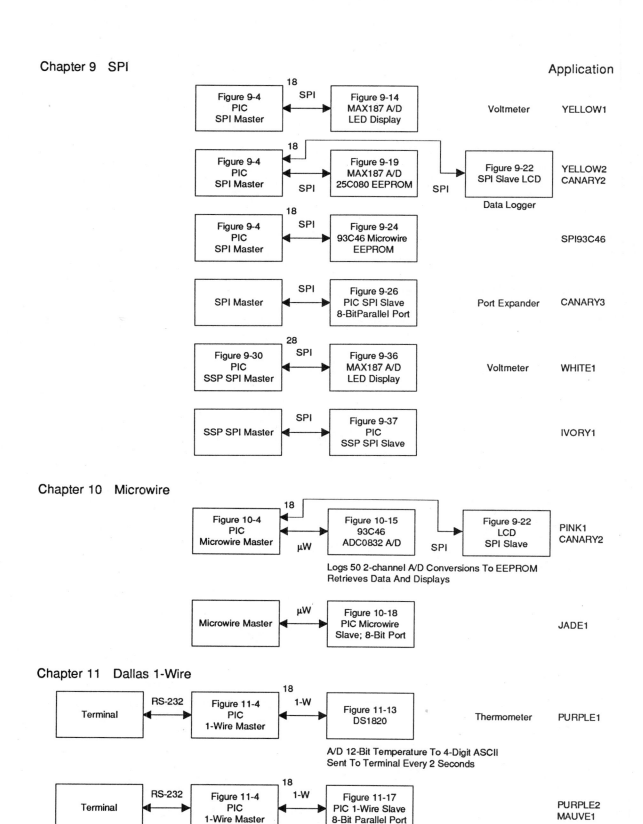

Chapter 10   Microwire

Chapter 11   Dallas 1-Wire

18 = 18 Pin PICmicro
28 = 28 Pin PICmicro

For Bruiser
Thanks For The Help

Chapter 1
PICmicro Serial Communications and This Book

1.1 Introduction to Serial Communications
1.2 About This Book

This book is for anyone who wants to learn a little about serial communications and a lot about serial communications using the PICmicro. The need for serial communications is found every-where in the digital domain. Every PICmicro programmer will at some time be called upon to design and write the software for serial communications to and from a PICmicro. On-board (meaning on a circuit board or within a specific hardware application) serial communications provide a cost effective solution to problems of hardware complexity and size constraints.

The goals of this book are threefold: to explain serial communications, to show how the PICmicro may be used to implement serial communications and to provide an easy to use collection of PICmicro serial communications routines.

1.1 Introduction to Serial Communications

When communicating serially, data to be communicated is disassembled into bits and transmitted bit-by-bit from a transmitting device to a receiving device and reassembled by the receiving device. The transmission distance may be no more than the centimeter separating two integrated circuits on a circuit board to as far as the distance separating the earth from a spacecraft approaching Jupiter, and even further. Although transmission to or from Jupiter requires more than two devices, the basic principles are identical.

Character Transmission

For the purposes of this book, the term *character* shall designate a minimum unit of multi-bit information. In other words, a character is any piece of data encoded with two or more bits. The term *byte* or *data byte* may be used interchangeably with character, but generally byte will be used to describe an eight bit character simply because the PICmicro unit of information is an eight bit byte.

In some cases a device may generate information units greater than 8 bits in length. Because the PICmicro is an eight bit device these long information units must be broken up into eight bit segments and each segment transmitted separately. The receiving device then re-assembles the segments to recover the original long information unit. The eight bit segments are treated as characters for the purposes of data transmission even though they are not a complete unit of information. The 12 or 14 or 16 bit binary values generated by analog to digital converters are examples of long information units.

When characters are serially transmitted, the bits that encode the characters are transmitted sequentially. The *bits* are distributed over *time*. When a transmitting device sends these bits distributed over time the receiving device must be able to determine at what point in time the bits will arrive. The receiver must recognize when the bit begins and when it ends. The receiver must also recognize when the series of bits encoding each character begins and ends. This bit recognition and character separation is a form of *synchronization*. Most serial communications use fixed length encoding because the number of bits can be easily counted once it is known that the first bit has been received. Two common methods of bit delimiting are clocking, (synchronous transmission), and framing, (asynchronous transmission). Framing may also be combined with clocking.

Synchronous Transmission

A common synchronous transmission method associates a clock pulse with each bit transmitted. This requires two communications media (usually wires), one for the data bits and one for the clock pulses. The receiver easily recognizes the data bits because they simultaneously occur (in *time*) with the clock pulses. The data bits will be different from bit to bit but the clock pulses are easily recognized because they are always the same for each bit time throughout the transmission. Since each data bit is associated with the clock pulse, the clock rate (bit time) does not have to be constant throughout the transmission. Each data bit is *synchronized* with the *clock*. When fixed length encoding is used, the receiver need only count bits, starting with the first bit received, to separate the characters from one another. In Chapter 9, covering the SPI bus, this *clocked synchronous* method is examined in detail. Special framing bits may be sent at the beginning or end of each character to further separate the data. In Chapter 8, covering the I²C bus, and Chapter 10, covering the Microwire Interface, this *clocked synchronous with frame bits* method is examined in detail.

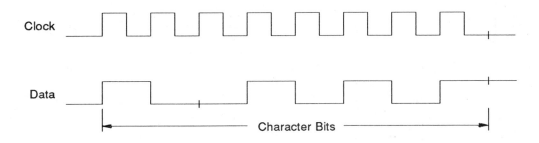

Figure 1-1   Typical Synchronous Serial Character

Asynchronous Transmission

A common asynchronous transmission method associates special framing bits with each character; one just before the character and in some cases one just after the character. All of the bits, including the framing bits, are transmitted at the same rate (constant bit period). After the receiver recognizes the first framing bit, each character data bit will be found at fixed time intervals after the framing bit. The first framing bit is the *synchronizing bit*; it synchronizes the receiver to the transmitter. The transmitter and receiver operate at the same bit rate. Since the first bit is the synchronizing bit and the character always has the same number of constant-period bits, the character may start at any time. This method is *character asynchronous* and *bit synchronous*. In Chapters 2, 5 and 6, covering asynchronous communications, this transmission method is examined in detail.

Another common asynchronous transmission method transmits at variable bit rates where the bit rate may change with each bit or may change over time. This *self clocking* method does not require fixed length characters and does not require framing bits. Even though fixed length characters and framing bits are not required for successful communications, most self clocking protocols do at least utilize framing bits. In Chapter 11 covering the Dallas 1-Wire Bus, one version of a *self clocking* method is examined in detail.

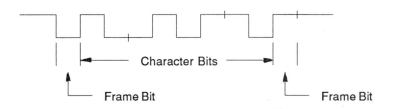

Figure 1-2   Typical Asynchronous Serial Character

1.2 About This Book

There are a number of synchronization and modulation methods employed with serial communications, but only the *clocked synchronous* and *character asynchronous-bit synchronous* schemes and the one *self clocked* scheme described above are found in most PICmicro serial communications applications. In this book, only these three methods and their variations will be examined.

PICmicro Serial Resources

Some PICmicros have on-chip dedicated hardware to perform serial communications, but many do not. When a project requiring serial communications uses a PICmicro that does not have the dedicated serial hardware, serial communications may be implemented with a few port pins and software.

Using microcomputer ports and software routines to simulate on-chip hardware is known as *bit-banging*. A bit-banged PICmicro can implement serial communications with both on-board and off-board peripheral devices. As well as implementing serial communications with peripheral devices, a bit-banged PIC micro may be used as a serial peripheral device. As a peripheral device it may execute a function otherwise unavailable as a dedicated device or may serve as an inexpensive functional substitute for a specific serial device. Bit-banging a serial interface is very cost effective both in terms of hardware and software flexibility. Bit-bang serial techniques for midrange PICmicros are extensively covered in Chapters 5, 8, 9, 10 and 11.

Applications using on-chip serial hardware are generally capable of operating at higher speeds than are bit-bang applications. The use of on-chip hardware replaces software complexity with hardware complexity but generally increases hardware cost. For some applications, the additional hardware cost is not significant because the software development is simpler when on-chip hardware is utilized. The application of on-chip serial hardware is covered in Chapters 6 and 9.

Physical and Protocol Layers

In this book we shall describe serial communications in terms of two layers: the *physical layer* and the *protocol layer*. The physical layer describes the hardware and the electrical signal characteristics and the protocol layer refers to the data format and the software necessary to implement the serial communications. The physical layers covered are the RS-232 interface, the I^{2}C bus, the SPI bus, the Microwire interface and the Dallas 1-Wire Bus. The RS-232 physical layer is covered in Chapter 3. The I^{2}C, SPI, Microwire and Dallas 1-Wire physical and protocol layers are covered in Chapters 8, 9, 10 and 11. A commonly used asynchronous protocol layer is fully described in Chapter 2.

Data and Character Encoding

The binary nature of serial communications requires that any transmitted data or characters must be encoded. The encoding may be standardized or application specific. The most commonly used standard character set is the ASCII Character Code. The ASCII Character Code is covered in Chapter 4. Application specific encoding is covered in Chapters 8 through 11.

Serial Communications Toolbox

Program source modules to implement specific serial communications subprograms and functions are included in Chapters 5, 6, 8, 9, 10 and 11. These modules address common serial communications tasks. The modules are not specific to a particular PICmicro. Most of the Toolbox Modules may be used unchanged with all 12 and 14 bit PICmicros and may be used with 16 bit PICmicros with minor changes. Some 12-bit-specific modules have been included.

Sample application programs using the Toolbox Modules are also included in Chapters 5, 6, 8, 9, 10 and 11. The sample applications use the PIC16C54, 16F84 and 16C63, but may be used with other devices with little or no change.

All of the modules may be used as include files. Some modules are presented as individual tasks while others are included in groups that perform related tasks. An entire group of related tasks, or only individual modules from the group, may be included in an application. The Toolbox includes 150 serial-communications-specific modules, 28 application programs and several other handy subprograms.

Programming Style

The modules and applications have been written to stress clarity and algorithmic simplicity. No attempt has been made to reduce code size or RAM usage at the expense of clarity. No macros and a minimum of assembler directives are used. The sample application programs are fairly well structured.

Standard Microchip assembler (MPASM) source code format and mnemonics are used. In most cases hexadecimal notation is of the form 0xNN, but for historical reasons and clarity, the form $NN is used in Chapter 4. The **TRIS** instruction is used in some modules for downward compatibility and simplicity.

A Short Comment on Comments

Source code commenting is a very important part of PICmicro programming. The comments serve to describe the function of the program or subprogram. Quite often the only source of information about a program, both for the author of the program and for others, is the comments. To be useful, the comments must provide information about the *function* of the program. Comments must describe the function from the point of view of the application, *not* from the point of view of the PICmicro. The instruction mnemonics provide the PICmicro point of view. Comments must be in English, not in computer lingo.

The following is an example of a useless form of commenting; it does not describe the function of the block of code:

```
bsf    status,c      ;set carry
btfss porta,rec       ;skip if porta,rec is set
bcf    status,c      ;clear carry
rrf    recreg,f      ;left rotate carry into recreg
```

The following is an example of a useful form of commenting; it describes the code in terms of the application. Note that the comment for *each* line describes the *function* of the line from the point of view of the application.

```
bsf    status,c      ;assume that received data bit is high
btfss porta,rec       ;get data bit. is it high? if yes, skip next
bcf    status,c      ;no. data bit is low. clear received data bit
rrf    recreg,f      ;rotate data bit into received data
```

Properly commented code is much easier to troubleshoot and maintain than is code with poor or no commenting. Notes, in addition to the line-by-line comments, scattered throughout the program further improve the readability of the source code. The source listings in this book are commented in this fashion.

Using the Toolbox Modules in Your Applications

In Chapters 5, 6, 8, 9, 10 and 11 are several sections titled: Using the Section ... Routines in Your Applications. These sections include additional information and applications hints about the Toolbox Modules. Some include discussions on functional expansion and modification of the modules.

The Toolbox Modules are not specific to a particular PICmicro. Most of the Toolbox Modules may be used unchanged with all 12 and 14 bit PICmicros and may be used with 16 bit PICmicros with minor changes. Most of the modules are subroutines that may be called by any application program having some degree of structure.

In the chapters covering synchronous and self clocking methods, PICmicro bit-bang routines for implementing both master and slave functions are covered in detail. The best way to gain a full understanding of a specific protocol is go through the process of developing bit-bang routines for the protocol. This is especially so for slave implementation. You will find that you have truly mastered the protocol once you have successfully implemented slave functions.

The Toolbox Modules may be downloaded from the Square 1 website (no charge) or they are available on disk.

Chapter 2
Asynchronous Serial Communications

Asynchronous Serial Communication

In this chapter asynchronous serial communications, character protocols and flow control are introduced. The coverage is general. Specific asynchronous applications will be covered in chapters 5 and 6.

2.1 Asynchronous Serial Overview

For the purposes of this book, we define *asynchronous serial communications* as the serial transmission of multi-bit characters at indeterminate intervals where each character has a fixed number of bits and each bit has a fixed period.

Serial transmission distributes the bits over time and the receiver must be able to recognize when a bit begins and when it ends. If the receiver can determine when the first bit of a character arrives, then, due to the fixed bit period, the receiver can anticipate when each successive bit will arrive. When no data is being transmitted the communication channel is in an idle state and the receiver is waiting for a bit to arrive. On the arrival of the bit (which must be the non-idle state) the receiver recognizes this as the first bit and waits for one bit period to elapse before reading the next bit. The receiver repeats this wait and read process until all bits have been read. The first bit is a *framing* bit or specifically the *synchronization* bit. The transmitter and receiver each have a clock for measuring the bit time. The two clocks cannot exactly match one another and after a period of time will drift out of phase. Then the receiver will be expecting a bit at the wrong time and will incorrectly read the received bit. This clock drift problem is compensated for by periodic re-synchronization. Periodic re-synchronization is accomplished by making the character length a fixed number of bits and re-transmitting the *synchronization* bit at the start of each fixed length character. Then the clocks need only remain in phase for a limited number of bit times because they are re-phased at each *synchronization* bit.

With a fixed number of bits per character the receiver counts bits to delineate each character allowing each character to be transmitted at irregular intervals (*asynchronous transmission*). Because the first framing bit is a change from the idle state to the non-idle state at least one bit time at the idle state should follow the last character bit. The *synchronization* bit is the starting *framing* bit for the character and the idle state bit following the last character bit is the ending *framing* bit for the character. The *framing* bits delineate the character *frame*.

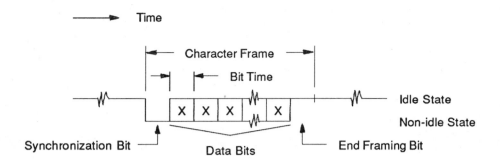

Figure 2-1   Character Frame

2.2 Asynchronous Serial Protocol

The asynchronous serial protocol as supported by most UARTs is the one used in this book. It is the most commonly used set of conventions for asynchronous serial telecommunications. All transmission is as described above: framed characters transmitted at indeterminate intervals at a fixed bit rate (character asynchronous, bit synchronous).

Under the protocol the idle state of the communications channel is at logic 1, or in a *marking* state. The non-idle state is at logic 0, or in a *spacing* state. The s*ynchronization* bit is termed the *start* bit and the ending framing bit the *stop* bit. The *start* bit is a transition from the *marking* state to the *spacing* state and the *stop* bit is the *marking* state. There may be only one start bit and one or more stop bits per character frame. The protocol specifies 1, 1 1/2 or 2 stop bits as a minimum. These are specified as a minimum because the stop bits are the marking state (idle state) which may have any length between character frames. There may be 5, 6, 7 or 8 character data bits. The character data is transmitted least significant bit first. There may be a special bit, called the *parity* bit following the last character data bit.

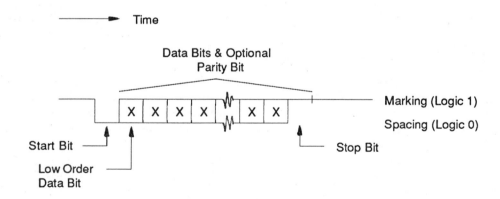

Figure 2-2   Character Format

The protocol allows a parity bit but does not require it. The parity bit provides limited error detection. Parity is a characteristic of the character data. It is determined by the number of logic 1's in the data. For *odd* parity, the number of 1's in the character data and the parity bit should be odd. The number of 1's in the character data are counted and if the count is odd then the parity bit is 0. If the number of 1's in the character data is even, then the parity bit is made 1 to make the total number of 1's odd. Similarly for *even* parity the parity bit is chosen to make the total number of 1's even. This single parity bit scheme will detect single bit errors in a character. Single bit parity will detect multiple bit errors only if the number of errors are odd. In addition to *odd* and *even* parity, three other ways of handling the parity bit are allowed: *none*, meaning the parity bit is not included in the character; *mark*, meaning the parity bit is always 1; *space*, meaning the parity bit is always 0.

2.3 The Communications Channel and Flow Control

Most communications are two way, requiring both a transmitter and a receiver at each end of the communications channel. For the purposes of this book, we shall designate the equipment at each end of the communications channel as a terminal and we shall speak of the data path as lines or circuits. We shall also use *terminal* as a general term for a piece of equipment at one end of a serial data path and *data terminal* as specifically a *terminal* with which humans can interface. A teleprinter, keyboard, printer or display are examples of data terminals. Two way communications require two lines; line A and line B, one for each direction of data travel. The transmitter of one terminal is connected via line A to the receiver of the second terminal and similarly the transmitter of the second terminal is connected via line B to the receiver of the first terminal (Figure 2-3).

In this two line communications channel, data may travel in both directions simultaneously or may travel in both directions but not simultaneously. A communications channel that is capable of operating in both directions simultaneously is termed a *full-duplex* channel and one capable of operating in both directions but not simultaneously a *half-duplex* channel. A single line channel capable of operating in one direction only is a *simplex* channel. For the *half-duplex* and *full-duplex* channels, the data rate must be the same for both directions.

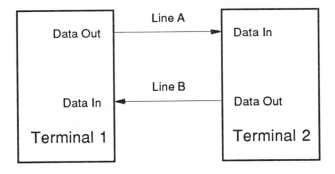

Figure 2-3   Two Line Serial Interface

For a half-duplex channel, provision must be made for some sort of control to prevent both terminals from attempting to transmit at the same time or one terminal from attempting to transmit when the other is unable to receive. This flow control requires at least two more lines; one used as a request-to-transmit line and the other as a permission-to-transmit line. Control using these extra control lines is termed *out-of-band* or *hardware* flow control.

A simplex channel with a slow receiving terminal will require flow control. In this case only one flow control line, from the receiving terminal to the transmitting terminal, is required. While the receiving terminal is processing the received character it is unable to receive another character and signals this fact to the transmitting terminal via the control line. In some cases an extra stop bit will give the receiving terminal enough time to process the character. This is why the protocol allows an additional 1/2 or 1 stop bit.

A full-duplex channel may also require flow control. Full-duplex flow control is implemented with extra control lines as in half-duplex control or with control characters transmitted on the data lines. The use of control characters is termed *in-band* or *software* flow control.

Several full-duplex and half-duplex demonstration applications are introduced in Chapters 5 and 6. Applications implementing both out-of-band and in-band flow control are included.

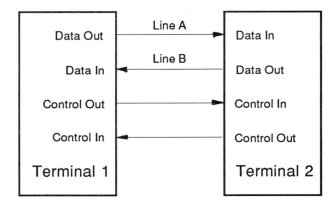

Figure 2-4   Two Line Serial Interface With Two Line Out-Of-Band Flow Control

Chapter 3
The RS-232 Standard

The RS-232 Standard

RS-232 is a physical layer standard. It is the only asynchronous physical layer that will be discussed in this book and is included for three reasons:

1. A great deal of misconception surrounds the application of the RS-232 Standard.
2. Many 'standard' RS-232 applications are in reality non-standard. To successfully apply the PICmicro to these applications, we must fully understand the standard.
3. It is the most common personal computer asynchronous serial interface. Most PICmicro applications that interface with a computer will do so via an RS-232 interface.

3.1 RS-232 Overview

In the section on asynchronous communications (Section 2.3), we described the serial communications channel as two terminals and a data path without addressing the physical characteristics of the terminals and path. In this section we shall address the physical characteristics and real world application of the asynchronous serial communications channel defined by the EIA RS-232 Standard. Note that RS-232 is a physical standard only. It defines the characteristics and functions of the data and control lines only and does not address the data format.

Formally, RS-232 is a standard for an: "Interface between Data Terminal Equipment and Data Communication Equipment Employing Serial Binary Data Interchange". Note that the standard makes the distinction between *Data Terminal Equipment* (DTE) and *Data Communications Equipment* (DCE); the terminals on either end of the channel are not the same.

NOTE: A more general definition of a communications channel would include the path from the DTE to the DCE to another mode of communication (such as a telephone line or radio link) to another DCE to a final DTE. We will limit this discussion to the DTE to DCE path and will use a computer configured as a data terminal as DTE and a modem as DCE. In the section on non-standard applications (most asynchronous serial PICmicro applications fall in the non-standard category) we shall address RS-232 based computer-to-computer and computer-to-peripheral communications.

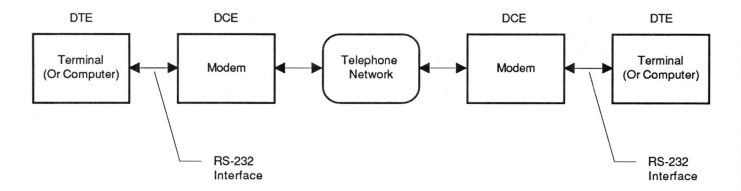

Figure 3-1   Typical Serial Communications Channel

3.2 Mechanical Interface

The RS-232 standard describes 25 interchange lines and assigns connector pin numbers to these lines. Of these 25 lines we shall consider only the 11 related to asynchronous communications (the balance of lines are either unassigned or are for synchronous communications or test). These 11 lines are summarized in Table 3-1. The standard also specifies that the DTE shall have a male connector and the DCE shall have a female connector. A 25 pin D-sub-miniature connector is generally used for RS-232 connections. A later revision of the standard describes a 9 pin connector for a limited subset of interchange lines. The pin number assignments in Tables 3-1 and 3-2 are the same for the DTE and the DCE.

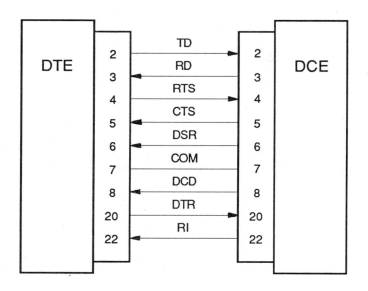

Note: Arrow heads on lines indicate
signal flow direction.

Figure 3-2   Typical DTE to DCE Connection

Table 3-1   RS-232 Lines (25 Pin Connector)

```
----------------------------------------------------------------------
                                 Direction
Pin          Name                DTE   DCE            Function
----------------------------------------------------------------------
  1    PG    Protective Ground    -     -     Safety Ground
  2    TD    Transmitted Data    Out    In    Outbound DTE Data
  3    RD    Received Data        In   Out    Inbound DTE Data
  4    RTS   Request To Send     Out    In    DTE Wants To Send
  5    CTS   Clear To Send        In   Out    OK For DTE To Send
  6    DSR   Data Set Ready       In   Out    DCE Ready To Communicate
  7    -     Signal Common        -     -     Signal Common (Ground)
  8    DCD   Data Carrier Detect  In   Out    Data Communications Link In Process
 20    DTR   Data Terminal Ready Out    In    DTE Ready For Communications Via Link
 22    RI    Ring Indicator       In   Out    Announces Incoming Call
 23    DSRD  Data Signal Rate    Either way   Data Rate Indicator
```

Table 3-2   IBM PC/AT 9 Pin RS-232 Connector

```
        ------------------------------
        Signal     RS-232     IBM PC/AT
        Line       25 pin      9 pin
        ------------------------------
          TD          2           3
          RD          3           2
          RTS         4           7
          CTS         5           8
          DSR         6           6
          Common      7           5
          DCD         8           1
          DTR        20           4
          RI         22           9

        IBM (tm), PC/AT (tm)
```

3.3 Functional Interface

The RS-232 lines are divided into two functional classifications: *data functions* and *control functions*. There are just two data functions: the transmitted data on pin 2 and the received data on pin 3. The other lines are control functions used for flow control and status.

The name of each line reflects the function from the point of view of the DTE. This is a very important point. On any device documentation, whether the device is DTE or DCE, this convention of naming the function of each line from the point of view of the DTE must be followed. For example, the transmitted data (TD) line (pin 2) is an *output* for the DTE and an *input* for the DCE and even though it is an input for the DCE it is labeled transmitted data (TD) on the DCE. As noted earlier: *The terminals on either end of the lines are not the same.* This is an important distinction. To avoid confusion, Table 3-1 tabulates the DTE and DCE inputs and outputs and signal flow directions. Following are functional descriptions of each line.

17

NOTE: The flow control functions and interactions are defined only for communications between DTE and DCE. In the descriptions below we assume the use of a computer operating some sort of communications software as the DTE and a modem connected to a telephone line as the DCE. A modem is always considered DCE, but the DCE may be any equipment capable of interfacing the RS-232 lines to some sort of communications link. Telephone specific signals referred to below will have equivalent functions for any type of DCE. The *asserted* state of a control function is a space, logic level 0 (see Section 3.5, Electrical Interface). Pin numbers are for the 25 pin connector.

Protective Ground (Pin 1)

This pin is connected physically to the chassis of the terminal.

Signal Common (Pin 7)

This is the common return for all lines and must be present on all terminals. This may be connected to Protective Ground (Pin 1).

Transmitted Data, TD (Pin 2)

The data signals on TD are transmitted from the DTE to the DCE. When no data is being transmitted, the DTE holds the line in the marking condition (logic level 1). The DTE *may not* transmit data unless the following four control lines are asserted (logic level 0):

1. RTS, Request to Send
2. CTS, Clear to Send
3. DSR, Data Set Ready
4. DTR, Data Terminal Ready

Received Data, RD (Pin 3)

The data signals on RD are transmitted from the DCE to the DTE. When no data is being transmitted the DCE holds the line in the marking condition (logic level 1). For half-duplex operation, the DCE *may not* transmit data when the RTS line is asserted and must wait briefly before beginning transmission when the RTS line transitions from asserted to not-asserted. This brief wait allows completion of any DTE transmission.

Request to Send, RTS (Pin 4)

This is used with CTS for` half-duplex flow control. When the DTE wishes to send data, it asserts (logic level 0) the RTS line, but the DTE must not start sending data to the DCE until the DCE allows it to do so. The DCE signals the DTE that it may start sending by asserting the CTS line.

Clear to Send, CTS (Pin5)

This is used with RTS for half-duplex flow control. In response to an RTS from the DTE, the DCE asserts (logic level 0) the CTS line when it is ready to receive data from the DTE.

There is no need for this RTS/CTS handshake protocol when the DCE is a full-duplex modem. For full-duplex modems the CTS pin is permanently asserted or tied to DCD. Modems are not limited to full-duplex operation and in fact there are many communications links that require half-duplex operation. For example, a half-duplex radio link, where the radio transmits and receives on a single frequency alternating between transmission and reception, clearly requires half-duplex operation between the DTE and the radio modem. In this case the RTS/CTS handshake protocol switches the half-duplex modem between transmit and receive.

Data Set Ready, DSR (Pin 6)

When asserted (logic level 0) by the DCE, this indicates to the DTE that the *data set* (telephone company term for a modem or DCE) is off hook (connected to the telephone line) and is ready to begin data communications. DSR may not be asserted until all call establishment procedures are completed and the modem is ready for *data* (not *voice*) communications over the telephone line and the DTE has asserted DTR (see DTR below).

Data Terminal Ready, DTR (Pin 20)

When asserted (logic level 0) by the DTE, the DCE *may* then assert DSR when it is ready to begin data communications over the telephone line. In originate mode, the modem cannot dial a phone number until DTE is asserted and in answer mode it cannot answer until DTE is asserted. This DTR/DSR protocol basically ensures that both the DTE and DCE are ready to communicate over the telephone line.

Ring Indicator, RI (Pin 22)

When asserted (logic level 0) by the DCE, this indicates that a ringing signal is on the telephone line.

Data Carrier Detect, DCD)Pin 8)

When asserted (logic level 0) by the DCE, this indicates that the modem is receiving a carrier signal from the telephone line.

Data Signal Rate Detector, DSRD (Pin 23)

If two data rates are possible, this line is asserted (logic level 0) for the higher rate. This line can be bi-directional if bi-directional DSDR is supported by the DTE and the DCE; the DTE may assert DSRD to force the modem to use the higher rate or the modem may assert DSRD to report that the data link is operating at the higher rate.

3.4 Non-Standard RS-232 Applications.

The ultimate aim of the RS-232 Standard was to standardize communications between two data terminals via a modem, a communications link and another modem (Figure 3-1).

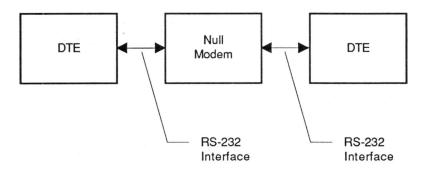

Figure 3-3   Serial Communications Channel With Null Modem

When the distance between terminals is short, we can eliminate the modems and communicate directly from terminal to terminal. This involves connecting two DTEs directly to one another, leading to problems because the RS-232 interface at each DTE is designed for connection to a DCE. One way to solve this connection problem is to have a dummy modem that presents a DCE type interface to each DTE. This dummy modem is called a *null modem* because the normally required modems are nonexistent. The null modem *replaces* the modems and telephone link of Figure 3-1. Both connectors on the null modem are of the DCE type so that standard RS-232 cables can be used to connect each DTE to it. Because both DTEs transmit data on pin 2 and receive data on pin 3 the null modem must be configured such that the transmit pin of the first DTE connects to the receive pin of the second DTE and similarly the transmit of the second connects to the receive of the first. Similar cross connections and pin to pin jumpering may be done to meet flow control and handshaking requirements.

Figure 3-4 illustrates a common null modem configuration. As is apparent from the figure, the null modem is nothing more than two DCE connectors appropriately wired one to the other.

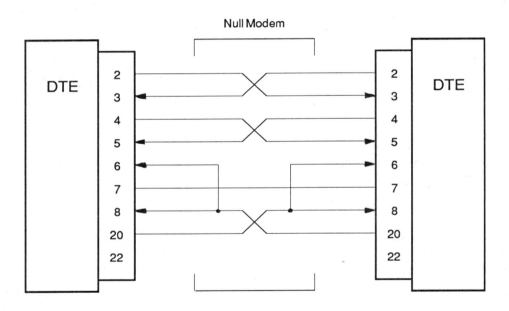

Note: Arrow heads on lines indicate
signal flow direction.

Figure 3-4   Typical DTE to DTE Connection Via Null Modem

The null modem in Figure 3-5 will generally satisfy the RS-232 control protocol, but may be too complex or will not work for some non-standard applications. Null modems are not included in the standard, so they may have any configuration that will work for a given application.

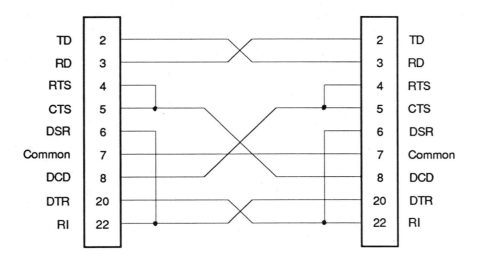

Figure 3-5   Null Modem

Figure 3-6 illustrates a typical serial interface between a personal computer, wired as DTE and a printer, wired as DTE. Most personal computers are wired as DTE (as they should be) and their terminal programs usually expect the required RS-232 control protocols (although these requirements can sometimes be relaxed through software). Printers are generally configured as DTE but do not always have the DTE specified male connectors. The computer to printer interface of Figure 3-6 is nothing more than another version of a null modem, thus the printer interface is DTE. Generally (but not always - after all we are considering non-standard applications) non-modem applications are configured as DTE.

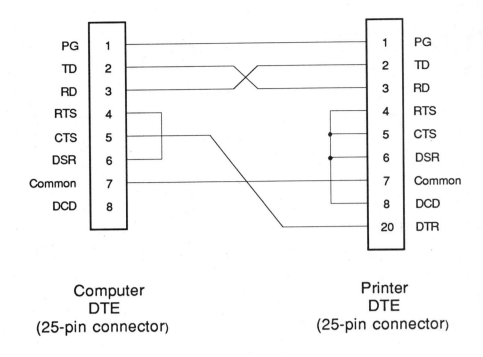

PG	1			1	PG	
TD	2			2	TD	
RD	3			3	RD	
RTS	4			4	RTS	
CTS	5			5	CTS	
DSR	6			6	DSR	
Common	7			7	Common	
DCD	8			8	DCD	
				20	DTR	

Computer
DTE
(25-pin connector)

Printer
DTE
(25-pin connector)

Figure 3-6   Typical Serial Computer to Printer Interface

The transmit and receive lines have been crossed as required for DTE to DTE communications. At the computer end of the link, RTS has a jumper to DSR to provide the data-set-ready handshake. The printer DTR is used as an error signal (ER) and is connected to CTS at the computer end. When the printer is capable of receiving data it asserts DTR which is recognized by the computer as an asserted CTS. Then when the computer wants to transmit data to the printer it asserts RTS, meeting all of the requirements (RTS, DSR, CTS and DTR all asserted) that allow it to transmit. When the printer buffer becomes nearly full it not-asserts DTR which is recognized by the computer as not-asserted CTS and the computer stops sending data until CTS is again asserted. This is a typical form of non-standard handshake and will be used in sample PICmicro programs in the following chapter.

Figure 3-7 illustrates the minimum connections required between a personal computer and a PICmicro based DTE peripheral operating in full-duplex mode. With this configuration, all flow control is in-band. If the computer operating system does not require the RS-232 controls, the pin jumpers on pins 4, 5, and 6 of the computer connector may be deleted. This is the simplest bi-directional null modem possible. It is also the simplest RS-232 asynchronous PICmicro to PICmicro link configuration.

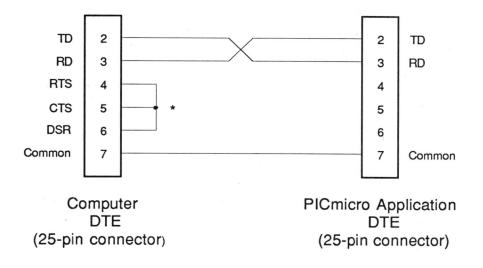

TD	2			2	TD
RD	3			3	RD
RTS	4			4	
CTS	5	*		5	
DSR	6			6	
Common	7			7	Common

Computer
DTE
(25-pin connector)

PICmicro Application
DTE
(25-pin connector)

* Note: If computer terminal program
does not require RS-232 flow
control, then RTS, CTS and DSR
jumper may be deleted.

Figure 3-7   Minimum Computer to PICmicro Full-Duplex Interface

The dominant asynchronous serial interface on personal computers is RS-232, therefore any PICmicro applications that communicate with personal computers must conform to the standard. By understanding the RS-232 rules we can work around all of the constraints the standard places on us and interface our PICmicro based applications to both standard and non-standard RS-232 interfaces. In Chapters 5 and 6 we will develop several PICmicro RS-232 asynchronous applications.

Many of the demonstration applications in the following chapters communicate via an RS-232 interface with a computer configured as a terminal (see Chapter 5). Some applications use a simple form of out-of-band flow control requiring at least one flow control line in the interface. The minimum necessary null modem for these applications is shown in Figure 3-8. With this configuration, standard terminal programs implementing out-of-band flow control may communicate with the PICmicro applications. Terminal programs expect the application to look like DCE. The null modem of Figure 3-8 serves this purpose. This null modem may be nothing more than two connectors wired together as shown in Figure 3-8.

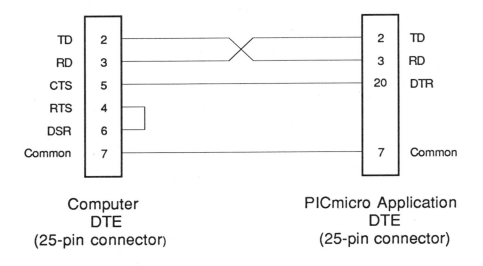

TD	2		2	TD
RD	3		3	RD
CTS	5		20	DTR
RTS	4			
DSR	6			
Common	7		7	Common

Computer
DTE
(25-pin connector)

PICmicro Application
DTE
(25-pin connector)

Figure 3-8   Minimum Computer to PICmicro Interface For Demonstration Applications

3.5 Electrical Interface

The RS-232 Standard applies to data rates from zero to 20,000 bits per second and puts a limitation of about 50 feet on cable length. This cable length may be exceeded provided the signal levels can be shown to meet the minimum specifications detailed below.

The standard applies only to binary communications, therefore only two signal states are defined: *mark* and *space*. A mark is a logic state 1 and is a signal voltage, measured with respect to the signal common line, in the range of minus 3 volts to minus 15 volts. A space is a logic state 0 and is a voltage in the range of plus 3 volts to plus 15 volts. The range from minus three volts to plus three volts is undefined. The plus and minus 3 volt values are minimum signal voltages to be presented to a *receiver*. To represent a mark condition, a transmit *driver* must apply a voltage between minus 5 volts and minus 15 volts. To represent a space, a transmit driver must apply a voltage between plus 5 volts and plus 15 volts. The 2 volt difference between the received signal minimum and the transmit minimum is a noise margin. A receiver must be able to correctly recognize a voltage as low as 3 volts. The open circuit voltage may not exceed 25 volts, and the driver circuit should be able to withstand a short circuit to any other wire in the cable without sustaining damage to itself or any other device attached to the cable.

The shunt capacitance of the terminator side of an RS-232 cable must not exceed 2500 pF including the capacitance of the cable. This rule primarily determines the approximately 50 feet cable length limit.

3.6 PICmicro to RS-232 Interface

When used in an RS-232 application, the PICmicro output port logic levels of approximately 0 and 5 volts must be converted to RS-232 output levels and the RS-232 input levels must be converted to PICmicro input port voltage levels. This conversion is done with an interface circuit that provides the logic levels, line drive capability and short circuit protection required by the RS-232 standard. Several manufacturers sell RS-232 interface ICs that provide this conversion. Some require plus and minus nominal 12 volt power supply voltages for the spacing and marking levels while others have built in voltage converters that allow the interfaces to operate from the 5 volt logic supply.

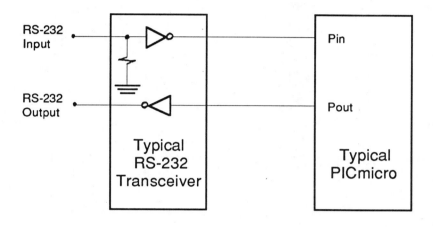

Logic	RS-232	PIC
Mark (1)	-3 to -12 Volts	5 Volts
Space (0)	+3 to +12 Volts	0 Volts

Figure 3-9   RS-232 to PICmicro Interface

Figure 3-10 illustrates a DTE to DCE connection using RS-232 transceivers from Linear Technology Corporation.

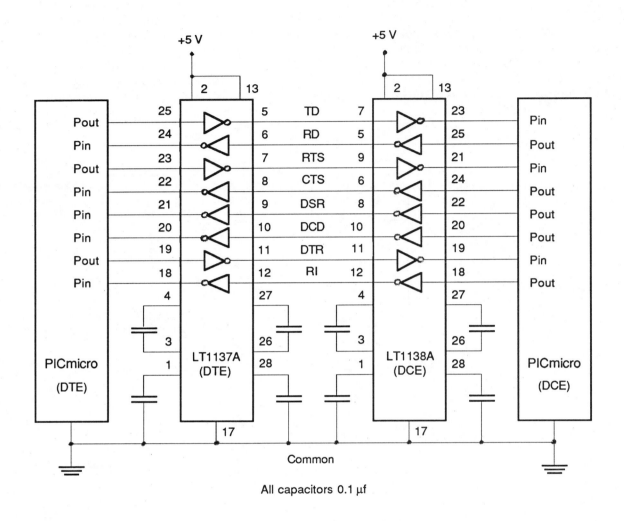

Figure 3-10   PICmicro DTE and DCE Application Using RS-232 Transceivers

Note that these parts generate the RS-232 levels on board the IC and require only 5 volt power. The PICmicro ports tie directly to the transceiver with a logic 1 level (5 volts) at the PICmicro port corresponding to the marking level and a logic 0 (0 volts) corresponding to the spacing level.

Within the transceiver, all RS-232 inputs are tied to ground through a resistor. This input termination ensures that any unconnected RS-232 input line generates a logic 1 (not asserted) at the PICmicro input port.

26

Chapter 4
The ASCII Character Code

4.1 Graphic Characters
4.2 Control Character Functions

The ASCII Character Code

The transmission of text (human readable characters) requires that the text characters be encoded using a combination of binary bits. The most widely accepted text code is ASCII, the American Standard Code for Information Interchange, supported by the American National Standards Institute (ANSI). ASCII is a 7-bit coded character set having 95 printable characters and 33 non-printable characters. The printable characters include 26 upper case letters, 26 lowercase letters, the numerals 0 through 9, punctuation characters and special characters. ANSI defines these printable ASCII characters as *graphic characters* and as such are human readable. The non-printable characters are defined by ANSI as *control characters*.

Table 4-1   ASCII Character Code

Low Nibble

		0	1	2	3	4	5	6	7	8	9	A	B	C	D	E	F
	0 |	NUL	SOH	STX	ETX	EOT	ENQ	ACK	BEL	BS	HT	LF	VT	FF	CR	SO	SI
	1 |	DLE	DC1	DC2	DC3	DC4	NAK	SYN	ETB	CAN	EM	SUB	ESC	FS	GS	RS	US
	2 |	SP	!	"	#	$	%	&	'	(	)	*	+	,	-	.	/
High	3 |	0	1	2	3	4	5	6	7	8	9	:	;	<	=	>	?
Nibble	4 |	@	A	B	C	D	E	F	G	H	I	J	K	L	M	N	O
	5 |	P	Q	R	S	T	U	V	W	X	Y	Z	[	\	]	^	_
	6 |	`	a	b	c	d	e	f	g	h	i	j	k	l	m	n	o
	7 |	p	q	r	s	t	u	v	w	x	y	z	{	|	}	~	DEL

The ASCII control characters are encoded as $00 through $1F and the DEL as $FF; the graphics characters as $20 through $7E. The layout of the table is significant and is optimized for the manipulation of textual data.

4.1 Graphic Characters

To appreciate the significance of the table layout, note that the only difference in the code for the characters in row 4 and row 6 is the logic level of bit 5. This is also the case for row 5 and row 7. The characters in row 4 are the shifted (uppercase) versions of those in row 6 and the characters in row 5 are the shifted versions of the characters in row 7. Thus changing from lower case to uppercase is a simple matter of changing bit 5 to a 0 level (subtracting $20) and similarly changing from uppercase to lowercase by simply changing bit 5 to a 1 level (adding $20). The numerals 0 through 9 are encoded as $30 through $39. Subtracting $30 from the code for a numeral results in the BCD representation of the numeral. Note that the ASCII codes for the numerals increase in numeric value as the numerals increase and similarly the codes for the letters increase in numeric value as the letters move toward the end of the alphabet. This increase in code value is the collating sequence and simplifies sorting and searching functions.

4.2 Control Character Functions

The control characters (except NUL) may be generated on a keyboard using the *Control key*. The *Control key-Character key* combinations for these control characters are listed in Table 4-2.

Table 4-2   ASCII Control Characters

HEX	CHAR	NAME	KEYBOARD
00	NUL	Null, Idle	^@
01	SOH	Start of header	^A
02	STX	Start of text	^B
03	ETX	End of text	^C
04	EOT	End of transmission	^D
05	ENQ	Enquiry	^E
06	ACK	Acknowledgement	^F
07	BEL	Bell or Beep	^G
08	BS	Backspace	^H
09	HT	Horizontal tab	^I
0A	LF	Line feed	^J
0B	VT	Vertical tab	^K
0C	FF	Form feed	^L
0D	CR	Carriage return	^M
0E	SO	Shift out	^N
0F	SI	Shift in	^O
10	DLE	Data link escape	^P
11	DC1	Device control 1 (XON)	^Q
12	DC2	Device control 2	^R
13	DC3	Device control3 (XOFF)	^S
14	DC4	Device control4	^T
15	NAK	Negative acknowledge	^U
16	SYN	Synchronous idle	^V
17	ETB	End of transmission block	^W
18	CAN	Cancel	^X
19	EM	End of medium	^Y
1A	SUB	Substitute	^Z
1B	ESC	Escape, Prefix, Altmode	^[
1C	FS	File separator	^\
1D	GS	Group separator	^]
1E	RS	Record separator	^^
1F	US	Unit separator	^-

NOTE: The leading ^ in the KEYBOARD column indicates the CONTROL key is to be held down when pressing the character key.

The ASCII control characters are categorized into *communication controls, format effectors,* and *information separators*. There are also some control characters that are not included in these categories and are treated as *general controls.*

Communications Control Characters

A *communication control* character controls or facilitates the transmission of information over the communication network. Following is a brief functional description of each *communication control* character:

NUL (Null)

Primarily used as a time-waster in the data stream, usually to give hardware time to do some function, such as carriage return on a printer. This is known as *media fill time*. Null has no information value and does not change the information content of the data stream.

SOH (Start of Heading)

Marks the beginning of the header block of a message.

STX (Start of Text)

Terminates the header block and marks the beginning of the text of a message.

ETX (End of Text)

Terminates the text of a message.

EOT (End of Transmission)

Indicates the conclusion of a transmission. EOT is usually transmitted where SOH would normally occur, telling the receiver that the transmission is over.

EOB (End of Transmission Block)

May be used in place of EOT. EOB is generally used when the data transmitted does not fill an expected block size (forced end of record).

ENQ (Enquiry)

Request for identification or status (who are you?, are you there?)

ACK (Acknowledge)

Transmitted by a receiver as a response to an error free reception of a message.

NAK (Negative Acknowledge)

Transmitted by a receiver when an error is detected in a message (see also SUB).

DLE (Data Link Escape)

Changes the meaning of a limited number of contiguously following characters. DLE is used exclusively to create supplemental control functions.

SYN (Synchronous Idle)

Used in *synchronous* systems to establish and maintain synchronization when no data is flowing.

Format Effector Characters

A *format effector* character controls the layout or positioning of information on a printing or display device. The ASCII specification was originally written with the teletypewriter in mind and as such only recognizes a display area defined by a continuous roll of paper. Thus, the format capabilities addressed by ASCII are quite limited. ASCII defines the current position to be printed as the 'active position'. Following is a brief functional description of each *format effector* character.

BS (Back Space)

Moves the active print position backwards one space on the same line. BS cannot be used to move from the beginning of one line to the end of the previous line.

HT (Horizontal Tab)

Advances the active position to the next predetermined character position on the same line.

LF (Line Feed)

Advances the active position to the same character position on the next line down.

VT (Vertical Tab)

Advances the active position to the same character position on the next predetermined line down.

FF (Form Feed)

Advances the active position to a predetermined line on the next page. The exact number of lines advanced must be determined by the device receiving the FF. On a video terminal, FF generally clears the screen.

CR (Carriage Return)

Moves the active position to the beginning of the same line. CR is used together with LF to move to the beginning of a new line.

Information Separator Characters

An *information separator* character is used to separate and qualify information. The separators impart hierarchical order to the information. The ASCII standard states "These information separators may be used with data in optional fashion, except that their hierarchical relationship shall be: FS as the most inclusive, then GS, then RS, and US as the least inclusive. The content and length of a file, group, record, or unit are not specified." Basically this means that the characters can have arbitrary meanings, but when they are used together the hierarchical order must be preserved. The four *information separators* are:

FS (File Separator)
GS (Group Separator)
RS (Record Separator)
US (Unit Separator)

General Control Characters

The control characters that do not fit the above three classifications are the *general control* characters. These *general control* characters provide physical device control and extended character activation. Following is a brief functional description of each *general control* character.

BEL (Bell)

This is a call for attention. It triggers some sort of attention-getting device, such as a bell.

DC1, DC2, DC3, DC4 (Device Control)

These device controls have no assigned meaning in the ASCII specification. They can be used for any purpose, but DC1 and DC3 used as a pair have become a de facto standard for flow control (XON / XOFF). See Section 5.2.2 for a discussion of XON/XOFF flow control.

CAN (Cancel)

Indicates that a predetermined number of preceding characters should be ignored. The exact meaning of CAN must be defined for each application.

EM (End of Medium)

Indicates that the preceding character was the last useable character on the medium. It does not necessarily indicate the physical end of the medium.

SUB (Substitute)

Substituted for a character that is found to be in error.

ESC, SI, SO

Used to activate alternate or extended character sets. Because the ASCII character set is not large enough to satisfy every need, an *Escape Sequence* is used to activate supplementary character sets. These supplementary character sets may include both text and control characters. An *Escape Sequence* is a string of characters, beginning with the ESC character, used to identify the supplementary character. SI (shift in) and SO (shift out) are used to invoke alternative sets of characters.

Chapter 5
Bit-Bang Asynchronous Communications

Bit-Bang Asynchronous Communications

The smaller PICmicros do not have on-chip UARTs. For these smaller and less expensive devices the UART functions can be performed in software. For cost sensitive applications, bit-banging the communications channel is a more cost effective solution than using on chip hardware. In the following sections, bit-banger software for using the PICmicro as an asynchronous half-duplex and full-duplex DTE device will be described.

Figure 5-1 is a schematic of the PICmicro circuit that we will use to demonstrate several bit-banger asynchronous applications. This circuit may be used with most of the 18 pin PICmicros, but the majority of the applications will use the 16F84. With little or no change, the software routines may be used with other PICmicros. In all of the applications, communications will be with a computer via RS-232. The computer will be configured as DTE. The computer will be running a program appropriate to the application and in most cases it will be a terminal program so we shall designate the computer as *the terminal*. The PICmicro application is also configured as DTE. In some of the applications, one or both of the flow control lines will not be used. This presents no difficulty because the RS-232 transceiver (in this case a Maxim MAX 232) presents a logic 1 (not asserted) at the port input for any non-connected RS-232 input line and the port state will be ignored by the software. The null modem cable in Figure 3-8 may be used with the demonstration applications.

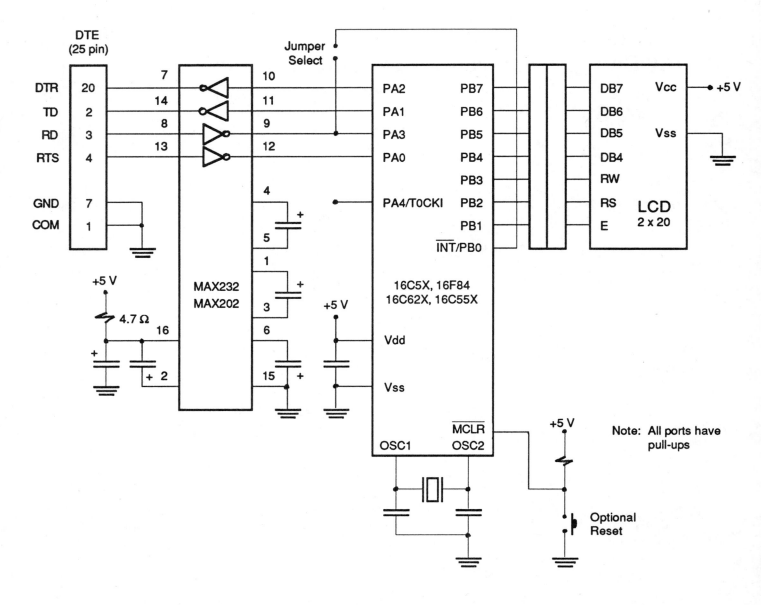

Figure 5-1   Schematic, Bit-Bang Asynchronous Applications

5.1 Bit-Bang Half-Duplex

Many applications require only half-duplex communications. Several half-duplex schemes are described in the following sections. The receive service in Section 5.1.1 waits in a loop for a character to arrive. While waiting in the loop for the character, the PICmicro cannot perform any other operation. For applications that have nothing to do until a character is received, this wait-in-a loop method is acceptable. But if an application has only a limited time to invest in waiting for a character, some other method must be implemented to recognize the arrival of a new character. Sections 5.1.2 and 5.1.3 address the solution to this problem using the loop-with-time-out and interrupt-driven reception methods.

34

5.1.1 Half-Duplex Receive and Transmit Services

The modules in HALF.GRP are all that are necessary to implement bit-bang half-duplex receive and transmit services. The character format is: 1 start bit, 8 data bits, no parity bit and 1 stop bit. The data rate is 2400 bits per second.

The modules are:

ASYREC   Half-Duplex Receive Service
ASYXMT   Half-Duplex Transmit Service
VDLY   Bit Timing Service

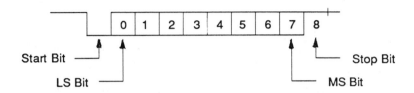

Figure 5-2   Asynchronous Character Format

Half-Duplex Receive (Module ASYREC and Figures 5-4 and 5-5)

Two receive error flags are defined: start error and framing error. On entry to ASYREC, the flags are cleared. The start error flag is set if the start bit is less than 1/2 bit time and is an indicator of a noisy communications channel. The framing error flag is set if the stop bit does not occur at the expected time (the ninth bit after the start bit).

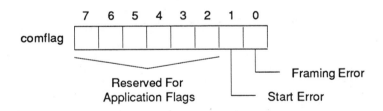

Figure 5-3   Communictions Flags; HALF.GRP

ASYREC watches for the start bit by testing the receive port for low (logic 0). If the port is not low, indicating that the start bit is absent, ASYREC then loops back to test the port again. If the start bit is present, then ASYREC waits for one-half of a bit period and again tests for low at the receive port. If the port is no longer low, the start error flag is set and ASYREC exits. If it is still low, then ASYREC waits for one bit period. At this point 1 1/2 bit periods have elapsed since the beginning of the start bit and the first data bit may be read. From this point on each succeeding data bit is read at one bit period intervals until all 9 bits are read. If the ninth bit is high (logic 1), ASYREC exits with the eight bit character in the parameter location **recreg**. If the ninth bit is not high, then the stop bit is not present, the framing error flag is set and ASYREC

35

exits with the character as received. It is then left to a higher level routine to decide what to do with the possibly corrupt character. Note that all data bit reads take place at the middle of the bit time due to the initial 1/2 bit wait after the beginning of the start bit. The data bits are read by moving the receive port value to the carry and rotating the carry into **recreg**. The data is received least significant bit first, requiring right rotation of the bit into **recreg**. ASREC exits at approximately the midpoint of the stop bit. If the calling module (the module that calls ASREC) requires more than a small part of a 1/2 bit period to process the received byte, it should inhibit DTR immediately upon return from ASYREC. DTR should remain inhibited until immediately before the next call to ASREC.

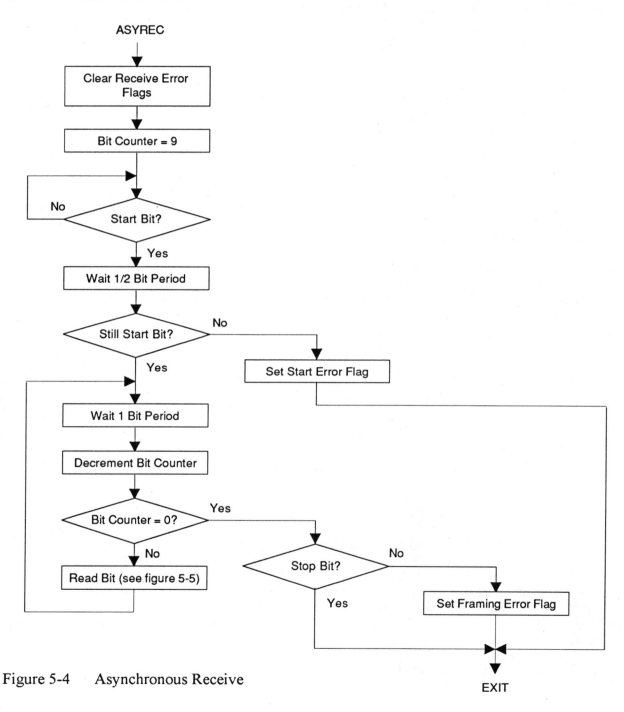

Figure 5-4   Asynchronous Receive

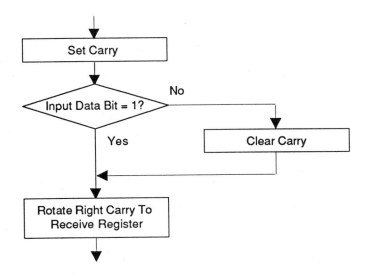

Figure 5-5   Read Receive Data Bit

The one-half and one bit time waits are generated by subroutines in the module VDLY. This is a nested loop (loop-within-a-loop) delay counter where the total delay is determined by two parameters: **acount** and **bcount**. These parameters are the starting value for the down counters in each loop. HALF and FULL are subroutines that call VDLY after having loaded **acount** and **bcount** with the starting values for the half-bit or full-bit wait times. A table of the count parameters for data rates of 110 bits/second to 19200 bits/second is included in the listing. Data rates other than 2400 bits/second may be used by simply replacing the 2400 bit/second count values in HALF and FULL with those from the table. The delays in the table are less than the bit times because the time used to read the data bit, call the delay routines, load the counters and return from the delay routines must be included in the total bit time. This becomes especially critical for the higher data rates.

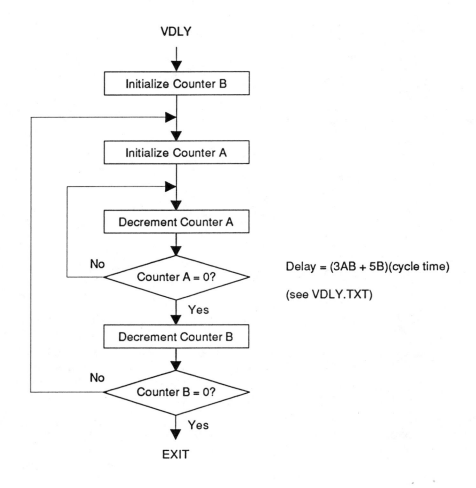

Delay = (3AB + 5B)(cycle time)

(see VDLY.TXT)

Figure 5-6   Nested Loop Delay

Table 5-1   Character Bit Times

```
-------------------------------------------------
   Rate     Bit Time   1/2 Bit Time   1/4 Bit Time
 Bits/Sec     μsec         μsec           μsec
-------------------------------------------------
    110      9090.9       4545.5         2272.7
    300      3333.3        166.7          833.3
    600      1666.6        833.3          416.7
   1200       833.3        416,7          208.3
   2400       416.7        208.3          104.2
   4800       208.3        104.2           52.1
   9600       104.2         52.1           26.0
  19200        52.1         26.0           13.0
```

Half-Duplex Transmit (Module ASYXMT and Figures 5-7 and 5-8)

The character format and data rate are the same as for the receive module. There are no transmit error flags. The character to be transmitted is in the parameter location **xmtreg**.

ASYXMT begins by taking the transmit port to a low (logic 0) for the start bit. After waiting for 1 bit period, the bit counter is loaded with 8 and the least significant data bit is rotated right to the carry. If the carry is low the transmit port is cleared (taken low) or if the carry is high the transmit port is set (taken high) and ASYXMT waits for 1 bit period. Then the bit counter is decremented and if all 8 bits have not been transmitted (bit counter not equal to 0), the routine loops back to rotate out the next data bit. When all data bits have been transmitted, the transmit port is set (for the stop bit) and ASYXMT waits for 1 bit period before exiting. To wait 1 bit period, ASYXMT calls the routine FULL.

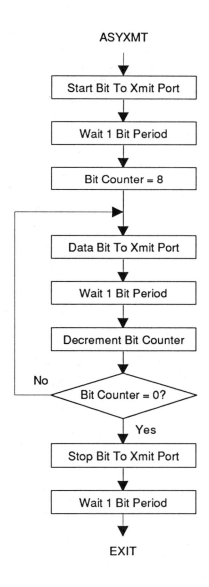

Figure 5-7   Asynchronous Transmit

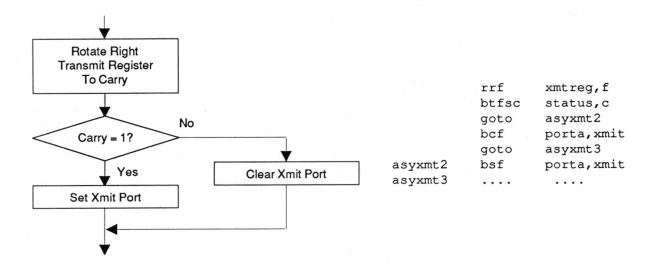

Figure 5-8   Current Data Bit to Xmit Port

```
;====== HALF.GRP ================================================================
;
;        Module: half.grp
;        Half-Duplex Asynchronous Bit-Bang Communications Routines.
;        14 bit PIC
;
;--------------------------------------------------------------------------------
;
;        REQUIRES Following Workspace:
;
;        chartr          data character received & xmitted
;        bitctr          bit counter
;        acount          delay count a
;        bcount          delay count b
;        comflag         communications flags
;        cntra           delay counter a
;        cntrb           delay counter b
;        recreg          received data character
;        xmtreg          transmitted data character
;
;        REQUIRES Following Equates:
;
;        xmit     equ     000x     ;port ax is transmit
;        dtr      equ     000y     ;port ay is DTR
;        rec      equ     000z     ;port az is receive
;
;        FLAG bit definitions:
;
;        comflag,0       set for framing error
;        comflag,1       set for start error
;
;        NOTE: port a is used for all communications lines. If a port other
```

```
;               than port a is used, all refrences to port a in this module
;               must be must be changed to the appropriate port.
;
;               Character protocol is 8 data bits, 1, start bit, 1 stop bit
;               and no parity. Bit rate is determined by the parameters
;               acount and bcount.
;
;               This module includes asyrec.txt, asyxmt.txt & vdly.txt
;
;               See INDIGO1.ASM and Section 5.1.1 for Initialization
;               and Application information.
;-----------------------------------------------------------------------
;        Module: asyrec.txt
;        Receive a character   8 bits, 1 start, 1 stop, no parity
;        On exit: character received is in recreg
;
;        Exits only after a character (or start error) has been received.
;        Start error is generated by a start bit that is less than 1/2 bit
;        time long. Framing error is generated if stop bit (marking) is not
;        ninth bit after start bit.
;
;        porta,rec is receive port
;-----------------------------------------------------------------------
asyrec  bcf     comflag,1       ;clear start error flag
        bcf     comflag,0       ;clear framing error flag
        movlw   09              ;8 data bits + stop bit
        movwf   bitctr
asyrec1 btfsc   porta,rec       ;start bit (rec port low)? if yes, skip
        goto    asyrec1         ;no. go try again
        call    half            ;wait 1/2 bit time
        btfss   porta,rec       ;still start bit ? if no, skip next
        goto    asyrec3         ;yes. go
        bsf     comflag,1       ;no. set start error flag
        goto    asyrecx         ;& go exit
asyrec3 call    full            ;yes. wait 1 bit time
        decfsz  bitctr,f        ;update bit counter. if all bits done, skip
        goto    asyrec4         ;not all done. go read bit
        btfss   porta,rec       ;all done. stop bit present ? if yes, skip
        bsf     comflag,0       ;no. set framing error flag
        goto    asyrecx         ;& go exit
;
asyrec4 bsf     status,c        ;set carry
        btfss   porta,rec       ;get data bit. is it 1 ? if yes,skip
        bcf     status,c        ;no. clear carry
        rrf     recreg,f        ;rotate carry to received character
        goto    asyrec3         ;go wait for next bit
;
asyrecx retlw   0               ;EXIT
;
;-----------------------------------------------------------------------
;        Module: asyxmt.txt
;        Send a character      8 bits, 1 start, 1 stop, no parity
;        On entry: character to be sent is in xmtreg & port a1 must be high
;        On exit: transmit port is high (marking)
```

41

```
;
;           porta,xmit   is transmit port
;-----------------------------------------------------------------
asyxmt   bcf      porta,xmit        ;start bit
         call     full              ;wait 1 bit time
         movlw    08                ;8 bit character length
         movwf    bitctr            ;to bit counter
asyxmt1  rrf      xmtreg,f          ;rotate bit out thru carry
         btfsc    status,c          ;carry = 0 ? IF YES, SKIP
         goto     asyxmt2           ;no. carry = 1. go set pa1
         bcf      porta,xmit        ;data bit = 0. clear pa1
         goto     asyxmt3           ;& go
asyxmt2  bsf      porta,xmit        ;data bit = 1. set pa1
;
asyxmt3  call     full              ;wait 1 bit time
         decfsz   bitctr,f          ;all 8 bits sent ? if yes, skip
         goto     asyxmt1           ;no, go do next bit
;
         bsf      porta,xmit        ;all bits done. do stop bit (marking)
         call     full              ;wait 1 bit time
         retlw    0                 ;EXIT
;-----------------------------------------------------------------
;           Module: vdly.txt
;           Delay used for bit timing
;-----------------------------------------------------------------
;           CYCLE TIME: 1 microsec (4 MHz xtal)
;           DELAY MODULE: vdly.txt
;
```

;	RATE	BIT TIME	— FOR 1 BIT —			— FOR 1/2 BIT —		
;		(uSec)	bcount	acount	delay (uS)	bcount	acount	delay
;								
;	110	9090.9	13	231	9074	13	115	4550
;	300	3333.3	13	81	3324	13	41	1654
;	600	1666.7	12	44	1644	6	44	822
;	1200	833.3	3	89	816	3	42	399
;	2400	416.7	3	43	402	3	20	191
;	4800	208.8	2	29	184	2	13	87
;	9600	104.2	1	27	86	1	11	35
;	19200	52.1	1	9	32	1	1	8

```
;
;-----------------------------------------------------------------
;
;           Variable time delay. Delay parameters are : acount & bcount
;
;           delay approx = (3)*(cycletime)*(acount)*(bcount)
;                        + (5)*(cycletime)*(bcount)
;
;           Total time from:   call full
;                        to:   next instruction   (return location)
;
;           is approximately = delay + (12)*(cycletime)
;
;
```

```
;          REQUIRES FOLLOWING WORKSPACE: acount    count parameter a
;                                        bcount    count parameter b
;                                        cntra     counter a
;                                        cntrb     counter b
;-----------------------------------------------------------------------
vdly    movf    bcount,w        ;b count to counter b
        movwf   cntrb
vdly0   movf    acount,w        ;a count to counter a
        movwf   cntra
vdly1   decfsz  cntra,f         ;dec counter a, skip if zero
        goto    vdly1           ;not zero. dec it again
        decfsz  cntrb,f         ;dec counter b, skip if zero
        goto    vdly0           ;not zero. do loop again
        retlw   0               ;exit
;-----------------------------------------------------------------------
half    movlw   d'3'            ;wait 1/2 bit time   (2400 bits per second)
        movwf   bcount
        movlw   d'20'
        movwf   acount
        call    vdly
        retlw   0
;-----------------------------------------------------------------------
full    movlw   d'3'            ;wait 1 bit time (2400 bits per second)
        movwf   bcount
        movlw   d'43'
        movwf   acount
        call    vdly
        retlw   0
;=======================================================================
```

INDIGO1.ASM: A Half-Duplex Bit-Bang Application
(See Figure 5-9 and INDIGO1.ASM)

INDIGO1.ASM is a bit-bang half-duplex application that receives a character byte from the terminal and echoes it (sends it back) to the terminal. Typical terminal programs print the echoed character to the screen. This simple demonstration program is ideal for developing and testing bit-bang transmit and receive routines. Ports A1 and A3 are TD and RD respectively and port A2 is DTR. RTS is not used with INDIGO1.

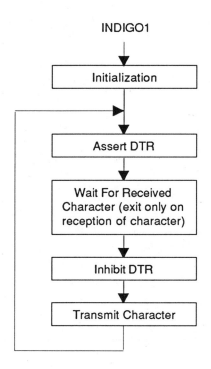

INDIGO1

Initialization

Assert DTR

Wait For Received
Character (exit only on
reception of character)

Inhibit DTR

Transmit Character

Figure 5-9   INDIGO1 and RED1 Main Program

When INDIGO1 is ready to receive a character, it asserts DTR then waits to receive the character. When a character has been received, INDIGO1 inhibits (not-asserts) DTR, then sends the character back to the terminal. Inhibiting DTR tells the terminal to stop sending characters because INDIGO1 is busy and cannot receive or because it wants to send a character to the terminal. After sending the character, INDIGO1 then asserts DTR and waits to receive the next character. This is a very simple form of half-duplex flow control where the application has full control of the communications channel. If INDIGO1 receives a character and a framing error has occurred, it sends the ASCII control character NAK to the terminal in place of the received character. The terminal then takes appropriate action, such as re-sending the character.

The main program loop of INDIGO1 asserts DTR to inform the terminal that it may transmit, then calls ASYREC to receive a character. ASYREC does not return until a character has been received. On reception of a character, DTR is inhibited and if there is no framing error, the received character **recreg** is moved to the transmit register **xmtreg** and is transmitted. If there is a framing error, NAK is transmitted. A one bit period wait is inserted immediately after DTR is inhibited and before the received character is echoed because ASYREC exits at approximately the middle of the stop bit. This one bit period wait gives the terminal time to respond to the inhibit DTR signal and also prevents INDIGO1 from transmitting while the terminal stop bit is still active. After the character has been echoed, the main program loops back to wait for the next character from the terminal.

INDIGO1 serves only as an example of how to apply the modules in HALF.GRP to an asynchronous half-duplex application. These modules may be used with any half-duplex application. For applications requiring data rates other than 2400 bits/second, the counter values in HALF and FULL need only be changed as per the table in VDLY. For other than 8 data bits, only the initialization of the bit counters in ASYREC and ASYXMT need be changed. In later sections these modules will be used in other application examples.

44

```
;====== INDIGO1.ASM =========================================================
;
;          FILE: indigo1.asm
;
;          16F84
;          Asynchronous serial communications loop
;          Waits for character from terminal, then
;          sends back (echoes) character received.
;          Uses 1 line flow control.
;          Configured as DTE
;
;----------------------------------------------------------------------------
;
;          INPUT:  RS 232
;                  2400 baud, 1 start bit, 8 data bits, 1 stop bit, no parity
;                  Port a3 is character IN (receive)
;
;          OUTPUT: RS 232
;                  2400 baud, 1 start bit, 8 data bits, 1 stop bit
;                  Port a1 is character OUT (transmit)
;
;          CONTROL: DTR only
;                  Asserts DTR only when ready to receive from terminal
;                  otherwise inhibits DTR
;                  Port a2 is DTR. Port a2 high for DTR asserted (OK to send)
;                  The DTR line should go to the CTS pin on the terminal.
;----------------------------------------------------------------------------
          radix   hex          ;RADIX is HEX
;
          list  p=16f84
;
c         equ     0            ;carry bit of status register (bit 0)
z         equ     2            ;zero flag bit of status register (bit 2)
w         equ     0            ;destination working
f         equ     1            ;destination file
rp0       equ     5            ;rp0 bit of status register (bit 5)
;
;----------------------------------------------------------------------------
;      CPU EQUATES   (memory map)
status    equ     03
porta     equ     05
portb     equ     06
trisa     equ     05           ;bank 1 (0x85)
trisb     equ     06           ;bank 1 (0x86)
;
;----------------------------------------------------------------------------
;      WORK AREA   (memory map)
chartr    equ     000c         ;data character received & xmitted
bitctr    equ     000d         ;bit counter
acount    equ     000e         ;delay count a
bcount    equ     000f         ;delay count b
comflag   equ     0010         ;communications flags
cntra     equ     0011         ;delay counter a
cntrb     equ     0012         ;delay counter b
```

```
recreg   equ      0013          ;received data character
xmtreg   equ      0014          ;transmitted data character
;
;
;-----------------------------------------------------------------------------
;         SYSTEM EQUATES
;
xmit     equ      0001          ;port a1 is transmit
dtr      equ      0002          ;port a2 is DTR
rec      equ      0003          ;port a3 is receive
;
;-----------------------------------------------------------------------------
;         FLAGS
;
;         comflag,0             set for framing error
;         comflag,1             set for start error
;
;=============================================================================
;         MAIN PROGRAM
;-----------------------------------------------------------------------------
         org      0x00          ;start of program memory
;
start    clrf     portb
         clrf     porta
         bsf      status,rp0    ;switch to bank 1
         movlw    00e9          ;a0 & a3 as inputs, a1, a2, a4 as outputs
         movwf    trisa
         movlw    0000          ;all port b as outputs
         movwf    trisb
         bcf      status,rp0    ;switch to bank 0
         bsf      porta,dtr     ;inhibit DTR (we are busy)
         bsf      porta,xmit    ;marking output
;
mloop    clrf     comflag       ;clear communications flags
         bcf      porta,dtr     ;assert DTR
         call     asyrec        ;wait for received character
         bsf      porta,dtr     ;inhibit DTR
         call     full          ;wait 1 bit period
         btfss    comflag,0     ;framing error ? if yes, skip
         goto     mloop1        ;no error. go
         movlw    15            ;yes. load NAK ($15)
         movwf    recreg        ;& send it back
mloop1   movf     recreg,w      ;move received character to...
         movwf    xmtreg        ;transmit register
         call     asyxmt        ;echo character back
         goto     mloop         ;& loop back for next character received
;-----------------------------------------------------------------------------
;         INCLUDES:
;         HALF.GRP          Half-Duplex Async Services
;-----------------------------------------------------------------------------
         include half.grp
;
;-----------------------------------------------------------------------------
         end                    ;END OF PROGRAM
;=============================================================================
```

12 Bit PICmicro Applications

INDIGO1 places calls three levels deep. If a 12 bit PICmicro is to be used for an INDIGO1 type application the call depth must be reduced to no more than 2 levels due to the 2 byte stack limitation for these smaller PICmicros. For a 12 bit application the *function* of the sub-modules HALF and FULL must be moved to the ASYREC and ASYXMT modules, reducing the call depth to 2. This has been done for REDHALF.GRP in RED1.ASM, which is a 16C54 version of INDIGO1. The modules ASYRECX.TXT, ASYXMTX.TXT and VDLYX.TXT in RED1.ASM may be used with any mid-range PICmicro half-duplex application but must be used for a 12 bit PICmicro application.

```
;====== RED1.ASM ================================================
;
;        FILE: red1.asm
;
;        Asynchronous serial communications loop.
;        Waits for character from terminal, then
;        sends back (echoes) character received.
;        For 12 bit PIC
;
;----------------------------------------------------------------
;
;        INPUT:    RS 232
;                  2400 baud, 1 start bit, 8 data bits, 1 stop bit, no parity
;                  Port a3 is character in (receive)
;
;        OUTPUT:   RS 232
;                  2400 baud, 1 start bit, 8 data bits, 1 stop bit
;                  Port a1 is character out (transmit)
;
;        CONTROL:  DTR only
;                  Asserts DTR only when ready to receive from terminal
;                  otherwise inhibits DTR.
;                  Port a2 is DTR. Port a2 high for DTR asserted (OK to send)
;                  The DTR line should go to the CTS pin on the terminal.
;----------------------------------------------------------------
        radix   hex         ;RADIX is HEX
;
        list p=16c54
;
c       equ     0           ;carry bit of status register (bit 0)
z       equ     2           ;zero flag bit of status register (bit 2)
w       equ     0           ;destination working
f       equ     1           ;destination file
;
;----------------------------------------------------------------
;    CPU EQUATES   (memory map)
status  equ     03
porta   equ     05
portb   equ     06
;
;----------------------------------------------------------------
```

```
;         WORK AREA    (memory map)
chartr  equ       0007        ;character received & xmitted
bitctr  equ       0008        ;bit counter
acount  equ       0009        ;delay count a
bcount  equ       000a        ;delay count b
comflag equ       000b        ;communications flags
cntra   equ       000c        ;delay counter a
cntrb   equ       000d        ;delay counter b
recreg  equ       000e        ;received data character
xmtreg  equ       000f        ;transmitted data character
;
;-----------------------------------------------------------------------
;         SYSTEM EQUATES
;
xmit    equ       0001        ;port a1 is transmit
dtr     equ       0002        ;port a2 is DTR
rec     equ       0003        ;port a3 is receive
;
;-----------------------------------------------------------------------
;         FLAG bit definitions
;
;         comflag,0        set for framing error
;         comflag,1        set for receive error
;
;=======================================================================
;         MAIN PROGRAM
;-----------------------------------------------------------------------
        org       0x00        ;start of program memory
;
start   clrf      portb
        clrf      porta
        movlw     00e9        ;a0 & a3 as inputs, a1, a2, a4 as outputs
        tris      porta
        bsf       porta,dtr   ;inhibit DTR (we are busy)
        bsf       porta,xmit  ;marking output
        movlw     0000        ; all port b as outputs
        tris      portb
;
mloop   clrf      comflag     ;clear communications flags
        bcf       porta,dtr   ;assert DTR
        call      asyrecx     ;wait for received character
        bsf       porta,dtr   ;inhibit DTR
        movlw     d'3'        ;wait 1 bit period:
        movwf     bcount
        movlw     d'20'
        movwf     acount
        call      vdly
        btfss     comflag,0   ;framing error ? if yes, skip
        goto      mloop1      ;no framing error.  go
        movlw     15          ;yes. load NAK ($15)
        movwf     recreg      ;& send it back
mloop1  movf      recreg,w    ;move received character to...
        movwf     xmtreg      ;transmit register
        call      asyxmtx     ;echo character back
```

48

```
        goto    mloop           ;& loop back for next character received
;
;====== REDHALF.GRP ============================================================
;       Module: redhalf.grp
;       Half-Duplex Asynchronous Bit-Bang Communications Routines
;       12 bit or 14 bit PIC
;
;       Requires WORK AREA:
;       chartr          character received & xmitted
;       bitctr          bit counter
;       acount          delay count a
;       bcount          delay count b
;       comflag         communications flags
;       cntra           delay counter a
;       cntrb           delay counter b
;       recreg          received data character
;       xmtreg          transmitted data character
;
;-------------------------------------------------------------------------------
;       Requires SYSTEM EQUATES:
;
;       xmit    equ     0001    ;port a1 is transmit
;       dtr     equ     0002    ;port a2 is DTR
;       rec     equ     0003    ;port a3 is receive
;
;       FLAG bit definitions
;
;       comflag,0       set for framing error
;       comflag,1       set for receive error
;
;       This module includes: asyrecx.txt, asyxmtx.txt and vdlyx.txt
;       See RED1.ASM and Section 5.1.1 for Initialization and Application
;       information.
;-------------------------------------------------------------------------------
;       Module: asyrecx.txt
;       Receive a character   8 bits, 1 start, 1 stop, no parity, 2400 baud
;       On exit: character received is in recreg
;       Exits only after a character (or start error) has been received.
;       Start error is generated by a start bit that is less than 1/2 bit
;       period long. Framing error is generated if stop bit (marking) is not
;       ninth bit after start bit.
;
;       porta,rec is receive port
;
;-------------------------------------------------------------------------------
asyrecx bcf     comflag,1       ;clear start error flag
        bcf     comflag,0       ;clear framing error flag
        movlw   09              ;8 bit character
        movwf   bitctr
;
asyrec1 btfsc   porta,rec       ;start bit low ? if yes, skip
        goto    asyrec1         ;no. go try again
        movlw   d'3'            ;yes. wait 1/2 bit time
        movwf   bcount
```

```
             movlw    d'22'
             movwf    acount
             call     vdly
;
             btfss    porta,rec          ;still start bit ? if no, skip next
             goto     asyrec3            ;yes. go
             bsf      comflag,1          ;no. set start error flag
             goto     asyrec5            ;& go exit
;
asyrec3 movlw    3                       ;wait 1 bit time
             movwf    bcount
             movlw    d'45'
             movwf    acount
             call     vdly
;
             decfsz   bitctr,f           ;update bit counter. if all bits done, skip
             goto     asyrec4            ;not all done. go read bit
             btfss    porta,rec          ;all done. stop bit present ? if yes, skip
             bsf      comflag,0          ;no. set framing error flag
             goto     asyrec5            ;& go exit
;
asyrec4 bsf      status,c                ;set carry
             btfss    porta,rec          ;get data bit. is it 1 ? if yes,skip
             bcf      status,c           ;no. clear carry
             rrf      recreg,f           ;rotate carry to received character
             goto     asyrec3            ;no. go get next bit
;
asyrec5 retlw    0                       ;EXIT
;
;------------------------------------------------------------------------
;        Module: asyxmtx.txt
;        Send a character     8 bits, 1 start, 1 stop, no parity, 2400 baud
;        On entry: character to be sent is in xmtreg & xmit port must be high
;        On exit: port a1 is high (marking)
;------------------------------------------------------------------------
asyxmtx bcf      porta,1                 ;start bit
             movlw    d'3'               ;wait 1 bit time (2400 baud)
             movwf    bcount
             movlw    d'45'
             movwf    acount
             call     vdly
             movlw    08                 ;8 bit character length
             movwf    bitctr             ;to bit counter
asyxmt1 rrf      xmtreg,f                ;rotate bit out thru carry
             btfsc    status,c           ;carry = 0 ? IF YES, SKIP
             goto     asyxmt2            ;no. carry = 1. go set xmit port
             bcf      porta,xmit         ;data bit = 0. clear xmit port
             goto     asyxmt3            ;& go
asyxmt2 bsf      porta,xmit             ;data bit = 1. set xmit port
;
asyxmt3 movlw    d'3'                    ;wait 1 bit time
             movwf    bcount
             movlw    d'45'
             movwf    acount
```

RED1.ASM

```
        call    vdly
        decfsz  bitctr,f        ;all 8 bits sent ? if yes, skip
        goto    asyxmt1         ;no, go do next bit
;
        bsf     porta,xmit      ;all bits done. do stop bit (marking)
        call    vdly            ;wait 1 bit time
        retlw   0               ;EXIT
;-------------------------------------------------------------------------
;       Module vdlyx.txt
;       Delay used for bit timing
;-------------------------------------------------------------------------
;       CYCLE TIME: 1 microsec (4 MHz xtal)
;       DELAY MODULE: vdly.txt
;
;       RATE    bcount  acount  approx          For 1/2 bit
;                               delay (uS)      bcount  acount
;
;       110     13      231     9074            13      115
;       300     13      81      3324            13      41
;       600     12      44      1644            6       44
;       1200    3       89      816             3       42
;       2400    3       43      402             3       20
;       4800    2       29      184             2       13
;       9600    1       27      86              1       11
;       19200   1       9       32              1       1
;
;-------------------------------------------------------------------------
;
;       Variable time delay. Delay parameters are : acount & bcount
;
;       delay approx = (3)*(cycletime)*(acount)*(bcount)
;                    + (5)*(cycletime)*(bcount)
;
;       REQUIRES FOLLOWING WORKSPACE: acount    count parameter a
;                                     bcount    count parameter b
;                                     cntra     counter a
;                                     cntrb     counter b
;-------------------------------------------------------------------------
vdly    movf    bcount,w        ;b count to counter b
        movwf   cntrb
vdly0   movf    acount,w        ;a count to counter a
        movwf   cntra
vdly1   decfsz  cntra,f         ;dec counter a, skip if zero
        goto    vdly1           ;not zero. dec it again
        decfsz  cntrb,f         ;dec counter b, skip if zero
        goto    vdly0           ;not zero. do loop again
        retlw   0               ;exit
;-------------------------------------------------------------------------
        end                     ;end of program
;=========================================================================
```

51

5.1.2 Receive Time-outs

When the receive modules ASYREC and ASYRECX are called, they do not return until a character has been received. Some applications may have only a limited time to wait for a character before going on to some other operation. In that case the receive module must return after a period of time even though it has not received a character. A simple timed out capability can be implemented by counting the start bit test loops and returning after a specific number of loops.

Module ASYRECT.TXT (Figure 5-10) uses a three byte down counter to count the start bit test loops. The counter is initialized by the calling program. Two additional flags are included: timed flag and timed-out flag. If the timed flag is not set the routine does not perform the timed out function and does not return until a character is received. If the timed flag is set and the counter times out (counts down to zero) the timed-out flag is set, DTR is asserted and ASYRECT returns. Immediately after the counter times out, one last start bit test is performed and if a start bit is received, the timed out flag is cleared and the character is received. This last start bit test is required in the event that a start bit arrived during the time that the counter was updating. Without this final test, a received character could be lost.

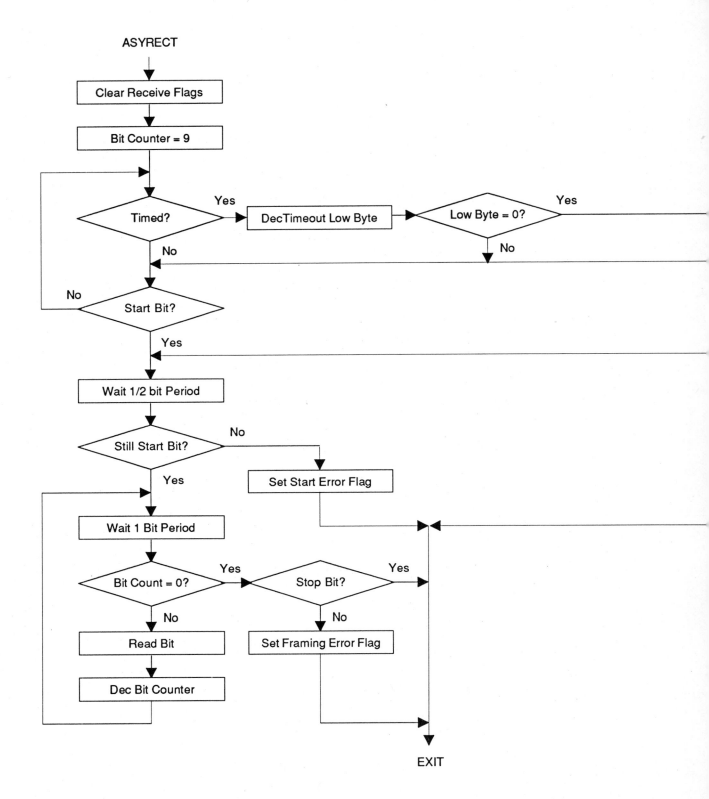

Figure 5-10   Receive With Time-out (ASYREC)

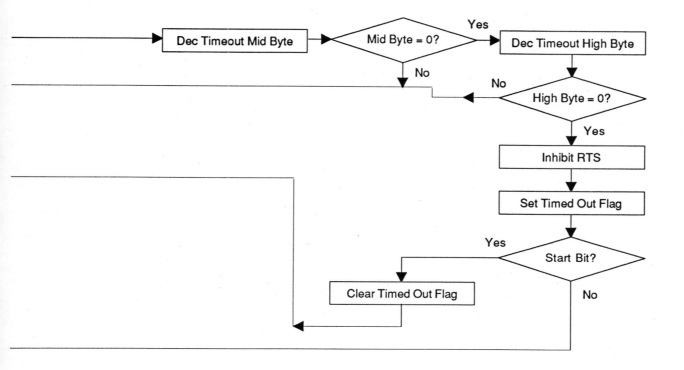

```
;====== ASYRECT.TXT ==========================================================
;
;        Module: asyrect.txt
;        Asynchronous receive with receive timeout
;
;        Receive a character   8 bits, 1 start, 1 stop, no parity
;        On exit: character received is in recreg
;
;        Exits after a character (or start error) has been received or, if
;        timed flag is set, then exits after timeout.
;
;        Start error is generated by a start bit that is less than 1/2 bit
;        time long. Framing error is generated if stop bit (marking) is not
;        ninth bit after start bit.
;
;        porta,rec is receive port
;
```

```
;            This is an extended version of module ASYREC.TXT in INDIGO1.ASM
;
;            ADDITIONAL PARAMETERS required by this version:
;
;            Timeout flags:  comflag,2 is timed out flag
;                            comflag,3 is timed flag (if set, timeout is active;
;                                      if not set then timeout test is not
;                                      performed)
;
;            Requires additional work area parameters:
;                            timcnt2   timeout counter high byte
;                            timcnt1                   mid byte
;                            timcnt                    low byte
;
;            Main program must set initial values of the timeout counter.
;            See section 5.1.2 for additional information.
;--------------------------------------------------------------------------
asyrect bcf      comflag,1          ;clear start error flag
        bcf      comflag,0          ;clear framing error flag
        bcf      comflag,2          ;clear timed out flag
        movlw    09                 ;8 data bits + stop bit
        movwf    bitctr
asyreca btfss    comflag,3          ;timed ? if yes, skip next
        goto     asyrec1            ;no. go test for start bit
        decfsz   tmcnt0,f           ;yes. dec low byte of timeout. if 0, skip
        goto     asyrec1            ;not 0. go test for start bit
        decfsz   tmcnt1,f           ;dec mid byte of timeout. if 0, skip
        goto     asyrec1            ;go
        decfsz   tmcnt2,f           ;dec high byte of timeout. if 0 , skip
        goto     asyrec1            ;go
        bsf      porta,dtr          ;timed out. inhibit DTR
;                                   ;a short delay (much less than a bit period)
;                                   ;may be inserted here to give the sending
;                                   ;terminal time to react to the DTR
        bsf      comflag,2          ;set timed out flag
;
;                                   ;In the event that a transmission was started
;                                   ;while the counter was updating, we make:
        btfsc    porta,rec          ;one last test for start bit. if start bit,
skip
        goto     asyrecx            ;no start bit. go exit
        bcf      comflag,2          ;start bit ! clear timed out flag
;
asyrec1 btfsc    porta,rec          ;start bit (rec port low)? if yes, skip
        goto     asyreca            ;no. go try again
        call     half               ;wait 1/2 bit time
        btfss    porta,rec          ;still start bit ? if no, skip next
        goto     asyrec3            ;yes. go
        bsf      comflag,1          ;no. set start error flag
        goto     asyrecx            ;& go exit
asyrec3 call     full               ;yes. wait 1 bit time
        decfsz   bitctr,f           ;update bit counter. if all bits done, skip
        goto     asyrec4            ;not all done. go read bit
        btfss    porta,rec          ;all done. stop bit present ? if yes, skip
```

```
        bsf     comflag,0       ;no. set framing error flag
        goto    asyrecx         ;& go exit
;
asyrec4 bsf     status,c        ;set carry
        btfss   porta,rec       ;get data bit. is it 1 ? if yes,skip
        bcf     status,c        ;no. clear carry
        rrf     recreg,f        ;rotate carry to received character
        goto    asyrec3         ;go wait for next bit
;
asyrecx retlw   0               ;EXIT
;===============================================================
```

5.1.3 Interrupt Driven Receive

An alternate method for avoiding the wait for a character is to make the receive function interrupt driven. With an interrupt driven receive the application program is interrupted by the start bit, passing control to the interrupt service. The interrupt service receives the character then returns control to the application program. For most applications an interrupt driven receive is the better method.

The modules in INTHALF.GRP are all that are necessary to implement bit-bang interrupt driven half-duplex receive and transmit services. The character format is: 1 start bit, 8 data bits, no parity bit and 1 stop bit. The data rate is 2400 bits per second.

The modules are:

ASYRECI   Interrupt Driven Half-Duplex Receive Service
ASYXMT   Half-Duplex Transmit Service
VDLY   Bit Timing Service

Interrupt Driven Receive (Module ASYRECI and Figure 5-11)

ASYRECI receives on the external interrupt pin, RB0/INT. RB0/INT is configured to interrupt on the high-to-low transition at the beginning of the start bit. ASRECI is an interrupt service and is the receive service module. It is similar to the receive module in HALF.GRP.

On entry, ASYRECI checks that the interrupt was external (on RB0/INT) and if not, it returns. If the main program enabled other types of interrupts, this is the point where they would be tested. Note: other interrupts must be enabled *only* when it is certain that a character will not be transmitted to the application, otherwise the character may be lost when the other interrupt function is being served. After the external interrupt is verified context is saved and RB0 is tested to verify the start bit. If the start bit is not found, then the start error flag is set and the service exits. As with previously discussed receive modules, this flag serves as an indicator of a noisy communications channel. It may be ignored by the main program or the start test may be deleted from the receive service to reduce code size. If there is no start error, the received character flag is set and the character is read as in the HALF.GRP receive service. At the beginning of the stop bit DTR is inhibited, further external interrupts are disabled (bit **INTE** of **INTCON** is cleared), a one bit period wait is implemented (to wait out the stop bit), the interrupt flag is cleared and the context is restored. The interrupt service then returns. The external interrupt is disabled so the main program can handle the received character before receiving any more characters. For the INDIGO2 application, this is only a safety measure since the inhibited DTR should prevent the terminal from transmitting any characters until DTR is re-asserted. A higher level service re-enables the interrupt and re-asserts DTR. As with the receive service in HALF.GRP, the counter values for

HALF and FULL may be changed for data rates other than 2400 bits per second and for other than 8 data bits the initialization value of the bit counter (**bitctr**) may be changed. With the above noted changes, this interrupt driven receive module may be used for the majority of half-duplex applications.

The transmit and bit timing modules ASYXMT and VDLY are identical to those in HALF.GRP. Only the receive module need be changed for interrupt driven receive applications.

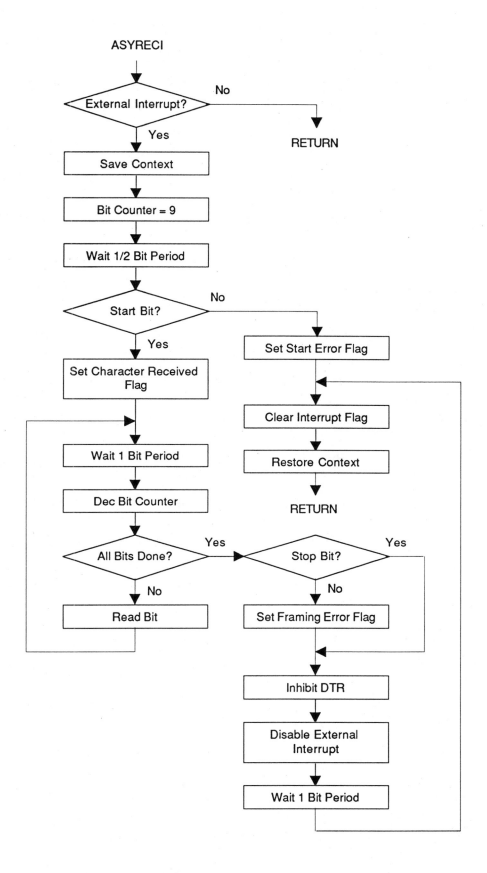

Figure 5-11   Receive Interrupt Service (ASYRECI)

```
;====== INTHALF.GRP ============================================================
;
;       Module: inthalf.grp
;       Interrupt driven asynchronous half-duplex bit-bang routines
;       14 bit PIC
;
;-------------------------------------------------------------------------------
;
;       Requires WORK AREA:
;       chartr          data character received & xmitted
;       bitctr          bit counter
;       acount          delay count a
;       bcount          delay count b
;       comflag         communications flags
;       cntra           delay counter a
;       cntrb           delay counter b
;       recreg          received data character
;       xmtreg          transmitted data character
;       tempw           temporary w
;       tempst          temporary status
;
;-------------------------------------------------------------------------------
;       Requires SYSTEM EQUATES:
;
;       tdport   equ    porta    ;port a is transmit port
;       xmit     equ    0001     ;port a1 is transmit
;       dtrport  equ    porta    ;port a is DTR port
;       dtr      equ    0002     ;port a2 is DTR
;       rdport   equ    portb    ;port b is receive port
;       rec      equ    0000     ;port b0 is receive
;-------------------------------------------------------------------------------
;       FLAG bit definitions
;
;       comflag,0       set for framing error
;       comflag,1       set for start error
;       comflag,2       character received flag
;
;       This module includes asyreci.txt, asyxmt.txt and vdly.txt
;       See INDIGO2.ASM and Section 5.1.3 for Initialization and
;       Application information
;-------------------------------------------------------------------------------
;       Module: asyreci.txt (interrupt service)
;       Interrupt Driven Receive
;
;       Character:   8 bits, 1 start, 1 stop, no parity
;
;       RB0/INT pin is receive port.(See system equates)
;       Low going edge on this pin triggers call to
;       interrupt service (this module).
;
;       Sets character received flag and exits after a character has been
;       received. Sets framing error flag if stop bit (marking) is not
;       ninth bit after start bit. Received character in recreg. On exit,
;       external interrupt is disabled.
```

```
;
;-----------------------------------------------------------------
asyreci btfss   intcon,intf     ;external interrupt ? if yes, skip next
        goto    asyrecx         ;no. go exit
        movwf   tempw           ;save context (w reg & status only):
        swapf   status,w
        bcf     status,rp0
        movwf   tempst
;
        movlw   09              ;8 data bits + stop bit
        movwf   bitctr
        call    half            ;wait 1/2 bit period
        btfss   rdport,rec      ;is it really start bit ? if no, skip next
        goto    asyrec2         ;yes. go receive character
        bsf     comflag,0       ;no. set start error flag
        goto    asyrec5         ;& go exit
;
asyrec2 bsf     comflag,2       ;set character received flag
asyrec3 call    full            ;wait 1 bit period
        decfsz  bitctr,f        ;update bit counter. if all bits done, skip
        goto    asyrec4         ;not all done. go read bit
        btfss   rdport,rec      ;all done. stop bit present ? if yes, skip
        bsf     comflag,0       ;no. set framing error flag
        bsf     dtrport,dtr     ;inhibit DTR
        bcf     intcon,inte     ;disable external interrupt
        call    full            ;wait 1 bit time
        goto    asyrec5         ;& go
;
asyrec4 bsf     status,c        ;set carry
        btfss   rdport,rec      ;get data bit. is it 1 ? if yes,skip
        bcf     status,c        ;no. clear carry
        rrf     recreg,f        ;rotate carry to received character
        goto    asyrec3         ;go wait for next bit
;
asyrec5 bcf     intcon,intf     ;clear interrupt flag
        swapf   tempst,w        ;restore context
        movwf   status
        swapf   tempw,f
        swapf   tempw,w
asyrecx retfie                  ;exit
;
;-----------------------------------------------------------------
;       Module: asyxmt.txt
;       Send a character    8 bits, 1 start, 1 stop, no parity
;       On entry: character to be sent is in xmtreg & transmit must be high
;       On exit: transmit port is high (marking)
;
;       tdport,xmit   is transmit port
;-----------------------------------------------------------------
asyxmt  bcf     tdport,xmit     ;start bit
        call    full            ;wait 1 bit time
        movlw   08              ;8 bit character length
        movwf   bitctr          ;to bit counter
asyxmt1 rrf     xmtreg,f        ;rotate bit out thru carry
```

```
        btfsc   status,c            ;carry = 0 ? IF YES, SKIP
        goto    asyxmt2             ;no. carry = 1. go set xmit port
        bcf     tdport,xmit         ;data bit = 0. clear xmit port
        goto    asyxmt3             ;& go
asyxmt2 bsf     tdport,xmit         ;data bit = 1. set xmit port
;
asyxmt3 call    full                ;wait 1 bit time
        decfsz  bitctr,f            ;all 8 bits sent ? if yes, skip
        goto    asyxmt1             ;no, go do next bit
;
        bsf     tdport,xmit         ;all bits done. do stop bit (marking)
        call    full                ;wait 1 bit time
        retlw   0                   ;EXIT
;----------------------------------------------------------------------
;       Module: vdly.txt
;       Delay used for bit timing
;----------------------------------------------------------------------
;       CYCLE TIME: 1 microsec (4 MHz xtal)
;       DELAY MODULE
;
;     RATE    BIT TIME    ---- FOR 1 BIT ----       -- FOR 1/2 BIT --
;             (uSec)    bcount   acount   delay (uS)   bcount   acount   delay
;
;     110     9090.9      13      231      9074          13      115     4550
;     300     3333.3      13       81      3324          13       41     1654
;     600     1666.7      12       44      1644           6       44      822
;     1200     833.3       3       89       816           3       42      399
;     2400     416.7       3       43       402           3       20      191
;     4800     208.8       2       29       184           2       13       87
;     9600     104.2       1       27        86           1       11       35
;    19200      52.1       1        9        32           1        1        8
;
;----------------------------------------------------------------------
;
;       Variable time delay. Delay parameters are : acount & bcount
;
;       delay approx = (3)*(cycletime)*(acount)*(bcount)
;                    + (5)*(cycletime)*(bcount)
;
;       Total time from:   call full
;                    to:   next instruction   (return location)
;
;       is approximately = delay + (12)*(cycletime)
;
;
;       REQUIRES FOLLOWING WORKSPACE: acount    count parameter a
;                                     bcount    count parameter b
;                                     cntra     counter a
;                                     cntrb     counter b
;----------------------------------------------------------------------
vdly    movf    bcount,w            ;b count to counter b
        movwf   cntrb
vdly0   movf    acount,w            ;a count to counter a
        movwf   cntra
```

```
vdly1    decfsz   cntra,f            ;dec counter a, skip if zero
         goto     vdly1              ;not zero. dec it again
         decfsz   cntrb,f            ;dec counter b, skip if zero
         goto     vdly0              ;not zero. do loop again
         retlw    0                  ;exit
;----------------------------------------------------------------------
half     movlw    d'3'               ;wait 1/2 bit time   (2400 bits per second)
         movwf    bcount
         movlw    d'20'
         movwf    acount
         call     vdly
         retlw    0
;----------------------------------------------------------------------
full     movlw    d'3'               ;wait 1 bit time (2400 bits per second)
         movwf    bcount
         movlw    d'43'
         movwf    acount
         call     vdly
         retlw    0
;======================================================================
```

INDIGO2.ASM: An Interrupt Driven Half-Duplex Bit-Bang Application
(See Figure 5-12 and INDIGO2.ASM)

INDIGO2.ASM is an example of an application using an interrupt driven receive routine. As with INDIGO1, it receives a character and echoes it back to the terminal, but unlike INDIGO1 it does not idly wait for the character to arrive. INDIGO2 executes a main application independently of any serial communications and only interrupts the main application when a character is to be received. After a character is received INDIGO2 echoes the character and returns to the main application. The echo is primarily used to test the program. A real application would certainly do more than echo the received character. Making the echo a part of the INDIGO2 main program serves to demonstrate how a received character is handled after the return from the interrupt.

The INDIGO2 main program flow is shown in Figure 5-12 and requires very little elaboration. The main point to note is that it is *only* the *application program* that is interrupted and the interrupt service returns with the external interrupt *disabled*. After having dealt with the received character the main program loops back and re-enables the external interrupt.

63

INDIGO2

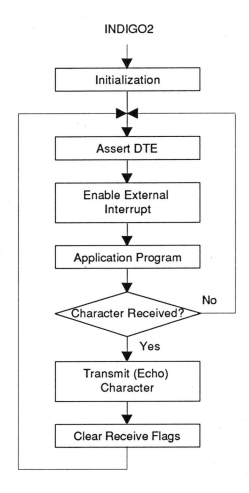

Figure 5-12   INDIGO2 Main Program

If the communications specification requires an extra stop bit (1 start, 8 data, 2 stop) this is easily handled in the main program: at the beginning of **echo** and just after the call to ASYXMT, a 1 bit period delay may be inserted. By handling the extra stop bit in the main program, the modules ASYRECI and ASYXMT may be used unchanged.

```
;====== INDIGO2.ASM ===========================================================
;
;       FILE: indigo2.asm
;
;       16F84
;       Asynchronous serial communications loop.
;       Waits for character from terminal, then
;       sends back (echoes) character received.
;       Receive is interrupt driven.
;       Uses 1 line flow control (DTR).
;       Configured as DTE
;
;------------------------------------------------------------------------------
;
```

```
;           INPUT:   RS 232
;                    2400 baud, 1 start bit, 8 data bits, 1 stop bit, no parity
;                    Port b0 is character IN (receive)
;
;           OUTPUT:  RS 232
;                    2400 baud, 1 start bit, 8 data bits, 1 stop bit
;                    Port a1 is character OUT (transmit)
;
;           CONTROL: DTR only
;                    Asserts DTR only when ready to receive from terminal,
;                    otherwise inhibits DTR.
;                    Port a2 is DTR. Port a2 high for DTR asserted (OK to send).
;                    The DTR line should go to the CTS pin on the terminal.
;-----------------------------------------------------------------------
        radix   hex         ;RADIX is HEX
;
        list p=16f84
;
c       equ     0           ;carry bit of status register (bit 0)
z       equ     2           ;zero flag bit of status register (bit 2)
w       equ     0           ;destination working
f       equ     1           ;destination file
rp0     equ     5           ;rp0 bit of status register (bit 5)
;
rbif    equ     0           ;intcon register bits:
intf    equ     1
toif    equ     2
rbie    equ     3
inte    equ     4
toie    equ     5
eeie    equ     6
gie     equ     7
;-----------------------------------------------------------------------
;     CPU EQUATES   (memory map)
;
;  BANK 0:
status  equ     03
porta   equ     05
portb   equ     06
intcon  equ     0b
;
;  BANK 1:
optreg  equ     01          ;bank 1 (0x81) option register
trisa   equ     05          ;bank 1 (0x85)
trisb   equ     06          ;bank 1 (0x86)
;
;-----------------------------------------------------------------------
;     WORK AREA   (memory map)
chartr        equ     000c          ;data character received & xmitted
bitctr        equ     000d          ;bit counter
acount        equ     000e          ;delay count a
bcount        equ     000f          ;delay count b
comflag       equ     0010          ;communications flags
cntra         equ     0011          ;delay counter a
```

65

```
cntrb          equ      0012          ;delay counter b
recreg         equ      0013          ;received data character
xmtreg         equ      0014          ;transmitted data character
tempw          equ      0015          ;temporary w
tempst         equ      0016          ;temporary status
;
;------------------------------------------------------------------------
;         SYSTEM EQUATES
;
tdport  equ      porta     ;port a is transmit port
xmit    equ      0001      ;port a1 is transmit
dtrport equ      porta     ;port a is DTR port
dtr     equ      0002      ;port a2 is DTR
rdport  equ      portb     ;port b is receive port
rec     equ      0000      ;port b0 is receive
;------------------------------------------------------------------------
;         FLAGS
;
;         comflag,0      set for framing error
;         comflag,1      set for start error
;         comflag,2      character received flag
;
;========================================================================
;         MAIN PROGRAM
;------------------------------------------------------------------------
        org      0x00          ;start of program memory
        goto     start         ;reset vector
;
;        locations 0x01 thru 0x03 are reserved for version number
;
        org      0x04          ;
        goto     asyreci       ;interrupt service vector
start   clrf     portb
        clrf     porta
        bsf      status,rp0    ;switch to bank 1
        movlw    00e9          ;a0 & a3 as inputs, a1, a2, a4 as outputs
        movwf    trisa
        movlw    0001          ;port b7-b1 as outputs, port b0 as input
        movwf    trisb
        bcf      optreg,6      ;select interrupt-on-down edge
        bcf      status,rp0    ;switch to bank 0
        bsf      dtrport,dtr   ;inhibit DTR (we are busy)
        bsf      tdport,xmit   ;marking output
        clrf     comflag       ;clear communications flags
;
mloop   bcf      dtrport,dtr   ;assert DTR
        bsf      intcon,inte   ;enable external interrupt
        bsf      intcon,gie    ;global enable interrupts
;        .....this is where the main loop application routine goes .......
;
;
        btfss    comflag,2     ;character received? if yes, skip next
        goto     mloop         ;no. go loop
;
```

```
echo      btfss    comflag,0      ;yes. framing error ? if yes, skip
          goto     echo1          ;no framing error. go
          movlw    15             ;yes. load NAK ($15)
          movwf    recreg         ;& send it back
echo1     movf     recreg,w       ;move received character to...
          movwf    xmtreg         ;transmit register
          call     asyxmt         ;echo character back
          bcf      comflag,2      ;clear received flags:
          bcf      comflag,1
          bcf      comflag,0
          goto     mloop          ;& go loop
;-------------------------------------------------------------------------
;         INCLUDES:
;         INTHALF.GRP      Interrupt driven half-duplex bit-bang services
;-------------------------------------------------------------------------
          include inthalf.grp
;
;-------------------------------------------------------------------------
          end                     ;END OF PROGRAM
;=========================================================================
```

5.1.4 Automatic Bit Rate Detection

When a serial communications session is initiated both terminals may not be operating at the same bit rate. In such cases provision must be made for one terminal to determine the rate of the other terminal and then perform subsequent communications at that rate.

A simple method for determination of the bit rate is to measure the period of the first received start bit. The start bit period will be correctly measured only if the next bit received (the least significant bit of the character code) is a logic 1. If this bit is not 1, a lower data rate will be selected and all subsequent data transfer will be erroneous . Since one-half of the character codes will have the LS (least significant) bit = 1, there is a 50 % chance that the data transfer will start correctly. If the communications protocol dictates that the first character transmitted has the LS bit set, then the correct rate will be selected. Examples of characters having the LS bit set are CR (Carriage Return), NAK, ESC, SOH and ENQ. If the initiating terminal is constrained to initially send a data byte having the LS bit = 1, then the rates will match after the first character. Of course, the first character received will be lost. The receiving terminal can then send a character as a form of handshake and acknowledgment of the initialization of communications. Other more complicated methods may be employed that will correctly determine the data rate for near-ly all character codes, but we will only examine the start bit method.

Bit Rate Detection
(See Module AUTORATE.GRP in INDIGO3.ASM and Figures 5-13 and 5-14)

AUTORATE.GRP (listed in INDIGO3.ASM) measures the start bit period in 15 microsecond increments. This 15 microsecond increment permits a one byte rate counter and the bit rate test counts to be powers of two as shown in Table 5-2. If the count is greater than 255 or less than 2, then the data rates are too low (110 bits per second or lower) or too high (greater than 19200 bits per second) respectively and the service returns with the rate error flag set. In the event of a rate error, INDIGO3 just calls the autorate service again, but another application could select a rate (such as 1200 bits per second) and send a handshake character (such as NAK) in an attempt to make the initiating terminal select the rate.

Table 5-2   Bit Rates For AUTORATE.GRP

Bit Rate	Bit Time (μsec)	15 μsec Counts	Test Count
300	3333	222	>128
600	1660	111	>64
1200	833	55	>32
2400	416	27	>16
4800	208	13	>8
9600	104	7	>4
19200	52	3	>2

Figures 5-13 and 5-14 are the flow diagrams for AUTORATE. Note that the interval counter test points determine the offset into the bit timing parameter tables. The timing parameters selected from the tables are moved to the data rate count block, FULLA through HALFB, and are used by the bit timing delay module VDLYAB.TXT. The autorate service does not exit until a full byte period for the lowest expected data rate has elapsed. AUTORATE can recognize all standard bit rates from 300 bits per second to 19200 bits per second.

If only the 7 bit ASCII codes are to be received and the character byte is 8 bits, the eighth bit will always be logic 0. The main program can test this bit and if it is not logic 0 then the incorrect bit rate has been selected (because the first character LS bit was not 1) and the autorate service can be called again. Eventually a data byte with the LS bit = 1 will be received and the correct bit rate will be selected. The alternate main loop service at the end of INDIGO3.ASM illustrates this special case.

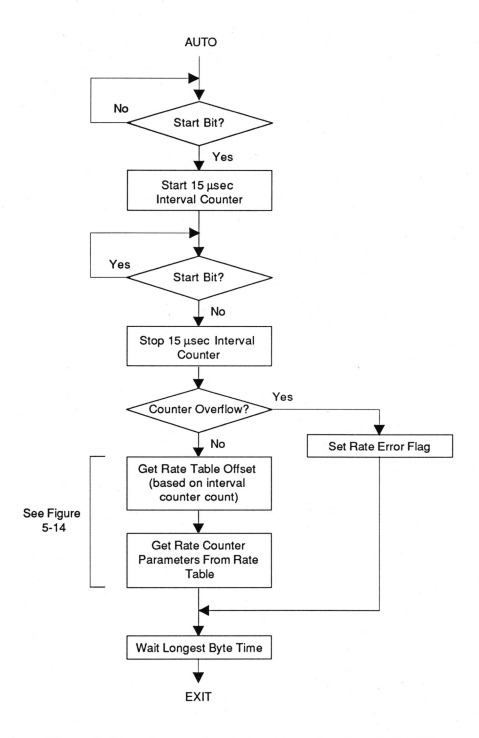

Figure 5-13   Automatic Bit Rate Detection (AUTORATE)

69

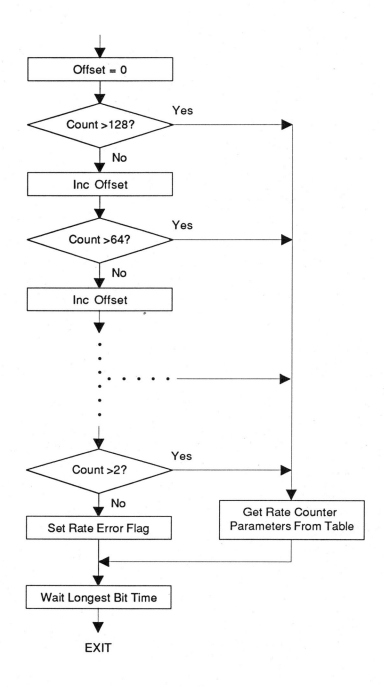

Figure 5-14   Determine Rate Counter Parameters (AUTORATE)

INDIGO3.ASM: An Automatic Bit Rate Detection Application

INDIGO3.ASM is a half-duplex demonstration of automatic bit rate detection based on the start bit period. After reset, the autorate service (module AUTORATE.GRP) waits for the first start bit of the first character received. The period of the start bit for this first character is measured, the data rate is selected based on the measured period and the autorate service exits. Then the main program transmits the character O followed by the character K at the selected rate. From this point on INDIGO3 then echoes any received characters. If the initiating terminal recognizes the OK the correct rate was selected.

```
;====== INDIGO3.ASM =========================================================
;
;       FILE: indigo3.asm
;
;       16F84
;       Asynchronous serial communications loop with automatic bit rate
;       selection. Waits for character from terminal, then sends back
;       (echoes) character received. Half-Duplex.
;
;       Automatic bit rate selection:
;
;       Bit rate is determined by measuring the length of the first
;       received start bit. The bit rate detection module (autorate)
;       accepts standard bit rates from 300 bits/sec to 19200 bits/sec.
;       For bit rates outside this range, autorate returns with the rate
;       error flag set. If the rate error flag is set, the main loop
;       again attempts to determine the rate at reception of the next
;       data byte.
;
;
;       Autorate expects the lowest significant bit of the 1st data byte
;       received to be 1. (This is the first bit following the start bit).
;       If the LS bit is not 1, then autorate selects a lower rate and all
;       subsequent data transfer will be erroneous. Since one half of the
;       127 ASCII data codes have the LS bit = 1, there is a 50 % chance that
;       data transfer will start correctly. If the first byte received is
;       always carriage return (0x0d), then the correct rate will be
;       selected.
;
;       After rate is selected, sends OK.  If the initiating terminal uses
;       the same auto rate method, the OK can be used as a handshake:
;       The initiator starts at the highest rate. If the initiator
;       correctly receives OK then the rates match; if not, then the
;       initiator selects the next lower rate. Eventually the rates will
;       match. If at all possible, the initiator should be constrained
;       to initially send a data byte having the LS bit = 1. Then the rates
;       will always match after the first data byte.
;
;       If only the 7 bit ASCII codes are to be received, the 8th bit
;       position can be tested for 0. If this bit position is not 0 then
;       the incorrect bit rate has been selected and autorate can be called
;       again. Eventually a data byte with the LS bit = 1 will be received
```

```
;              and the correct bit rate will be selected. See the ALTERNATE MAIN
;              LOOP section at the bottom of this listing.
;
;-------------------------------------------------------------------------------
;
;       INPUT:   RS 232
;                1 start bit, 8 data bits, 1 stop bit, no parity
;                Port a3 is character IN (receive)
;
;       OUTPUT:  RS 232
;                1 start bit, 8 data bits, 1 stop bit
;                Port a1 is character OUT (transmit)
;
;       CONTROL: DTR only
;                Asserts DTR only when ready to receive from terminal,
;                otherwise inhibits DTR.
;                Port a2 is DTR. Port a2 low for DTR asserted (OK to send).
;-------------------------------------------------------------------------------
         radix    hex          ;RADIX is HEX
;
         list p=16f84
;
c        equ      0            ;carry bit of status register (bit 0)
z        equ      2            ;zero flag bit of status register (bit 2)
w        equ      0            ;destination working
f        equ      1            ;destination file
rp0      equ      5            ;rp0 bit of status register (bit 5)
;
;-------------------------------------------------------------------------------
;    CPU EQUATES   (memory map)
pcl      equ      02           ;program counter
status   equ      03           ;status register
porta    equ      05
portb    equ      06
trisa    equ      05           ;bank 1 (0x85)
trisb    equ      06           ;bank 1 (0x86)
;
;-------------------------------------------------------------------------------
;    WORK AREA   (memory map)
;
bitctr   equ      000d         ;bit counter
acount   equ      000e         ;delay count a
bcount   equ      000f         ;delay count b
comflag  equ      0010         ;communications flags
cntra    equ      0012         ;delay counter a
cntrb    equ      0013         ;delay counter b
recreg   equ      0014         ;received data character
xmtreg   equ      0015         ;transmitted data character
fulla    equ      0016         ;data rate count a (full bit time)
fullb    equ      0017         ;data rate count b (full bit time)
halfa    equ      0018         ;data rate count a (half bit time)
halfb    equ      0019         ;data rate count b (half bit time)
;
```

```
;              SHARED WORK AREA:
;
counter set       acount      ;autorate time counter
delctr  set       bcount      ;autorate time delay counter
offset  set       bitctr      ;autorate table offset
;
;
;-------------------------------------------------------------------
;              SYSTEM EQUATES
;
tdport  equ       porta       ;port a1 is transmit
xmit    equ       1
rdport  equ       porta       ;port a3 is receive
rec     equ       3
dtrport equ       porta       ;port a2 is DTR
dtr     equ       2
;-------------------------------------------------------------------
;              FLAGS
;
;       comflag,0         set for framing error
;       comflag,1         set for start error
;       comflag,7         set for rate counter error
;
;
;===================================================================
;              MAIN PROGRAM
;-------------------------------------------------------------------
        org       0x00                ;start of program memory
;
start   clrf      portb
        clrf      porta
        bsf       status,rp0          ;switch to bank 1
        movlw     00e9                ;a0 & a3 as inputs, a1, a2, a4 as outputs
        movwf     trisa
        movlw     0000                ;all port b as outputs
        movwf     trisb
        bcf       status,rp0          ;switch to bank 0
        bsf       dtrport,dtr         ;inhibit DTR (we are busy)
        bsf       tdport,xmit         ;marking output
;
mloop   clrf      comflag             ;clear communications flags
mloop0  call      auto                ;wait for 1st start bit to determine rate
        btfsc     comflag,7           ;rate error ? if no, skip next
        goto      mloop0              ;yes. go try again
        clrf      comflag
        movlw     4f                  ;send 'OK'
        movwf     xmtreg
        call      asyxmt
        movlw     4b
        movwf     xmtreg
        call      asyxmt
mloop1  bcf       dtrport,dtr         ;assert DTR
        clrf      comflag             ;clear all communications flags
        call      asyrec              ;wait for received character
        bsf       dtrport,dtr         ;inhibit DTR (busy)
```

```
                btfss   comflag,0       ;framing error ? if yes, skip next
                goto    mloop2          ;no. go
                movlw   15              ;yes. load NAK (0x15)
                movwf   recreg          ;& send it
mloop2          movf    recreg,w        ;move received character to...
                movwf   xmtreg          ;transmit register
                call    asyxmt          ;echo character back
                goto    mloop1          ;& loop back for next character received
;------------------------------------------------------------------------
;       Module: asyrec.txt
;       Receive a character   8 bits, 1 start, 1 stop, no parity
;       On exit: character received is in recreg
;------------------------------------------------------------------------
asyrec  bcf     comflag,1       ;clear start error flag
        bcf     comflag,0       ;clear framing error flag
        movlw   09              ;8 data bits + stop bit
        movwf   bitctr
asyrec1 btfsc   rdport,rec      ;start bit (port a3 low)? if yes, skip
        goto    asyrec1         ;no. go try again
        call    half            ;wait 1/2 bit time
        btfss   rdport,rec      ;still start bit ? if no, skip next
        goto    asyrec3         ;yes. go
        bsf     comflag,1       ;no. set start error flag
        goto    asyrecx         ;& go exit
asyrec3 call    full            ;yes. wait 1 bit time
        decfsz  bitctr,f        ;update bit counter. if all bits done, skip
        goto    asyrec4         ;not all done. go read bit
        btfss   rdport,rec      ;all done. stop bit present ? if yes, skip
        bsf     comflag,0       ;no. set framing error flag
        goto    asyrecx         ;& go exit
;
asyrec4 bsf     status,c        ;set carry
        btfss   rdport,rec      ;get data bit. is it 1 ? if yes,skip
        bcf     status,c        ;no. clear carry
        rrf     recreg,f        ;rotate carry to received character
        goto    asyrec3         ;go wait for next bit
;
asyrecx retlw   0               ;EXIT
;
;------------------------------------------------------------------------
;       Module: asyxmt.txt
;       Send a character   8 bits, 1 start, 1 stop, no parity
;       On entry: character to be sent is in xmtreg & port a1 must be high
;       On exit: port a1 is high (marking)
;------------------------------------------------------------------------
asyxmt  bcf     tdport,xmit     ;start bit
        call    full            ;wait 1 bit time
        movlw   08              ;8 bit character length
        movwf   bitctr          ;to bit counter
asyxmt1 rrf     xmtreg,f        ;rotate bit out thru carry
        btfsc   status,c        ;carry = 0 ? IF YES, SKIP
        goto    asyxmt2         ;no. carry = 1. go set pa1
        bcf     tdport,xmit     ;data bit = 0. clear pa1
        goto    asyxmt3         ;& go
```

```
asyxmt2 bsf     tdport,xmit      ;data bit = 1. set pa1
;
asyxmt3 call    full             ;wait 1 bit time
        decfsz  bitctr,f         ;all 8 bits sent ? if yes, skip
        goto    asyxmt1          ;no, go do next bit
;
        bsf     tdport,xmit      ;all bits done. do stop bit (marking)
        call    full             ;wait 1 bit time
        retlw   0                ;EXIT
;==============================================================================
;         Module: autorate.grp
;
;         Measures bit time for first start bit received then uses
;         lookup tables to determine parameters for delay used for
;         bit timing. Lowest significant bit of data byte MUST be 1
;         (such as carriage return (0x0d)). If LS bit is not 1,
;         then will select a lower rate. Limited to 300 bits/sec to
;         19200 bits/second.
;
;         ON EXIT: DTR inhibited
;                  rate error flag set if bit time is out of range
;         14 bit PIC
;------------------------------------------------------------------------------
;     Required WORK AREA:
;
;         bitctr          bit counter
;         acount          delay count a
;         bcount          delay count b
;         comflag         communications flags
;         cntra           delay counter a
;         cntrb           delay counter b
;         recreg          received data character
;         xmtreg          transmitted data character
;         fulla           data rate count a (full bit time)
;         fullb           data rate count b (full bit time)
;         halfa           data rate count a (half bit time)
;         halfb           data rate count b (half bit time)
;
;         SHARED WORK AREA:
;
;         counter set     acount   ;autorate time counter
;         delctr  set     bcount   ;autorate time delay counter
;         offset  set     bitctr   ;autorate table offset
;
;         Required SYSTEM EQUATES:
;
;         tdport  equ     porta    ;port a1 is transmit
;         xmit    equ     1
;         rdport  equ     porta    ;port a3 is receive
;         rec     equ     3
;         dtrport equ     porta    ;port a2 is DTR
;         dtr     equ     2
;
```

```
;           FLAG DEFINITIONS
;
;       comflag,0        set for framing error
;       comflag,1        set for start error
;       comflag,7        set for rate counter error
;
;       This module includes auto.txt and vdlyab.txt
;       See INDIGO3.ASM and Section 5.1.4 for Initialization and
;       Application information
;------------------------------------------------------------------------
;       Module: auto.txt
;       Determines bit rate and sets delay counter parameters
;       If bit rate is out of range, then exits with rate error flag set
;------------------------------------------------------------------------
auto    clrf    counter         ;rate counter
        clrf    comflag         ;clear all communications flags
        bcf     dtrport,dtr     ;assert DTR
auto1   btfsc   rdport,rec      ;start bit ? if yes, skip next
        goto    auto1           ;no. go try again
;
;    start of 15 uSec loop
auto2   btfsc   rdport,rec      ;still start bit ? if yes, skip next
        goto    auto4           ;no. go
        movlw   02              ;delay parameter
        movwf   delctr
auto3   decfsz  delctr,f
        goto    auto3
        nop
        incf    counter,f       ;update counter
        btfsc   status,z        ;overflow ? if no, skip next
        goto    autoe           ;yes. go error exit
        goto    auto2           ;15 uSec completed. go
;    end of 15 uSec loop
;
auto4   decf    counter,f       ;counter adjustment
        clrf    offset          ;initialize table pointer
        btfsc   counter,7       ;counter = or greater than 128 ? if no, skip
        goto    auto5           ;yes. go
        incf    offset,f        ;no. update pointer
        btfsc   counter,6       ;counter = or greater than 64 ? if no, skip
        goto    auto5           ;yes. go
        incf    offset,f        ;no. update pointer
        btfsc   counter,5       ;counter = or greater than 32 ? if no, skip
        goto    auto5           ;yes. go
        incf    offset,f        ;no. update pointer
        btfsc   counter,4       ;counter = or greater than 16 ? if no, skip
        goto    auto5           ;yes. go
        incf    offset,f        ;no. update pointer
        btfsc   counter,3       ;counter = or greater than 8 ? if no, skip
        goto    auto5           ;yes. go
        incf    offset,f        ;no. update pointer
        btfsc   counter,2       ;counter = or greater than 4 ? if no, skip
        goto    auto5           ;yes. go
        incf    offset,f        ;no. update pointer
        btfsc   counter,1       ;counter = or greater than 2 ? if no, skip
                                ;next
```

```
              goto     auto5                  ;yes. go
autoe   bsf      comflag,7              ;set rate error flag
              goto     auto6                  ;go wait longest byte time, then exit
;
auto5   movf     offset,w               ;get pointer (offset into table)
              call     ftaba                  ;get full bit time acount
              movwf    fulla                  ;& keep it
              movf     offset,w
              call     ftabb                  ;get full bit time bcount
              movwf    fullb                  ;& keep it
              movf     offset,w
              call     htaba                  ;get half bit time acount
              movwf    halfa                  ;& keep it
              movf     offset,w
              call     htabb                  ;get half bit time bcount
              movwf    halfb                  ;& keep it
;
auto6   bsf      dtrport,dtr            ;inhibit DTR (busy)
              movlw    d'115'                 ;wait longest byte time (approx 40 mSec)
              movwf    acount                 ;
              movwf    bcount
              call     vdly
;
autox   retlw    0                      ;exit
;
;------------------------------------------------------------------------
;       DELAY LOOK UP TABLES
;
;       full bit time acount table:
ftaba   addwf    pcl,f                  ;offset to program counter
              retlw    d'81'                  ;300 bits/sec
              retlw    d'44'                  ;600 bits/sec
              retlw    d'89'                  ;1200 bits/sec
              retlw    d'43'                  ;2400 bits/sec
              retlw    d'29'                  ;4800 bits/sec
              retlw    d'27'                  ;9600 bits/sec
              retlw    d'9'                   ;19200 bits/sec
;
;       full bit time bcount table:
ftabb   addwf    pcl,f
              retlw    d'13'
              retlw    d'12'
              retlw    d'3'
              retlw    d'3'
              retlw    d'2'
              retlw    d'1'
              retlw    d'1'
;
;       half bit time acount table
htaba   addwf    pcl,f
              retlw    d'41'
              retlw    d'44'
              retlw    d'42'
```

```
                retlw   d'20'
                retlw   d'13'
                retlw   d'11'
                retlw   d'1'
;
;       half bit time bcount table
htabb   addwf   pcl,f
                retlw   d'13'
                retlw   d'6'
                retlw   d'3'
                retlw   d'3'
                retlw   d'2'
                retlw   d'1'
                retlw   d'1'
;
;-----------------------------------------------------------------------
;       Module: vdlyab    (for automatic bit rate detect only)
;       Delay used for bit timing
;       This is a part of autorate.grp.  To be called by autorate ONLY
;-----------------------------------------------------------------------
;       CYCLE TIME: 1 microsec (4 MHz xtal)
;       Delay Module: vdly
;
```

RATE	BIT TIME (uSec)	— FOR 1 BIT —			— FOR 1/2 BIT —		
		bcount	acount	delay (uS)	bcount	acount	delay
110	9090.9	13	231	9074	13	115	4550
300	3333.3	13	81	3324	13	41	1664
600	1666.7	12	44	1644	6	44	822
1200	833.3	3	89	816	3	42	399
2400	416.7	3	43	402	3	20	191
4800	208.8	2	29	184	2	13	87
9600	104.2	1	27	86	1	11	35
19200	52.1	1	9	32	1	1	8

```
;-----------------------------------------------------------------------
;
;       Variable time delay. Delay parameters are : acount & bcount
;
;       delay approx = (3)*(cycletime)*(acount)*(bcount)
;                       + (5)*(cycletime)*(bcount)
;
;       Total time from:   call full
;                    to:    next instruction    (return location)
;
;       is approximately = delay + (12)*(cycletime)
;
;
;       REQUIRES FOLLOWING WORKSPACE: acount    count parameter a
;                                     bcount    count parameter b
;                                     cntra     counter a
;                                     cntrb     counter b
;-----------------------------------------------------------------------
```

```
vdly    movf    bcount,w        ;b count to counter b
        movwf   cntrb
vdly0   movf    acount,w        ;a count to counter a
        movwf   cntra
vdly1   decfsz  cntra,f         ;dec counter a, skip if zero
        goto    vdly1           ;not zero. dec it again
        decfsz  cntrb,f         ;dec counter b, skip if zero
        goto    vdly0           ;not zero. do loop again
        retlw   0               ;exit
;---------------------------------------------------------------
half    movfw   halfb           ;wait 1/2 bit time
        movwf   bcount
        movfw   halfa
        movwf   acount
        call    vdly
        retlw   0
;---------------------------------------------------------------
full    movfw   fullb           ;wait 1 bit time
        movwf   bcount
        movfw   fulla
        movwf   acount
        call    vdly
        retlw   0
;---------------------------------------------------------------
        end                     ;END OF PROGRAM
;
;===============================================================
;
;       ALTERNATE MAIN LOOP
;
;       Seven bit ASCII data codes with 8 bit data byte
;
;       Autorate expects the lowest significant bit of the 1st data byte
;       received to be 1. (This is the first bit following the start bit).
;       If the LS bit is not 1, then autorate selects a lower rate and all
;       subsequent data transfer will be erroneous. Since one half of the
;       127 ASCII data codes have the LS bit = 1, there is a 50 % chance that
;       data transfer will start correctly. If the first byte received is
;       always carriage return (0x0d), then the correct rate will be
;       selected.
;
;       If only the 7 bit ASCII codes are to be received, the 8th bit
;       position can be tested for 0. If this bit position is not 0 then
;       the incorrect bit rate has been selected and autorate can be called
;       again. Eventually a data byte with the LS bit = 1 will be received
;       and the correct bit rate will be selected. After the correct rate is
;       selected, the 8th bit position will always be 0 unless a transmission
;       error causes it to be 1. In that case, autorate is called again.
;       all data bytes received while attempting to determine the bit rate
;       are lost.
;
;---------------------------------------------------------------
```

```
;mloop   clrf    comflag              ;clear communications flags
;mloop0  call    auto                 ;wait for 1st start bit to determine rate
;        btfsc   comflag,7            ;rate error ? if no, skip next
;        goto    mloop0               ;yes. go try again
;        clrf    comflag
;        movlw   4f                   ;send 'OK'
;        movwf   xmtreg
;        call    asyxmt
;        movlw   4b
;        movwf   xmtreg
;        call    asyxmt
;mloop1  bcf     dtrport,dtr          ;assert DTR
;        clrf    comflag              ;clear all communications flags
;        call    asyrec               ;wait for received character
;        bsf     dtrport,dtr          ;inhibit DTR (busy)
;        btfss   comflag,0            ;framing error ? if yes, skip next
;        goto    mloop2               ;no. go
;        movlw   15                   ;yes. load NAK (0x15)
;        movwf   recreg               ;& send it
;
;        beginning of changes to main loop for 7 bit ASCII test:
;mloop2  btfsc   recreg,7             ;MS bit set ? if no, skip next
;        goto    mloop                ;yes. go try auto rate again
;        end of changes
;
;        movf    recreg,w             ;no. move received character to...
;        movwf   xmtreg               ;transmit register
;        call    asyxmt               ;echo character back
;        goto    mloop1               ;& loop back for next character received
;===============================================================================
```

5.1.5 Using the Section 5.1 Routines in Your Applications

Generally all of the routines can be used in your applications as written or with minor changes. For all routines, the entry and exit conditions, variables, port definitions and flag definitions are described in the individual xx.ASM, xx.GRP and xx.TXT listings. With the exception of the receive line for the interrupt driven receive, all port assignments are arbitrary and may be changed to suit your application.

The sample applications demonstrate how the routines are applied. With the exception of RED1, the sample applications use the PIC16F84 but the routines may be used with other PICmicros with little or no change.

All of the xx.TXT and xx.GRP modules may be used as include files.

The routines introduced in sections 5.1.1, 5.1.2 and 5.1.3 are:

HALF.GRP   Bit-Bang Half-Duplex Receive and Transmit Routines
REDHALF.GRP   12 bit PICmicro Bit-Bang Half-Duplex Routines
ASYRECT.TXT   Receive a Character (with time-out)
ASYRECI.TXT   Interrupt Driven Receive

If the number of bits per character is to be changed, the number loaded into the bit counter (**bitctr**) must be changed within the receive and transmit routines. If more than 1 stop bit is to be used, the call to FULL at the end of the transmit routines must also be repeated an appropriate number of times.

If a different bit rate is to be used, the value loaded into the delay counter (**bcount** and **acount**) must be changed as shown in the table in the selectable time delay routine.

If a cycle time other than 1 microsecond is to be used, the acount and bcount values in the table in the selectable time delay routine (VDLY.TXT or VDLYX.TXT) must be recalculated. Note that the delays generated by the subroutine VDLY are less than a full bit time (or half bit time) because the time used to read the data bit, call the delay routines, load the counters and return from the delay must be included in the total bit time. Be sure to take this into account when calculating the values.

The routines introduced in section 5.1.4 are in:

AUTORATE.GRP   Automatic Bit Rate Detection

The selectable time delay subroutine VDLYAB (including HALF and FULL) is a part of the module AUTORATE.GRP and is to be called only by AUTORATE. The subroutine VDLYAB differs from VDLY because AUTORATE rather than the programmer selects the baud rate delay counter parameters. All of the transmit and receive routines from sections 5.1.1, 5.1.2, and 5.1.3, with the exception of those in RED1.ASM, may be used with AUTORATE because the bit times are implemented with calls to HALF and FULL. Be sure to use the AUTORATE version of HALF and FULL.

If a cycle time other than 1 microsecond is to be used, the values in the VDLYAB delay lookup table must be recalculated. Note that the delays generated by the subroutine VDLY are less than a full bit time (or half bit time) because the time used to read the data bit, call the delay routines, load the counters and return from the delay must be included in the total bit time. Be sure to take this into account when calculating the values.

5.2 Bit-Bang Full-Duplex

Full-duplex communication is characterized by simultaneous receive and transmit, but a full-duplex bit-bang application must be divided into separate receive and transmit tasks because the PICmicro cannot execute more than one instruction at a time. Since the basic time interval for asynchronous communications is the bit time, simultaneous receive and transmit may be simulated by dividing each bit time into several discrete time slots and executing each receive and transmit task in separate time slots. All communications timing is determined by software loop times. The modules in TASKFULL.GRP (Section 5.2.1) implement this time-slot-task method of bit-bang full duplex communication. The applications INDIGO4 (Section 5.2.1) and INDIGO5 (Section 5.2.2) demonstrate the application of the task modules.

Simultaneous receive and transmit may also be simulated with interrupt driven receive and transmit services. All communication takes place within the interrupt service and timing is determined by a hardware timer. This interrupt driven bit-bang full-duplex method is covered in Section 5.3.

5.2.1 Full-Duplex Receive and Transmit Tasks

The module TASKFULL.GRP includes the receive and transmit tasks. Each *user task* is unique to an application and thus is not included in TASKFULL. The application INDIGO4 demonstrates a simple user task to be used with the transmit and receive tasks in TASKFULL.

INDIGO4 receives a character from the terminal and echoes it (sends it back) to the terminal. When the terminal sequentially sends characters they are sequentially returned and the system is operating full-duplex. The character format for INDIGO4 is 8 data bits, no parity bit, and 1 stop bit. The data rate is 2400 bits per second for a crystal frequency of 4.0 MHz.

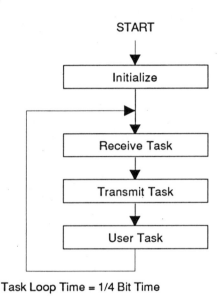

Figure 5-15   INDIGO4 Task Loop

The program is divided into 3 tasks: receive task and transmit task (in TASKFULL) and the user task USER. These tasks are each executed in turn in a loop. The loop executes in exactly one-fourth of a bit time (an iso-synchronous loop), dividing the bit time into 4 discrete time slots. Any application using the TASKFULL tasks must loop in this manner. See Figures 5-15 and 5-16. For INDIGO4 the user task does little more than transfer the character received by the receive task to the transmit task for transmission back to the terminal. No flow control is used. This simple user task serves only to demonstrate the minimum procedures required to successfully apply the receive and transmit tasks found in the module TASKFULL.GRP. This module may be used in any bit-bang full-duplex application with an appropriate user task. In Section 5.2.2, a full-duplex application having a more complex user task (INDIGO5) and including in-band flow control is demonstrated.

82

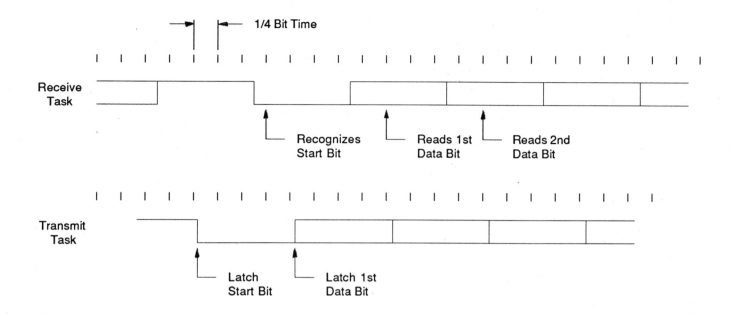

Figure 5-16   Task Loop Data Timing

The task loop must execute in exactly one-fourth of a bit time. This constant time task loop is said to be iso-synchronous. At 2400 bits per second the bit time is 416.66 microseconds, thus the task loop time is 104.17 microseconds. For an instruction cycle time of 1 microsecond (4.0 MHz crystal) the task loop must execute in 104 instruction cycles. For the following discussion, execution times are in terms of instruction cycles. The receive and transmit tasks have fixed execution times of 22 and 20 cycles respectively, forcing the user task to be 62 cycles at 2400 bits per second with a crystal frequency of 4.0 MHz. Table 5-3 tabulates the required user task cycles for several bit rates and crystal frequencies. Bit times are determined by counting task loops. One bit time is 4 task loops, starting with the loop within which the bit started. Four counters are used for bit timing. The receive loop counter counts the four task loops making up the receive bit time and the receive bit counter counts the bits making up the received character byte. These counters are controlled only by the receive task. The transmit loop counter and transmit bit counter have analogous functions for the transmit character byte. They are controlled only by the transmit task. A communications flags register (**comflg**) is used to indicate receive and transmit task status (Table 5-4).

Table 5-3   User Cycles For FULLDUP.TXT

Crystal (MHz)	Bit Rate	Cycles Per Task Loop	User Task Cycles
4	2400	104	62
4	4800	52	10
4	9600	26	4
8	2400	208	164
8	4800	104	62
8	9600	52	10
12	9600	78	36
16	9600	104	62
20	9600	130	88

Table5-4   FULLDUP.TXT Flags (comflg)

BIT	FLAG	FUNCTION
	Receive Flags:	
0	RECEIVING (recflg)	SET at reception of start bit CLEARED at reception of stop bit
1	LAST BIT (lbflg)	SET at reception of last data bit CLEARED at reception of stop bit
2	FRAMING ERROR (feflg)	SET if no stop bit at bit 10 time CLEARED by user
3	NEW DATA RECEIVED (ndrflg)	SET at reception of stop bit CLEARED by user
4	RECEIVE OVERRUN (roflg)	SET at last data bit if new-data-received flag is not clear CLEARED by user
	Transmit Flags:	
5	TRANSMITTING (xmtflg)	SET at beginning of start bit CLEARED at end of stop bit
6	TRANSMIT DATA READY (xdrflg)	SET by user when new data in xmit register CLEARED at beginning of start bit
7	TRANSMIT COMPLETED (xcflg)	SET at end of stop bit CLEARED by user

For any application using TASKFULL, the user task must check for new data received (by testing the new-data-received flag) and if a new character has been received, must move it from the user received data register. This makes the user received data register available for the next character to be received. If the user does not do this within 9 bit times, the next received character may overwrite the current character. Similarly the user must not attempt to move a character to be transmitted to the transmit register until the transmit task has signaled the completion of transmission via the transmit-complete flag. All flags are available to the user, but the user must *only* clear the framing-error, new-data-received, receive-overrun and transmit-completed flags and *only* set the transmit-data-ready flag. All other flags are the property of the receive and transmit tasks. After any branch in the user task program a delay must be inserted before exiting the user task. These delays are required to make the total number of instruction cycles through the user equal to that required by Table 5-3. The last instruction in the user must be: **goto frec**. This last instruction passes control to the receive task. Any user task program *must* conform to the above requirements.

The INDIGO4 user task (Figure 5-17) tests for new data received. If no new data is received it waits until the required cycle times have been completed then passes control to the receive task with the **goto frec** instruction. If new data has been received, the received character is moved from the user received data register to the user transmit data register and the new-data-received flag is cleared to indicate to the user in subsequent loop passes that the new character has been fetched. If the transmitter is not busy (indicated by the xmit-completed-flag being set), the xmit-data-ready flag is set, indicating to the transmit task that new data is available to transmit, and control is passed to the receive task after waiting the necessary number of cycles. If the transmitter is busy, INDIGO4 passes control to the receive task after waiting the necessary number of cycles. During a subsequent task loop, the transmitter will no longer be busy and the character will then be transmitted. Note that after each branch a delay is inserted before the final **goto** instruction. These are instruction cycle fillers to make the user task execute exactly 62 instruction cycles regardless of which branch is selected.

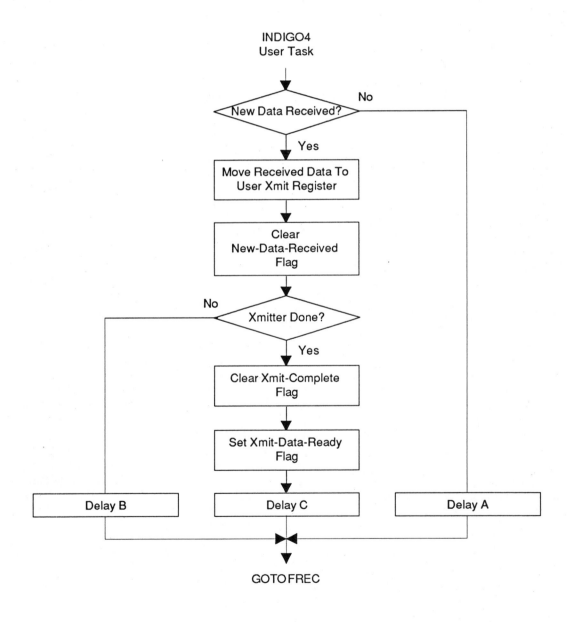

Figure 5-17   INDIGO4 User Task

The receive task (FREC.TSK in TASKFULL.GRP) receives an incoming data byte and signals to the user that a byte has been received and is available to the user. The receiver executes exactly 22 instruction cycles regardless of which branches are executed within the task. After detecting a start bit condition the task waits for 5 one-quarter-bit-time slots before reading the first data bit. All subsequent data bits are read at 4 time slot increments after the first bit. This one time slot shift into the data bit serves to move the bit read away from the bit transition point. FREC recognizes and flags two errors: If the tenth bit (stop bit) is not marking (logic 1) then the framing-error flag is set. If the new-data-received flag is not clear when the ninth bit (last data bit) is read, the receive-overrun flag is set. Both of these flags must be cleared by the user task. The FREC flow diagram (Figure 5-18) details the receive task implementation.

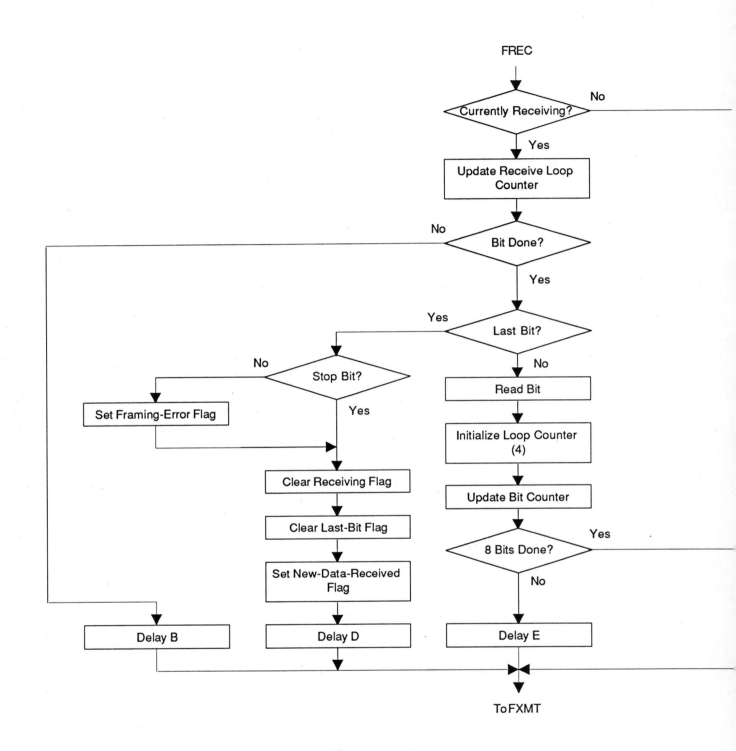

Figure 5-18   Receive Task (FREC)

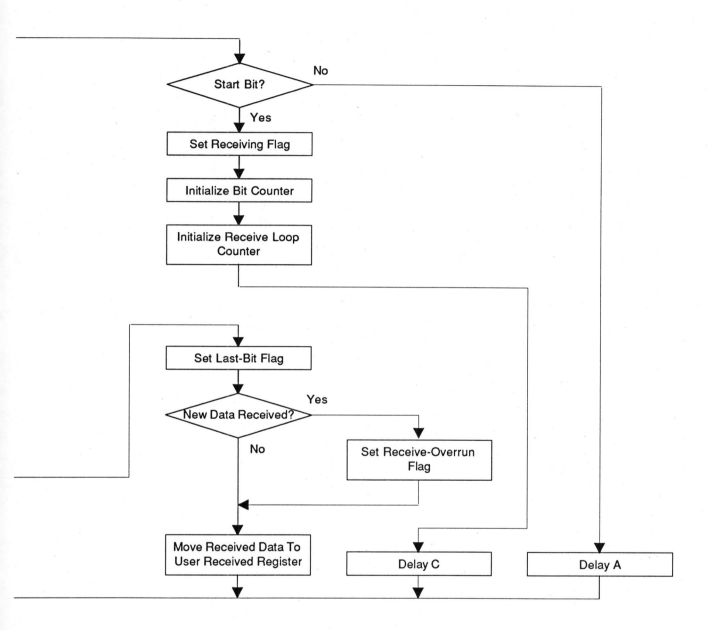

89

The transmit task (FXMT.TSK in TASKFULL.GRP) transmits a data byte and signals to the user when the transmission has been completed. The transmitter executes exactly 20 instruction cycles. FXMT recognizes no errors. The FXMT flow diagram (Figure 5-19) details the transmit task implementation.

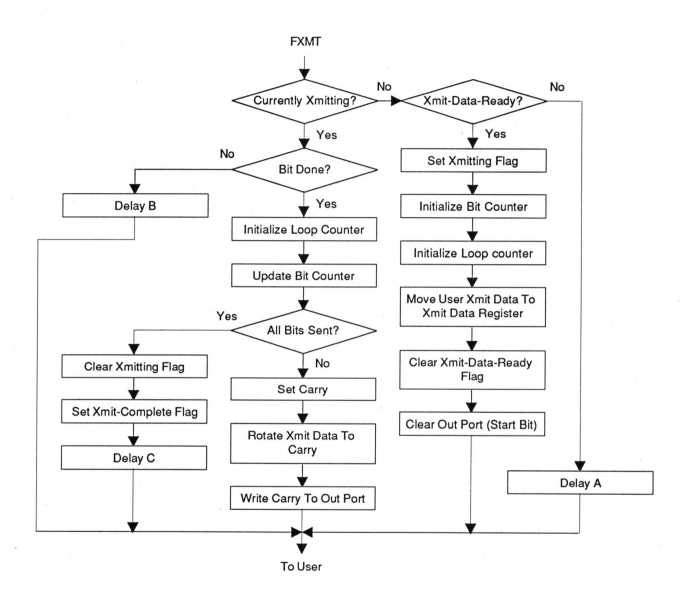

Figure 5-19   Transmit Task (FXMT)

```
;====== TASKFULL.GRP =========================================================
;
;         TASK BASED FULL-DUPLEX BIT-BANG MODULE
;         File: TASKFULL.TXT
;         14 Bit PIC
;         This module includes two of the three required tasks: receive
;         task and transmit task. The Application must include the User task.
;
;         See INDIGO4.ASM, INDIGO5.ASM and Sections 5.2 through 5.2.3 for
;         User Requirements and Constraints and Initialization and
;         Application information.
;
;-----------------------------------------------------------------------------
;
;     Required  WORK AREA:
;
;     Communications variables:
;         comflg          communications flags
;         dlyctr          delay counter
;         recreg          receive register
;         recuse          receive user register
;         rloop           receive loop counter
;         rbit            receive bit counter
;         xmtreg          transmit register
;         xmtuse          transmit user register
;         xloop           transmit loop counter
;         xbit            transmit bit counter
;
;     User variables:
;         useflg          user flags
;
;-----------------------------------------------------------------------------
;         Required SYSTEM EQUATES:
;
;         Communications Flags Bits (comflg):
;         recflg   equ     00      ;receiving flag
;         lbflg    equ     01      ;last-bit flag
;         feflg    equ     02      ;framing-error flag
;         ndrflg   equ     03      ;new-data-received flag
;         roflg    equ     04      ;receive-overrun flag
;         xmtflg   equ     05      ;xmitting flag
;         xdrflg   equ     06      ;xmit-data-ready flag
;         xcflg    equ     07      ;xmit-completed flag
;
;         Port Functions:
;         outport equ     porta    ;xmit is port a1
;         outpin  equ     01
;         inport  equ     porta    ;receive is port a3
;         inpin   equ     03
;
;         This module includes  frec.tsk, fxmt.tsk and dloop.txt
;
;-----------------------------------------------------------------------------
;         RECEIVE TASK
```

91

```
;            File: FREC.TSK
;            Uses total of 22 cycles
;
;            ON EXIT: IF new-data-received flag is set, THEN received byte is in
;                     recuse.
;------------------------------------------------------------------
rdeld   set     rdele               ;delay entrance rdeld same as entrance rdele
;
frec    btfss   comflg,recflg       ;receiving ? if yes, skip next
        goto    frec2               ;no. go
        decfsz  rloop,f             ;yes. update loop counter. if bit
                                     completed, skip
        goto    rdelb               ;bit not completed. go delay
        btfsc   comflg,lbflg        ;last bit flag set? if no, skip next
        goto    frec3               ;yes. go
        bsf     status,c            ;no. read bit  (set carry)
        btfss   inport,inpin        ;is b3 = 1 ? if yes, skip
        bcf     status,c            ;no. clear carry
        rrf     recreg,f            ;rotate carry to received byte
        movlw   04                  ;initialize loop counter
        movwf   rloop
        decfsz  rbit,f              ;update rbit counter.skip if all 8 bits done
        goto    rdele               ;all 8 not done. go delay
        btfss   comflg,ndrflg       ;new-data-received flag clear ? if yes, skip
        bsf     comflg,roflg        ;no. set receive-overrun flag
        bsf     comflg,lbflg        ;set last-bit flag
        movf    recreg,w            ;move received byte to user received register
        movwf   recuse
        goto    rdelf               ;& go delay
;
frec2   btfsc   inport,inpin        ;start bit ? if yes, skip next
        goto    rdela               ;no. go delay
        bsf     comflg,recflg       ;yes. set receiving flag
        movlw   08                  ;initialize receive bit counter
        movwf   rbit
        movlw   05                  ;initialize receive loop counter
        movwf   rloop
        goto    rdelc               ;& go delay
;
frec3   btfsc   inport,inpin        ;stop bit ? if no, skip next
        goto    frec4               ;yes. go
        bsf     comflg,feflg        ;no. set framing-error flag
frec4   bcf     comflg,recflg       ;clear receiving flag
        bcf     comflg,lbflg        ;clear last-bit flag
        bsf     comflg,ndrflg       ;set new-data-received flag
        goto    rdeld               ;& go delay
;
rdelb   nop                         ;delay 17 cycle entrance
rdela   goto    rda1                ;delay 16 cycles entrance
rda1    goto    rda2                ;delay 14 cycles entrance
rda2    goto    rdelc
rdelc   nop                         ;delay 10 cycles entrance
        goto    rdele
rdele   goto    rda3                ;delay 7 cycles entrance
```

```
rda3      goto     rda4
rda4      goto     rdelf
;
rdelf     nop                          ;delay 1 cycle entrance & END of receive
;
;-----------------------------------------------------------------------
;         TRANSMIT TASK
;         File: FXMT.TSK
;         Uses total of 20 cycles
;
;         Data byte to be transmitted is in xmituse
;-----------------------------------------------------------------------
;
fxmt      btfss    comflg,xmtflg       ;transmitting ? If yes, skip next
          goto     fxmt2               ;no. go
          decfsz   xloop,f             ;yes. update loop counter. If bit completed,
skip
          goto     xdlyb               ;bit not completed. go delay, then exit
          movlw    04                  ;timed out. initialize loop counter
          movwf    xloop
          decfsz   xbit,f              ;update bit counter. skip if done
          goto     fxmt4               ;all bits not sent. go send next bit
          bcf      comflg,xmtflg       ;all bits sent. clear transmiting flag
          bsf      comflg,xcflg        ;set xmit-complete flag
          goto     xdlyc               ;go delay, then exit
;
fxmt2     btfss    comflg,xdrflg       ;xmit data ready ? if yes, skip next
          goto     xdlya               ;not ready. go delay
          bsf      comflg,xmtflg       ;data ready. set xmiting flag
          movlw    0a                  ;initialize bit counter (10)
          movwf    xbit
          movlw    04                  ;initialize loop counter
          movwf    xloop
          movf     xmtuse,w            ;move user data to xmit register
          movwf    xmtreg
          bcf      comflg,xdrflg       ;clear xmit-data-ready flag
          goto     fxd1                ;cycle equalizer
fxd1      bcf      outport,outpin      ;start bit
          goto     fxmt8               ;& go  exit
;
;
fxmt4     bsf      status,c            ;set carry
          rrf      xmtreg,f            ;move data bit to carry
;
;         This is data bit write to output port:
fxmt5     btfsc    status,c            ;carry (data bit) = 0 ? if yes, skip next
          goto     fxmt6               ;no. data bit =1. go set port a1
          bcf      outport,outpin      ;yes. data bit = 0. clear port a1
          goto     fxmt7               ;& go
fxmt6     bsf      outport,outpin      ;set port a1
          nop                          ;cycle equalizer
fxmt7     goto     fxmt8               ;go end of transmit
;
xdlyb     nop
```

93

```
xdlya     goto     fxd2
fxd2      goto     fxd3
fxd3      goto     xdlyc
xdlyc     goto     fxd4
fxd4      goto     fxd5
fxd5      goto     fxmt8
;
fxmt8     nop                           ;transmit EXIT
;
;-----------------------------------------------------------------------
;         delay loop subroutine    dloop.txt
;
;         When used with following routine,
;         generates delay (in cycles) = 3n + 5
;
;                  movlw    n
;                  movwf    dlyctr
;                  call     dloop
;
;-----------------------------------------------------------------------
dloop     decfsz   dlyctr,f
          goto     dloop
          retlw    0
;=======================================================================




;====== INDIGO4.ASM =====================================================
;
;         FILE: indigo4.asm
;
;         16F84
;         Full-duplex bit-bang asynchronous communications.
;         Waits for character from terminal then sends back (echoes)
;         character. No flow control. Uses task loop having 3 tasks:
;         Receive Task, Transmit Task and User Task.
;
;-----------------------------------------------------------------------
          radix    hex          ;RADIX is HEX
;
          list p=16f84
;
;         STATUS REGISTER BIT DEFINITIONS:
c         equ      0            ;carry bit of status register (bit 0)
z         equ      2            ;zero flag bit of status register (bit 2)
dc        equ      1            ;digit carry
pd        equ      3            ;power down bit
to        equ      4            ;time out bit
rp0       equ      5            ;program page preselect, low bit
rp1       equ      6            ;program page preselect, high bit
;
```

```
;        DESTINATION BIT DEFINITIONS:
w        equ     0          ;destination working
f        equ     1          ;destination file
;
;----------------------------------------------------------------------
;      CPU EQUATES   (special function register memory map)
indf     equ     00         ;indirect file register
tmr0     equ     01         ;timer
pcl      equ     02         ;program counter (low byte)
status   equ     03         ;status register
fsr      equ     04         ;indirect data pointer
porta    equ     05         ;port a
portb    equ     06         ;port b
eedata   equ     08         ;eeprom data
eeadr    equ     09         ;eeprom address
pclath   equ     0a         ;write buffer for program counter (high byte)
intcon   equ     0b         ;interrupt control register
;
;  BANK 1:
optreg   equ     01         ;option register                 bank 1 (0x81)
trisa    equ     05         ;data direction register port a  bank 1 (0x85)
trisb    equ     06         ;data direction register port b  bank 1 (0x86)
eecon1   equ     08         ;eeprom control register         bank 1 (0x88)
;
;----------------------------------------------------------------------
;      WORK AREA   (memory map)
;
;    Communications variables:
comflg   equ     000c          ;communications flags
dlyctr   equ     000d          ;delay counter
recreg   equ     000e          ;receive register
recuse   equ     000f          ;receive user register
rloop    equ     0010          ;receive loop counter
rbit     equ     0011          ;receive bit counter
xmtreg   equ     0012          ;transmit register
xmtuse   equ     0013          ;transmit user register
xloop    equ     0014          ;transmit loop counter
xbit     equ     0015          ;transmit bit counter
;
;    User variables:
useflg   equ     0016          ;user flags
;
;----------------------------------------------------------------------
;         SYSTEM EQUATES
;
;       Communications Flags Bits (comflg):
recflg   equ     00         ;receiving flag
lbflg    equ     01         ;last-bit flag
feflg    equ     02         ;framing-error flag
ndrflg   equ     03         ;new-data-received flag
roflg    equ     04         ;receive-overrun flag
xmtflg   equ     05         ;xmitting flag
xdrflg   equ     06         ;xmit-data-ready flag
xcflg    equ     07         ;xmit-completed flag
```

```
;
;         Port Functions:
outport  equ      porta     ;xmit is port a1
outpin   equ      01
inport   equ      porta     ;receive is port a3
inpin    equ      03
;-------------------------------------------------------------------
         org      0x00               ;start of program memory
;
start    clrf     porta
         bsf      outport,outpin     ;output marking
         clrf     portb
         bsf      status,rp0         ;switch to bank 1
         movlw    00e9               ;a0 & a3 as inputs. a1, a2, a4 as outputs
         movwf    trisa
         bcf      status,rp0         ;switch back to bank 0
         clrf     comflg             ;clear comms flags
         bsf      comflg,xcflg       ;set xmit-completed flag (MUST DO !)
         goto     frec               ;go start with receive task
;-------------------------------------------------------------------
;        INCLUDES:
;        TASKFULL.GRP    Task Based bit-bang full-duplex services
;-------------------------------------------------------------------
         include taskfull.grp
;
;===================================================================
;        USER TASK (For INDIGO4.ASM)
;        Echoes back received byte
;        2400 baud (4 MHz xtal)
;
;        This module MUST use 62 cycles
;-------------------------------------------------------------------
echo     btfss    comflg,ndrflg      ;new data recived ? if yes, skip next
         goto     udlya              ;no. go delay & exit
         movf     recuse,w           ;yes. get received data
         movwf    xmtuse             ;& move it to user xmit
         bcf      comflg,ndrflg      ;clear new-data-received flag
         btfss    comflg,xcflg       ;xmit completed ? if yes, skip next
         goto     udlyb              ;no. go delay & exit
         bcf      comflg,xcflg       ;clear xmit-completed flag
         bsf      comflg,xdrflg      ;set xmit-data-ready flag
         goto     udlyc              ;go delay & exit
;
udlya    goto     udlyb              ;59 cycle delay entrance
         goto     uda1
uda1     nop
udlyb    nop                         ;54 cycle delay entrance
         goto     udlyc
udlyc    movlw    d'14'              ;51 cycle delay entrance
         movwf    dlyctr
         call     dloop
         goto     uda3
uda3     goto     frec               ;LAST LINE OF USER
;-------------------------------------------------------------------
         end                         ;end of program
;===================================================================
```

5.2.2 Full-Duplex Receive and Transmit Tasks with In-Band Flow Control

INDIGO5.ASM (Figure 5-20) demonstrates a full duplex application with in-band flow control implemented with the full-duplex module TASKFULL.GRP. It receives characters from a terminal, places the characters in a buffer, and when the buffer is full signals the terminal to stop sending characters. The characters are then written to a two line by 20 character LCD display, emptying the buffer. The terminal is then signaled to resume sending characters. Figure 5-1 is the schematic of the circuit for this application.

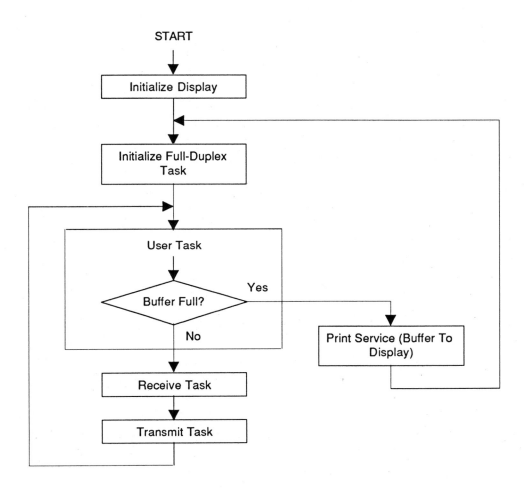

Figure 5-20   INDIGO5

A common in-band flow control protocol is known as XON/XOFF. Within this protocol special meanings are assigned to two control characters: DC3 and DC1. The control character DC3 functions as XOFF and DC1 functions as XON. The receiver sends the XOFF character when it wants the sender to pause in sending data and sends the XON character when it wants the sender to resume sending. Most PC terminal programs recognize the XON/XOFF protocol. DC3 and DC1 may be sent from the keyboard as CONTROL-S and CONTROL-Q respectively.

The character buffer in INDIGO5 is 16 bytes deep. When the buffer is nearly full (14 bytes) INDIGO5 sends XOFF, waits until the buffer is full or until 2 character byte periods have elapsed then exits the USER task and prints the buffer contents to the display. XOFF is sent 2 bytes prior to buffer full to prevent the loss of any characters sent before the terminal can respond to the XOFF. If the buffer contains character data but is not nearly full and if no characters are received for approximately 25 character byte periods, INDIGO5 sends XOFF and prints the buffer contents. After printing the buffer contents, INDIGO5 re-initializes the full-duplex interface, enters the USER task and sends XON, requesting the terminal to resume sending.

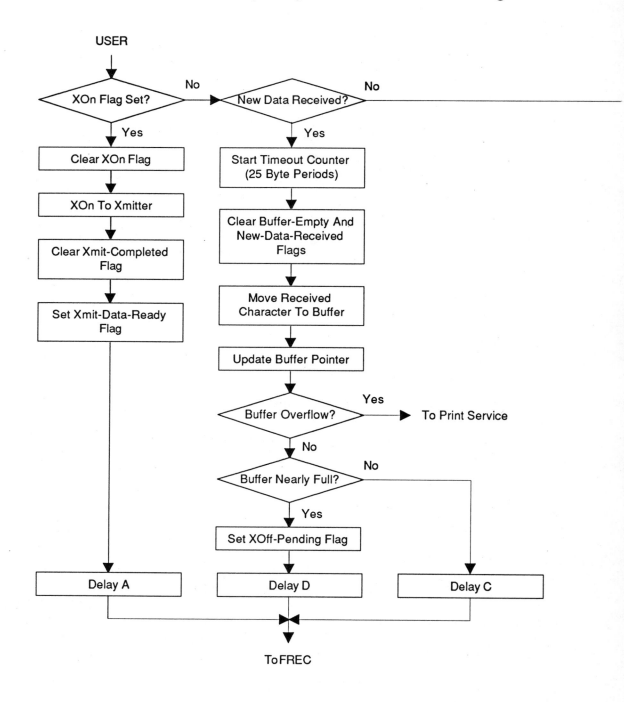

Figure 5-21   INDIGO5 User Task

Figures 5-20 through 5-23 detail the implementation of INDIGO5.

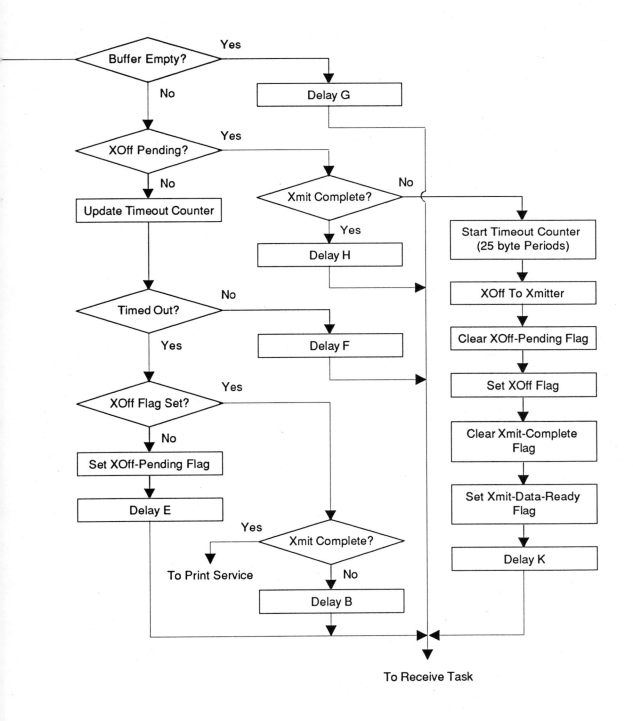

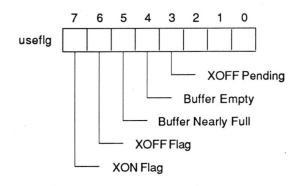

Figure 5-22   User Flags, (INDIGO5)

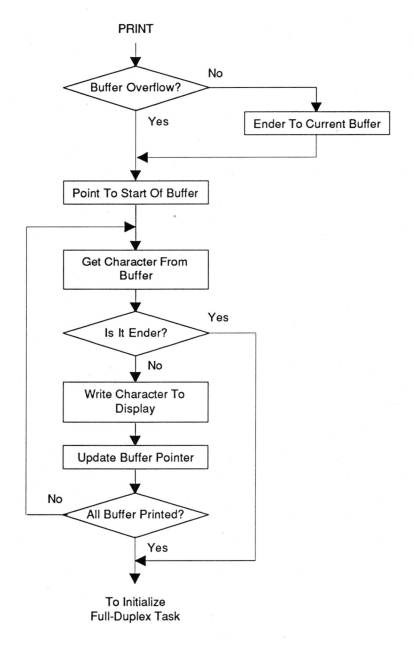

Figure 5-23   PRINT - INDIGO5

```
;====== INDIGO5.ASM ========================================================
;
;          FILE: indigo5.asm
;
;          Bit-Bang Full Duplex Asynchronous Communications
;
;          Receives a block of data from a terminal, then writes the block
;          to 2 line by 20 character LCD display.
;
;          Demonstrates use of In-Band handshake (XON/XOFF).
;
;          2400 baud, 1 start bit, 8 data bits, 1 stop bit (4 MHz XTAL)
;
;--------------------------------------------------------------------------
           radix    hex          ;RADIX is HEX
;
           list p=16f84
;
;          STATUS REGISTER BIT DEFINITIONS:
c          equ      0            ;carry bit of status register (bit 0)
z          equ      2            ;zero flag bit of status register (bit 2)
dc         equ      1            ;digit carry
pd         equ      3            ;power down bit
to         equ      4            ;time out bit
rp0        equ      5            ;program page preselect, low bit
rp1        equ      6            ;program page preselect, high bit
;
;          DESTINATION BIT DEFINITIONS:
w          equ      0            ;destination working
f          equ      1            ;destination file
;
;--------------------------------------------------------------------------
;     CPU EQUATES   (special function register memory map)
indf       equ      00           ;indirect file register
tmr0       equ      01           ;timer
pcl        equ      02           ;program counter (low byte)
status     equ      03           ;status register
fsr        equ      04           ;indirect data pointer
porta      equ      05           ;port a
portb      equ      06           ;port b
eedata     equ      08           ;eeprom data
eeadr      equ      09           ;eeprom address
pclath     equ      0a           ;write buffer for program counter (high byte)
intcon     equ      0b           ;interrupt control register
;
;  BANK 1:
optreg     equ      01           ;option register                  bank 1 (0x81)
trisa      equ      05           ;data direction register port a   bank 1 (0x85)
trisb      equ      06           ;data direction register port b   bank 1 (0x86)
eecon1     equ      08           ;eeprom control register          bank 1 (0x88)
;
;--------------------------------------------------------------------------
;     WORK AREA   (memory map)  Starts at 000c
;
```

```
;       Communications variables:
comflg  equ     000c                    ;communications flags
dlyctr  equ     000d                    ;delay counter
recreg  equ     000e                    ;receive register
recuse  equ     000f                    ;receive user register
rloop   equ     0010                    ;receive loop counter
rbit    equ     0011                    ;receive bit counter
xmtreg  equ     0012                    ;transmit register
xmtuse  equ     0013                    ;transmit user register
xloop   equ     0014                    ;transmit loop counter
xbit    equ     0015                    ;transmit bit counter
;
;       User variables:
useflg  equ     0016                    ;user flags
timout  equ     0017                    ;timeout counter
;
;       Display Variables:
dispflg equ     0018                    ;display flags
dispdat equ     0019                    ;display data
dispstat equ    001a                    ;display status
temp    equ     001b                    ;temporary storage
acount  equ     001c                    ;delay count a
bcount  equ     001d                    ;delay countb
cntra   equ     001e                    ;delay counter a
cntrb   equ     001f                    ;delay counter b
;------------------------------------------------------------------------
;       SYSTEM EQUATES
;
;       Communications Flags Bits (comflg):
recflg  equ     00      ;receiving flag
lbflg   equ     01      ;last-bit flag
feflg   equ     02      ;framing-error flag
ndrflg  equ     03      ;new-data-received flag
roflg   equ     04      ;receive-overrun flag
xmtflg  equ     05      ;xmitting flag
xdrflg  equ     06      ;xmit-data-ready flag
xcflg   equ     07      ;xmit-completed flag
;
;       User Flags Bits (useflg):
uxpnd   equ     03      ;xoff pending flag
ubfe    equ     04      ;buffer empty flag
ubnf    equ     05      ;buffer nearly full flag
uxoff   equ     06      ;XOFF flag
uxon    equ     07      ;XON flag
;
;       Port Functions
outport equ     porta   ;output port a1
outpin  equ     01      ;
inport  equ     porta   ;input port a3
inpin   equ     03
;
;       Buffer:
buffer  equ     0020    ;buffer starts at register 0x20
;       Display:
```

```
dispen  equ     01      ;(PB1)
disprs  equ     02      ;(PB2)
disprw  equ     03      ;(PB3)
;-----------------------------------------------------------------
        org     0x00            ;start of program memory
;
start   goto    start0          ;start (jumps over version & int vector)
        dw      0072            ;version code
        dw      006c
        dw      0073
        dw      0000            ;reserved for hardware interrupt vector
start0  clrf    portb
        clrf    porta
        bsf     outport,outpin  ;output marking
        clrf    portb
        bsf     status,rp0      ;switch to bank 1
        movlw   00e9            ;a0 & a3 as inputs. a1, a2, a4 as outputs
        movwf   trisa
        movlw   0000            ;all port b outputs
        movwf   trisb

        bcf     status,rp0      ;switch to bank 0
        call    initdis         ;initialize display
;
initcom movlw   buffer          ;clear buffer
        movwf   fsr
        clrf    useflg          ;clear user flags
        bsf     useflg,4        ;set buffer empty flag
        clrf    comflg          ;clear comms flags
        bsf     comflg,7        ;set xmit-completed flag (MUST DO !)
;
;       Start communications by sendimg XON
        bsf     useflg,7        ;set XON flag
        goto    user            ;go to user
;
;-----------------------------------------------------------------
;       INCLUDES:
;       TASKFULL.GRP    Task based bit-bang full-duplex services
;       DISSRV.GRP      Two Line by 20 Character LCD display services
;-----------------------------------------------------------------
        include taskfull.grp
        include dissrv.grp
;
;-----------------------------------------------------------------
;       USER MODULE   (For INDIGO5.ASM)
;
;-----------------------------------------------------------------
;
;       Places received data byte in buffer. When  buffer is nearly
;       full (14 bytes), sends XOFF. After sending XOFF, waits until buffer
;       is full (16 bytes) OR until two byte times have elapsed then exits
;       full-duplex-loop and goes to print service to write buffer data to
;       display.
;
```

```
;           If buffer contains data, but no new data is received in a period of
;           approximately 25 byte times, then also sends XOFF and goes to
;           print service.   fsr is buffer pointer.
;
;           If XON flag is set at entry, then sends XON then waits for received
;           data. If XON flag not set, then waits for received data.
;
;           On entry from initcom, buffer pointer (fsr) contains start address
;           of buffer, XON flag is set and buffer-empty flag is set. All other
;           user flags are cleared.
;
;           This user module MUST use 62 cycles
;-------------------------------------------------------------------------------
usdlyG  set     usdlyA          ;delay G same as delay A
usdlyE  set     usdlyC          ;delay E same as delay C
;
user    btfss   useflg,uxon     ;XON flag set ? if yes, skip next
        goto    userb           ;no.go
        bcf     useflg,uxon     ;yes. clear XON flag
        movlw   011             ;XON (control-Q)
        movwf   xmtuse          ;to xmitter
        bcf     comflg,xcflg    ;clear xmit-completed flag
        bsf     comflg,xdrflg   ;set xmit-data-ready flag
        goto    usdlyA          ;& go delay, then loop
;
userb   btfss   comflg,ndrflg   ;new-data-received ? if yes, skip next
        goto    userc           ;no. go
        clrf    timout          ;yes. start timeout counter
        bcf     useflg,ubfe     ;clear buffer-empty-flag
        bcf     comflg,ndrflg   ;clear new-data-received flag
        movf    recuse,w        ;get received data
        movwf   indf            ;& move to new buffer location
        incf    fsr,f           ;update buffer pointer
        btfsc   fsr,4           ;buffer overflow ? if no, skip next
        goto    print           ;yes. exit user & go display buffer contents
        movlw   buffer + 0e     ;no. buffer nearly full ?
        subwf   fsr,w           ;pointer - (buffer + 14)
        btfsc   status,c        ;if yes, skip next
        goto    usdlyC          ;no. go delay, then loop
        bsf     useflg,uxpnd    ;yes. set XOFF-pending flag
        goto    usdlyD          ;& go delay, then loop
;
userc   btfsc   useflg,ubfe     ;buffer empty ? if no, skip next
        goto    usdlyG          ;yes. go delay
        btfsc   useflg,uxpnd    ;XOFF pending ? if no, skip next
        goto    userd           ;yes, go
        decfsz  timout,1        ;no update timeout counter. if timed out,
skip
        goto    usdlyF          ;not timed out. go delay, then loop
        btfss   useflg,uxoff    ;timed out. XOFF flag set ? if yes, skip next
        goto    userc1          ;no, go
        btfss   comflg,xcflg    ;yes. xmit completed ? if yes,skip next
        goto    usdlyB          ;no. go delay, then loop
        goto    print           ;yes. exit user & go display buffer contents
```

```
;
userc1  bsf     useflg,uxpnd     ;set XOFF-pending
        goto    usdlyE           ;& go delay, then loop
;
;
userd   btfss   comflg,xcflg     ;yes. xmitter done ? if yes, skip next
        goto    usdlyH           ;no. go delay, then loop
        movlw   055              ;start timeout counter (approx 2 byte times)
        movwf   timout
        movlw   013              ;XOFF (control S)
        movwf   xmtuse           ;to xmitter
        bcf     useflg,uxpnd     ;clear XOFF-pending flag
        bsf     useflg,uxoff     ;set XOFF flag
        bcf     comflg,xcflg     ;clear xmit-completed-flag
        bsf     comflg,xdrflg    ;set xmit-data-ready flag
        goto    usdlyk           ;go delay, then loop
;
;
usdlyA  nop                      ;53 cycle delay entrance
        nop
        nop
        nop
usdlyF  nop                      ;49 cycle delay entrance
usdlyH  nop                      ;48 cycle delay entrance
        nop
        nop
usdlyB  nop                      ;45 cycle delay entrance
usdlyC  nop                      ;44 cycle delay entrance
        nop
usdlyD  nop                      ;42 cycle delay entrance
usdlyk  nop                      ;41 cycle delay entrance
        movlw   d'11'            ;40 cycle delay entrance
        movwf   dlyctr
        call    dloop
        goto    frec             ;LAST LINE OF USER
;
;-------------------------------------------------------------------------
;       print
;
;       Write buffer to display
;
;       16 bit buffer beginning at register 0020
;       Current buffer pointer in fsr
;
;-------------------------------------------------------------------------
print   btfsc   fsr,4            ;buffer overflow ? if no, skip next
        goto    print1           ;yes. go
        movlw   0ff              ;no. place ender in current buffer location
        movwf   indf
print1  movlw   buffer           ;point to start of buffer
        movwf   fsr
print2  movf    indf,w           ;get data from buffer
        movwf   dispdat          ;& move to display data register
        movlw   0ff              ;is data ender ?
```

```
        subwf   dispdat,w
        btfsc   status,c         ;if no, skip next
        goto    printx           ;yes. go
        call    dissrv           ;no. display it
        incf    fsr,f            ;point to next buffer location
        btfss   fsr,4            ;overflow ? if yes, skip next
        goto    print2           ;no. go do next buffer data
printx  goto    initcom          ;go re-start communications
;
        end                      ;end of program
;===============================================================================


;====== DISSRV.GRP =============================================================
;
;       Write to 2 line by 20 character LCD display (Optrex DMC20261)
;
;-------------------------------------------------------------------------------
;
;       PORT B interfaces with display:
;       PB7-PB4:  data
;       PB3    :  read/not write  (disprw)
;       PB2    :  character/not instruction (disprs)
;       PB1    :  enable  (dispen)
;
;       DISPLAY VARIABLES: (work area)
;        dispflg         display flags
;        dispdat         display data
;        dispstat        display status (current address & busy flag)
;        temp            temporary storage
;        acount          for delay counter
;        bcount
;        cntra
;        cntrb
;
;       DISPLAY FLAGS: (dispflg)
;        Bit 0: Current line (0=line 1, 1=line 2)
;        Bit 1: reserved for displays with more than 2 lines
;        Bit 2: Char/not instruction (0=instruction,1=character)
;        Bit 3: Read/not write (0=write, 1=read)
;        Bit 6: Nibble flag (0=high nibble, 1=low nibble)
;
;       DISPLAY STATUS: (dispstat)
;        Bit 0 - Bit 6: Current address (cursor location)
;        Bit 7:         Busy flag
;
;       REQUIRED DISPLAY EQUATES:
;        dispen  equ     01              (PB1)
;        disprs  equ     02              (PB2)
;        disprw  equ     03              (PB3)
;
;-------------------------------------------------------------------------------
;       Display Service
;
```

```
;           Write Character code to display
;
;           ON ENTRY: 1. Display MUST be ready for new data
;                     2. Character code in dispdat
;
;           On EXIT:  1. Current address (cursor location) in dispstat
;                     2. Display is ready for new data
;-----------------------------------------------------------------------
dissrv   movlw    20                  ;char code greater than or equal 20 ?
         subwf    dispdat,w
         btfsc    status,c            ;if no skip next
         goto     dissrv4             ;yes. go display character
         movlw    1b                  ;char code for ESC (x1b) ?
         subwf    dispdat,w
         btfsc    status,z            ;if no, skip next
         goto     dissrv3             ;yes. go reset display
         movlw    0d                  ;no. char code for CR (x0d) ?
         subwf    dispdat,w
         btfsc    status,z            ;if no, skip next
         goto     dissrv2             ;yes. go do carriage return
         movlw    0a                  ;no. char code for LF (x0a) ?
         subwf    dispdat,w
         btfsc    status,z            ;if no, skip next
         goto     dissrv1             ;yes. go do line feed
         goto     dissrvx             ;no. go exit (ignore char code)
dissrv1  movf     dispstat,w          ;LINE FEED:
         movwf    dispdat             ;current address to display data
         bcf      dispdat,6           ;assume moving to line 1
         btfss    dispstat,6          ;current line = line 2 ? if yes skip next
         bsf      dispdat,6           ;no. bad assumption. moving to line 2
         bsf      dispdat,7           ;DD Ram address (bit7 = 1)
         goto     dissrv5             ;write instruction to display
dissrv2  movlw    02                  ;CARRIAGE RETURN: assume current line 1
         btfsc    dispstat,6          ;current line 1 ? if yes, skip next
         movlw    0c0                 ;current not line 1. must be line 2
         movwf    dispdat
         goto     dissrv5             ;write instruction to display
dissrv3  call     initdis             ;CLEAR DISPLAY: initialize display
         goto     dissrvx             ;& go exit
dissrv4  bsf      dispflg,2           ;set character flag
dissrv5  call     sendis              ;write data to display
dissrvx  retlw    0                   ;return
;-----------------------------------------------------------------------
;        Initialize display
;
;        Required to initialize display at start up.
;        Clears display and moves cursor to start of line 1.
;
;        initdis is entry point for FULL software initialization
;        initalt is entry point for optional POWER ON HARDWARE initialization
;
;-----------------------------------------------------------------------
initdis  movlw    30
         movwf    dispdat             ;required by display for initialization
```

107

```
          call     senint
          call     senint
          call     senint
;
;         At this point INSTRUCTIONS are to be sent to the display. initalt is
;         an alternate entry point that may be used if display is initialized
;         by POWER ON internal reset circuit
;
initalt   movlw    20             ;selects 4 bit operation
          movwf    dispdat
          call     senint
;
;         From this point on the display is operating in 4 bit mode & the
;         BUSY flag test is functional. senint is no longer required & all
;         writes to the display are made by calling sendis.
;
          clrf     dispflg        ;clear display flags
          movlw    28             ;Function Set: 4 bits (DL=0), 2 lines (N=1),
          movwf    dispdat        ;5x7 dot font (F=0)
          call     sendis
          movlw    08             ;display off
          movwf    dispdat
          call     sendis
          movlw    01             ;clear display, cursor home
          movwf    dispdat
          call     sendis
          movlw    06             ;Entry mode: Increment (ID=1),
          movwf    dispdat        ;no display shift (S=0)
          call     sendis
          movlw    0e             ;display on, cursor on, cursor not blinking
          movwf    dispdat
          call     sendis
          retlw    0              ;init complete. return
;-------------------------------------------------------------------------
senint    movf     dispdat,w
          movwf    portb
          bsf      portb,dispen   ;clock it to display
          nop
          bcf      portb,dispen
          movlw    d'13'          ;approx 9 mSec delay
          movwf    bcount
          movlw    d'231'
          movwf    acount
          call     vdly
senint3   retlw    0              ;return
;-------------------------------------------------------------------------
;         Write a character or instruction to display.
;         NOTE: 4 bit interface ONLY. Eight bit word sent as two 4 bit
;               nibbles (PB7-PB4), high nibble first
;
;         ON ENTRY: 1. Character or instruction data in dispdat
;                   2. Display enable (PB1) MUST be low
;                   3. Read/not write flag cleared
;                   4. If character write, then char/not instruction flag set
```

```
;                              If instruction write, then char/not instruction flag
;                              clear
;                      5. Display MUST be ready to receive (not busy)
;
;          ON EXIT:    1. Display enable low
;                      2. All display flags except current line flag are cleared
;                      3. Display ready to receive new character or instruction
;-----------------------------------------------------------------------------
sendis   movlw   0f0           ;high nibble mask (low nibble = 0000)
         andwf   dispdat,w     ;data nibble to data high nibble
         movwf   portb         ;write it to port b
         btfsc   dispflg,2     ;char flag set ? if no, skip next
;                                (write inst)
         bsf     portb,disprs  ;yes. set disprs bit of port b (write
;                                character)
         bsf     portb,dispen  ;take clock high
         nop                   ;clock time waster
         bcf     portb,dispen  ;take clock low (xfers data to display)
         btfsc   dispflg,6     ;both nibbles done ? if no skip next
         goto    sendis1       ;yes. go
         bsf     dispflg,6     ;no set low nibble  flag
         rlf     dispdat,f     ;move data low nibble to bits 7 thru 4
         rlf     dispdat,f
         rlf     dispdat,f
         rlf     dispdat,f
         goto    sendis        ;& go send it
;
sendis1 call     busy          ;wait until display not busy
         movlw   03            ;clear display flags (except current line
flags)
         andwf   dispflg,f
         retlw   0             ;exit
;-----------------------------------------------------------------------------
;         Test for busy & get current address
;
;         Gets busy flag (bit 7 of display status) & current address
;         (bit 6 thru bit 0 of display status)
;         Remains in routine UNTIL display NO LONGER busy.
;
;         ON ENTRY: 1. dispen MUST be low
;
;         ON EXIT:  1. dispen is low
;                   2. disprs is low
;                   3. disprw is low
;                   4. Display status (current address & busy flag) is in
;                      dispstat
;
;         Returns ONLY when display is NOT busy.
;
;-----------------------------------------------------------------------------
busy     bcf     portb,disprs            ;configure for display status read
         bsf     portb,disprw
busy1    clrf    dispstat                ;clear display status
         movlw   0f0                     ;pb7-pb4 as inputs
```

```
        bsf     status,rp0              ;switch to bank 1
        movwf   trisb
        bcf     status,rp0              ;switch to bank 0
        bsf     portb,dispen           ;clock-in high nibble
        movlw   0f0                    ;nibble mask
        andwf   portb,w                ;read nibble
        movwf   dispstat               ;& move to display status
        bcf     portb,dispen           ;un-clock
        nop                            ;time waster
        bsf     portb,dispen           ;clock-in low nibble
        movlw   0f0                    ;nibble mask
        andwf   portb,w                ;read nibble
        movwf   temp                   ;keep it for now
        bcf     portb,dispen           ;un-clock
        rrf     temp,f                 ;low nibble to low bits
        rrf     temp,f                 ;of display status
        rrf     temp,f
        rrf     temp,f
        movlw   0f                     ;mask for low nibble
        andwf   temp,f                 ;clear high nibble
        movf    temp,w                 ;low nibble to display status
        iorwf   dispstat,f
        btfsc   dispstat,7             ;busy ? if no, skip next
        goto    busy1                  ;yes. go try again
        bcf     portb,disprw           ;no. re-config for write
        clrw                           ;all port b outputs
        bsf     status,rp0             ;switch to bank1
        movwf   trisb                  ;data direction register
;                                       (for all out)
        bcf     status,rp0             ;switch to bank0
        retlw   0                      ;and exit
;------------------------------------------------------------------------
;       Module: vdly.txt
;
;       Variable time delay. Delay parameters are : acount & bcount
;
;       delay approx = (3)*(cycletime)*(acount)*(bcount)
;                    + (5)*(cycletime)*(bcount)
;
;       REQUIRES FOLLOWING WORKSPACE: acount    count parameter a
;                                     bcount    count parameter b
;                                     cntra     counter a
;                                     cntrb     counter b
;------------------------------------------------------------------------
vdly    movf    bcount,w               ;b count to counter b
        movwf   cntrb
vdly0   movf    acount,w               ;a count to counter a
        movwf   cntra
vdly1   decfsz  cntra,f                ;dec counter a, skip if zero
        goto    vdly1                  ;not zero. dec it again
        decfsz  cntrb,f                ;dec counter b, skip if zero
        goto    vdly0                  ;not zero. do loop again
        retlw   0                      ;exit
;========================================================================
```

5.2.3 Using the Section 5.2 Routines in Your Applications

Generally all of the routines can be used in your applications as written or with minor changes. For all routines, the entry and exit conditions, variables, port definitions and flag definitions are described in the individual xx.ASM, xx.TXT and xx.GRP listings. All port assignments are arbitrary and may be changed to suit your application.

The sample applications demonstrate how the routines are applied. They use the PIC16F84 but the routines may be used with other PICmicros with little or no change. All of the xx.GRP and xx.TXT modules may be used as include files.

The routines introduced in sections 5.2.1 and 5.2.2 are:

TASKFULL.GRP   Full Duplex Receive and Transmit Tasks
DISSRV.GRP   Write to Two Line LCD Display

The TASKFULL.GRP module contains three sub modules: FREC.TSK, the receive task; FXMT.TSK, the transmit task; and DLOOP, a delay loop subroutine. The FREC and FXMT tasks *do not* call the DLOOP subroutine but the user task may call it. An application using TASKFULL must have at least three tasks: FREC.TSK, FXMT.TSK and a user task. The user task deals with the received characters and the characters to be transmitted. The tasks *cannot* be called. The user task *must* follow the transmit task and *must* loop back to the receive task. These three tasks form the task loop that executes in a fixed time (Figure 5-15). The total task loop time must be as shown in Table 5-3. The FREC and FXMT tasks use a total of 42 cycles. In any application, the user task *must be made* to execute in the number of cycles as shown in Table 5-3. Note that an increase in the bit rate or a decrease in clock (crystal) rate results in fewer available cycles for the user task.

An application may enter the task loop at the beginning of any task. Prior to initial entry to the task loop, the output *must* be marking (**outport** pin **outpin** set) and the transmit- completed flag *must* be set. See section 5.2.1 for a detailed description of FREC and FXMT. FULLDUP is configured for 8 data bits and one stop bit. If an application requires other than 8 data bits, the receive bit counter (**rbit**) initialization in FREC must be changed to the new number of data bits (change the third line below **frec2** in FREC.TSK). The transmit bit counter (**xbit**) initialization in FXMT must also be changed (change the third line below **fxmt2** in FXMT.TSK). The transmit bit counter must be initialized as the number of bits plus 2. The INDIGO4 sample application has no flow control. If flow control is to be used, it must be placed in the user task and the application should *not* stop the flow until a full character is completely received. Likewise, a transmitted character should *not* be stopped until it is completed. Any exit from the task loop generally should not take place until the currently received character and the currently transmitted character have been completed. Any return to the task loop *must* be preceded by an initialization as discussed above. See section 5.2.2 for an example of an application using flow control and exit from and re-entry to the task loop.

Because all tasks must be iso-synchronous, the tasks FREC and FXMT have time fillers at the end. These fillers ensure that the task will consume a fixed number of cycles regardless of any branching within the task. A user task will also require these time fillers. The time fillers may be constructed with the subroutine DLOOP or **nop** instructions. Two cycle fillers may be made with **goto** instructions of the form:

```
            goto   there      ;two cycle filler
    there   xxxx              ;next instruction
```

111

If your assembler recognizes the operand $ as meaning current program counter value (MPASM does), the two cycle delays may be made more readable with the form:

```
goto  $+1
```

Then the last few lines of FREC.TSK will be:

```
rdelb nop                       ;entrance to 17 cycle filler
rdela goto  $+1                 ;entrance to 16 cycle filler
      goto  $+1
      goto  $+1
rdelc nop                       ;entrance to 10 cycle filler
      goto  $+1
rdele goto  $+1                 ;entrance to 7 cycle filler
      goto  $+1
      goto  $+1
rdelf nop                       ;entrance to 1 cycle filler and end
                                ;of receive task
```

which is easier to read. Be careful when using `goto $+1` because `goto $` is an infinite loop with no possible escape!

INDIGO5.ASM is a sample application illustrating in band flow control and exit from and re-entry to the task loop. See section 5.2.2 for a detailed description of INDIGO5. Note that the user task exits the task loop when the buffer is full. After the buffer has been printed to the display, re-entry to the task loop is via **initcom**. Among other things, **initcom** performs the communications task initialization as discussed above. All of the above discussion regarding the use of the FREC and FXMT tasks applies also to INDIGO5. The LCD display service DISSRV.GRP may be used unchanged (with the possible exception of changes to the port assignments) with any application.

5.3 Interrupt Driven Bit-Bang Full-Duplex

The iso-synchronous task oriented bit-bang full-duplex communications described in Section 5.2 place several constraints on the user program including cycle counting, task sequencing, task looping and careful attention to task loop entrance and exit timing. The interrupt driven method described in this section eliminates all of these constraints and makes the application interface look very much like that of a hardware (UART) interface.

Both external and timer interrupts are employed. TMR0 overflow interrupts are used to delineate transmit bit times. Each overflow period of the timer (256 timer ticks) corresponds to one bit time and at each overflow the serial output line is updated with the next character bit. The external interrupt (RB0/INT) is the serial receive line. Transitions on this serial receive line are detected by the external interrupt and the arrival time of the transitions (time stamps) are determined by the timer. The time stamps are used in building the received character.

The module INTFULL.GRP includes all of the routines necessary for full-duplex communications with 8 data bits, one stop bit and no parity bit. INTFULL.GRP is the interrupt service. To send a character, the application simply writes a character byte to a transmit register. INTFULL then takes care of sending the character. When a character has been received, INTFULL notifies the application and the application reads the character from a receive register. Other than occasional interrupts, the character transmission and reception is transparent to the application. All flow control is the responsibility of the application.

112

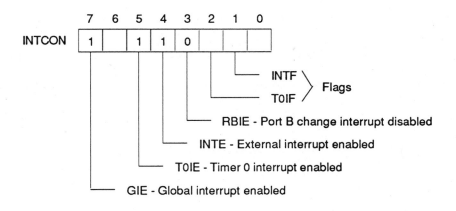

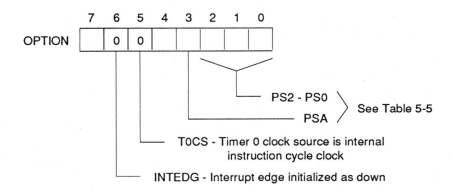

Figure 5-24   Special Registers; INTFULL

Transmit Service

TMR0 overflow triggers a timer interrupt. When a character is being transmitted, a timer overflow interrupt defines the beginning of each transmission bit. The timer uses the internal instruction cycle as a clock. The timer overflow period (256 counts), and therefore the transmission bit rate, is a function of the instruction clock rate and the prescaler settings. Bit rates as a function of crystal frequency and prescaler settings are shown in Table 5-5.

Table 5-5   Bit-rate - INTFULL.GRP

XTAL (MHz)	Bit Rate	PSA	PS2	PS1	PS0
19.6608	19200	1	x	x	x
	9600	0	0	0	0
	4800	0	0	0	1
	2400	0	0	1	0
	1200	0	0	1	1
	600	0	1	0	0
9.8304	9600	1	x	x	x
	4800	0	0	0	0
	2400	0	0	0	1
	1200	0	0	1	0
	600	0	0	1	1
4.9152	4800	1	x	x	x
	2400	0	0	0	0
	1200	0	0	0	1
	600	0	0	1	0

The transmit service, XMITSRV.TXT, is the timer overflow service (Figure 5-25). When the application wants to transmit a character it checks that the transmit register is empty (transmit-register-empty flag is set) and if so, writes the character to the transmit register (**txreg**) and clears the transmit-register-empty flag. On the next timer interrupt the transmit service recognizes the cleared flag and takes the transmit line low to send the start bit. On the following eight timer interrupts, the character data is shifted onto the transmit line and on the tenth timer interrupt the transmit service takes the transmit line high for the stop bit. Immediately after initiating the start bit XMITSRV fetches the character data from the transmit register and sets the transmit-register-empty flag, making the transmit register again available to the application. The transmit-register-empty flag is the only transmit flag available to the application and should be only tested by and cleared by the application. All of the other transmit flags are for XMITSRV use only. Table 5-6 lists the INTFULL flags.

114

Table 5-6   INTFULL Flags

BIT	FLAG	FUNCTION
	RECEIVE FLAGS (rxflgs):	
0	RECEIVING (rxing)	SET at reception of start bit CLEARED at character to receive register
1	RECEIVE OVERRUN (rxover)	SET at receive register overrun CLEARED at character to receive register
2	FRAMING ERROR (rxframe)	SET at received framing error CLEARED by Application
3	NEW CHARACTER RECEIVED (rxnew)	SET at new character to buffer CLEARED by Application
4	RECEIVED BIT VALUE (rxbit)	SET and CLEARED by various
6	RECEIVE EDGE (rxedg)	TOGGLED at external interrupt CLEARED at Case C ending
	TRANSMIT FLAGS (txflgs):	
0	TRANSMITTING (txing)	SET at beginning of start bit CLEARED at completion of stop bit
1	DOING STOP BIT (txstop)	SET at beginning of stop bit CLEARED at completion of stop bit
2	TRANSMIT REGISTER EMPTY (txmty)	SET shortly after beginning of start bit CLEARED by Application

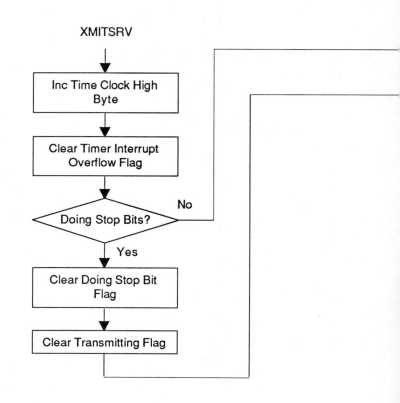

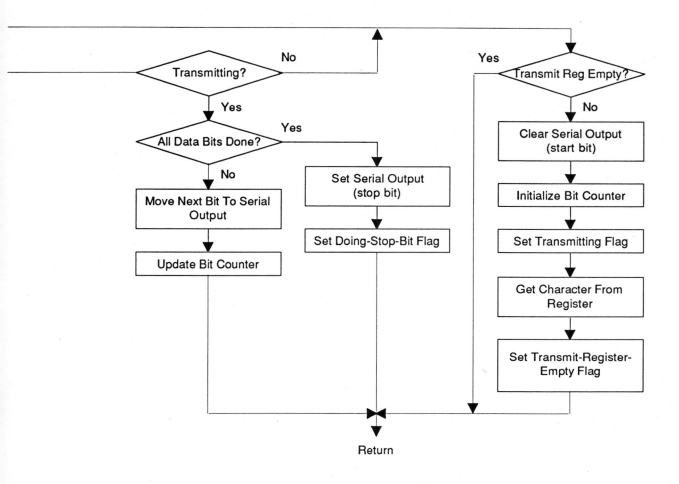

Figure 5-25   INTFULL Transmit Service

Receive Service

The external interrupt (RB0/INT) is the serial receive line. Transitions on this serial receive line are detected by the external interrupt and the real time of the transitions are recorded as time stamps. The PICmicro external interrupt is edge sensitive and edge selective, allowing the software to determine the direction of the transition that triggers the interrupt. See Figure 5-26 for the following general description of the receive service. Rather than watch for the arrival of individual bits, the receive service watches for changes in bit level and determines the time elapsed (in terms of bit periods) between these changes. For example, if two bit periods elapsed between a high-to-low transition and a low-to-high transition on the serial input line, then two zero value bits were received. The next transition would then be high-to-low and the bits received would be ones. With each transition the receive service tabulates these bits until a full character is received. The bit counter keeps a count of the remaining bits to be received (including the stop bit) and is used to resolve character ending issues. Figure 5-28 illustrates the receive service in greater detail.

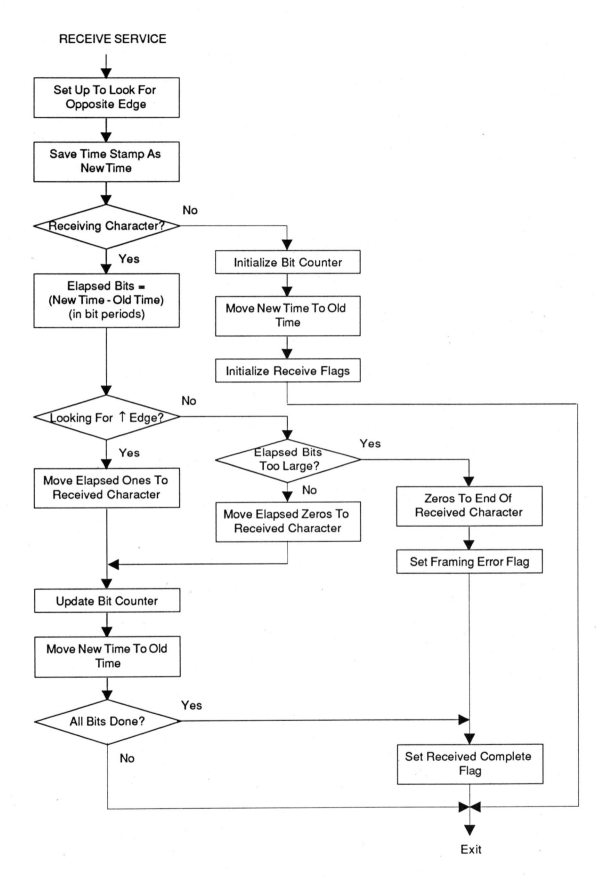

Figure 5-26   Simplified Receive Service

Each serial input transition triggers a call (via interrupt) to the receive service (INTSRV.TXT). The TMR0 register along with a timer overflow counter forms a two byte real-time clock. When TMR0 overflows the overflow counter (**time1**) is incremented. **time1** is the high byte and the TMR0 register is the low byte of the real-time clock. This clock has a precision of 1 in 256 parts of a bit period. At each transition, the value of this real-time counter is the time stamp for the transition. The number of bit periods between the transitions are calculated by subtracting the earlier time stamp (old-time) from the later time stamp (new-time). A bit period is nominally one overflow period, but because the received bits will not necessarily arrive at overflow time, a two byte time stamp is required. The new-time minus old-time result is rounded to the nearest full bit period. This two byte precision and rounding also compensates for bit jitter and sender bit-clock errors.

Because the receive service watches for transitions rather than bits, the end of a character cannot always be precisely determined. If the sender does not immediately send another character or a character having a framing error is received, some mechanism must be provided to complete the character. A time-out based on approximately two bit periods beyond the expected 10 bit periods for a character provides this mechanism. The state of the serial receive line and the value of the bit-counter at time-out are used to determine the final bits of the character and whether the character is good or erroneous. The only error recognized is a framing error and it is defined as the serial receive line not being at logic one at the time that the stop bit is expected. All characters are completed as received including erroneous characters. The time-out counter is updated at each timer overflow.

Figure 5-27 illustrates all of the possible ending scenarios and Figure 5-28 provides a more detailed description of the receive service showing how the endings are resolved. For the Case A ending another character follows immediately or very shortly after the stop bit and time-out does not occur. The value of the bit counter and the number of bit periods between the previous transition and the new start transition determines the value (1 or 0) and number of bits to complete the character. For the Case B ending an up edge occurs after the stop bit is expected but before time-out. This means that a stop bit was not received and the framing-error flag is set.

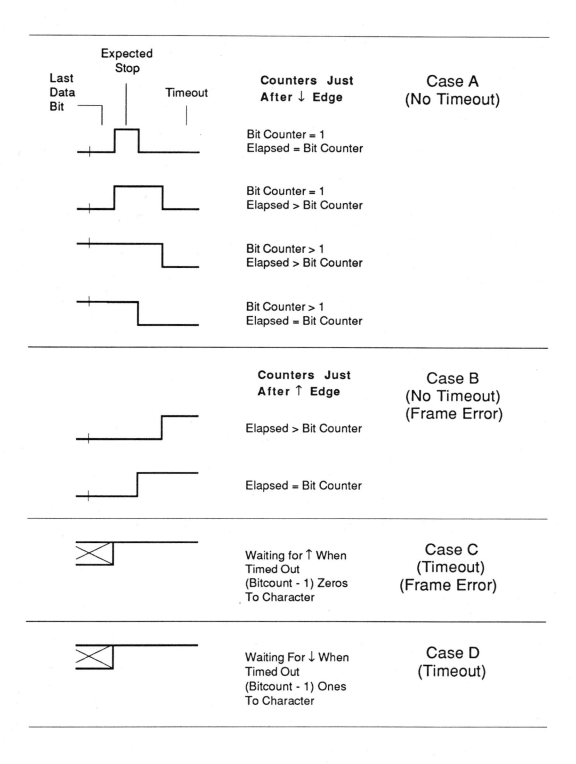

Figure 5-27   Receive Endings

Case C and D endings have no transitions between the expected stop bit time and time-out. If the serial receive line is logic one at time-out (Case C), the stop bit is correct and the final character bits are ones. If the serial receive line is logic zero at time-out (Case D), the stop bit has not been received and the framing-error flag is set. When communicating with a terminal, most endings will be Case C because the time between characters is relatively long. When blocks of data are received most endings will be Case A.

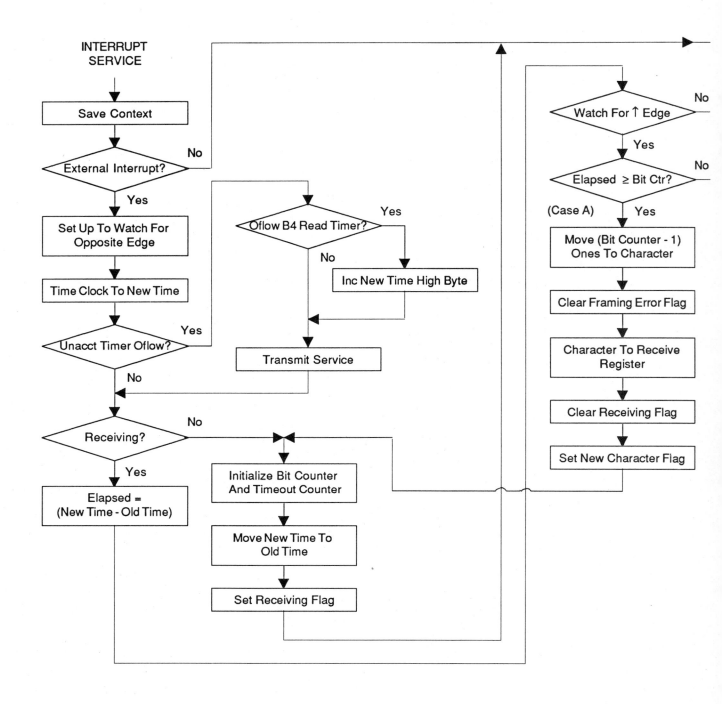

Figure 5-28   INTFULL Interrupt Service

122

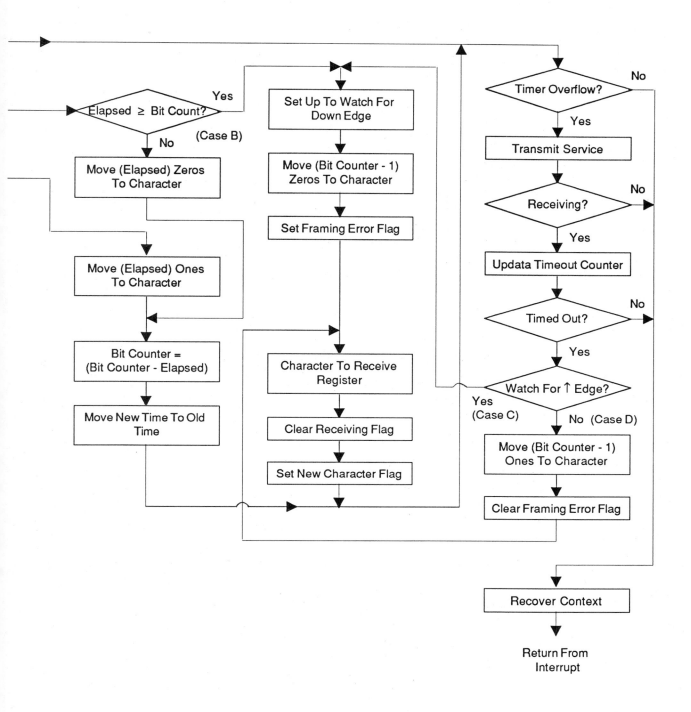

See Figure 5-28 and INTFULL.GRP for the following discussion. The external interrupt (receive) has priority over the timer interrupt (transmit) in order to preserve the best possible time-stamp precision. If a timer overflow were to occur shortly after entering the receive service, the transmit could not be serviced until the entire receive service was completed. This would result in transmit bit period jitter. To reduce this possible jitter, the receive service tests for timer overflow after recording the time-stamp, and in the case of overflow, calls the transmit service, then returns to the receive service. This reduces transmit jitter without effecting the receive service. If the timer overflow occurred between the entry to the receive service and the point in time that the TMR0 register was read for the time-stamp, the high byte of the time-stamp would be one count too low. In this case the high byte is incremented to correct the time-stamp.

123

When a character has been received the receive service writes the character to the receive register (**rxreg**) and sets the new-character-received flag (**rxnew**). The application should then fetch the character from the receive register and clear the new-character-received flag. If the application does not fetch the character and clear the flag before the next character is completely received, the receive service overwrites the old character with the new character and sets the receive-register-overflow flag (**rxover**). The framing-error flag (**rxframe**), new-character-received flag (**rxnew**) and receive-register-overflow flag (**rxover**) are the only receive flags available to the application. These flags should be tested only and must be cleared by the application. The framing-error flag (**rxframe**) is cleared by the receive service, but may be cleared by the application. All of the other receive flags are for receive service use only. See Table 5-6 for the receive flags.

```
;====== INTFULL.GRP ===========================================================
;
;        File: INTFULL.GRP                        See Section 5.3
;
;        Full-Duplex Asynchronous Communications.
;        14 bit PIC
;
;------------------------------------------------------------------------------
;
;        REQUIRES Following Workspace:
;
;        time1            time clock high byte
;        time0                       low byte
;        rtnew1           time stamp high byte
;        rtnew0                      low byte
;        rtold1           time stamp high byte
;        rtold0                      low byte
;        rxreg            receive character buffer (user accessible)
;        recdat           received data byte
;        rbitctr          receive bit counter
;        rlapctr          receive elapsed bit period counter
;        rtmout           receive timeout counter
;        filler           0 or 1 fill counter
;
;        txreg            transmit character buffer (user accessible)
;        xmtdat           transmit data byte
;        tbitctr          transmit bit counter
;
;        rxflgs           receive flags
;        txflgs           transmit flags
;
;        tempst           temporary status
;        tempw            temporary working
;------------------------------------------------------------------------------
;        REQUIRES following equates;
;
;        receive flags bits (rxflgs)
;        rxing    equ     00      ;receiving flag
;        rxover   equ     01      ;receive buffer overflow flag
;        rxframe equ      02      ;receive framing error flag
```

```
;           rxnew    equ      03          ;new character to receive buffer flag
;           rxbit    equ      04          ;received bit value
;           rxedg    equ      06          ;receive interrupt edge (DO NOT CHANGE
;                                         ;THIS BIT ASSIGNMENT)
;
;           transmit flag bits (txflgs)
;           txing    equ      00          ;transmitting flag
;           txstop   equ      01          ;doing stop bit flag
;           txmty    equ      02          ;transmit buffer empty flag
;
;           port assignments
;           comport equ       portx       ;communications port (port x)
;           xmtp     equ       0y          ;port bit y of port x is transmit
;
;           See Section 5.3 for Initialization and Application information.
;           All flow control is external to these modules.
;-------------------------------------------------------------------------
;           module: intsrv.txt
;
;           Full-Duplex Interrupt service
;
;           This module performs all of the communications operations.
;           It is called in the event of an external interupt or a timer
;           overflow interrupt.
;
;           This module calls: XMITSRV, RXTOBUF & FILLIT.
;-------------------------------------------------------------------------
intsrv  movwf    tempw              ;save context
        swapf    status,w
        bcf      status,rp0
        movwf    tempst
        btfss    intcon,intf        ;external interrupt ? if yes, skip next
        goto     intovfl            ;no. go
        bcf      intcon,intf        ;yes. clear flag
        movlw    0x40               ;now set up to watch for opposite edge
        bsf      status,rp0         ;switch to bank 1
        xorwf    optreg,f           ;opposite edge
        bcf      status,rp0         ;switch back to bank 0
        xorwf    rxflgs,f           ;shadow the edge flag
        movf     time1,w            ;time clock to new-time (time stamp)
        movwf    rtnew1
        movf     tmr0,w
        movwf    rtnew0
        btfss    intcon,toif        ;un-accounted-for timer overflow ? if yes,
skip
        goto     intsrv1            ;no. go
        btfss    rtnew0,7           ;yes. Overfld before read timer ? if no, skip
        incf     rtnew1,f           ;yes. correct time stamp
        call     xmitsrv            ;service the overflow
intsrv1 btfsc    rxflgs,rxing       ;receiving ? if no, skip next
        goto     intsrv3            ;yes. go
intsrv2 movlw    0x0a               ;no. initialize receive bit counter
        movwf    rbitctr
        movlw    0x0c               ;initialize timeout counter
```

125

```
                movwf    rtmout
                movf     rtnew1,w       ;move new time to old time
                movwf    rtold1
                movf     rtnew0,w
                movwf    rtold0
                bsf      rxflgs,rxing   ;set receiving flag
                goto     intovfl        ;& go
;
;       Here we calculate the number of bit periods that have elapsed
;       since the last receive data line transition
intsrv3 comf    rtold0,f               ;compliment the old time stamp
                comf     rtold1,f
                incf     rtold0,f
                btfsc    status,z
                incf     rtold1,f
                movf     rtnew0,w       ;add it to new time stamp (new - old)
                addwf    rtold0,f       ;(result to old time stamp location)
                btfsc    status,c
                incf     rtold1,f
                movf     rtnew1,w
                addwf    rtold1,f
                btfsc    rtold0,7       ;round the msb (if lsb < 128 then
;                                        msb unchanged
                incf     rtold1,f       ;or if lsb => 128 then msb incremented)
                movf     rtold1,w       ;result to elapsed counter
                movwf    rlapctr
;
                btfss    rxflgs,rxedg   ;watching for up edge ? if yes, skip
                goto     intsrv7        ;no. go
                movf     rbitctr,w      ;yes. elapsed < bit counter ?
                subwf    rlapctr,w
                btfsc    status,c       ;if yes, skip next
                goto     intsrv5        ;no. go
                bsf      rxflgs,rxbit   ;yes. (elapsed) ones to character
                movf     rlapctr,w
                movwf    filler
                call     fillit
intsrv4 movf    rlapctr,w              ;update bit counter (bit counter - elapsed)
                subwf    rbitctr,f
                movf     rtnew1,w       ;move new time to old time
                movwf    rtold1
                movf     rtnew0,w
                movwf    rtold0
                goto     intovfl        ;& go
intsrv5 decf    rbitctr,f              ;(bit counter - 1) ones to character
                btfsc    status,z       ;any ones for character? if yes, skip next
                goto     intsrv6        ;no. nothing to character
                bsf      rxflgs,rxbit   ;yes. do ones
                movf     rbitctr,w
                movwf    filler
                call     fillit
intsrv6 bcf     rxflgs,rxframe         ;clear framing error flag
                call     rxtobuf        ;move character to buffer
                goto     intsrv2        ;& go set up for new character
```

126

```
intsrv7 movf    rbitctr,w        ;elapsed < bit counter ?
        subwf   rlapctr,w
        btfss   status,c         ;if no, skip next
        goto    intsrvB          ;yes. go
intsrv8 bsf     status,rp0
        bcf     optreg,intedg    ;set up to watch for down edge
        bcf     status,rp0
        bcf     rxflgs,rxedg     ;shadow the edge flag
        decf    rbitctr,f        ;(bit counter - 1) zeros to character
        btfsc   status,z         ;any zeros for character ? if yes, skip next
        goto    intsrv9          ;no. nothing to character
        bcf     rxflgs,rxbit     ;yes. do zeros
        movf    rbitctr,w
        movwf   filler
        call    fillit
intsrv9 bsf     rxflgs,rxframe   ;set framing error flag
intsrvA call    rxtobuf          ;move character to buffer
        goto    intovfl          ;& go
intsrvB bcf     rxflgs,rxbit     ;(elapsed) zeros to character
        movf    rlapctr,w
        movwf   filler
        call    fillit
        goto    intsrv4          ;& go
;
intovfl btfss   intcon,toif      ;timer overflow ? if yes, skip next
        goto    intsrvx          ;no. go exit
        call    xmitsrv          ;yes. service it
        btfss   rxflgs,rxing     ;receiving ? if yes, skip next
        goto    intsrvx          ;no. go exit
        decf    rtmout,f         ;yes. update timed out counter
        btfss   status,z         ;timed out ? if yes, skip next
        goto    intsrvx          ;no. go exit
        btfsc   rxflgs,rxedg     ;yes. watching for up edge ? if no, skip
        goto    intsrv8          ;yes. go
        decf    rbitctr,f        ;no. (bit counter - 1) ones to character
        btfsc   status,z         ;any ones for character ? if yes, skip next
        goto    intsrvC          ;no. nothing to character
        bsf     rxflgs,rxbit     ;yes. do ones
        movf    rbitctr,w
        movwf   filler
        call    fillit
intsrvC bcf     rxflgs,rxframe   ;clear framing error
        goto    intsrvA          ;& go move character to buffer
intsrvx swapf   tempst,w         ;recover context
        movwf   status
        swapf   tempw,f
        swapf   tempw,w
        retfie                   ;return
;
;--------------------------------------------------------------------------
;       module: xmitsrv.txt
;       Timer overflow service. Synchronizes xmit bits and places xmit
;       bits on xmit line.
;--------------------------------------------------------------------------
```

```
xmitsrv incf    time1,f              ;update time
        bcf     intcon,toif          ;clear timer interrupt
        btfss   txflgs,txstop        ;doing stop bit ? If yes, skip next
        goto    xmit1                ;no. go
        bcf     txflgs,txstop        ;yes. clear doing stop bit flag
        bcf     txflgs,txing         ;clear doing xmit flag
        goto    xmit1a               ;& go
xmit1   btfsc   txflgs,txing         ;transmitting ? if no, skip next
        goto    xmit2                ;yes. go
xmit1a  btfsc   txflgs,txmty         ;xmit buffer empty ? if no, skip next
        goto    xmitx                ;yes. go exit
        bcf     comport,xmtp         ;no. clear output (start bit)
        movlw   0x08                 ;initialize bit counter
        movwf   tbitctr
        bsf     txflgs,txing         ;set transmitting flag
        movf    txreg,w              ;get character from buffer
        movwf   xmtdat
        bsf     txflgs,txmty         ;set buffer empty flag
        goto    xmitx                ;& go exit
xmit2   movf    tbitctr,f            ;all bits sent ?
        btfss   status,z             ;if yes, skip next
        goto    xmit3                ;no. go
        bsf     comport,xmtp         ;yes. set output (stop bit)
        bsf     txflgs,txstop        ;set stop bit flag
        goto    xmitx                ;& go exit
xmit3   rrf     xmtdat,f             ;data bit to output
        btfsc   status,c             ;is it zero ? if yes, skip
        goto    xmit4                ;no. go
        bcf     comport,xmtp         ;yes. clear output
        goto    xmit5                ;& go
xmit4   bsf     comport,xmtp         ;bit is one. set output
xmit5   decf    tbitctr,f            ;update bit counter
xmitx   return                       ;exit
;-------------------------------------------------------------------------
;
;       module: rxtobuf.txt
;
;       moves received character to receive buffer
;
;-------------------------------------------------------------------------
rxtobuf movf    recdat,w             ;received character
        movwf   rxreg                ;to receive buffer
        btfsc   rxflgs,rxnew         ;buffer overflow ? if no, skip next
        bsf     rxflgs,rxover        ;yes. set buffer overflow flag
        bsf     rxflgs,rxnew         ;set new received character flag
        bcf     rxflgs,rxing         ;clear receiving flag
        return
;-------------------------------------------------------------------------
;
;       module: fillit.txt
;
;       Moves ones or zeros into received character. On entry the number
;       of ones or zeros is in filler and if rxedg flag of rxflgs is 1,
;       then fills ones otherwise fills zeros.
```

```
;
;---------------------------------------------------------------------
fillit  bcf     status,c        ;clear carry
        btfsc   rxflgs,rxbit    ;zeros to data ? if yes skip next
        bsf     status,c        ;no. ones to data
        rrf     recdat,f
        decfsz  filler,f        ;update counter. All done ? if yes, skip
        goto    fillit
        return                  ;exit
;=====================================================================
```

5.3.1 INDIGO6.ASM: Bit-Bang Full-Duplex Application

INDIGO6 is a simple demonstration application illustrating how an application interfaces with
INTFULL. It begins by sending the ASCII characters OK to the terminal. Subsequently any
characters received from the terminal are sent back (echoed) to the terminal. INDIGO6 communicates at 2400 bits per second with 8 data bits, one stop bit and no parity with a 4.9152 MHz
crystal. Figure 5-1 is the hardware schematic for INDIGO6. The serial input, RB0/INT, must be
jumpered to port A3.

The interrupt control and option registers must be configured as shown in Figure 5-24. Prior to
receiving a character the external interrupt edge must be configured to interrupt on a down going
edge. The application must initially make sure the down edge is selected (clear bit 6, **INTEDG**,
of the option register). After receiving the first character the receive service subsequently handles this requirement. The **PSA** bit and **PS2** through **PS0** bits of the option register are configured as per Table 5-5 for 2400 bits per second and a crystal frequency of 4.9152 MHz. The global, timer and external interrupts are enabled (**GIE**, **T0IE** and **INTE** bits of **INTCON** are set).

INDIGO6 waits for a received character by polling the new-character-received flag, **rxnew**, of
the receive flags byte **rxflgs** until the flag is set, indicating that a character has been received.
INDIGO6 then fetches the character from the receive register, **rxreg**, clears the **rxnew** flag,
writes the character to the transmit register, **txreg**, and clears the transmit-register-empty flag,
txmty of the transmit flags byte **txflgs**.

```
;====== INDIGO6.ASM ==================================================
;
;       14 Bit PIC
;       Full-Duplex Interrupt Driven Bit-Bang Asynchronous Communications
;
;       Demonstrates use of INTFULL.GRP Full-Duplex modules.
;       Waits for character from terminal then echoes character
;       back to terminal.
;
;       2400 bits per second, 1 start bit, 8 data bits, no parity
;       and 1 stop bit.
;       RB0/INT is input and Port A1 is output.
;       See Section 5.3
;
;---------------------------------------------------------------------
        radix   hex             ;RADIX is HEX
;
        list p=16f84
```

```
;
;              STATUS REGISTER ( status) BIT DEFINITIONS:
c       equ       0          ;carry bit of status register (bit 0)
z       equ       2          ;zero flag bit of status register (bit 2)
dc      equ       1          ;digit carry
pd      equ       3          ;power down bit
to      equ       4          ;time out bit
rp0     equ       5          ;program page preselect, low bit
rp1     equ       6          ;program page preselect, high bit
;
;              INTERRUPT CONTROL & STATUS (intcon) REGISTER BIT DEFINITIONS:
rbif    equ       0          ;port change int flag
intf    equ       1          ;RB0/INT flag
toif    equ       2          ;TMR0 overflow flag
rbie    equ       3          ;port change int enable
inte    equ       4          ;RB0/INT int enable
toie    equ       5          ;TMR0 overflow int enable
eeie    equ       6          ;EE write complete int enable
gie     equ       7          ;global int enable
;
;              OPTION REGISTER (optreg) BIT DEFINITIONS
ps0     equ       0          ;prescaler rate select
ps1     equ       1
ps2     equ       2
psa     equ       3          ;prescaler assignment
tose    equ       4          ;TMR0 source edge select
tocs    equ       5          ;TMR0 clock source select
intedg  equ       6          ;interrupt edge select bit
rbpu    equ       7          ;port b pullup enable
;
;              DESTINATION BIT DEFINITIONS:
w       equ       0          ;destination working
f       equ       1          ;destination file
;
;-----------------------------------------------------------------------
;      CPU EQUATES   (special function register memory map)
;
;   BANK 0:
indf    equ       00         ;indirect file register
tmr0    equ       01         ;timer
pcl     equ       02         ;program counter (low byte)
status  equ       03         ;status register
fsr     equ       04         ;indirect data pointer
porta   equ       05         ;port a
portb   equ       06         ;port b
eedata  equ       08         ;eeprom data
eeadr   equ       09         ;eeprom address
pclath  equ       0a         ;write buffer for program counter (high byte)
intcon  equ       0b         ;interrupt control register
;
;   BANK 1:
optreg  equ       01         ;option register                    bank 1 (0x81)
trisa   equ       05         ;data direction register port a     bank 1 (0x85)
trisb   equ       06         ;data direction register port b     bank 1 (0x86)
```

```
eecon1   equ      08       ;eeprom control register           bank 1 (0x88)
;
;-----------------------------------------------------------------------
;        WORK AREA  (memory map)   Starts at 000c
;
;-----------------------------------------------------------------------
;
;        Communications variables:
;
time1    equ      000c     ;time clock high byte
time0    equ      000d     ;           low byte
rtnew1   equ      000e     ;time stamp high byte
rtnew0   equ      000f     ;           low byte
rtold1   equ      0010     ;time stamp high byte
rtold0   equ      0011     ;           low byte
rxreg    equ      0012     ;receive character register (user accessable)
recdat   equ      0013     ;received data byte
rbitctr  equ      0014     ;receive bit counter
rlapctr  equ      0015     ;receive elapsed bit period counter
rtmout   equ      0016     ;receive timeout counter
filler   equ      0017     ;0 or 1 fill counter
;
txreg    equ      0018     ;transmit character register (user accessable)
xmtdat   equ      0019     ;transmit data byte
tbitctr  equ      001a     ;transmit bit counter
;
rxflgs   equ      001c     ;receive flags
txflgs   equ      001d     ;transmit flags
;
tempst   equ      001e     ;temporary status
tempw    equ      001f     ;temporary working
;
;        User (application) variables
;
utemp    equ      0020     ;user general parameter
counter  equ      0021     ;user general counter
;
;-----------------------------------------------------------------------
;        COMMUNICATIONS EQUATES
;
;        receive flags bits (rxflgs)
rxing    equ      00       ;receiving flag
rxover   equ      01       ;receive buffer overflow flag
rxframe  equ      02       ;receive framing error flag
rxnew    equ      03       ;new character to receive buffer flag
rxbit    equ      04       ;received bit value
rxedg    equ      06       ;receive interrupt edge
;
;        transmit flag bits (txflgs)
txing    equ      00       ;transmitting flag
txstop   equ      01       ;doing stop bit flag
txmty    equ      02       ;transmit buffer empty flag
;
;        port assignments
```

```
comport equ       porta      ;communications port
xmtp    equ       01         ;port a1 is transmit
;
;-------------------------------------------------------------------
;
        org       0x00                ;start of program memory
;
start   goto      start0              ;jumps over version code & int vector
ver     dw        0072                ;version code
        dw        006c
        dw        0073
        goto      intsrv              ;interrupt service vector
start0  movlw     0xfe
        movwf     porta               ;output marking
        movwf     portb
        bsf       status,rp0          ;switch to bank 1
        movlw     0x09                ;pa0 & pa3 as inputs, pa1 & pa3 as outputs
        movwf     trisa
        movlw     0x01                ;pb0 (INT) as input, pb1 - pb7 output
        movwf     trisb
        movlw     0x90                ;waiting for down edge
                                      ;timer on internal clock
                                      ;2400 bits per second (4.9152 MHz Xtal)
        movwf     optreg
        bcf       status,rp0          ;switch to bank 0
        movlw     0x30                ;timer & external ints enabled, global
;                                      disabled
        movwf     intcon
        clrf      rxflgs              ;clear communications flags
        clrf      txflgs
        bsf       txflgs,txmty        ;transmit buffer empty
        bsf       intcon,gie          ;enable global interrupts
;
test    movlw     004f                ;send OK
        movwf     utemp
        call      sendit
        movlw     004b
        movwf     utemp
        call      sendit
;
main    btfss     rxflgs,rxnew        ;new character received ? if yes, skip next
        goto      main                ;no. go try again
        movf      rxreg,w             ;yes. get character
        movwf     utemp               ;save it for now  (to send it)
        bcf       rxflgs,rxnew        ;clear new character received flag
;
        call      sendit              ;echo character back
        goto      main                ;and wait for next character
;
;-------------------------------------------------------------------
sendit  btfss     txflgs,txmty        ;xmitter ready for new character ? if yes,
skip
        goto      sendit              ;no. go try again
        movf      utemp,w             ;yes. character to be sent...
```

```
        movwf    txreg              ;to xmit buffer
        bcf      txflgs,txmty       ;clear xmit buffer empty flag
        return
;
;-----------------------------------------------------------------------
;       INCLUDES:
;       INTFULL.GRP       Bit-Bang Full-Duplex Interrupt Driven Services
;-----------------------------------------------------------------------
        include intfull.grp
;
;-----------------------------------------------------------------------
        end                        ;end of program
;=======================================================================
```

5.3.2 Using the Section 5.3 Routines in Your Applications

Generally all of the routines can be used in your applications as written or with minor changes. For all routines the entry and exit conditions, variables, port definitions and flag definitions are described in the individual xx.ASM, xx.GRP and xx.TXT listings. All port assignments (except serial receive, RB0/INT) are arbitrary and may be changed to suit your application.

The sample application uses the PIC16F84, but the routines may be used with other PICmicros with little or no change. All of the xx.GRP and xx.TXT routines may be used as include files.

The routines introduced in Section 5.3 are in:

INTFULL.GRP   Full-Duplex Receive and Transmit

The INTFULL.GRP module is an *interrupt* service and contains four sub-modules: INTSRV.TXT, XMITSRV.TXT, RXTOBUF.TXT and FILLIT.TXT. The sub-module INTSRV.TXT calls the other three sub-modules. If your application requires additional interrupt services, they should be placed at the end of INTSRV.TXT just before the context recovery. If additional interrupt services must have higher priority than the external and timer interrupts, they may cause receive errors and bit jitter in the transmitted character.

Prior to enabling the global interrupt, your application must initialize the communications flag registers as shown in Figure 5-29.

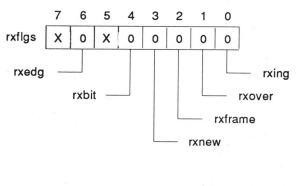

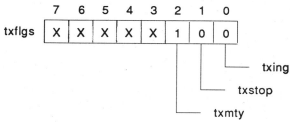

Figure 5-29   Communications Flags Initial Values

When receiving or sending characters, follow the procedure illustrated in Figure 5-30.
The flags must be cleared each time a character is received or sent. The application INDIGO6
calls the subroutine **sendit** to write to the transmit register. Note that **sendit** does not return until
the transmit register is available to accept a new character. If your application cannot tolerate
this wait, the register ready test may be moved outside the subroutine. In either case it is good
practice to provide subroutines for reading characters from and writing characters to the receive
and transmit registers because the subroutines will always 'remember' to clear the flags. When
reading the receive register *always* clear the **rxnew** flag *after* reading the register. When writing
to the transmit register *always* clear the **txmty** flag *after* writing to the register. If a character is
received before the application fetches the previously received character it replaces the previous
character and the receive overrun flag (**rxover**) is set. This flag *must* be cleared by the
application.

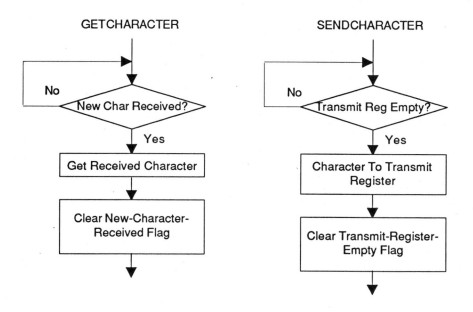

Figure 5-30   Application Character Transfer

If the communications protocol for your application calls for other than 8 data bits the initialization of the receive bit counter (**rbitctr**) and the receive time out counter (**rtmout**) must be changed. The receive bit counter must be initialized to (number of data bits + 2) and the receive time-out counter to (number of data bits + 4). For fewer than 8 data bits it is a good idea to clear the receive data register (**rxreg**) as part of the receive initialization. The transmit bit counter (**tbitctr**) must be initialized to the number of data bits.

If blocks or packets of data are to be sent or received the application will require multi-byte buffers to store the blocks of data. These buffer operations will generally be a part of the applications program. See Sections 5.2.2 and 6.3 for examples of multi-byte buffers. If it would better suit the application to have the buffer operations as a part of the INTFULL service, the module RXTOBUF.TXT may be replaced with a receive multi-byte buffer routine. A transmit multi-byte buffer routine will have to be added to the INTFULL service. This routine should be called by the transmit service. The unused flag bits in **rxflgs** and **txflgs** may be used as buffer related flags.

Chapter 6
On-Chip UART

On-Chip UART

Several of the PIC16Cxxx, 16Fxxx and 17Cxxx series micro-controllers have an on-chip Universal Synchronous Asynchronous Receiver Transmitter (USART). The on-chip USART is capable of full-duplex asynchronous or half-duplex synchronous communications. Implementation of this hardware USART unloads the data communications burden from the application software resulting in simpler software and more program memory available to the non-communications part of the application.

6.1 Using the On Chip USART

For the following asynchronous applications, the USART will be referred to as an UART (Universal Asynchronous Receiver Transmitter). The UART data format is 1 start bit, 8 or 9 data bits and 1 stop bit. Parity is not supported, but the ninth bit may be used as the parity bit with parity generated and tested in software. The format for all of the following demonstration applications will be 2400 bits per second, 1 start bit, 8 data bits and 1 stop bit. Figure 6-1 is the schematic of the circuit that will be used for the demonstration UART applications. The applications communicate with a computer. The null modem cable in Figure 3-8 may be used for the applications. The PIC16C63 is used for all of the applications, but most of the routines may be used with other PICmicro devices having the on-chip UART with little or no change.

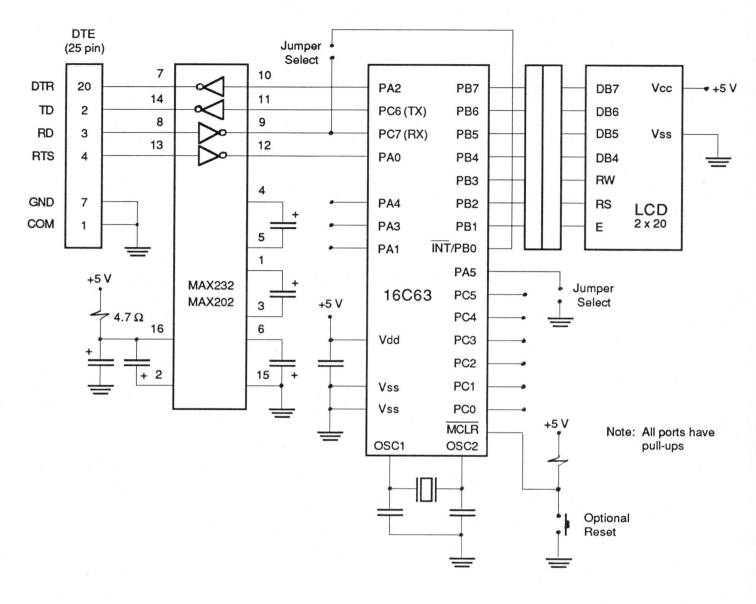

Figure 6-1   Schematic; UART Applications

There are 8 special registers associated with the UART. A ninth special register is required if the communications are to be interrupt driven. The special registers implement the control, status and data interface required by the program software.

Register **SPBRG** is used to set the transmission rate (bits per second). The contents of this register are determined by the following formula and the HEX value of BRG must be written to the **SPBRG** register prior to enabling the UART.

$$BRG = \frac{F_{osc} - 64(Rate)}{64(Rate)}$$

NOTE: When using this formula the UART Low Speed Mode *must* be selected (**BRGH** of register **TXSTA** set).

F_{osc} is the oscillator frequency in MHz
Rate is the data rate in bits per second

Port pins TX (transmit) and RX (receive) must be configured as inputs (via **TRISC**) for UART operation. (NOTE: The port C transmit pin, TX, is an output, but the **TRISC** bit corresponding to the TX pin *must* be set.) Registers **RCSTA** and **TXSTA** implement receive status and control and transmit status and control respectively. Registers **RCSTA, RXSTA** and **PIR1** provide communications status. Registers **RCREC** and **TXREC** are the receive and transmit data registers. Registers **PIE1** and **INTCON** implement interrupt control for interrupt driven communications.

Figure 6-2 illustrates the required control register bit settings for 8 data bit communications at 2400 bits per second (4 MHz clock) and Figure 6-3 the required interrupt control register settings for interrupt driven receive. Figure 6-4 locates the UART status flag bits.

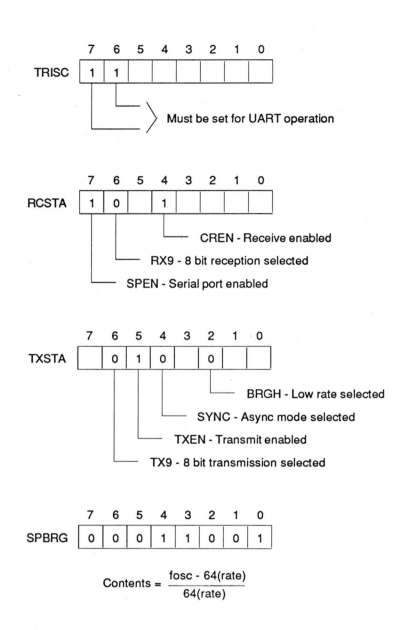

Figure 6-2   UART Control Register Settings: Full - Duplex, Async, 8 Data Bits, 2400 BPS

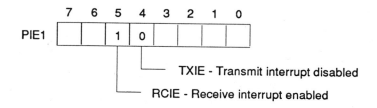

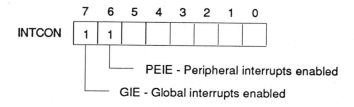

Figure 6-3   Control Register Settings - UART Interrupt Driven Receive

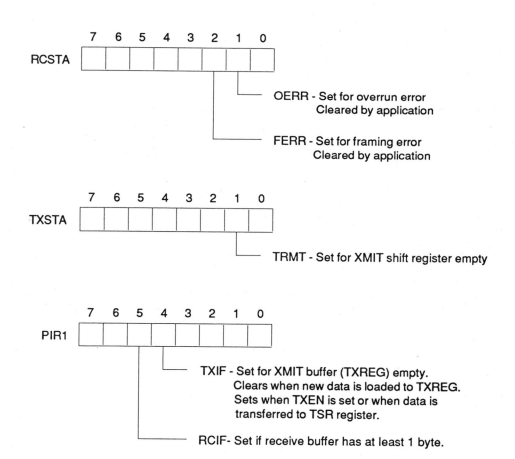

Figure 6-4   UART Status Registers

For 9 bit data communications bit 6 of **RCSTA** and **TXSTA** must be set. The received and transmitted ninth data bits are found at bit 0 of **RCSTA** and **TXSTA** respectively.

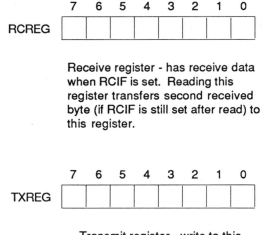

RCREG

| 7 | 6 | 5 | 4 | 3 | 2 | 1 | 0 |

Receive register - has receive data
when RCIF is set. Reading this
register transfers second received
byte (if RCIF is still set after read) to
this register.

TXREG

| 7 | 6 | 5 | 4 | 3 | 2 | 1 | 0 |

Transmit register - write to this
register only when TXIF is set.

Figure 6-6   UART Data Registers

6.2 UART Full-Duplex Receive and Transmit Services

The UART transmit and receive hardware are independent of one another making full-duplex communications very simple to implement. Full-duplex communications requires only writing a byte to the transmit data register and reading a byte from the receive data register. Data transfer is done entirely by the UART hardware.

The UART communications software, UCOMS.GRP, is implemented in three modules: UXMT, UREC and INTSRV. These modules may be used unchanged (with the possible exception of INTSRV) in many applications and with any 16CXXX having an on-chip USART. For 17CXXX applications, the Special Register addresses must be changed.

Because the UART receive and transmit hardware operate independently of one another, the distinction between full-duplex, half-duplex and simplex is made only in the application software. Therefore the modules may be applied to any of these data transfer schemes. The data byte to be transmitted is placed in the parameter **xmtuse** and the byte received is placed in one of two parameters **recuse1** or **recuse2**. The UART receive is interrupt driven.

6.2.1 UART Transmit

The transmit module, UXMT tests for an empty transmit register by checking the **TXIF** flag of register **PIR1**. If the register is empty, the flag will be set. If the register is not empty (flag cleared) the flag is tested until it is set, then the byte in **xmtuse** is placed in the register and the module exits. An empty register indicates that the previous byte to be transmitted has been transferred to the transmit shift register. If the transmit interrupt is enabled (bit **TXIE** of **PIE1** set), the interrupt will occur when the register is emptied. If the transmit shift register is empty, the register contents are immediately transferred to the shift register and transmission of the byte begins. If the shift register is not empty, transmission of the new register contents does not begin until the previous byte has been completely transmitted. In this case, if UXMT is again called shortly after it returns, the wait for an empty transmit register will be nearly as long as the full data byte transmission time and the program will remain in the UXMT module for this time. If this wasted time presents a problem to the application program, the test for an empty transmit register may be placed outside the transmit module and the module called only when the register is empty. Then, while the register is not empty, the application program can be tending to other business. If the transmit interrupt is enabled, UXMT may be called as part of the interrupt service. The transmit interrupt occurs immediately after the transmit register is emptied.

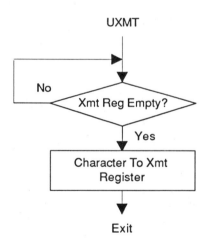

Figure 6-6   UXMT

6.2.2 UART Receive

With asynchronous communications, the arrival time of a character is not predictable. To receive a character, the application program may (1) wait for the character, (2) poll the receiver to see if a character has been received or (3) may be notified when a character has been received. Unless the application is very simple, waiting for a received character is not an option because no other operations may be performed during the wait. Polling for a received character is a valid option, but if the polling period is too long, some characters may be lost. Notification of a received character via an interrupt is generally the best scheme for most applications. When configured for interrupt on receive the UART generates an interrupt after a complete character byte has been received. The interrupt service must then fetch the character from the receive register. The receive software described below uses the third option: notification of character received via interrupt.

The interrupt service module, INTSRV, determines if the interrupt was the result of a character having been received. If not, then the interrupt service returns. If it was a receive interrupt, the received character is fetched by the UREC module, then the interrupt returns.

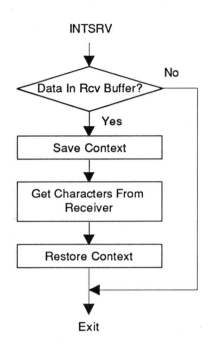

Figure 6-7   GREEN1 Interrupt Service

The UREC module fetches the received character from the receive register. The UART receive register is a two byte deep first in first out buffer. Thus two characters may be received before the receive register must be read. For most applications, two character periods are more than enough to deal with any latencies introduced by large interrupt services having complex priority issues or by disabled global interrupts that cause a delay in servicing the interrupt (see Section 6.2.4). If the receive registers are read before a third character is completely received, no characters will be lost. If the receive registers are not read in time, an overrun error occurs (data is lost) and the **OERR** flag in **RCSTA** is set to indicate the overrun. The **RCIF** flag in **PIR1** is set if there is any data in the receive register buffer. If this flag is set the receive register must be read prior to the completion of the third character to prevent character loss. The received characters are placed in the user parameters **recuse1** and **recuse2**. If the stop bit for a received character is clear (0), a framing error has occurred and the **FERR** flag in **RCSTA** is set. This flag and the ninth data bit are also buffered in the receive buffer, so the **FERR** flag and ninth bit must be read before the receive register is read.

144

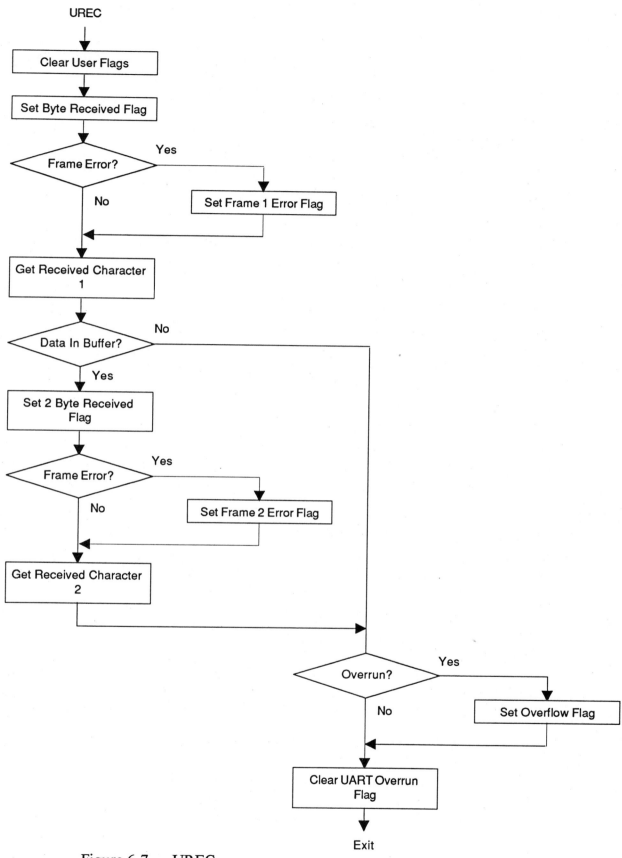

Figure 6-7   UREC

145

The UART error flags **OERR** and **FERR** must be cleared by software. Reading the receive buffer for each received byte clears the framing error flag, **FERR**, for that byte. If the **OERR** flag is not cleared any subsequently received characters will not be placed in the receive buffer. **OERR** is cleared by clearing and setting the receive enable flag, **CREN**, in the receive control and status register **RCSTA**.

The UREC module generates receive related flags for use by the application program. Table 6-1 describes these receive user flags. All of the flags are in the user flag register **recflg**. If an overrun error occurs, the user overflow flag is set. If a framing error occurs for any received character, the corresponding user framing error flag is set. All **recflg** flags are cleared at the beginning of the UREC module and may be cleared by the user.

Table 6-1   UREC.TXT User Receive Flags (**recflg**)

BIT	FLAG	FUNCTION
0	BYTE RECEIVED (**newbyt**)	SET at reception of a byte CLEARED at entry or by user
1	TWO BYTES RECEIVED (**twobyt**)	SET at reception of two bytes CLEARED at entry or by user
2	Reserved	
3	FRAMING ERROR BYTE 1	SET for first byte framing error CLEARED at entry or by user
4	FRAMING ERROR BYTE 2	SET for second byte framing error CLEARED at entry or by user
5	Reserved	
6	OVERFLOW ERROR (**overerr**)	SET for receiver overrun CLEARED at entry or by user
7	Reserved	

```
;====== UCOMS.GRP =========================================================
;
;       UART ASYNCHRONOUS COMMUNICATIONS GROUP           UCOMS.GRP
;       Module ucoms.grp
;
;       On chip UART    See Section 6.2
;
;--------------------------------------------------------------------------
;       Requires WORK AREA:
;       System variables:
;       tempst              temporary status (for context save)
;       tempw               temporary w (for context save)
;
```

```
;        Communications variables:
;        recflg          communications receive flags
;        recuse1         user receive character 1
;        recuse2         user receive character 2
;        xmtuse          user xmit character
;--------------------------------------------------------------------
;        Requires SYSTEM EQUATES:
;
;        recflg bit definitions (receive flags):
;        newbyt  equ     0       ;byte received flag
;        twobyt  equ     1       ;two bytes received flag
;        threbyt equ     2       ;three bytes received flag
;        frmerr1 equ     3       ;framing error 1 flag
;        frmerr2 equ     4       ;framing error 2 flag
;        overerr equ     6       ;overflow error flag
;
;        All communications parameters are established at program
;        initialization.
;        See Sections 6.2 through 6.3.1 and GREEN1.ASM and GREEN2.ASM for
;        initialization and application information.
;
;--------------------------------------------------------------------
;        TRANSMIT MODULE
;        Module: uxmt.txt
;
;        On entry, if xmit buffer is NOT empty, this module will require
;        up to one character time to execute. If buffer is empty, execution
;        time is approx 6 instruction cycles.
;--------------------------------------------------------------------
uxmt    btfss   pir1,txif       ;xmit buffer empty ? if yes, skip next
        goto    uxmt            ;no. go try again
        movf    xmtuse,w        ;yes. get character to xmit
        movwf   txreg           ;xmit it
        return                  ;& exit
;--------------------------------------------------------------------
;        RECEIVE MODULE
;        Module: urec.txt
;
;        Receives 1 or 2 bytes from UART receiver
;
;--------------------------------------------------------------------
urec    clrf    recflg          ;clear communications receive flags
        bsf     recflg,newbyt   ;set byte received flag
        btfsc   rcsta,ferr      ;framing error ? if no, skip next
        bsf     recflg,frmerr1  ;yes set user frame error 1 flag
        movf    rcreg,w         ;get received character
        movwf   recuse1         ;& move to user received byte 1
        btfss   pir1,rcif       ;data still in buffer (2nd byte) ? if yes,
skip
        goto    urecx           ;no. go
        bsf     recflg,twobyt   ;yes. set two bytes received flag
        btfsc   rcsta,ferr      ;framing error ? if no, skip next
        bsf     recflg,frmerr2  ;yes. set user frame error 2
        movf    rcreg,w         ;get 2nd received character
        movwf   recuse2         ;& move to user received byte 2
```

```
;
urecx   btfsc   rcsta,oerr        ;overrun error ? if no, skip next
        bsf     recflg,overerr    ;yes. set overflow flag
        bcf     rcsta,cren        ;clear UART overrun flag
        bsf     rcsta,cren
        return                    ;& exit
;-----------------------------------------------------------------------
;       INTERRUPT service
;       Module: intsrv
;       Interrupt service for receive.
;-----------------------------------------------------------------------
intsrv  btfss   pir1,rcif         ;data in receive buffer ? if yes, skip
        goto    intsrvx           ;no. not receive interrupt. go exit
        movwf   tempw             ;yes. save context
        swapf   status,w
        bcf     status,rp0
        movwf   tempst
;
        call    urec              ;get received data
intsrv1 swapf   tempst,w          ;restore context
        movwf   status
        swapf   tempw,f
        swapf   tempw,w
intsrvx retfie                    ;return from interrupt (exit)
;-----------------------------------------------------------------------
;       END OF MODULE UCOMS.GRP
;=======================================================================
```

6.2.3 GREEN1.ASM: A Simple Full-Duplex Application

GREEN1.ASM is a full-duplex UART application that receives a character from a terminal and echoes the character back to the terminal. This program serves to demonstrate the software interface between the UART and an application program. GREEN1 is written for the 16C63, but will work on any 16CXXX with an on-chip USART.

GREEN1 (Figure 6-9) begins by sending the ASCII characters OK to the terminal. Any characters received from the terminal are then sent back to the terminal (echoed). If a received character generates a framing error, the ASCII control code SUB is returned in place of the received character. This serves to alert the terminal of the error and the terminal can resend the character. If an overflow error is generated the received bytes are echoed followed by the control character NAK. The terminal may then be able to determine which characters were lost and can resend them. This is a very rudimentary error detection system.

148

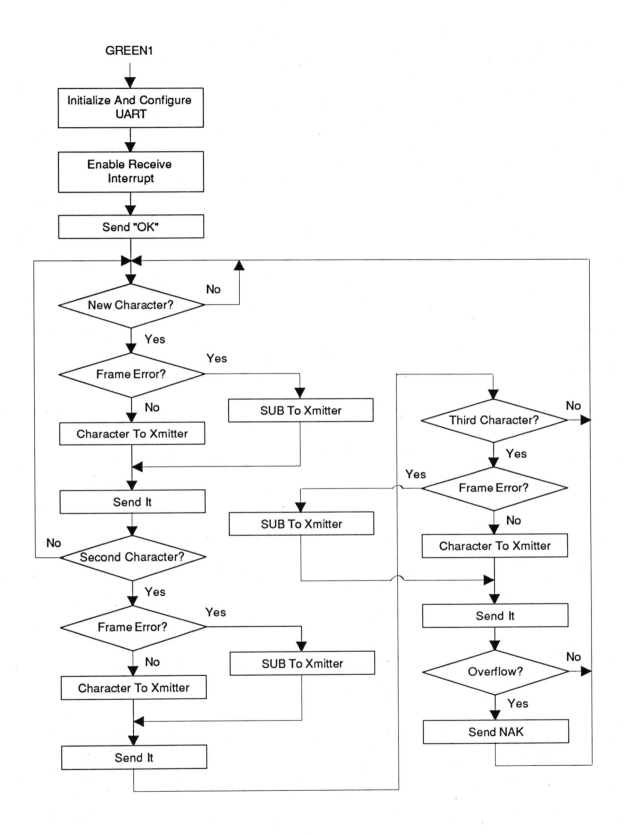

Figure 6-9   GREEN1

149

GREEN1 waits for a received character in a short loop. When a character is received by the UART, the UART issues an interrupt and the interrupt service calls the module UREC. UREC gets the received character (or characters) from the UART receiver, sets the new-byte flag (**new-byt**) and returns. The interrupt service then returns with the character (or characters). The loop recognizes the new-byte flag and exits to continue with the echo application. If no receive error flags are set the received character is echoed (sent back) to the terminal. If a second character was received by UREC, it is also echoed.

In general, this loop, interrupt, return to loop and exit loop procedure will apply to most programs using an interrupt driven UART receive. Of course the loop is seldom as short as in this example and the interrupt service may in many cases be a significant portion of the program.

```
;====== GREEN1.ASM =========================================================
;
;        FILE: green1.asm
;
;        On chip UART full-duplex demo of UART routines UCOMS.GRP
;        Echoes received characters
;
;---------------------------------------------------------------------------
         radix   hex        ;RADIX is HEX
;
         list    p=16c63
;
;        STATUS REGISTER BIT DEFINITIONS:
c        equ     0          ;carry bit of status register (bit 0)
z        equ     2          ;zero flag bit of status register (bit 2)
dc       equ     1          ;digit carry
pd       equ     3          ;power down bit
to       equ     4          ;time out bit
rp0      equ     5          ;program page preselect, low bit
rp1      equ     6          ;program page preselect, high bit
;
;        DESTINATION BIT DEFINITIONS:
w        equ     0          ;destination working
f        equ     1          ;destination file
;
;---------------------------------------------------------------------------
;        CPU EQUATES   (special function register memory map)
;
;   BANK 0:
indf     equ     00         ;indirect file register
tmr0     equ     01         ;timer
pcl      equ     02         ;program counter (low byte)
status   equ     03         ;status register
fsr      equ     04         ;indirect data pointer
porta    equ     05         ;port a
portb    equ     06         ;port b
portc    equ     07         ;port c
pclath   equ     0a         ;write buffer for program counter (high byte)
intcon   equ     0b         ;interrupt control register
pir1     equ     0c         ;peripheral interrupt flags
```

```
pir2     equ     0d
tmr1l    equ     0e          ;TMR1 register low byte
tmr1h    equ     0f          ;              high byte
t1con    equ     10          ;timer 1 control register
tmr2     equ     11          ;timer 2
t2con    equ     12          ;timer 2 control register
sspbuf   equ     13          ;SSP receive/xmit register
sspcon   equ     14          ;SSP control register
ccpr1l   equ     15          ;CCP 1 low byte
ccpr1h   equ     16          ;       high byte
ccp1con  equ     17          ;CCP 1 control register
rcsta    equ     18          ;UART receive status & control register
txreg    equ     19          ;UART xmit data register
rcreg    equ     1a          ;UART receive register
ccpr2l   equ     1b          ;CCP 2 low byte
ccpr2h   equ     1c          ;       high byte
ccp2con  equ     1d          ;CCP 2 control register
;
;   BANK 1:
optreg   equ     01          ;option register                bank 1 (0x81)
trisa    equ     05          ;data direction register port a bank 1 (0x85)
trisb    equ     06          ;data direction register port b bank 1 (0x86)
trisc    equ     07          ;data direction register port c bank 1 (0x87)
pie1     equ     0c          ;peripheral interrupt enable    bank 1 (0x8c)
pie2     equ     0d          ;                               bank 1 (0x8d)
pcon     equ     0e          ;power control register         bank 1 (0x8e)
pr2      equ     12          ;timer 2 period register        bank 1 (0x92)
sspadd   equ     13          ;SSP address register           bank 1 (0x93)
sspstat  equ     14          ;SSP status register            bank 1 (0x94)
txsta    equ     18          ;UART xmit status & control     bank 1 (0x98)
spbrg    equ     19          ;UART baud rate generater       bank 1 (0x99)
;
;-------------------------------------------------------------------------
;          SPECIAL REGISTER BIT DEFINITIONS
;
;       Register PIR1:
rcif     equ     5
txif     equ     4
;       Register PIE1:
rcie     equ     5
txie     equ     4
;       Register TXSTA:
csrc     equ     7
tx9      equ     6
txen     equ     5
sync     equ     4
brgh     equ     2
trmt     equ     1
tx9d     equ     0
;       Register RCSTA:
spen     equ     7
rx9      equ     6
sren     equ     5
cren     equ     4
ferr     equ     2
```

```
oerr     equ     1
rx9d     equ     0
;       Register INTCON:
gie      equ     7
peie     equ     6
toie     equ     5
inte     equ     4
rbie     equ     3
toif     equ     2
intf     equ     1
rbif     equ     0
;
;
;-------------------------------------------------------------------
;        FULL DUPLEX    8 DATA BITS, 1 STOP BIT,  2400 BITS PER SECOND
;
;        Receives a character and echoes it back to sender.
;        Uses on-chip UART
;-------------------------------------------------------------------
;        WORK AREA (Memory Map)  Starts at 0020
;        System variables:
tempst   equ     0020    ;temporary status (for context save)
tempw    equ     0021    ;temporary w (for context save)
;
;        Communications variables:
recflg   equ     0022    ;communications receive flags
recuse1  equ     0023    ;user receive character 1
recuse2  equ     0024    ;user receive character 2
xmtuse   equ     0026    ;user xmit character
;
;        User variables:


;-------------------------------------------------------------------
;        SYSTEM EQUATES
;
;        recflg bit definitions (receive flags):
;
newbyt   equ     0       ;byte received flag
twobyt   equ     1       ;two bytes received flag
threbyt  equ     2       ;three bytes received flag
frmerr1  equ     3       ;framing error 1 flag
frmerr2  equ     4       ;framing error 2 flag
overerr  equ     6       ;overflow error flag
;
;        ascii character codes:
OH       equ     04f     ;"O'
KAY      equ     04b     ;"K"
SUB      equ     01a     ;SUB
NAK      equ     015     ;NAK


;-------------------------------------------------------------------
         org     0x00                    ;start of program memory
start    goto    start0                  ;jump over version and int vector
```

```
        dw      0072            ;version code
        dw      006c
        dw      0073
        goto    intsrv          ;interrupt service vector
start0  clrf    porta
        clrf    portb
        clrf    portc
        bsf     status,rp0      ;switch to bank 1
        movlw   0c0             ;pc7,6 as inputs (required for UART
;                                operation)
        movwf   trisc           ;& other pc as outputs
        movlw   000             ;all port b as outputs
        movwf   trisb
        movlw   001             ;port a0 as input
        movwf   trisa           ;& all others as outputs
        movlw   080             ;config UART xmitter
        movwf   txsta
        movlw   019             ;2400 bits per second
        movwf   spbrg
        bcf     status,rp0      ;switch to bank 0
        movlw   010             ;configure UART receiver (set cren)
        movwf   rcsta
;
;       at this point the UART is configured, but NOT on.
;
;       here we turn On the UART:
        bsf     rcsta,spen      ;enable serial port
        bsf     status,rp0      ;switch to bank 1
        bsf     txsta,txen      ;enable xmit
        bsf     pie1,rcie       ;enable receive interrupt
        bcf     status,rp0      ;switch to bank 0
        bsf     intcon,peie     ;enable all unmasked peripheral interrupts
;
;       at this point the UART is ON, but will not receive because
;       global interrupt is still inhibited.
;
        clrf    recflg          ;clear receive flags
        bsf     intcon,gie      ;enable interrupts
;
;       at this point, UART will receive because interrupts are enabled
;
        movlw   OH              ;send OK to terminal
        movwf   xmtuse          ;(this will require a little over 1 character
        call    uxmt            ; period because uxmt will not accept a new
        movlw   KAY             ; character until any currently transmitting
        movwf   xmtuse          ; character has been completely transmitted)
        call    uxmt
mloop   btfss   recflg,newbyt   ;byte received ? if yes, skip next
        goto    mloop           ;no. go try again
        bcf     recflg,newbyt   ;yes. clear byte received flag
        btfss   recflg,frmerr1  ;framing error ? if yes, skip next
        goto    mloop1          ;no. go
        movlw   SUB             ;prepare to echo SUB
        movwf   recuse1
```

153

```
mloop1  movf    recuse1,w       ;echo received character
        movwf   xmtuse
        call    uxmt
        btfss   recflg,twobyt   ;2nd byte received ? if yes, skip next
        goto    mloop           ;no. go loop (wait for next byte)
        btfss   recflg,frmerr2  ;yes. framing error ? if yes, skip
        goto    mloop2          ;no error. go
        movlw   SUB             ;prepare to echo SUB
        movwf   recuse2
mloop2  movf    recuse2,w       ;echo received character
        movwf   xmtuse
        call    uxmt
        btfss   recflg,overerr  ;over flow ? if yes, skip
        goto    mloop           ;no. go loop
        movlw   NAK             ;yes. send NAK
        movwf   xmtuse
        call    uxmt
        goto    mloop           ; & go loop
;
;----------------------------------------------------------------------
;       INCLUDES:
;       UCOMS.GRP       UART Communications Services
;----------------------------------------------------------------------
        include         ucoms.grp
;
;----------------------------------------------------------------------
        end                     ;end of program
;======================================================================
```

6.2.4 Using the Section 6.2 Routines in Your Applications

Generally all of the routines can be used in your applications as written or with minor changes. For all routines, the entry and exit conditions, variables, port definitions and flag definitions are described in the individual xx.ASM , xx.GRP and xx.TXT listings. All port assignments (except RX and TX) are arbitrary and may be changed to suit your application.

The sample applications demonstrate how the UART routines are applied. They use the PIC16C63 but may be used with other 16CXX PICmicros with little or no change. For 17CXXX applications the Special Register addresses must be changed. All of the xx.GRP and xx.TXT modules may be used as include files.

Configuring the UART

UINIT.TXT (immediately below) configures the UART for 2400 bits per second, 8 data bits, 1 stop bit and interrupt driven receive. If two stop bits are required, select 9 bit transmission and reception and set the ninth bit. For other bit rates, change the value loaded to **SPBRG** as per the equation in Section 6.1. For the GREEN applications, the UINIT function is not a called routine, but may be implemented as a called routine in your applications:

```
;====== UINIT.TXT ============================================================
;
;       INITIALIZE UART
;       UART is configured for 2400 bits per second, 8 data bits,
;       1 stop bit and interrupt driven reception.
;       See Sections 6.1, 6.2 and 6.2.4
;
;----------------------------------------------------------------------------
        clrf    portc
        bsf     status,rp0      ;switch to bank 1
        movlw   0c0             ;port c7, c6 as inputs (required for
                                ;UART operation)
        movwf   trisc           ;& other portc as outputs
        movlw   80              ;config UART xmitter
        movwf   txsta
        movlw   019             ;2400 bits per second
        movwf   spbrg
        bcf     status,rp0      ;switch to bank 0
        movlw   010             ;configure UART receiver
        movwf   rcsta
;
;       At this point the UART is configured, but NOT on.
;       Here we turn On the UART:
;
        bsf     rcsta,spen      ;enable serial port
        bsf     status,rp0      ;switch to bank 1
        bsf     txsta,txen      ;enable xmit
        bsf     pie1,rcie       ;enable receive interrupt
        bcf     status,rp0      ;switch to bank 0
        bsf     intcon,peie     ;enable peripheral interrupts
;
```

```
;        At this point the UART is ON, but will not receive because
;        global interrupt is still inhibited.
;
;        Global Interrupt must be enabled prior to the point in the
;        application where reception is expected.
;==============================================================================
```

See the Microchip PICmicro Manual and Sections 6.1 and 6.2 for information on alternate configurations.

Section 6.2 Routines

The routines introduced in section 6.2 are:

UXMT.TXT   UART Transmit a Character
UREC.TXT   UART Receive a Character
INTSRV   Receive Interrupt Service
The above modules are included in UCOMS.GRP

See Sections 6.1, 6.2, and 6.2.1 through 6.2.3 for detailed descriptions of the UART routines. Also see the appropriate Microchip PICmicro Manual for further details about the UART.

UXMT.TXT is a called routine that finds the character to be transmitted in the application transmit buffer, **xmtuse**, and transmits it. If the transmit buffer is not empty at the time of entry into UXMT, the routine waits until it is empty. This wait can be as long as a full character time. If the application cannot tolerate this wait, move the test for empty transmit buffer outside UXMT and only call UXMT when the buffer is empty.

In GREEN1, the receive is interrupt driven (which will be the case for most applications) and UREC.TXT is called by the interrupt service when a UART receive interrupt occurs. On exit, the received character(s) are in **recuse1** and **recuse2** (see Section 6.2.2). If the application requires 9 bit reception, the ninth bit read must be added to UREC. The ninth bit is found at bit 0 of the receive status register. Be sure to read this bit immediately *before* reading the Receive Register (see the PICmicro Manual for details). A buffer must be provided for 2 of these ninth bits.

If the interrupt service, INTSRV, was triggered by the UART *receive* interrupt it calls UREC. If not, it exits. If interrupts other than receive are enabled, the interrupt service must verify that the interrupt was triggered by receive before calling UREC. Some of your applications may have a far more complex interrupt service than INTSRV, but the service still must include the function of INTSRV. See GREEN3.ASM (Section 6.3.2) for an example of a more complex interrupt service.

The UREC module fetches the received character from the receive register. The UART receive register is a two byte deep first in first out buffer. Two characters may be received before the receive register must be read. If the receive register is read before a third character is completely received, no characters will be lost. If the receive register is not read in time, an overrun error occurs (data is lost) and the **OERR** flag in **RCSTA** is set to indicate the overrun. The **RCIF** flag in **PIR1** is set if there is any data in the receive register buffer. If this flag is set the receive register must be read prior to the completion of the third character to prevent character loss. If the buffer contains one byte, UREC exits after reading the byte. If the buffer contains two bytes, UREC exits after reading the second byte.

156

If the call to UREC is delayed sufficiently for the top of the receive buffer to be read just before the completion of the third character the third character will be placed in the buffer and is available for reading. Normally this third character will be read when UREC is next called. The receive service may be made to read this third character before exiting. UREC3.TXT (see below) is a receive module capable of reading this third character. The third character is placed in parameter **recuse3**. Since a full character period will elapse before a fourth character arrives, it is not productive to make the receive service capable of reading this fourth character before exiting.

```
;===============================================================================
;
          RECEIVE MODULE
          Module: UREC3.TXT
;
;-------------------------------------------------------------------------------
urec      clrf     recflg          ;clear communications receive flags
          bsf      recflg,newbyt   ;set byte received flag
          btfsc    rcsta,ferr      ;framing error ? if no, skip next
          bsf      recflg,frmerr1  ;yes set user frame error 1 flag
          movf     rcreg,w         ;get received character
          movwf    recuse1         ;& move to user received byte 1
          btfss    pir1,rcif       ;data still in buffer (2nd byte) ? if yes,
                                   ;skip
          goto     urecx           ;no. go
          bsf      recflg,twobyt   ;yes. set two bytes received flag
          btfsc    rcsta,ferr      ;framing error ? if no, skip next
          bsf      recflg,frmerr2  ;yes. set user frame error 2
          movf     rcreg,w         ;get 2nd received character
          movwf    recuse2         ;& move to user received byte 2
          btfss    pir1,rcif       ;data still in buffer (3rd byte) ? if yes,
                                   ;skip
          goto     urecx           ;no. go
          bsf      recflg,threbyt  ;yes. set three bytes received flag
          btfsc    rcsta,ferr      ;framing error ? if no, skip next
          bsf      recflg,frmerr3  ;yes. set user frame eror 3
          movf     rcreg,w         ;get 3rd received character
          movwf    recuse3         ;& move to user received byte 3
;
urecx     btfsc    rcsta,oerr      ;overrun error ? if no, skip next
          bsf      recflg,overerr  ;yes. set overflow flag
          bcf      rcsta,cren      ;clear UART overrun flag
          bsf      rcsta,cren
          return                   ;& exit
;===============================================================================
```

6.3 UART Applications

The following applications demonstrate block data transfer and packet data transfer using the UART.GRP routines described in section 6.2.

For block data transfer a group of bytes is sent without interruption. The block transfers may be full-duplex or half-duplex and flow control may be either in-band or out-of-band. Block size (number of bytes) is either fixed or the block is delineated by special characters embedded within the block. The application GREEN2 demonstrates a half-duplex block transfer with in-band flow control and embedded-character block delineation.

Packet data transfer is similar to embedded-character-delineated block transfer, but much more information about the block is embedded within the block. Packet transfer is half-duplex and flow control is always in-band. Packet data transfer is commonly used for file transfer over a network. The file is broken into blocks and each block is individually transmitted as a packet. At the receiving end the embedded characters are stripped from the packet and the file is rebuilt a data block at a time. Packet data transfer protocols provide error detection, error correction and a mechanism for any corrupted packet to be resent. Packet protocols are quite robust, resulting in the transfer of very large amounts of information with a very low probability of error. Examples of common packet protocols are XMODEM, ZMODEM and KERMIT. The application GREEN3 demonstrates a simple packet data transfer protocol.

6.3.1 Half-Duplex Block Data Transfers

GREEN2 (Figure 6-10) demonstrates an application where a block of data is sent to a terminal or another PICmicro application via an asynchronous half-duplex link.

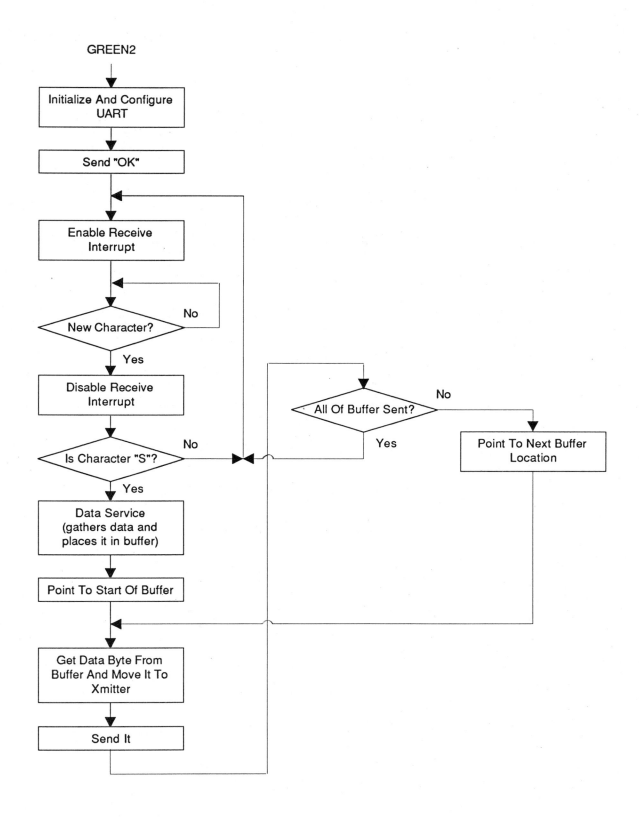

Figure 6-10   GREEN2

In a typical application the data may have been generated by a series of measurements made with one or more analog to digital converters. This application program uses the UART communications modules (UREC,UXMT and INTSRV) as described in Section 6.2. For the purposes of this demonstration application the data is generated from a table rather than by an analog to digital converter.

At power up GREEN2 sends the ASCII characters OK to indicate to the terminal that it is ready for communications. The terminal then sends the ASCII character S to tell GREEN2 to send the block of data. The block is terminated with the ASCII control code for Carriage Return (CR) followed by the code for Line Feed (LF). The CR and LF combination tells the terminal that the full block has been sent. The OK, S, CR & LF are used as in-band control characters for the necessary half-duplex flow control. In addition, the terminating CR & LF allow variable length blocks to be sent.

The use of ASCII CR and LF characters for flow control limits the data in the block transfer to the seven bit ASCII character set. If eight bit binary data must be sent, the simplest protocol is to use fixed length data blocks, circumventing the need for the block terminator. If variable length blocks better fit the application, then the binary data can be converted to hexadecimal and transferred as a two byte ASCII representation of the hexadecimal value. This simple block transfer protocol affords no form of error detection. The packet data transfer protocol described in Section 6.3.2 provides some measure of error detection and correction along with the ability to transfer variable length blocks of 8 bit binary data.

```
;====== GREEN2.ASM =========================================================
;
;        File: green2.asm
;
;        On chip UART. Sends a block of characters
;
;---------------------------------------------------------------------------
         radix   hex         ;RADIX is HEX
;
         list p=16c63
;
;        STATUS REGISTER BIT DEFINITIONS:
c        equ     0           ;carry bit of status register (bit 0)
z        equ     2           ;zero flag bit of status register (bit 2)
dc       equ     1           ;digit carry
pd       equ     3           ;power down bit
to       equ     4           ;time out bit
rp0      equ     5           ;program page preselect, low bit
rp1      equ     6           ;program page preselect, high bit
;
;        DESTINATION BIT DEFINITIONS:
w        equ     0           ;destination working
f        equ     1           ;destination file
;
;---------------------------------------------------------------------------
;     CPU EQUATES   (special function register memory map)
;
;   BANK 0:
indf     equ     00          ;indirect file register
```

```
tmr0     equ     01        ;timer
pcl      equ     02        ;program counter (low byte)
status   equ     03        ;status register
fsr      equ     04        ;indirect data pointer
porta    equ     05        ;port a
portb    equ     06        ;port b
portc    equ     07        ;port c
pclath   equ     0a        ;write buffer for program counter (high byte)
intcon   equ     0b        ;interrupt control register
pir1     equ     0c        ;peripheral interrupt flags
pir2     equ     0d        ;
tmr1l    equ     0e        ;TMR1 register low byte
tmr1h    equ     0f        ;                high byte
t1con    equ     10        ;timer 1 control register
tmr2     equ     11        ;timer 2
t2con    equ     12        ;timer 2 control register
sspbuf   equ     13        ;SSP receive/xmit register
sspcon   equ     14        ;SSP control register
ccpr1l   equ     15        ;CCP 1 low byte
ccpr1h   equ     16        ;     high byte
ccp1con  equ     17        ;CCP 1 control register
rcsta    equ     18        ;UART receive status & control register
txreg    equ     19        ;UART xmit data register
rcreg    equ     1a        ;UART receive register
ccpr2l   equ     1b        ;CCP 2 low byte
ccpr2h   equ     1c        ;     high byte
ccp2con  equ     1d        ;CCP 2 control register
;
;   BANK 1:
optreg   equ     01        ;option register               bank 1 (0x81)
trisa    equ     05        ;data direction register port a bank 1 (0x85)
trisb    equ     06        ;data direction register port b bank 1 (0x86)
trisc    equ     07        ;data direction register port c bank 1 (0x87)
pie1     equ     0c        ;peripheral interrupt enable    bank 1 (0x8c)
pie2     equ     0d        ;                               bank 1 (0x8d)
pcon     equ     0e        ;power control register         bank 1 (0x8e)
pr2      equ     12        ;timer 2 period register        bank 1 (0x92)
sspadd   equ     13        ;SSP address register           bank 1 (0x93)
sspstat  equ     14        ;SSP status register            bank 1 (0x94)
txsta    equ     18        ;UART xmit status & control     bank 1 (0x98)
spbrg    equ     19        ;UART baud rate generator       bank 1 (0x99)
;
;----------------------------------------------------------------------
;        SPECIAL REGISTER BIT DEFINITIONS
;
;       Register PIR1:
rcif     equ     5
txif     equ     4
;       Register PIE1:
rcie     equ     5
txie     equ     4
;       Register TXSTA:
csrc     equ     7
tx9      equ     6
```

```
txen       equ      5
sync       equ      4
brgh       equ      2
trmt       equ      1
tx9d       equ      0
;        Register RCSTA:
spen       equ      7
rx9        equ      6
sren       equ      5
cren       equ      4
ferr       equ      2
oerr       equ      1
rx9d       equ      0
;        Register INTCON:
gie        equ      7
peie       equ      6
toie       equ      5
inte       equ      4
rbie       equ      3
toif       equ      2
intf       equ      1
rbif       equ      0
;
;========================================================================
;        GREEN2.ASM     Main Program
;        Sends a block of data to a terminal upon receipt of
;        ASCII character S from the terminal.
;        Uses on-chip UART with interrupt driven receive
;
;        FULL DUPLEX    8 DATA BITS, 1 STOP BIT,  2400 BITS PER SECOND
;
;------------------------------------------------------------------------
;        WORK AREA (Memory Map)   Starts at 0020
;        System variables:
tempst     equ      0020      ;temporary status (for context save)
tempw      equ      0021      ;temporary w (for context save)
;
;        Communications variables:
recflg     equ      0022      ;communications receive flags
recuse1    equ      0023      ;user receive character 1
recuse2    equ      0024      ;user receive character 2
recuse3    equ      0025
xmtuse     equ      0026      ;user xmit character
;
;        User variables:
bufctr     equ      0030      ;buffer position counter
;
bufstrt    equ      0050      ;start of buffer

;------------------------------------------------------------------------
;        SYSTEM EQUATES
;
;        recflg bit definitions (receive flags):
newbyt     equ      0         ;byte received flag
```

```
twobyt  equ     1               ;two bytes received flag
threbyt equ     2               ;three bytes received
frmerr1 equ     3               ;framing error 1 flag
frmerr2 equ     4               ;framing error 2 flag
frmerr3 equ     5               ;framing error 3 flag
overerr equ     6               ;overflow error flag
;
;       ascii character codes:
ESS     equ     053     ;"S"
OH      equ     04f     ;"O"
KAY     equ     04b     ;"K"
CR      equ     00d     ;carraige return
LF      equ     00a     ;line feed
;
bufdeep equ     d'14'   ;buffer is 14 bytes deep
;--------------------------------------------------------------------------
        org     0x00            ;start of program memory
start   goto    start0          ;jump over version and int vector
        dw      0072            ;version code
        dw      006c
        dw      0073
        goto    intsrv          ;interrupt service vector
start0  clrf    porta
        clrf    portb
        clrf    portc
        bsf     status,rp0      ;switch to bank 1
        movlw   0c0             ;pc7,6 as inputs (required for UART
;                                 operation)
        movwf   trisc           ;& other pc as outputs
        movlw   000
        movwf   trisb           ;all port b as outputs
        movlw   001             ;port a0 as input
        movwf   trisa           ;& all others as outputs
        movlw   080
        movwf   txsta           ;config UART xmitter
        movlw   019
        movwf   spbrg           ;2400 bits per second
        bcf     status,rp0      ;switch to bank 0
        movlw   010
        movwf   rcsta           ;configure UART receiver
;
;       at this point the UART is configured, but NOT on.
;
;       here we turn On the UART:
        bsf     rcsta,spen      ;enable serial port
        bsf     status,rp0      ;switch to bank 1
        bsf     txsta,txen      ;enable xmit
        bsf     pie1,rcie       ;enable receive interrupt
        bcf     status,rp0      ;switch to bank 0
        bsf     intcon,peie     ;enable peripheral interrupts
;
;       at this point the UART is ON, but will not receive because
;       global interrupt is still inhibited.
;
```

163

```
          movlw    OH              ;send OK
          movwf    xmtuse
          call     uxmt
          movlw    KAY
          movwf    xmtuse
          call     uxmt
          movlw    CR
          movwf    xmtuse
          call     uxmt
          movlw    LF
          movwf    xmtuse
          call     uxmt
;
mloop     clrf     recflg          ;clear receive flags
          bsf      intcon,gie      ;enable global interrupts
mloop1    btfss    recflg,newbyt   ;byte received ? if yes, skip next
          goto     mloop1          ;no. go try again
          bcf      intcon,gie      ;disable interrupts
          movlw    ESS             ;is it ascii S ?
          subwf    recuse1,w
          btfss    status,z        ;if yes, skip next
          goto     mloop           ;no. go wait for next received character
          call     datsrv          ;yes. generate data
          movlw    bufstrt         ;point to start of buffer
          movwf    fsr
          movlw    bufdeep         ;buffer depth
          movwf    bufctr
mloop2    movf     indf,w          ;get data character
          movwf    xmtuse          ;move to xmitter
          call     uxmt            ;& xmit it
          decf     fsr,f           ;point to next buffer location.
          decfsz   bufctr,f        ;skip if all done
          goto     mloop2          ;not done. get next character
          goto     mloop           ;all done. go start over
;
;----------------------------------------------------------------------
;         INCLUDES:
;         UCOMS.GRP        UART Communications Services
;----------------------------------------------------------------------
          include ucoms.grp
;
;======================================================================
;         DATA service
;         Module: datsrv
;
;         For the purposes of this demo program, this module moves a
;         string of ascii characters from a data table into a buffer.
;         The buffer contents form the data block transmitted to the terminal
;         For a real-world application, this module would be replaced
;         with some sort of service that gets data from peripheral devices
;         such as several A/D converters and places the data in the buffer.
;
;         This buffer has a fixed length of 14 characters. The buffer size may
;         be fixed or dynamic. The parameter bufdeep defines the buffer size.
```

```
;
;           The buffer is read by the main program.
;-----------------------------------------------------------------------------
datsrv   movlw   bufstrt                ;start of buffer
         movwf   fsr                    ;to fsr
         movlw   bufdeep                ;data table & buffer depth
         movwf   bufctr                 ;offset into data table
datsrv1  movf    bufctr,w
         call    dattbl                 ;get data from table
         movwf   indf                   ;& put it in buffer
         decf    fsr,f                  ;point to next buffer location
         decfsz  bufctr,f               ;next table location. if all done, skip next
         goto    datsrv1                ;not all done. get next table byte
         return                         ;exit
;
;
dattbl   addwf   pcl,f                  ;data table ("Hello World!")
         nop                            ;dummy place filler (because NOT using
;                                        offset = 0)
         retlw   00a                    ;LF    (offset = 1)
         retlw   00d                    ;CR
         retlw   021                    ;!
         retlw   064                    ;d
         retlw   06c                    ;l
         retlw   072                    ;r
         retlw   06f                    ;o
         retlw   057                    ;W
         retlw   020                    ;
         retlw   06f                    ;o
         retlw   06c                    ;l
         retlw   06c                    ;l
         retlw   065                    ;e
         retlw   048                    ;H    (offset = 14)
;-----------------------------------------------------------------------------
         end
;=============================================================================
```

6.3.2 Packet Data Transfer

Packet data transfer is primarily used to transfer data files over a serial communications circuit. This means that data is sent without the possibility of human intervention. For example, the data does not appear on a screen where a human can control the transfer and watch for and intervene in case of transmission errors. Packet data transfer substitutes a machine protocol for the human watching the screen. For the following discussion, *file transfer* refers to a complete data transfer session where a complete set of data is transferred from a sender to a receiver.

Packet data protocols transfer data by breaking it into pieces and placing the pieces into packets. A packet is a sequence of characters arranged such that the beginning, the end, and the location of control and data fields can be unambiguously identified. The control fields are used for synchronization, sequencing and error detection. The data fields are usually a subset of the data to be transferred. Synchronization is used to identify the beginning of a packet. Sequencing serves to identify each packet sequentially so that if any packet is lost or hopelessly mangled, the receiving terminal can tell the sender which packet was lost. The sender can then re-send the lost packet. Error detection is a means of determining if any errors were introduced into the packet during transmission.

GREEN3 is an application program demonstrating packet communications. As with the other programs in the GREEN series, this program uses the UART modules UREC and UXMT. The interrupt service in GREEN3 is vastly different from that in GREEN1 and GREEN2 mainly because the interrupt service and the modules called by it make up the majority of the communications part of the program. The communications modules in GREEN3 may be used unchanged in other applications. These modules are included in the group of modules PACKET.GRP in the GREEN3.ASM source file. The packet format, packet transmission and packet reception part of the GREEN3 protocol have been standardized for this book and are denoted as the GREENPK packet. The packet design is sufficiently general to accommodate a wide range of protocols that might be used in any PICmicro based application. The GREENPK packet is defined in Figure 6-11.

| HEAD | LEN | TYPE | SEQ | Data | CHECK |

Figure 6-11   GREENPK Packet

The HEAD identifies the beginning of the packet. The LEN specifies how long the rest of the packet is. The TYPE indicates the purpose or contents of the packet. The SEQ (sequence number) is used to detect lost or duplicated packets. The CHECK contains a quantity that is derived from all of the other characters in the packet. The sender computes this value and places it in CHECK. The receiver also computes the value and compares it with the value in CHECK. If the receiver computed value does not match the value in CHECK then the packet has probably been corrupted and the receiver requests a retransmission of the packet. This is a form of error detection and correction. The DATA field contains the data subset and can be any length from one byte up to a maximum defined by the protocol. All of the packet bytes are 8 bits wide; accommodating protocols using binary or ASCII characters.

The length of the packet (LEN) is a count of all of the bytes in the packet beginning at the TYPE byte and the CHECK is computed using all of the bytes beginning with the LEN byte and ending with the last DATA byte (Figure 6-12). The format of the LEN and CHECK bytes is determined by the protocol (binary, ASCII, ASCII mod x, ASCII decimal, etc.). The GREEN3 protocol specifies LEN and CHECK as 8 bit binary.

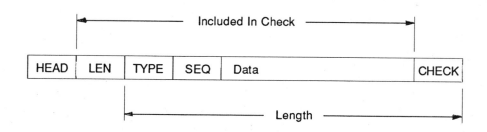

Figure 6-12   GREENPK Packet Length And Check

Packet communications systems are synchronized in that the sender waits for a response to each packet sent before sending the next packet. After having received a packet, the receiver sends a response packet. This gives the receiver time to process the received data by controlling when the sender can send the next packet. If the received packet appears to be error-free, the response packet indicates that the packet transfer was successful. If the received packet was corrupted, the response packet indicates an erroneous reception and the sender is expected to resend the original packet.

A typical file transfer starts with the sender transmitting an *initialization* packet and the receiver responding with an *initialization response* packet. These initialization packets are used to establish an agreement between the sender and the receiver about any optional or variable parameters allowed by the protocol. The sender then transmits any packets necessary to name the file or otherwise identify the data, followed by as many data packets as necessary to send the complete file. After all data packets are sent some sort of *end-of-file* or *end-of-transmission* packet (or both) is transmitted by the sender to terminate the transmission. Each packet transmitted by the sender is acknowledged by a response packet from the receiver and any corrupted or lost packets are resent.

If a packet is lost in transit or damaged so badly that it is unrecognizable as a packet, both the sender and the receiver are waiting for a packet; the sender is waiting for an acknowledgment and the receiver is waiting for the packet that it will acknowledge. This is a deadlock and some method must be in place to break it. A *time-out* is used to break the deadlock. The sender or receiver (or both) start a timer after transmitting a packet. If a packet is not received before the timer times out a deadlock is assumed and the program breaks the deadlock by sending an error packet or re-transmitting the last packet sent. The timer period must be longer than the time required for any type of packet to arrive. If several time-outs occur without a response, the transfer session is usually terminated. For communications over a network, the timer period should include anticipated delays due to routing and congestion.

GREEN3 Protocol

GREEN3 receives a packet of ASCII data and prints the data to a two line by 20 character display. GREENPK transfers are not limited to ASCII data and in most cases would be used with binary data transfer. ASCII data is used here because the display requires ASCII characters. For example, if the data received by GREEN3 were to be sent to a disk file, all of the modules in GREEN3, with the exception of the display related modules, may be used with 8 bit binary data.

The GREEN3 protocol defines the HEAD as the ASCII control character SOH and defines only 6 packet TYPES: ASCII control codes ACK, NAK, ENQ and EOT and ASCII character codes S and D. The maximum data field length for GREEN3 is 48 bytes. LEN is the binary representation of the length and CHECK is the binary modulo 256 sum of all of the bytes included in the CHECK computation.

GREEN3 Packet TYPES:

ACK   Acknowledgment.
NAK   Negative Acknowledgment
ENQ   Initialization
EOT   Termination
S   Send
D   Data type

For the control TYPES (ACK, NAK, ENQ EOT, and S) the DATA field is 1 byte and the contents of the DATA field and SEQ have no significance.

For the data TYPE, the DATA field is 1 to 48 bytes. The contents of SEQ has no significance (for GREEN3 the packets have a SEQ byte, but the value of SEQ is meaningless).

When GREEN3 receives an ENQ packet, it responds with an S packet, telling the sender to begin transmitting data packets. If the next packet received is a data packet, GREEN3 places the data bytes into a buffer, writes the buffer contents to the display and then sends an ACK packet. If another data byte is received, it is similarly displayed and an ACK packet is sent. This process is repeated until an EOT packet is received at which time GREEN3 sends an ACK packet and starts over at the beginning of the program.

As each byte of a packet is received, starting with the LEN byte and continuing through the last data byte, the value of each byte is added (binary add without carry; modulo 256) to compute a checksum. Each checksum is unique to each packet and should equal the value of the CHECK byte. If the checksum equals CHECK it is assumed that the packet has been received without error. If a received packet is corrupted (check sum does not equal CHECK) then GREEN3 responds by sending a NAK packet as a request for a resend. NOTE: both the checksum and CHECK are binary. The sender must compute CHECK in the same way that GREEN3 does.

If a packet is not received within the time-out period after a response packet has been sent by GREEN3, a time-out occurs and it repeats the last packet sent. GREEN3 does not terminate the transfer session after a certain number of consecutive time-outs.

If a packet HEAD byte is incorrectly received or if a LEN byte is out of range, GREEN3 restarts the time-out counter and waits for a new HEAD byte. If the beginning of a head byte was sensed due to noise on the circuit (false HEAD) rather than as a result of a corrupted real HEAD, a real HEAD may arrive before time-out and transfer will continue normally. If a real HEAD does not arrive before the time-out (not very likely if the time-outs are set correctly), GREEN3 will retransmit the last byte sent. If it was a corrupted real HEAD byte, there will be a deadlock, resulting in a time-out and GREEN3 will retransmit the last byte sent to get the transfer going again. In any case the sender will know how to interpret the packet from the receiver. If the sender was not expecting the packet, it will know it represents a false HEAD error and will ignor it. If the sender was expecting a packet, it will retransmit the last packet sent. Because GREEN3 uses very simple control packets and no significant SEQ data, the time-out periods must be long enough to account for any delays and *only* one end of the communications circuit should have time-out capability. Port A5 (see schematic, Figure 6-1) enables or disables the GREEN3 time-outs: a jumper from Port A5 to ground disables the time-out.

GREEN3 Program Summary

For the following functional description of the GREEN3 program modules, see Figures 6-13 through 6-16 and GREEN3.ASM.

The main program waits in a timing loop (for time-outs) for an interrupt on reception of a byte. If a time-out occurs, the time-out service, TIMSRV, is called and the last response is retransmitted. At program initialization, time-outs are inhibited until at least one byte has been received.

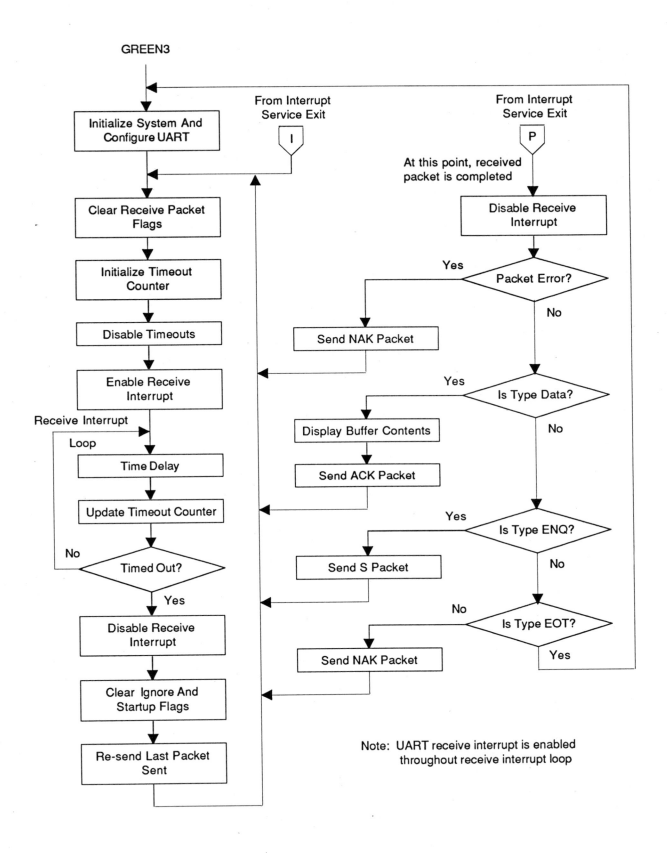

Figure 6-13   GREEN3 Main Program

169

When a byte is received, the interrupt service, INTSRV, is called. INTSRV fetches the received byte via a call to UREC, calls PACREC to build the received packet and then restarts the time-out counter and returns to the main timing loop. INTSRV also checks Port A5 to determine if the time-outs have been disabled. If the received packet is complete, INTSRV does not return, but goes to the user area PACSRV. If a false HEAD has been received or LEN is out of range, INTSRV does not return, but goes to the beginning of the main timing loop.

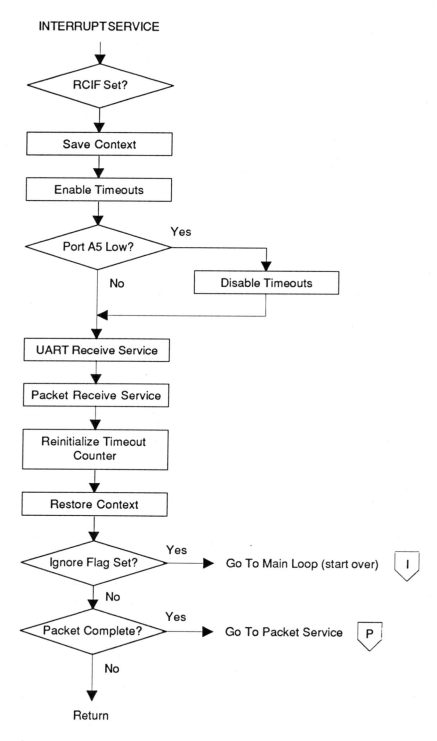

Figure 6-14   GREEN3 Interrupt Service

PACREC builds the received packet one byte at a time. It is called each time a byte is received until a packet is completed. It uses the value of LEN and a byte counter to determine when all of the packet bytes have been received. As data bytes are received, PACREC places them in the data buffer. PACREC also computes the checksum.

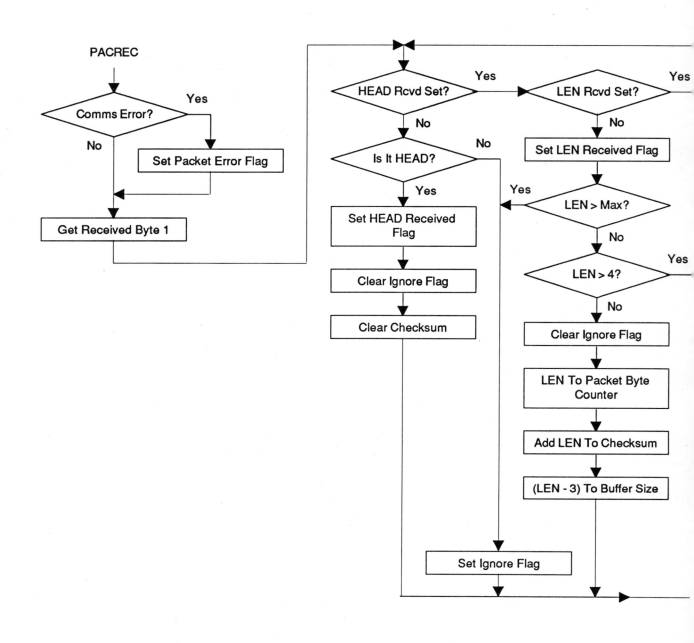

Figure 6-15   PACREC; Packet Receive Service

172

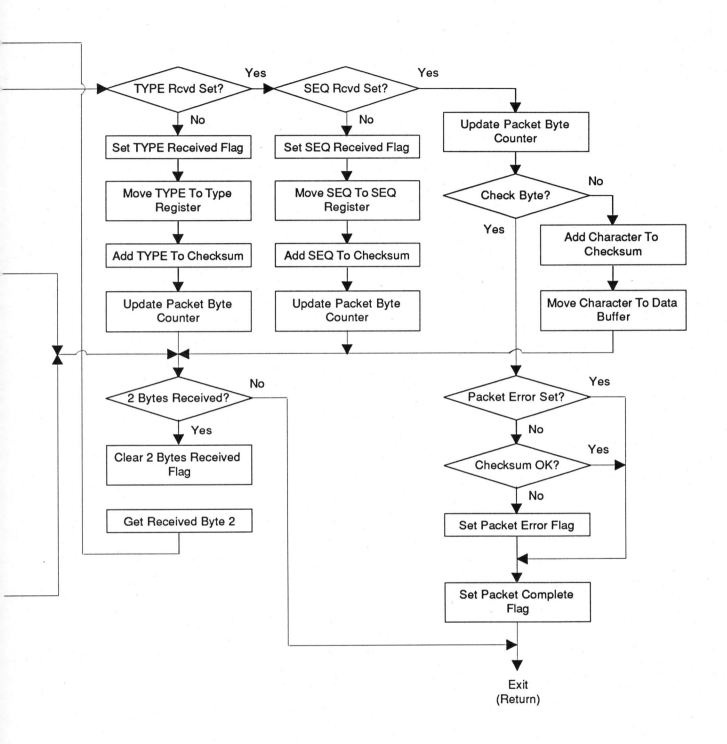

173

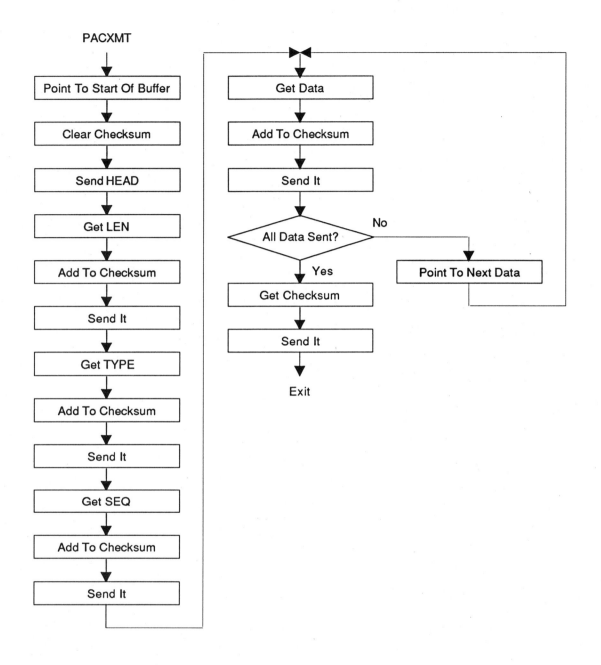

Figure 6-16   PACXMT; Packet Transmit Service

The user part of the main program, PACSRV, checks the completed packet. If the packet is corrupted, or is not one of the defined TYPES, it sends the NAK response packet. If the packet is an ENQ type, PACSRV sends the S response packet or if it is an EOT type, sends an ENQ response packet. The responses are sent via calls to alternate entrances of the CTLPAC module. IF the packet is a D type (data), PACSRV calls the PRINT module. PRINT writes the data buffer contents to the display and returns. PACSRV then sends the ACK packet and goes to the beginning of the main timing loop.

Table 6-2   GREENPK - Receive Packet Flags (rflgs)

BIT	FLAG	FUNCTION
0	PACKET ERROR (pakerr)	SET for packet error
1	PACKET COMPLETE (newpac)	SET when CHECK byte is received
2	reserved	
3	reserved	
4	TYPE RECEIVED (newtype)	SET when TYPE byte is received
5	SEQUENCE RECEIVED (newseq)	SET when SEQ byte is rceived
6	LENGTH RECEIVED (newlen)	SET when LEN byte is received
7	HEAD RECEIVED (newhead)	SET when HEAD byte is received

Table 6-3   GREEN3 - System Flags (sysflg)

BIT	FLAG	FUNCTION
0	reserved	
1	STARTUP (startup)	SET at initialize, CLEARED at 1ST send
2	BAD HEAD or LEN(ignore)	SET for bad HEAD or LEN out of range
3	reserved	
4	reserved	
5	TIMED OUT (timout)	SET when timeout counter times out
6	reserved	
7	TIMEOUT ENABLED (timen)	SET when timeout is enabled

```
;======GREEN3.ASM===============================================================
;
;;        File: green3.asm
;
;        On chip UART
;        Packet communications with in-band flow control
;        See Section 6.3.2
;
;-------------------------------------------------------------------------------
          radix   hex        ;RADIX is HEX
;
          list p=16c63
;
;-------------------------------------------------------------------------------
;     CPU DEFINITIONS
;
;        STATUS REGISTER BIT DEFINITIONS:
c         equ     0          ;carry bit of status register (bit 0)
z         equ     2          ;zero flag bit of status register (bit 2)
dc        equ     1          ;digit carry
pd        equ     3          ;power down bit
to        equ     4          ;time out bit
rp0       equ     5          ;program page preselect, low bit
rp1       equ     6          ;program page preselect, high bit
;
;        DESTINATION BIT DEFINITIONS:
w         equ     0          ;destination working
f         equ     1          ;destination file
;
;-------------------------------------------------------------------------------
;     CPU EQUATES   (special function register memory map)
;
;   BANK 0:
indf      equ     00         ;indirect file register
tmr0      equ     01         ;timer
pcl       equ     02         ;program counter (low byte)
status    equ     03         ;status register
fsr       equ     04         ;indirect data pointer
porta     equ     05         ;port a
portb     equ     06         ;port b
portc     equ     07         ;port c
pclath    equ     0a         ;write buffer for program counter (high byte)
intcon    equ     0b         ;interrupt control register
pir1      equ     0c         ;peripheral interrupt flags
pir2      equ     0d         ;
tmr1l     equ     0e         ;TMR1 register low byte
tmr1h     equ     0f         ;              high byte
t1con     equ     10         ;timer 1 control register
tmr2      equ     11         ;timer 2
t2con     equ     12         ;timer 2 control register
sspbuf    equ     13         ;SSP receive/xmit register
sspcon    equ     14         ;SSP control register
ccpr1l    equ     15         ;CCP 1 low byte
ccpr1h    equ     16         ;      high byte
```

```
ccp1con equ      17          ;CCP 1 control register
rcsta   equ      18          ;UART receive status & control register
txreg   equ      19          ;UART xmit data register
rcreg   equ      1a          ;UART receive register
ccpr2l  equ      1b          ;CCP 2 low byte
ccpr2h  equ      1c          ;        high byte
ccp2con equ      1d          ;CCP 2 control register
;
;   BANK 1:
optreg  equ      01          ;option register                   bank 1 (0x81)
trisa   equ      05          ;data direction register port a    bank 1 (0x85)
trisb   equ      06          ;data direction register port b    bank 1 (0x86)
trisc   equ      07          ;data direction register port c    bank 1 (0x87)
pie1    equ      0c          ;peripheral interrupt enable       bank 1 (0x8c)
pie2    equ      0d          ;                                  bank 1 (0x8d)
pcon    equ      0e          ;power control register            bank 1 (0x8e)
pr2     equ      12          ;timer 2 period register           bank 1 (0x92)
sspadd  equ      13          ;SSP address register              bank 1 (0x93)
sspstat equ      14          ;SSP status register               bank 1 (0x94)
txsta   equ      18          ;UART xmit status & control        bank 1 (0x98)
spbrg   equ      19          ;UART baud rate generator          bank 1 (0x99)
;
;-----------------------------------------------------------------------------
;       CPU SPECIAL REGISTER BIT DEFINITIONS
;
;       Register PIR1:
rcif    equ      5
txif    equ      4
;       Register PIE1:
rcie    equ      5
txie    equ      4
;       Register TXSTA:
csrc    equ      7
tx9     equ      6
txen    equ      5
sync    equ      4
brgh    equ      2
trmt    equ      1
tx9d    equ      0
;       Register RCSTA:
spen    equ      7
rx9     equ      6
sren    equ      5
cren    equ      4
ferr    equ      2
oerr    equ      1
rx9d    equ      0
;       Register INTCON:
gie     equ      7
peie    equ      6
toie    equ      5
inte    equ      4
rbie    equ      3
toif    equ      2
```

```
intf      equ     1
rbif      equ     0
;
;================================================================
;         GREEN3
;
;         Full-Duplex Packetized Data Transfer System
;         Uses on-chip UART
;----------------------------------------------------------------
;         WORK AREA (Memory Map)   Starts at 0020
;
;         System variables:
tempst    equ     0020      ;temporary status (for context save)
tempw     equ     0021      ;temporary w (for context save)
temp      equ     0022      ;temporary storage
cntra     equ     0023      ;time delay counter
cntrb     equ     0024      ;time delay counter
timctr    equ     0025      ;time out counter
acount    equ     0026      ;time delay counter parameter a
bcount    equ     0027      ;time delay counter parameter b
sysflg    equ     0028      ;system flags
;
;         Communications (uart) variables:
recflg    equ     0030      ;communications receive flags
recuse1   equ     0031      ;user receive character 1
recuse2   equ     0032      ;user receive character 2
xmtuse    equ     0034      ;user xmit character
;
;         Packet variables
rflgs     equ     0036      ;packet receive flags
rhead     equ     0037      ;   "        "     head
rlen      equ     0038      ;   "        "     len (used as receive data
;                                            byte counter)
rseq      equ     0039      ;   "        "     seq
rtype     equ     003a      ;   "        "     type
rcheck    equ     003b      ;   "        "     check
rdat      equ     003c      ;current received packet byte
;
xflgs     equ     003f      ;packet xmit flags
xhead     equ     0040      ;packet xmit head (reserved)
xlen      equ     0041      ;   "      "    len
xseq      equ     0042      ;   "      "    seq
xtype     equ     0043      ;   "      "    type
xdat      equ     0044      ;   "      "    data
;
cksum     equ     0048      ;check sum
;
;         Buffer variables:
bufptr    equ     0050      ;buffer position pointer
buflen    equ     0051      ;buffer length
bufdat    set     rdat      ;buffer data (shares memory with rdat and xdat)
;
;
;
```

178

```
;           Buffer Literals
rbufst   equ        007f      ;start of receive buffer - Bank 1 (00ff)
xbufst   equ        004f      ;start of xmit buffer    - Bank 1 (00cf)
;
;           Display variables
dispflg  equ        0055      ;display flags
dispdat  equ        0056      ;display data
dispstat equ        0057      ;display status
;
;           Display Equates
dispen   equ        01
disprs   equ        02
disprw   equ        03
;-------------------------------------------------------------------------
;           SYSTEM EQUATES
;
;           recflg bit definitions (uart receive flags):
newbyt   equ        0         ;byte received flag
twobyt   equ        1         ;two bytes received flag
threbyt  equ        2         ;three bytes received flag
frmerr1  equ        3         ;framing error 1 flag
frmerr2  equ        4         ;framing error 2 flag
overerr  equ        6         ;overflow error flag
;
;           rflgs bit definitions (packet receive flags):
pakerr   equ        0         ;packet error
newpac   equ        1         ;packet completed
newtype  equ        4         ;type received
newseq   equ        5         ;seq received
newlen   equ        6         ;len received
newhead  equ        7         ;head received
;
;           sysflg bit definitions (system flags)
timen    equ        7         ;timeouts enabled
timout   equ        5         ;timed out flag
ignore   equ        2         ;bad head or len
;
;           System Literals
timeout  equ        d'50'     ;timeout is 10 seconds (0.2 seconds per count)
maxbuf   equ        d'48'     ;max buffer depth (max len = maxbuf + 3)
;
;           ascii character codes (literals):
SOH      equ        001       ;ascii SOH
ACK      equ        006       ;ascii ACK
NAK      equ        015       ;ascii NAK
EOT      equ        004       ;ascii EOT
ENQ      equ        005       ;ascii ENQ
DEE      equ        044       ;ascii D
ESS      equ        053       ;ascii S
OH       equ        04f       ;ascii O
KAY      equ        04b       ;ascii K
CR       equ        00d       ;ascii carriage return
LF       equ        00a       ;ascii line feed
head     set        SOH       ;head is SOH
```

```
;-----------------------------------------------------------------
;          MAIN PROGRAM
;
;-----------------------------------------------------------------
          org       0x00            ;start of program memory
start     goto      start0          ;jump over version and int vector
          dw        0072            ;version code
          dw        006c
          dw        0073
          goto      intsrv          ;interrupt service vector
start0    clrf      porta
          clrf      portb
          clrf      portc
          bsf       status,rp0      ;switch to bank 1
          movlw     0c0             ;port c7, c6 as inputs (required for UART
;                                    operation)
          movwf     trisc           ;& other portc as outputs
          movlw     000
          movwf     trisb           ;all port b as outputs
          movlw     021             ;port a0, a5 as inputs
          movwf     trisa           ;& all others porta as outputs
          movlw     080             ;config UART xmitter
          movwf     txsta
          movlw     019             ;2400 bits per second
          movwf     spbrg
          bcf       status,rp0      ;switch to bank 0
          movlw     010
          movwf     rcsta           ;configure UART receiver
;
;         at this point the UART is configured, but NOT on.
;
;         here we turn On the UART:
          bsf       rcsta,spen      ;enable serial port
          bsf       status,rp0      ;switch to bank 1
          bsf       txsta,txen      ;enable xmit
          bsf       pie1,rcie       ;enable receive interrupt
          bcf       status,rp0      ;switch to bank 0
          bsf       intcon,peie     ;enable peripheral interrupts
;
;         at this point the UART is ON, but will not receive because
;         global interrupt is still inhibited.
;
          call      initdis         ;initialize display
;
          bcf       sysflg,timen    ;disable timeouts (until 1st byte received)
;
          movlw     OH              ;display "OK"
          movwf     dispdat
          call      dissrv
          movlw     KAY
          movwf     dispdat
          call      dissrv
          movlw     CR
```

```
                movwf    dispdat
                call     dissrv
                movlw    LF
                movwf    dispdat
                call     dissrv
        ;
        mloop   clrf     rflgs           ;clear packet receive flags
                movlw    timeout         ;timeout to time out counter
                movwf    timctr          ;(in 200 mSec increments)
                movlw    rbufst          ;point to start of receive buffer
                movwf    bufptr
        ;       this is the start of the receive interrupt loop:
        ;
        mloop1  bsf      intcon,gie      ;enable interrupts (enables receive)
                movlw    0ff             ;delay approx 200 mSec
                movwf    cntrb
        mloop2  movlw    0ff
                movwf    cntra
        mloop3  decfsz   cntra,f
                goto     mloop3
                decfsz   cntrb,f         ;delay completed ? if yes,skip next
                goto     mloop2          ;no. go
                bcf      intcon,gie      ;yes. disable interrupts
                btfss    sysflg,timen    ;timeouts enabled ? if yes, skip next
                goto     mloop1          ;no. go loop
                decfsz   timctr,f        ;yes. timed out ? if yes, skip next
                goto     mloop1          ;no.go loop
                bsf      sysflg,timout   ;yes. set timed out flag
                call     timsrv          ;timeout service
                goto     mloop           ;go receive next packet
        ;
        ;===============================================================================
        ;
        ;       USER AREA STARTS HERE
        ;
        ;       This is the destination for the completed packet alternate exit
        ;       from the interrupt service. At this point a complete packet has
        ;       been received. This is the beginning of the USER area.
        ;       This is NOT a called service.
        ;
        pacsrv  btfss    rflgs,pakerr    ;receive packet error ? if yes, skip next
                goto     pacsrv0         ;no. go
                call     senNAK          ;yes. send NAK packet
                goto     mloop           ;& go receive next packet
        ;
        pacsrv0 movlw    DEE             ;no. is it data type ?
                subwf    rtype,w
                btfss    status,z        ;if yes, skip next
                goto     pacsrv1         ;no. go test for other types
                call     print           ;write buffer to display
                call     senACK          ;send ACK packet
                goto     mloop           ;& go receive next packet
        ;
        pacsrv1 movlw    ENQ             ;is it ENQ ?
```

```
          subwf    rtype,w
          btfss    status,z        ;if yes, skip next
          goto     pacsrv2         ;no. go
          call     senESS          ;yes. send S type packet
          goto     mloop           ;& go receive next packet
;
pacsrv2 movlw      EOT             ;is it EOT ?
          subwf    rtype,w
          btfss    status,z        ;if yes, skip next
          goto     pacsrve         ;no. illegal packet. go send NAK packet
          call     senACK          ;yes. send ACK
          goto     start           ;& go reinitialize
;
pacsrve call       senNAK          ;send NAK packet
          goto     mloop           ;& go receive next packet
;------------------------------------------------------------------
;         TIMEOUT SERVICE
;         Module:timsrv.txt
;
;         This is part of USER area. This is a called service.
;         This service is called if more than approx 10 seconds between
;         received bytes. See mloop1 through mloop3 above.
;         The GREEN3 response to a timeout is to re-send the last
;         packet sent.
;         The packet receive service sets the ignore flag if a bad head
;         is received or if the packet length is incorrect. If the ignore
;         flag is set, the GREEN3 response is to send NAK.
;         NOTE: It is the users responsibility to clear any timeout
;               related flags in sysflg.
;
;------------------------------------------------------------------
timsrv  bcf        sysflg,timout   ;clear timed out flag (flag is redundant for
;                                    this application (GREEN3)
          btfss    sysflg,ignore   ;ignore flag set ? if yes, skip next
          goto     timsrv1         ;no. go repeat last packet sent
          bcf      sysflg,ignore   ;yes. clear it
          call     senNAK          ;send NAK
          goto     timsrvx         ;& go exit
;
timsrv1 call pacxmt                ;repeat last packet sent
timsrvx return                     ;exit
;
;------------------------------------------------------------------
;         This is the end of the MAIN program.
;         The USER AREA continues with the module PRINT (located after the
;         PACKET GROUP) and includes all modules from PRINT to the end of
;         the program.
;
;====== PACKET.GRP ================================================
;
;         PACKET GROUP - File: PACKET.GRP
;         Module packet.grp
;         These Modules are required for packet communications.
;         The Modules are: pacrec, pacxmt, ctlpac, urec, uxmt, ldbuf,
```

```
;                                   getbuf, intsrv
;
;-----------------------------------------------------------------------------
;         Required WORK AREA:
;
;         System variables:
;         tempst              temporary status (for context save)
;         tempw               temporary w (for context save)
;         temp                temporary storage
;         timctr              time out counter
;         sysflg              system flags
;
;         Communications (uart) variables:
;         recflg              communications receive flags
;         recuse1             user receive character 1
;         recuse2             user receive character 2
;         xmtuse              user xmit character
;
;         Packet variables
;         rflgs               packet receive flags
;         rhead                  "      "    head
;         rlen                   "      "    len (used as receive data byte
;                                            counter)
;         rseq                   "      "    seq
;         rtype                  "      "    type
;         check                  "      "    check
;         rdat                current received packet byte
;         xflgs               packet xmit flags
;         xhead               packet xmit head (reserved)
;         xlen                   "      "   len
;         xseq                   "      "   seq
;         xtype                  "      "   type
;         xdat                   "      "   data
;         cksum               check sum
;
;         Buffer variables:
;         bufptr              buffer position pointer
;         buflen              buffer length
;         bufdat              buffer data (shares memory with rdat and xdat)
;
;         Buffer Literals
;         rbufst              start of receive buffer - Bank 1 (00ff)
;         xbufst              start of xmit buffer    - Bank 1 (00cf)
;
;-----------------------------------------------------------------------------
;         SYSTEM EQUATES
;
;         recflg bit definitions (uart receive flags):
;         newbyt  equ     0       ;byte received flag
;         twobyt  equ     1       ;two bytes received flag
;         threbyt equ     2       ;three bytes received flag
;         frmerr1 equ     3       ;framing error 1 flag
;         frmerr2 equ     4       ;framing error 2 flag
;         overerr equ     6       ;overflow error flag
```

183

```
;
;           rflgs bit definitions (packet receive flags):
;           pakerr  equ     0          ;packet error
;           newpac  equ     1          ;packet completed
;           newtype equ     4          ;type received
;           newseq  equ     5          ;seq received
;           newlen  equ     6          ;len received
;           newhead equ     7          ;head received
;
;        sysflg bit definitions (system flags)
;           timen   equ     7          ;timeouts enabled
;           timout  equ     5          ;timed out flag
;           ignore  equ     2          ;bad head or len
;
;           System Literals
;           timeout equ     d'50'      ;timeout is 10 seconds (0.2 seconds per
;                                       count)
;           maxbuf  equ     d'48'      ;max buffer depth (max len = maxbuf + 3)
;
;           ascii character codes (literals):
;           SOH     equ     001        ;ascii SOH
;           ACK     equ     006        ;ascii ACK
;           NAK     equ     015        ;ascii NAK
;           EOT     equ     004        ;ascii EOT
;           ENQ     equ     005        ;ascii ENQ
;           DEE     equ     044        ;ascii D
;           ESS     equ     053        ;ascii S
;           OH      equ     04f        ;ascii O
;           KAY     equ     04b        ;ascii K
;           CR      equ     00d        ;ascii carriage return
;           LF      equ     00a        ;ascii line feed
;           head    set     SOH        ;head is SOH
;
;        All communications parameters are established at program
;        initialization. See Sections 6.2 and 6.3.2 and GREEN3.ASM
;        for initialization and application information.
;-------------------------------------------------------------------------
;        RECEIVE PACKET BYTE
;        Module: pacrec
;
;-------------------------------------------------------------------------
pacrec  movlw   078             ;frame or overflow error ?
        andwf   recflg,w
        btfss   status,z        ;if no (result = 0), skip next
        bsf     rflgs,pakerr    ;yes. set packet error flag
        movf    recuse1,w       ;no. get received byte
        movwf   rdat
pacrecA btfsc   rflgs,newhead   ;head already received ? if no, skip next
        goto    pacrec2         ;yes. go
        movlw   head            ;no. is it correct head ?
        subwf   rdat,w
        btfss   status,z        ;if yes, skip next
        goto    pacrec1         ;no. go set packet ignore flag
        bsf     rflgs,newhead   ;yes. set head received flag
```

```
        bcf       sysflg,ignore    ;clear ignore flag
        clrf      cksum            ;clear check sum
        goto      pacrecB          ;& go
;
pacrec1 bsf       sysflg,ignore    ;set packet ignore flag
        goto      pacrecB          ;& go
;
pacrec2 btfsc     rflgs,newlen     ;len already received ? if no, skip next
        goto      pacrec3          ;yes. go
        bsf       rflgs,newlen     ;no. set len received flag
        movlw     maxbuf           ;max buffer depth
        movwf     temp             ;max len = maxbuf + 3
        incf      temp,f
        incf      temp,f
        incf      temp,f
        movf      rdat,w
        subwf     temp,w           ;len > max len ?
        btfss     status,c         ;len too large ? if no, skip next
        goto      pacrec1          ;yes. go to ignore exit
        movlw     04               ;no. len < 4 ?
        subwf     rdat,w
        btfss     status,c         ;if no, skip next
        goto      pacrec1          ;yes. go to ignore exit
        bcf       sysflg,ignore    ;no. clear ignore flag
        movf      rdat,w           ;len to packet data byte counter
        movwf     rlen
        addwf     cksum,f          ;add len to checksum
        movwf     buflen           ;buffer length is len-3
        decf      buflen,f
        decf      buflen,f
        decf      buflen,f         ;number of data bytes (used by print)
        goto      pacrecB          ;go
;
pacrec3 btfsc     rflgs,newtype    ;type already received ? if no, skip next
        goto      pacrec4          ;yes. go
        bsf       rflgs,newtype    ;no. set type received flag
        movwf     rtype            ;save type
        addwf     cksum,f          ;add it to check sum
        decf      rlen,f           ;update byte counter
        goto      pacrecB          ;& go
;
pacrec4 btfsc     rflgs,newseq     ;seq already received ? if no, skip next
        goto      pacrec5          ;yes. go
        bsf       rflgs,newseq     ;no. set seq received flag
        movwf     rseq             ;save seq
        addwf     cksum,f          ;add it to check sum
        decf      rlen,f           ;update byte counter
        goto      pacrecB          ;& go
;
pacrec5 decfsz    rlen,f           ;update byte counter. skip if check byte
        goto      pacrec6          ;not check. then it is data. go
        goto      pacrec7          ;is check. go test check against check sum
;
pacrec6 addwf     cksum,f          ;add it to check sum
```

```
                movwf    bufdat            ;move it to bufdat
                call     ldbuf             ;& place it in buffer
;
pacrecB btfss   recflg,twobyt             ;2 bytes in uart ? if yes, skip
        goto    pacrecx                   ;no. go exit
        bcf     recflg,twobyt             ;yes. clear 2 byte flag
        movf    recuse2,w                 ;get 2nd byte
        movwf   rdat                      ;save it for now
        goto    pacrecA                   ;& go
;
pacrec7 btfsc   rflgs,pakerr              ;packet error ? if no, skip
        goto    pacrec8                   ;yes. go packet completed exit
        movf    rdat,w                    ;no. get check
        subwf   cksum,w                   ;same as check sum ?
        btfss   status,z                  ;if yes, skip next
pacrecC bsf     rflgs,pakerr              ;no. check sum NOT ok. set packet error flag
pacrec8 bsf     rflgs,newpac              ;set packet completed flag
;
pacrecx return                           ;EXIT
;-----------------------------------------------------------------------
;       SEND PACKET
;       Module: pacxmt
;       Sends a complete packet
;
;-----------------------------------------------------------------------
pacxmt  movlw   xbufst                    ;point to start of xmit buffer
        movwf   bufptr
        clrf    cksum                     ;clear checksum
        movlw   head                      ;send head
        movwf   xmtuse
        call    uxmt
        movf    xlen,w                    ;get len
        movwf   cksum                     ;1st value of checksum
        movwf   xmtuse                    ;move it to xmitter
        movwf   buflen                    ;data byte counter
        decf    buflen,f
        decf    buflen,f
        decf    buflen,f
        call    uxmt                      ;send len
        movf    xtype,w                   ;get type
        addwf   cksum,f                   ;add it to checksum
        movwf   xmtuse                    ;move it to xmitter
        call    uxmt                      ;send it
        movf    xseq,w                    ;get seq
        addwf   cksum,f                   ;add it to checksum
        movwf   xmtuse                    ;move it to xmitter
        call    uxmt                      ;send it
pacxmt1 call    getbuf                    ;get data from buffer
        movf    bufdat,w
        addwf   cksum,f                   ;add it to checksum
        movwf   xmtuse                    ;move it to xmitter
        call    uxmt                      ;send it
        decfsz  buflen,f                  ;update data byte counter. skip if
;                                          all data done
```

```
        goto    pacxmt1             ;go get next data byte
        movf    cksum,w             ;all data done. get checksum
        movwf   xmtuse              ;move it to xmitter
        call    uxmt                ;send it
        return                      ;exit
;-------------------------------------------------------------------
;       CONTROL PACKET SERVICE
;       Module:ctlpac
;
;       Sends Control Packets
;-------------------------------------------------------------------
senNAK  movlw   NAK                 ;send NAK packet
        movwf   xtype
        goto    senbal
senACK  movlw   ACK                 ;send ACK packet
        movwf   xtype
        goto    senbal
senESS  movlw   ESS                 ;send 'S' packet
        movwf   xtype
        goto    senbal
;
senbal  movlw   04                  ;len = 4
        movwf   xlen
        clrf    xseq                ;(seq not significant for green3)
        clrf    xdat                ;xdat = 0 for NAK, ACK & ESS packet
        movf    xdat,w              ;xdat to buffer:
        movwf   bufdat
        movlw   xbufst              ;beginning of xmit buffer
        movwf   bufptr              ;point to beginning of buffer
        call    ldbuf               ;xdat to buffer
        call    pacxmt              ;send packet
        return                      ;exit
;
;-------------------------------------------------------------------
;       RECEIVE MODULE
;       Module: urec
;
;       Receives 1 or 2 bytes from UART receiver
;
;===================================================================
;       The following two modules (UREC and UXMT) are the same as in
;       UCOMS.GRP
;-------------------------------------------------------------------
urec    clrf    recflg              ;clear communications receive flags
        bsf     recflg,newbyt       ;set byte received flag
        btfsc   rcsta,ferr          ;framing error ? if no, skip next
        bsf     recflg,frmerr1      ;yes set user frame error 1 flag
        movf    rcreg,w             ;get received character
        movwf   recuse1             ;& move to user received byte 1
        btfss   pir1,rcif           ;data still in buffer (2nd byte) ? if yes,
skip
        goto    urecx               ;no. go
        bsf     recflg,twobyt       ;yes. set two bytes received flag
        btfsc   rcsta,ferr          ;framing error ? if no, skip next
```

```
        bsf     recflg,frmerr2  ;yes. set user frame error 2
        movf    rcreg,w         ;get 2nd received character
        movwf   recuse2         ;& move to user received byte 2
;
urecx   btfsc   rcsta,oerr      ;overrun error ? if no, skip next
        bsf     recflg,overerr  ;yes. set overflow flag
        bcf     rcsta,cren      ;clear UART overrun flag
        bsf     rcsta,cren
        return                  ;& exit
;--------------------------------------------------------------------
;       TRANSMIT MODULE
;       Module: uxmt
;       Transmitts 1 byte via UART
;
;--------------------------------------------------------------------
uxmt    btfss   pir1,txif       ;xmit buffer empty ? if yes, skip next
        goto    uxmt            ;no. go try again
        movf    xmtuse,w        ;yes. get character to xmit
        movwf   txreg           ;xmit it
        return                  ;& exit
;====================================================================
;       LOAD BUFFER BYTE
;       Module: ldbuf
;
;       Loads current buffer location with bufdat
;       ON ENTRY, bufptr points to current buffer location
;
;--------------------------------------------------------------------
ldbuf   movf    bufptr,w        ;point to current buffer location
        movwf   fsr
        movf    bufdat,w        ;get data
        bsf     status,rp0      ;switch to bank 1
        movwf   indf            ;data to buffer
        bcf     status,rp0      ;switch to bank 0
        decf    bufptr,f        ;point to next buffer location
        return
;--------------------------------------------------------------------
;       GET BUFFER BYTE
;       Module getbuf
;
;       Gets contents of current buffer location and places in bufdat.
;       ON ENTRY, bufptr points to current buffer location
;
;       Buffer is located in bank 1
;--------------------------------------------------------------------
getbuf  movf    bufptr,w        ;point to current buffer location
        bsf     status,rp0      ;switch to bank 1
        movwf   fsr
        movf    indf,w          ;get data byte
        bcf     status,rp0      ;switch to bank 0
        movwf   bufdat
        decf    bufptr,f        ;point to next location
        return
```

```
;---------------------------------------------------------------
;        INTERRUPT service
;        Module: intsrv
;        This receive interrupt service is specific to the GREEN3 application
;
;---------------------------------------------------------------
intsrv  btfss   pir1,rcif       ;data in receive buffer ? if yes, skip
        goto    intsrvx         ;no. not receive interrupt. go exit
        movwf   tempw           ;yes. save context
        swapf   status,w
        bcf     status,rp0
        movwf   tempst
;
        call    urec            ;get received byte
        bsf     sysflg,timen    ;enable timeouts
        btfss   porta,5         ;port a5 high ? if yes, skip next
        bcf     sysflg,timen    ;no. disable timeouts
        call    pacrec          ;packet service for received byte
        movlw   timeout         ;reinitialize time out counter
        movwf   timctr
intsrv1 swapf   tempst,w        ;restore context
        movwf   status
        swapf   tempw,f
        swapf   tempw,w
        btfsc   sysflg,ignore   ;ignore flag set ? if no, skip next
;
        goto    mloop           ;yes. Go start over ! ALTERNATE EXIT.
;                                Does NOT return from interrupt. Ignores
;                                received byte and goes to wait for NEW head.
;
        btfss   rflgs,newpac    ;packet completed ? if yes, skip next
;
intsrvx retfie                  ;no. return from interrupt. NORMAL EXIT
;
        goto    pacsrv          ;ALTERNATE EXIT from interrupt. Does NOT
;                                RETURN from interrupt. Global interrupts
;                                remain inhibited. Full packet has been
;                                received. pacsrv is beginning of USER area.
;---------------------------------------------------------------
;
;     This is the end of the PACKET GROUP
;===============================================================
;
;        ALL OF THE FOLLOWING MODULES ARE PART OF THE USER AREA
;---------------------------------------------------------------
;        DISPLAY BUFFER CONTENTS
;        Module print.txt
;
;
;---------------------------------------------------------------
print   movlw   rbufst          ;point to start of receive buffer
        movwf   bufptr
print1  call    getbuf          ;get character from buffer
        movf    bufdat,w        ;move it to display character parameter
```

189

```
        movwf    dispdat
        call     dissrv              ;display it
        decfsz   buflen,f            ;all characters displayed? if yes, skip next
        goto     print1              ;no. get next from buffer
        return                       ;yes. exit
;--------------------------------------------------------------------------
;       INCLUDES:
;       DISSRV.TXT                   Two line by 20 character LCD Display service
;--------------------------------------------------------------------------
        include          dissrv.grp       ;LCD Display
;
;--------------------------------------------------------------------------
        end                          ;end of program
;==========================================================================
```

6.3.3   Using the Section 6.3 Routines in Your Applications

Generally all of the routines can be used in your applications as written or with minor changes. For all routines, the entry and exit conditions, variables, port definitions and flag definitions are described in the individual xx.ASM, xx.GRP and xx.TXT listings. All port assignments (except RX and TX) are arbitrary and may be changed to suit your application.

The sample applications demonstrate how the UART routines are applied to communications applications. They use the PIC16C63 but may be used with other 16Cxxx devices or with 16Fxxx devices with little or no change. For 17Cxxx applications the Special Register addresses must be changed. All of the xx.TXT and xx.GRP modules may be used as include files.

If data rates and data formats differing from the sample applications are required, the special register settings will have to be changed. See Section 6.1 and the Microchip Product manuals.

The GREEN2 sample application sends a block of characters, but does not receive a block. PACKET.GRP in GREEN3.ASM demonstrates block data reception. GREEN3 demonstrates packet communications with in-band flow control.

The Packet Communications routines introduced in section 6.3 are in:

PACKET.GRP A set of modules required for packet communications

The modules in PACKET.GRP are:

PACREC	Receive a Packet Byte
INTSRV	Packet Receive Interrupt Service (builds a received packet)
PACXMT	Send a Complete Packet
CTLPAC	Send Control Packet
LDBUF	Load One Byte to Buffer
GETBUF	Get One Byte From Buffer
UREC	UART Receive a Character
UXMT	UART Transmit a Character

If the GREENPK packet format is retained for your application, all of the PACKET.GRP modules (with the possible exception of INTSRV) may be used unchanged.

If time-outs are enabled, and your application does not initiate communications, the application main program must disable time-outs until the first byte is received. Generally the best place to enable the time-outs is in the receive interrupt service as in GREEN3. A startup flag has also been provided for distinguishing between startup and active communication states (bit 1 of **sysflg**). This startup flag is not used in GREEN3. All of the GREEN3 flags (except the display flags) must be retained for any application. Note that the packet receive service sets the packet receive flags and the ignore flag. Your application is responsible for clearing these flags. See sections 6.1 and 6.2 for a discussion of the UART, UREC and UXMT related flags.

The interrupt service returns after a byte has been received. If the received byte completes the packet, the service does not return, but jumps to the packet service which is the beginning of the USER area. The USER treats the packet as required by the application then goes to some restart point in the application. GREEN3 prints the packet to the display and if it was not the last packet (type EOT), jumps to the beginning of the USER area to await the next packet. If the received packet was an EOT type, GREEN3 jumps to the beginning (**reset**) of the program and queries the sender for a new file.

If your application must service other interrupts, the UART receive interrupt should have highest priority. If the application requires interrupts having higher priority than the UART be sure that they can be serviced in less than one character period. The UART two byte receive buffer will handle this multiple interrupt latency.

If the ignore flag is set, as a result of a bad head or incorrect packet length, the interrupt service jumps to the beginning of the main loop, ignoring any previously received characters. It is possible that the interrupt service will continue this looping until all characters of the corrupted packet have been received. A time out will then restart the communication and the lost packet will be re-sent. GREENPK defines a SEQ field which may be used to number the packet. GREEN3 assigns no significance to this field, but your application may use it to determine when communications were garbled or lost and indicate to the sender which packet was last correctly received. The sender may then re-start at the packet following the last good packet.

Packet types other than those defined for GREEN3 may be defined for your application and handled in the USER area. As long as the format of the GREENPK packet is unchanged, the Packet Group modules may be used unchanged (with the exception of CTLPAC) with your packet types.

GREEN3 receives both control and data packets, but only sends control packets. Your application may send both control and data packets using the Packet Group modules. Simply build the data packet, then send it with the PACXMT module.

The modules PACXMT and PACREC calculate the checksum on the fly: The checksum is updated as each byte is transmitted or received. The checksum update takes place within the modules, so any protocol using these modules must use the checksum as defined for GREEN3. The modules in ALTCHECK.GRP demonstrate how you can move the error checking function out of the PACXMT and PACREC modules. Replacing the modules with those in ALTCHECK will let you use a check algorithm different from the GREEN3 checksum and only the module CHKSRV will have to be replaced by a module implementing your check algorithm. Note that CHKSRV has two entrances: one for updating the check and one for verifying the check. Your version of CHKSRV will have to retain that format.

The GREENPK packet format specifies a one byte check field. If you wish to use a two byte check field (for example, a 16 bit CRC), the PACKET.GRP modules will have to be modified to accommodate the two byte check.

```
;====== ALTCHECK.GRP ==========================================
;
;        ALTERNATE CHECK SERVICE
;        Module: altcheck.grp
;
;        This module relocates the check service out of the receive and
;        transmit services. The check service is no longer done on the fly
;        allowing the module chksrv.txt to be re-written for any type of check
;        algorithm. See Section 6.3.3 for further explanation.
;
;        The modules alpacrec.txt and alpacxmt.txt replace the
;        modules pacrec.txt and pacxmt.txt in module packet.grp.
;        The module chksrv.txt is to be added to packet.grp.
;
;--------------------------------------------------------------
;        RECEIVE PACKET BYTE
;        Module: alpacrec.txt
;
;--------------------------------------------------------------
pacrec   movlw    078              ;frame or overflow error ?
         andwf    recflg,w
         btfss    status,z         ;if no (result = 0), skip next
         bsf      rflgs,pakerr     ;yes. set packet error flag
         movf     recuse1,w        ;no. get received byte
         movwf    rdat
pacrecA  btfsc    rflgs,newhead    ;head already received ? if no, skip next
         goto     pacrec2          ;yes. go
         movlw    head             ;no. is it correct head ?
         subwf    rdat,w
         btfss    status,z         ;if yes, skip next
         goto     pacrec1          ;no. go set packet ignore flag
         bsf      rflgs,newhead    ;yes. set head received flag
         bcf      sysflg,ignore    ;clear ignore flag
         clrf     cksum            ;clear check sum
         goto     pacrecB          ;& go
;
pacrec1  bsf      sysflg,ignore    ;set packet ignore flag
         goto     pacrecB          ;& go
;
pacrec2  btfsc    rflgs,newlen     ;len already received ? if no, skip next
         goto     pacrec3          ;yes. go
         bsf      rflgs,newlen     ;no. set len received flag
         movlw    maxbuf           ;max buffer depth
         movwf    temp             ;max len = maxbuf + 3
         incf     temp,f
         incf     temp,f
         incf     temp,f
         movf     rdat,w
         subwf    temp,w           ;len > max len ?
         btfss    status,c         ;len too large ? if no, skip next
         goto     pacrec1          ;yes. go to ignore exit
         movlw    04               ;no. len < 4 ?
         subwf    rdat,w
         btfss    status,c         ;if no, skip next
```

192

```
            goto     pacrec1          ;yes. go to ignore exit
            bcf      sysflg,ignore    ;no. clear ignore flag
            movf     rdat,w           ;len to packet data byte counter
            movwf    rlen
            movwf    buflen           ;buffer length is len-3
            decf     buflen,f
            decf     buflen,f
            decf     buflen,f         ;number of data bytes (used by print)
            call     chksrv           ;update checksum
            goto     pacrecB          ;go
;
pacrec3     btfsc    rflgs,newtype    ;type already received ? if no, skip next
            goto     pacrec4          ;yes. go
            bsf      rflgs,newtype    ;no. set type received flag
            movwf    rtype            ;save type
            decf     rlen,f           ;update byte counter
            call     chksrv           ;update checksum
            goto     pacrecB          ;& go
;
pacrec4     btfsc    rflgs,newseq     ;seq already received ? if no, skip next
            goto     pacrec5          ;yes. go
            bsf      rflgs,newseq     ;no. set seq received flag
            movwf    rseq             ;save seq
            decf     rlen,f           ;update byte counter
            call     chksrv           ;update checksum
            goto     pacrecB          ;& go
;
pacrec5     decfsz   rlen,f           ;update byte counter. skip if check byte
            goto     pacrec6          ;not check. then it is data. go
            goto     pacrec7          ;is check. go test check against check sum
;
pacrec6     addwf    cksum,f          ;add it to check sum
            movwf    bufdat           ;move it to bufdat
            call     ldbuf            ;& place it in buffer
;
pacrecB     btfss    recflg,twobyt    ;2 bytes in uart ? if yes, skip
            goto     pacrecx          ;no. go exit
            bcf      recflg,twobyt    ;yes. clear 2 byte flag
            movf     recuse2,w        ;get 2nd byte
            movwf    rdat             ;save it for now
            goto     pacrecA          ;& go
;
pacrec7     btfsc    rflgs,pakerr     ;packet error ? if no, skip
            goto     pacrec8          ;yes. go packet completed exit
            movf     rdat,w           ;no. get check
            call     chksrv           ;update checksum
pacrec8     bsf      rflgs,newpac     ;set packet completed flag
;
pacrecx     return                    ;EXIT
;-------------------------------------------------------------------------
;       SEND PACKET
;       Module: alpacxmt.txt
;       Sends a complete packet
;
```

```
;-----------------------------------------------------------------------
pacxmt  movlw   xbufst          ;point to start of xmit buffer
        movwf   bufptr
        clrf    cksum           ;clear checksum
        movlw   head            ;send head
        movwf   xmtuse
        call    uxmt
        movf    xlen,w          ;get len
        movwf   xmtuse          ;move it to xmitter
        movwf   buflen          ;data byte counter
        decf    buflen,f
        decf    buflen,f
        decf    buflen,f
        call    chksrv          ;update checksum
        call    uxmt            ;send len
        movf    xtype,w         ;get type
        movwf   xmtuse          ;move it to xmitter
        call    chksrv          ;update checksum
        call    uxmt            ;send type
        movf    xseq,w          ;get seq
        movwf   xmtuse          ;move it to xmitter
        call    chksrv          ;update checksum
        call    uxmt            ;send seq
pacxmt1 call    getbuf          ;get data from buffer
        movf    bufdat,w
        movwf   xmtuse          ;move it to xmitter
        call    chksrv          ;update checksum
        call    uxmt            ;send data
        decfsz  buflen,f        ;update data byte counter. skip if all data
done
        goto    pacxmt1         ;go get next data byte
        movf    cksum,w         ;all data done. get checksum
        movwf   xmtuse          ;move it to xmitter
        call    uxmt            ;send it
        return                  ;exit
;-----------------------------------------------------------------------
;       CHECK SUM SERVICE
;       Module: chksrv.txt
;
;       ON ENTRY:
;       If the call is to chksrv, the value to be added to checksum is
;       in the working register.
;
;       If the call is to chkfin, the value to be compared with the
;       checksum is in the working register.
;-----------------------------------------------------------------------
chksrv  addwf   cksum,f         ;update checksum
        goto    chksrx          ;and go exit
;
chkfin  subwf   cksum,w         ;same as check sum ?
        btfss   status,z        ;if yes, skip next
        bsf     rflgs,pakerr    ;no. check sum NOT ok. set packet error flag
chksrx  return
;=======================================================================
```

Chapter 7
Synchronous Serial Communications

Synchronous Serial Communications

For the purposes of this book, we define synchronous serial communications as the serial transfer of multi-bit data where each bit transmitted is associated with a clock pulse transmitted on a line separate from the data line. Synchronous transfer may or may not have framing bits and these framing bits may or may not be associated with the clock.

7.1 Synchronous Serial Overview

Serial transmission distributes the bits over time and the receiver must be able to recognize when a bit begins and when it ends (delimit the bit). When a clock is sent along with the data (actually the clock can be thought of as being sent alongside the data), the receiver easily delimits the bits because they simultaneously occur (in *time*) with the clock bits. The data bits will be different from bit to bit but the clock bits always have the same *form* for each bit time throughout the transmission and as such are easily recognized. *Form* refers to some aspect of the clock, such as the high or low state or the transition between states. Within certain limits, imposed by the hardware and the application, we are not concerned with the clock rate. Because each data bit is associated with the *form* of the clock, the clock rate (bit time) is not significant and does not have to be constant throughout the transmission. Each data bit is *synchronized* to one or more aspects of the clock.

The sample synchronous serial data protocol shown in Figure 7-1 defines the clock transitions as being the significant aspects of the clock. The bits are synchronized to the clock transitions. A new bit is placed on the data line at an up-going clock transition and is considered to be valid at the down-going clock transition. The receiver will accept (read) the bit at the down-going transition, when it is expected to be valid. Note that the receiver correctly recognizes the bit regardless of the clock rate or even the clock asymmetry.

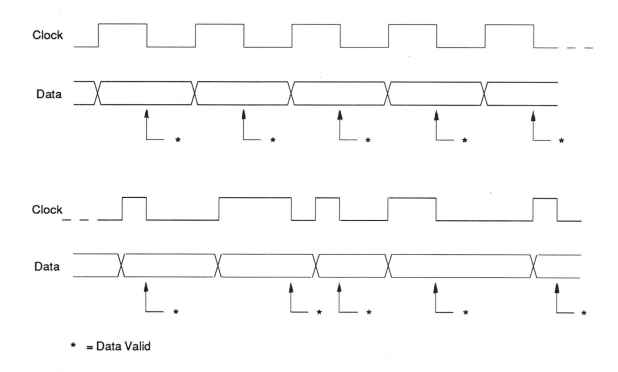

Clock

Data

Clock

Data

* = Data Valid

Figure 7-1   Sample Synchronous Serial Protocol

When fixed length encoding (fixed byte length) is used, the receiver need only count bits, starting with the first bit received, to delimit the data bytes. The SPI synchronous serial bus, covered in Chapter 9, employs this *fixed-length-encoding*.

Special framing bits may be sent at the beginning or end of each character byte to further delimit the data. The I^2C synchronous serial bus as well as the Microwire bus, covered in Chapters 8 and 10, employ this *synchronous-with-frame-bits* method.

7.2 Embedded Systems and Synchronous Serial Communications

Synchronous serial communications find their greatest advantage in embedded systems where a micro-controller must communicate with on board peripheral devices and offers several distinct advantages over parallel (byte wide) communications. The primary advantage is a significant reduction in the number of controller port lines necessary to transfer data to multiple peripheral devices. This advantage is paid for with slower transmission rates, but many peripheral devices do not constantly communicate with the micro-controller, thus the application is not greatly affected by the slower rates. A large number of serial devices may be included in an application with a very small increase in hardware complexity. In many applications, this significant reduction of board space, port lines and addressing complexity is well worth the reduction in communications rate.

Synchronous serial communications may increase software complexity, but this only increases the one-time development cost. The additional software may also require additional program memory. Even with the additional program memory and cost of development, the trade-off between parallel and synchronous serial communications will generally be in favor of serial communications.

Asynchronous serial communications schemes (requiring no clock line) may be used within an embedded system, but are a good deal slower than synchronous serial communications and require more complexity (resulting in higher cost) within the peripherals. Even though asynchronous schemes eliminate the need for a clock line, the speed afforded by synchronous communications and the reduced device complexity makes the synchronous serial method more attractive.

7.3 Synchronous Serial Protocol

The actions of the devices on a serial bus are constrained by the bus protocol. The protocol is the set of rules and procedures necessary to ensure successful data transfers. A protocol defines the data bit format (and in some cases the data byte format), clock form and arbitration procedures that protect against all possibilities of data loss, confusion and communications blockage. Only one device at a time may be in control of the bus; this device is the *master*. The other devices on the bus are *slaves*. The master initiates and terminates a transfer, addresses the slave devices and generates the clock signal. Some serial protocols allow multiple masters on a bus, but allow only one device at a time to function as a master. In a multi-master application, master devices may also function as slaves. The serial protocol includes arbitration procedures that ensure that only one master is allowed to control the bus for a given transfer. Arbitration procedures are not addressed in this book.

Generally the microcontroller in an embedded system acts as the master device and controls the communications with the slave peripheral devices. The microcontroller may have on-chip hardware to implement the serial protocol. In the absence of on-chip hardware, the protocol may be modeled in software.

7.4 Synchronous Serial Peripheral Devices

Synchronous serial hardware devices generally implement a specific peripheral function. Some of the functions available as hardware devices are:

1. Memory devices (EEPROM and other non-volatile technologies and RAM).
2. Analog-to-Digital Converters.
3. Digital-to-Analog Converters.
4. Switches and Multiplexers.
5. Display Drivers.
6. Real Time Clocks and Calendars.
7. Input/Output Ports (including Shift registers).
8. Tone Generators (including DTMF and Musical-tone).
9. Consumer-Product-Specific Functions (these are mostly I^2C devices).

When a specific function is not available as a serial hardware device (or is too costly), the peripheral function and serial interface may be modeled with a microcontroller. The microcontroller serves as the slave device.

Alternatively, the microcontroller may model only the serial interface and act as an intermediary between the serial bus and other hardware implementing the peripheral function. The hardware may be multi-functional and the microcontroller may act as both a master and a slave.

The 12 and 14 bit PICmicros are ideal for modeling serial peripheral functions that are not available as hardware devices. Board to board communication within an embedded system is an unparalleled (pun intended!) application of a PICmicro-to-PICmicro synchronous serial interface. The PICmicro serial applications may be bit-bang software or, for some devices, on-chip-hardware driven. In chapters 8, 9 and 10 we shall describe several PICmicro synchronous serial applications. Both master-to-slave communications and slave function applications will be described.

7.5 Three Synchronous Serial Communications Standards

Several inter-chip serial communications schemes have been developed. Three of the most common are the Philips I^2C (Inter IC), the Motorola SPI (Serial Peripheral Interface) and the National Semiconductor Microwire Interface. A large number of peripheral devices for these busses are available from several manufacturers. All of these schemes are intended for on-board communications between microcontrollers and a plurality of peripheral devices. The I^2C and SPI busses may be applied to multi-master systems where several devices may operate as either master or slave. These three synchronous standards will be examined in detail in the following chapters.

I^2C Bus

The I^2C bus requires only two lines: clock and data. These devices are half-duplex because the one data line is shared for data in and data out. Each peripheral device is software addressed so no chip select lines are required. I^2C is truly a two wire bus. The pertinent clock aspects for I^2C are the clock states: Data is valid for clock high and data may change for clock low.

SPI Bus

The SPI bus requires three lines: data in, data out and clock. An additional chip select line is required for each peripheral device on the bus, but all communications are full duplex. The pertinent clock aspects for SPI are the clock transitions between clock states. SPI defines several synchronization schemes but basically data is valid at one transition and it may change on the opposite transition. SPI uses fixed length data bytes although QSPI (Queued SPI), a variant of SPI, allows variable length data bytes.

Microwire Interface

The Microwire Interface is similar to the SPI bus: It requires the three lines and the chip select lines of the SPI bus, but is somewhat less versatile. The pertinent clock aspect for the Microwire Interface is the clock transition from the low state to the high state: The data must be valid around this transition. Microwire is basically a fixed length data byte implementation, but it provides a means of using a framing bit to delineate short bytes.

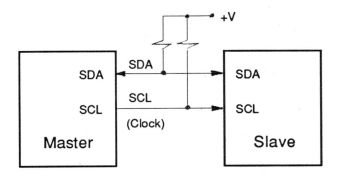

I²C Bus

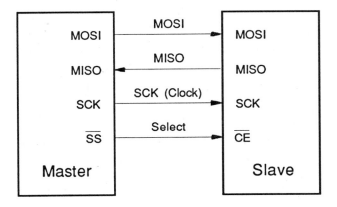

SPI Bus

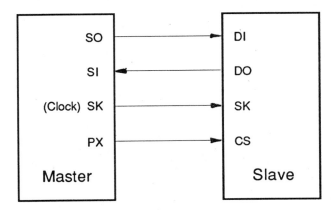

Microwire Interface

Figure 7-2   Three Synchronous Serial Schemes

Chapter 8
The I²C Serial Bus

The I²C Serial Bus

I²C (Inter-Integrated Circuit) is a two wire serial bus for eight bit data transfer applications. The two wires (serial clock and serial data) carry information between the devices connected to the bus. The serial data wire is bi-directional but data may flow in only one direction at a given time. Each device on the bus can operate as either a transmitter or receiver, but not simultaneously. Some devices may be only transmitters while others only receivers. An example of a receive only device is a display, while a memory would both receive and transmit information.

Devices on the bus are defined as masters or slaves. A master is the device that initiates an information transfer on the bus and generates the clock and control signals. All control signals are placed on the data wire. A slave is the device controlled by the master. Both masters and slaves may operate as transmitters and receivers. Each device on the bus has a unique address called the slave address. Only when acting as a slave may a device be addressed. When the master wants to initiate communications with a slave device it transmits the slave address and the addressed slave responds via a handshake sequence with the master. Only the master and the *addressed* slave are active on the bus and the slave remains active until the master de-activates it. The I²C bus is a multi-master bus. Multi-master means that more than one device capable of controlling the bus may be connected to it. At any given time, only one device may be functioning as a master. All other devices on the bus are considered to be slaves. Microcontrollers are generally masters but may also function as slaves.

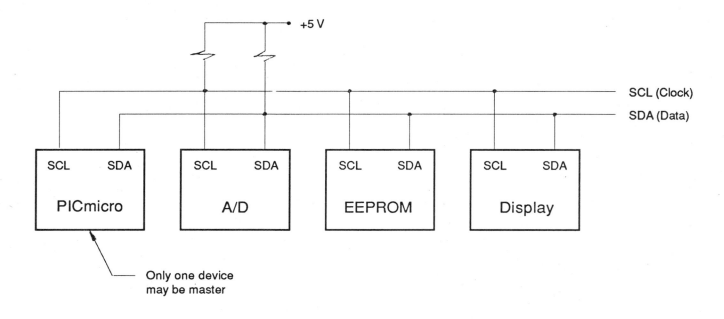

Figure 8-1   Typical I²C Bus Configuration

8.1 I²C Bus Specification

Both the serial clock (SCL) and serial data (SDA) are bi-directional lines, connected to a positive supply voltage via pull-up resistors. When the bus is free, both lines are HIGH (released). This is a wired-AND connection. The output stages of devices connected to the bus must be open drain or open collector in order to implement the wired-AND function. Information on the I²C bus may be transferred at a rate of near zero bits/second up to 100 kbit/second. Generation of the clock and control signals is always the responsibility of the master device. The master generates the clock signal when any information is transferred on the bus. The handshake signals are generated by both the master and the slave, but are clocked only by the master. Handshake is implemented with an acknowledgment (ACK) bit. With multi-masters on a bus, an arbitration procedure is necessary to prevent the possibility of two or more masters attempting to control information transfer at the same time. The I²C CLOCK is a LOW to HIGH to LOW transition on the SCL line. The LOW and HIGH clock periods must be a minimum of approximately 5 microseconds.

The START and STOP conditions are control signals. They are generated ONLY by the master. The bus is considered to be busy after the START condition. The bus is considered to be free again a short time after the STOP condition. Every data transfer must begin with a START, followed by a slave address, followed by any number of data bytes, followed by a STOP.
A START condition is a HIGH-to-LOW transition of the SDA line while the SCL line is HIGH.
A STOP condition is a LOW-to-HIGH transition of the SDA line while the SCL line is HIGH.

Every byte put on the SDA line must be 8 bits long. Any number of bytes may be transmitted per transfer. Each byte must be followed by an acknowledge (ACK) bit (with special exceptions) generated by the receiver. An ACK indicates that the receiver received the byte and can act on it. Data is transferred with the most significant bit (MSB) first. Data is valid (must be stable) during the clock HIGH period and may be changed during the clock LOW period.

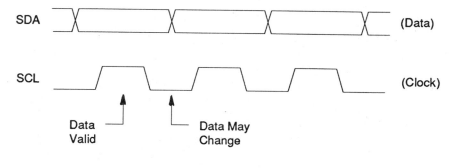

I^2C Bit Transfer

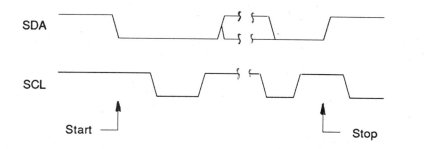

I^2C Start And Stop Conditions

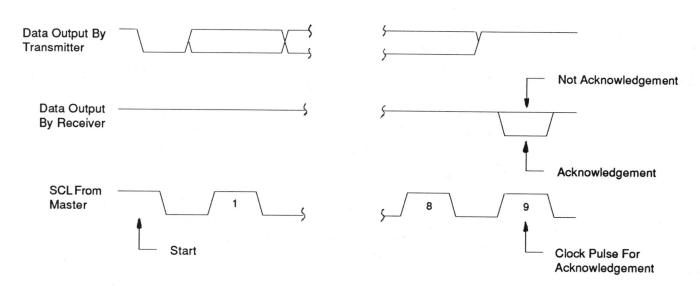

I^2C Acknowledgement

Figure 8-2 I^2C Bus Conditions

The clock for the ACK bit is generated by the master. The transmitting device must release the SDA line (take it HIGH) during the acknowledge so that the receiving device can take the SDA line LOW (pull it down). This LOW on the SDA line during the clock HIGH is the acknowledgement of reception. On receipt of an ACK the transmitting device continues with the transaction.

If a device is unable to continue to receive or act on the byte it will leave the SDA line HIGH (negative acknowledgment, NOACK). If a NOACK is sent by a slave, the master must generate a STOP condition to terminate (or abort) the transaction. A NOACK is generally an indication that the receiver no longer wants to receive any more data. If a NOACK is sent by a master, the master should follow it with a STOP.

If a receiving device cannot receive another complete byte of data until it has performed some other function it can hold the SCL line low to force the transmitter into a wait state. Data transfer then continues when the receiver releases the SCL line, indicating that it is ready for another byte of data.

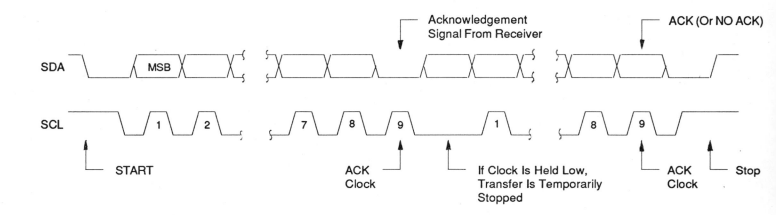

Figure 8-3   I²C Data Transfer

After the START, the first byte sent by the master is the slave address. This address determines which slave will be selected and the direction of information flow for the following bytes. Each slave device has an unique address. The 7 most significant bits of the slave address are the device address and the least significant bit (LSB) determines information flow direction for the following bytes. A zero in the LSB means that the master will write information to the slave (master transmits); a one in the LSB means that the master will read information from the slave (slave transmits). An ACK (generated by the slave) follows the slave address. Then the transmitter sends any data bytes, each followed by an ACK (generated by the receiver). If the direction of information flow is to be changed, a START and slave address must be sent by the master to implement the change. Communication with the slave is terminated with a STOP (Figures 8-2 and 8-3).

204

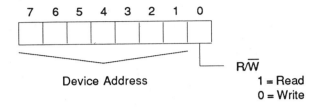

Figure 8-4   Slave Address format

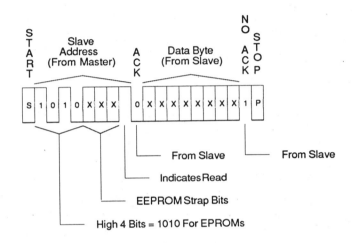

Figure 8-5   Simple I²C Transaction (EEPROM Address Read)

8.2 The PICmicro as a Bit-Bang I²C Master

As of the date of writing, there are no 12 or 14 bit PICmicros with on chip fully functional I²C hardware. PICmicro to I²C device communications must be implemented using software services. All of the PICmicro serial communications described in this chapter are modeled in software (bit-bang models). In the following subsections, software for using the PICmicro as a bit-bang I²C master device is described.

8.2.1 I²C Bit-Bang Master Bus Services

IICOMS.GRP is a collection of routines necessary to perform all of the master bus functions. These functions are: generate START and STOP conditions, generate I²C clock, send and receive a data byte and send and recognize ACK conditions.

Two lines of port B are used for SCL and SDA (Figure 8-6). These lines have pull-up resistors to Vpp. The I²C specifications require that SCL and SDA be wire-AND (open drain). The PICmicro ports are not open drain in the output mode, but can be simulated as open drains by configuring a port line as an input (releasing the line) for output data bit =1 and as an output (pulled LOW) for output data bit = 0. For data bit = 1 the pull-ups will ensure that the line is HIGH. The slave may then pull the line down without causing bus level contention. The input/output configuration of these two port lines will be changed a great many times throughout the program, so a register (labeled **dirb**) is defined as port b data direction register. **dirb** will match the contents of the port b **TRIS** register and will be used to load the **TRIS** register. Using **dirb**, the data input/output configuration may be changed with bit set and bit clear instructions without causing unintended changes to the other lines on the port.

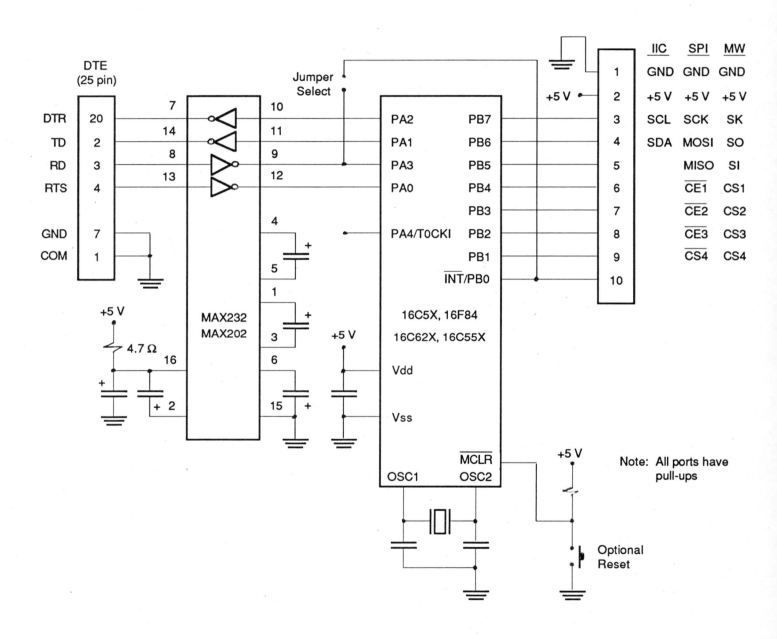

Figure 8-6   Schematic; Bit-Bang Master Applications

To change SDA to an input (release it) or an output with value 1:
(sda defines the PORT B bit for SDA)

```
bsf     dirb,sda    ;SDA bit to be an input
movf    dirb,w      ;move it to working
tris    portb       ;sda now an input
```

At the completion of the **TRIS** instruction, SDA is HIGH

To change SDA to an output with value 0:

```
bcf     portb,sda   ;take SDA low
bcf     dirb,sda    ;make it an output
movf    dirb,w
tris    portb
```

At the completion of the **TRIS** instruction, SDA is LOW.

NOTE: The setup and clock high and clock low periods must not be less than the minimum specified for the I^2C Bus. These are approximately 5 micro-seconds. These program modules generate all delays in software and assume the use of a 4 MHz crystal. If a faster system clock is used, the delay routines have to be changed to keep all delays greater than 5 microseconds. See Module FILLER.TXT.

The modules in IICOMS.GRP are all that are necessary to model an I^2C MASTER with the PICmicro. These are the I^2C *bus* services. They are all *called* functions. The modules are:

IISTRT   Generate START
IISTOP   Generate STOP
IICLK   Generate SCL and read SDA line at high clock
IIIN   Receives an 8 bit byte from a slave device
IIOUT   Sends an 8 bit byte to a slave device
NACK   Tests for an ACK from a slave device
SACK   Send an ACK to a slave device
FILLER   Determines clock period and set-up time

Throughout these I^2C modules, the carry bit serves several functions:
The CARRY:
1. Passes the SDA line state from the IICLK module. See Module IICLK.

2. Moves the bit received from the SDA line into the data byte by rotating it into the data byte. Since data transfer is MSB first, the carry is rotated left into the data byte. See Modules IICLK and IIIN.

3. Moves the bit to be transmitted from the data byte to the SDA line. The data byte rotates left to the carry. See Modules IICLK and IIOUT.

4. Passes the ACK status from the NACK module. See Modules IICLK and NACK.

5. Passes an error flag from the IISTRT and IISTOP modules. See Modules IISTRT and IISTOP.

Module Descriptions:

Generate START (Module IISTRT and Figure 8-7)

The I^{2}C specification requires that the SDA and SCL lines both be high (released) when the bus is free. The Master should generate a START condition only if the bus is free. IISTRT begins by testing the bus. If it is not free, then IISTRT exits with the error flag (carry) set. If the bus is free, SDA is asserted LOW and a short time later SCL is asserted LOW.

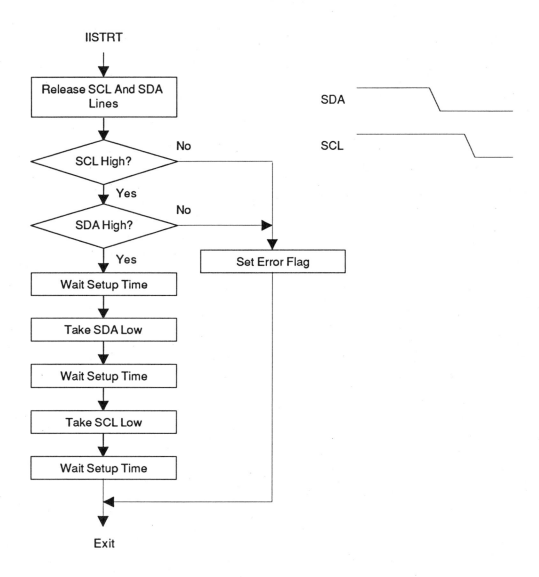

Figure 8-7   IICOMS Start

Generate STOP (Module IISTOP and Figure 8-8)

IISTOP begins by asserting the SDA line LOW while SCL is LOW, then asserting the SCL line HIGH (releases it). Then the stop condition is generated by asserting SDA HIGH (releases it) while SCL is HIGH. At this point, both SDA and SCL should be HIGH (bus free). It is possible that some hardware problem or a slow slave device that was not tested for busy is holding either line LOW. If the bus is not free at this point IISTOP exits with the error flag (carry) set.

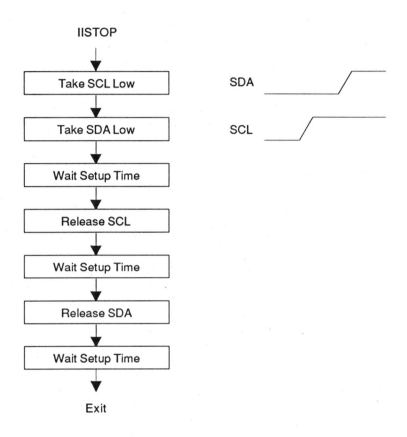

Figure 8-8   IICOMS Stop

Generate CLOCK and read SDA line (Module IICLK and Figure 8-9)

IICLK begins with testing the SCL line for LOW. If it is LOW, it is tested until it goes high. Then SCL is asserted HIGH (released). During the SCL HIGH period the data bit on the SDA line is transferred to the carry. Then SCL is then asserted LOW. If a slave device is holding SCL low, the routine does not return until the slave releases SCL and the clock sequence is completed.

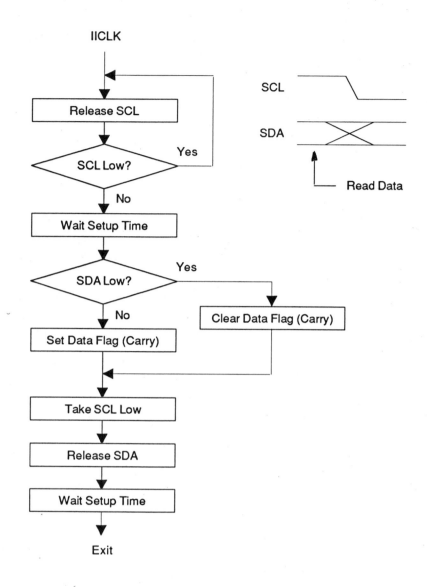

Figure 8-9   IICOMS Clock

Receive eight bit byte from slave device (Module IIIN and Figure 8-10)

IIIN initializes the bit counter for 8 bits, configures SDA as an input (releases it) and calls IICLK. IICLK reads the SDA line and passes the SDA level (1 or 0) back via the carry. The carry is rotated left into the received data byte (**iidata**). Rotation is to left because I^{2}C transfers all data MSB first. The bit counter is then decremented. If the counter is not zero, IIIN then loops back to the call to IICLK to get the next bit. If the counter is zero, then all 8 bits have been received and IIIN exits. The received data is passed out via the data byte **iidata**.

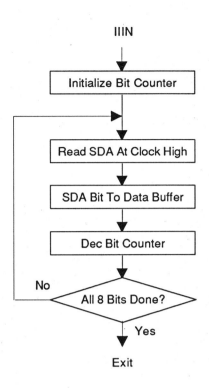

Figure 8-10   IICOMS Receive Byte

Transmit 8 bit byte to slave device (Module IIOUT and Figure 8-11)

The byte to be transmitted is passed in via **iidata**. IIOUT loads the bit counter with 8, then rotates to the left a bit from **iidata** into carry. Rotation is to left because I^{2}C transfers all data MSB first. The carry value determines if SDA is to be set or cleared: If carry is 0, then SDA is asserted LOW. If carry is 1 then SDA is released. IIOUT then calls IICLK to clock the SDA line to the slave. The bit counter is then decremented. If the counter is not zero, then it loops back to rotate the next bit out of **iidata** and transmit it. If the bit counter is zero, then all bits have been transmitted. IIOUT then makes sure that SDA is an input (released) and exits.

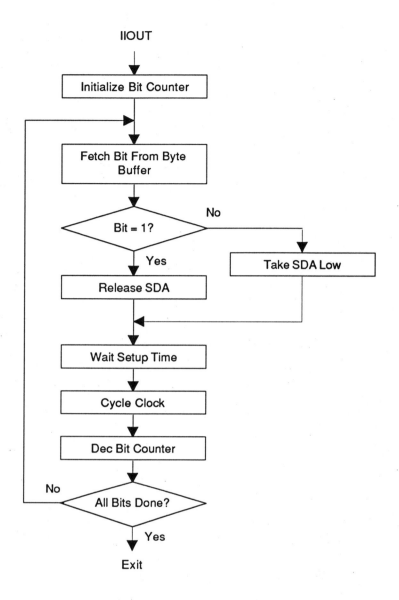

Figure 8-11   IICOMS Send Byte

Test for ACK from receiving device. (Module NACK and Figure 8-12)

NACK configures SDA as an input (releases it) and calls IICLK to test the SDA line. IICLK passes the state of the SDA line back to NACK via carry. If carry is 0, then ACK was received. If carry is 1, then ACK was not received. On exit, NACK passes this ACK status back via the carry.

Send an ACK to a slave device. (Module SACK and Figure 8-12)

SACK configures SDA as an output, takes it low, calls IICLK to clock it out then makes SDA an input (releases SDA). No error tests are made.

212

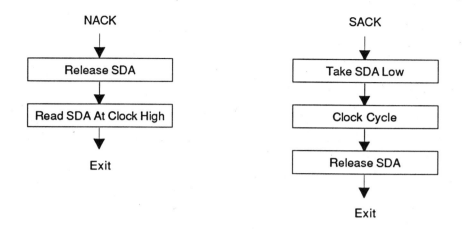

Figure 8-12   IICOMS NACK and SACK

See Section 8.2.4 for application information for these modules and Sections 8.4 and 8.5 for demonstration applications using these modules.

```
;====== IICOMS.GRP =============================================================
;
;         IICOMS.GRP
;         Bit-Banger routines to read from and write to devices on the IIC Bus
;
;         PICmicro is MASTER
;         IIC Bus uses 2 lines: scl & sda on PORT B
;
;-------------------------------------------------------------------------------
;
;         Requires the following work space:
;             dirb        direction register for PORT B
;             iidata      data byte to be sent to or received from IIC device
;             bitctr      bit counter
;             fillctr     clock period counter
;
;         Requires following equates:
;             sda      equ      nn      (PORT B bit for data line)
;             scl      equ      nn      (PORT B bit for clock line)
;             iicrate  equ      nn      (Determines IIC clock rate. See filler.txt)
;                                       (CANNOT be less than 1)
;
;         To simulate IIC wired-AND, any module that drives the scl or sda
;         line HIGH (line released) does so by making the scl or sda port
;         an input.
;
;         In some modules, carry is used as an error flag:
;                 If carry =1 then error condition
;                 If carry =0 then no error
;
;         All modules except IISTOP exit with clock line held low.
```

```
;
;              All modules except IISTRT exit with data line released.
;
;              Module IISTRT exits with data line held low.
;
;              Module IICLK exits with unpredictable data level.
;
;              IIC clock period is determined by Module FILLER. The clock period
;              is adjustable in 6 cycle increments in the range from approximately
;              30 cycles to 1554 cycles. (See module FILLER)
;
;--------------------------------------------------------------------------------
;              Module: IISTRT
;              Generates START Condition
;              Data line goes low while clock line is high.
;
;              On entry: Expects both clock and data lines to be high. At start
;                        attempts to release them. If both are not high,
;                        then error condition and sets carry and exits with
;                        start error code (0x01) in w.
;
;              On exit: Clock and data lines are held low.
;
;--------------------------------------------------------------------------------
iistrt  bsf     dirb,sda        ;release clock and data lines
        bsf     dirb,scl
        movf    dirb,w
        tris    portb
        bcf     status,c        ;clear carry
        btfss   portb,scl       ;clock high ? if yes, skip next
        goto    iistrte         ;no. go error exit
        btfss   portb,sda       ;data high ? if yes, skip next
        goto    iistrte         ;no. go error exit
        call    filler          ;time filler
;       at this point both clock and data lines are high
        bsf     portb,scl       ;reads clock and data to port register (high)
        bcf     dirb,sda        ;make data line an output
        movf    dirb,w
        tris    portb
        bcf     portb,sda       ;take data line low (START)
        call    filler          ;time filler
        bcf     dirb,scl        ;make clock line an output
        movf    dirb,w
        tris    portb
        bcf     portb,scl       ;take clock line low
        call    filler          ;time filler
        goto    iistrtx         ;go exit
;
iistrte bsf     status,c        ;set carry (error flag)
;
iistrtx retlw   01              ;exit with module code 0x01
;--------------------------------------------------------------------------------
;              Module: IISTOP
;              Generates STOP Condition
```

```
;         Data line goes high while clock line is high.
;         On entry: scl is expected to be low
;
;         On exit: sda & scl are high (bus free)
;------------------------------------------------------------------------
iistop    bcf     dirb,scl      ;make clock an output (safety)
          movf    dirb,w
          tris    portb
          bcf     portb,scl     ;take clock low in preparation for ...
          goto    iistopa       ;short wait
iistopa   bcf     dirb,sda      ;sda as output (don't care if high or low)
          movf    dirb,w
          tris    portb
          bcf     portb,sda     ;make sure data line is low
          call    filler        ;set up time
          bsf     dirb,scl      ;take clock high (make it an input)
          movf    dirb,w
          tris    portb
          call    filler        ;time filler (set up time)
          bsf     dirb,sda      ;take data line high (make it an input)
          movf    dirb,w
          tris    portb
          call    filler        ;time filler
          retlw   02            ;exit with module code 0x02
;------------------------------------------------------------------------
;         Module: IICLK
;         Generates clock & reads data line at clock high
;
;         On entry: Master is holding clock line low. Just after entry
;                   releases clock line and expects it to be high.
;                   If clock line is held low by another device on
;                   the bus, then waits until clock line is released
;                   by the other device then remains released for approx
;                   one-half clock period. While clock is high we do not
;                   care if data line is released (reading) or held low
;                   by master (writing). Data line is released shortly
;                   after clock line goes low.
;
;         On exit:  Carry is set if data clocked = 1
;                   Carry is cleared if data clocked = 0
;                   The clock line is held low
;                   The data line is released
;------------------------------------------------------------------------
iiclk     bsf     dirb,scl      ;release clock line (make it an input)
          movf    dirb,w
          tris    portb
iiclk1    btfss   portb,scl     ;scl still low ? if no, skip next
          goto    iiclk1        ;yes. go try again
          bcf     status,c      ;no. clock now released. clear carry
          call    filler        ;time filler
          btfsc   portb,sda     ;data line 0 ? if yes, skip next
          bsf     status,c      ;no. set carry
;         at this point, clock line is still high.
          bsf     portb,scl     ;reads clock line to port register (high)
```

215

IICOMS.GRP

```
          bcf     dirb,scl         ;make scl an output (still high)
          movf    dirb,w
          tris    portb
          bcf     portb,scl        ;take clock line low
          nop
          bsf     dirb,sda         ;release data line
          movf    dirb,w
          tris    portb
          call    filler           ;time filler
          retlw   0                ;exit
;-------------------------------------------------------------------
;         Module: IIIN
;         Receives 8 bit byte from slave device
;         Places received byte in iidata
;         (Module IICLK receives bit & places it in carry)
;
;         On exit: Data line is released (as an input)
;                  Clock line is held low
;-------------------------------------------------------------------
iiin      movlw   d'8'             ;8 bits
          movwf   bitctr           ;to bit counter
          bsf     dirb,sda         ;data line as input
          movf    dirb,w
          tris    portb
iiin1     call    iiclk            ;clock in a bit (into carry)
          rlf     iidata,f         ;rotate it (carry) into iidata
          decfsz  bitctr,f         ;dec bit ctr. is it 0 ? if yes, skip
          goto    iiin1            ;no. go get next bit
          retlw   0                ;yes. exit
;-------------------------------------------------------------------
;         Module: IIOUT
;         Sends 8 bit byte to slave device
;         Byte to be sent is in iidata
;
;         If data bit is high, then data line released (made an input).
;         If data bit is low, then data line is held low.
;
;         On entry: Clock line is held low
;
;         On exit: Data line is released (as an input)
;                  Clock line is held low
;-------------------------------------------------------------------
iiout     movlw   d'8'             ;8 bits
          movwf   bitctr           ;to bit counter
iiout1    rlf     iidata,f         ;rotate data bit to carry
          btfss   status,c         ;bit = 1 ? if yes, skip
          goto    iiout2           ;no. go clear sda line
          bsf     dirb,sda         ;yes. release data line (make it an input)
          movf    dirb,w
          tris    portb
          goto    iiout3           ;& go
;
iiout2    bcf     dirb,sda         ;make it an output
          movf    dirb,w
```

216

```
          tris    portb
          bcf     portb,sda        ;take data line low
iiout3    goto    iiouta           ;setup time
iiouta    call    iiclk            ;clock it out
          decfsz  bitctr,f         ;dec bit ctr. all bits done ? if yes, skip
          goto    iiout1           ;no. go do next bit
          retlw   0                ;exit
;--------------------------------------------------------------------------
;         Module: NACK     Tests for ACK from receiver.
;
;         On Exit: If ACK received, then carry = 0
;                  If ACK not received, then carry = 1
;                  Data line is released
;                  Clock line is held low
;--------------------------------------------------------------------------
nack      bsf     dirb,sda         ;data line as input
          movf    dirb,w
          tris    portb
          call    iiclk            ;clock it (data line tested in iiclk)
          retlw   0                ;exit
;--------------------------------------------------------------------------
;         Module: SACK
;         Sends ACK to slave (clocks low onto data line)
;
;         On entry: Expects clock line to be low.
;
;         On exit: Clock line is held low and data line is released.
;--------------------------------------------------------------------------
sack      bcf     dirb,sda         ;make data line an output
          movf    dirb,w
          tris    portb
          bcf     portb,sda        ;take data line low
          goto    sacka            ;short wait
sacka     call    iiclk            ;clock it out
          bsf     dirb,sda         ;release data line
          movf    dirb,w
          tris    portb
          goto    sackb            ;short wait
sackb     retlw   0                ;exit
;--------------------------------------------------------------------------
;         Module: FILLER
;
;         Determines IIC clock period.
;
;         Clock period (in instruction cycles) is approximately = (6*n + 24)
;         where n is the literal in the first line of the routine below.
;--------------------------------------------------------------------------
filler    movlw   iicrate          ;determines clock rate
          movwf   fillctr
filler1   decfsz  fillctr,f
          goto    filler1
          retlw   0
;==========================================================================
```

8.2.2 I²C Bit-Bang Master Bus Services Using FET Drivers.

The I²C specification requires that the SDA and SCL lines be wired-AND. The routines described in section 8.2.1 accomplished this requirement by configuring the SDA and SCL ports as inputs for the logic 1 condition (line released) and outputs for the logic 0 condition. An alternate method is to drive FET buffers with output ports and sense SDA and SCL with input ports as shown in Figure 8-13. A disadvantage to this method is that four rather than two port lines are required for SDA and SCL. The advantages are that the bit-bang routines are shorter and the maximum realized clock rate is higher. IFCOMS.GRP is the set of routines for the FET driven configuration. The IFCOMS routines are similar to those in IICOMS. The major differences are that the SDA and SCL port configuration is not switched between input and output and the SDA and SCL output port logic levels must be inverted.

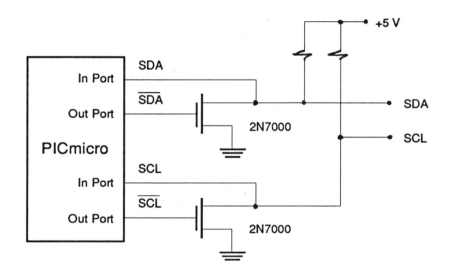

Figure 8-13   I²C Bus With FET Drivers

```
;====== IFCOMS.GRP ===========================================================
;
;       IFCOMS.GRP
;       Bit-Banger routines to read from and write to devices on the IIC Bus
;       using FET drivers.
;       See Section 8.2.2


;-----------------------------------------------------------------------------
;       PICmicro is MASTER      14 Bit family
;
;       The IIC specification requires that the sda and scl lines be
;       wired-AND. This wired-AND is simulated by inverting data OUT and
;       placing it on port line sdo. Port line sdo drives a FET which drives
;       the sda line. The same technique is used on the scl line. The
;       wired-AND clock line is necessary with multi-master systems or when a
;       slave device capable of pulling down the scl line is used.
;
```

```
;      Requires the following work space:
;          iidata     data byte to be sent to or received from IIC device
;          bitctr     bit counter
;
;      Requires following equates:
;          sda    equ    nn          PORT B bit for data line
;                                     MUST be configured as INPUT
;          scl    equ    nn          PORT B bit for clock line
;                                     MUST be configured as INPUT
;          sdo    equ    nn          PORT B bit for data out
;                                     MUST be configured as OUTPUT
;          sco    equ    nn          PORT B bit for clock out
;                                     MUST be configured as OUTPUT
;
;      In some modules, carry is used as an error flag:
;              If carry =1 then error condition
;              If carry =0 then no error
;
;      All modules except IISTOP exit with clock line held low.
;
;      All modules except IISTRT exit with data line released.
;
;      (Module IICLK exits with unpredictable data level, but is called
;      only by the other IIxxx modules).
;      Clock period is approx 20 instruction cycles. (Approx 50 KHz
;      clock rate with 4 MHz crystal).
;-------------------------------------------------------------------------
;      Module: IISTRTF.TXT    (FET Version)
;      Generates START Condition
;      Data line goes low while clock line is high.
;
;      On entry: Expects both clock and data lines to be high. At start
;                attempts to release them. If both are then not high,
;                then error condition and sets carry and exits with
;                start error code (0x01) in w.
;
;      On exit: Clock and data lines are held low.
;
;-------------------------------------------------------------------------
;      FET version of iistrt
;
iistrt  bcf     portb,sdo       ;release data line
        bcf     portb,sco       ;release clock line
        bcf     status,c        ;clear carry
        btfss   portb,scl       ;clock high ? if yes, skip next
        goto    iistrte         ;no. go error exit
        btfss   portb,sda       ;data high ? if yes, skip next
        goto    iistrte         ;no. go error exit
;
;      At this point, both clock and data lines are high
        bsf     portb,sdo       ;take data line low (START)
        goto    iistrta         ;set up time
iistrta goto    iistrtb
iistrtb goto    iistrtc
```

219

```
iistrtc bsf      portb,sco      ;take clock line low
        goto     iistrtd        ;set up time
iistrtd goto     iistrte
iistrte goto     iistrtx        ;go exit
;
iistrte bsf      status,c       ;set carry (error flag)
;
iistrtx retlw    01             ;exit with module code 0x01
;----------------------------------------------------------------------
;        Module: IISTOPF.TXT  (FET Version)
;        Generates STOP Condition
;        Data line goes high while clock line is high.
;        On entry: scl is expected to be low
;
;        On exit: sda & scl are high (bus free)
;----------------------------------------------------------------------
;        FET version of iistop
iistop  bsf      portb,sco      ;take clock low (safety)
        goto     iistopa        ;set up time
iistopa bsf      portb,sdo      ;make sure data line is low
        goto     iistopb        ;set up time
iistopb goto     iistopc
        bcf      portb,sco      ;take clock high
        goto     iistopc
iistopc goto     iistopd        ;set up time
iistopd bcf      portb,sdo      ;take data line high
        goto     iistope        ;set up time
goto    iistopf
iistopf retlw    02             ;exit with module code 0x02
;----------------------------------------------------------------------
;        Module: IICLKF.TXT  (FET Version)
;        Generates clock & reads data line at clock high
;
;        On entry: Master is holding clock line low. Then releases
;                  clock line and expects it to be high.
;                  If clock line is held low by another device on
;                  the bus, then waits until clock line is released.
;                  We do not care if data line is released (reading or
;                  writing) or held low by master (writing).
;
;        On exit:  Carry is set if data clocked = 1
;                  Carry is cleared if data clocked = 0
;                  The clock line is held low
;----------------------------------------------------------------------
;        FET version of iiclk
iiclk   bcf      portb,sco      ;release clock line
iiclk1  btfss    portb,scl      ;clock line still low ? if no, skip next
        goto     iiclk1         ;yes. go try again
        bcf      status,c       ;no. clear carry
        goto     iiclka         ;set up time
iiclka  btfsc    portb,sda      ;data line 0 ? if yes, skip next
        bsf      status,c       ;no. set carry
        nop
        bsf      portb,sco      ;take clock line low
```

```
          goto    iiclkb              ;clock low time
iiclkb  goto    iiclkc
iiclkc  goto    iiclkd
iiclkd  retlw   0                   ;exit
;------------------------------------------------------------------
;       Module: IIINF.TXT (FET Version)
;       Receives 8 bit byte from slave device
;       Places received byte in iidata
;       (Called module IICLK receives bit & places it in carry)
;
;       On exit: Data line is released
;                Clock line is held low
;                Data byte in iidata
;------------------------------------------------------------------
;       FET version of iiin
iiin    movlw   d'8'                ;8 bits
        movwf   bitctr              ;to bit counter
        bcf     portb,sdo           ;release data line
iiin1   call    iiclk               ;clock in a bit (into carry)
        rlf     iidata,f            ;rotate it (carry) into iidata
        decfsz  bitctr,f            ;dec bit ctr. is it 0 ? if yes, skip
        goto    iiin1               ;no. go get next bit
        retlw   0                   ;yes. exit
;------------------------------------------------------------------
;       Module: IIOUTF.TXT  (Fet Version)
;       Sends 8 bit byte to slave device
;       Byte to be sent is in iidata
;
;       If data bit is 1, then data line released
;       If data bit is 0, then data line is held low
;
;       On entry: Clock line is held low
;
;       On exit: Data line is released
;                Clock line is held low
;------------------------------------------------------------------
;       FET version od iiout
iiout   movlw   d'8'                ;8 bits
        movwf   bitctr              ;to bit counter
iiout1  rlf     iidata,f            ;rotate data bit to carry
        btfss   status,c            ;bit = 1 ? if yes, skip
        goto    iiout2              ;no. go
        bcf     portb,sdo           ;yes. release data line
        goto    iiout3              ;& go
;
iiout2  bsf     portb,sdo           ;take data line low
iiout3  goto    iiouta              ;setup time
iiouta  goto    iioutb
iioutb  call    iiclk               ;clock it out
        decfsz  bitctr,f            ;dec bit ctr. all bits done ? if yes, skip
        goto    iiout1              ;no. go do next bit
        bcf     portb,sdo           ;yes. release data line
        goto    iioutc
iioutc  retlw   0                   ;exit
```

```
;----------------------------------------------------------------------
;         Module: NACKF.TXT   (FET Version)
;         Tests for ACK from receiver.
;
;         On Exit: If ACK received, then carry = 0
;                  If ACK not received, then carry = 1
;                  Data line is released
;                  Clock line is held low
;----------------------------------------------------------------------
;         FET version of nack
nack     bcf     portb,sdo       ;release data line
         goto    nacka           ;set up time
nacka    call    iiclk           ;clock it (data line tested in iiclk)
         retlw   0               ;exit
;----------------------------------------------------------------------
;         Module: SACK.TXT   (FET version)
;         Sends ACK to slave (clocks low onto data line)
;
;         On entry: Expects clock line to be low.
;
;         On exit: Clock line is held low and data line is released.
;----------------------------------------------------------------------
;         FET version of sack
sack     bsf     portb,sdo       ;take data line low
         goto    sacka           ;set up time
         nop
sacka    call    iiclk           ;clock it out
         bcf     portb,sdo       ;release data line
         goto    sackb
sackb    retlw   0               ;exit
;======================================================================
```

8.2.3 Bit-Banging the I^{2}C Bus with the 12 Bit PICmicro Family

The 12 bit family of PICmicro devices have a two-level deep hardware stack. This limits any program to just two call levels. To reserve these calls for upper level modules, the I^{2}C bus modules must make no calls to lower level modules. In IICOMS, all of the modules make calls to either IICLK or FILLER and IICLK calls FILLER. For 12 bit PICmicro applications these modules must have all clock related functions internal to each module. The modules in IXCOMS.GRP are the 12 bit versions of those in IICOMS. They should be used for all 12 bit PICmicro bit-banger applications but are not limited to the 12 bit device.

The modules in IXCOMS.GRP require approximately 28 % more program memory than do those in IICOMS.GRP. Reduced call depth has resulted in increased program complexity. This program memory requirement may be reduced by trading program complexity for hardware complexity. For IXCOMS the SCL and SDA wired-AND requirement of the I^{2}C bus was met by configuring the SCL and SDA lines as inputs for high output levels (line released) and outputs for low levels. Rather than switching a port line between input and output configurations, two ports can be used for the I^{2}C line as shown in Figure 8-13. The data to be transmitted is inverted and written to the port driving the FET gate (as described in Section 8.2.2) and data received is read at the port connected directly to the SDA line. The same technique may be used for the SCL line. The modules in ISCOMS.GRP use this hardware wired-AND method only on the

222

SDA line. If the application does not have multi-master capability or uses only slaves incapable of pulling down the SCL line, wired-AND is not required on the SCL line. ISCOMS.GRP requires even fewer bytes of program memory than does IICOMS.GRP. Thus a small increase in hardware complexity has resulted in a substantial reduction in software complexity.

```
;====== IXCOMS.GRP ==============================================
;
;       IXCOMS.GRP
;       Bit-Banger routines to read from & write to devices on the IIC Bus
;
;       May be used with 12 bit PICmicro because these modules are bottom
;       level (they make no calls). The main program calls the modules that
;       call these modules, thus making them compatible with the 12 bit PIC
;       two-level stack. See Section 8.2.3
;
;----------------------------------------------------------------
;
;       PIC is MASTER
;       IIC Bus uses 2 lines: scl & sda on PORT B
;
;       Requires the following work space:
;           dirb        direction register for PORT B
;           iidata      data byte to be sent to or received from IIC device
;           bitctr      bit counter
;
;       Requires following equates:
;           sda    equ    nn         (PORT B bit for data line)
;           scl    equ    nn         (PORT B bit for clock line)
;
;       To simulate IIC wired-AND, any module that drives the scl or sda
;       line HIGH does so by making the scl or sda port an input.
;
;       In some modules, carry is used as an error flag:
;               If carry =1 then error condition
;               If carry =0 then no error
;----------------------------------------------------------------
;       Module: IXSTRT
;       Generates START Condition
;       Data line goes low while clock line is high.
;
;       At entry, tests both scl and sda lines for high. If not high
;       then error condition. Sets carry and exits.
;
;       On exit, sda & scl are low
;       Error exit: carry set
;----------------------------------------------------------------
ixstrt  bsf     dirb,sda        ;release clock and data lines
        bsf     dirb,scl
        movf    dirb,w
        tris    portb
        bcf     status,c        ;clear carry
        btfss   portb,scl       ;scl high ? if yes, skip next
```

```
        goto    ixstrt1         ;no. go error exit
        btfss   portb,sda       ;sda high ? if yes, skip next
        goto    ixstrt1         ;no. go error exit
        goto    ixstrta         ;short wait
ixstrta goto    ixstrtb
ixstrtb bsf     portb,scl
        bcf     dirb,sda        ;read scl and sda to port
        movf    dirb,w          ;make sda an output
        tris    portb
        bcf     portb,sda       ;take data line low (START)
        goto    ixstrtc         ;set up time
ixstrtc goto    ixstrtd
ixstrtd goto    ixstrte
ixstrte bcf     dirb,scl        ;make scl an output
        movf    dirb,w
        tris    portb
        bcf     portb,scl       ;take scl low
        goto    ixstrtf         ;set up time
ixstrtf goto    ixstrtg
ixstrtg goto    ixstrth
ixstrth goto    ixstrtx         ;go exit
;
ixstrt1 bsf     status,c        ;set carry (error flag)
;
ixstrtx retlw   0               ;exit
;-------------------------------------------------------------------
;       Module: IXSTOP
;       Generates STOP Condition
;       Data line goes high while clock line is high.
;       On entry, scl is low
;
;       On exit, sda & scl are high (bus free)
;       If both sda and scl are NOT high, then hardware error. Exits with
;       carry set.
;-------------------------------------------------------------------
ixstop  bcf     dirb,scl        ;make clock an output (safety)
        movf    dirb,w
        tris    portb
        bcf     portb,scl       ;take clock low
        goto    ixstopa         ;short wait
ixstopa bcf     dirb,sda        ;sda as output
        movf    dirb,w
        tris    portb
        bcf     portb,sda       ;make sda is low
        goto    ixstopb
ixstopb goto    ixstopc
ixstopc goto    ixstopd         ;set up time
ixstopd bsf     dirb,scl        ;take clock high (make it an input)
        movf    dirb,w
        tris    portb
        goto    ixstope         ;set up time
ixstope goto    ixstopf
ixstopf goto    ixstopg
ixstopg bsf     dirb,sda        ;take data line high (make it an input)
```

```
        movf     dirb,w
        tris     portb
        goto     ixstoph          ;set up time
ixstoph goto     ixstopi
ixstopi goto     ixstopj
ixstopj retlw    0                ;exit
;------------------------------------------------------------------------
;        Module: IXIN
;        Receives 8 bit byte from slave device
;        Places received byte in iidata
;
;------------------------------------------------------------------------
ixin    movlw    d'8'             ;8 bits
        movwf    bitctr           ;to bit counter
        bsf      dirb,sda         ;sda as input
        movf     dirb,w
        tris     portb
ixin1   goto     ixina            ;short delay
ixina   bsf      dirb,scl         ;release scl (make it an input)
        movf     dirb,w
        tris     portb
ixin2   btfss    portb,scl        ;scl still low ? if no, skip next
        bcf      status,c         ;clear carry
        goto     ixin2            ;yes. go try again
        goto     ixinb            ;wait
ixinb   goto     ixinc
ixinc   goto     ixind
ixind   btfsc    portb,sda        ;data line 0 ? if yes, skip
        bsf      status,c         ;no. set carry
        bsf      portb,scl        ;read clock line to port register
        bcf      dirb,scl         ;make it an output
        movf     dirb,w
        tris     portb
        bcf      portb,scl        ;take clock low
        nop
        bsf      dirb,sda         ;release data line
        movf     dirb,w
        tris     portb
        goto     ixine
ixine   goto     ixinf
ixinf   goto     ixing
ixing   rlf      iidata,f         ;rotate it(carry) into iidata
        decfsz   bitctr,f         ;all bits done 0 ? if yes, skip
        goto     ixin1            ;no. go get next bit
        retlw    0                ;yes. exit
;------------------------------------------------------------------------
;        Module: IXOUT
;        Sends 8 bit byte to slave device
;        Byte to be sent is in iidata
;
;        If data bit is high, then data line is made an input.
;------------------------------------------------------------------------
ixout   movlw    d'8'             ;8 bits
        movwf    bitctr           ;to bit counter
```

225

```
ixout1    rlf      iidata,f      ;rotate data bit to carry
          btfss    status,c      ;bit = 1 ? if yes, skip
          goto     ixout2        ;no. go clear sda line
          bsf      dirb,sda      ;yes. release sda (make it an input)
          movf     dirb,w
          tris     portb
          goto     ixout3        ;& go
ixout2    bcf      dirb,sda      ;make sda an output
          movf     dirb,w
          tris     portb
          bcf      portb,sda     ;take sda low
ixout3    goto     ixouta        ;short delay
ixouta    bsf      dirb,scl      ;release scl (make it an input)
          movf     dirb,w
          tris     portb
ixout4    btfss    portb,scl     ;scl held low ? if no, skip next
          goto     ixout4        ;yes. go try again
          goto     ixoutb        ;clock high time
ixoutb    goto     ixoutc
ixoutc    goto     ixoutd
ixoutd    bsf      portb,scl     ;reads scl to port register
          bcf      dirb,scl      ;make scl an output
          movf     dirb,w
          tris     portb
          bcf      portb,scl     ;take scl low
          goto     ixoute        ;clock low time
ixoute    goto     ixoutf
ixoutf    goto     ixoutg
ixoutg    decfsz   bitctr,f      ;dec bit ctr. all bits done ? if yes, skip
          goto     ixout1        ;no. go do next bit
          retlw    0             ;yes. exit
;------------------------------------------------------------------------
;         Module: XNACK
;         Tests for ACK from receiver.
;
;         On Exit: if ACK received, then carry = 0
;                  if ACK not received, then carry = 1
;------------------------------------------------------------------------
xnack     bsf      dirb,sda      ;data line as input
          movf     dirb,w
          tris     portb
          nop
          bsf      dirb,scl      ;release scl (make it an input)
          movf     dirb,w
          tris     portb
          bcf      status,c      ;clear carry
          goto     xnacka        ;clock high time
xnacka    goto     xnackb
xnackb    goto     xnackc
xnackc    btfsc    portb,sda     ;data line 0 ? if yes, skip
          bsf      status,c      ;no. set carry
          bcf      dirb,scl      ;make it an output
          movf     dirb,w
          tris     portb
```

```
            bcf     portb,scl       ;take clock low
            goto    xnackd          ;clock low time
xnackd      goto    xnacke
xnacke      goto    xnackf
xnackf      retlw   0               ;exit
;-------------------------------------------------------------------
;           Module: xsack
;           Sends ACK to slave (clocks low onto data line)
;
;           On entry: Expects Clock line to be low
;
;           On exit:  Clock line is held low and data line is released
;-------------------------------------------------------------------
xsack       bcf     dirb,sda        ;make data line an output
            movf    dirb,w
            tris    portb
            bcf     portb,sda       ;take data line low
            goto    xsacka
xsacka      bsf     dirb,scl        ;release scl
            movf    dirb,w
            tris    portb
xsack1      btfss   portb,scl       ;scl held low ? if no, skip next
            goto    xsack1          ;yes. go try again
            goto    xsackb          ;no. clock high time
xsackb      goto    xsackc
xsackc      goto    xsackd
xsackd      bsf     portb,scl       ;reads scl to port register
            bcf     dirb,scl        ;make scl an output
            movf    dirb,w
            tris    portb
            bcf     portb,scl       ;take scl low
            goto    xsacke
xsacke      goto    xsackf
xsackf      bsf     dirb,sda        ;release data line
            movf    dirb,w
            tris    portb
            goto    xsackg
xsackg      retlw   0               ;exit
;===================================================================
```

```
;====== ISCOMS.GRP =============================================================
;
;           ISCOMS.GRP     12 Bit PICmicro IIC Master (FET drivers)
;           Master Routines to read & write to devices on the IIC Bus
;           May be used with 12 Bit PICmicros. Leaves both call levels available
;           to the application.   See Sections 8.2.2 and 8.2.3.
;
;           The IIC specification requires that the sda and scl lines be
;           wired-AND. This wired-AND is simulated by inverting data OUT and
;           placing it on port line sdo. Port line sdo drives an FET which drives
;           the sda line. The same technique may be used on the scl line, but is
;           necessary only with multi-master systems or when a slave device
;           capable of pulling down the scl line is used. This version DOES NOT
;           simulate wired-AND on the scl line.
;
;           Requires following workspace:
;                   timctr             timout counter
;                   eeddr1             EEPROM address high byte
;                   eeddr0             EEPROM address low byte
;                   data0              data to be sent to or received from EEPROM
;                   iidata             data byte to be sent to or received from
;                                      IIC device
;                   bitctr             bit counter
;                   comstat            IIC communications status flag register
;
;         comstat flag definitions:
;                   bit 0 is scl flag
;                   bit 1 is sda flag
;                   all other bits reserved for application communications flags
;
;           Requires following equates:
;            sda       equ       nn        (PORT B bit for data line)
;            scl       equ       nn        (PORT B bit for clock line)
;            sdo       equ       nn        (PORT B bit for data out (drives FET))
;            eeslv     equ       nn        (slave address)
;                                          (for read bit0 =1, for write bit0 =0)
;
;           All TIMING is based on 1 microsecond cycle time (4 MHz xtal)
;           For shorter cycle times ALL clock & setup time code MUST be
;           rewritten so that times are the same as for 1 uS cycle time.
;           For longer cycle times (slower processor clock) the clock & setup
;           time code need not be changed.
;
;-------------------------------------------------------------------------------
;           Module: ISSTRT.TXT
;           Generates START Condition
;           Data line goes low while clock line is high.
;
;           At entry, tests both scl and sda lines for high. If either are not
;           high, then error condition: Sets carry and and copies sda and scl
;           to sda and scl flags in comstat.
;
;           On exit, for no error condition, sda & scl are low.
;           Error exit: carry set and sda and scl copied to sda and scl flags
```

```
;-------------------------------------------------------------------------
isstrt  bcf     status,c        ;clear carry
        bsf     comstat,0       ;initialize scl and sda flags
        bsf     comstat,1
        btfss   portb,scl       ;scl high ? if yes, skip next
        goto    isstre1         ;go scl error exit
        btfss   portb,sda       ;yes. sda high ? if yes, skip next
        goto    isstre2         ;no. go sda error exit
        goto    isstrt1         ;yes. short wait
isstrt1 nop
        bsf     portb,sdo       ;take data low
        goto    isstrt2         ;set up time
isstrt2 goto    isstrt3
isstrt3 nop
        bcf     portb,scl       ;take clock low
        goto    isstrt4         ;set up time
isstrt4 goto    isstrt5
isstrt5 nop
        goto    isstrtx         :go exit
;
isstre1 bcf     comstat,0       ;error service (scl error flag)
        btfss   portb,sda       ;sda error ? if no, skip
isstre2 bcf     comstat,1       ;yes. sda error flag
        bsf     status,c        ;set carry (error flag)
;
isstrtx retlw   0               ;exit
;-------------------------------------------------------------------------
;       Module: ISSTOP.TXT
;       Generates STOP Condition
;       Data line goes high while clock line is high.
;       On entry, scl is low
;
;       On exit, sda & scl are high (bus free)
:       If sda is NOT high, then hardware error. Exits with carry set.
;-------------------------------------------------------------------------
isstop  bsf     portb,sdo       ;make sure data line low
        goto    iistop1         ;set up time
iistop1 goto    iistop2
iistop2 nak
        bsf     portb,scl       ;take clock high
        goto    iistop3         ;set up time
iistop3 goto    iistop4
iistop4 nop
        bcf     portb,sdo       ;take data line high
        goto    iistop5         ;set up time
iistop5 goto    iistop6
iistop6 nop
        bcf     status,c        ;clear carry
        btfss   portb,sda       ;sda high ? if yes, skip next
        bsf     status,c        ;no. set carry
        retlw   0               ;exit
;-------------------------------------------------------------------------
;       Module: ISIN.TXT
;       Receives 8 bit byte from slave device
```

```
;           Places received byte in iidata
;
;----------------------------------------------------------------
isin     movlw   d'8'               ;8 bits
         movwf   bitctr             ;to bit counter
isin1    nop                        ;short delay
         nop
         bsf     portb,scl          ;take clock high
         bcf     status,c           ;clear carry
         goto    issin1             ;set up time
issin1   goto    issin2
issin2   btfsc   portb,sda          ;data line 0 ? if yes, skip
         bsf     status,c           ;no. set carry
         bcf     portb,scl          ;take clock low
         goto    issin3             ;set up time
issin3   goto    issin4
issin4   nop
         rlf     iidata,f           ;rotate it (carry) into iidata
         decfz   bitctr,f           ;dec bit ctr. all bits done ? if yes, skip
next
         goto    isin1              ;no. go get next bit
         retlw   0                  ;yes. exit
;----------------------------------------------------------------
;        Module: ISOUT.TXT
;        Sends 8 bit byte to slave device
;        Byte to be sent is in iidata
;
;----------------------------------------------------------------
isout    movlw   d'8'               ;8 bits
         movwf   bitctr             ;to bit counter
isout1   rlf     iidata             ;rotate data bit to carry
         btfss   status,c           ;bit = 1 ? if yes, skip
         goto    isout2             ;no. go clear sda line
         bcf     portb,sdo          ;yes. set sda line
         goto    isout3             ;& go
isout2   bsf     portb,sdo          ;clear sda line
isout3   goto    isout4             ;short delay
isout4   bcf     portb,scl          ;take clock high
         goto    isout5             ;clock high time
isout5   goto    isout6
isout6   goto    isout7
isout7   bcf     portb,scl          ;take clock low
         goto    isout8             ;clock low time
isout8   goto    isout9
isout9   goto    isouta
isouta   decfsz  bitctr,f           ;dec bit ctr. all bits done ? if yes, skip
         goto    isout1             ;no. go do next bit
         retlw   0                  ;yes. exit
;----------------------------------------------------------------
;        Module: SNACK.TXT
;        Tests for ACK from receiver.
;
;        On Exit: if ACK received, then carry = 0
;                 if ACK not received, then carry = 1
```

```
;---------------------------------------------------------------------------
snack    goto     snack1          ;short wait
snack1   bsf      portb,scl       ;take clock high
         bcf      status,sc       ;clear carry
         goto     snack2          ;clock high time
snack2   goto     snack3          ;time filler
snack3   btfsc    portb,sda       ;data line 0 ? if yes, skip
         bsf      status,sc       ;no. set carry
         bcf      portb,scl       ;take clock low
         goto     snack4          ;clock low time
snack4   goto     snack5
snack5   retlw    0               ;exit
;===========================================================================
```

8.2.4 Using the Section 8.2 Routines in Your Applications

Generally all of the routines can be used in your applications as written or with minor changes. For all routines, the entry and exit conditions, variables, port definitions and flag definitions are described in the xx.GRP and xx.TXT listings. All port assignments are arbitrary and may be changed to suit your application. See Sections 8.4 and 8.5 for sample applications using the routines. The sample applications use the PIC16F84 but the routines may be used with other PICmicros with little or no change. For the 12 bit family use the routines in IXCOMS.GRP or ISCOMS.GRP.

The routines introduced in Section 8.2 are:

IICOMS.GRP	I²C Master Bus Communications Services
IFCOMS.GRP	FET Buffered I²C Master Bus Communications Services
IXCOMS.GRP	12 Bit Family I²C Master Bus Communications Services
ISCOMS.GRP	12 Bit Family FET I²C Master Bus Communications Services

The routines in these groups are all *called* functions. A bit-bang I²C application using these functions is little more than a sequence of calls to these functions interspersed with specific application services.

Most of your applications will generally use the I²C bit-bang routines to communicate with standard I²C hardware slave devices. These devices are capable of operating at the maximum I²C clock rate of 100 KHz. The bit-bang services generate the clock timing with software routines and are thus sensitive to crystal frequency. The modules in all four of the groups operate at less than 100 KHZ when a 4 MHz crystal is used. The I²C clock period for the modules in IICOMS is determined by the literal **iicrate** in the subroutine FILLER (see modules IICLK and FILLER) and may range from approximately 30 to 1554 instruction cycles. The clock period for IFCOMS, IXCOMS and ISCOMS is a function of crystal frequency only. See the individual listings for these groups for more detailed information about the clock rate. IFCOMS may be modified to include a FILLER type of adjustable clock rate. IXCOMS and ISCOMS may be modified by placing a time waster similar to FILLER at the setup or clock period area within each module.

When using the bit-bang master bus services with a device using the bit-bang slave bus services (Section 8.3), pay close attention to the clock rates because the bit-bang slave routines are generally slower than the master routines (see Section 8.3.2 and listings ORANGE4.ASM and ORANGE5.ASM).

The modules in IIPROM.GRP (Section 8.4.1) serve as excellent application examples of the I²C bus services because serial EEPROMS implement most of the common transaction protocols.

8.3 The PICmicro as a Bit-Bang I²C Slave

All slave devices sit on the I²C bus and do nothing until a start condition is recognized. Following the start they all receive the slave address. Each slave then compares the slave address to its own address. The device with the matching address becomes the active slave and remains active until a stop condition. All other slaves do nothing but wait for another start condition.

A PICmicro used as a bit-bang slave device must be programmed with routines for communication with the I²C bus and routines for the device application. The routines for slave I²C bus communication are described in this section. See section 8.6 for bit-bang slave demonstration applications.

8.3.1 I²C Bit-Bang Slave Bus Services

The modules in IISLAVE.GRP are all that are required for a bit-banger PICmicro slave to communicate with the I²C bus. These are the I²C *slave bus* modules. The modules are:

IIWAIT   Waits for bus activity and determines type of activity.
SLREC   Receives an 8 bit byte from the master.
ACK   Sends an ACK to the master.
SLVOUT   Transmits an 8 bit byte to the master.
NOACK   Does nothing for 1 clock period (1 bit time).
SLVLP   Main control loop. Calls the above 5 modules and
              calls slave application program.
HOLD   Holds clock line low to temporarily stop communications.
              (HOLD includes RELEASE which releases clock line).
BACK   Combines ACK and NOACK in one module.

At entry and exit, all modules configure the SDA and SCL lines as inputs (lines released).

Module Descriptions:

Wait for bus activity (Module IIWAIT and Figure 8-14)

This is a *wait* and *see* module: wait for bus activity and see what it is. Other than the trivial bus-free state, there are three bus states that the slave must uniquely recognize: start condition, stop condition and data byte. The start and stop conditions are recognized as a change of level on the data line during the clock high period while a data bit is recognized as a stable level during the entire clock high period. The start condition is SDA going low while SCL is high and the stop condition is SDA going high while SCL is high. The data bit is the stable SDA level during the clock high period. The bus state is passed from the routine via the receive flags byte (**recflg**). If a start condition is detected the start flag (bit 1 of **recflg**) is set and the routine exits. If a stop condition is detected the stop flag (bit 2 of **recflg**) is set and the routine exits. If the data line is stable throughout the clock high period the routine exits at the time that the clock goes low, passing the data bit through the data flag (bit 3 of **recflg**).

On entry, all receive flags are cleared. At the time that the clock goes high, the data line level is transferred to the data flag bit. Throughout the clock high period the data line is sampled, compared with the data flag, and if the compare is true (data line = data flag) the routine loops back to sample the data again. If the compare remains true until the clock goes low, the routine exits with the data bit in the data flag. If at any time while the clock is high the compare is *not* true (indicating a change on the data line), the stop flag is set if the data line changes to low or the start flag is set if the data line changes to high and the routine exits. Note that in the case of a start or stop condition, the routine exits immediately upon detecting the condition.

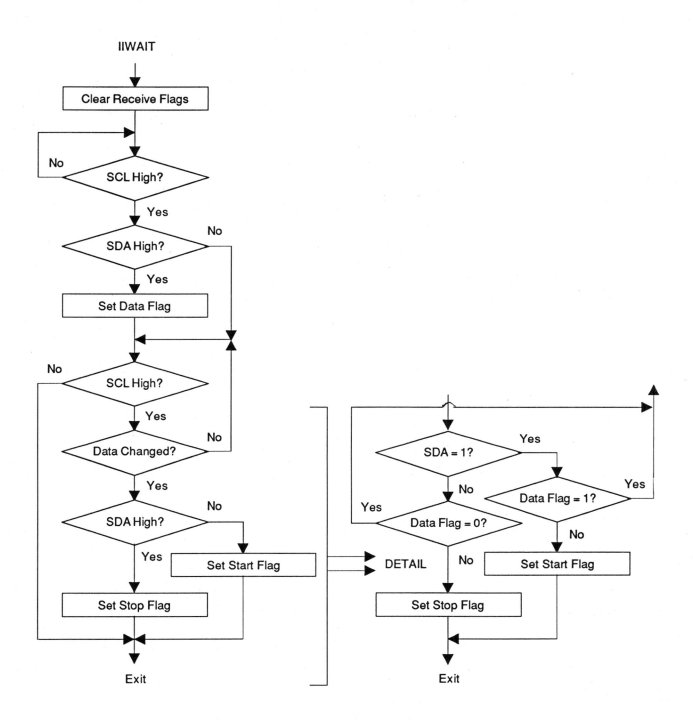

Figure 8-14   IISLAVE Wait For Bus Activity

`Receive a Byte of Data From the Master (Module SLVREC and Figure 8-15)

This routine receives the 8 bit byte clocked onto the bus by the master. On entry, the bit counter is initialized to 8 bits then IIWAIT is called. IIWAIT receives the data bit and passes it back via the data bit of the receive flags byte. The data bit is then rotated (via the carry) into the data byte IIDATA. The routine loops back to the call to IIWAIT to get the next bit. After all 8 bits are received, the routine exits. If a stop or start condition is received, the routine exits, passing the condition via the start or stop bit of the receive flags byte. Note that in the case of a start or stop condition, the routine exits immediately upon detecting the condition.

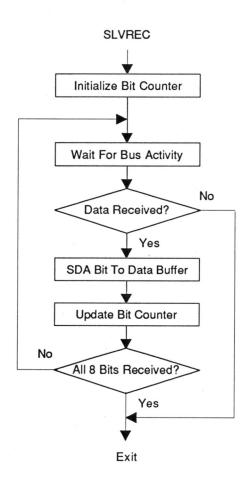

Figure 8-15   IISLAVE Receive Byte

Send an acknowledge (Module ACK and Figure 8-16)

This routine places an ACK bit on the bus. The ACK signals to the master that the slave received the byte transmitted by the master. When the clock line is low, the data line is brought low and held low until the clock has gone high and back low. When the clock goes low the data line is released (taken high) and the routine exits.

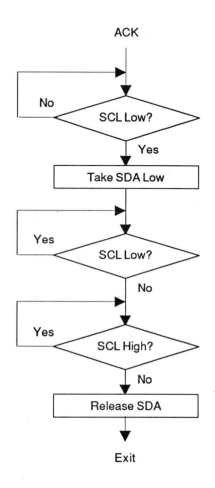

Figure 8-16   IISLAVE Send ACK

Transmit a Byte of Data to the Master (Module SLVOUT and Figure 8-17)

Data transmitted to the master by the slave is clocked onto the data line by the master. The slave must change the data line only when the clock line is low. On entry, the bit counter is initialized to 8 bits. If the clock line is low, the data bit is placed on the data line. If the data is a 1, the data line is made an input; if it is 0, the data line is made an output and taken low. The data line then remains unchanged until the clock has gone high and back low. The bit counter is updated and if all the bits have not been sent, the routine loops back to send the next bit. If all bits have been sent, then the data line is made an input and the routine exits.

235

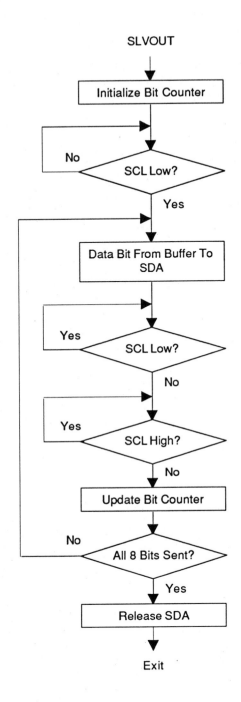

Figure 8-17   IISLAVE Send Byte

Release Data Bus for One Bit Time (Module NOACK and 8-18)

A NOACK releases the data line for one bit time. The NOACK is controlled by the slave. It is required when modeling some I²C slave devices. When the clock line is low, the data line is released (made an input) and remains unchanged until the clock has gone high and back low. When the clock goes low the routine exits.

The module BACK is included in IISLAVE.GRP. This module combines the ACK and NOACK functions. The function is selected by bit 2 of the system flags byte (**systat**). Combining the functions results in a 4 byte savings in program memory, but if the module is called from several locations in the application program the need to set or clear the flag may negate any savings in program memory. If the NOACK function is not used by the application program, delete NOACK and BACK from IISLAVE.GRP.

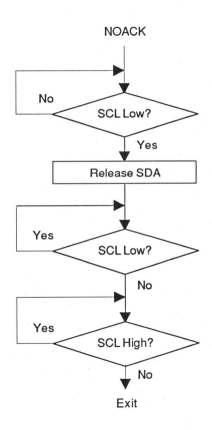

Figure 8-18   IISLAVE Send NO ACK

Main Control Loop (Module SLVLP and figure 8-19)

This module passes control to the slave application program when the device is addressed. When not addressed it does little more than watch the bus. On entry the bus is monitored for a start condition. After the start condition, the slave address is received and compared with the device slave address. If the addresses match, an ACK is sent and control is passed to the application program. Upon return from the application program, the routine loops back to the entry point.

If the addresses do not match, the routine monitors the bus until a stop condition is recognized, then loops back to the entry. See the module SLVLP.TXT in IISLAVE.GRP for more information about the relationship between the application and SLVLP. See also Section 8.6 for demonstration slave applications.

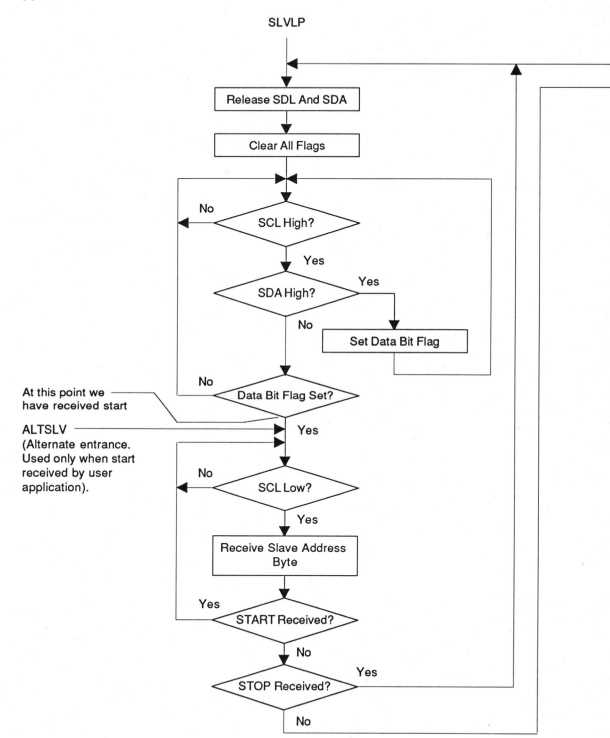

Figure 8-19   IISLAVE Main Slave Loop

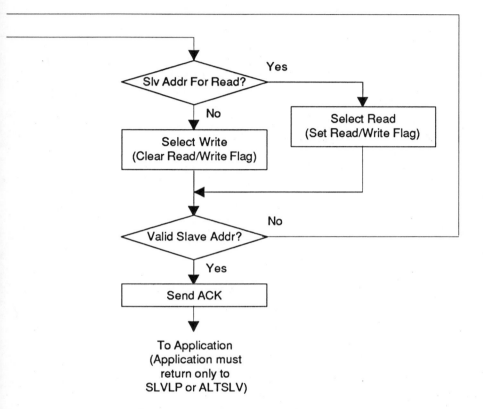

```
              Yes
   Slv Addr For Read?  ─────────────┐
          │                         │
          │ No                      ▼
          ▼                 ┌─────────────────────┐
  ┌─────────────────────┐   │    Select Read      │
  │    Select Write     │   │ (Set Read/Write Flag)│
  │ (Clear Read/Write Flag)│ └─────────────────────┘
  └─────────────────────┘            │
          │◄───────────────────────────┘
          ▼
                    No
   Valid Slave Addr?  ─────────────────────►
          │
          │ Yes
          ▼
  ┌─────────────────────┐
  │     Send ACK        │
  └─────────────────────┘
          │
          ▼
      To Application
    (Application must
      return only to
    SLVLP or ALTSLV)
```

The application program may call any of the above slave modules except SLVLP. When using the 12 bit PICmicro family, note that only one call level is allowed within the application program because the application program is called by SLVLP. For the 12 bit PICmicro family SLVREC will have to be modified because it calls IIWAIT.

```
;====== IISLAVE.GRP===========================================================
;
;       IISLAVE.GRP        14 Bit PICmicro
;
;       Bit-Banger SLAVE routines for PICmicro on IIC bus.
;       PIC is slave. IIC Bus uses two lines: scl and sda on PORT A
;       See Section 8.3
;
;-----------------------------------------------------------------------------
```

```
;
;              REQUIRES Work space:
;                     dira    direction register for PORT A
;                     iidata  data byte received or transmitted
;                     bitctr  bit counter
;                     systat  system flags
;                     recflg  receive flags
;
;              REQUIRES the following literals:
;                     slvaddr          slave address NOTE: Bit 0 MUST be 0
;
;              REQUIRES Following equates:
;                     sda     equ     nn       (PORT A bit for data line)
;                     scl     equ     nn       (PORT A bit for clock line)
;
;                     recflg bit definitions:
;                     stflg   equ     01       start flag
;                     spflg   equ     02       stop flag
;                     datflg  equ     03       data flag
;                     datbit  equ     04       data bit
;
;                     systat flag definitions:
;                     rw      equ     00       read/write flag rw = 0 for write
;                                                              rw = 1 for read
;                     fb      equ     01       first byte flag
;                     anoa    equ     02       ack/no ack flag anoa = 0 for no ack
;                                                              anoa = 1 for ack
;
;         To simulate IIC wired-AND, any module that drives the scl or sda
;         line HIGH does so by making the line an input.
;
;         At the entry and exit of all modules scl and sda lines are INPUTS.
;
;         At RESET or POWER UP, Application program may do any initialization
;         operations, BUT MUST then goto slvlp. The PIC DOES NOT become an IIC
;         slave until the program gets to slvlp !
;
;         Maximum IIC clock rate is approximately 20 KHz when using 4 MHz
;         crystal. Higher crystal frequencies will allow proportionatly
;         higher IIC clock rates. Master MUST NOT exceed this clock rate.
;         See Section 8.3 and FAWN1.ASM & FAWN2.ASM for initialization
;         and application information.
;-----------------------------------------------------------------------
;         Module: slvlp.txt
;         Slave Main loop (main program)
;         Waits for start condition, tests slave address, calls application
;         program if slave address is a match.
;-----------------------------------------------------------------------
slvlp   bsf     dira,scl         ;sda & scl as inputs
        bsf     dira,sda
        movf    dira,w
        tris    porta
        clrf    recflg           ;clear receive flags
slvlp1  btfss   porta,scl        ;clock high ? if yes, skip
```

```
            goto    slvlp1          ;no. go try again
            btfss   porta,sda       ;yes. data line high ? if yes, skip next
            goto    slvlp2          ;no. go
            bsf     recflg,datbit   ;yes. set data bit flag
            goto    slvlp1          ;& go
slvlp2      btfss   recflg,datbit   ;data bit flag set ? if yes, skip
            goto    slvlp1          ;no. go
;
;           At this point, a START has been recognized.
altslv      clrf    systat          ;yes. clear iic system flags. This is also
                                    ;an alternate entrance (used only when a
                                    ;START has been recognized in the user
;                                    application).
            btfsc   porta,scl       ;is clock low ? if yes, skip next
            goto    altslv          ;go try for low clock again
            call    slvrec          ;receive the slave address
            btfsc   recflg,stflg    ;START received ? if no, skip next
            goto    altslv          ;yes. go alternate entrance
            btfsc   recflg,spflg    ;no. STOP recieved ? if no, skip next
            goto    slvlp           ;yes. go start over
            btfsc   iidata,0        ;no. is slave address for read ? if no, skip
            bsf     systat,rw       ;yes. select read (default is write)
            bcf     iidata,0        ;clear bit 0 of received slave address
            movlw   slvaddr         ;test slave address
            subwf   iidata,w        ;my address ?
            btfss   status,z        ;if yes, skip next
            goto    slvlp           ;no. go start over
;
            call    ack             ;yes. send ACK
;
            goto    SLAVEAP         ;GO TO APPLICATION module
                                    ;The FIRST line of the APPLICATION Module
                                    ;MUST be labeled: SLAVEAP
                                    ;
                                    ;The Application module MUST terminate with
                                    ;ONLY a goto slvlp or a goto altslv.
                                    ;------------------------------------------
                                    ;The application may be called but then
                                    ;the application program MUST terminate
                                    ;with a RETURN and THIS module
                                    ;MUST terminate with goto slvlp:
                                    ;Example:
                                    ;    ....
                                    ;          call   someapp
                                    ;          goto   slvlp
;
;---------------------------------------------------------------------------
;           Module: iiwait.txt
;           Waits for a stop or start condition or a data bit.
;
;           On exit, flags in recflg indicate what was received.
;           If start condition, then sets start flag (stflg) & exits. If stop
;           condition, then sets stop flag (spflg) & exits. If data bit, then
```

```
;          data bit is placed in data bit (datbit) flag and data flag (datflg)
;          is set and exits after end of clock high period. NOTE: Data bit has
;          no significance if start or stop flag is set or data flag is not set.
;-----------------------------------------------------------------------------
iiwait  clrf    recflg          ;clear receive flags
iiwait1 btfss   porta,scl       ;scl high ? if yes, skip next
        goto    iiwait1         ;no. go try again
        btfsc   porta,sda       ;yes. sda high ? if no, skip next
        bsf     recflg,datbit   ;yes. set data bit
iiwait2 btfss   porta,scl       ;clock high ? if yes, skip next
        goto    iiwait4         ;clock now low. must be data. go
        btfss   porta,sda       ;sda high ? if yes, skip next
        goto    iiwait3         ;no. go
        btfsc   recflg,datbit   ;data bit flag high ? if no, skip next
        goto    iiwait2         ;yes. go try again
        bsf     recflg,spflg    ;no.set stop flag
        goto    iiwait5         ;& go exit
;
iiwait3 btfss   recflg,datbit   ;data bit flag low ? if no, skip next
        goto    iiwait2         ;yes. go try again
        bsf     recflg,stflg    ;no. set start flag
        goto    iiwait5         ;& go exit
iiwait4 bsf     recflg,datflg   ;set data flag
iiwait5 retlw   0               ;exit
;-----------------------------------------------------------------------------
;       Module slvrec.txt
;       Receives a byte of data (or STOP or START) from master.
;
;       Received data byte placed in iidata, then exits.
;       If Start or Stop condition received, then exits with receive
;       flags (recflg) intact as determined by iiwait.
;-----------------------------------------------------------------------------
slvrec  movlw   d'8'            ;initialize bit counter
        movwf   bitctr
slvrec1 call    iiwait          ;wait & see what is on bus
        bcf     status,c        ;clear carry
        btfss   recflg,datflg   ;was data received ? if yes, skip next
        goto    slvrec2         ;no. go exit
        btfsc   recflg,datbit   ;data bit = 1 ? if no, skip next
        bsf     status,c        ;yes. set carry
        rlf     iidata,f        ;rotate carry into data byte
        decfsz  bitctr,f        ;update bit counter. skip if all done
        goto    slvrec1         ;go get next receive bit
slvrec2 retlw   0               ;exit
;-----------------------------------------------------------------------------
;       Module: acl.txt
;       Sends ACK
;
;       When scl is low, takes sda low and keeps it low until clock has
;       gone high and returned to low. When clock has returned to low,
;       releases sda line and exits.
;-----------------------------------------------------------------------------
ack     btfsc   porta,scl       ;clock low ? if yes, skip next
        goto    ack             ;no. go try again
```

242

```
            bcf     dira,sda        ;yes. make sda an output
            movf    dira,w
            tris    porta
            bcf     porta,sda       ;& take sda low
ack1        btfss   porta,scl       ;clock still low ? if no, skip next
            goto    ack1            ;yes. go try again
ack2        btfsc   porta,scl       ;no. clock still high ? if no, skip
            goto    ack2            ;yes. go try again
            bsf     dira,sda        ;no. release sda
            movf    dira,w
            tris    porta
            retlw   0               ;exit
;-------------------------------------------------------------------
;           Module: noack.txt
;           Sends NOACK
;
;           When scl is low, takes sda high. Exits after full clock cycle.
;-------------------------------------------------------------------
noack       btfsc   porta,scl       ;clock low ? if yes, skip next
            goto    noack           ;no. go try again
            bsf     dira,sda        ;release sda
            movf    dira,w
            tris    porta
noack1      btfss   porta,scl       ;clock still low ? if no, skip next
            goto    noack1          ;yes. go try again
noack2      btfsc   porta,scl       ;no. clock still high ? if no, skip
            goto    noack2          ;yes. go try again
            retlw   0               ;no. exit
;-------------------------------------------------------------------
;           Module: slvout.txt
;           Slave transmits a byte of data
;           Byte to be transmitted in iidata
;-------------------------------------------------------------------
slvout      movlw   d'8'            ;initialize bit counter
            movwf   bitctr
slvout1     btfss   porta,scl       ;clock low ? if yes, skip next
            goto    slvout1         ;no. go try again
            rlf     iidata,f        ;yes. data bit to carry
            btfss   status,c        ;data bit =1 ? if yes, skip next
            goto    slvout2         ;no. go clear sda line
            bsf     dira,sda        ;yes. make sda line an input
            goto    slvout3         ;and go
slvout2     bcf     dira,sda        ;make it an output
slvout3     movf    dira,w
            tris    porta
slvout4     btfss   porta,scl       ;clock still low ? if no, skip next
            goto    slvout4         ;yes. go try again
slvout5     btfsc   porta,scl       ;clock still high ? if no, skip next
            goto    slvout5         ;yes. go try again
            decfsz  bitctr,f        ;update bit counter. skip if all done
            goto    slvout1         ;not done. do next bit
            bsf     dira,sda        ;release sda
            movf    dira,w
            tris    porta
```

```
        retlw   0                   ;done. exit
;--------------------------------------------------------------------
;       Modules: hold.txt and release.txt
;
;       HOLD: Slave holds clock line low to temporarily stop communications
;             until an application function is finished.
;       RELEASE: Slave releases clock line to resume communications
;--------------------------------------------------------------------
hold    btfsc   porta,scl           ;clock low ? if yes, skip next
        goto    hold                ;no. go try again
        bcf     dira,scl            ;yes. make scl an output
        movf    dira,w
        tris    porta
        bcf     porta,scl           ;and take scl low
        retlw   0                   ;& exit
;--------------------------------------------------------------------
release bsf     dira,scl            ;make scl an input
        movf    dira,w
        tris    porta
        retlw   0
;--------------------------------------------------------------------
;       Module: back.txt
;       Sends ACK or NOACK
;       This module may be used as a replacement for ACK and NOACK
;       If bit 2 of SYSTAT is set then sends ACK, otherwise sends NOACK
;
;       For ACK:
;       When scl is low, takes sda low and keeps it low until clock has
;       gone high and returns back to low. When clock has gone low,
;       releases sda line and exits.
;
;       For NOACK:
;       When scl is low, takes sda high. Exits after full clock cycle.
;--------------------------------------------------------------------
back    btfsc   porta,scl           ;clock low ? if yes, skip next
        goto    back                ;no. go try again
        btfss   systat,anoa         ;ACK flag set ? if yes, skip next
        goto    back0               ;no. go send NOACK
        bcf     dira,sda            ;yes. send ACK. make sda an output
        movf    dira,w
        tris    porta
        bcf     porta,sda           ;take sda low
        goto    back1               ;& go
back0   bsf     dira,sda            ;NO ACK. release sda
        movf    dira,w
        tris    porta
back1   btfss   porta,scl           ;clock still low ? if no, skip next
        goto    back1               ;yes. go try again
back2   btfsc   porta,scl           ;no. clock still high ? if no, skip
        goto    back2               ;yes. go try again
        bsf     dira,sda            ;no. release sda
        movf    dira,w
        tris    porta
        retlw   0                   ;exit
;====================================================================
```

8.3.2 Using the Section 8.3 Routines in Your Applications

Generally all of the routines can be used in your applications as written or with minor changes. For all routines, the entry and exit conditions, variables, port definitions and flag definitions are described in the xx.GRP and xx.TXT listings. All port assignments are arbitrary and may be changed to suit your application. See FAWN1.ASM and FAWN2.ASM (Section 8.6) for sample applications using the IISLAVE routines. The sample applications use the PIC16F84 but the routines may be used with other PICmicros with little or no change.

The routines introduced in Section 8.3 are in:

IISLAVE.GRP   Slave I^2C Bus Services

The Bit-Bang slave routines are relatively slow, so be sure that the Master I^2C clock rate does not override the routines. See IISLAVE.GRP for clock rate details.

At power on or RESET, the slave program may do any necessary initialization, but then must go to SLVLP. The program is not a slave until it gets to SLVLP. The slave application service is controlled by SLVLP. It calls (or jumps to) the application. The application must ultimately return to SLVLP. The START condition and slave address are watched for and recognized by SLVLP. When the application service is completed, control must return to SLVLP. If the recognition of a START must be within the application service, the application can return control to SLVLP via ALTSLV. See SLVLP in IISLAVE.GRP for further details. The application may call any of the IISLAVE modules, but use care when directly calling IIWAIT (see Figure 8-19).

When assigning a slave address to your application be sure that all slaves on the bus have different addresses. No more than one device on the bus may have a given slave address.

When using IISLAVE.GRP with the 12 bit family, SLVLP should jump to the application and SLVREC should be modified by moving the IIWAIT function into it. This reserves both call levels for use by the application.

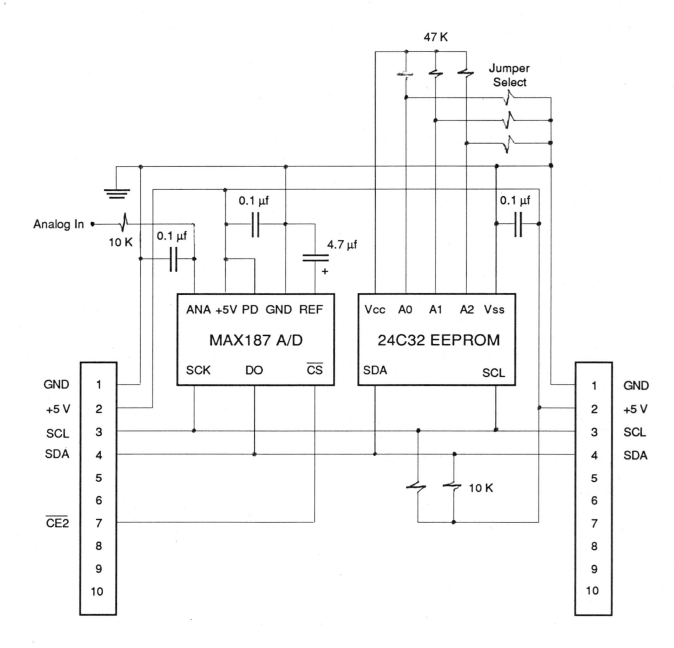

Figure 8-20   SlaveSchematic; I²C Applications

8.4 Communicating With an I²C Serial EEPROM

The Microchip 24C32 serial EEPROM is typical of most I²C Serial Bus Electrically Erasable PROMS. It is a 32K bit device configured as 4K bytes of 8 bits each. The 24C32 I²C interface conforms to the standard I²C protocol. The 24C32 is organized as a continuous 32K bit block of memory, however, for multi-byte writes, it looks like 512 pages of 8 bytes each. The significance of this distinction will be covered in the discussion below on page and cache write. Data writes may be one byte at a time to a specific memory address or sequentially to a limited block of contiguous memory. Reads may be one byte or multi-byte. The EEPROM device protocols are covered in more detail in Sections 8.4.1 and 8.4.2.

8.4.1 Bit-Banging the 24C32 EEPROM
See Source Listings IIPROM.GRP and IICOMS.GRP.

The modules in the IIPROM.GRP, along with the IICOMS modules, are all that are needed to communicate with an I²C EEPROM. The modules are all *called* functions and are called by the application. The IIPROM modules perform the specific EEPROM operations and call the I²C bus modules in IICOMS.GRP. These are the I²C *EEPROM* modules. The modules are:

EEPRE	Sends slave address and memory address to EEPROM
EEWRIT	Writes a byte to the EEPROM
EEPOLL	Polls the EEPROM for completion of write cycle
EEREAD	Reads byte from the EEPROM
EECUR	Reads a byte from the EEPROM current address
EESQWR	Multi-byte write to EEPROM
EESQRD	Multi-byte read from EEPROM
EESEQ	Multi-byte write to and read from EEPROM

I²C EEPROM Description

Functional address lines (strap downs) on the 24C32 allow up to eight of the devices to be on the same bus. The device address is determined by the strapping on the A0, A1 and A2 inputs of each device (Figure 8-20). The I²C protocol requires that the first byte sent after a START condition be the slave address. For the EEPROM, the slave address is (beginning with MS bit): 1010 followed by A2,A1,A0, followed by the read/write bit. If the following byte is a write to the EEPROM, the read/write bit is 0. If the following byte is to be read from the EEPROM, the read/write bit is 1 (Figure 8-21). The Microchip data book uses the term 'control byte' for the slave address byte. To be consistent with the I²C specification, the term 'slave address' is used throughout this book. The specific EEPROM operations are covered in the module descriptions below.

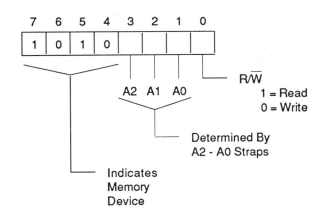

Figure 8-21   EEPROM Slave Address

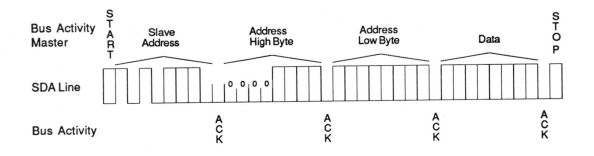

Byte Write

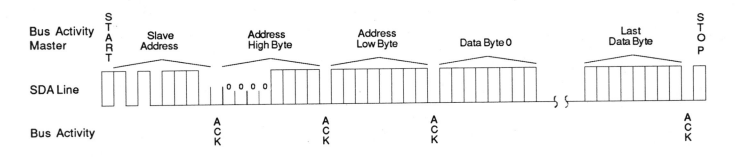

Page Write

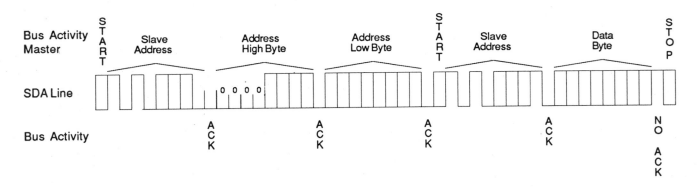

Random Read

Figure 8-22   I²C EEPROM Transactions

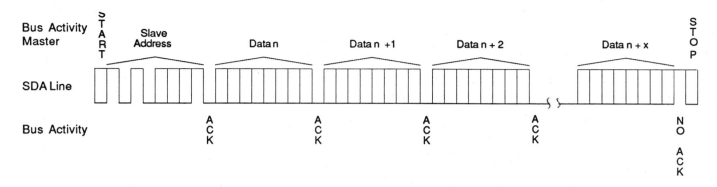

Sequential Read

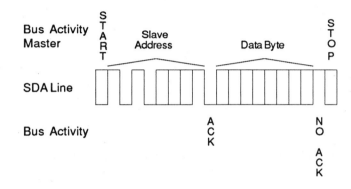

Current Address Read

Module Descriptions

Slave Address and Memory Location Address (Module EEPRE and Figure 8-23)

Because nearly every command to the EEPROM begins with the slave address followed by a two byte memory location address, this part of the command string is implemented as a called module. It is treated as a preamble and called by the modules requiring it. Following the start condition, the master transmits the slave address for a *write*, the high order memory address and the low order memory address. If any ACK is not received by EEPRE when expected, the error flag (carry) is set and the routine exits. Note that the error flag (carry) is actually set or cleared by the IIIN routine which was called by the NACK routine which was called by EEPRE. The flow diagram for EEPRE shows the error flag being set by EEPRE, but this is for functional clarity only. This note also applies to some of the other EEPROM routines.

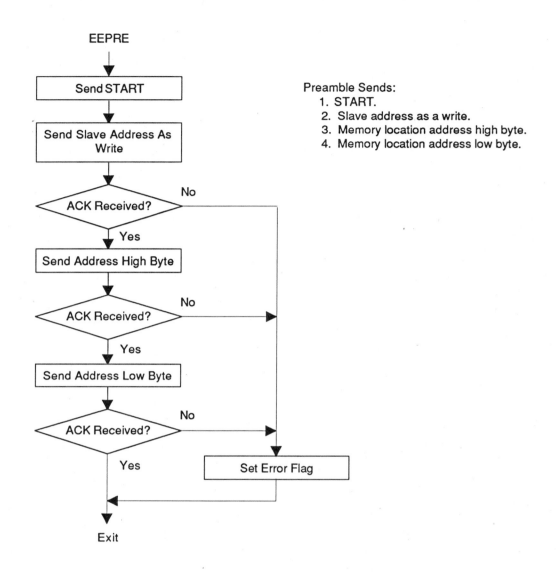

EEPRE

Send START

Send Slave Address As Write

ACK Received? — No

Yes

Send Address High Byte

ACK Received? — No

Yes

Send Address Low Byte

ACK Received? — No

Yes

Set Error Flag

Exit

Preamble Sends:
1. START.
2. Slave address as a write.
3. Memory location address high byte.
4. Memory location address low byte.

Figure 8-23   Send EEPROM Preamble

Byte Write (Module EEWRIT and Figure 8-24)

Following the start condition, the master transmits the slave address for a *write*, the high order memory location address, the low order memory location address and the data byte to be written, followed by the stop condition. Note that all command transmissions follow the: .. byte, wait for ACK, byte, wait for ACK, .. I²C protocol. After receiving the STOP, the EEPROM initiates the internal write cycle. During the internal memory write cycle the EEPROM will not generate acknowledge signals. If at any time during the transmission, ACK is not received from the EEPROM when expected, EEWRIT sets the error flag (carry), sends a stop condition and exits. EEWRIT calls EEPRE to send the slave and memory addresses.

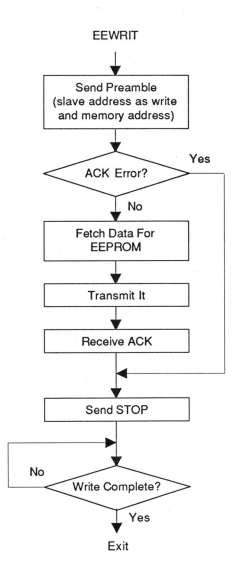

Figure 8-24   Write Byte To EEPROM

Acknowledge Polling (Module EEPOLL and Figure 8-25)

The EEPROM requires a variable time period to complete byte, page or cache writes. For the 24C32 this time can be up to 5 milliseconds for byte and page writes and longer for cache writes. The write cycle time for some EEPROMS can be as long as 25 mS. During the write cycle, the EEPROM cannot be accessed for read or write operations. Rather than wait for the longest possible cycle time before further access, EEPOLL tests the EEPROM to determine if it has completed the cycle. The test attempts to make the EEPROM generate an ACK. The EEPROM will not acknowledge during the write cycle, indicating that it is still busy. When the write has been completed, the EEPROM will generate the ACK. The master sends a start condition followed by the slave address for a *write*. If the device is still busy with the write cycle, then no

ACK is returned. If the cycle is complete, then the EEPROM returns an ACK and the master can then proceed with the next read or write. The master repeats this polling until an ACK is received. If an ACK is not received after 256 attempts (approximately 30 mS), the routine times out, sets the error flag and returns. This acknowledgment polling significantly increases the bus throughput rate. This module is usually called by other IIPROM.GRP modules, but may be called by the application. All of the EEPROM write modules call EEPOLL.

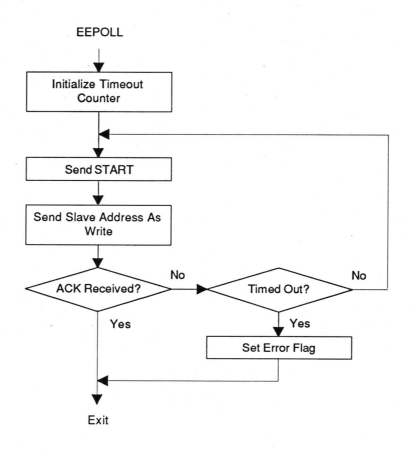

Figure 8-25   Poll EEPROM For Completed Write Cycle

Byte Read (Module EEREAD and Figure 8-26)

Following the start condition, the master transmits the slave address for a *write* followed by the high order memory address and the low order memory address. The master then sends the start condition followed by the slave address as a *read*. The master then receives the data byte transmitted by the EEPROM. After the EEPROM transmits the data it does *not* acknowledge. The master must wait 1 bit time (where the acknowledge would have been) before sending the stop condition. This is the NO ACK time. It does this by testing for the ACK and ignoring the result of the test. To generate this NO ACK time, the acknowledge test is called rather than calling the I²C clock routine because the acknowledge test routine ensures that the data line is high. If any ACK is not received by EEREAD when it is expected, the error flag (carry) is set and the routine exits.

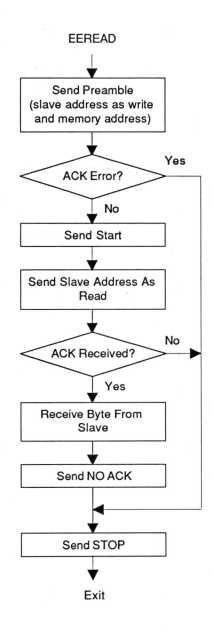

EEREAD

Send Preamble
(slave address as write
and memory address)

ACK Error? — Yes

No

Send Start

Send Slave Address As
Read

ACK Received? — No

Yes

Receive Byte From
Slave

Send NO ACK

Send STOP

Exit

Figure 8-26   Random Read EEPROM

Current Address Read (Module EECUR and Figure 8-27)

Quite often an application must retrieve a data byte from the EEPROM, act on the data, retrieve the next data byte, act on it and so on through several iterations. This sequence can be accomplished without the need to maintain a record of the last address read because the 24C32 address counter always points to the address of the byte following the last byte accessed. The address counter is said to be at the *current* address. The current address read command is very simple: after the start condition the master transmits the slave address for a *read*, then reads in the data byte followed by a stop condition (no address is transmitted). As with the random read, the master must wait one bit time (NO ACK) before sending the stop condition. If an ACK is not received by EECUR after it sends the slave address, the error flag is set and the routine exits.

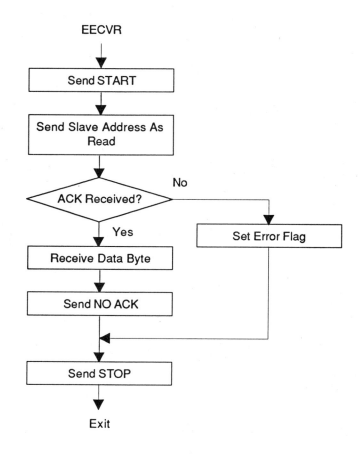

EECVR

Send START

Send Slave Address As
Read

ACK Received? — No

Yes

Set Error Flag

Receive Data Byte

Send NO ACK

Send STOP

Exit

Figure 8-27   Read Data At Current EEPROM Address

Multi-byte Transactions

Sequential Multi-byte Write and Multi-byte Read (Module EESEQ and Figure 8-28)

The byte write module (EEWRIT) may be repeated any number of times to write multiple bytes to the EEPROM. Likewise the random byte read module (EEREAD) may be repeated for multiple reads. Multiple read and write to sequential address locations are common application requirements. Multiple writes using EEWRIT would be very slow. The 24C32 is capable of performing a page write (eight bytes) to sequential memory in the same time as a one byte write. This capability is used to reduce the write cycle for up to 64 bytes. These multi-byte writes are performed with a single command, further reducing write time and code complexity.

Any number of bytes may be read from the EEPROM sequentially. The sequential read command is like the random read command, except that after the 24C32 transmits the first data byte the master issues an ACK rather than a stop condition. This ACK directs the 24C32 to transmit the next sequentially addressed byte. Every time the master sends an ACK, the EEPROM transmits the next byte in memory. Following the final byte transmitted to the master, the master does not generate an acknowledge, but generates a stop condition (See Sequential Read, Figure 8-22).

A page write may write up to 8 bytes in one write cycle time. The page write command is like the byte write command, except that after the master transmits the first data byte to the 24C32 it transmits up to 7 more bytes before sending the stop condition (See Page Write, Figure 8-22). In the discussion below on page and cache write, multi-byte writes of greater than 8 bytes is covered.

An application that requires multi-byte write or read usually will move data in blocks from or to PICmicro data memory. The module EESEQ moves a block of data in RAM to the EEPROM or moves the block from the EEPROM to RAM. These two functions have been combined in one module because they share some code. Combining functions that share code in a single module will generally, but not always, reduce the size of the program. In this case, as will be seen below, no significant reduction in code size was realized, but it serves as a good example of how to combine functions. For read the block size can range from 1 byte to 255 bytes limited only by available RAM. For write the block size can range from 1 to 64 bytes with some caveats as discussed below in the section on page and cache write. A one byte block size makes this module a replacement for the EEWRIT and EEREAD modules described above. For an application requiring both block moves and single byte write and read, using EESEQ in place of EEWRIT and EEREAD reduces program size.

The RAM block starts at data memory address **block.** The size of the block is stored in the parameter **datctr**. The parameter **datctr** is used to count the bytes being transferred and to generate the offset (pointer) into the block. The block data is transferred starting at the high end of the block because **datctr** is decremented each time a byte is transferred and the pointer is generated by adding the current value of **datctr** to **block**. A system flag register, **systat**, is used to determine whether the move is EEPROM write or EEPROM read. Bit 0 of **systat** is reserved for this function. If bit 0 is 1, then the block operation is read from EEPROM. If it is 0, then write to EEPROM. On entry the number of bytes to move is in **datctr** and the flag indicates the operation.

As can be seen from the EESEQ flow diagram (Figure 8-28) the send preamble routine and generate pointer function are shared by both the read and write loops and branches (other than error service) are determined only by the read/write flag and the current value of the byte counter. The ACK test (after the read-all-done? test) serves only to insert the NO ACK bit time, as in EEREAD.

The pointer into the block of RAM is generated by adding the byte counter, **datctr**, to the start address of the block, **block**. The pointer is placed in the *indirect data memory address pointer* register (FSR). At each block access, it is adjusted by 1 because current address = **(block + datctr -1)**. (When the byte counter = 1, the address in the FSR register must be **block**):

```
eeseq3   movlw    block        ;block start address to w
         addwf    datctr,w     ;add byte counter to block start and place
                               ;result in w
         movwf    fsr          ;move pointer to FSR
```

Prior to each block access, FSR is adjusted by 1:

```
         decf     fsr,f        ;adjust by 1 and place back into FSR
```

At this point the address in FSR is the address of the next block byte.

When the instruction: `movf indf,w` is encountered, the contents of the next block byte are moved into w or, when the instruction: `movwf indf` is encountered, the contents of w are placed in the next block byte.

The multi-byte write and read functions were combined in the module EESEQ. The modules EESQWR and EESQRD break these functions out to separate modules. Combining functions that share code in a single module will generally, but not always, reduce the size of the program. EESQWR and EESQRE are presented as a test of this statement for the case of the multi-byte read and write functions. For PICmicro programs, counting source code lines is the same as counting program memory bytes:

EESQWR	17 lines
EESQRD	24 lines
EESEQ	37 lines

Thus the combined module saves 4 bytes of program memory. Not a very significant savings, but if the application does not require both of the multi-byte functions, the module EESEQ would be replaced with EESQWR or EESQRE the savings would be 13 or 20 bytes.

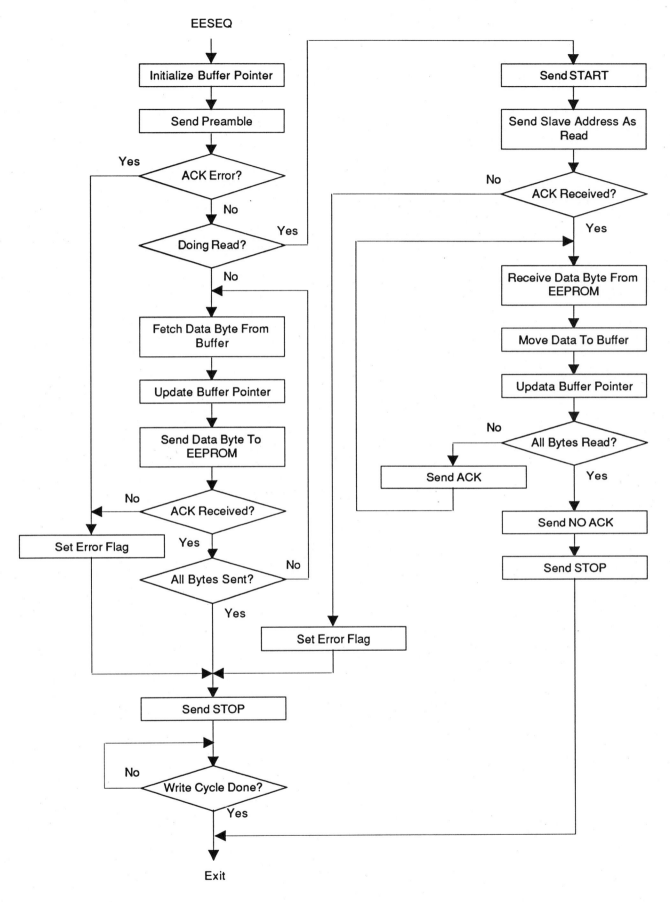

Figure 8-28   Sequential Write And Read EEPROM Data

257

Page and Cache Writes

A page is an 8 byte block of EEPROM memory. A page begins at a page boundary. Page boundaries are every address for which memory address bits A2, A1 and A0 are zero. The cache is an 8 page (64 byte) FIFO buffer. All multi-byte writes are processed through the cache.

Multi-byte writes start at the address transmitted by the master as part of the write command (See Page Write, Figure 8-22) and *do not* have to begin on a page boundary. But the start of the 64 byte buffer does map to a page boundary. Thus if a multi-byte write does not start at a page boundary, the first data byte transmitted by the master does not go into the first byte of the buffer but is offset into the buffer by as many places as it is offset into the page. For example, if the write start address is 0x2B (byte 3 of page 5) the first data byte transmitted will be placed in the byte 3 position of the buffer and buffer bytes 0, 1, and 2 will be empty. If the entire 64 byte buffer is used, then the buffer address will wrap around and the last 3 bytes transmitted will be placed in the first 3 buffer locations and will be written to the first 3 bytes of page 5, overwriting any data in these locations. When the write starts at a page boundary (3 LS address bits = 0) all 64 bytes will map into the 8 pages and no unexpected overwrites will occur. If a multi-byte write starts at a page boundary and if more than 64 bytes are written to the buffer, it will wrap and the last bytes sent will overwrite the first bytes sent. BE CAREFUL WHEN WRITING A LARGE NUMBER OF BYTES !

```
;====== IIPROM.GRP ==============================================================
;
;         IIPROM.GRP
;         Routines to write to & read from IIC EEPROM type 25C32 or similar
;         NOTE: CANNOT be used with 12 bit PICmicro because requires more than
;               2 level stack. See IXPROM.TXT for 12 bit family routines.
;         See Section 8.4
;
;--------------------------------------------------------------------------------
;
;         Requires following workspace:
;                 All workspace as required by IICOMS.TXT and...
;
;                 timctr          timout counter
;                 eeddr1          EEPROM address high byte
;                 eeddr0          EEPROM address low byte
;                 data0           data to be sent to or received from EEPROM
;
;         Also required for EESEQ, EESQWR & EESQRD:
;                 datctr          data counter
;                 comstat         communications status register
;                                 (bit 0 reserved for IIPROM.TXT modules,
;                                 others may be used by application).
;                 bufstrt         Data buffer. This block must be as many
;                                 contiguous bytes long as number of bytes
;                                 to read or write.
;
;         Requires following equates:
;                 eeslv   equ     nn       (slave address of EEPROM)
;
;         All TIMING is based on 1 microsecond cycle time (4 mHz xtal)
```

```
;           For shorter cycle times ALL clock & setup time code MUST be
;           rewritten so that times are the same as for 1 uS cycle time.
;           For longer cycle times (slower processor clock) the clock & setup
;           time code need not be changed.
;
;           NOTE: All modules are not necessary for EEPROM communication. The
;                 module EESEQ may be used for most read and write operations.
;                 All modules called by EESEQ must be present. All IICOMS.TXT
;                 modules must be present.
;-------------------------------------------------------------------------
;           Module: EEWRIT
;           Random write a byte to EEPROM memory
;
;           On entry: Data to be written is in data0
;                     EEPROM location is eeddr1, eeddr0
;
;           ERROR EXIT: If carry is set at exit, indicates error occurred
;                       and a stop was sent to EEPROM.
;-------------------------------------------------------------------------
eewrit  call    eepre           ;send addresses
        btfsc   status,c        ;eepre error ? if no, skip next
        goto    ewerr           ;yes. go error
        movf    data0,w         ;data to be written to memory
        movwf   iidata          ;send it ...
        call    iiout
        call    nack
ewerr   call    iistop          ;send stop
        call    eepoll          ;wait until EEPROM finished writing
        retlw   0               ;exit
;-------------------------------------------------------------------------
;           Module:  EEREAD
;           Random read a byte from memory
;
;           On entry: EEPROM location is eeddr1, eeddr0
;
;           On exit: Data read from EEPROM is in data0
;
;           ERROR EXIT: If carry is set on exit, indicates error occurred
;                       and stop was sent to EEPROM
;-------------------------------------------------------------------------
eeread  call    eepre           ;send address
        btfsc   status,c        ;eepre error ? if no, skip next
        goto    erderr          ;yes. go error
        call    iistrt          ;send start
        movlw   eeslv           ;slave address...
        movwf   iidata
        bsf     iidata,0        ;as read
        call    iiout
        call    nack
        btfsc   status,c        ;ACK received ? if yes, skip next
        goto    erderr          ;no ! go error
        call    iiin            ;receive the byte from memory
        movf    iidata,w        ;move it to data0
```

```
        movwf   data0
        call    nack            ;NO ACK bit time
        bcf     status,c        ;clear error flag
erderr  call    iistop          ;send stop
        retlw   0               ;exit
;------------------------------------------------------------------------
;       Module: EEPRE
;       Sends slave address & EEPROM memory location address
;       On entry: eeslv is slave address
;                 location low byte is in eeddr0
;                 location high byte is in eeddr1
;
;       On exit: Carry is set for an ACK error, cleared otherwise
;------------------------------------------------------------------------
eepre   call    iistrt          ;send start
        movlw   eeslv           ;slave (EEPROM) address
        movwf   iidata          ;to ii data register
        bcf     iidata,0        ;clear bit 0 (as write)
        call    iiout           ;send it
        call    nack            ;test for ACK from slave
        btfsc   status,c        ;ACK received ? if yes, skip next
        goto    eeprex          ;no ! go exit
        movf    eeddr1,w        ;address high byte
        movwf   iidata          ;send it ...
        call    iiout
        call    nack
        btfsc   status,c        ;ACK received ? if yes, skip next
        goto    eeprex          ;no ! go exit
        movf    eeddr0,w        ;address low byte
        movwf   iidata          ;send it ...
        call    iiout
        call    nack
eeprex  retlw   0               ;exit
;------------------------------------------------------------------------
;       Module: EEPOLL
;       Polls EEPROM to determine if it has completed write
;       cycle. Attempts to send slave address to EEPROM. If
;       ACK received from EEPROM, then it has completed write
;       cycle. Attempts 256 times, (approx 30 mS) then times
;       out if no ACK received.
;
;       On entry: slave address is eeslv
;
;       On exit: if ACK received, then carry = 0
;                if timed out (no ACK), then carry = 1
;------------------------------------------------------------------------
eepoll  clrf    timctr          ;start timeout counter
eepoll0 call    iistrt          ;send start
        movlw   eeslv           ;EEPROM slave address
        movwf   iidata          ;to ii data register
        bcf     iidata,0        ;clear bit 0 (for write)
        call    iiout           ;send it to eeprom
eepoll1 call    nack            ;test for ACK from slave
        btfss   status,c        ;carry = 0 (ACK received) ? if no, skip next
```

```
          goto    eepollx         ;yes. ACK received. go exit
          decfsz  timctr,f        ;no. timed out ? if yes, skip next
          goto    eepoll0         ;no. go try again
eepollx   retlw   0               ;exit
;-------------------------------------------------------------------
;         Module: EECUR
;         Reads data at current address of EEPROM
;
;         The current address is one more than the last address accessed
;         for either a read or write operation.
;         On entry: Slave address is eeslv
;
;         On exit: The data read from the EEPROM is in data0.
;                  If carry is 1 then error occured.
;-------------------------------------------------------------------
eecur     call    iistrt          ;send start
          movlw   eeslv           ;slave address
          movwf   iidata          ;to ii data register
          bsf     iidata,0        ;as a read
          call    iiout           ;send it
          call    nack
          btfsc   status,c        ;ACK received ? if yes, skip next
          goto    eecurx          ;no ! go error exit
          call    iiin            ;receive the byte from memory
          movf    iidata,w        ;move it to data0
          movwf   data0
          call    nack            ;NO ACK time filler
          bcf     status,c        ;clear error
eecurx    call    iistop          ;send stop
          retlw   0               ;exit
;-------------------------------------------------------------------
;         Module:  EESEQ
;         Sequentially read or write one or more bytes from or to memory.
;         For read, the bytes received from the EEPROM are placed in a data
;         memory buffer starting at data address: bufstrt. The first byte
;         received is placed at bufstrt. The buffer grows to higher memory.
;         For write, the bytes to be written to the EEPROM are retrieved from
;         the same buffer.
;
;         On entry:
;         READ or WRITE selection is determined by bit 0 of the system flags
;         register: systat.       systat bit 0=1 for read
;                                 systat bit 0=0 for write.
;
;         The number of bytes to read or write is in datctr.
;         The eeprom starting location is eeddr1, eeddr0.
;
;         The write block MUST BE HANDLED WITH CARE. CROSSING PAGE BOUNDRIES
;         CAN BE DANGEROUS. SEE Section 8.4.1.
;         Any number of bytes may be read sequentialy, but reads
;         cannot wrap arround from the end of memory.
;
;         On exit: datctr is corrupted (equals 0)
;
```

261

```
;          ERROR EXIT: If carry is set on exit, indicates error occurred
;                      and stop was sent to EEPROM
;
;          The following workspace must be added:
;                   comstat        Communications status flag register
;                   datctr         Data counter
;                   bufstrt        Data buffer. This block must be as many
;                                  contiguous bytes long as number of bytes
;                                  to read or write.
;--------------------------------------------------------------------------
eeseq    movlw   bufstrt         ;pointer to start of buffer
         movwf   fsr
         call    eepre           ;send preamble
         btfsc   status,c        ;eepre error ? if no, skip next
         goto    eeseqe          ;yes. go error
         btfss   comstat,0       ;read flag ? if yes, skip next
         goto    eeseq4          ;no. go do write
         call    iistrt          ;send start
         movlw   eeslv           ;slave address
         movwf   iidata
         bsf     iidata,0        ;send slave address as read
         call    iiout
         call    nack
         btfsc   status,c        ;ACK received ? if yes, skip next
         goto    eeseqe          ;no. go error
eeseq2   call    iiin            ;receive the byte from eeprom
         movf    iidata,w        ;received data byte to w
         movwf   indf            ;& to next location in buffer
         incf    fsr,f           ;point to next buffer location
         decfsz  datctr,f        ;all bytes done ? if yes, skip next
         goto    eeseq3          ;no. go read next byte
         call    nack            ;yes. NO ACK bit time
         bcf     status,c        ;clear error flag
         call    iistop          ;send stop
         goto    eeseqa          ;go exit
;
eeseq3   call    sack            ;send ACK
         goto    eeseq2          ;get next byte
;
eeseq4   movf    indf,w          ;get byte from buffer
         movwf   iidata          ;& move to iidata
         incf    fsr,f           ;update buffer pointer
         call    iiout           ;write data byte to eeprom
         call    nack
         btfsc   status,c        ;ACK received ? if yes, skip next
         goto    eeseqe          ;no ! go error exit
         decfsz  datctr,f        ;all bytes done ? if yes, skip next
         goto    eeseq4          ;no. go do next byte
eeseqx   bcf     status,c        ;clear error flag
eeseqe   call    iistop          ;send stop
         call    eepoll          ;wait until EEPROM finished writing
;
eeseqa   retlw   0               ;exit
;--------------------------------------------------------------------------
```

```
;           Module EESQWR
;           Sequentially writes one or more bytes of data to EEPROM. The bytes
;           to write are found in a data buffer beginning at bufstrt. The buffer
;           grows to higher memory.
;
;           ON ENTRY: The number of bytes to write is in datctr.
;                     The bytes are written to EEPROM starting at the EEPROM
;                     location eeaddr1, eeaddr0. The write block MUST BE HANDLED
;                     WITH CARE. IT IS DANGEROUS TO CROSS PAGE BOUNDRIES.
;                     See Section 8.4.1
;           ON EXIT: datctr is corrupted (equals 0)
;-------------------------------------------------------------------------------
eesqwr  movlw   bufstrt         ;pointer to start of buffer
        movwf   fsr
        call    eepre           ;send preamble
        btfsc   status,c        ;errror ? if no,skip next
        goto    eesqwrx         ;yes. go exit
eesqwr1 movf    indf,w          ;get byte from buffer
        movwf   iidata          ;& write to EEPROM
        incf    fsr,f           ;point to next buffer location
        call    iiout
        call    nack
        btfsc   status,c        ;ACK received ? if yes, skip next
        goto    eesqwrx         ;no. go error exit
        decfsz  datctr,f        ;all bytes done ? if yes, skip next
        goto    eesqwr1         ;No. go do next byte
eesqwrx call    iistop          ;Yes. send stop
        call    eepoll          ;wait until EEPROM finished writing
        retlw   0               ;exit
;-------------------------------------------------------------------------------
;           Module EESQRD
;           Sequentaly read one or more bytes from EEPROM. The bytes read from
;           the EEPROM are placed in a data buffer starting at bufstrt. The
;           buffer grows to higher memory.
;
;           ON ENTRY: The number of bytes to read is in datctr.
;                     The bytes are read from the EEPROM starting at
;                     eeprom location eeddr1, eeddr0.
;           ON EXIT: datctr is corrupted (equals 0)
;-------------------------------------------------------------------------------
eesqrd  movlw   bufstrt         ;pointer to start of buffer
        movwf   fsr
        call    eepre           ;send preamble
        btfsc   status,c        ;error ? if no, skip next
        goto    eesqrdx         ;yes. go error exit
        call    iistrt          ;no. send start
        movlw   eeslv           ;slave address
        movwf   iidata          ;to ii data register
        bsf     iidata,0        ;as a read
        call    iiout           ;send it
        call    nack
        btfsc   status,c        ;ACK received ? if yes, skip next
        goto    eesqrdx         ;no. go error exit
```

```
eesqrd1 call    iiin             ;receive data from EEPROM
        movf    iidata,w         ;data to buffer...
        movwf   indf
        incf    fsr,f            ;point to next buffer location
        decfsz  datctr,f         ;all done ? if yes, skip next
        goto    eesqrd2          ;no. go
        call    nack             ;NO ACK bit time
        bcf     status,c         ;clear error flag
        goto    eesqrdx          ;& go exit
;
eesqrd2 call    sack             ;send ACK
        goto    eesqrd1          ;& go do next byte
eesqrdx call    iistop           ;send stop
        retlw   0                ;exit
;=============================================================================
```

8.4.2 Bit Banging the 24C32 EEPROM with the 12 Bit PICmicro Family
See Source Listing IXPROM.GRP.

The 12 bit family of PICmicro devices have a two-level deep hardware stack. This limits any program to just two call levels. To reserve one call for the top level module (main program), the EEPROM modules must make calls to bottom level modules only. As the I²C bus modules must be at the bottom level, they must make no calls. The modules in IXCOMS.GRP, developed for the 12 bit PICmicro, make no calls and are used for all 12 bit I²C applications. IXPROM.GRP is a set of modules suitable for 12 bit PICmicro bit-banger communications with the 24C32 EEPROM. These modules call only the bottom level and are to be called only by the top level (main program). Use of the modules in IXPROM.GRP is not limited to the 12 bit family.

```
;====== IXPROM.GRP =========================================================
;
;          IXPROM.GRP
;          Routines to write to & read from IIC EEPROM type 24C32 or similar
;
;          MUST INCLUDE:
;                  IXCOMS.GRP
;
;          May be used with 12 bit PICmicros. (When the modules EXCUR, EXSEQ and
;          EXPOLL are called from the main program, only two levels of calls are
;          required which makes these routines compatible with the 12 bit PIC
;          two level stack.)  See Section 8.4.2
;
;---------------------------------------------------------------------------
;
;          The IIC specification requires that the SDA and scl lines be
;          wired-AND. This wired-AND is simulated by configuring the SDA and
;          scl lines as inputs for output data =1. For output data =0, the lines
;          are configured as outputs and are asserted low.
;
;          24C32 uses 2 line IIC bus: scl and sda from PORT B
;                                     ; scl is clock line
;                                     ; sda is data line
```

```
;
;        Requires following workspace:
;                timctr              timout counter
;                eeddr1              EEPROM address high byte
;                eeddr0              EEPROM address low byte
;                data0               data to be sent to or received from EEPROM
;                dirb                direction register for PORT B
;                iidata              data byte to be sent to or received from
;                                    IIC device
;                bitctr              bit counter
;                comstat             communications status flag register
;                datctr              Data counter
;                bufstrt             Data buffer. This block must be as many
;                                    contigious bytes long as number of bytes
;                                    to be read. Block begining address is: block
;                                    (see required equates below).
;
;        Requires following equates:
;          sda      equ      nn      (PORT B bit for data line)
;          scl      equ      nn      (PORT B bit for clock line)
;          eeslv    equ      nn      (slave address of EEPROM)
;                                    (for read bit0 =1,for write bit0 =0)
;          block    equ      nn      (beginning address of block)
;
;        All TIMING is based on 1 microsecond cycle time (4 mHz xtal)
;        For shorter cycle times ALL clock & setup time code MUST be
;        rewritten so that times are the same as for 1 uS cycle time.
;        For longer cycle times (slower processor clock) the clock & setup
;        time code need not be changed.
;
;        NOTE: Does not have all modules equivalent to all modules in
;              IIPROM.TXT. The module EXSEQ may be used for most read and
;              write operations. All of the IXCOMS.TXT modules are required.
;
;        NOTE: The write polling function IS NOT included in EXSEQ. After
;              writing to the EEPROM, the main program MUST call EXPOLL
;              before attempting another write to the EEPROM.
;
;-----------------------------------------------------------------------
;        Module: EXCUR
;        Reads data at current address of EEPROM
;
;        The current address is one more than the last address accessed
;        for either a read or write operation.
;        On entry: Slave address is eeslv
;
;        On exit: The data read from the EEPROM is in data0.
;                 If carry is 1 then error occurred.
;
;-----------------------------------------------------------------------
excur    call    ixstrt          ;send start
         movlw   eeslv           ;slave address
         movwf   iidata          ;to ii data register
         bcf     iidata,0        ;as a write
```

265

```
          call    ixout               ;send it
          call    xnack
          btfsc   status,c            ;ACK received ? if yes, skip next
          goto    excurx              ;no ! go error exit
          call    ixin                ;receive the byte from memory
          movf    iidata,w            ;received byte to data0
          movwf   data0
          call    xnack               ;NO ACK time filler
          bcf     status,c            ;clear error
excurx    call    ixstop              ;send stop
          retlw   0                   ;exit
;-----------------------------------------------------------------------
;         Module: EXSEQ
;         Sequentialy read or write one or more bytes from or to memory.
;         For read, the bytes received from the EEPROM are placed in a block
;         of data memory starting at data address: block. The first byte
;         received is placed at the bottom (higher address) of the block.
;         For write, the bytes to be written to the EEPROM are retrieved from
;         the same block (also starting with the higher address).
;
;         READ or WRITE selection is determined by bit 0 of the communications
;         flags register: comstat.        comstat bit 0=1 for read
;                                          comstat bit 0=0 for write.
;
;         On entry: The number of bytes to read or write is in datctr.
;                   Datctr is also used to generate the offset into the
;                   data block.
;
;         The write block MUST BE HANDLED WITH CARE. CROSSING PAGE BOUNDRIES
;         CAN BE DANGEROUS. SEE Section 8.4.1.
;         Any number of bytes may be read sequentialy, but reads
;         cannot wrap arround from the end of memory.
;
;         ERROR EXIT: If carry is set on exit, indicates error occurred
;                     and stop was sent to EEPROM
;
;-----------------------------------------------------------------------
exseq     movlw   bufstrt             ;block start address to w
          addwf   datctr,w            ;(block start + data counter) to w
          movwf   fsr                 ;to pointer
          call    ixstrt              ;send start
          movlw   eeslv               ;slave (EEPROM) address
          movwf   iidata              ;to ii data register
          bcf     iidata,0            ;clear bit 0 (as write)
          call    ixout               ;send it
          call    xnack               ;test for ACK from slave
          btfsc   status,c            ;ACK received ? if yes, skip next
          goto    exseqx              ;no ! go exit
          movf    eeddr1,w            ;address high byte
          movwf   iidata              ;send it ...
          call    ixout
          call    xnack
```

```
        btfsc   status,c        ;ACK received ? if yes, skip next
        goto    exseqx          ;no ! go error exit
        movf    eeddr0,w        ;address low byte
        movwf   iidata          ;send it ...
        call    ixout
        call    xnack
        btfsc   status,c        ;ACK received ? if yes, skip next
        goto    exseqx          ;yes. go error
exseq1  btfss   comstat,0       ;read flag ? if yes, skip next
        goto    exseq3          ;no. go point to data to write
        call    ixstrt          ;send start
        movlw   eeslv           ;slave address
        movwf   iidata
        bsf     iidata,0        ;send slave address as read
        call    ixout
exseq2  call    xnack
        btfsc   status,c        ;ACK received ? if yes, skip next
        goto    exseqx          ;no ! go error
exseq3  call    ixin            ;receive the byte from memory
        movf    iidata,w        ;received byte...
        movwf   indf            ;to next location in buffer
        incf    fsr,f           ;point to next location
        decfsz  datctr,f        ;all bytes done ? if yes, skip next
        goto    exseq3a         ;no. go read next byte
        call    xnack           ;yes. send NO ACK bit time
        bcf     status,c        ;clear error flag
        call    ixstop          ;send STOP
        goto    exseqx          ;go exit
;
exseq3a call    xsack           ;send ACK
        goto    exseq3          ;get next byte
;
exseq4  movf    indf,w          ;get byte from block
        movwf   iidata          ;& move to iidata
        incf    fsr,f           ;update buffer pointer
        call    ixout           ;write it to memory
        call    xnack
        btfsc   status,c        ;ACK received ? if yes, skip next
        goto    exseqx          ;no ! go error exit
        decfsz  datctr,f        ;all bytes done ? if yes, skip next
        goto    exseq4          ;no. go do next byte
;
exseqx  call    ixstop          ;send stop
        retlw   0               ;exit
;------------------------------------------------------------------------
;       Module: EXPOLL
;       Polls EEPROM to determine if it has completed write
;       cycle. Attempts to send slave address to EEPROM. If
;       ACK received from EEPROM, then it has completed write
;       cycle. Attempts 256 times, (approx 30 mS) then times
;       out if no ACK received.
;
;       On entry: slave address is eeslv
;
```

```
;           On exit: if ACK received, then carry = 0
;                    if timed out (no ACK) then carry = 1
;-------------------------------------------------------------------------
expoll  clrf    timctr          ;start timeout counter
expoll0 call    ixstrt          ;send start
        movlw   eeslv           ;EEPROM slave address
        movwf   iidata          ;to ii data register
        bcf     iidata,0        ;clear bit 0 (for write)
        call    ixout           ;send it to eeprom
expoll1 call    xnack           ;test for ACK from slave
        btfss   status,c        ;carry = 0 (ACK received) ? if no, skip next
        goto    expollx         ;yes. ACK received. go exit
        decfsz  timctr,f        ;no. timed out ? if yes, skip next
        goto    expoll0         ;no. go try again
expollx retlw   0               ;exit
;=========================================================================
```

8.4.3 ORANGE1.ASM: I²C Bit-Bang EEPROM Application

ORANGE1 demonstrates the application of the IIPROM.GRP modules. Using each of the read and write methods it writes ASCII data to various locations in the EEPROM and then reads back the data and sends the read data to a terminal. ORANGE1 uses the bit-bang routines in IICOMS and IIPROM. It also uses the asynchronous routine ASYXMT.TXT from Chapter 5 to communicate with the terminal.

```
;====== ORANGE1.ASM ======================================================
;
;       Demonstrates application of IICOMS.GRP and IIPROM.GRP
;       Writes data to EEPROM and reads data from EEPROM
;
;-------------------------------------------------------------------------
        radix   hex         ;RADIX is HEX
;
        list p=16f84
;
;       STATUS REGISTER BIT DEFINITIONS:
c       equ     0           ;carry bit of status register (bit 0)
z       equ     2           ;zero flag bit of status register (bit 2)
dc      equ     1           ;digit carry
pd      equ     3           ;power down bit
to      equ     4           ;time out bit
rp0     equ     5           ;program page preselect, low bit
rp1     equ     6           ;program page preselect, high bit
;
;       DESTINATION BIT DEFINITIONS:
w       equ     0           ;destination working
f       equ     1           ;destination file
;
;-------------------------------------------------------------------------
;     CPU EQUATES  (special function register memory map)
;
;   BANK 0:
```

```
indf      equ     00         ;indirect file register
tmr0      equ     01         ;timer
pcl       equ     02         ;program counter (low byte)
status    equ     03         ;status register
fsr       equ     04         ;indirect data pointer
porta     equ     05         ;port a
portb     equ     06         ;port b
eedata    equ     08         ;eeprom data
eeadr     equ     09         ;eeprom address
pclath    equ     0a         ;write buffer for program counter (high byte)
intcon    equ     0b         ;interrupt control register
;
;   BANK 1:
optreg    equ     01         ;option register                  bank 1 (0x81)
trisa     equ     05         ;data direction register port a   bank 1 (0x85)
trisb     equ     06         ;data direction register port b   bank 1 (0x86)
eecon1    equ     08         ;eeprom control register          bank 1 (0x88)
;
;-------------------------------------------------------------------------
;        WORK AREA   (memory map)   Starts at 000c
;
;        For IIC applications:
dirb      equ     000c       ;direction register for port B
iidata    equ     000d       ;data byte to be written to or read from IIC bus
bitctr    equ     000e       ;bit counter
datctr    equ     000f       ;byte counter
data0     equ     0010       ;data byte for eeprom
eeddr1    equ     0011       ;eeprom location (address) high byte
eeddr0    equ     0012       ;eeprom location (address) low byte
timctr    equ     0013       ;timeout counter
comstat   equ     0014       ;communications flags
fillctr   equ     0015       ;clock period counter
;
;        For terminal communications:
xmtreg    equ     0016       ;character xmitted to terminal
cntrb     equ     0017       ;delay counter parameters
cntra     equ     0018
;        For buffer:
bufstrt   equ     0020       ;start of buffer block
;-------------------------------------------------------------------------
;        SYSTEM EQUATES
;
eeslv     equ     0a0        ;eeprom address
sda       equ     06         ;port B6 is IIC data
scl       equ     07         ;port B7 is IIC clock
xmit      equ     01         ;port A1 is async out
iicrate   equ     01         ;IIC clock rate
;
OH        equ     04f        ;ascii O
KAY       equ     04b        ;ascii K
EE        equ     045        ;ascii E
TEE       equ     054        ;ascii T
ESS       equ     053        ;ascii S
ee        equ     065        ;ascii e
```

```
LF        equ      00a        ;ascii line feed
CR        equ      00d        ;ascii carriage return
;
;-------------------------------------------------------------------
          org      0x00       ;start of program memory
start     movlw    0ff
          movwf    portb
          clrf     porta
          bsf      status,rp0 ;switch to bank 1
          movlw    00e9       ;a0 & a3 inputs, a1, a2, a4 as outputs
          movwf    trisa
          movlw    00c0       ;initialize b7 & b6 as input,
;                              others as outputs
          movwf    trisb
          bcf      status,rp0 ;switch to bank 0
          movwf    dirb       ;initialize port b data direction register
          bsf      porta,xmit ;marking output
          movlw    00c0
          movwf    portb
          movlw    OH         ;OK followed by CR & LF to terminal
          movwf    xmtreg
          call     asyxmt
          movlw    KAY
          movwf    xmtreg
          call     asyxmt
          movlw    CR
          movwf    xmtreg
          call     asyxmt
          movlw    LF
          movwf    xmtreg
          call     asyxmt
;
          bsf      portb,scl  ;initialize scl high
          bsf      portb,sda  ;initialize sda high
;
;         The following demonstrates the use of the eeprom communications
;         modules in EEPROM.GRP. We write data to the eeprom, then
;         read back the data and send it to the terminal for display.
;
;         Write ascii 1 to an eeprom location using
;         module ESWRITE and read the location using module ESREAD.
;         Data to write is in data0.
;         Read data is in data0.
;
demo1     call     iistrt         ;START
          btfsc    status,0       ;error ? if no skip next
          goto     errsrv
          movlw    031
          movwf    data0          ;write ascii 1
          clrf     eeddr1         ;to location 0x16
          movlw    016
          movwf    eeddr0
          call     eewrit
          btfsc    status,c
```

```
        goto    errsrv
;
        call    eeread              ;read the eeprom (same location)
        btfsc   status,c
        goto    errsrv
        movf    data0,w             ;send read data to display
        movwf   xmtreg
        call    asyxmt
;
;
;       Write the ascii characters "TE" to  eeprom locations
;       0x08 and 0x09 using ESSEQ to write ONE byte at a time
;       Data to write is in bufstrt
;
demo2   movlw   TEE                 ;ascii "T"
        movwf   bufstrt
        movlw   008
        movwf   eeddr0              ;to write to eeprom location (address) 0x18
        clrf    eeddr1
        movlw   01                  ;ONE byte
        movwf   datctr
        bcf     comstat,0           ;select write
        call    eeseq               ;write it
        btfsc   status,c            ;error ? if no, skip next
        goto    errsrv              ;yes. go error service
;
        call    eepoll              ;no. wait for eeprom to complete write
        movlw   EE                  ;ascii "E" to eeprom location 0x09
        movwf   bufstrt
        incf    eeddr0,f            ;eeprom location 0x09
        movlw   01                  ;ONE byte
        movwf   datctr
        bcf     comstat,0           ;select write
        call    eeseq               ;write it
        btfsc   status,c            ;error ? if no, skip next
        goto    errsrv              ;yes. go error service
;
;       Read the contents of eeprom using EEREAD for each byte
;       Read data is in data0
;
demo3   movlw   008                 ;eeprom location 0x08
        movwf   eeddr0
        clrf    eeddr1
        call    eeread              ;read it
        btfsc   status,c
        goto    errsrv
        movf    data0,w             ;display it
        movwf   xmtreg
        call    asyxmt
        incf    eeddr0,f            ;eepom location 0x09
        call    eeread              ;read it
        btfsc   status,c
        goto    errsrv
        movf    data0,w             ;display it
```

```
              movwf    xmtreg
              call     asyxmt
;
;        Write the ascii characters "ST" to eeprom locations
;        0x08 and 0x09 using ESSEQ to write both characters with only
;        one call to ESSEQ.
;
demo4    movlw    ESS              ;ascii S
         movwf    bufstrt          ;to beginning of buffer
         movlw    TEE              ;ascii T
         movwf    bufstrt+1        ;to next location in buffer
         movlw    008              ;first eeprom location is 0x08
         movwf    eeddr0
         clrf     eeddr1
         movlw    02               ;two bytes to write
         movwf    datctr
         bcf      comstat,0        ;select WRITE flag
         call     eeseq
         btfsc    status,c         ;error ? if no, skip next
         goto     errsrv           ;yes. go error
;
;        Read the contents of eeprom location 0x08 and 0x09
;        using ESSEQ to read the first byte and using ESCUR to read the second
;        byte and send them to the terminal:
;        Data retrieved by EESEQ is in bufstrt
;        Data retrieved by ESCUR is in data0
;
demo5    movlw    ee               ;clear buffer
         movwf    bufstrt
         clrf     eeddr1           ;eeprom loc 0x08
         movlw    008
         movwf    eeddr0
         movlw    01               ;read ONE byte
         movwf    datctr
         bsf      comstat,0        ;select read
         call     eeseq            ;read  byte
         btfsc    status,c         ;error ? if no, skip next
         goto     errsrv           ;yes. go error service
         movf     bufstrt,w        ;received eeprom data to terminal
         movwf    xmtreg
         call     asyxmt
;
         call     eecur            ;read the next byte (0x09)
         btfsc    status,c         ;error ? if no, skip next
         goto     errsrv           ;yes. go error service
         movf     data0,w          ;eeprom data to terminal
         movwf    xmtreg
         call     asyxmt
;
;        Write the numerals 0 through 9 to a block of
;        10 locations beginning at eeprom location 0x10 using ESSEQ.
;        First we load the numerals into the buffer (buffer starts
;        at bufstrt):
;
```

272

```
demo6    call     load              ;load 0 thru 9 into buffer
;
;        Now we write the buffer contents to the eeprom block using EESEQ:
;
         clrf     eeddr1            ;eeprom block start location is 0x10
         movlw    010
         movwf    eeddr0
         movlw    d'10'             ;10 characters in the buffer
         movwf    datctr
         bcf      comstat,0         ;select WRITE flag
         call     eeseq             ;write buffer to block
         btfsc    status,c          ;error ? if no, skip next
         goto     errsrv            ;yes. go error service
;
;        Read the contents of the eeprom block into the buffer
;        using ESSEQ, then send buffer contents to the terminal:
;        First clear the buffer (required only for TESTING block read modules
;        because same buffer used for write and read).
;
demo7    call     clear             ;load buffer with ascii e
;
;        Here we read the eeprom block to the buffer using ESSEQ
;
         clrf     eeddr1            ;block start location = 0x10
         movlw    010
         movwf    eeddr0
         movlw    d'10'             ;10 byte block
         movwf    datctr
         bsf      comstat,0         ;select READ flag
         call     eeseq             ;read the block
         btfsc    status,c          ;error ? if no, skip next
         goto     errsrv            ;yes. go error service
;
;        Send the buffer contents to the terminal
;
         call     trans
;
;        Write the first 8 characters received above
;        to a block of eeprom starting at location 0x0120 using EESQWR.
;
demo8    movlw    00                ;eeprom location 0x0120
         movwf    eeddr1
         movlw    20
         movwf    eeddr0
         movlw    d'8'              ;8 characters
         movwf    datctr
         call     eesqwr
         btfsc    status,c          ;error ? if no, skip next
         goto     errsrv            ;yes. go error
;
;        Read the 8 byte block to the buffer using EESQRD
;
demo9    call     clear             ;load buffer with ascii "e" (testing only)
;
```

273

```
               movlw    00
               movwf    eeddr1
               movlw    20
               movwf    eeddr0
               movlw    d'8'              ;8 characters
               movwf    datctr
               call     eesqrd
               btfsc    status,c
               goto     errsrv
;
;              Here we will send the buffer contents to the terminal
               call     trans
;
dead   goto    dead              ;all done. dead loop
;
errsrv movlw   EE                        ;ascii E
       movwf   xmtreg                    ;send ascii E to terminal
       call    asyxmt
       goto    dead                      ;dead loop
;-------------------------------------------------------------------
;       Load buffer:    loads buffer with numerals 0 thru 9
;
load   movlw   d'10'             ;10 bytes
       movwf   datctr
       movlw   bufstrt           ;start of buffer
       movwf   fsr               ;to fsr
       movlw   030               ;ascii for "0"
       movwf   data0
ldloop movf    data0,w           ;ascii character to buffer
       movwf   indf
       incf    fsr,f             ;point to next location in buffer
       incf    data0,f           ;next numeral
       decfsz  datctr,f          ;all 10 numerals done ? if yes, skip next
       goto    ldloop            ;no. go do next numeral
       return
;-------------------------------------------------------------------
;       Load buffer with ascii e
;
clear  movlw   d'10'             ;10 bytes in buffer
       movwf   datctr
       movlw   bufstrt
       movwf   fsr
clloop movlw   ee                ;ascii e to each buffer location
       movwf   indf
       incf    fsr,f
       decfsz  datctr,f
       goto    clloop
       return
;------------------------------------------------------------
;       Send buffer contents to terminal
;
trans  movlw   d'10'             ;10 bytes in buffer
       movwf   datctr
```

```
              movlw     bufstrt               ;start of buffer
              movwf     fsr
trloop        movf      indf,w                ;get character
              movwf     xmtreg                ;send it to terminal
              call      asyxmt
              incf      fsr,f                 ;point to next buffer location
              decfsz    datctr,f              ;all bytes done ? if yes, skip next
              goto      trloop                ;no. go do next
              return
;-------------------------------------------------------------------------
;             INCLUDED FILES:
;
;             IICOMS.GRP   IIC communications services  See Section 8.2.1
;             IIPROM.GRP   IIC EEPROM communications services  See Section 8.4.1
;-------------------------------------------------------------------------
              include iicoms.grp
              include iiprom.grp
;
;=========================================================================
;             Module: asyxmt.txt
;             Send a character     8 bits, 1 start, 1 stop, no parity
;             On entry: character to be sent is in xmtreg & port a1 must be high
;             On exit: transmit port is high (marking)
;
;             porta,xmit  is transmit port
;-------------------------------------------------------------------------
asyxmt        bcf       porta,xmit            ;start bit
              call      full                  ;wait 1 bit time
              movlw     08                    ;8 bit character length
              movwf     bitctr                ;to bit counter
asyxmt1       rrf       xmtreg,f              ;rotate bit out thru carry
              btfsc     status,c              ;carry = 0 ? IF YES, SKIP
              goto      asyxmt2               ;no. carry = 1. go set pa1
              bcf       porta,xmit            ;data bit = 0. clear pa1
              goto      asyxmt3               ;& go
asyxmt2       bsf       porta,xmit            ;data bit = 1. set pa1
;
asyxmt3 call  full                            ;wait 1 bit time
              decfsz    bitctr,f              ;all 8 bits sent ? if yes, skip
              goto      asyxmt1               ;no, go do next bit
;
              bsf       porta,xmit            ;all bits done. do stop bit (marking)
              call      full                  ;wait 1 bit time
              retlw     0                     ;EXIT
;-------------------------------------------------------------------------
full          movlw     d'3'                  ;wait 1 bit time (2400 bits per second)
              movwf     cntrb
vdly0         movlw     d'43'
              movwf     cntra
vdly1         decfsz    cntra,f               ;dec counter a, skip if zero
              goto      vdly1                 ;not zero. dec it again
              decfsz    cntrb,f               ;dec counter b, skip if zero
              goto      vdly0                 ;not zero. do loop again
              retlw     0                     ;exit
```

275

```
; ----------------------------------------------------------------------
          end                       ;END OF PROGRAM
; ======================================================================
```

8.4.4 Using The Section 8.4 Routines in Your Applications

Generally all of the routines can be used in your applications as written or with minor changes. For all routines, the entry and exit conditions, variables, port definitions and flag definitions are described in the xx.GRP and xx.TXT listings. All port assignments are arbitrary and may be changed to suit your application. See ORANGE1.ASM and ORANGE3.ASM (Section 8.5) for sample applications using the EEPROM routines. The sample applications use the PIC16F84 but the routines may be used with other PICmicros with little or no change. For the 12 bit family use the routines in IXPROM.GRP.

The EEPROM services in IIPROM.GRP will communicate with most I^{2}C EEPROMS as written. No changes to the services are necessary.

The routines introduced in Section 8.4 are:

IIPROM.GRP	I^{2}C EEPROM Services
IXPROM.GRP	12 Bit Family I^{2}C EEPROM Services

The routines in these groups are all *called* functions. Routines in these groups call the I^{2}C bus services in IICOMS.GRP or in the case of 12 bit PICmicros, IXCOMS.GRP. Your application must include the I^{2}C bus services.

The EEPROM demonstrations, **demo1** through **demo9**, in ORANGE1 illustrate how easy it is to use the IIPROM modules: it is simply a matter of placing the data and EEPROM addresses in the proper register and calling the module. All of the modules may not be required in your application. See especially the discussion of EESEQ above. Generally the modules EEPOLL and EEPRE must be included in your application. The EEPROM write modules all test for write cycle completion by calling EEPOLL. The modules do not exit until the write cycle is completed. If your application cannot tolerate waiting for the write cycle to complete and can do other operations while the EEPROM is in the write cycle, you may remove the call to EEPPOLL at the end of the write modules and call it from your application.

See also KEEP.TXT in Section 8.5.3 for a discussion of allocated EEPROM memory blocks.

8.5 The I²C Bus and Serial Analog to Digital Converters

Several vendors manufacture, collectively, a great variety of serial bus analog to digital converters (A/D), but very few of these are for the I²C bus. The majority of serial A/D converters use a three wire bus compatible with the SPI and Microwire configurations. An application that would otherwise use I²C bus peripheral devices would be either limited to the few available I²C A/Ds or would have to include at least two bus configurations in the application hardware. The nature of the I²C bit-bang services introduced in Section 8.2.1 are such that we must deal with the details of the I²C bus software and hardware protocols to successfully apply the services. This seeming disadvantage becomes an advantage when we must mix serial protocols in an application. With care we can use some of the bit-bang I²C services (unchanged) to communicate with SPI or Microwire devices. Thus for an application that has several I²C devices on the I²C bus, but requires an A/D converter that may be available as SPI only, we can implement it with little or no additional software and hardware. In section 8.5.1 below, a short routine using some of the IICOMS services to communicate with a Maxim MAX187 SPI/Microwire A/D converter is described. At a cost of only 25 lines of code and no additional hardware this routine allows an SPI/Microwire A/D to be used with an otherwise all I²C application.

8.5.1 Using an SPI/Microwire A/D on the I²C Bit-Bang Bus

The Maxim MAX187 is a 12 bit resolution analog to digital converter configured for operation on the 3 wire SPI or Microwire busses. It features an internal 4.096 volt reference which may be disabled for applications requiring an external reference. The MAX187 uses only two of the three SPI lines: serial clock and slave serial output. We can use the bit-bang I²C bus services for MAX187 communications because only one data line (data out) is used. We can use the I²C SDA line for the MAX187 data out line (DO) and read the A/D data via bit-bang I²C receive.

Figure 8-29 illustrates the serial communications signaling and timing necessary for MAX187 operation. The SPI and Microwire bus protocol does not address a device on the bus via software as with the I²C protocol. Instead, a separate device enable line (chip select) is required for each device on the bus. When the MAX187 is not selected, the A/D DO is released (high impedance). When the A/D is selected (chip select brought low) the conversion process begins and the data line goes low. When the conversion is completed the data line goes high. At this point the data may be clocked out of the A/D. Data bits are clocked onto the data line at the down going clock edge and are valid at clock high. The initial data high (which signaled the end-of-conversion) is read at the first high clock. This initial leading high bit is not a part of the conversion value and will be discarded. The next 12 clocks place the 12 A/D conversion bits on the data line. Any following clocks place low bits on the data line. Thus a minimum of 13 clock cycles are required to read the A/D. Since the I²C protocol calls for data valid at clock high just as is required for the A/D, we may use the IICOMS service IIIN to clock the data bits into the PICmicro.

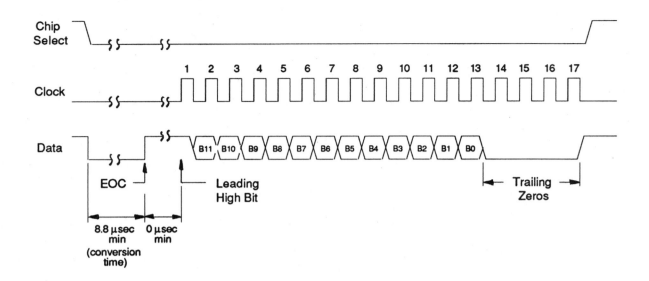

Figure 8-29   MAX187 A/D SPI Timing

See Figures 8-30 and 8-31 and IIATOD.TXT for the following discussion. IIATOD calls IISTOP to ensure that all of the I²C devices on the line are in the idle mode and the SDA line is released. Then IICLK is called to ensure that the clock line is low. These are the necessary conditions prior to MAX187 chip select. IIIN is called to clock in 8 bits of data. It is called twice to clock in a total of 16 data bits beginning with the initial leading high bit and ending with three zero bits. After clocking in these 16 bits, the chip select line is made high to place the A/D in the idle mode (release DO). The 16 data bits received via IIIN are placed in two bytes, **data1** and **data0** (see Figure 8-31, top illustration). The data bits in **data1** and **data0** are then shifted right 3 places to normalize the data and the high 4 bits of **data1** are cleared to discard the initial high bit (see Figure 8-31, middle and bottom illustrations). **data1** and **data0** now hold the MAX187 A/D result as a 12 bit binary value.

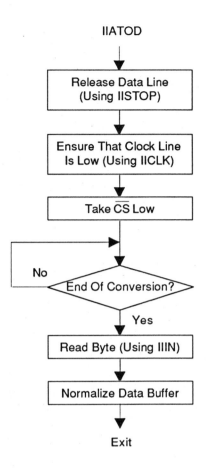

Figure 8-30   IIATOD Read A/D Using I²C Services

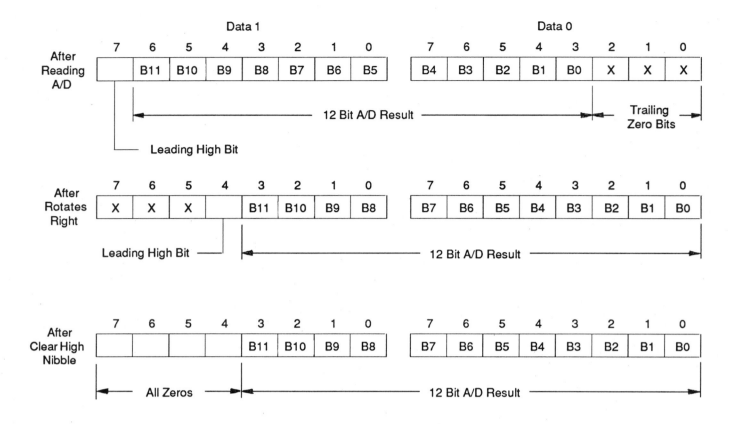

Figure 8-31   Normalizing The IIATOD Data Buffer

```
;====== IIATOD.TXT ================================================
;
;       Module IIATOD.TXT
;       Analog to digital converter: MAX 187
;       A/D control and communications via IIC bus.
;
;       On exit: A/D count in data1, data0
;       Note: The MAX 187 serial interface is compatible with the SPI and
;             Microwire protocol, but with care, we can use the bit-bang IIC
;             routines from IICOMS.GRP to interface with the A/D.
;             See Section 8.5.1
;
;-----------------------------------------------------------------
iiatod  bsf     portb,adcs      ;make sure A to D not enabled
        call    iistop          ;make sure data line released
        call    iiclk           ;make sure clock line down
        bcf     portb,adcs      ;select A/D (starts conversion)
        nop
iiatod1 btfss   portb,sda       ;end of conversion ? if yes, skip next
        goto    iiatod1         ;no. go try again
        call    iiin            ;yes. read high byte using IIC read service
        movf    iidata,w        ;received byte to...
        movwf   data1           ;data1
```

```
        call    iiin            ;read low byte
        movf    iidata,w        ;received byte to...
        movwf   data0           ;data0
        bsf     portb,adcs      ;deselect A/D
        call    iistop          ;return IIC bus to idle
;
;       Here we arrange the 12 A/D bits into the 12 lower bit positions of
;       (data1,data0)
;
        rrf     data1,f         ;DB5 to c
        rrf     data0,f         ;DB5 to data0
        rrf     data1,f         ;DB6 to c
        rrf     data0,f         ;DB6 to data0
        rrf     data1,f         ;DB7 to c
        rrf     data0,f         ;DB7 to data0. data0 has low 8 bits of A/D
;                                data
        movlw   0f              ;clear high 4 bits of data1
        andwf   data1,f         ;data1 low nibble has high 4 bits of A/D data
        retlw   0               ;exit
;=====================================================================
```

8.5.2 ORANGE2.ASM: I²C Bit-Bang A/D Application

ORANGE2.ASM serves primarily to demonstrate IIATOD and the MAX187 analog to digital
converter. ORANGE2 measures a voltage at the A/D, converts it to ASCII decimal and transmits
it to a terminal. This sequence is repeated with a period of approximately one second. The hardware is configured as in Figures 8-6 and 8-20 but the 24C32 EEPROM is not accessed. The A/D
is configured to use the internal reference and has a measurement range of 0 to 4.095 volts.

ORANGE2 calls IIATOD to read the voltage at the MAX187 input. The voltage is passed from
IIATOD via **data1** and **data0** as a 12 bit binary number ranging from \$00 to \$FFF (0 to 4095
milli-volts). ORANGE2 then calls ASVERT to convert the 12 bit value to ASCII decimal (0 to
4095) then transmits the four digit number to a terminal, along with some formatting characters,
using ASYXMT. This process is repeated approximately once every second. The value printed at
the terminal is the voltage on the A/D input ANALOG IN.

```
;====== ORANGE2.ASM =====================================================
;
;       Demonstrates application of Bit-Bang IIC Modules IICOMS.TXT
;       to communicate IIC Bus with SPI/MICROWIRE Analog to Digital Converter
;       type MAX 187. Illustrates how Bit-Bang IIC routines may be used
;       to communicate with Non-IIC device.
;       Converts A/D 12 bit binary output to 4 digit ASCII and sends
;       to terminal.
;
;-----------------------------------------------------------------------
        radix   hex         ;RADIX is HEX
;
        list p=16f84
;
;       STATUS REGISTER BIT DEFINITIONS:
c       equ     0           ;carry bit of status register (bit 0)
```

```
z          equ      2          ;zero flag bit of status register (bit 2)
dc         equ      1          ;digit carry
pd         equ      3          ;power down bit
to         equ      4          ;time out bit
rp0        equ      5          ;program page preselect, low bit
rp1        equ      6          ;program page preselect, high bit
;
;          DESTINATION BIT DEFINITIONS:
w          equ      0          ;destination working
f          equ      1          ;destination file
;
;-------------------------------------------------------------------------
;          CPU EQUATES   (special function register memory map)
;
;   BANK 0:
indf       equ      00         ;indirect file register
tmr0       equ      01         ;timer
pcl        equ      02         ;program counter (low byte)
status     equ      03         ;status register
fsr        equ      04         ;indirect data pointer
porta      equ      05         ;port a
portb      equ      06         ;port b
eedata     equ      08         ;eeprom data
eeadr      equ      09         ;eeprom address
pclath     equ      0a         ;write buffer for program counter (high byte)
intcon     equ      0b         ;interrupt control register
;
;   BANK 1:
optreg     equ      01         ;option register                  bank 1 (0x81)
trisa      equ      05         ;data direction register port a   bank 1 (0x85)
trisb      equ      06         ;data direction register port b   bank 1 (0x86)
eecon1     equ      08         ;eeprom control register          bank 1 (0x88)
;
;-------------------------------------------------------------------------
;          WORK AREA   (memory map)   Starts at 000c
;
dirb       equ      000c       ;direction register for port B
iidata     equ      000d       ;data byte to be written to or read from IIC bus
bitctr     equ      000e       ;bit counter
datctr     equ      000f       ;byte counter
counter    equ      0010       ;general counter
eeddr1     equ      0011       ;eeprom location (address) high byte
eeddr0     equ      0012       ;eeprom location (address) low byte
timctr     equ      0013       ;timeout counter
comstat    equ      0014       ;communications and system flags
temp       equ      0015       ;temporary storage
xmtreg     equ      0016       ;character xmitted to terminal
cntrb      equ      0017       ;delay counter parameters
cntra      equ      0018
;
data1      equ      0019       ;high data byte
data0      equ      001a       ;low data byte
sum1       equ      001b       ;sum high byte
sum0       equ      001c       ;sum low byte
```

```
fillctr equ        001d      ;iic clock period counter
;
;        for asvert:
asc4    equ        0020
asc3    equ        0021
asc2    equ        0022
asc1    equ        0023
asc0    equ        0024
pten1   equ        0025
pten0   equ        0026
index   equ        0027
;----------------------------------------------------------------
;        SYSTEM EQUATES
;
sda     equ        06        ;port B6 is IIC data
scl     equ        07        ;port B7 is IIC clock
xmit    equ        01        ;port A1 is async out
adcs    equ        03        ;port B3 is A/D chip select
iicrate equ        01        ;IIC clock rate
;
ovrfl   equ        07        ;flag for asvert (bit 7 of comstat)
;
OH      equ        04f       ;ascii O
KAY     equ        04b       ;ascii K
AY      equ        041       ;ascii A
DEE     equ        044       ;ascii D
SLS     equ        02f       ;ascii /
VEE     equ        056       ;ascii V
ee      equ        065       ;ascii e
LF      equ        00a       ;ascii line feed
CR      equ        00d       ;ascii carriage return
SP      equ        020       ;ascii space
DOT     equ        02e       ;ascii dot
;
;----------------------------------------------------------------
        org        0x00      ;start of program memory
        goto       start     ;jump over tables
;
;----------------------------------------------------------------
tbl1    addwf      pcl,f               ;tables for asvert
        retlw 027
        retlw 003
        retlw 000
        retlw 000
;
tbl0    addwf      pcl,f
        retlw 010
        retlw 0e8
        retlw 064
        retlw 00a
;----------------------------------------------------------------
;
start   movlw      0ff
        movwf      portb
```

```
            clrf     porta
            bsf      status,rp0      ;switch to bank 1
            movlw    00e9            ;a0 & a3 inputs, a1, a2, a4 as outputs
            movwf    trisa
            movlw    00e0            ;initialize b7, b6, b5 inputs, others outputs
            movwf    trisb
            bcf      status,rp0      ;switch to bank 0
            movwf    dirb            ;initialize port b data direction register
            bsf      porta,xmit      ;marking output
            movlw    00c0
            movwf    portb
            movlw    OH              ;OK followed by CR & LF to terminal
            movwf    xmtreg
            call     asyxmt
            movlw    KAY
            movwf    xmtreg
            call     asyxmt
            call     nline
;
            bsf      portb,scl       ;initialize clock line high
            bsf      portb,sda       ;initialize data line high
mloop       call     iiatod          ;measure voltage (Read A to D)
            call     asvert          ;convert 12 bit binary to bcd ascii
            movlw    AY              ;display A/D
            movwf    xmtreg
            call     asyxmt
            movwf    SLS
            movwf    xmtreg
            call     asyxmt
            movlw    DEE
            movwf    xmtreg
            call     asyxmt
            call     dispval         ;display voltage
            movlw    SP
            movwf    xmtreg
            call     asyxmt
test        call     nline
            movlw    09              ;approx 1 second wait
            movwf    temp
sec1        clrf     counter
sec2        call     full
            decfsz   counter,f
            goto     sec2
            decfsz   temp,f
            goto     sec1
            goto     mloop           ;go loop
;==============================================================================
;           Module IIATOD.TXT
;           Analog to digital converter: MAX 187
;           A/D control and communications via IIC bus.
;
;           On exit: A/D count in data1, data0
;           Note. The MAX 187 serial interface is compatible with the SPI and
;                 Microwire protocol, but with care, we can use the bit-bang IIC
```

284

```
;                   routines from IICOMS.GRP to interface with the A/D.
;                   See Section 8.5.1
;
;-------------------------------------------------------------------------
iiatod    bsf       portb,adcs        ;make sure A to D not enabled
          call      iistop            ;make sure data line released
          call      iiclk             ;make sure clock line down
          bcf       portb,adcs        ;select A/D (starts conversion)
          nop
iiatod1   btfss     portb,sda         ;end of conversion ? if yes, skip next
          goto      iiatod1           ;no. go try again
          call      iiin              ;yes. read high byte using IIC read service
          movf      iidata,w          ;received byte to...
          movwf     data1             ;data1
          call      iiin              ;read low byte
          movf      iidata,w          ;received byte to...
          movwf     data0             ;data0
          bsf       portb,adcs        ;deselect A/D
          call      iistop            ;return IIC bus to idle
;
;         Here we arrange the 12 A/D bits into the 12 lower bit positions of
;         (data1,data0)
;
          rrf       data1,f           ;DB5 to c
          rrf       data0,f           ;DB5 to data0
          rrf       data1,f           ;DB6 to c
          rrf       data0,f           ;DB6 to data0
          rrf       data1,f           ;DB7 to c
          rrf       data0,f           ;DB7 to data0. data0 has low 8 bits of
;                                      A/D data
          movlw     0f                ;clear high 4 bits of data1
          andwf     data1,f           ;data1 low nibble has high 4 bits of A/D data
          retlw     0                 ;exit
;=========================================================================
;         SUBSET of IICOMS
;         ORANGE2.ASM uses only the following modules from IICOMS.TXT:
;
;                   IISTOP
;                   IICLK
;                   IIIN
;                   FILLER
;
;         See IICOMS.TXT (Section 8.2.1) for details on the above modules
;-------------------------------------------------------------------------
;         Module: IISTOP
;         Generates STOP Condition
;         Data line goes high while clock line is high.
;         On entry: scl is expected to be low
;
;         On exit: sda & scl are high (bus free)
;-------------------------------------------------------------------------
iistop    bcf       dirb,scl          ;make clock an output (safety)
          movf      dirb,w
          tris      portb
```

ORANGE2.ASM

```
                bcf      portb,scl         ;take clock low in preparation for ...
                goto     iistopa           ;short wait
iistopa bcf     dirb,sda                   ;sda as output (don't care if high or low)
                movf     dirb,w
                tris     portb
                bcf      portb,sda          ;make sure data line is low
                goto     iistopb            ;set up time
iistopb goto    iistopc
iistopc goto    iistopd
iistopd bsf     dirb,scl                   ;take clock high (make it an input)
                movf     dirb,w
                tris     portb
                call     filler             ;time filler (set up time)
                bsf      dirb,sda           ;take data line high (make it an input)
                movf     dirb,w
                tris     portb
                call     filler             ;time filler
                retlw    02                 ;exit with module code 0x02
;-------------------------------------------------------------------------
;       Module: IICLK
;       Generates clock & reads data line at clock high
;
;       On entry: Master is holding clock line low. Just after entry
;                 releases clock line and expects it to be high.
;                 If clock line is held low by another device on
;                 the bus, then waits until clock line is released
;                 by the other device then remains released for approx
;                 one-half clock period. While clock is high we do not
;                 care if data line is released (reading) or held low
;                 by master (writing). Data line is released shortly
;                 after clock line goes low.
;
;       On exit:  Carry is set if data clocked = 1
;                 Carry is cleared if data clocked = 0
;                 The clock line is held low
;                 The data line is released
;-------------------------------------------------------------------------
iiclk   bsf     dirb,scl                   ;release clock line (make it an input)
                movf     dirb,w
                tris     portb
iiclk1  btfss   portb,scl                  ;scl still low ? if no, skip next
                goto     iiclk1             ;yes. go try again
                bcf      status,c           ;no. clock now released. clear carry
                call     filler             ;time filler
                btfsc    portb,sda          ;data line 0 ? if yes, skip next
                bsf      status,c           ;no. set carry
;       at this point, clock line is still high.
                bsf      portb,scl          ;reads clock line to port register (high)
                bcf      dirb,scl           ;make scl an output (still high)
                movf     dirb,w
                tris     portb
                bcf      portb,scl          ;take clock line low
                nop
                bsf      dirb,sda           ;release data line
```

286

```
        movf    dirb,w
        tris    portb
        call    filler          ;time filler
        retlw   0               ;exit
;------------------------------------------------------------------------
;       Module: IIIN
;       Receives 8 bit byte from slave device
;       Places received byte in iidata
;       (Module IICLK receives bit & places it in carry)
;
;       On exit: Data line is released (as an input)
;                Clock line is held low
;------------------------------------------------------------------------
iiin    movlw   d'8'            ;8 bits
        movwf   bitctr          ;to bit counter
        bsf     dirb,sda        ;data line as input
        movf    dirb,w
        tris    portb
iiin1   call    iiclk           ;clock in a bit (into carry)
        rlf     iidata,f        ;rotate it (carry) into iidata
        decfsz  bitctr,f        ;dec bit ctr. is it 0 ? if yes, skip
        goto    iiin1           ;no. go get next bit
        retlw   0               ;yes. exit
;------------------------------------------------------------------------
;       Module: FILLER
;
;       Deternimes IIC clock period.
;
;       Clock period (in instruction cycles) is approximately = (6*n + 24)
;       where n is the literal in the first line of the routine below.
;------------------------------------------------------------------------
filler  movlw   iicrate         ;approx 30 instruction cycle
;                                    clock period (n=1)
        movwf   fillctr
filler1 decfsz  fillctr,f
        goto    filler1
        retlw   0
;========================================================================
;       Module: ASVERT.TXT
;       Convert 12 BIT A/D result to 4 digit ascii
;       (data1, data0) => (asc3,asc2,asc1,asc0)
;
;       NOTE: This Module PLACES CALLS TWO LEVELS DEEP
;             The called routines asvert4 and asvert5 are part of this module
;------------------------------------------------------------------------
asvert  clrf    index           ;convert to bcd, then to ascii
asvert1 clrf    counter
asvert2 movf    index,w
        call    asvert4
        call    asvert5
        btfss   status,c
        goto    asvert3
        incf    counter,f
        goto    asvert2
```

```
asvert3 movf    index,w
        call    asvert4
        call    asvert6
        movlw   asc4
        movwf   fsr
        movf    index,w
        addwf   fsr,f
        movlw   030             ;convert to ascii
        addwf   counter,w
        movwf   indf            ;and place in ascii block
        incf    index,f
        btfss   index,2
        goto    asvert1
        movlw   30
        addwf   data0,w
        movwf   asc0
        retlw   0
;-------------------------------------------------------------------
asvert4 call    tbl1            ;read table
        movwf   pten1
        movf    index,w
        call    tbl0
        movwf   pten0
        return
;-------------------------------------------------------------------
asvert5 comf    pten1,f         ;convert to bcd
        comf    pten0,f
        movf    pten0,w
        addlw   01
        movwf   pten0
        btfsc   status,c
        incf    pten1,f
asvert6 movf    pten0,w
        addwf   data0,f
        bcf     comstat,ovrfl
        btfsc   status,c
        bsf     comstat,ovrfl
        movf    pten1,w
        addwf   data1,f
        btfss   comstat,ovrfl
        goto    asvertx
        btfsc   status,c
        goto    asvert7
        movlw   01
        addwf   data1,f
        goto    asvertx
asvert7 incf    data1,f
asvertx return
;-------------------------------------------------------------------
;       Module DISPVAL
;       Displays voltage to terminal
;-------------------------------------------------------------------
dispval movlw   SP              ;display space
```

```
            movwf    xmtreg
            call     asyxmt
            movf     asc3,w          ;display ascii of voltage
            movwf    xmtreg
            call     asyxmt
            movlw    DOT             ;decimal point
            movwf    xmtreg
            call     asyxmt
            movf     asc2,w
            movwf    xmtreg
            call     asyxmt
            movf     asc1,w
            movwf    xmtreg
            call     asyxmt
            movf     asc0,w
            movwf    xmtreg
            call     asyxmt
            movlw    SP              ;display space
            movwf    xmtreg
            call     asyxmt
            movlw    VEE             ;display V
            movwf    xmtreg
            call     asyxmt
            return
;------------------------------------------------------------------------
;       Module NLINE
;       Start new line
;
;       Sends carriage return and line feed to terminal
;------------------------------------------------------------------------
nline       movlw    CR
            movwf    xmtreg
            call     asyxmt
            movlw    LF
            movwf    xmtreg
            call     asyxmt
            return
;========================================================================
;       Module: asyxmt.txt
;       Send a character    8 bits, 1 start, 1 stop, no parity
;       On entry: character to be sent is in xmtreg & port a1 must be high
;       On exit: transmit port is high (marking)
;
;       porta,xmit  is transmit port
;------------------------------------------------------------------------
asyxmt      bcf      porta,xmit      ;start bit
            call     full            ;wait 1 bit time
            movlw    08              ;8 bit character length
            movwf    bitctr          ;to bit counter
asyxmt1     rrf      xmtreg,f        ;rotate bit out thru carry
            btfsc    status,c        ;carry = 0 ? IF YES, SKIP
            goto     asyxmt2         ;no. carry = 1. go set pa1
            bcf      porta,xmit      ;data bit = 0. clear pa1
            goto     asyxmt3         ;& go
```

```
asyxmt2 bsf     porta,xmit      ;data bit = 1. set pa1
;
asyxmt3 call    full            ;wait 1 bit time
        decfsz  bitctr,f        ;all 8 bits sent ? if yes, skip
        goto    asyxmt1         ;no, go do next bit
;
        bsf     porta,xmit      ;all bits done. do stop bit (marking)
        call    full            ;wait 1 bit time
        retlw   0               ;EXIT
;-------------------------------------------------------------------
full    movlw   d'3'            ;wait 1 bit time (2400 bits per second)
        movwf   cntrb
vdly0   movlw   d'43'
        movwf   cntra
vdly1   decfsz  cntra,f         ;dec counter a, skip if zero
        goto    vdly1           ;not zero. dec it again
        decfsz  cntrb,f         ;dec counter b, skip if zero
        goto    vdly0           ;not zero. do loop again
        retlw   0               ;exit
;-------------------------------------------------------------------
        end                     ;END OF PROGRAM
;===================================================================
```

8.5.3 ORANGE3.ASM: I²C Bit-Bang A/D and EEPROM Application

ORANGE3.ASM combines the IICOMS.GRP, IIPROM.GRP and IIATOD.TXT modules in an I²C application mixing I²C and SPI A/D hardware on the same bus (Figure 8-20). A total of 128 voltage measurements are made, each at an interval of approximately 1 second, using the A/D converter. Each conversion result is stored in the EEPROM at contiguous memory locations. After the 128 measurements have been completed, they are retrieved from memory, converted to decimal ASCII and sent to a terminal. The terminal display format is done within ORANGE3. The conversion results are formatted as rows and columns and are displayed as *n.mmm* volts. The A/D is read as in ORANGE2.ASM (Section 8.5.2).

The Module KEEP.TXT either writes the conversion result (two bytes) to the EEPROM or reads the result from the EEPROM. Write or read is determined by the state of the **comstat** read/write bit (see IICOMS, Section 8.2.1). KEEP has allocated 256 bytes of EEPROM for the conversions (128 conversions at 2 bytes per conversion). See Module KEEP.TXT in ORANGE3.ASM for further information about KEEP.

The Module DISPLAY.TXT formats the conversion data fetched from the EEPROM as 16 lines of 8 columns. Formatting is done on the fly because each two byte conversion result is converted to ASCII decimal and transmitted individually.

```
;====== ORANGE3.ASM ================================================
;
;       BIT-BANG IIC APPLICATION
;       Demonstrates IIC EEPROM and Analog to Digital converter (MAX 187)
;       application. Once per second performs an A/D conversion and places
;       conversion result into a block of memory of EEPROM. After completing
;       128 conversions, reads EEPROM block and displays all 128 conversions
;       to the terminal. Terminal display is formatted within this
```

```
;         application.
;
;----------------------------------------------------------------
          radix    hex          ;RADIX is HEX
;
          list p=16f84
;
;         STATUS REGISTER BIT DEFINITIONS:
c         equ      0            ;carry bit of status register (bit 0)
z         equ      2            ;zero flag bit of status register (bit 2)
dc        equ      1            ;digit carry
pd        equ      3            ;power down bit
to        equ      4            ;time out bit
rp0       equ      5            ;program page preselect, low bit
rp1       equ      6            ;program page preselect, high bit
;
;         DESTINATION BIT DEFINITIONS:
w         equ      0            ;destination working
f         equ      1            ;destination file
;
;----------------------------------------------------------------
;     CPU EQUATES   (special function register memory map)
;
;   BANK 0:
indf      equ      00           ;indirect file register
tmr0      equ      01           ;timer
pcl       equ      02           ;program counter (low byte)
status    equ      03           ;status register
fsr       equ      04           ;indirect data pointer
porta     equ      05           ;port a
portb     equ      06           ;port b
eedata    equ      08           ;eeprom data
eeadr     equ      09           ;eeprom address
pclath    equ      0a           ;write buffer for program counter (high byte)
intcon    equ      0b           ;interrupt control register
;
;   BANK 1:
optreg    equ      01           ;option register                    bank 1 (0x81)
trisa     equ      05           ;data direction register port a     bank 1 (0x85)
trisb     equ      06           ;data direction register port b     bank 1 (0x86)
eecon1    equ      08           ;eeprom control register            bank 1 (0x88)
;----------------------------------------------------------------
;      WORK AREA  (memory map)   Starts at 000c
;
dirb      equ      000c         ;direction register for port B
iidata    equ      000d         ;data byte to be written to or read from IIC bus
bitctr    equ      000e         ;bit counter
datctr    equ      000f         ;byte counter
counter   equ      0010         ;general counter
eeddr1    equ      0011         ;eeprom location (address) high byte
eeddr0    equ      0012         ;eeprom location (address) low byte
timctr    equ      0013         ;timeout counter
comstat   equ      0014         ;communications and system flags
temp      equ      0015         ;temporary storage
```

```
xmtreg  equ     0016    ;character xmitted to terminal
cntrb   equ     0017    ;delay counter parameters
cntra   equ     0018
;
data1   equ     0019    ;high data byte
data0   equ     001a    ;low data byte
anacnt  equ     001b    ;block counter
fillctr equ     001c    ;iic clock period counter
dispctr equ     001d    ;display column counter
;
asc4    equ     0020    ;used by ASVERT
asc3    equ     0021
asc2    equ     0022
asc1    equ     0023
asc0    equ     0024
pten1   equ     0025
pten0   equ     0026
index   equ     0027
;
bufstrt equ     0028    ;beginning of buffer
;-------------------------------------------------------------------
;       SYSTEM EQUATES
;
eeslv   equ     0a0     ;eeprom address
sda     equ     06      ;port B6 is IIC data
scl     equ     07      ;port B7 is IIC clock
iicrate equ     01      ;IIC clock rate
xmit    equ     01      ;port A1 is async out
adcs    equ     03      ;port B3 is A/D chip select
anast1  equ     00      ;beginning of A/D eeprom memory area (high byte)
anast0  equ     20      ;                                    (low byte)
anamax  equ     80      ;A/D eeprom allocated memory block size
;
;       comstat flag bit definitions:
rw      equ     00      ;read/write select flag for EESEQ (bit 0)
done    equ     01      ;all-memory-block-used flag for KEEP (bit1)
bkerr   equ     02      ;EEPROM block error flag (see KEEP) (bit 2)
ovrfl   equ     07      ;flag for ASVERT (bit 7)
;

OH      equ     04f     ;ascii O
KAY     equ     04b     ;ascii K
DEE     equ     044     ;ascii D
ESS     equ     053     ;ascii S
VEE     equ     056     ;ascii V
ee      equ     065     ;ascii e
LF      equ     00a     ;ascii line feed
CR      equ     00d     ;ascii carriage return
SP      equ     020     ;ascii space
DOT     equ     02e     ;ascii dot
;
;-------------------------------------------------------------------
        org     0x00            ;start of program memory
        goto    start           ;jump over tables
```

```
;
;-------------------------------------------------------------------
tbl1    addwf   pcl,f               ;tables for asvert
        retlw 027
        retlw 003
        retlw 000
        retlw 000
;
tbl0    addwf   pcl,f
        retlw 010
        retlw 0e8
        retlw 064
        retlw 00a
;-------------------
;
start   movlw   0ff
        movwf   portb
        clrf    porta
        bsf     status,rp0          ;switch to bank 1
        movlw   00e9                ;a0 & a3 inputs, a1, a2, a4 as outputs
        movwf   trisa
        movlw   00e0                ;initialize b7, b6, b5 inputs, others outputs
        movwf   trisb
        bcf     status,rp0          ;switch to bank 0
        movwf   dirb                ;initialize port b data direction register
        bsf     porta,xmit          ;marking output
        movlw   00c0
        movwf   portb
        movlw   OH                  ;OK followed by CR & LF to terminal
        movwf   xmtreg
        call    asyxmt
        movlw   KAY
        movwf   xmtreg
        call    asyxmt
        call    nline
;
        bsf     portb,scl           ;initialize scl high
        bsf     portb,sda           ;initialize sda high
;
mloop   clrf    anacnt              ;initialize block counter
        clrf    comstat             ;clear comms flags
;
mloop1  movlw   09                  ;wait approx 1 second
        movwf   temp
sec1    clrf    counter
sec2    call    full
        decfsz  counter,f
        goto    sec2
        decfsz  temp,f
        goto    sec1
;
        call    iiatod              ;measure voltage
        movf    data1,w             ;A/D data to buffer
        movwf   bufstrt
```

293

```
        movf    data0,w
        movwf   bufstrt+1
        bcf     comstat,rw          ;select EEPROM write
        call    keep                ;store it to memory
        btfss   comstat,done        ;all A/D conversions done ? if yes, skip
        goto    mloop1              ;no. go do next conversion
;
        clrf    anacnt              ;yes. initialize block counter (for reads)
        bcf     comstat,done        ;clear all done flag
mloop3  bsf     comstat,rw          ;select EEPROM read
        call    keep                ;read voltage from memory
        movf    bufstrt,w           ;buffer contents to data
        movwf   data1
        movf    bufstrt+1,w
        movwf   data0
        call    asvert              ;convert it to ascii
        call    display             ;format and send it to terminal
        btfss   comstat,done        ;all of memory block read ? if yes, skip next
        goto    mloop3              ;no. go read next
dead    goto    dead                ;yes. all done. dead loop
;------------------------------------------------------------------------
;       Module IIATOD
;       Analog to digital converter MAX 187
;
;       On Exit: A/D count in (data1,data0)
;       Note. The MAX 187 serial interface is compatible with the SPI and
;             Microwire protocol, but with care, we can use the bit-bang IIC
;             routines from IICOMS.TXT to interface with the A/D.
;             See Section 8.5.1
;------------------------------------------------------------------------
iiatod  bsf     portb,adcs          ;make sure A to D not enabled
        call    iistop              ;make sure data line released
        call    iiclk               ;make sure clock line down
        bcf     portb,adcs          ;select A/D (starts conversion)
        nop
iiatod1 btfss   portb,sda           ;end of conversion ? if yes, skip next
        goto    iiatod1             ;no. go try again
        call    iiin                ;yes. read high byte
        movf    iidata,w            ;received byte to...
        movwf   data1               ;data1
        call    iiin                ;read low byte
        movf    iidata,w            ;received byte to...
        movwf   data0               ;data0
        bsf     portb,adcs          ;deselect A/D
        call    iistop              ;return ii bus to idle
;
;       Here we arrange the 12 bits in the 12 lower bit positions of
;       data1, data0
        rrf     data1,f             ;DB5 to c
        rrf     data0,f             ;DB5 to data0
        rrf     data1,f             ;DB6 to c
        rrf     data0,f             ;DB6 to sata0
        rrf     data1,f             ;DB7 to c
        rrf     data0,f             ;DB7 to data0. data0 has low byte of A/D data
```

294

```
        movlw   00f             ;clear high 4 bits of data1
        andwf   data1,f         ;data1 has high 4 bits of A/D data
                                ;data0 has low byte of A/D data
        retlw   0               ;exit
;-----------------------------------------------------------------------
;       INCLUDED FILES:
;
;       IICOMS.GRP  IIC communications services  See Section 8.2.1
;       IIPROM.GRP  IIC EEPROM communications services  See Section 8.4.1
;-----------------------------------------------------------------------
        include iicoms.grp
        include iiprom.grp
;
;=======================================================================
;       Module KEEP.TXT
;
;       Stores two byte A/D data to EEPROM  (24C32)
;       Reads two bytes of stored A/D data from EEPROM
;       The two byte values are stored sequentially in an allocated block of
;       EEPROM memory (256 bytes MAX)
;
;       The A/D data is stored to EEPROM  beginning at EEPROM location
;       (anast1, anast0). Each successive two byte A/D data value is stored
;       sequentially in the EEPROM. The EEPROM location is maintained by a
;       counter (anacnt) that counts the two byte A/D data value.
;       The location is determined by doubling the count and adding it to
;       anastrt. If all bytes of the block have been written to,
;       (or read from) exits with done flag set. Make sure (anast1, anast0) +
;       twice anamax does not exceed maximum EEPROM address.
;
;       The A/D data is read from the EEPROM beginning at EEPROM location
;       (anast1,anast0). Each successive two byte block is read sequentially
;       from the EEPROM. If all bytes of block have been read, exits with
;       done flag set.
;
;       If KEEP is called with done flag set, exits with block-error flag
;       set.
;
;       If called for write, data must be in buffer at entry. If called
;       for read, data in buffer at exit.
;
;       comstat flags:
;               rw bit of comstat: read/write select (=1 for read)
;                                                    (=0 for write)
;               done bit of comstat: all-memory-block-done flag
;               bkerr bit of comstat: block-error flag
;
;       Required literals:
;               anast1          Beginning of A/D memory area (High Byte)
;
;               anast0          Beginning of A/D memory area (Low Byte)
;                               This MUST be an even value (bit 0 = 0)
;               anamax          Maximum number of conversions stored in A/D
;                               memory area of EEPROM (cannot exceed 0x7f)
```

```
;
;           Required parameters:     All parameters required by IICOMS.TXT
;           and:
;
;               anacnt               A/D block counter (number of conversions)
;
;               eeddr1               EEPROM location, High Byte (used by IIPROM)
;               eeddr0               EEPROM location, Low Byte  (used by IIPROM)
;               datctr               number of bytes to write   (used by IIPROM)
;
;-------------------------------------------------------------------------
keep    btfsc    comstat,done    ;all of block done ? if no skip
        goto     keepe           ;yes. go error exit
        movf     anacnt,w        ;no. get current data count
        movwf    temp            ;temp anacnt
        bcf      status,c        ;double it
        rlf      temp,f
        movlw    anast1          ;add doubled count to start location
        movwf    eeddr1
        movlw    anast0
        movwf    eeddr0
        movf     temp,w          ;doubled data count
        addwf    eeddr0,f
        btfsc    status,c
        incf     eeddr1,f
        movlw    02              ;two bytes to read or write
        movwf    datctr
        call     eeseq           ;read or write them
        incf     anacnt,f        ;set up for next read or write
        movlw    anamax          ;all of allocated block used ?
        movwf    temp
        movf     anacnt,w
        subwf    temp,w
        btfsc    status,z        ;if no skip next
        bsf      comstat,done    ;yes. set done flag
keepx   return                   ;no. exit
;
keepe   bsf      comstat,bkerr   ;set block-error flag
        goto     keepx           ;& go exit
;
;-------------------------------------------------------------------------
;           Module: ASVERT.TXT
;           Convert 12 BIT A/D result to 4 digit ascii
;           (data1, data0) => (asc3,asc2,asc1,asc0)
;
;           NOTE: This Module PLACES CALLS TWO LEVELS DEEP
;                 The called routines asvert4 and asvert5 are part of
;                 this module.
;           comstat flag: ovrfl (bit 7)
;-------------------------------------------------------------------------
asvert  clrf     index           ;convert to bcd, then to ascii
asvert1 clrf     counter
asvert2 movf     index,w
        call     asvert4
        call     asvert5
```

```
            btfss   status,c
            goto    asvert3
            incf    counter,f
            goto    asvert2
asvert3 movf    index,w
            call    asvert4
            call    asvert6
            movlw   asc4
            movwf   fsr
            movf    index,w
            addwf   fsr,f
            movlw   030             ;convert to ascii
            addwf   counter,w
            movwf   indf            ;and place in ascii block
            incf    index,f
            btfss   index,2
            goto    asvert1
            movlw   30
            addwf   data0,w
            movwf   asc0
            retlw   0
;--------------------------------------------------------------------
asvert4 call    tbl1            ;read table
            movwf   pten1
            movf    index,w
            call    tbl0
            movwf   pten0
            return
;--------------------------------------------------------------------
asvert5 comf    pten1,f
            comf    pten0,f
            movf    pten0,w
            addlw   01
            movwf   pten0
            btfsc   status,c
            incf    pten1,f
asvert6 movf    pten0,w
            addwf   data0,f
            bcf     comstat,ovrfl
            btfsc   status,c
            bsf     comstat,ovrfl
            movf    pten1,w
            addwf   data1,f
            btfss   comstat,ovrfl
            goto    asvertx
            btfsc   status,c
            goto    asvert7
            movlw   01
            addwf   data1,f
            goto    asvertx
asvert7 incf    data1,f
asvertx return
;--------------------------------------------------------------------
```

```
;            Module DISPLAY
;            Displays voltage to terminal
;            Formats for display as 8 columns per line
;            NOTE: The ASYNC comms with the terminal have no flow control, so if
;            terminal buffer overflows, strange results may show up on screen
;            toward the end of the block of readings.
;-------------------------------------------------------------------------
display movf     asc3,w              ;display ascii of voltage
        movwf    xmtreg
        call     asyxmt
        movlw    DOT                 ;decimal point
        movwf    xmtreg
        call     asyxmt
        movf     asc2,w
        movwf    xmtreg
        call     asyxmt
        movf     asc1,w
        movwf    xmtreg
        call     asyxmt
        movf     asc0,w
        movwf    xmtreg
        call     asyxmt
        decfsz   dispctr,f           ;all 8 columns done ? if yes, skip next
        goto     displ1              ;no. go display 5 spaces
        call     nline               ;yes. start new line
        goto     displx              ;& go exit
;
displ1  call     spaces              ;display 5 spaces
displx  return                       ;exit
;-------------------------------------------------------------------------
;            Module NLINE
;            Start new line
;
;            Sends carriage return and line feed to terminal and
;            initializes column counter
;-------------------------------------------------------------------------
nline   movlw    CR
        movwf    xmtreg
        call     asyxmt
        movlw    LF
        movwf    xmtreg
        call     asyxmt
        call     spaces              ;left margin
        movlw    08
        movwf    dispctr
        return
;-------------------------------------------------------------------------
;            Module: SPACES
;            Sends 4 spaces to terminal
;
;-------------------------------------------------------------------------
spaces  movlw    04
        movwf    temp
spaces1 movlw    SP
```

```
                movwf     xmtreg
                call      asyxmt
                decfsz    temp,f
                goto      spaces1
                return
;---------------------------------------------------------------------
;         Module: asyxmt.txt
;         Send a character      8 bits, 1 start, 1 stop, no parity
;         On entry: character to be sent is in xmtreg & port a1 must be high
;         On exit: transmit port is high (marking)
;
;         porta,xmit  is transmit port
;---------------------------------------------------------------------
asyxmt    bcf       porta,xmit      ;start bit
          call      full            ;wait 1 bit time
          movlw     08              ;8 bit character length
          movwf     bitctr          ;to bit counter
asyxmt1   rrf       xmtreg,f        ;rotate bit out thru carry
          btfsc     status,c        ;carry = 0 ? IF YES, SKIP
          goto      asyxmt2         ;no. carry = 1. go set pa1
          bcf       porta,xmit      ;data bit = 0. clear pa1
          goto      asyxmt3         ;& go
asyxmt2   bsf       porta,xmit      ;data bit = 1. set pa1
;
asyxmt3   call      full            ;wait 1 bit time
          decfsz    bitctr,f        ;all 8 bits sent ? if yes, skip
          goto      asyxmt1         ;no, go do next bit
;
          bsf       porta,xmit      ;all bits done. do stop bit (marking)
          call      full            ;wait 1 bit time
          retlw     0               ;EXIT
;---------------------------------------------------------------------
full      movlw     d'3'            ;wait 1 bit time (2400 bits per second)
          movwf     cntrb
vdly0     movlw     d'43'
          movwf     cntra
vdly1     decfsz    cntra,f         ;dec counter a, skip if zero
          goto      vdly1           ;not zero. dec it again
          decfsz    cntrb,f         ;dec counter b, skip if zero
          goto      vdly0           ;not zero. do loop again
          retlw     0               ;exit
;---------------------------------------------------------------------
          end                       ;END OF PROGRAM
;=====================================================================
```

8.5.4 Using the Section 8.5 Routines in Your Application.

Generally all of the routines can be used in your applications as written or with minor changes. For all routines, the entry and exit conditions, variables, port definitions and flag definitions are described in the xx.GRP and xx.TXT listings. All port assignments are arbitrary and may be changed to suit your application. The sample applications use the PIC16F84 but the routines may be used with other PICmicros with little or no change.

The routines introduced in Section 8.5 are:

IIATOD.TXT	SPI A/D applied to the I^{2}C Bus
ASVERT.TXT	Convert 12 bit binary to 4 byte ASCII decimal
KEEP.TXT	Write to and read from allocated EEPROM block

The module IIATOD is very easy to use: just call it when you want to read the A/D. The techniques used in IIATOD may be applied to communications with other non-I^{2}C serial devices providing they conform to the data-valid-at-clock-high requirement and require only data out or only data in. An example of an only data in device is the Motorola MC14489 SPI Multi-character LED Display/Lamp Driver. This device can drive a 5 digit LED display or 25 lamps. Serial communications require 8 bit and 24 bit transfers, eliminating the need for byte normalization.

KEEP is configured for two-byte data writes to EEPROM and is limited to a maximum block size of 128 two-byte entries. Each EEPROM address is calculated by doubling the entry number (because it is two bytes) and adding it to the block start address. The number of entries are limited to 128 because twice the number of entries may be no more than a one byte value. If you want a block larger than 128 entries or more than 2 bytes per entry you will have to modify KEEP to use a two byte entry counter and use two byte add and subtract for address calculations and the all-done test.

The demonstration program ORANGE3.ASM does not trap errors. Any of your applications should include error traps using the error flags provided by the individual modules. ORANGE3, without error traps, and *without* an EEPROM in the circuit, will display to the terminal 128 readings all having the *correct* value of the last (128 th) reading. Without error traps, the missing EEPROM is not noticed. Error traps are important!

8.6 I^{2}C Bit-Bang Slave Applications

The two I^{2}C slave applications in this section serve to demonstrate the use of the I^{2}C slave bus services described in Section 8.3.1. FAWN1.ASM receives an ASCII upper case character from the master, converts it to lower case and sends it back to the master as lower case. FAWN2.ASM receives an ASCII character from the master and writes the character to a two line by 20 character LCD display. Because the display is relatively slow, the slave does not ACK the master until the display is finished and ready for the next character. The master thus must poll the slave for the ACK as in the case of writing to an EEPROM. The master programs that communicate with the slave applications use the I^{2}C bit-bang bus services described in Section 8.2.

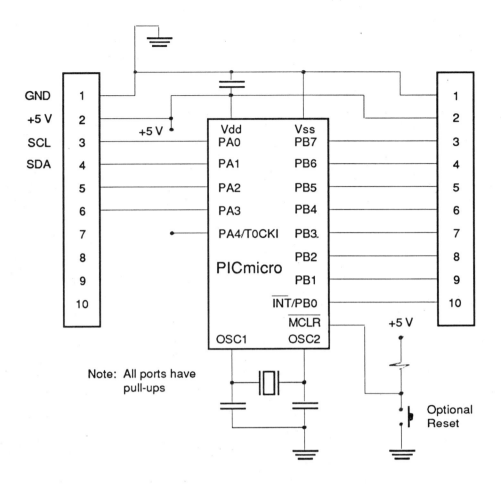

Note: All ports have pull-ups

Figure 8-32   Schematic I²C Bit Bang Slave Applications

8.6.1 FAWN1.ASM: I²C Bit-Bang Slave Application

The sample slave application program FAWN1.ASM receives a byte from the master, adds hexadecimal 20 to the byte and transmits the result back to the master. If the byte received by the slave happens to be the ASCII code for a capitalized letter, adding hexadecimal 20 serves to convert the letter to lower case. The master program that communicates with FAWN1 is ORANGE4.ASM. See Figure 8-32 for the FAWN1 application hardware.

The master and slave sequence of operations is:
The master:
1. Sends a start condition.
2. Sends the slave address as a write.
3. Receives ACK from slave.
4. Sends the byte.
5. Receives ACK from slave.
6. Receives the byte from the slave.
7. Receives NOACK from the slave.
8. Sends the stop condition.

The slave:
>   1. Receives start condition.
>   2. Receives and confirms slave address.
>   3. Sends ACK.
>   4. Receives data byte.
>   5. Adds hex 20 (makes data lower case).
>   6. Sends ACK.
>   7. Sends data byte.
>   8. Sends NOACK.
>   9. Waits for stop.

The above sequence of events follows the I²C bus protocol and is the device protocol for a 'LOWERCASER'. If the master sends a slave address (**slvaddr**) that does not match that of FAWN1, the slave main loop, SLVLP, does not respond to the master and patiently waits for another START condition. If the correct address is received, SLVLP sends an ACK and passes control to the application. The application, LOWSRV, then receives the data byte that is sent by the master in response to the ACK from the slave. Having successfully received the byte, LOWSRV then sends an ACK, converts it to lower case, sends it back to the master and sends a NOACK. In response to the NOACK, the master sends a STOP and control is given back to SLVLP. The slave then waits for the next START.

Note that LOWSRV does not specifically test for the STOP from the master. Instead it tests for data and if no data is received it assumes that a STOP was received. This is acceptable because a 'LOWERCASER' may only respond to data or STOP. STOP is also a fail safe condition. As can be seen from the above discussion, the IISLAVE modules allow the application to be entirely defined by the application service; the IISLAVE modules simply provide the I²C slave bus services.

```
;======= FAWN1.ASM ============================================================
;
;           BIT-BANG IIC SLAVE APPLICATION
;           Demonstrates application of IIC SLAVE Module IISLAVE.TXT.
;           Receives ASCII upper case letter and converts to ascii lower case
;           and sends back the lower case letter. See Section 8.6.1
;           Master program is ORANGE4.ASM.
;           14 Bit PIC
;
;------------------------------------------------------------------------------
            radix   hex         ;RADIX is HEX
;
            list p=16f84
;
;           STATUS REGISTER BIT DEFINITIONS:
c           equ     0           ;carry bit of status register (bit 0)
z           equ     2           ;zero flag bit of status register (bit 2)
dc          equ     1           ;digit carry
pd          equ     3           ;power down bit
to          equ     4           ;time out bit
rp0         equ     5           ;program page preselect, low bit
rp1         equ     6           ;program page preselect, high bit
;
;           DESTINATION BIT DEFINITIONS:
```

```
w        equ     0           ;destination working
f        equ     1           ;destination file
;
;------------------------------------------------------------------------
;        CPU EQUATES   (special function register memory map)
;
;   BANK 0:
indf     equ     00          ;indirect file register
tmr0     equ     01          ;timer
pcl      equ     02          ;program counter (low byte)
status   equ     03          ;status register
fsr      equ     04          ;indirect data pointer
porta    equ     05          ;port a
portb    equ     06          ;port b
eedata   equ     08          ;eeprom data
eeadr    equ     09          ;eeprom address
pclath   equ     0a          ;write buffer for program counter (high byte)
intcon   equ     0b          ;interrupt control register
;
;   BANK 1:
optreg   equ     01          ;option register              bank 1 (0x81)
trisa    equ     05          ;data direction register port a    bank 1 (0x85)
trisb    equ     06          ;data direction register port b    bank 1 (0x86)
eecon1   equ     08          ;eeprom control register       bank 1 (0x88)
;
;------------------------------------------------------------------------
;        WORK AREA   (memory map)   Starts at 000c
;
dira     equ     000c        ;direction register for port A
iidata   equ     000d        ;data byte to be written to or read from IIC bus
bitctr   equ     000e        ;bit counter
systat   equ     000f        ;system flags
recflg   equ     0010        ;receive flags
;
;------------------------------------------------------------------------
;          SYSTEM EQUATES
;
slvaddr  equ     070         ;slave address for this application (0x70)
sda      equ     01          ;port A1 is IIC data
scl      equ     00          ;port A0 is IIC clock
;
;        recflg flag bit definitions:
stflg    equ     01          ;start flag
spflg    equ     02          ;stop flag
datflg   equ     03          ;data flag
datbit   equ     04          ;data bit
;
;        systat flag bit definitions:
rw       equ     00          ;read/write flag rw = 0 for write
;                                            rw = 1 for read
fb       equ     01          ;first byte flag
anoa     equ     02          ;ack/no ack flag anoa = 0 for NO ACK
;                                            anoa = 1 for ACK
;
;------------------------------------------------------------------------
```

303

```
        org     0x00                ;start of program memory
;------------------------------------------------------------------------------
;
start   movlw   0ff                 ;INITIALIZE:
        movwf   porta
        movwf   portb
        bsf     status,rp0          ;switch to bank 1
        movlw   00ff                ;all port a inputs
        movwf   trisa
        movlw   0000                ;initialize all port b as outputs
        movwf   trisb
        bcf     status,rp0          ;switch to bank 0
        movlw   0003                ;initialize port a data direction register
        movwf   dira
        goto    slvlp               ;go to slave loop (wait for something on bus)
;
;==============================================================================
;       Module: LOWSRV.TXT
;       This is the application module. Control is passed to it
;       by SLVLP. It must pass control to SLVLP via a jump to SLVLP.
;       Converts an upper case ASCII to lower case.
;       This application does not use the Modules BACK, HOLD & RELEASE.
;       IISLAVE.GRP must be included.
;------------------------------------------------------------------------------
SLAVEAP nop                         ;REQUIRED label for application module
lowsrv  btfsc   systat,rw           ;is slave address as write ? if yes, skip
next
        goto    lowsrvx             ;no. ERROR. go exit
lowsrv1 call    slvrec              ;yes. receive the data byte
        btfss   recflg,datflg       ;was data received ? if yes, skip next
        goto    lowsrvx             ;no. go exit
        movlw   020                 ;add 0x20 to the data (makes it lower case)
        addwf   iidata,f
        call    ack                 ;send ACK
        call    slvout              ;send lower case data
        call    noack               ;do nothing for one clock cycle
        goto    lowsrv1             ;& go wait for next data
;
lowsrvx goto    slvlp               ;go start over
;
;       End of application module
;------------------------------------------------------------------------------
;       INCLUDED FILES:
;
;       IISLAVE.GRP  IIC Bit-Bang services  See Section 8.3.1
;------------------------------------------------------------------------------
        include iislave.grp
;
;------------------------------------------------------------------------------
        end                         ;END OF PROGRAM
;==============================================================================
```

```
;====== ORANGE4.ASM ============================================
;
;        Demonstrates Bit-Bang MASTER IIC and Bit-Bang SLAVE IIC application.
;        This is Master Program. Sends upper case ASCII letter to IIC slave.
;        Slave returns ASCII lower case of the letter. Master then sends
;        the received lower case to the terminal.
;
;        Slave program is FAWN1.ASM.
;        See Section 8.6.1
;---------------------------------------------------------------
        radix   hex         ;RADIX is HEX
;
        list p=16f84
;
;        STATUS REGISTER BIT DEFINITIONS:
c       equ     0           ;carry bit of status register (bit 0)
z       equ     2           ;zero flag bit of status register (bit 2)
dc      equ     1           ;digit carry
pd      equ     3           ;power down bit
to      equ     4           ;time out bit
rp0     equ     5           ;program page preselect, low bit
rp1     equ     6           ;program page preselect, high bit
;
;        DESTINATION BIT DEFINITIONS:
w       equ     0           ;destination working
f       equ     1           ;destination file
;
;---------------------------------------------------------------
;     CPU EQUATES  (special function register memory map)
;
;   BANK 0:
indf    equ     00          ;indirect file register
tmr0    equ     01          ;timer
pcl     equ     02          ;program counter (low byte)
status  equ     03          ;status register
fsr     equ     04          ;indirect data pointer
porta   equ     05          ;port a
portb   equ     06          ;port b
eedata  equ     08          ;eeprom data
eeadr   equ     09          ;eeprom address
pclath  equ     0a          ;write buffer for program counter (high byte)
intcon  equ     0b          ;interrupt control register
;
;   BANK 1:
optreg  equ     01          ;option register                  bank 1 (0x81)
trisa   equ     05          ;data direction register port a   bank 1 (0x85)
trisb   equ     06          ;data direction register port b   bank 1 (0x86)
eecon1  equ     08          ;eeprom control register          bank 1 (0x88)
;
;---------------------------------------------------------------
;     WORK AREA  (memory map)  Starts at 000c
;
;        For IIC applications:
dirb    equ     000c        ;direction register for port B
```

305

ORANGE4.ASM

```
iidata   equ     000d        ;data byte to be written to or read from IIC bus
bitctr   equ     000e        ;bit counter
datctr   equ     000f        ;byte counter
data0    equ     0010        ;data byte to send or receive
fillctr  equ     0011        ;clock period counter
comstat  equ     0012        ;communications flags
;
;        For terminal communications:
xmtreg   equ     0016        ;character xmitted to terminal
cntrb    equ     0017        ;delay counter parameters
cntra    equ     0018
;        For buffer:
;---------------------------------------------------------------------
;        SYSTEM EQUATES
;
addslv   equ     070         ;slave address
sda      equ     06          ;port B6 is IIC data
scl      equ     07          ;port B7 is IIC clock
xmit     equ     01          ;port A1 is async out
iicrate  equ     04          ;approx 48 inst cycle IIC clock period
;
OH       equ     04f         ;ascii O
KAY      equ     04b         ;ascii K
EE       equ     045         ;ascii E
TEE      equ     054         ;ascii T
ESS      equ     053         ;ascii S
ee       equ     065         ;ascii e
LF       equ     00a         ;ascii line feed
CR       equ     00d         ;ascii carriage return
;
;---------------------------------------------------------------------
         org     0x00                ;start of program memory
start    movlw   0ff
         movwf   portb
         clrf    porta
         bsf     status,rp0          ;switch to bank 1
         movlw   00e9                ;a0 & a3 inputs, a1, a2, a4 as outputs
         movwf   trisa
         movlw   00c0                ;initialize b7 & b6 as input,
;                                     others as outputs
         movwf   trisb
         bcf     status,rp0          ;switch to bank 0
         movwf   dirb                ;initialize port b data direction register
         bsf     porta,xmit          ;marking output
         movlw   00c0
         movwf   portb
         movlw   OH                  ;OK followed by CR & LF to terminal
         movwf   xmtreg
         call    asyxmt
         movlw   KAY
         movwf   xmtreg
         call    asyxmt
         movlw   CR
         movwf   xmtreg
```

306

```
                call    asyxmt
                movlw   LF
                movwf   xmtreg
                call    asyxmt
;
                bsf     portb,scl       ;initialize scl high
                bsf     portb,sda       ;initialize sda high
;
                call    iistrt          ;send START
                movlw   addslv          ;slave address as write
                movwf   iidata
                call    iiout           ;send it
                call    nack            ;ACK ?
                movlw   030             ;error 0
                btfsc   status,c        ;ACK received ? if yes, skip next
                goto    errsrv          ;no. go error exit
                movlw   TEE             ;yes. send character and receive character
                movwf   iidata
                call    sendit
                movlw   EE
                movwf   iidata
                call    sendit
                movlw   ESS
                movwf   iidata
                call    sendit
                movlw   TEE
                movwf   iidata
                call    sendit
                call    iistop          ;send STOP
dead            goto    dead            ;dead loop
;
errsrv          movwf   xmtreg          ;error service
                call    asyxmt
                movlw   ee
                movwf   xmtreg
                call    asyxmt
                goto    dead
;--------------------
sendit  call    iiout           ;send ascii character
                call    nack            ;ACK ?
                movlw   031             ;error 1
                btfsc   status,c        ;Ack received ? if yes, skip next
                goto    errsrv
                call    iiin            ;receive converted ascii character
                movf    iidata,w
                movwf   xmtreg
                call    sack            ;send ACK
                bcf     status,c        ;clear error
                call    asyxmt          ;display received character to terminal
                return
;--------------------
;-------------------------------------------------------------------------
;       INCLUDED FILES:
;
```

307

```
;           IICOMS.GRP   IIC communications services  See Section 8.2.1
;-----------------------------------------------------------------------
          include iicoms.grp
;
;=======================================================================
;         Module: asyxmt.txt
;         Send a character      8 bits, 1 start, 1 stop, no parity
;         On entry: character to be sent is in xmtreg & port al must be high
;         On exit: transmit port is high (marking)
;
;         porta,xmit  is transmit port
;-----------------------------------------------------------------------
asyxmt    bcf        porta,xmit      ;start bit
          call       full            ;wait 1 bit time
          movlw      08              ;8 bit character length
          movwf      bitctr          ;to bit counter
asyxmt1   rrf        xmtreg,f        ;rotate bit out thru carry
          btfsc      status,c        ;carry = 0 ? IF YES, SKIP
          goto       asyxmt2         ;no. carry = 1. go set pal
          bcf        porta,xmit      ;data bit = 0. clear pal
          goto       asyxmt3         ;& go
asyxmt2   bsf        porta,xmit      ;data bit = 1. set pal
;
asyxmt3   call       full            ;wait 1 bit time
          decfsz     bitctr,f        ;all 8 bits sent ? if yes, skip
          goto       asyxmt1         ;no, go do next bit
;
          bsf        porta,xmit      ;all bits done. do stop bit (marking)
          call       full            ;wait 1 bit time
          retlw      0               ;EXIT
;-----------------------------------------------------------------------
full      movlw      d'3'            ;wait 1 bit time (2400 bits per second)
          movwf      cntrb
vdly0     movlw      d'43'
          movwf      cntra
vdly1     decfsz     cntra,f         ;dec counter a, skip if zero
          goto       vdly1           ;not zero. dec it again
          decfsz     cntrb,f         ;dec counter b, skip if zero
          goto       vdly0           ;not zero. do loop again
          retlw      0               ;exit
;-----------------------------------------------------------------------
          end                        ;END OF PROGRAM
;=======================================================================
```

8.6.2 FAWN2.ASM I²C Bit-Bang Slave Application with ACK Polling

The sample slave application program FAWN2.ASM receives an ASCII byte from the master then writes the byte to a two line by 20 character LCD display. The master program that communicates with FAWN2 is ORANGE5.ASM. See Figure 8-33 for the FAWN2 application hardware.

The master and slave sequence of operations is:
The master:
      1. Sends a start condition.
      2. Sends the slave address as a write.
      3. Receives ACK from slave.
      4. Sends the data byte.
      5. Receives ACK from slave.
      6. Sends the STOP condition.

The slave:
      1. Receives start condition.
      2. Receives and confirms slave address.
      3. Sends ACK.
      4. Receives data byte.
      5. Writes data byte to buffer.
      6. Sends ACK.
      7. Waits for STOP.
      8. Writes buffer character to display.

The above sequence of events follows the I²C protocol and is the device protocol for a 'FAWN DISPLAY'. If the master sends a slave address (**slvaddr**) that does not match that of FAWN2, the slave main loop, SLVLP, does not respond to the master and patiently waits for another START condition. If the correct address is received, SLVLP sends an ACK and passes control to the application FAWNSR.

FAWNSR then receives the character byte, sends an ACK and receives the STOP. FAWNSR then calls the display service. Control does not return to FAWNSR until the display service has written the character to the display screen. This will require several milliseconds. If the master attempts to send another character to the FAWN DISPLAY device, the device will not respond to the master with an ACK. The master will continue to send START followed by the FAWN2 slave address and the FAWN DISPLAY device will not respond until the display service has returned control to FAWNSR which in turn returns control to SLVLP. SLVLP then recognizes the START and slave address and responds with an ACK and a new character is transferred to the FAWN DISPLAY. This is an example of acknowledgment polling as described in Section 8.4.2.

The FAWN DISPLAY device protocol specifies that only one character byte is to be sent by the master for each transaction. Because the master is aware of the protocol (it better be!) the slave handshake does not need to include NOACK.

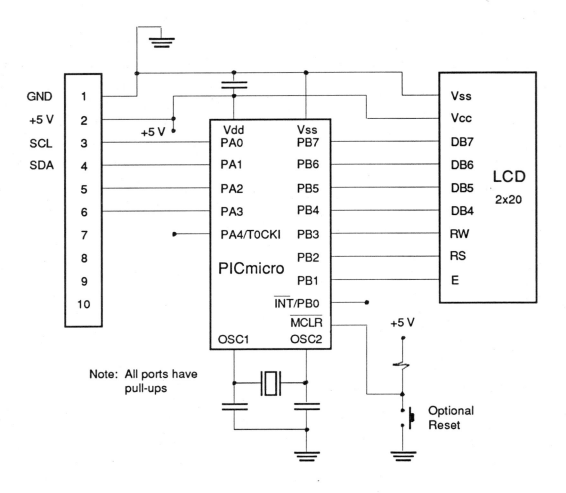

Figure 8-33   Schematic; FAWN2 Bit-Bang Slave Display

```
;======= FAWN2.ASM ============================================================
;
;       BIT-BANG IIC SLAVE APPLICATION
;       Receives a character and writes it to LCD display.
;       Demonstrates use of delayed ACK while slave is busy (master
;       polls for ACK).  See section 8.6.2
;       Master program is ORANGE5.ASM
;       14 Bit PIC
;
;------------------------------------------------------------------------------
        radix   hex         ;RADIX is HEX
;
        list p=16f84
;
;       STATUS REGISTER BIT DEFINITIONS:
c       equ     0           ;carry bit of status register (bit 0)
z       equ     2           ;zero flag bit of status register (bit 2)
dc      equ     1           ;digit carry
pd      equ     3           ;power down bit
```

```
to        equ      4          ;time out bit
rp0       equ      5          ;program page preselect, low bit
rp1       equ      6          ;program page preselect, high bit
;
;         DESTINATION BIT DEFINITIONS:
w         equ      0          ;destination working
f         equ      1          ;destination file
;
;------------------------------------------------------------------------
;         CPU EQUATES   (special function register memory map)
;
;   BANK 0:
indf      equ      00         ;indirect file register
tmr0      equ      01         ;timer
pcl       equ      02         ;program counter (low byte)
status    equ      03         ;status register
fsr       equ      04         ;indirect data pointer
porta     equ      05         ;port a
portb     equ      06         ;port b
eedata    equ      08         ;eeprom data
eeadr     equ      09         ;eeprom address
pclath    equ      0a         ;write buffer for program counter (high byte)
intcon    equ      0b         ;interrupt control register
;
;   BANK 1:
optreg    equ      01         ;option register                bank 1 (0x81)
trisa     equ      05         ;data direction register port a bank 1 (0x85)
trisb     equ      06         ;data direction register port b bank 1 (0x86)
eecon1    equ      08         ;eeprom control register        bank 1 (0x88)
;
;------------------------------------------------------------------------
;         WORK AREA   (memory map)   Starts at 000c
;
dira      equ      000c       ;direction register for port A
iidata    equ      000d       ;data byte to be written to or read from IIC bus
bitctr    equ      000e       ;bit counter
systat    equ      000f       ;system flags
recflg    equ      0010       ;receive flags
;
;         Display variables
dispflg   equ      0015       ;display flags
dispdat   equ      0016       ;display data
dispstat  equ      0017       ;display status
temp      equ      0018       ;temporary storage
acount    equ      0019
bcount    equ      001a
cntra     equ      001b
cntrb     equ      001c
;------------------------------------------------------------------------
;         SYSTEM EQUATES
;
slvaddr   equ      070        ;slave address for this application (0x70)
sda       equ      01         ;port A1 is IIC data
scl       equ      00         ;port A0 is IIC clock
```

```
;
;         recflg flag bit definitions:
stflg    equ     01        ;start flag
spflg    equ     02        ;stop flag
datflg   equ     03        ;data flag
datbit   equ     04        ;data bit
;
;         systat flag bit definitions:
rw       equ     00        ;read/write flag rw = 0 for write
;                                          rw = 1 for read
fb       equ     01        ;first byte flag
anoa     equ     02        ;ack/no ack flag anoa = 0 for NO ACK
;                                          anoa = 1 for ACK
;         display equates:
dispen   equ     01        ;PB1
disprs   equ     02        ;PB2
disprw   equ     03        ;PB3
;----------------------------------------------------------------------
         org     0x00               ;start of program memory
;----------------------------------------------------------------------
;
start    movlw   0ff                ;INITIALIZE:
         movwf   porta
         movwf   portb
         bsf     status,rp0         ;switch to bank 1
         movlw   00ff               ;all port a inputs
         movwf   trisa
         movlw   0000               ;initialize all port b as outputs
         movwf   trisb
         bcf     status,rp0         ;switch to bank 0
         movlw   0003               ;initialize port a data direction register
         movwf   dira
;
         call    initdis            ;initialize display
         goto    slvlp              ;go wait for somthing to happen on the bus
;
;======================================================================
;         Module: FAWNSR
;         This is the application program called by SLVLP
;
;         This application does not use the Modules BACK, HOLD & RELEASE
;----------------------------------------------------------------------
SLAVEAP nop                         ;REQUIRED label for application module
fawnsr  btfsc   systat,rw           ;is slave address as write ? if yes,
;                                    skip next
        goto    fawnsrx             ;no. ERROR. go exit
fawnsr1 call    slvrec              ;yes. receive the data byte
        btfss   recflg,datflg       ;was data received ? if yes, skip next
        goto    fawnsrx             ;no. go exit
        movf    iidata,w            ;character to display parameter
        movwf   dispdat
        call    ack                 ;send ACK
        call    slvrec              ;wait for STOP
        btfss   recflg,spflg        ;STOP received ? if yes, skip next
```

```
        goto    fawnsrx         ;no. go error exit (ignore previous data)
        call    dissrv          ;write character to display
;
;       Returns from dissrv only after character has been written to display
;       screen. Will require several mSec. Thus master must poll for ACK.
;       Master repeatedly sends START followed by slave address until ACK
;       is received. When ACK is received, master then sends next character.
;
fawnsrx goto    slvlp           ;go start over for next character
;
;       End of application module
;-------------------------------------------------------------------------
;       INCLUDED FILES:
;
;       IISLAVE.GRP   IIC Bit-Bang services   See Section 8.3.1
;       DISSRV.GRP    LCD Display Service     See Section 5.2.2
;-------------------------------------------------------------------------
        include iislave.grp
        include dissrv.grp
;
;-------------------------------------------------------------------------
        end                     ;END OF PROGRAM
;=========================================================================




;====== ORANGE5.ASM ======================================================
;
;       Writes characters received to bit-bang IIC slave that then writes to
;       LCD Display. Uses Acknowledging Polling to determine when slave
;       is ready to receive.  See Section 8.6.2
;       Slave program is FAWN2.ASM
;       14 bit PICmicro
;
;-------------------------------------------------------------------------
        radix   hex        ;RADIX is HEX
;
        list p=16f84
;
;       STATUS REGISTER BIT DEFINITIONS:
c       equ     0          ;carry bit of status register (bit 0)
z       equ     2          ;zero flag bit of status register (bit 2)
dc      equ     1          ;digit carry
pd      equ     3          ;power down bit
to      equ     4          ;time out bit
rp0     equ     5          ;program page preselect, low bit
rp1     equ     6          ;program page preselect, high bit
;
;       DESTINATION BIT DEFINITIONS:
w       equ     0          ;destination working
f       equ     1          ;destination file
;
```

313

```
;-------------------------------------------------------------------------
;       CPU EQUATES   (special function register memory map)
;                     ;   BANK 0:
indf     equ    00        ;indirect file register
tmr0     equ    01        ;timer
pcl      equ    02        ;program counter (low byte)
status   equ    03        ;status register
fsr      equ    04        ;indirect data pointer
porta    equ    05        ;port a
portb    equ    06        ;port b
eedata   equ    08        ;eeprom data
eeadr    equ    09        ;eeprom address
pclath   equ    0a        ;write buffer for program counter (high byte)
intcon   equ    0b        ;interrupt control register
timctr   equ    0c        ;timeout counter for poll
;
;   BANK 1:
optreg   equ    01        ;option register                    bank 1 (0x81)
trisa    equ    05        ;data direction register port a     bank 1 (0x85)
trisb    equ    06        ;data direction register port b     bank 1 (0x86)
eecon1   equ    08        ;eeprom control register            bank 1 (0x88)
;
;-------------------------------------------------------------------------
;       WORK AREA   (memory map)   Starts at 000c
;
;       For IIC applications:
dirb     equ    000c      ;direction register for port B
iidata   equ    000d      ;data byte to be written to or read from IIC bus
bitctr   equ    000e      ;bit counter
datctr   equ    000f      ;byte counter
data0    equ    0010      ;data byte to send or receive
fillctr  equ    0011      ;time filler counter
comstat  equ    0012      ;communications flags
;
;       For terminal communications:
xmtreg   equ    0016      ;character xmitted to terminal
cntrb    equ    0017      ;delay counter parameters
cntra    equ    0018
;       For buffer:
;-------------------------------------------------------------------------
;       SYSTEM EQUATES
;
addslv   equ    070       ;slave address
sda      equ    06        ;port B6 is IIC data
scl      equ    07        ;port B7 is IIC clock
iicrate  equ    04        ;IIC clock rate
xmit     equ    01        ;port A1 is async out
;
OH       equ    04f       ;ascii O
KAY      equ    04b       ;ascii K
EE       equ    045       ;ascii E
TEE      equ    054       ;ascii T
ESS      equ    053       ;ascii S
STAR     equ    02a       ;ascii *
```

314

```
LF        equ      00a        ;ascii line feed
CR        equ      00d        ;ascii carriage return
;
;------------------------------------------------------------------
          org      0x00       ;start of program memory
start     movlw    0ff
          movwf    portb
          clrf     porta
          bsf      status,rp0 ;switch to bank 1
          movlw    00e9       ;a0 & a3 inputs, a1, a2, a4 as outputs
          movwf    trisa
          movlw    00c0       ;initialize b7 & b6 as input,
                              ;others as outputs
          movwf    trisb
          bcf      status,rp0 ;switch to bank 0
          movwf    dirb       ;initialize port b data direction register
          bsf      porta,xmit ;marking output
          movlw    00c0
          movwf    portb
;
          bsf      portb,scl  ;initialize scl high
          bsf      portb,sda  ;initialize sda high
;
          movlw    OH         ;OK followed by CR & LF to display
          movwf    data0
          call     sendit
          movlw    KAY
          movwf    data0
          call     sendit
          movlw    CR
          movwf    data0
          call     sendit
          movlw    LF
          movwf    data0
          call     sendit
          movlw    TEE        ;yes. send TEST to display
          movwf    data0
          call     sendit
          movlw    EE
          movwf    data0
          call     sendit
          movlw    ESS
          movwf    data0
          call     sendit
          movlw    TEE
          movwf    data0
          call     sendit
          call     iistop     ;send STOP
dead      goto     dead       ;dead loop
;
errsrv    goto     dead       ;NO REAL error service for this demo
;----------------------
sendit    call     iistrt     ;send START
          movlw    addslv     ;slave address as write
```

315

```
        movwf    iidata
        call     iiout              ;send it
        call     nack               ;ACK ?
        btfsc    status,c           ;ACK received ? if yes, skip next
        goto     sendit             ;no. go try again (poll for slave ready)
        movf     data0,w            ;yes. get character
        movwf    iidata
        call     iiout              ;send ascii character
        call     nack               ;ACK ?
        btfsc    status,c           ;Ack received ? if yes, skip next
        goto     errsrv             ;no.go error
        call     iistop             ;yes. send STOP
        btfsc    status,c           ;ACK received ? if yes, skip next
        goto     errsrv             ;No. go error
        return                      ;yes. do next character
;--------------------
;------------------------------------------------------------------------
;
;       INCLUDED FILES:
;
;       IICOMS.GRP   IIC communications services   See Section 8.2.1
;------------------------------------------------------------------------
        include iicoms.grp
;
;------------------------------------------------------------------------
        end                        ;END OF PROGRAM
;========================================================================
```

Buffered Fawn Display

If a multi-byte buffer is added to FAWNSR the master can continuously send data bytes until the buffer is full. When the buffer fills, the master stops sending and the buffer contents are written to the display. The following describes the procedures necessary to implement a buffer version of the FAWN display.

When the buffer fills, the master must be signaled to stop sending characters until all of the characters in the buffer have been displayed. The slave signals the full buffer condition to the master with NOACK. After every character, except the last one, is received the slave will respond with ACK. After the last character is received it will respond with NOACK and the master will respond with STOP. The master will then poll for ACK until all of the characters in the buffer have been displayed. Unlike LOWSRV, FAWNSR actually tests for the stop bit after it sends the final ACK. For this buffered display scheme the application must be changed to test for a data byte, as is done in LOWSRV. After sending the NOACK, the slave application will assume that the master sent the STOP and will no longer be active on the bus until all buffer characters have been displayed.

Chapter 9
The SPI Serial Bus

The SPI Serial Bus

SPI (Serial Peripheral Interface) is a three wire serial bus for eight bit data transfer applications. The three wires carry information between devices connected to the bus. Each device on the bus acts simultaneously as a transmitter and a receiver. Two of the three lines transfer data (one line for each direction) and the third is the serial clock. Some devices may be only transmitters while others only receivers. Generally a device that transmits will also receive. An SPI display is an example of a receive-only device while an EEPROM is a receive and transmit device.

Devices on the bus are defined as masters and slaves. A master is the device that initiates an information transfer on the bus and generates the clock and control signals. A slave is the device controlled by the master. Each slave device on the bus is controlled by a slave select (chip enable) line. The slave is active only when selected. Generally a dedicated select line is required for each slave device. Some devices may act as either masters or slaves. When not selected as a slave, these dual-role devices are masters. At any given time only one master may be on the bus. Any slave device that is not selected must release (make it high impedance) the slave output line.

The SPI bus employs a simple shift register data transfer scheme: Data is clocked out of and into the active devices in a first-in, first-out fashion (see Figure 9.1). It is in this manner that SPI devices simultaneously transmit and receive (full duplex capability).

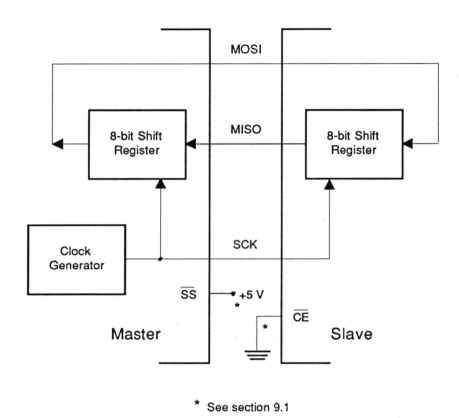

* See section 9.1

Figure 9-1   SPI Bus

9.1 SPI Bus Specification

All lines on the SPI bus are one-directional: The signal on the clock line (SCK) is generated by the master and synchronizes the data transfer. The master-out, slave-in (MOSI) line carries data from the master to the slave and the master-in, slave-out (MISO) line carries data from the slave to the master. Each slave device is selected by the master via the individual select lines (see Figure 9.2). An SPI slave device is selected by a low (logic 0) on the select ($\overline{CE}$) line. Devices capable of being masters or slaves are selected as masters by a high (logic 1) on the slave select ($\overline{SS}$) line. Information on the SPI bus can be transferred at a rate of near zero bits/second to 1 Mbits/second. Data is transferred in 8 bit blocks, most significant bit (MSB) first.

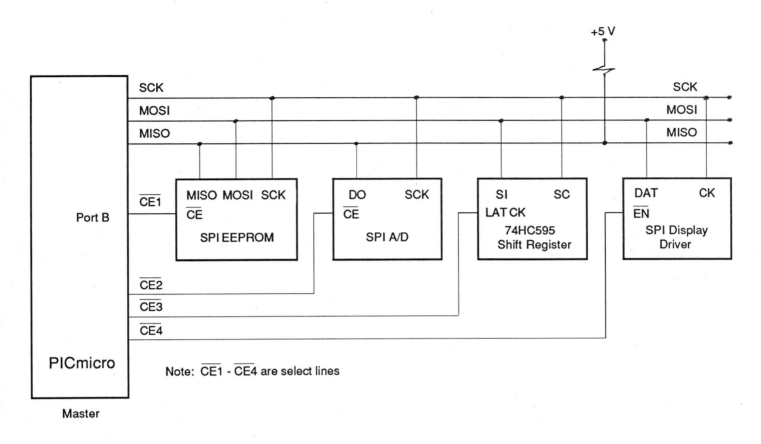

Figure 9-2   Typical SPI Bus Application

Clock Modes

All data transfer is synchronized by the serial clock (SCK). One bit of data is transferred for each clock cycle. Four versions of the clock to data relationship are defined for the SPI bus. These versions (Modes A through D) are determined by the value of the clock polarity (CPOL) and clock phase (CPHA) bits. Any hardware device capable of operation in more than one mode will have some means of selecting the value of these bits. The four possible modes are illustrated in Figure 9.3. The clock polarity determines the level of the clock idle state and the clock phase determines which clock edge places new data on the bus. The mode required for a given application is generally determined by the slave. This multi-mode capability combined with the simple shift register architecture makes the SPI bus very versatile. Due to this versatility many non-SPI serial devices, including most shift registers, may be used as SPI slaves.

Clock Polarity (CPOL)

If CPOL is cleared (logic 0) and no data is being transferred (idle state), the master holds the SCK line low. If CPOL is set (logic 1) the master idles the SCK line high.

Clock Phase (CPHA)

CPHA, in conjunction with CPOL, controls when new data is placed on the bus (shifted out). If CPHA is set (logic 1), data is shifted onto the MOSI line as determined by the value of CPOL. For CPHA set: If CPOL is set, new data is placed on the line at the down-going clock and is read at the up-going clock and if CPOL is cleared, new data is placed on the line at the up-going clock and is read at the down-going clock.

If CPHA is cleared (logic 0), the shift clock is the OR of SCK with $\overline{SS}$: As soon as $\overline{SS}$ goes low, new data is placed on the line and the first edge of the clock reads the data. If CPOL is set, the first clock edge is down-going and subsequent data bits are read at each down-going clock. Each new bit is placed on the line at the up-going clock. If CPOL is cleared, the first clock edge is up-going and subsequent data bits are read at each up-going clock. Each new bit is placed on the line at the down-going clock.

In summary: if CPHA is logic 1, the transfer (valid data read by receiver) begins at the second clock edge. If CPHA is logic 0, the transfer begins at the first clock edge. All subsequent transfers within the byte take place at every other clock edge. See Figure 9-6. In all cases, data is read one-half clock cycle after it is placed on the data line.

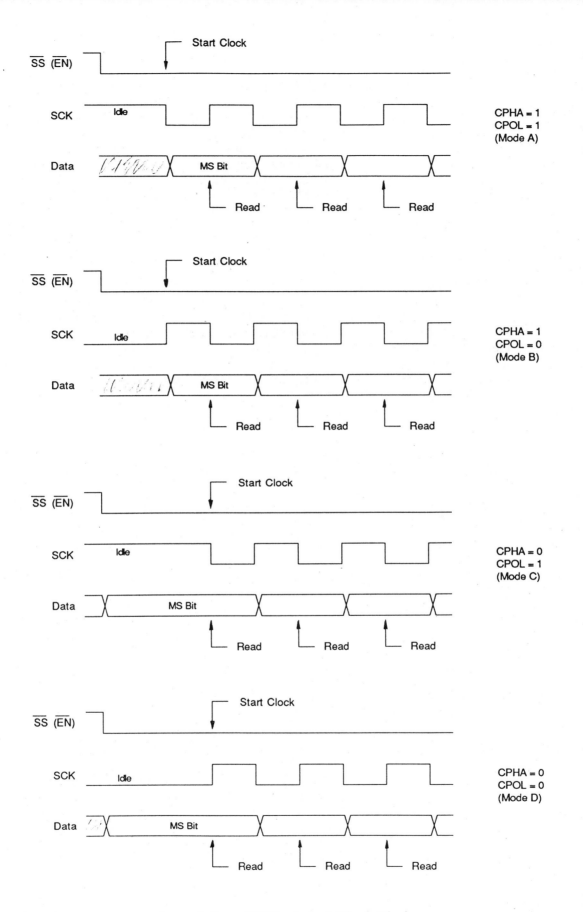

Figure 9-6   SPI Data And Clock Timing

9.2 The PICmicro as a Bit-Bang SPI Master and Slave

As of the date of writing, some of the 14 bit and 16 bit PICmicros have on-chip SPI hardware. For those not having the SPI hardware and the 12 bit PICmicros, SPI communications may be implemented in software. In Section 9.2.1 software for using the PICmicro as a bit-bang SPI master device is described. SPICOMS.GRP is a collection of four routines necessary to execute the four modes of SPI master transactions. In section 9.2.2 software for using the PICmicro as a bit-bang SPI slave device is described. SPISLAVE.GRP contains routines to execute the Mode A and Mode D slave transactions. See Figures 9-4 and 9-9 for the master and slave schematics.

9.2.1 SPI Bit-Bang Master Bus Services

Two lines of port B are used for master MOSI and MISO and a third line is used for SCK (Figure 9-4). These lines should have pull-ups, but are not wired AND as with the I²C bus because the SPI bus uses separate lines for data out and data in. When configured as a bit-bang master, the output port (MOSI) and the clock (SCK) will be configured as outputs and the input port (MISO) as an input. The setup and clock high and low periods must not be less than the minimum specified for the SPI bus. These are approximately 200 and 400 nano-seconds respectively. The timing for the bit-bang routines is far in excess of these minimums.

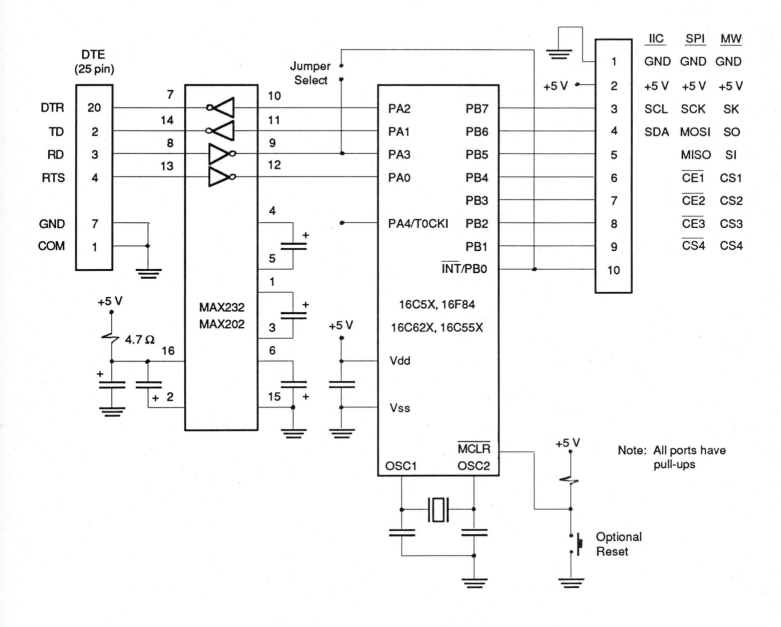

Figure 9-4   Schematic; Bit-Bang Master Applications

The modules in SPICOMS.GRP are all that are necessary to model an SPI MASTER with the PICmicro. These are the SPI *bus* services. They are all *called* functions. The modules are:

SPIMA   SPI Master Mode A byte transfer
SPIMB   SPI Master Mode B byte transfer
SPIMC   SPI Master Mode C byte transfer
SPIMD   SPI Master Mode D byte transfer

Throughout these modules the data to be transmitted is found in the parameter **datout** and the data received in the parameter **datin** (the eight bit shift register is modeled with two 8 bit bytes).

The data bits for each byte are counted by **bitctr**. When a module is called and subsequently returns, the **datout** byte is corrupted and the newly received data byte is found in **datin** (the previously received byte is lost).

Mode A Transaction (Module SPIMA and Figure 9-5)

On entry, SPIMA initializes the bit counter and takes SCK low. Immediately after the clock goes low, the first transmit data bit is placed on the MOSI line. One-half clock period later the clock is taken high and the MISO line is read. The read bit is placed in the receive data register. The data is moved from and to the registers via right rotates through the carry. One-half clock period after the low to high clock transition the above process is repeated until all eight bits have been transferred and the routine exits. The clock remains high (idle state) at exit. In summary: MOSI is updated just after SCK goes low and MISO is read just after SCK returns high. At entry and exit SCK is high.

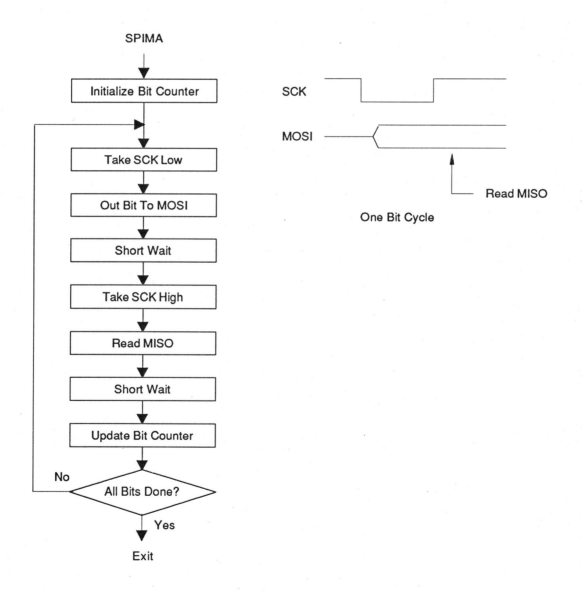

Figure 9-5   SPIMA - Mode A Service

Mode B Transaction (Module SPIMB and Figure 9-6)

On entry, SPIMB initializes the bit counter and takes SCK high. Immediately after the clock goes high, the first transmit data bit is placed on the MOSI line. One-half clock period later the clock is taken low and the MISO line is read. The read bit is placed in the receive data register. The data is moved from and to the registers via right rotates through the carry. One-half clock period after the high to low clock transition the above process is repeated until all eight bits have been transferred and the routine exits. The clock remains low (idle state) at exit. In summary: MOSI is updated just after SCK goes high and MISO is read just after SCK returns low. At entry and exit the SCK is low.

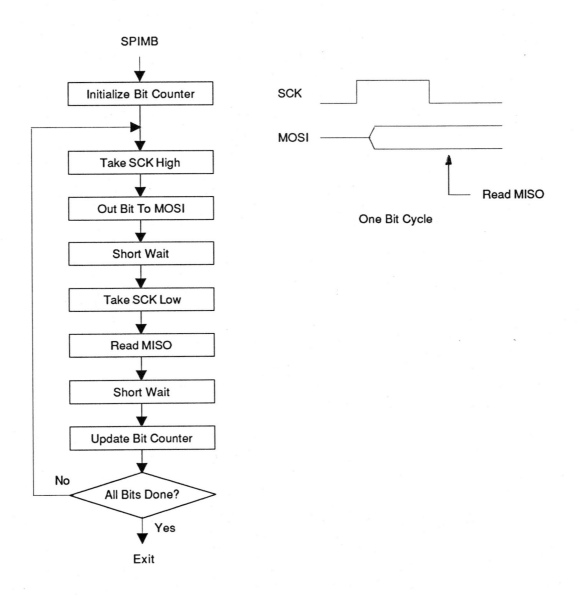

Figure 9-6   SPIMB - Mode B Service

Mode C Transaction (Module SPIMC and Figure 9-7)

On entry, SPIMC initializes the bit counter and places the first transmit data bit on the MOSI line. One-half clock period later the clock is taken low and the MISO line is read. The read bit is placed in the receive data register. The data is moved from and to the registers via right rotates through the carry. One-half clock period after the high to low clock transition the clock is taken high and the above process is repeated until all eight bits have been transferred and the routine exits. The clock remains high (idle state) at exit. In summary: MOSI is updated just after entry and MISO is read just after SCK goes low. One-half clock period later, SCK returns high. At entry and exit SCK is high.

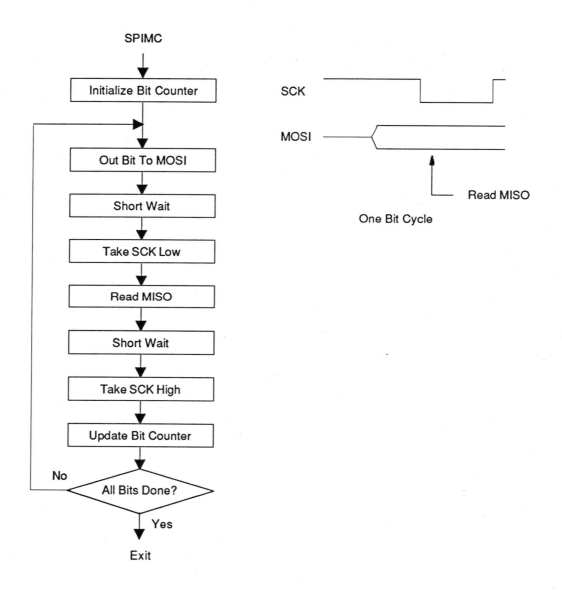

Figure 9-7   SPIMC - Mode C Service

Mode D Transaction (Module SPIMD and Figure 9-8)

On entry, SPIMD initializes the bit counter and places the first transmit data bit on the MOSI line. One-half clock period later the clock is taken high and the MISO line is read. The read bit is placed in the receive data register. The data is moved from and to the registers via right rotates through the carry. One-half clock period after the low to high clock transition the clock is taken low and the above process is repeated until all eight bits have been transferred and the routine exits. The clock remains low (idle state) at exit. In summary: MOSI is updated just after entry and MISO is read just after SCK goes high. One-half clock period later, SCK returns low. At entry and exit SCK is low.

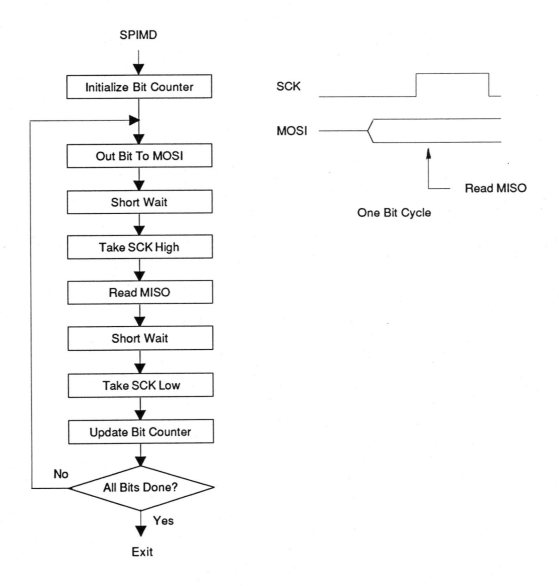

Figure 9-8   SPIMD - Mode D Service

Note that any one of these routines (21 lines of code) is all that is necessary to accomplish an SPI bit-bang data transfer. In contrast, an I²C transfer requires eight modules totaling approximately 111 lines of code. This is an example of trading hardware complexity (4 hardware lines for SPI, 2 for I²C) for software complexity.

These routines are very easy to apply. The application:

1. Loads data to be transmitted into **datout**.
2. Takes the appropriate device-select line low.
3. Calls the appropriate mode service (SPIMA, SPIMB, SPIMC or SPIMD).
4. Reads received data from **datin**.
5. Repeats the above until all bytes have been transferred.
6. Releases the device-select line.

```
;====== SPICOMS.GRP ============================================================
;
;          Bit-Bang Master SPI communications routines
;
;-------------------------------------------------------------------------------
;
;          SPI Bus uses 3 lines on Port B:
;               SCK     Clock
;               MOSI    Master Out Slave In Data Line
;               MISO    Master In Slave Out data Line
;
;          Requires following workspace:
;               bitctr  bit counter
;               datout  data out
;               datin   data in
;
;          Requires following equates:
;               sck     equ     nn      (Port B bit for SCK line)
;               mosi    equ     nn      (Port B bit for MOSI line)
;               miso    equ     nn      (Port B bit for MISO line)
;
;-------------------------------------------------------------------------------
;          Module: SPIMA
;          Transfers 1 byte over SPI bus.
;          (Clock Mode A: CPHA = 1, CPOL = 1)
;
;          On Entry:  SCK line must be high
;                     Data to be sent is in datout
;
;          On Exit:   SCK line is high
;                     Data received is in datin
;-------------------------------------------------------------------------------
spima      movlw   d'8'            ;8 data bytes
           movwf   bitctr
spima0     bcf     portb,sck       ;take clock low
           rlf     datout,f        ;data out bit to MOSI
           btfss   status,c        ;bit = 1 ? if yes, skip next
           goto    spima1          ;no. go
```

```
           bsf     portb,mosi         ;yes. set MOSI
           goto    spima2             ;& go
spima1     bcf     portb,mosi         ;clear MOSI
spima2     nop
           nop
           bsf     portb,sck          ;take clock high
           bcf     status,c           ;clear carry
           btfsc   portb,miso         ;MISO set ? if no skip
           bsf     status,c           ;yes. set carry
           rlf     datin,f            ;MISO level to data in
           nop
           nop
           decfsz  bitctr,f           ;all bits done ? if yes skip next
           goto    spima0             ;no. go do next bit
           retlw   0                  ;yes. exit
;----------------------------------------------------------------------
;          Module: SPIMB
;          Transfers 1 byte over SPI bus.
;          (Clock Mode B: CPHA = 1, CPOL = 0)
;
;          On Entry:  SCK line must be low
;                     Data to be sent is in datout
;
;          On Exit:   SCK line is low
;                     Data received is in datin
;----------------------------------------------------------------------
spimb      movlw   d'8'               ;8 data bytes
           movwf   bitctr
spimb0     bsf     portb,sck          ;take clock high
           rlf     datout,f           ;data out bit to MOSI
           btfss   status,c           ;bit = 1 ? if yes, skip next
           goto    spimb1             ;no. go
           bsf     portb,mosi         ;yes. set MOSI
           goto    spimb2             ;& go
spimb1     bcf     portb,mosi         ;clear MOSI
spimb2     nop
           nop
           bcf     portb,sck          ;take clock low
           bcf     status,c           ;clear carry
           btfsc   portb,miso         ;MISO set ? if no skip
           bsf     status,c           ;yes. set carry
           rlf     datin,f            ;MISO level to data in
           nop
           nop
           decfsz  bitctr,f           ;all bits done ? if yes skip next
           goto    spimb0             ;no. go do next bit
           retlw   1                  ;yes. exit
;----------------------------------------------------------------------
;          Module: SPIMC
;          Transfers 1 byte over the SPI bus
;          (Clock Mode C: CPHA = 0, CPOL = 1)
;
;          On Entry:  SCK line must be high
;                     Data to be sent is in datout
```

```
;
;        On Exit:    SCK line is high
;                    Data received is in datin
;-----------------------------------------------------------------------
spimc    movlw    d'8'            ;8 data bytes
         movwf    bitctr
spimc0   rlf      datout,f        ;data out bit to MOSI
         btfss    status,c        ;bit = 1 ? if yes, skip next
         goto     spimc1          ;no. go
         bsf      portb,mosi      ;yes. set MOSI
         goto     spimc2          ;& go
spimc1   bcf      portb,mosi      ;clear MOSI
spimc2   nop
         nop
         bcf      portb,sck       ;take SCK low
         bcf      status,c        ;clear carry
         btfsc    portb,miso      ;MISO set ? if no, skip next
         bsf      status,c        ;set carry
         rlf      datin,f         ;MISO level to datin
         nop
         nop
         bsf      portb,sck       ;take clock high
         decfsz   bitctr,f        ;all bits done ? if yes, skip next
         goto     spimc0          ;no. go do next bit
         retlw    2               ;yes. exit
;-----------------------------------------------------------------------
;        Module: SPIMD
;        Transfers 1 byte over the SPI bus
;        (Clock Mode D: CPHA = 0, CPOL = 0)
;
;        On Entry:   SCK line must be low
;                    Data to be sent is in datout
;
;        On Exit:    SCK line is low
;                    Data received is in datin
;-----------------------------------------------------------------------
spimd    movlw    d'8'            ;8 data bytes
         movwf    bitctr
spimd0   rlf      datout,f        ;data out bit to MOSI
         btfss    status,c        ;bit = 1 ? if yes, skip next
         goto     spimd1          ;no. go
         bsf      portb,mosi      ;yes. set MOSI
         goto     spimd2          ;& go
spimd1   bcf      portb,mosi      ;clear MOSI
spimd2   nop
         nop
         bsf      portb,sck       ;take SCK high
         bcf      status,c        ;clear carry
         btfsc    portb,miso      ;MISO set ? if no, skip next
         bsf      status,c        ;set carry
         rlf      datin,f         ;MISO level to datin
         nop
         nop
         bcf      portb,sck       ;take SCK low
```

```
        decfsz  bitctr,f        ;all bits done ? if yes, skip next
        goto    spimd0          ;no. go do next bit
        retlw   2               ;yes. exit
;=============================================================================
```

The clock rate for these Bit-Bang modules is approximately 70 KHz with a 4 MHz crystal. If an application requires a slower SPI clock (as may be necessary when communicating with a bit-bang slave) a time delay may be inserted into each clock phase to stretch the clock period as in SPIFA.TXT.

```
;====== SPIFA.TXT ============================================================
;
;       Module: SPIFA
;       Transfers 1 byte over SPI bus.
;       (Clock Mode A: CPHA = 1, CPOL = 1)
;
;       VARIABLE CLOCK RATE VERSION   (Clock rate determined by called
;                                      subroutine: filler)
;       Note: This routine places calls 1 level down (calls filler).
;
;       On Entry:  SCK line must be high
;                  Data to be sent is in datout
;
;       On Exit:   SCK line is high
;                  Data received is in datin
;-----------------------------------------------------------------------------
spifa   movlw   d'8'            ;8 data bytes
        movwf   bitctr
spifa0  bcf     portb,sck       ;take clock low
        rlf     datout,f        ;data out bit to MOSI
        btfss   status,c        ;bit = 1 ? if yes, skip next
        goto    spifa1          ;no. go
        bsf     portb,mosi      ;yes. set MOSI
        goto    spifa2          ;& go
spifa1  bcf     portb,mosi      ;clear MOSI
spifa2  call    filler          ;time filler
        bsf     portb,sck       ;take clock high
        bcf     status,c        ;clear carry
        btfsc   portb,miso      ;MISO set ? if no skip
        bsf     status,c        ;yes. set carry
        rlf     datin,f         ;MISO level to data in
        call    filler          ;time filler
        decfsz  bitctr,f        ;all bits done ? if yes skip next
        goto    spifa0          ;no. go do next bit
        retlw   0               ;yes. exit
;
;-----------------------------------------------------------------------------
;       When called adds approx   ((dlyctr)*(3) + 3) cycles
;
filler  movlw   6               ;add approx 21 cycles
        movwf   dlyctr
filler1 decfsz  dlyctr,f
```

```
        goto    filler1
        retlw   0
;=============================================================================
```

9.2.2 SPI Bit-Bang Slave Bus Services

Two lines of port A are used for slave MOSI and MISO and a third line is used for SCK (Figure 9-9). These lines should have pull-ups, but are not wired AND as with the I²C bus because the SPI bus uses separate lines for data out and data in. When configured as a bit-bang slave, the output port (MISO) must be configured as an output *only* when the slave is selected. When not selected, the slave MISO *must* be an input (to release the line). The input port (MOSI) and clock (SCK) are configured as inputs. The bit-bang setup and clock high and low periods are significantly longer than the minimum specified for the SPI bus; so much so that successful communications requires clock stretching of the bit-bang master routines as described at the end of Section 9.2.1. The maximum clock rate for the slave routines in SPISLAVE.GRP (with 4 MHz crystal) is approximately 25 KHz.

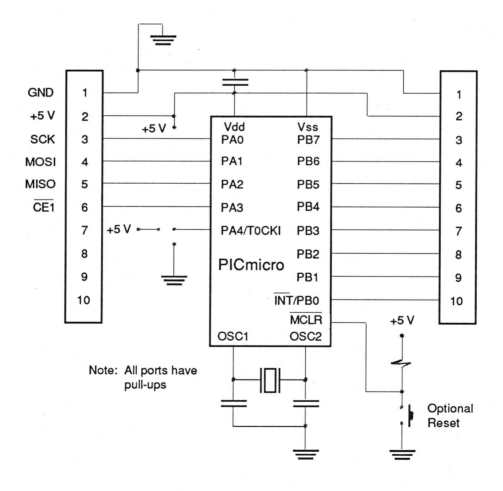

Figure 9-9   Schematic; SPI Bit-Bang Slave

The modules in SPISLAVE.GRP model an SPI SLAVE for Mode A and Mode D. These are the most commonly used modes. Bit-bang slave routines for all four modes are not required because SPI master devices can implement any SPI mode required by the slave. The modules in SPISLAVE.GRP are the SPI *slave bus* services and are all *called* functions. The modules are:

SPISMA   SPI Slave Mode A byte transfer
SPISMD   SPI Slave Mode D byte transfer
DESELCT   Places the slave in the de-selected configuration

Throughout these modules the data to be transmitted is found in the parameter **datout** and the data received in the parameter **datin** (the eight bit shift register is modeled with two 8 bit bytes). The data bits for each byte are counted by **bitctr**. After calling the module (actually after it returns), the **datout** byte is corrupted and the newly received data byte is found in **datin** (the previously received byte is lost).

Mode A Slave Transaction (Module SPISMA, Figure 9-10)

On entry SPISMA initializes the bit counter then waits for a low clock. If, during the wait for the low clock the slave device is de-selected, SPISMA calls DESELCT, sets the de-selected flag and exits. Immediately after the clock goes low SPISMA places the first transmit data bit on the MISO line and waits for the clock to return high. During this wait it again tests for de-select as described above. Immediately after the clock goes high it reads the receive data bit. SPISMA repeats the above process until all 8 bits have been transferred. In summary: MISO is updated just after SCK goes low and MOSI is read just after SCK returns high. On entry SPISMA expects SCK to be high (idle state).

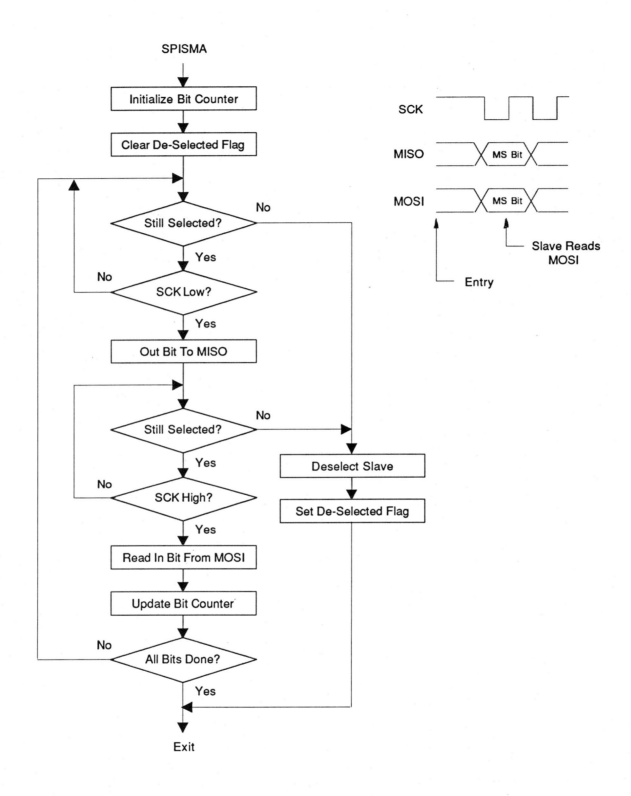

Figure 9-10   SPISMA - Mode A Slave Service

334

Mode D Slave Transaction (Module SPISMD and Figure 9-11)

On entry SPISMD initializes the bit counter, places the first transmit bit on the MISO line then waits for a high clock. If, during the wait for the high clock the slave device is de-selected, SPISMD calls DESELCT, sets the de-selected flag and exits. Immediately after the clock goes high SPISMD reads the first bit on the MOSI line and waits for the clock to return low. During this wait it again tests for de-select as described above. Immediately after the clock goes low it places the next transmit bit on the MISO line and repeats the above process until all 8 bits have been transferred. In summary: MISO is updated just after SCK goes low and MOSI is read just after SCK goes high. On entry SPISMD expects SCK to be low (idle state).

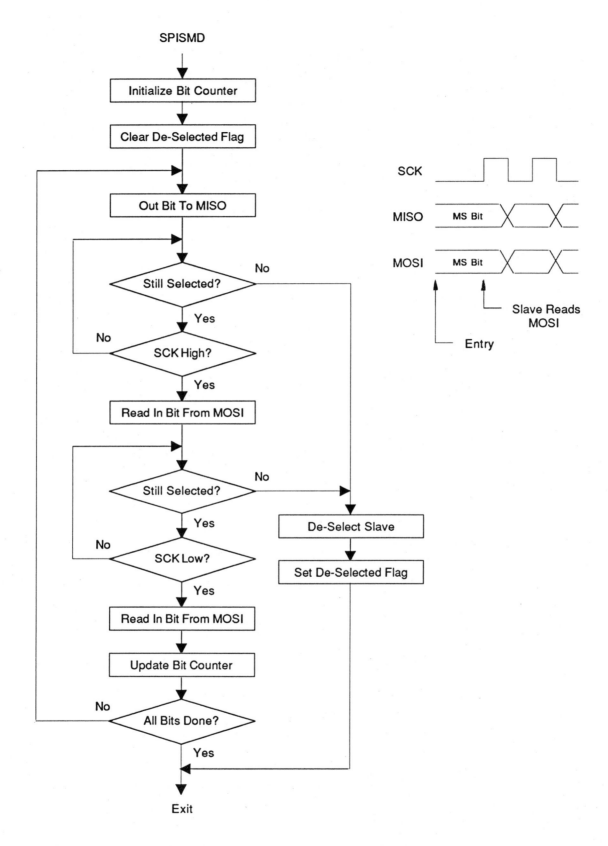

Figure 9-11   SPISMD - Mode D Slave Service

336

Configure Slave as De-Selected (Module DESELCT and Figure 9-12)

DESELCT configures the MISO port as an input and sets the de-selected flag. The de-selected flag signals the de-selected state to the application program. It is the responsibility of the application program to return to the slave-idle (wait-to-be-selected) state. DESELCT is called by the above two modules and may be called by the application. It is important that the application monitor the select line and release the MISO line as soon as possible after recognizing the select line de-select.

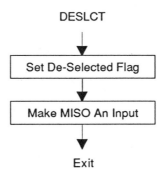

Figure 9-12   DESELCT - De-Select Slave

```
;====== SPISLAVE.GRP =========================================================
;
;         SPISLAVE.GRP
;         Bit-Banger Routines for slave SPI communications
;         See Section 9.2.2
;
;-----------------------------------------------------------------------------
;
;         SPI Bus uses 4 lines: MISO, MOSI, SCK and SEL on Port A.
;               MOSI, SCK and SEL MUST be configured as INPUTS.
;               When slave application is NOT selected, MOSI
;               MUST be configured as input. When selected, MOSI
;               is an output.
;
;         Requires the following work space:
;               datin    data received on MOSI line
;               datout   data sent on MISO line
;               bitctr   bit counter
;               slvflg   slave system flag (bit 7 reserved for de-selected
;                        flag)
;               dira     port a data direction register
;
;         Requires the following Equates:
;               sel      equ    xx      port a bit for select line
;               miso     equ    xx      port a bit for MISO line
```

```
;               mosi   equ    xx         port a bit for MOSI line
;               sck    equ    xx         port a bit for SCK line
;               desel  equ    07         de-selected flag bit
;                                        (bit 7 of slvflg)
;
;       Bits 0 through 6 of slvflg may be used by application.
;
;-----------------------------------------------------------------------
;       Module: SPISMA.TXT
;       Bit-Bang SPI Slave data transfer
;
;       CPHA=1, CPOL=1 (SPI Mode A)
;       On entry: Expects SCK to be HIGH
;                 Data to write to MISO in datout
;
;       On exit: Data read from MOSI in datin. If slave de-selected while
;                in this routine, then exits with de-selected flag set.
;
;-----------------------------------------------------------------------
spisma  movlw   d'8'            ;8 bit byte
        movwf   bitctr
        bcf     slvflg,desel    ;clear de-selected flag
spisma1 btfss   porta,sel       ;still selected ? if no, skip next
        goto    spismaa         ;yes. go test clock
        call    deselct         ;no. de-select slave
        goto    spismax         ;& go  exit
;
spismaa btfss   porta,sck       ;clock low ? if no, skip next
        goto    spismas         ;yes. go send bit
        goto    spisma1         ;no. go try again
;
spismas rlf     datout,f        ;rotate bit out
        btfss   status,c        ;bit = 1 ? if yes, skip next
        goto    spisma2         ;no. go take MISO low
        bsf     porta,miso      ;yes. take MISO high
        goto    spisma3         ;& go
spisma2 bcf     porta,miso      ;take MISO low
spisma3 btfss   porta,sel       ;still selected ? if no, skip next
        goto    spismab         ;yes. go test clock
        call    deselct         ;no. de-select slave
        goto    spismax         ;& go exit
;
spismab btfsc   porta,sck       ;clock high ? if no, skip next
        goto    spismar         ;yes. go receive bit
        goto    spisma3         ;no. go try again
;
spismar bcf     status,c        ;clear data bit
        btfsc   porta,mosi      ;MOSI high ? if no, skip next
        bsf     status,c        ;yes. set data bit
        rlf     datin,f         ;rotate it into data
        decfsz  bitctr,f        ;all bits done ? if yes, skip next
        goto    spisma1         ;no. go do next bit
spismax retlw   0               ;yes. exit
;-----------------------------------------------------------------------
```

```
;          Module: SPISMD.TXT
;          Bit-Bang SPI Slave data transfer
;
;          CPHA=0, CPOL=0 (SPI Mode D)
;          On entry: Expects SCK to be LOW
;                    Data to write to MISO in datout
;
;          On exit: Data read from MOSI in datin. If slave de-selected while
;                   in this routine, then exits with de-selected flag set.
;
;-------------------------------------------------------------------------
spismd   movlw    d'8'            ;8 bit byte
         movwf    bitctr
         bcf      slvflg,desel    ;clear de-selected flag
spismds  rlf      datout,f        ;rotate bit out
         btfss    status,c        ;bit = 1 ? if yes, skip next
         goto     spismd2         ;no. go take MISO low
         bsf      porta,miso      ;yes. take MISO high
         goto     spismd1         ;& go
spismd2  bcf      porta,miso      ;take MISO low
spismd1  btfss    porta,sel       ;still selected ? if no, skip next
         goto     spismda         ;yes. go test clock
         call     deselct         ;no. de-select slave
         goto     spismdx         ;& go  exit
;
spismda  btfss    porta,sck       ;clock high ? if yes, skip next to
                                  ;receive bit
         goto     spismd1         ;no. go try again
spismdr  bcf      status,c        ;clear data bit
         btfsc    porta,mosi      ;MOSI high ? if no, skip next
         bsf      status,c        ;yes. set data bit
         rlf      datin,f         ;rotate it into data
spismd3  btfss    porta,sel       ;still selected ? if no, skip next
         goto     spismdb         ;yes. go test clock
         call     deselct         ;no. de-select slave
         goto     spismdx         ;& go exit
;
spismdb  btfsc    porta,sck       ;clock low ? if yes, skip next
         goto     spismd3         ;no. go try again
spsmd4   decfsz   bitctr,f        ;all bits done ? if yes, skip next
         goto     spismds         ;no. go do next bit
spismdx  retlw    0               ;yes. exit
;-------------------------------------------------------------------------
;          Module DESELCT.TXT
;          Bit Bang SPI Slave De-Selected (Release MISO line)
;
;          Called by SPISMA & SPISMD. May be called by application.
;          On exit: de-selected flag set and port a MISO line
;                   configured as an input.
;-------------------------------------------------------------------------
deselct  bsf      slvflg,desel    ;set de-selected flag
```

339

```
        bsf     dira,miso          ;make MISO an input
        movf    dira,w
        tris    porta
        retlw   0                  ;exit
;========================================================================
```

9.2.3 Using the Section 9.2 Routines in Your Applications

Generally all of the routines can be used in your applications as written or with minor changes. For all routines, the entry and exit conditions, variables, port definitions and flag definitions are described in the xx.GRP and xx.TXT listings. All port assignments are arbitrary and may be changed to suit your application. See Sections 9.3 through 9.8 for sample applications using the routines. The sample applications use the PIC16F84 but the routines may be used with other PICmicros with little or no change. The MISO line should have a pull-up to eliminate the possibility of a floating input when all bit-bang slave devices are de-selected.

The routines introduced in Section 9.2 are:

SPICOMS.GRP   SPI Master Bit-Bang Bus Communications Services
SPISLAVE.GRP   SPI Slave Bit-Bang Bus Communications Services
SPIFA.TXT   SPI Communications Service with Stretched Clock

The routines in these groups are all *called* functions. A bit-bang SPI application using these functions is little more than a sequence of calls to these functions interspersed with specific application services.

Master Services

Most of your applications will generally use the SPI bit-bang master services to communicate with standard SPI hardware slave devices. These devices are capable of operating at the maximum SPI clock rate of 1 MHz. The SPI bit-bang services generate the clock timing with software routines and are thus sensitive to crystal frequency. The modules in SPICOMS clock at less than 100 KHZ when a 4 MHz crystal is used. This presents no problem because the hardware devices generally can tolerate clock rates approaching zero bits per second. The clock period for the SPICOMS modules is a function of crystal frequency only. See the listing for this group for more detailed information about the clock rate. The Module SPIFA.TXT illustrates the use of an added time delay to stretch the clock period if even slower SPI clock rates are required by an application.

When using the SPI bit-bang master bus services to communicate with a device using the SPI bit-bang slave bus services, pay close attention to the clock rates because the bit-bang slave routines are generally slower than the master routines.

Be very careful to select the correct SPI Mode when communicating with a slave. The most common slave modes are Mode A and Mode D. SPI slave device data sheets generally specify these as mode (1,1) and mode (0,0) respectively. Careful study of the device timing diagrams is the best way to determine the mode. Microwire devices may be placed on the SPI bus if you pay careful attention to the timing (see Section 9.7). Devices having different SPI modes may be placed on the same bus provided you communicate with each device using the appropriate mode.

The SPI bit-bang master bus services are very easy to apply: Simply place the data byte to be sent in **datout**, select the device, call the service, then read the received data byte at **datin**. If you are communicating with a receive-only slave then ignore the received byte. Repeat the call to the service until all bytes are transferred then deselect the device. If you are communicating with a transmit-only slave then the contents of **datout** have no significance.

Slave Services

When writing an application for a bit-bang slave your most important concern should be the state of the MISO line. When the slave is *not* selected, the MISO port *must* be configured as an input. Only configure the port as an output when you are anticipating sending a data byte. A slave application that only receives should *never* configure MISO as an output. The modules SPISMA and SPISMD monitor the select line when waiting for the clock edge. If a de-select is detected, the modules call DESLCT to ensure that the MISO line is released (made an input). If your application has MISO configured as an output and is not currently executing SPISMA or SPISMD you must frequently test the select line for a de-select state and immediately respond to a de-select by calling DESELCT or otherwise releasing the MISO line. Because of the software induced delay in response to de-select, your master program should wait a while after de-selecting the bit-bang slave before selecting another slave. See CANARY3.ASM (Section 9.8) for an example of how the slave application handles an asynchronous de-select.

Bit-bang slave applications are relatively slow. To ensure successful communications, slow the master clock rate down to a little below the maximum rate of the slave application. The maximum clock rate for SPISMA and SPISMD (with a 4 MHz crystal) is approximately 25 KHz. Also leave ample response time between selecting the slave and sending a byte of data to it. This response time and the necessary delay between bytes sent to the slave is primarily a function of the application.

9.3 SPI Analog to Digital Converter

In section 8.5.1 we were able to fit the Maxim MAX187 SPI A/D to a bit-bang I^2C bus. In this section we shall use the MAX187 on the bus for which it was designed. Figure 9-13 illustrates the clock and data timing necessary for MAX187 operation: the clock must idle low, the data must change on the down going clock and is read on the up going clock. Examining Figure 9-3 we find that these requirements are met by SPI Mode D (CPHA=0, CPOL=0). All SPI communications with the Max187 A/D may be implemented with the SPIMD service.

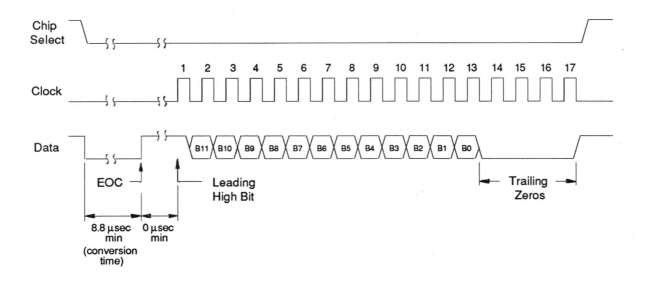

Figure 9-13   MAX187 A/D SPI Timing

When the MAX187 A/D is selected (chip select brought low) the conversion process begins and the data line (MISO) goes low. When the conversion is completed MISO returns high. At this point the data may be clocked out of the A/D. After selecting the A/D, MISO must be monitored for a high level. Only after detecting the high level on MISO, may the data be transferred. The initial data high (which signaled the end-of-conversion) is read as the first bit. This initial leading high bit is not a part of the conversion value. The next 12 clocks place the 12 A/D conversion bits on the data line. Any following clocks place low bits on the data line. Thus a minimum of 13 clock cycles are required to read the A/D. Since the SPI protocol calls for 8 bit bytes we must transfer two bytes (16 bits) from the A/D beginning with the leading high bit and ending with the last of the three trailing low bits (Figure 8-3, Section 8.5.1). As with the I^{2}C application in Section 8.5.1, this two byte result must be normalized to a 12 bit value.

The Module SPIATOD.TXT executes the above described conversion process. Note that the normalization process is exactly as in IIATOD.TXT.

On entry, SPIATOD ensures that the clock line is in the low idle state, as required by mode D, before enabling the A/D. If an application includes slave devices that operate under differing SPI timing modes, the SCK line may be idling at an incorrect level when a given device is to be enabled. For example, if a volt meter uses an SPI A/D operating as a Mode D device and an SPI display driver operating as a Mode C device, the clock line will be idling low after the A/D is read. The next SPI transaction will be a write to the display driver. The Mode C display driver expects the clock to idle high, but the A/D has left the SCK low. This potential for disaster is prevented by having *all* SPI bit-bang device services ensure that the SCK idle state is correct before the device is enabled.

The MAX187 is just one of many A/D converters that may be used on the SPI bus. Most of the converters require multi-byte transfer and some sort of received data normalization. Some shift out the result of the previous conversion while instructions (such as multiplexer channel selection) for the current conversion are being shifted in. In general, the software necessary to handle the result of the conversion is far more complex than the SPI communications software.

```
;====== SPIATOD.TXT ============================================================
;
;        Module SPIATOD.TXT
;        SPI analog to digital converter MAX 187
;        Bit-Bang SPI
;
;-------------------------------------------------------------------------------
;
;        Max 187 requires SPI Clock Mode D (CPHA=0, CPOL=0)
;
;        A/D select line is port B bit adcen
;
;        On Exit: A/D count in (data1,data0)
;
;-------------------------------------------------------------------------------
spiatod bsf      portb,adcen      ;make sure A to D not enabled
        bcf      portb,sck        ;make sure clock idles down (Mode D)
        bcf      portb,adcen      ;select A/D (starts conversion)
        nop
spiad1  btfss    portb,miso       ;end of conversion ? if yes, skip next
        goto     spiad1           ;no. go try again
        call     spimd            ;yes. transfer data byte (CPHA=0, CPOL=0)
        movf     datin,w          ;received byte to...
        movwf    data1            ;data1
        clrf     data0
        call     spimd            ;read low byte
        movf     datin,w          ;received byte to...
        movwf    data0            ;data0
        bsf      portb,adcen      ;deselect A/D
;
;        Here we arrange the 12 bits in the 12 lower bit positions of
;        data1, data0
        rrf      data1,f          ;DB5 to c
        rrf      data0,f          ;DB5 to data0
        rrf      data1,f          ;DB6 to c
        rrf      data0,f          ;DB6 to data0
        rrf      data1,f          ;DB7 to c
        rrf      data0,f          ;DB7 to data0. data0 has low byte of A/D data
        movlw    0f               ;clear high 4 bits of data1
        andwf    data1,f          ;data1 has high 4 bits of A/D data
;
        retlw    0                ;exit
;===============================================================================
```

9.4 SPI Display Driver

The Motorola MC14489 is an SPI five digit LED display driver (Figure 9-14). It provides a simple hardware interface to what would otherwise require an extensive utilization of hardware resources. The MC14489 may be cascaded for applications requiring a greater number of display digits. It features built-in seven segment and special character decoders and an LED or lamp mode capable of driving 25 individual LEDs or lamps. The LED current source is built in - no LED series resistors are required.

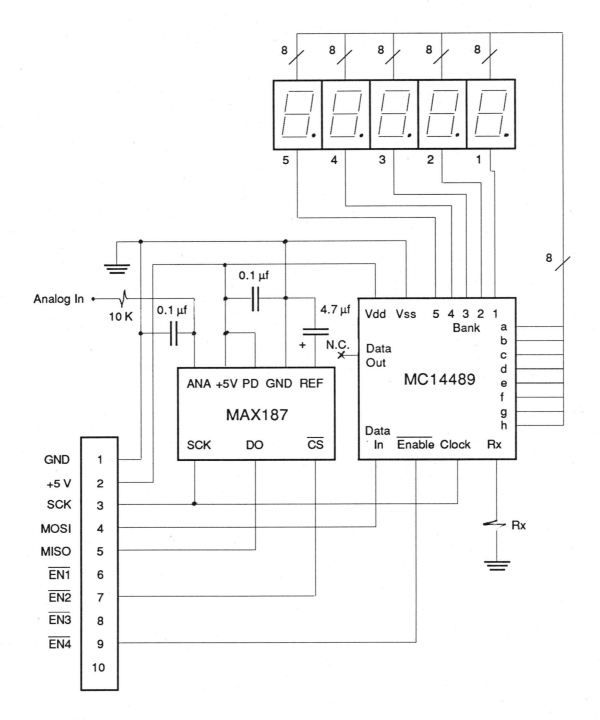

Figure 9-14   Slave Schematic; YELLOW1 And WHITE1 Applications

The MC14489 SPI timing is shown in Figure 9-15. Note that SCK idles low and MOSI is read on the up-going clock; indicating that it communicates as an SPI Mode D (CPHA=0, CPOL=0) device. The display driver has an eight bit configuration register and a 24 bit data register (Figure 9-15). As with all SPI devices, data is clocked in MSB first. The configuration data must be sent to the device prior to sending any display data. The configuration data is sent only when the configuration is to be changed.

344

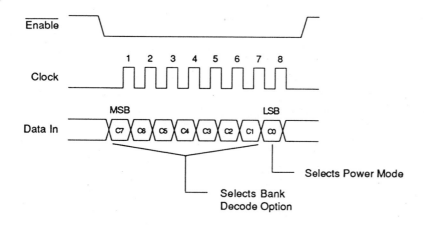

Configuration Register Format

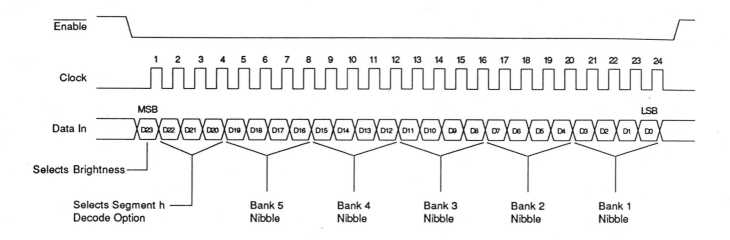

Display Register Format

Figure 9-15   Timing Diagram - MC14489

The SPI module DISP89.TXT is the master driver service for the MC14489. On entry, DISP89 ensures that SCK is low as required by Mode D. It then enables the MC14489, sequentially sends the three data bytes and de-selects the device. CONFIG89 does the same except only one byte, the configuration word, is sent. This is a very simple to use yet very versatile display driver. See the Motorola product literature for more information on configuring the MC14489.

```
;====== DISP89.TXT ============================================================
;
;        Module DISP89.TXT
;        Writes to MC14489 LED Display Driver
;        Bit-Bang SPI
;        Display Driver select line is Port B, Bit dispen
;        Display Driver requires SPI Clock Mode D (CPHA=0, CPOL=0)
;
;        Requires the following equates:
;
;                dispen  equ  nn  (nn is port B bit for MC14489 select)
;
;        Requires the following work space:
;
;        Display Block:
;                discon              Configuration word
;                disdat0             Low Byte   (bank2, bank1)
;                disdat1             Mid Byte   (bank4, bank3)
;                disdat2             High Byte  (dp, bank5)
;
;        This Module consists of two called subroutines. They are to be called
;        by the application.
;
;        Subroutine DISP89 sends digit data (5 digits) and decimal point
;        information to the device. On entry it expects the data to be in
;        disdat0, disdat1 and disdat2.
;
;        Subroutine CONFG89 sends the configuration word to the device. On
;        entry it expects the configuration word to be in discon.
;-------------------------------------------------------------------------------
disp89  bcf      portb,sck       ;make sure clock idles low (Mode D)
        bcf      portb,dispen    ;select display
        movf     disdat2,w       ;high display byte
        movwf    datout          ;to SPI out register
        call     spimd           ;send it (Mode D)
        movf     disdat1,w       ;mid display byte
        movwf    datout
        call     spimd           ;send it
        movf     disdat0,w       ;low display byte
        movwf    datout
        call     spimd           ;send it
        bsf      portb,dispen    ;de-select display
        retlw    0               ;exit
;
;
confg89 bcf      portb,sck       ;make sure clock idles low (Mode D)
        bcf      portb,dispen    ;select display
        movf     discon,w        ;configuration word
        movwf    datout          ;to SPI out register
        call     spimd           ;send it (Mode D)
        bsf      portb,dispen    ;de-select display
        retlw    0               ;exit
;==============================================================================
```

9.4.1 YELLOW1.ASM: An SPI Bit-Bang A/D and Display Application.

See Figure 9-14 and YELLOW1.ASM.

The demonstration program YELLOW1 utilizes the bit-bang SPI bus, MAX187 and MC14489 master service routines in a voltmeter application. Because the volt meter range is 0.000 to 4.096 volts, only four of the possible five 7-segment LED displays are used. All four display digits use the MC14489 built-in decoder. The application main loop simply calls three services: read the A/D, convert the reading to packed BCD and send the BCD to the display. Both the A/D and the display driver are SPI Mode D devices, so only the SPI bus service SPIMD is necessary.

```
;====== YELLOW1.ASM =========================================================
;
;        SPI Analog to Digital Converter to SPI 4 Digit LED Display
;
;        Maxim MAX 187 SPI A/D
;        Motorola MC14489 SPI 5 Digit LED Display Decoder-Driver
;
;        Bit-Bang PIC SPI Communications
;        14 Bit PIC
;
;----------------------------------------------------------------------------
         radix   hex          ;RADIX is HEX
;
         list p=16f84
;
;        STATUS REGISTER BIT DEFINITIONS:
c        equ     0            ;carry bit of status register (bit 0)
z        equ     2            ;zero flag bit of status register (bit 2)
dc       equ     1            ;digit carry
pd       equ     3            ;power down bit
to       equ     4            ;time out bit
rp0      equ     5            ;program page preselect, low bit
rp1      equ     6            ;program page preselect, high bit
;
;        DESTINATION BIT DEFINITIONS:
w        equ     0            ;destination working
f        equ     1            ;destination file
;
;----------------------------------------------------------------------------
;     CPU EQUATES   (special function register memory map)
;
;   BANK 0:
indf     equ     00           ;indirect file register
tmr0     equ     01           ;timer
pcl      equ     02           ;program counter (low byte)
status   equ     03           ;status register
fsr      equ     04           ;indirect data pointer
porta    equ     05           ;port a
portb    equ     06           ;port b
eedata   equ     08           ;eeprom data
eeadr    equ     09           ;eeprom address
```

347

```
pclath   equ     0a          ;write buffer for program counter (high byte)
intcon   equ     0b          ;interrupt control register
;
;   BANK 1:
optreg   equ     01          ;option register                    bank 1 (0x81)
trisa    equ     05          ;data direction register port a     bank 1 (0x85)
trisb    equ     06          ;data direction register port b     bank 1 (0x86)
eecon1   equ     08          ;eeprom control register            bank 1 (0x88)
;
;------------------------------------------------------------------------
;       WORK AREA  (memory map)  Starts at 000c
;
datin    equ     000c        ;data byte read from MISO line
datout   equ     000d        ;data byte to be written to MOSI line
bitctr   equ     000e        ;bit counter
systat   equ     000f        ;system status
counter  equ     0010        ;general counter
disdat0  equ     0011        ;display data
disdat1  equ     0012
disdat2  equ     0013
discon   equ     0014        ;display configuration word
;
data1    equ     0019        ;high data byte
data0    equ     001a        ;low data byte
;
;       for vert:
bcd4     equ     0020
bcd3     equ     0021
bcd2     equ     0022
bcd1     equ     0023
bcd0     equ     0024
pten1    equ     0025
pten0    equ     0026
index    equ     0027
;------------------------------------------------------------------------
;       SYSTEM EQUATES
;
dispen   equ     01          ;port B1 is display select
adcen    equ     03          ;port B3 is A/D select
miso     equ     05          ;port B5 is SPI MOSI
mosi     equ     06          ;port B6 is SPI MOSI
sck      equ     07          ;port B7 is SPI SCK
;
ovrfl    equ     07          ;flag for asvert (bit 7 of systat)
;
;------------------------------------------------------------------------
         org     0x00        ;start of program memory
         goto    start       ;jump over tables
;
;------------------
tbl1     addwf   pcl,f       ;tables for asvert
         retlw   027
         retlw   003
         retlw   000
```

```
        retlw   000
;
tbl0    addwf   pcl,f
        retlw   010
        retlw   0e8
        retlw   064
        retlw   00a
;------------------
;
start   movlw   0ff
        movwf   porta
        movwf   portb           ;de-select all SPI devices
        bsf     status,rp0      ;switch to bank 1
        movlw   0000            ;all port A as outputs
        movwf   trisa
        movlw   0020            ;initialize b5 as input, others as outputs
        movwf   trisb
        bcf     status,rp0      ;switch to bank 0
;
        movlw   00e1            ;display configuration word
        movwf   discon          ;(digit 5 blank and digits 4 thru 1
;                                hex decode)
        call    confg89         ;write it to display config register
;
mloop   call    spiatod         ;measure voltage
        call    vert            ;convert 12 bit binary to packed bcd
        call    disp89          ;display measured voltage
        goto    mloop           ;go loop
;-----------------------------------------------------------------------------
;       INCLUDED FILES:
;
;       SPIATOD.TXT             SPI A/D
;       DISP89.TXT              SPI Display Driver MC14489
;-----------------------------------------------------------------------------
        include spiatod.txt
        include disp89.txt
;-----------------------------------------------------------------------------
;       Module: SPIMD.TXT     (part of SPICOMMS.GRP)
;       Transfers 1 byte over the SPI bus
;       (Clock Mode D: CPHA = 0, CPOL = 0)
;
;       On Entry:  SCK line must be low
;                  Data to be sent is in datout
;
;       On Exit:   SCK line is low
;                  Data received is in datin
;-----------------------------------------------------------------------------
spimd   movlw   d'8'            ;8 data bytes
        movwf   bitctr
spimd0  rlf     datout,f        ;data out bit to MOSI
        btfss   status,c        ;bit = 1 ? if yes, skip next
        goto    spimd1          ;no. go
        bsf     portb,mosi      ;yes. set MOSI
        goto    spimd2          ;& go
```

```
spimd1    bcf       portb,mosi      ;clear MOSI
spimd2    nop
          nop
          bsf       portb,sck       ;take SCK high
          bcf       status,c        ;clear carry
          btfsc     portb,miso      ;MISO set ? if no, skip next
          bsf       status,c        ;set carry
          rlf       datin,f         ;MISO level to datin
          nop
          nop
          bcf       portb,sck       ;take SCK low
          decfsz    bitctr,f        ;all bits done ? if yes, skip next
          goto      spimd0          ;no. go do next bit
          retlw     2               ;yes. exit
;==============================================================================
;         Module: VERT89.TXT
;
;         For Use with Bit-Bang SPI
;         Convert 12 BIT A/D result to 4 digit packed BCD
;         (data1, data0) => (bcd3,bcd2,bcd1,bcd0)
;         (bcd3,bcd2,bcd1,bcd0) => (disdat1,disdat0)
;
;         Display Block:
;                   discon          Configuration word
;                   disdat0         Low Byte   (bank2, bank1)
;                   disdat1         Mid Byte   (bank4, bank3)
;                   disdat2         High Byte (dp, bank5)
;
;         NOTE: This Module PLACES CALLS TWO LEVELS DEEP
;               The called routines vert4 and vert5 are part of this module
;------------------------------------------------------------------------------
vert      clrf      index           ;convert to bcd
vert1     clrf      counter
vert2     movf      index,w
          call      vert4
          call      vert5
          btfss     status,c
          goto      vert3
          incf      counter,f
          goto      vert2
vert3     movf      index,w
          call      vert4
          call      vert6
          movlw     bcd4
          movwf     fsr
          movf      index,w
          addwf     fsr,f
          movf      counter,w
          movwf     indf
          incf      index,f
          btfss     index,2
          goto      vert1
          movf      data0,w
          movwf     bcd0
```

```
;
;           Here we pack the BCD data into the display block
;
        movf    bcd3,w              ;MS digit to Mid Byte..
        movwf   disdat1
        swapf   disdat1,f           ;& to high nibble of Mid Byte
        movf    bcd2,w              ;next digit to low nibble of Mid Byte
        iorwf   disdat1,f
        movf    bcd1,w              ;next digit to Low Byte..
        movwf   disdat0
        swapf   disdat0,f           ;& to high nibble of Low Byte
        movf    bcd0,w              ;LS digit to low nibble of Low Byte
        iorwf   disdat0,f
        movlw   00c0                ;decimal point and digit 5 (0) to high byte
        movwf   disdat2
        retlw   0                   ;exit
;-----------------------------------------------------------------------
vert4   call    tbl1                ;read table
        movwf   pten1
        movf    index,w
        call    tbl0
        movwf   pten0
        return
;-----------------------------------------------------------------------
vert5   comf    pten1,f
        comf    pten0,f
        movf    pten0,w
        addlw   01
        movwf   pten0
        btfsc   status,c
        incf    pten1,f
vert6   movf    pten0,w
        addwf   data0,f
        bcf     systat,ovrfl
        btfsc   status,c
        bsf     systat,ovrfl
        movf    pten1,w
        addwf   data1,f
        btfss   systat,ovrfl
        goto    vertx
        btfsc   status,c
        goto    vert7
        movlw   01
        addwf   data1,f
        goto    vertx
vert7   incf    data1,f
vertx   return
;-----------------------------------------------------------------------
        end                         ;END OF PROGRAM
;=======================================================================
```

351

9.5 Communicating With an SPI EEPROM

The Microchip 25C080 serial EEPROM is typical of most SPI serial bus electrically erasable PROMS. It is an 8K bit device configured as 1024 bytes of eight bits each. The 25C080 SPI interface conforms to the standard SPI protocol. The 25C080 is organized as a continuous 8K bit block of memory, however for multi-byte writes, it looks like 512 pages of 16 bytes each. This importance of this distinction will be covered in the discussion below on page write. Data writes may be one byte at a time to a specific memory address or sequentially to a limited block of contiguous memory. Reads may be one byte or multiple byte beginning at a specified address and continuing sequentially through contiguous memory.

Data to the EEPROM (MOSI) is clocked in on the SI line and data from the EEPROM (MISO) is clocked out on the SO line (Figure 9-19). All data transfers are MSB first. As with all SPI devices, the EEPROM is selected by pulling down the $\overline{CE}$ pin. Two other inputs ($\overline{WP}$ and $\overline{HOLD}$) provide system flexibility. Communications to the device can be paused by pulling down the $\overline{HOLD}$ input. While the EEPROM is paused, transitions on all inputs (except $\overline{CE}$) will be ignored. Write operations to the status register and certain blocks of memory can be disabled by pulling down the write protect ($\overline{WP}$) input. For the applications in this book, $\overline{HOLD}$ and $\overline{WP}$ are not used (held high). See the Microchip 25C080 product literature for more information on the $\overline{HOLD}$ and $\overline{WP}$ inputs.

In addition to the 1024 byte memory array, the 25C080 contains an eight bit instruction register and an eight bit status register. Instructions, written to the instruction register, configure the EEPROM for a specific operation. Table 9-1 lists all of the instructions. The status register (Figure 9-16) indicates the status of certain operations and may be used to select one of four protection (block write disable) options. The status register may be read at any time, even during a write cycle.

Table 9-1   25Cxxx Instruction set

```
----------------------------------------------------
Instruction    Code         Description
----------------------------------------------------
   WREN        0x06     Enable write
   WRDI        0x04     Disable write
   RDSR        0x05     Read status register
   WRSR        0x01     Write status register
   READ        0x03     Read data from memory array
   WRITE       0x02     Write data to memory array
```

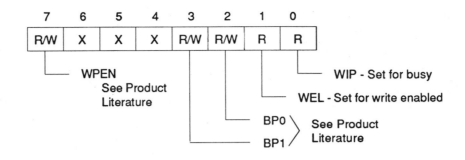

Figure 9-16   25Cxxx EEPROM Status Register

The Status register *write-in-process* bit (**wip**) indicates whether the EEPROM is busy with a write cycle. When **wip** is set (logic 1), a write cycle is in progress; when cleared (logic 0), no write cycle is in progress. This bit is read-only. When a write cycle is in progress, the status register may be repeatedly read and the **wip** bit tested until the write cycle is completed. A completed write cycle is signaled by a cleared **wip** bit (see module POLL below).

The *write-enable-latch* bit (**wel**) indicates the status of the write enable latch. When set, writes to the status register and memory array are allowed. When cleared, writes to the status register and memory array are dis-allowed. This bit is read-only and is controlled by the WREN and WRDI instructions. The WREN (write enable) instruction sets the write enable latch. The WRDI (write disable) instruction clears the latch. To successfully set the latch the $\overline{CE}$ line *must* be returned high after the WREN instruction byte is sent. The only way to set the latch is via a WREN instruction. After any successful byte write, page write or status register write, the write enable latch is cleared. The latch must be reset with the WREN instruction prior to any subsequent writes. The internal write cycle starts when the $\overline{CE}$ line goes high. To initiate the write cycle the $\overline{CE}$ line *must* go high after the proper number of clock cycles (to clock in the data) have been completed. Any attempted access to the memory array during the write cycle will be ignored.

The other bits of the status register are used in conjunction with the $\overline{WP}$ input pin. See the 25C080 product literature for more information on these bits.

9.5.1 SPI EEPROM Bit-Bang Communications Services

The modules in EE25C.GRP, along with the SPICOMS module SPIMD, are all that are needed to communicate with an SPI EEPROM. The modules are all *called* functions and are called by the application. The EE25C modules perform the specific EEPROM operations and call the SPI bus service SPIMD. These are the SPI *EEPROM* modules. The modules in EE25C.GRP are:

WRITESR   Write to EEPROM status register
READSR   Read EEPROM status register
CLOSE   Disable all EEPROM write operations
POLL   Polls the EEPROM for completion of write cycle
PREWRT   Send preamble for EEPROM data write
ONEOUT   Write one byte to EEPROM
MLTOUT   Multiple byte (page) write to EEPROM
PRERD   Send preamble for EEPROM data read
ONEIN   Read one byte from EEPROM
MLTIN   Multiple byte read from EEPROM

Module Descriptions

See Figure 9-18 and EE25C.GRP

The 25C080 EEPROM is compatible with SPI timing Mode D (CPHA=0, CPOL=0). The modules in 25C080.GRP treat the EEPROM as a Mode D device. As with other SPI devices, the SPICOM service SPIMD is slow enough to ensure that the setup and de-select hold times are well above the minimums for the EEPROM (see Section 9.2.1).

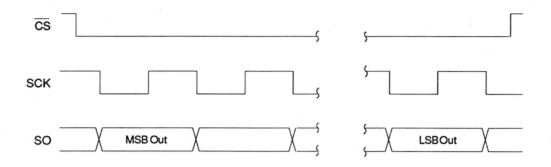

EEPROM Serial Output Timing

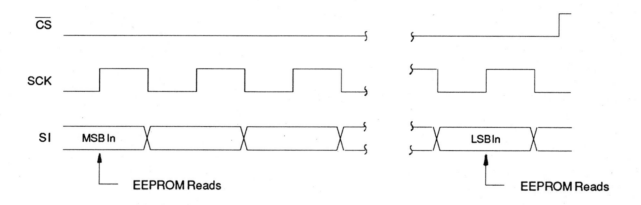

EEPROM Serial Input Timing

Figure 9-17   25Cxxx EEPROM Clock And Data Timing

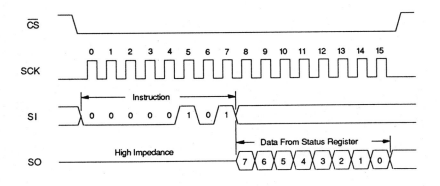

Read Status Register

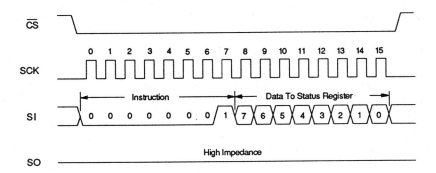

Write Status Register

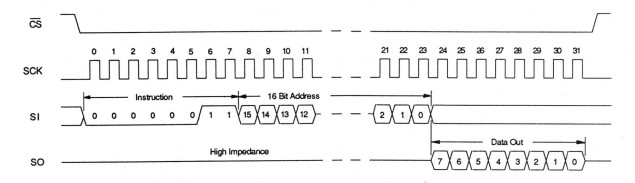

Read

Figure 9-18   25Cxxx Transactions

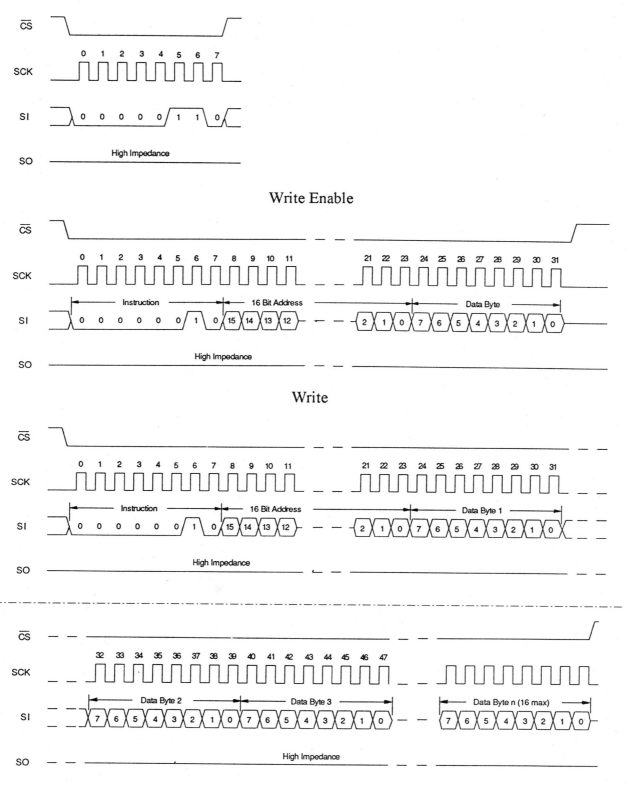

Write Enable

Write

Page Write

Figure 9-18   25Cxxx Transactions

Write to EEPROM Status Register (Module WRITESR)

After selecting the device, WRITESR sends the WREN (write enable) instruction followed by a device de-select. This sets the write enable bit in anticipation of the following WRSR instruction and status bytes. The device is again selected and the WRSR (write status register) instruction and status bytes are sent. The device is de-selected and polled for completion of the write cycle. When the write cycle is completed WRITESR exits. The initial write enable instruction is required prior to any write to the status register or memory array. This requirement for all writes to the memory array is handled by the module PREWRT.

Read EEPROM Status Register (Module READSR)

After selecting the device, READSR sends the RDSR (read status register) instruction followed by another byte. The second byte clocks the status register data out on the SO line. Note that the contents of the second byte sent to the EEPROM are not significant. This is a dummy byte. Here the RDSR instruction is simply sent twice. The EEPROM is then de-selected.

Disable All EEPROM Write Operations (Module CLOSE)

This module sends the WRDI (write disable) instruction to the EEPROM to clear the write enable latch, prohibiting any writes to the status register or memory array. The main reason for this module is to ensure that the EEPROM is not left with an unexpected write capability after an EEPROM communications session is completed. This module should be called by the application after completing any series of EEPROM transactions.

Poll the EEPROM for Completed Write Cycle (Module POLL)

POLL repeatedly reads the status register and tests the state of the **wip** (write in process) bit until the **wip** is cleared, indicating the end of the write cycle. POLL is called after any write sequence. POLL exits only after the **wip** bit is cleared.

Send Preamble for EEPROM Data Write (Module PREWRT)

All writes to the memory array must be initialized with a write enable instruction followed by a write instruction followed by an array address. Because this initial sequence is the same for both byte write and page write it is a separate module and is called by the byte and page write modules. PREWRT enables writing with the: select EEPROM, send WREN, de-select sequence described above. It then re-selects the EEPROM, sends the WRITE (write data) instruction followed by the two byte array address and exits. This module is called by ONEOUT and MLTOUT. These modules send the data. Note that PREWRT does *not* de-select the EEPROM. On exit, the EEPROM remains selected. The next EEPROM operation following PREWRT must be one or more send operations followed by a de-select (see ONEOUT and MLTOUT below).

Write One Byte to EEPROM (Module ONEOUT)

ONEOUT writes one byte to the EEPROM. ONEOUT write addresses the EEPROM by calling the write preamble module PREWRT. After calling PREWRT, ONEOUT simply sends the data byte, de-selects the EEPROM and then polls it for completed write cycle. ONEOUT exits when the write cycle is completed.

Multiple Byte or Page write to EEPROM (Module MLTOUT)

MLTOUT writes one to 16 bytes to the EEPROM. The bytes to write are in a buffer and are sequentially moved from the buffer and sent to the EEPROM. MLTOUT write addresses the EEPROM by calling the write preamble module PREWRT. After calling PREWRT, the data bytes are sent. When all bytes have been sent the EEPROM is de-selected and polled for completed write cycle. MLTOUT exits when the write cycle is completed.

A page is a maximum of 16 bytes. Page boundaries are at array addresses having the four lower bits equal to zero. Multiple byte writes may begin at any address but if the write crosses a page boundary, the address counter wraps around and any bytes sent after crossing the boundary are written beginning at the start of the page. BE CAREFUL with PAGE writes! Make sure that a write does not cross a page boundary.

Send Preamble for EEPROM Data Read (Module PRERD)

All reads from the memory array must be initialized with a read instruction followed by an array address. Because this initial sequence is the same for both single and multiple byte reads, it is a separate module and is called by the single byte and multiple byte read modules. PRERD selects the EEPROM, sends the READ (read data) instruction followed by the two byte array address and exits. This module is called by ONEIN or MLTIN. Note that PRERD does *not* de-select the EEPROM. On exit, the EEPROM remains selected. The next EEPROM operation following PRERD must be one or more receive operations followed by a de-select (see ONEIN and MULTIN below).

Read One Byte from EEPROM (Module ONEIN)

ONEIN reads one byte from the EEPROM. It read addresses the EEPROM by calling PRERD. After calling PRERD, ONEIN simply sends a dummy data byte to clock in the read data then de-selects the EEPROM.

Multiple Byte read from EEPROM (Module MLTIN)

MLTIN reads one to 256 bytes from EEPROM. The received bytes are sequentially read and placed in a buffer. MLTIN read addresses the EEPROM by calling PRERD. After calling PRERW, MLTIN sends dummy bytes to clock in the read data until all bytes have been received. The EEPROM is then de-selected. Any number of bytes may be sequentially read from the 25C080 but the maximum number is generally limited by the application buffer size. MULTIN is limited to 256 bytes because the buffer counter is only one byte. See section 9.5.2 for more on multiple byte reads.

```
;====== EE25C.GRP ==============================================================
;
;        COMMUNICATIONS WITH 25CXX SPI EEPROM  Using SPI Bit-Bang modules
;        in SPICOMS.GRP
;
;-------------------------------------------------------------------------------
;
;        Required workspace:
;                Workspace required by SPICOMS.TXT
;                and:
;                datctr          data byte counter
;                data0           data byte
;                addr1           EEPROM address high byte
;                addr0           EEPROM address low byte
;
;        Required equates:
;                Equates required by SPICOMS.TXT
;                and:
;                WREN    equ     0x06    write enable instruction
;                WRDI    equ     0x04    write disable instruction
;                RDSR    equ     0x05    read status register instruction
;                WRSR    equ     0x01    write status register instruction
;                READ    equ     0x03    Read data from memory instruction
;                WRITE   equ     0x02    Write data to memory instruction
;                cs      equ     nn      Port B bit for eeprom chip select
;                wip     equ     0x00    write in progress bit of EEPROM
;                                        status
;
;        All communications via SPI Address Mode D (CHPA=0,CPOL=0)
;        (SPICOMS.TXT Module SPIMD)
;-------------------------------------------------------------------------------
;        Module: WRITESR
;        Write to EEPROM status register
;
;        On entry: data to write to status register is in data0
;        Note: To disable all array protection: data0 = 0x00
;
;-------------------------------------------------------------------------------
writesr bsf     portb,cs        ;idle clock for Mode D
        bcf     portb,sck
        bcf     portb,cs        ;select eeprom
        movlw   WREN            ;write enable instruction
        movwf   datout          ;send it
        call    spimd
        bsf     portb,cs        ;de-select eeprom
        nop
        bcf     portb,cs        ;select eeprom
        movlw   WRSR            ;write to status register instruction
        movwf   datout          ;send it
        call    spimd
        movf    data0,w         ;data to status register
        movwf   datout          ;send it
        call    spimd
        bsf     portb,cs        ;de-select eeprom
```

```
                call    poll                ;wait while eeprom busy
                retlw   0                   ;exit
;------------------------------------------------------------------
;       Module: READSR
;       Read EEPROM status register
;
;       On exit: Status register contents in data0
;
;------------------------------------------------------------------
readsr  bsf     portb,cs            ;idle clock for Mode D
        bcf     portb,sck
        bcf     portb,cs            ;select eeprom
        movlw   RDSR                ;read status register instruction
        movwf   datout
        call    spimd               ;send it
        call    spimd               ;read register
        movf    datin,w             ;register contents to data0
        movwf   data0
        bsf     portb,cs            ;de-select eeprom
        retlw   0                   ;exit
;------------------------------------------------------------------
;       Module: CLOSE
;       Disable all write operations
;
;------------------------------------------------------------------
close   bsf     portb,cs            ;idle clock for Mode D
        bcf     portb,sck
        bcf     portb,cs            ;select eeprom
        movlw   WRDI                ;write disable instruction
        movwf   datout              ;send it
        call    spimd
        bsf     portb,cs            ;de-select eeprom
        call    poll                ;wait until EEPROM finished
        retlw   0                   ;exit
;------------------------------------------------------------------
;       Module: POLL
;       Poll EEPROM for busy
;
;------------------------------------------------------------------
poll    bsf     portb,cs            ;idle clock for Mode D
        bcf     portb,sck
poll1   bcf     portb,cs            ;select eeprom
        movlw   RDSR                ;read status register instruction
        movwf   datout
        call    spimd               ;send the instructon
        call    spimd               ;send dummy to read status
        bsf     portb,cs            ;de-select EEPROM
        btfsc   datin,wip           ;still busy ? if no, skip next
        goto    poll1               ;yes. go try again
        retlw   0                   ;no. exit
;------------------------------------------------------------------
;       Module: PREWRT
;       Send preamble for data write
;
```

```
;         On entry: EEPROM address in (addr1, addr0)
;
;         On exit: EEPROM selected and SCK low
;-----------------------------------------------------------------------
prewrt  bsf     portb,cs        ;idle clock for Mode D
        bcf     portb,sck
        bcf     portb,cs        ;select eeprom
        movlw   WREN            ;write enable instruction
        movwf   datout          ;send it
        call    spimd
        bsf     portb,cs        ;de-select eeprom
        nop
        bcf     portb,cs        ;select eeprom
        movlw   WRITE           ;write instruction
        movwf   datout          ;send it
        call    spimd
        movf    addr1,w         ;eeprom address high byte
        movwf   datout          ;send it
        call    spimd
        movf    addr0,w         ;eeprom address low byte
        movwf   datout          ;send it
        call    spimd
        retlw   0               ;exit
;-----------------------------------------------------------------------
;         Module: ONEOUT
;         One byte data write
;
;         On entry: EEPROM address in (addr1, addr0)
;                   Data byte in data0
;
;-----------------------------------------------------------------------
oneout  call    prewrt          ;send write preamble
        movf    data0,w         ;data to write
        movwf   datout          ;send it
        call    spimd
        bsf     portb,cs        ;de-select eeprom
        call    poll            ;wait while eeprom busy
        retlw   0               ;exit
;-----------------------------------------------------------------------
;         Module: MLTOUT
;         Multiple byte (page write) write
;
;         On entry: EEPROM start address in (addr1, addr0)
;                   Data bytes in buffer beginning at bufstrt
;                   Number of bytes to write in datctr
;
;         NOTE: Page is MAXIMUM of 16 bytes. Pages begin at EEPROM addresses
;               having lowest 4 bits = 0. Page writes may begin at any location
;               within the page, but CROSSING PAGE BOUNDRIES IS DANGEROUS.
;               See Section 9.5.1.
;-----------------------------------------------------------------------
mltout  call    prewrt          ;send write preamble
        movlw   bufstrt         ;pointer to start of buffer
        movwf   fsr
```

361

```
mltout1 movf    indf,w          ;data byte from buffer
        movwf   datout          ;send it
        call    spimd
        incf    fsr,f           ;point to next data
        decfsz  datctr,f        ;all bytes done ? if yes, skip next
        goto    mltout1         ;no. go send next byte
        bsf     portb,cs        ;de-select eeprom
        call    poll            ;wait while eeprom busy
        retlw   0               ;exit
;----------------------------------------------------------------------------
;       Module:PRERD
;       Send preamble for data read
;
;       On entry: EEPROM address in (addr1, addr0)
;
;       On exit: EEPROM selected and SCK low
;----------------------------------------------------------------------------
prerd   bsf     portb,cs        ;idle clock for mode D
        bcf     portb,sck
        bcf     portb,cs        ;select eeprom
        movlw   READ            ;read instruction
        movwf   datout          ;send it
        call    spimd
        movf    addr1,w         ;eeprom address high byte
        movwf   datout          ;send it
        call    spimd
        movf    addr0,w         ;eeprom address low byte
        movwf   datout          ;send it
        call    spimd
        retlw   0               ;exit
;----------------------------------------------------------------------------
;       Module: ONEIN
;       One byte data read
;
;       On entry: EEPROM address in (addr1, addr0)
;
;       On exit: Read data byte in data0
;----------------------------------------------------------------------------
onein   call    prerd           ;send read preamble
        call    spimd           ;read byte from eeprom
        movf    datin,w         ;read byte to data0
        movwf   data0
        bsf     portb,cs        ;de-select eeprom
        retlw   0               ;exit
;----------------------------------------------------------------------------
;       Module: MLTIN
;       Multiple byte read
;
;       On entry: EEPROM start address in (addr1,addr0)
;                 Number of bytes to read in datctr
;
;       On exit; Bytes read in buffer beginning at bufstrt
;
;----------------------------------------------------------------------------
```

```
mltin    call    prerd           ;send read preamble
         movlw   bufstrt         ;pointer to start of buffer
         movwf   fsr
mltin1   call    spimd           ;read byte
         movf    datin,w         ;move it to buffer
         movwf   indf
         incf    fsr,f           ;point to next buffer location
         decfsz  datctr,f        ;all bytes done ? if yes, skip next
         goto    mltin1          ;no. go read next byte
         bsf     portb,cs        ;de-select eeprom
         retlw   0               ;exit
;===============================================================================
```

9.5.2 Using the Section 9.5 Routines in Your Applications

Generally all of the routines can be used in your applications as written or with minor changes. For all routines, the entry and exit conditions, variables, port definitions and flag definitions are described in the xx.GRP and xx.TXT listings. All port assignments are arbitrary and may be changed to suit your application. See Section 9.6 for a sample application using the EEPROM routines.

The routines introduced in Section 9.5 are in:

EE25C.GRP   SPI Master Bit-Bang EEPROM Services

The routines in this group are all *called* functions. All of the routines in this group call the SPI bit-bang communications service SPIMD (see SPICOMS.GRP, Section 9.2.1). Any of the EE25C functions not required by your application may be deleted.

These routines may be used with all 25xxx series 16 bit address SPI EEPROMS. The major differences between members of the 16 bit address 25xxx families are total memory array size and page size. The versions with smaller memory size tend to have smaller page size or no paging. Page size also varies by manufacturer. The very small 25xxx series devices have eight bit addressing. The EE25C.GRP routines may be applied to these small devices by modifying PREWRT and PRERD to send only one address byte.

The module POLL tests the **wip** bit in the status register to determine when the write cycle is completed. All EEPROM applications require the POLL function but many do not need to read any other bits in the status register. For this reason POLL directly reads the status register and the read-status-register service READSR need not be included in your application. If your application requires READSR and code space is an issue, POLL may be changed to:

```
poll     call    readsr
         btfsc   datin,wip
         goto    poll
         retlw   0
```

Note that POLL continuously loops until the **wip** bit is cleared. If for some reason a cleared **wip** is not recognized, POLL will become an infinite loop. As a safety factor, a time-out and error flag may be added to POLL. If a time-out occurs POLL should exit passing the error condition via the flag. See EEPOL.TXT, Section 8.4.1, for an example of polling with time-out.

If an application requires a large number of sequential reads (too many for a RAM buffer) from contiguous memory, such as a memory dump to a PC, you can use the HOLD feature. Using the HOLD allows your application to keep the device enabled and pointing to the next EEPROM memory location while the application services the data transmission to the PC. This eliminates the need for the application to keep a record of the current EEPROM address and re-addressing the device for read (via calls to PREWRT). See the manufacturers product literature for more information on the HOLD feature. A sequential read that reads to the end of the memory array will wrap around and continue reading at the start of memory.

9.6 Putting It All Together: A Data Logger Application Using the Bit-Bang SPI Master and Slave Services, the A/D Services and the EEPROM Services

This application is a simple data logger that periodically measures a voltage, stores it in EEP-ROM and after a number of measurements have been logged, displays the data sequentially to an LCD display. The A/D and EEPROM are hardware slave devices and the LCD display is a PICmicro bit-bang slave device. The master program uses services from Sections 9.2.1, 9.3 and 9.5. The slave program uses services from Section 9.2.2. Figure 9-19 illustrates the MAX 187 A/D and 25C080 EEPROM hardware, Figure 9-22 the slave display hardware and Figure 9-4 the master hardware.

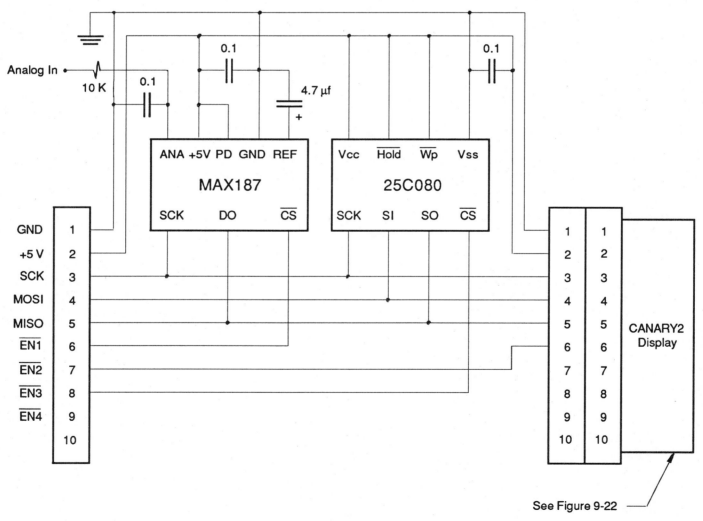

Figure 9-19   Slave Schematic; YELLOW2 Application

9.6.1 YELLOW2.ASM: Bit-Bang SPI Data Logger Master Application

See Figure 9-20 and YELLOW2.ASM

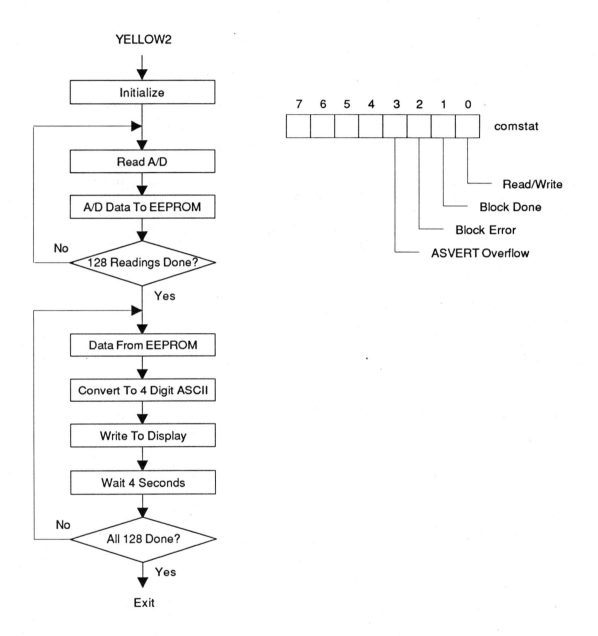

Figure 9-20   YELLOW2

YELLOW2 accesses the A/D to measure a voltage at its input and writes the A/D result (as two byte binary) to the EEPROM. The measurements are made at a rate of approximately 5 times per second. Each A/D measurement is written to successive two byte blocks of EEPROM until 100 measurements are completed. After having completed the 100 measurements, YELLOW2 accesses each result, beginning with the first and ending with the last, from the EEPROM and displays it to the LCD display. Each measurement is retrieved from the EEPROM at approximately four second intervals. This simplistic data logger serves primarily to demonstrate the application of the previously introduced SPI services and the slave LCD display CANARY2 (Section 9.6.2).

YELLOW2 applies the previously discussed modules: SPICOMS.GRP (Section 9.2.1), SPIATOD.TXT (Section 9.3), EE25C.GRP (Section 9.5.1) and ASVERT.TXT (Section 8.5.2) and introduces two new modules: SPIKEEP.TXT and SPIDISP.TXT. SPIKEEP is an SPI version of the I^2C two-byte EEPROM data log service KEEP (Section 8.5.3). SPIDISP is the service required for communications with the slave LCD display application CANARY2 (Section 9.6.2).

YELLOW2 implements two main loops: the read A/D and store to EEPROM loop and the read EEPROM and write to display loop. See Figure 9-20.

SPIKEEP is similar to the I^2C EEPROM data log service KEEP (Section 8.5.3). It writes a two-byte data block to the EEPROM or reads a two-byte data block from the EEPROM. Write or read is determined by the state of the **comstat** read/write bit. SPIKEEP allocates 200 bytes of contiguous memory for 100 two-byte blocks. The allocated memory must start at a block boundary. SPIKEEP may be modified to write blocks larger than two byes, but the block size must be limited to 4, 8, or 16 bytes to prevent page boundary problems. See the module SPIKEEP.TXT in YELLOW2.ASM for further information.

SPIDISP follows the protocol required by CANARY2 (Section 9.6.2): It repeatedly sends a character until it is informed by the slave that the character was accepted. SPIDISP does not exit (return) until the character is accepted. The character is passed to the module via **dispdat**.

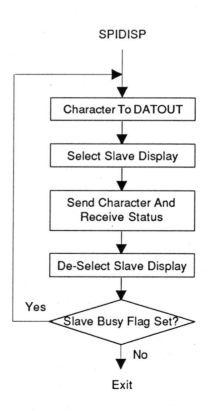

Figure 9-21   SPIDISP - Write To CANARY2

```
;====== YELLOW2.ASM ================================================
;
;          BIT-BANG SPI  APPLICATION  -  DATA LOGGER
;          Demonstrates SPI Analog to Digital converter (MAX 187), SPI EEPROM
;          SPI slave display. Continuously performs an A/D conversion and places
;          conversion result into a block of memory of EEPROM. After completing
;          128 conversions, reads EEPROM block and displays all 128 conversions
;          to the LCD display at approx 4 second intervals.
;
;          Bit-Bang SPI salve application is CANARY2
;          See Sections 9.6, 9.6.1 and 9.6.2
;
;------------------------------------------------------------------
            radix    hex        ;RADIX is HEX
;
            list p=16f84
;
;          STATUS REGISTER BIT DEFINITIONS:
c           equ      0          ;carry bit of status register (bit 0)
z           equ      2          ;zero flag bit of status register (bit 2)
dc          equ      1          ;digit carry
pd          equ      3          ;power down bit
to          equ      4          ;time out bit
rp0         equ      5          ;program page preselect, low bit
rp1         equ      6          ;program page preselect, high bit
;
;          DESTINATION BIT DEFINITIONS:
w           equ      0          ;destination working
f           equ      1          ;destination file
;
;------------------------------------------------------------------
;     CPU EQUATES  (special function register memory map)
;
;   BANK 0:
indf        equ      00         ;indirect file register
tmr0        equ      01         ;timer
pcl         equ      02         ;program counter (low byte)
status      equ      03         ;status register
fsr         equ      04         ;indirect data pointer
porta       equ      05         ;port a
portb       equ      06         ;port b
eedata      equ      08         ;eeprom data
eeadr       equ      09         ;eeprom address
pclath      equ      0a         ;write buffer for program counter (high byte)
intcon      equ      0b         ;interrupt control register
;
;   BANK 1:
optreg      equ      01         ;option register                bank 1 (0x81)
trisa       equ      05         ;data direction register port a  bank 1 (0x85)
trisb       equ      06         ;data direction register port b  bank 1 (0x86)
eecon1      equ      08         ;eeprom control register         bank 1 (0x88)
;------------------------------------------------------------------
;     WORK AREA  (memory map)  Starts at 000c
;
```

```
datout   equ      000c       ;data byte to write to MOSI
datin    equ      000d       ;data byte read from MISO
bitctr   equ      000e       ;bit counter
datctr   equ      000f       ;byte counter
counter  equ      0010       ;general counter
addr1    equ      0011       ;eeprom location (address) high byte
addr0    equ      0012       ;eeprom location (address) low byte
timctr   equ      0013       ;timeout counter
comstat  equ      0014       ;communications and system flags
temp     equ      0015       ;temporary storage
dispdat  equ      0016       ;character to display
cntrb    equ      0017       ;delay counter parameters
cntra    equ      0018
dlyctr   equ      0019
;
data1    equ      001a       ;high data byte
data0    equ      001b       ;low data byte
anacnt   equ      001c       ;block counter
;
asc4     equ      0020       ;used by ASVERT
asc3     equ      0021
asc2     equ      0022
asc1     equ      0023
asc0     equ      0024
pten1    equ      0025
pten0    equ      0026
index    equ      0027
;
bufstrt  equ      0028       ;beginning of buffer
;-------------------------------------------------------------------------
;          SYSTEM EQUATES
;
dispen   equ      04         ;port B4 is display enable
miso     equ      05         ;port B5 is MISO
mosi     equ      06         ;port B6 is MOSI
sck      equ      07         ;port B7 is IIC clock
adcen    equ      03         ;port B3 is A/D enable
anast1   equ      00         ;beginning of A/D eeprom memory area (high byte)
anast0   equ      20         ;                                    (low byte)
anamax   equ      64         ;A/D eeprom allocated memory block size
;
;          comstat flag bit definitions:
rw       equ      00         ;read/write select flag for EESEQ (bit 0)
done     equ      01         ;all-memory-block-used flag for SPIKEEP (bit1)
bkerr    equ      02         ;EEPROM block error flag (see SPIKEEP) (bit 2)
ovrfl    equ      07         ;flag for ASVERT (bit 7)
;
;        equates required by EE25C.TXT
WREN     equ      0x06       ;write enable instruction
WRDI     equ      0x04       ;write disable instruction
RDSR     equ      0x05       ;read status register instruction
WRSR     equ      0x01       ;write status register instruction
READ     equ      0x03       ;Read data from memory instruction
WRITE    equ      0x02       ;Write data to memory instruction
```

```
cs        equ       0x02          ;Port B bit for eeprom chip select
wip       equ       0x00          ;write in progress bit of EEPROM status
;
busy      equ       00            ;display status busy flag bit

SOH       equ       01            ;ascii SOH
DEE       equ       44            ;ascii D
EE        equ       45            ;ascii E
GEE       equ       47            ;ascii G
EYE       equ       49            ;ascii I
ELL       equ       4c            ;ascii L
ENN       equ       4e            ;ascii N
OH        equ       4f            ;ascii O
VEE       equ       56            ;ascii V
SP        equ       20            ;ascii space
DOT       equ       2e            ;ascii dot
;
;----------------------------------------------------------------------
          org       0x00          ;start of program memory
          goto      start         ;jump over tables
;
;------------------
tbl1      addwf     pcl,f         ;tables for asvert
          retlw     027
          retlw     003
          retlw     000
          retlw     000
;
tbl0      addwf     pcl,f
          retlw     010
          retlw     0e8
          retlw     064
          retlw     00a
;------------------
DOING     addwf     pcl,f         ; "DOING" table
          retlw     GEE
          retlw     ENN
          retlw     EYE
          retlw     OH
          retlw     DEE
;------------------
LOGGED    addwf     pcl,f         ; "LOGGED" table
          retlw     DEE
          retlw     EE
          retlw     GEE
          retlw     GEE
          retlw     OH
          retlw     ELL
;------------------
DONE      addwf     pcl,f         ; "DONE" table
          retlw     EE
          retlw     ENN
          retlw     OH
          retlw     DEE
```

369

```
;-------------------------------------------------------------------
;
start   movlw   0ff
        movwf   portb
        movwf   porta
        bsf     status,rp0      ;switch to bank 1
        movlw   00e9            ;all port a as outputs
        movwf   trisa
        movlw   0020            ;portb 5 input, others outputs
        movwf   trisb
        bcf     status,rp0      ;switch to bank 0
;
        call    second          ;wait 1 second
        movlw   SOH             ;initialize and clear display
        movwf   dispdat
        call    spidisp
        call    dly             ;wait approx 200 mS for initialize
;
        movlw   05              ;display DOING
        movwf   index
strt1   decf    index,w
        call    DOING
        movwf   dispdat
        call    spidisp
        decfsz  index,f
        goto    strt1
        clrf    data0           ;init EEPROM for NO protection
        call    writesr
        call    close
;
mloop   clrf    anacnt          ;initialize block counter
        clrf    comstat         ;clear comms flags
;
mloop1  call    dly             ;wait approx 200 mS
        call    spiatod         ;measure voltage
;
        movf    data1,w         ;A/D data to buffer
        movwf   bufstrt
        movf    data0,w
        movwf   bufstrt+1
        bcf     comstat,rw      ;select EEPROM write
        call    keep            ;store voltage to memory
        btfss   comstat,done    ;all A/D conversions done ? if yes, skip
        goto    mloop1          ;no. go do next conversion
        clrf    anacnt          ;yes. initialize block counter (for reads)
        bcf     comstat,done    ;clear all done flag
;
        movlw   SOH             ;clear display
        movwf   dispdat
        call    spidisp
        call    dly             ;wait approx 200 mS
        movlw   06              ;display "LOGGED"
        movwf   index
strt2   decf    index,w
```

```
            call      LOGGED
            movwf     dispdat
            call      spidisp
            decfsz    index,f
            goto      strt2
;
mloop2      call      foursec         ;wait 4 seconds
            movlw     SOH             ;clear display
            movwf     dispdat
            call      spidisp
            call      dly             ;wait approx 200 mS
            bsf       comstat,rw      ;select EEPROM read
            call      keep            ;read voltage from memory
            movf      bufstrt,w       ;buffer contents to data
            movwf     data1
            movf      bufstrt+1,w
            movwf     data0
            call      asvert          ;convert it to ascii
            call      display         ;format and send it to slave display
            btfss     comstat,done    ;all of memory block read ? if yes, skip next
            goto      mloop2          ;no. go read next
            bcf       comstat,done    ;clear done flag
;
            movlw     SOH             ;clear display
            movwf     dispdat
            call      spidisp
            call      dly             ;wait approx 200 mS
            movlw     04              ;display "DONE"
            movwf     index
strt3       decf      index,w
            call      DONE
            movwf     dispdat
            call      spidisp
            decfsz    index,f
            goto      strt3
;
dead        goto      dead            ;all done. dead loop
;-------------------------------------------------------------------------
;           INCLUDED FILES
;
;           EE25C.GRP       SPI EEPROM Communications Services
;           SPIATOD.TXT     SPI A/D
;           SPICOMMS.GRP    Bit-Bang SPI Communications Services
;-------------------------------------------------------------------------
            include ee25c.grp
            include spiatod.txt
            include spicoms.grp
;-------------------------------------------------------------------------
;           Module: SPIFA
;           Transfers 1 byte over SPI bus.
;           (Clock Mode A: CPHA = 1, CPOL = 1)
;
;           VARIABLE CLOCK RATE VERSION   (Clock rate determined by called
;                                           subroutine: filler)
```

371

```
;              Note: This routine places calls 1 level down (calls filler).
;
;              On Entry:   SCK line must be high
;                          Data to be sent is in datout
;
;              On Exit:    SCK line is high
;                          Data received is in datin
;--------------------------------------------------------------------------
spifa   movlw   d'8'              ;8 data bytes
        movwf   bitctr
spifa0  bcf     portb,sck         ;take clock low
        rlf     datout,f          ;data out bit to MOSI
        btfss   status,c          ;bit = 1 ? if yes, skip next
        goto    spifa1            ;no. go
        bsf     portb,mosi        ;yes. set MOSI
        goto    spifa2            ;& go
spifa1  bcf     portb,mosi        ;clear MOSI
spifa2  call    filler            ;time filler
        bsf     portb,sck         ;take clock high
        bcf     status,c          ;clear carry
        btfsc   portb,miso        ;MISO set ? if no skip
        bsf     status,c          ;yes. set carry
        rlf     datin,f           ;MISO level to data in
        call    filler            ;time filler
        decfsz  bitctr,f          ;all bits done ? if yes skip next
        goto    spifa0            ;no. go do next bit
        retlw   0                 ;yes. exit
;
;--------------------------------------------------------------------------
;              When called adds approx    ((dlyctr)*(3) + 3) cycles
;
filler  movlw   6                 ;add approx 21 cycles
        movwf   dlyctr
filler1 decfsz  dlyctr,f
        goto    filler1
        retlw   0
;==========================================================================
;              Module SPIKEEP.TXT
;
;              Stores two byte A/D data to EEPROM  (25xxx) or
;              reads two bytes of stored A/D data from EEPROM.
;              The two byte values are stored sequentially in an allocated block of
;              EEPROM memory (256 bytes MAX).
;
;              The A/D data is stored to EEPROM  beginning at EEPROM location
;              (anast1, anast0). Each successive two byte A/D data value is stored
;              sequentially in the EEPROM. The EEPROM location is maintained by a
;              counter (anacnt) that counts the two byte A/D data value. The
;              location is determined by doubling the count and adding it to
;              anastrt. If all bytes of the block have been written to, (or read
;              from) exits with done flag set. Make sure (anast1, anast0) +
;              twice anamax does not exceed maximum EEPROM address.
;
;              The A/D data is read from the EEPROM beginning at EEPROM location
```

```
;             (anast1,anast0). Each successive two byte block is read sequentially
;             from the EEPROM. If all bytes of block have been read, exits with
;             done flag set.
;
;             If KEEP is called with done flag set, exits with block-error
;             flag set.
;
;             If called for write, data must be in buffer at entry. If called
;             for read, data in buffer at exit.
;
;             comstat flags:
;                     rw bit of comstat: read/write select (=1 for read)
;                                                          (=0 for write)
;                     done bit of comstat: all-memory-block-done flag
;                     bkerr bit of comstat: block-error flag
;
;             Required literals:
;                     anast1          Beginning of A/D memory area (High Byte)
;                     anast0          Beginning of A/D memory area (Low Byte)
;                                     This MUST be an even value (bit 0 = 0)
;                     anamax          Maximum number of conversions stored in A/D
;                                     memory area of EEPROM (cannot exceed 0x7f)
;
;             Required parameters:    All parameters required by SPICOMS.TXT and
;                     anacnt          A/D block counter (number of conversions)
;                     addr1           EEPROM location, High Byte (used by EE25C)
;                     addr0           EEPROM location, Low Byte  (used by EE25C)
;                     datctr          number of bytes to write   (used by EE25C)
;                     comstat         spi status
;-----------------------------------------------------------------------------
keep    btfsc   comstat,done    ;all of block done ? if no skip
        goto    keepe           ;yes. go error exit
        bsf     portb,cs        ;make sure de-selected
        bsf     portb,sck       ;make sure clock idling high (Mode A)
        movf    anacnt,w        ;no. get current data count
        movwf   temp            ;temporary anacnt
        bcf     status,c        ;double it
        rlf     temp,f
        movlw   anast1          ;add doubled count to start location
        movwf   addr1
        movlw   anast0
        movwf   addr0
        movf    temp,w          ;doubled data count
        addwf   addr0,f
        btfsc   status,c
        incf    addr1,f
        movlw   02              ;two bytes to read or write
        movwf   datctr
        btfss   comstat,rw      ;for read ? if yes skip next
        goto    keep1           ;no. go write
        call    mltin           ;yes. read it
```

373

```
        goto    keep2           ;& go
keep1   call    mltout          ;write it
keep2   incf    anacnt,f        ;set up for next read or write
        movlw   anamax          ;all of allocated block used ?...
        movwf   temp
        movf    anacnt,w
        subwf   temp,w
        btfsc   status,z        ;if no skip next
        bsf     comstat,done    ;yes. set done flag
keepx   call    close           ;disable all EEPROM writes
        return                  ;no. exit
;
keepe   bsf     comstat,bkerr   ;set block-error flag
        goto    keepx           ;& go exit
;
;------------------------------------------------------------------
;       Module: ASVERT.TXT
;       Convert 12 BIT A/D result to 4 digit ascii
;       (data1, data0) => (asc3,asc2,asc1,asc0)
;
;       NOTE: This Module PLACES CALLS TWO LEVELS DEEP
;             The called routines asvert4 and asvert5 are part of this
;             module.
;       comstat flag: ovrfl (bit 7)
;------------------------------------------------------------------
asvert  clrf    index           ;convert to bcd, then to ascii
asvert1 clrf    counter
asvert2 movf    index,w
        call    asvert4
        call    asvert5
        btfss   status,c
        goto    asvert3
        incf    counter,f
        goto    asvert2
asvert3 movf    index,w
        call    asvert4
        call    asvert6
        movlw   asc4
        movwf   fsr
        movf    index,w
        addwf   fsr,f
        movlw   030             ;convert to ascii
        addwf   counter,w
        movwf   indf            ;and place in ascii block
        incf    index,f
        btfss   index,2
        goto    asvert1
        movlw   30
        addwf   data0,w
        movwf   asc0
        retlw   0
;------------------------------------------------------------------
asvert4 call    tbl1            ;read table
        movwf   pten1
```

```
        movf    index,w
        call    tbl0
        movwf   pten0
        return
;-----------------------------------------------------------------------
asvert5 comf    pten1,f
        comf    pten0,f
        movf    pten0,w
        addlw   01
        movwf   pten0
        btfsc   status,c
        incf    pten1,f
asvert6 movf    pten0,w
        addwf   data0,f
        bcf     comstat,ovrfl
        btfsc   status,c
        bsf     comstat,ovrfl
        movf    pten1,w
        addwf   data1,f
        btfss   comstat,ovrfl
        goto    asvertx
        btfsc   status,c
        goto    asvert7
        movlw   01
        addwf   data1,f
        goto    asvertx
asvert7 incf    data1,f
asvertx return
;-----------------------------------------------------------------------
;       Module DISPLAY
;       Formats display voltage to SPI slave LCD display
;       Slave application is CANARY2
;-----------------------------------------------------------------------
display movf    asc3,w          ;display ascii of voltage
        movwf   dispdat
        call    spidisp
        movlw   DOT             ;decimal point
        movwf   dispdat
        call    spidisp
        movf    asc2,w
        movwf   dispdat
        call    spidisp
        movf    asc1,w
        movwf   dispdat
        call    spidisp
        movf    asc0,w
        movwf   dispdat
        call    spidisp
displx  return                  ;exit
;-----------------------------------------------------------------------
;       Module SPIDISP.TXT
;       Writes a character to the slave display application CANARY2 via
;       the SPI bus. CANARY2 is an SPI Mode A device.
;
```

```
;           On entry the character to display is in dispdat.
;           On exit the character is not corrupted.
;           Exits after slave accepts the character. If slave is busy, does not
;           exit until slave accepts the character.  See Section 9.6.2
;           NOTE: Uses stretched clock Mode A service SPIFA
;           Requires workspace:
;                   As for SPICOMS.GRP and:
;                   dispdat            character to be displayed
;
;           Requires equates:
;                   dispen  equ     nn      port B bit that enables slave display
;                   busy    equ     00      display status busy bit (bit 0)
;--------------------------------------------------------------------------
spidisp movf    dispdat,w       ;get character
        movwf   datout          ;character to spi out register
        bsf     portb,dispen    ;make sure CANARY2 device not enabled
        bsf     portb,sck       ;make sure clock idles high (Mode A)
        bcf     portb,dispen    ;enable CANARY2 device
        call    spifa           ;send character & receive status
        bsf     portb,dispen    ;de-select slave
        btfsc   datin,busy      ;slave busy ? if no, skip next
        goto    spidisp         ;yes. go try again
        return                  ;exit
;--------------------------------------------------------------------------
;           APPROX 4 Second and 1 Second delay
;--------------------------------------------------------------------------
foursec movlw   020             ;4 second entrance
        goto    four0
second  movlw   005             ;1 second entrance
four0   movwf   counter
four1   call    dly
        decfsz  counter,f
        goto    four1
        return
;--------------------------------------------------------------------------
dly     clrf    cntrb           ;approx 200 ms delay
dly0    clrf    cntra
dly1    decfsz  cntra,f         ;dec counter a, skip if zero
        goto    dly1            ;not zero. dec it again
        decfsz  cntrb,f         ;dec counter b, skip if zero
        goto    dly0            ;not zero. do loop again
        retlw   0               ;exit
;--------------------------------------------------------------------------
        end                     ;END OF PROGRAM
;==========================================================================
```

9.6.2 CANARY2.ASM: Bit-Bang SPI Slave LCD Display for YELLOW2

See Figures 9-22 and 9-23 and CANARY2.ASM.

CANARY2 implements a bit-bang SPI slave LCD two line by 20 character display. The slave receives and displays characters one at a time. When receiving a character from the master, the slave sends a status byte to the master. If the slave is busy, this status byte is all ones (0xFF) indicating to the master that it cannot accept the character just sent. The master must re-send the character until it is accepted and the master may attempt to send the next character. This sort of slave busy polling is quite efficient because the master is told that the character was or was not accepted. Rather than poll for acceptability (slave not busy) and then send the character if the slave can accept it, the master simply sends the character and if it was accepted moves on. If the character was not accepted, the master simply re-sends it until it is accepted.

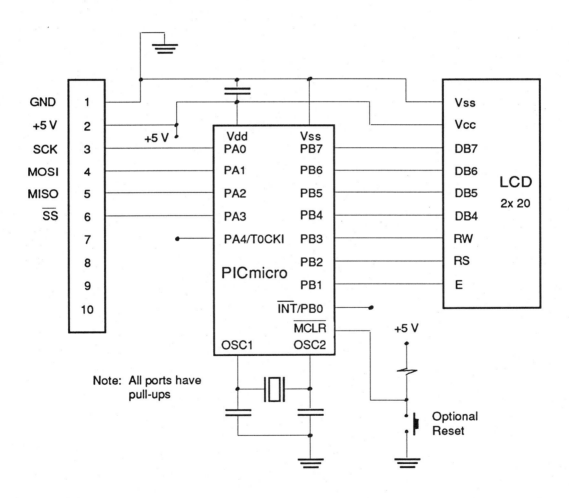

Figure 9-22   Schematic; CANARY2 Bit-Bang Slave Display

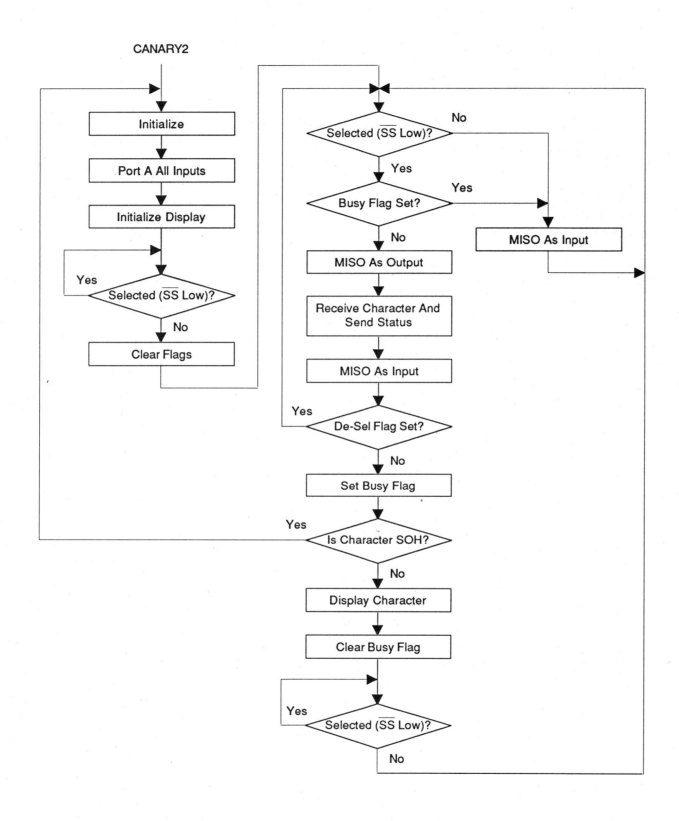

Figure 9-23   CANARY2 Display

378

If CANARY2 is busy and cannot accept new characters it makes the MISO line an input, in effect placing all ones on the MISO line; the master will received all ones. If CANARY2 is not busy (capable of accepting a new character), the **busy** bit of the slave flags register (**slvflg**) is cleared and when the slave is selected, the MISO line is made an output. When the master sends the character, the slave flags register is sent to the master as the slave status. The master uses the **busy** bit of the status byte to determine if the character was or was not accepted. A low **busy** bit indicates that the character was accepted.

The master must de-select the slave display between each byte sent. This de-select serves to re-synchronize the communications to prevent the slave from receiving partial data in the event that it ceases to be busy in the middle of a transmission from the master. If it is selected at the time that it comes out of the busy state, it will ignore all data until it has been de-selected and subsequently re-selected.

If the character sent to the slave display is SOH (0x01), this is treated as a software RESET and CANARY2 starts over at the beginning of the program. This re-initializes the LCD display: clearing the display and moving the cursor to the beginning of the line.

CANARY2 is an SPI Mode A device. See module SPIDISP in YELLOW2.ASM (Section 9.6.1) for an example of a master write-to-CANARY2 service.

```
;====== CANARY2.ASM ============================================================
;
;       SPI Bit-Bang Slave Application - LCD Display driver
;       Writes To 20 character by 2 line LCD display
;       14 Bit PIC
;
;       When slave selected (select line low):
;
;       1. If Display NOT busy receives character and sends status (slvflg)
;          back to master and writes character to display. (If busy flag
;          of status is clear, then master knows character was accepted).
;       2. If Display is busy does not accept character and sends
;          data = 0xFF back to master.
;       3. Master must de-select slave between each byte sent.
;       4. If character received is SOH (start of heading) (0x01), then
;          program starts over at START. This re-initializes display.
;       5. Slave is a SPI Mode A device.
;
;       When slave not selected (select line high): MISO line is tristate
;       (configured as an input)
;
;       See Section 9.6.2
;-------------------------------------------------------------------------------
        radix   hex        ;RADIX is HEX
;
        list p=16f84
;
```

```
;           STATUS REGISTER BIT DEFINITIONS:
c         equ     0           ;carry bit of status register (bit 0)
z         equ     2           ;zero flag bit of status register (bit 2)
dc        equ     1           ;digit carry
pd        equ     3           ;power down bit
to        equ     4           ;time out bit
rp0       equ     5           ;program page preselect, low bit
rp1       equ     6           ;program page preselect, high bit
;
;           DESTINATION BIT DEFINITIONS:
w         equ     0           ;destination working
f         equ     1           ;destination file
;
;------------------------------------------------------------------------
;       CPU EQUATES   (special function register memory map)
;
;   BANK 0:
indf      equ     00          ;indirect file register
tmr0      equ     01          ;timer
pcl       equ     02          ;program counter (low byte)
status    equ     03          ;status register
fsr       equ     04          ;indirect data pointer
porta     equ     05          ;port a
portb     equ     06          ;port b
eedata    equ     08          ;eeprom data
eeadr     equ     09          ;eeprom address
pclath    equ     0a          ;write buffer for program counter (high byte)
intcon    equ     0b          ;interrupt control register
;
;   BANK 1:
optreg    equ     01          ;option register              bank 1 (0x81)
trisa     equ     05          ;data direction register port a    bank 1 (0x85)
trisb     equ     06          ;data direction register port b    bank 1 (0x86)
eecon1    equ     08          ;eeprom control register      bank 1 (0x88)
;
;------------------------------------------------------------------------
;       WORK AREA   (memory map)   Starts at 000c
;
;
datin     equ     000c        ;data received on MOSI line
datout    equ     000d        ;data sent on MISO line
bitctr    equ     000e        ;bit counter
slvflg    equ     000f        ;slave system flags
dira      equ     0010        ;direction register a
;
;           Display Variables
;
dispflg   equ     011         ;display flags
dispdat   equ     012         ;display data
dispstat  equ     013         ;display status
temp      equ     014         ;temporary storage
bcount    equ     015
acount    equ     016
cntrb     equ     017
cntra     equ     018
```

```
;------------------------------------------------------------------------
;          System Equates
;
sel     equ     03          ;port a3 is select line
miso    equ     02          ;port a2 is MISO line
mosi    equ     01          ;port a1 is MOSI line
sck     equ     00          ;port a0 is CLOCK line
;
ambusy  equ     00          ;display-busy bit of slvflg (busy flag)
desel   equ     07          ;slave de-selected bit of slvflg (de-selected flag)
;
;          Display Equates
;
dispen  equ     01
disprs  equ     02
disprw  equ     03
;========================================================================
;          Main Program
;------------------------------------------------------------------------
        org     0x00        ;start of program memory
start   clrf    porta
        clrf    portb
        movlw   0ff
        tris    porta       ;all port a input
        tris    portb       ;all port b input
        movwf   dira        ;initialize data direction register a
        clrw
        tris    portb       ;all port b as outputs
        call    initdis     ;initialize display
sloop   btfss   porta,sel   ;currently selected ? if no, skip next
        goto    sloop       ;yes. go try again until no longer selected
        clrf    slvflg      ;clear all flags
        movf    slvflg,w
        movwf   datout      ;ready to send status
;
mloop   btfss   porta,sel   ;am I selected ? if no, skip next
        goto    mloop2      ;yes. go
mloop1  call    hizee       ;no. make MISO input
        goto    mloop       ;& go start over
;
mloop2  btfsc   slvflg,ambusy ;busy ? if no, skip next
        goto    mloop1      ;yes. go make MISO an input & start over
        bcf     dira,miso   ;no. make MISO an output
        movf    dira,w
        tris    porta
        movf    slvflg,w    ;status to datout for sending it
        movwf   datout
        call    spisma      ;receive character & send status
        call    hizee       ;make MISO an input
        btfsc   slvflg,desel ;deselected while receiving ? if no skip
        goto    mloop       ;yes. start over
        bsf     slvflg,ambusy ;set busy flag ('cause I am now busy)
        movf    datin,w     ;no. get character to...
```

```
         movwf    dispdat            ;write to display
         movwf    temp               ;before writing it: is it SOH ?
         decfsz   temp,f             ;if yes, skip next
         goto     mloop3             ;no. go display it
         goto     start              ;yes. Go Re-Initialize Slave
;
mloop3   call     dissrv             ;write it to display
         bcf      slvflg,ambusy      ;no longer busy: clear busy flag
mloop4   btfss    porta,sel          ;currently selected ? if no, skip next
         goto     mloop4             ;yes. go try again until no longer selected
         goto     mloop              ;no. go start over
;
hizee    bsf      dira,miso          ;make MISO an input
         movf     dira,w
         tris     porta
         retlw    00                 ;& return
;
;--------------------------------------------------------------------------
;        NOTE: SPISMA and DESELCT are part of SPISLAVE.GRP
;--------------------------------------------------------------------------
;        Module: SPISMA
;        Bit-Bang SPI Slave data transfer
;
;        CPHA=1, CPOL=1 (SPI Mode A)
;        On entry: Expects SCK to be HIGH
;                  Data to write to MISO in datout
;
;        On exit: Data read from MOSI in datin. If slave de-selected while
;                 in this routine, then exits with de-selected flag set.
;--------------------------------------------------------------------------
spisma   movlw    d'8'               ;8 bit byte
         movwf    bitctr
         bcf      slvflg,desel       ;clear de-selected flag
spisma1  btfss    porta,sel          ;still selected ? if no, skip next
         goto     spismaa            ;yes. go test clock
         call     deselct            ;no. de-select slave
         goto     spismax            ;& go  exit
;
spismaa  btfss    porta,sck          ;clock low ? if no, skip next
         goto     spismas            ;yes. go send bit
         goto     spisma1            ;no. go try again
;
spismas  rlf      datout,f           ;rotate bit out
         btfss    status,c           ;bit = 1 ? if yes, skip next
         goto     spisma2            ;no. go take MISO low
         bsf      porta,miso         ;yes. take MISO high
         goto     spisma3            ;& go
spisma2  bcf      porta,miso         ;take MISO low
spisma3  btfss    porta,sel          ;still selected ? if no, skip next
         goto     spismab            ;yes. go test clock
         call     deselct            ;no. de-select slave
         goto     spismax            ;& go exit
;
spismab  btfsc    porta,sck          ;clock high ? if no, skip next
```

```
                goto    spismar         ;yes. go receive bit
                goto    spisma3         ;no. go try again
;
spismar bcf     status,c        ;clear data bit
        btfsc   porta,mosi      ;MOSI high ? if no, skip next
        bsf     status,c        ;yes. set data bit
        rlf     datin,f         ;rotate it into data
        decfsz  bitctr,f        ;all bits done ? if yes, skip next
        goto    spisma1         ;no. go do next bit
spismax retlw   0               ;yes. exit
;--------------------------------------------------------------------
;       Module DESELCT
;       Bit Bang SPI Slave De-Selected (Release MISO line)
;
;       Called by SPISMA & SPISMD. May be called by application.
;       On exit: de-selected flag set and port a MISO line
;                configured as an input.
;--------------------------------------------------------------------
deselct bsf     slvflg,desel    ;set de-selected flag
        bsf     dira,miso       ;make MISO an input
        movf    dira,w
        tris    porta
        retlw   0               ;exit
;--------------------------------------------------------------------
;       INCLUDED FILES:
;
;       DISSRV.GRP      LCD Display Services    See Section 5.2.2
;--------------------------------------------------------------------
        include dissrv.grp
;
;--------------------------------------------------------------------
        end                     ;end of program
;====================================================================
```

9.7 Using a Microwire EEPROM on the SPI Bit-Bang Bus

The versatility of the SPI timing protocols and the similarity of the Microwire and SPI busses permits us to mix SPI and Microwire devices on the SPI bus. With care, most Microwire bus devices may be used on the SPI bus.

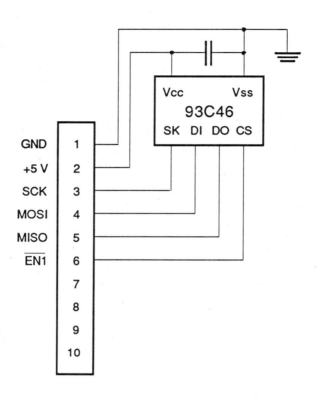

Figure 9-24   93C46 On SPI Bus

The 93xxx series Microwire EEPROMS are an attractive substitute for the SPI 25xxx series because they are generally less expensive. If an application requires a smaller memory, the cost savings can be significant and the increased software complexity is minimal. The 93C46 is typical of most Microwire EEPROMS. It is configured as 64 words of 16 bits each. Most 93xxx series devices have 16 bit word lengths and some feature selectable word lengths of 8 or 16 bits.

The 93C46 Microwire timing is shown in Figure 9-25. Note that SCK idles low and DI (MOSI) is read on the up-going clock, indicating that it receives as an SPI Mode D (CPHA=0, CPOL=0) device. Also note that DO (MISO) is valid at the down going clock, indicating that it transmits as an SPI Mode B (CPHA=1, CPOL=0) device.

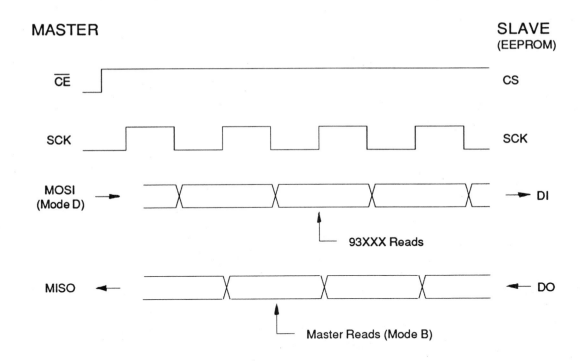

MASTER   SLAVE
                                                          (EEPROM)

$\overline{CE}$ CS

SCK   SCK

MOSI   → DI
(Mode D)

                        └── 93XXX Reads

MISO ←   ← DO

                        └── Master Reads (Mode B)

Figure 9-25   93xxx EEPROM - SPI Clock And Data Timing

The SPI to Microwire EEPROM modules in SPI93C46.GRP are similar to the Microwire EEP-
ROM modules in Section 10.3.1. Note that all writes to the 93C46 are done as if it is an SPI
Mode D device and all reads as if it is an SPI Mode B device. The Routines in SPI93C46.GRP
are:

EEOPEN	Enables EEPROM erase and write
EECLOSE	Disables EEPROM erase and write
EEWRITE	Writes 16 bits to EEPROM
EEREAD	Reads 16 bits from EEPROM
EERASE	Erase all registers

See Section 10.3.1 for functional descriptions of the modules.

```
;====== SPI93C46.GRP =======================================================
;
;       SPI93C46.GRP
;       Communicating with MICROWIRE EEPROM via the SPI bus
;       EEPROM is Type 93C46 or similar
;       See Section 9.7
;
;---------------------------------------------------------------------------
;
;       Requires following workspace:
;               Workspace required by SPICOMS.TXT
;               and:
;               eeaddr   eeprom address
```

385

```
;                     data1    data high byte write to or read from eeprom
;                     data0    data low byte
;
;         Requires following equates:
;                     equates required by SPICOMS.TXT
;                     and:
;                     ee       equ      nn       (Port B Bit for EEPROM Chip Enable)
;
;-----------------------------------------------------------------------------
;         Module: EEOPEN
;         Enable EEPROM Erase and Write
;
;         Note: Polling for 'write completed ?' is included in this module.
;
;-----------------------------------------------------------------------------
eeopen  bcf      portb,ee           ;de-select eeprom
        bcf      portb,sck          ;make sure SCK is low
        bsf      portb,ee           ;select eeprom
        movlw    01                 ;start bit
        movwf    datout
        call     spimd              ;send it
        movlw    30                 ;enable erase & write instruction
        movwf    datout
        call     spimd              ;send it
        bcf      portb,ee           ;de-select
        call     eepoll             ;wait for eeprom to finish
        retlw    0                  ;exit
;-----------------------------------------------------------------------------
;         Module: EECLOSE
;         Disable EEPROM Erase and Write, then De-select EEPROM
;
;-----------------------------------------------------------------------------
eeclose bsf      portb,ee           ;select eeprom
        movlw    01                 ;start bit
        movwf    datout
        call     spimd              ;send it
        clrf     datout             ;disable instruction
        call     spimd              ;send it
        bcf      portb,ee           ;de-select eeprom
        retlw    0                  ;exit
;-----------------------------------------------------------------------------
;         Module: EEPOLL
;         Poll eeprom DO pin for ready level
;
;-----------------------------------------------------------------------------
eepoll  bsf      portb,ee           ;select eeprom
eepoll1 clrf     datout             ;dummy data to send
        call     spimb              ;send it
        movf     datin,f            ;test returned data
        btfsc    status,z           ;00 returned ? if no, skip next
        goto     eepoll1            ;yes. go try again
        bcf      portb,ee           ;yes. de-select eeprom
        retlw    0                  ;exit
;-----------------------------------------------------------------------------
```

386

```
;          Module: EEWRITE
;          Write 16 bits to EEPROM
;
;          Note: Erase is included because some 93C46 EEPROMS do not feature
;                automatic erase before write. If not required, delete from
;                race1 to race2
;
;          Note: Polling for 'write completed ?' is included in this module.
;          Note: Each memory location is 16 bits with the most significant
;                bit in bit position 15. The 16 bit memory word is made up of
;                two 8 bit bytes (data1, data0) with the most siginificant
;                bit of data1 placed in bit position 15 and the least
;                significant bit of data0 placed in bit position 0.
;--------------------------------------------------------------------------
eewrite bsf     portb,ee            ;select eeprom
;
;race1    Here we send the erase instruction: (if not required, delete
;         from here)
         movlw   01                 ;start bit                    |
         movwf   datout             ;                             |
         call    spimd              ;send it                      |
         movlw   0c0                ;erase instruction            |
         iorwf   eeaddr,w           ;or with address              |
         movwf   datout             ;                             |
         call    spimd              ;send it                      |
         bcf     portb,ee           ;de-select eeprom             |
         call    eepoll             ;wait for ready               V
;race2    At this point the erase has been completed     (to here)
;
         bsf     portb,ee           ;select eeprom
         movlw   01                 ;start bit
         movwf   datout
         call    spimd              ;send it
         movlw   40                 ;write instruction
         iorwf   eeaddr,w           ;or with address
         movwf   datout
         call    spimd              ;send it
         movf    data1,w            ;data high byte
         movwf   datout
         call    spimd              ;send it
         movf    data0,w            ;data low byte
         movwf   datout
         call    spimd              ;send it
         bcf     portb,ee           ;de-select
         call    eepoll             ;wait for ready
         retlw   0                  ;exit
;--------------------------------------------------------------------------
;          Module: EEREAD
;          Read 16 bits from EEPROM
;
;          Reads 16 bit memory word as (data1, data0)
;--------------------------------------------------------------------------
eeread  bsf     portb,ee           ;select eeprom
        movlw   01                 ;start bit
```

387

```
          movwf     datout
          call      spimd
          movlw     80              ;read instruction
          iorwf     eeaddr,w        ;or with address
          movwf     datout
          call      spimd           ;send it
          clrf      datout          ;dummy byte to clock out read bytes
          call      spimb           ;send dummy byte (mode b)
          movf      datin,w
          movwf     data1           ;high byte to data1
          clrf      datout          ;dummy byte to clock out read bytes
          call      spimb           ;send dummy byte (mode b)
          movf      datin,w
          movwf     data0           ;low byte to data0
          bcf       portb,ee        ;de-select eeprom
          retlw     0               ;exit
;------------------------------------------------------------------------
;         Module: EERASE
;         Erase all registers
;
;         Note: Polling for 'write completed ?' is included in this module.
;------------------------------------------------------------------------
eerase    bsf       portb,ee        ;select eeprom
          movlw     01              ;start bit
          movwf     datout
          call      spimd           ;send it
          movlw     20              ;erase all instruction
          movwf     datout
          call      spimd           ;send it
          bcf       portb,ee        ;de-select eeprom
          call      eepoll          ;wait for ready
          retlw     0               ;exit
;========================================================================
```

9.8 An SPI Bit-Bang Slave Port Expander Application

Serial busses are generally employed in an application to reduce the number of controller port lines necessary to implement the application. In addition to the function specific serial peripherals, there is often a need for additional input and output ports . In some cases this requirement may be met with shift registers capable of communicating on the SPI bus. In other cases, devices with configurable input and output ports are required. The SPI to eight bit parallel input/output port described in this section fulfills the latter requirement. It is implemented as the SPI bit-bang slave application CANARY3.

9.8.1 CANARY3.ASM: SPI Bit-Bang Slave Port Expander

The CANARY3 port expander provides a configurable eight bit input/output port capable of operation on the SPI bus. Each port bit may be configured individually as an input or output. See Figure 9-26 for the schematic of the port expander. Port B is the eight bit input/output port.

388

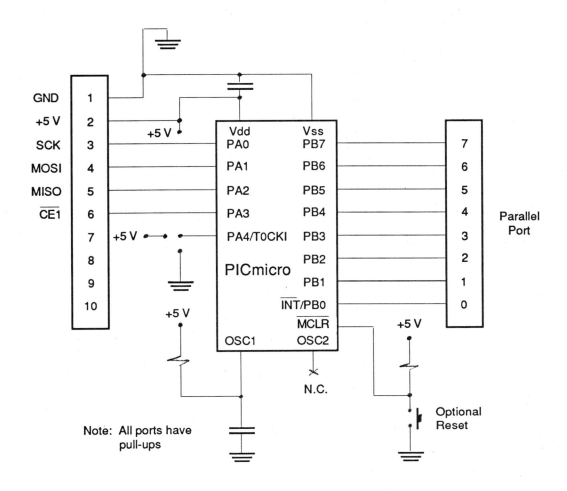

Figure 9-26   Schematic; CANARY3 Port Expander

See Figure 9-27 and CANARY3.ASM for the following discussion. All SPI port expander trans-actions are one or two bytes. The first byte is an instruction and the second byte is data to or from the port expander. Three two-byte instructions and one one-byte instruction are supported (see Figure 9-28): READ reads the eight bit port and sends the data byte read from the port back to the master as the second byte of the transaction. WRITE writes the second byte of the transaction to the port. CONFIG writes a configuration byte to a data direction register and to the port B **TRIS** register. When the master sends the first byte (the instruction) of the transaction, the slave sends the current copy of the port B **TRIS** register (slave status) to the master. Note that for the READ transaction, the second byte sent by the master is a dummy and for the WRITE and CONFIG transactions, the second byte sent by the slave is also a dummy. An exception to the two byte transaction is the STAT one-byte instruction. The slave sends a copy of the port B **TRIS** register just as with the first byte of the above described two-byte commands, but does not expect a second byte from the master.

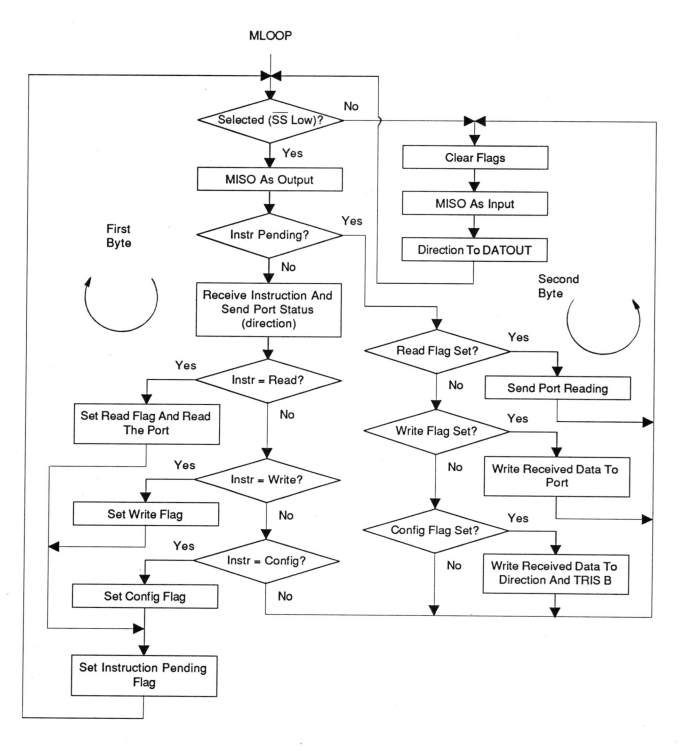

Figure 9-27   CANARY3 Port Expander

390

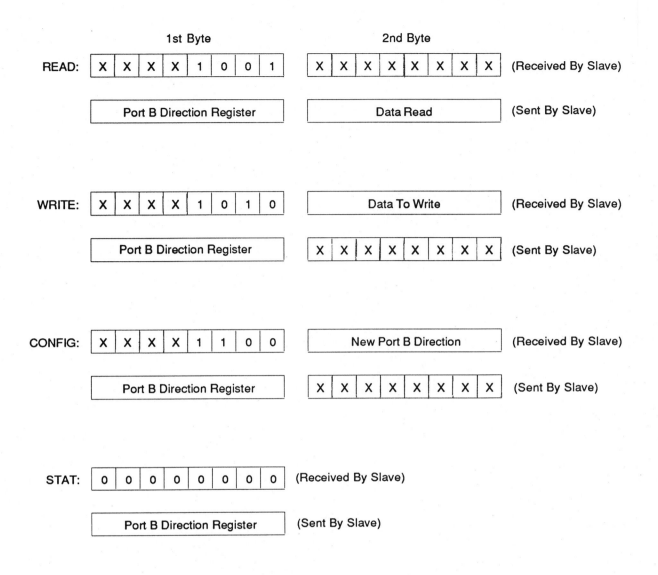

Figure 9-28   CANARY3 Transactions

Table 9-2   CANARY3 Slave Flags (**slvflg**)

BIT	FLAG	FUNCTION
0	READ (**read**)	Instruction *read* bit
1	WRITE (**write**)	Instruction *write* bit
2	CONFIGURE (**config**)	Instruction *configure* bit
3	INSTRUCTION PENDING (**inst**)	SET for valid instruction received CLEARED after instruction executed
4	Reserved	
5	Reserved	
6	Reserved	
7	DESELECTED (**desel**)	SET when slave is active CLEARED after instruction executed

NOTE: All flags are cleared prior to entry to main loop and after an instruction is executed.

Prior to beginning the transaction, the master must bring the slave port expander enable line low and it must remain low until the entire transaction is completed. If the enable returns high during the transaction, the instruction will not be processed and the slave will release the MISO line.

```
;====== CANARY3.ASM ===========================================================
;
;       SPI Bit-Bang Slave Application - PORT EXPANDER
;       SPI Serial to 8 Bit Parallel Port
;       Writes To or Reads From Port B.
;       12 or 14 Bit PIC
;
;       When slave selected (select line low):
;
;       1. If receives WRITE instruction (0x09), then writes next
;          received byte to port B.
;       2. If receives READ instruction (0x0a), then reads
;          port B and sends result as next byte.
;       3. If receives CONFIG instruction (0x0c), then writes next
;          received byte to Port B tris register.
;       4. If instruction is not READ or WRITE or CONFIG, then ignores it.
;          See Figure 9-27.
;       5. When receiving an instruction, the slave sends the current
;          status of port B (Sends copy of Port B tris register).
;       6. If instruction is 0x00, then only sends port status as in
;          5 above and does not expect second byte.
;
```

```
;           NOTE: all transactions, except number 6 above, are two bytes.
;
;           When slave not selected (select line high): MISO line is tristate
;           (configured as an input)
;
;-------------------------------------------------------------------------
            radix   hex         ;RADIX is HEX
;
            list p=16f84
;
;           STATUS REGISTER BIT DEFINITIONS:
c           equ     0           ;carry bit of status register (bit 0)
z           equ     2           ;zero flag bit of status register (bit 2)
dc          equ     1           ;digit carry
pd          equ     3           ;power down bit
to          equ     4           ;time out bit
rp0         equ     5           ;program page preselect, low bit
rp1         equ     6           ;program page preselect, high bit
;
;           DESTINATION BIT DEFINITIONS:
w           equ     0           ;destination working
f           equ     1           ;destination file
;
;-------------------------------------------------------------------------
;     CPU EQUATES  (special function register memory map)
;
;   BANK 0:
indf        equ     00          ;indirect file register
tmr0        equ     01          ;timer
pcl         equ     02          ;program counter (low byte)
status      equ     03          ;status register
fsr         equ     04          ;indirect data pointer
porta       equ     05          ;port a
portb       equ     06          ;port b
eedata      equ     08          ;eeprom data
eeadr       equ     09          ;eeprom address
pclath      equ     0a          ;write buffer for program counter (high byte)
intcon      equ     0b          ;interrupt control register
;
;   BANK 1:
optreg      equ     01          ;option register                 bank 1 (0x81)
trisa       equ     05          ;data direction register port a  bank 1 (0x85)
trisb       equ     06          ;data direction register port b  bank 1 (0x86)
eecon1      equ     08          ;eeprom control register         bank 1 (0x88)
;
;-------------------------------------------------------------------------
;     WORK AREA  (memory map)  Starts at 000c
;
;
datin       equ     000c        ;data received on MOSI line
datout      equ     000d        ;data sent on MISO line
bitctr      equ     000e        ;bit counter
slvflg      equ     000f        ;slave system flags
```

```
dira      equ     010          ;port a data direction register
dirb      equ     011          ;port b data direction register
;------------------------------------------------------------------------
;         System Equates
;
sel       equ     03           ;port a3 is select line
miso      equ     02           ;port a2 is MISO line
mosi      equ     01           ;port a1 is MOSI line
sck       equ     00           ;port a0 is CLOCK line
;
read      equ     00           ;read flag bit of slvflg & read bit of instruction
write     equ     01           ;write flag bit of slvflg & write bit of instruction
config    equ     02           ;config flag bit of slvflg & config bit of
                               ;instruction
inst      equ     03           ;instruction pending flag bit of slvflg
desel     equ     07           ;slave de-selected flag
;========================================================================
;         Main Program
;------------------------------------------------------------------------
          org     0x00         ;start of program memory
          clrf    porta
          clrf    portb
          movlw   0ff
          tris    porta        ;all port a input
          tris    portb        ;all port b input
          movwf   dira         ;initialize port a data direction register
          movwf   dirb         ;initialize port b data direction register
          movf    dirb,w       ;direction port b to SPI data out
          movwf   datout
          clrf    slvflg       ;clear flags
;
mloop     btfsc   porta,sel    ;am I selected ? if yes, skip next
          goto    cloop        ;no. go clear flags and go try again
          bcf     dira,miso    ;yes. make MISO an output
          movf    dira,w
          tris    porta
          btfsc   slvflg,inst  ;instruction pending ? if no, skip next
          goto    iloop        ;yes. go implement instruction
          call    spisma       ;receive an instruction
          btfsc   slvflg,desel ;was I deselected ? If no. skip next
          goto    cloop        ;yes. go start over
          movlw   0x0f         ;set instruction flags
          andwf   datin,w
          iorwf   slvflg,f
          btfss   slvflg,read  ;is it read instruction ? if yes, skip next
          goto    mloop1       ;no. go
          movf    portb,w      ;yes. port b data to SPI data out
          movwf   datout
mloop1    btfsc   slvflg,inst  ;instruction pending set ? if no skip next
          goto    mloop        ;yes.  go wait for next byte
;
cloop     clrf    slvflg       ;clear all flags except de-select
          bsf     dira,miso    ;make MISO an input (tristate it)
          movf    dira,w
```

```
            tris    porta
            movf    dirb,w          ;port direction register
            movwf   datout          ;direction to SPI data out
            goto    mloop           ;and go wait for next enable
;
iloop       btfsc   slvflg,read     ;read flag set ? if no, skip
            goto    rloop           ;yes. go read
            btfsc   slvflg,write    ;write flag set ? if no, skip
            goto    wloop           ;yes. go write
            btfsc   slvflg,config   ;config flag set ? if no, skip
            goto    tloop           ;yes. go change port directions
            goto    cloop           ;no. go start over
;
rloop       call    spisma          ;send port reading
            goto    cloop           ;go start over
;
wloop       call    spisma          ;receive data to write
            btfsc   slvflg,desel    ;was I de-selected ? if no, skip
            goto    cloop           ;yes. go start over
            movf    datin,w         ;write data to port b
            movwf   portb
            goto    cloop           ;and go start over
;
tloop       call    spisma          ;receive data to change direction
            btfsc   slvflg,desel    ;was I de-selected ? if no, skip
            goto    cloop           ;yes. go start over
            movf    datin,w         ;write direction data to port b tris
            tris    portb
            movwf   dirb            ;& to data direction register
            goto    cloop           ;go start over
;-----------------------------------------------------------------------
;       NOTE: SPISMA and DESELCT are a subset of SPISLAVE.GRP
;-----------------------------------------------------------------------
;       Module: SPISMA
;       Bit-Bang SPI Slave data transfer
;
;       CPHA=1, CPOL=1 (SPI Mode A)
;       On entry: Expects SCK to be HIGH
;                 Data to write to MISO in datout
;
;       On exit: Data read from MOSI in datin. If slave de-selected while
;                in this routine, then exits with de-selected flag set.
;-----------------------------------------------------------------------
spisma      movlw   d'8'            ;8 bit byte
            movwf   bitctr
            bcf     slvflg,desel    ;clear de-selected flag
spisma1     btfss   porta,sel       ;still selected ? if no, skip next
            goto    spismaa         ;yes. go test clock
            call    deselct         ;no. de-select slave
            goto    spismax         ;& go  exit
;
spismaa     btfss   porta,sck       ;clock low ? if no, skip next
            goto    spismas         ;yes. go send bit
            goto    spisma1         ;no. go try again
```

```
;
spismas  rlf     datout,f        ;rotate bit out
         btfss   status,c        ;bit = 1 ? if yes, skip next
         goto    spisma2         ;no. go take MISO low
         bsf     porta,miso      ;yes. take MISO high
         goto    spisma3         ;& go
spisma2  bcf     porta,miso      ;take MISO low
spisma3  btfss   porta,sel       ;still selected ? if no, skip next
         goto    spismab         ;yes. go test clock
         call    deselct         ;no. de-select slave
         goto    spismax         ;& go exit
;
spismab  btfsc   porta,sck       ;clock high ? if no, skip next
         goto    spismar         ;yes. go receive bit
         goto    spisma3         ;no. go try again
;
spismar  bcf     status,c        ;clear data bit
         btfsc   porta,mosi      ;MOSI high ? if no, skip next
         bsf     status,c        ;yes. set data bit
         rlf     datin,f         ;rotate it into data
         decfsz  bitctr,f        ;all bits done ? if yes, skip next
         goto    spisma1         ;no. go do next bit
spismax  retlw   0               ;yes. exit
;-----------------------------------------------------------------------
;        Module DESELCT
;        Bit Bang SPI Slave De-Selected (Release MISO line)
;
;        Called by SPISMA & SPISMD. May be called by application.
;        On exit: de-selected flag set and port a MISO line
;                 configured as an input.
;-----------------------------------------------------------------------
deselct  bsf     slvflg,desel    ;set de-selected flag
         bsf     dira,miso       ;make MISO an input
         movf    dira,w
         tris    porta
         retlw   0               ;exit
;-----------------------------------------------------------------------
         end                     ;end of program
;=======================================================================
```

9.8.2 Using the CANARY3 Port Expander in Your Applications

The CANARY3 Slave Port expander may be used unchanged with 12 or 14 bit PICmicros. When the slave is selected, be sure to leave enough set up time in your master application for the slave main loop to get to the first call to SPISMA before you begin the transaction. Likewise wait a while before re-selecting after de-selecting the slave.

Note that the instruction decoding only makes a bit test to determine if the read, write or configure bit of the instruction is set. The bits are tested in the order: read, write, configure; giving the read instruction the highest priority and configure the lowest priority. For example, if both the read bit and the write bit are set (or even the read, write and configure bits) in the instruction byte, the instruction is interpreted as read or if the read bit is cleared and the write and configure bits are set, the instruction is interpreted as write:

Instruction	Interpreted As
xxxx1000	ignore following byte
xxxx1001	read
xxxx1010	write
xxxx1011	read
xxxx1100	configure
xxxx1101	read
xxxx1110	write
xxxx1111	read
xxxx0xxx	status

If bit 3 of the instruction is not set the instruction is treated as the one byte status instruction. If the read, write or configure bit are not set but bit 3 is set, the slave will ignore the next received byte. To avoid confusion it is best to define and send only the following instruction bytes from the master:

xxxx1001	read
xxxx1010	write
xxxx1100	configure
xxxx0000	status

Note from Figure 9-27, multiple one or two byte transactions may be sent by the master without an intervening de-select. Thus the master can read the status, reconfigure the port, write to it and read from it all without disturbing the enable line after the initial enable.

From Figure 9-26 it is apparent that one port A pin is not used. This pin may be used as a device address pin so that two CANARY3 slave devices may be on the same enable line and addressed via an SPI transaction. For one of the devices the port pin would be tied low, assigning it to address 0, and for the other device tied high, assigning it address 1. CANARY3 will have to be modified in such a way that it expects two or three byte transactions and the first byte received is an address byte. Only the correctly addressed device will configure MISO as an output and will respond to the following bytes. The other slave will ignore the following bytes because its output is in effect turned off (because its MISO remains as an input). Each two or three byte transaction must be separated from the next with a de-select. The de-select will be used by the slave to reset the byte counter used to recognize the first byte.

Most of the device RAM is not used for CANARY3. This RAM may be made available as serial RAM by adding to CANARY3 additional instruction decoding and routines for addressing, writing and reading RAM. Only the RAM not used by CANARY3 is available for use as serial RAM and you must be sure to include error traps to prevent access to the RAM used by CANARY3.

You may implement any sort of peripheral function by using the techniques illustrated in CANARY3. The 12 and 14 bit PICmicros are ideal for implementing serial bit-bang peripheral functions that are not available as hardware devices.

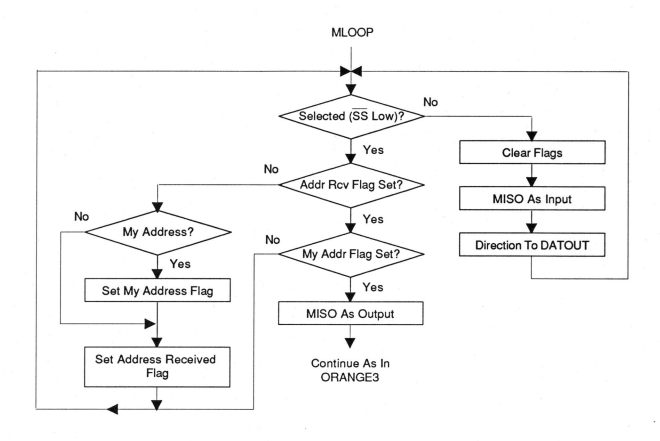

Figure 9-29   CANARY3 Modification For Addressable Port Expander

9.9 On-Chip SPI Hardware

Several of the PIC16Cxxx, 16Fxxx and 17Cxxx series microcontrollers have an on-chip Synchronous Serial Port (SSP). The on-chip SSP is capable of supporting the SPI protocol as both a master device and a slave device. The SPI support is entirely in hardware. Implementation of this hardware SPI unloads the data communications burden from the application software resulting in simpler software and more program memory available to the non-communications part of the application. An SPI master transaction is initiated by a write to an SSP buffer. No other operation is necessary; the hardware executes the entire transaction. A slave transaction is equally simple.

9.9.1 Using the On Chip SSP based SPI Hardware

The SPI portion of the SSP hardware module implements only SPI Modes A and B. In 1997 Microchip upgraded the SSP to implement all four SPI modes. This upgraded four-mode SSP retains the designation SSP and the old two-mode version has been re-designated the BSSP (Basic Synchronous Serial Port). The upgraded SSP is implemented only on new PICmicros released after the upgrade and any product literature published prior to the upgrade will refer to the BSSP as SSP. To avoid confusion about the SSP versions, all references in this book to the SSP will be understood to be the two-mode version. For our purposes, the main difference between the versions is that applications requiring Modes C and D are easier to handle with the four-mode version (see Sections 9.9.2.and 9.9.5).

For the following applications, the SSP based SPI will be referred to as the SPI or SSP SPI. Figure 9-30 is the schematic of the circuit that will be used for the demonstration SSP SPI applications. The PIC16C63 is used for all of the applications, but all of the routines may be used with other PICmicro devices with little or no change.

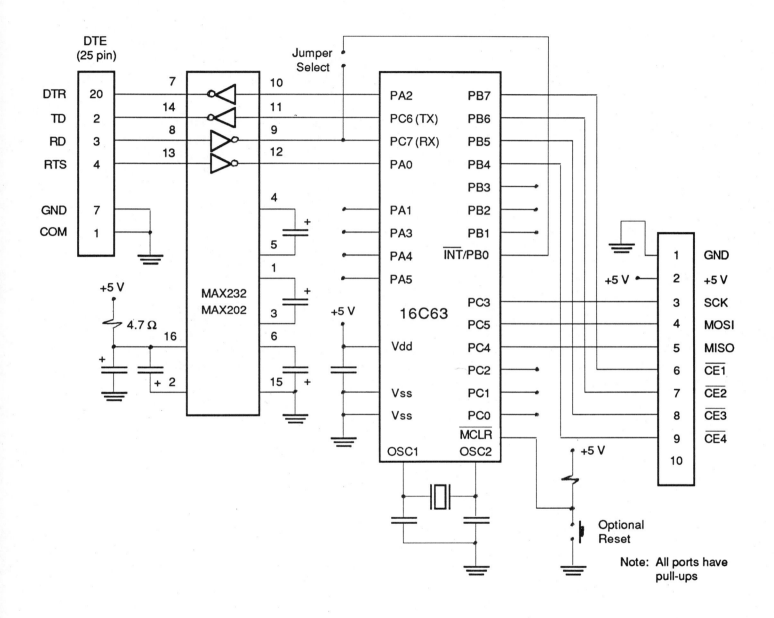

Figure 9-30   Schematic - SSP SPI Master Applications

The hardware SPI includes a transmit/receive shift register, **SSPSR**, and a buffer register **SSPBUF**. Data is passed to the application from the SPI via **SSPBUF** and from the SPI to the application via **SSPBUf**. The register **SSPSR** is not available to the application.

Data to be transmitted is written to **SSPBUF** and shadowed in **SSPSR**. In master mode, SPI data transfer begins immediately after the write to **SSPBUF**: current **SSPSR** data is clocked out of **SSPSR** while new received data is clocked into **SSPSR**. In slave mode, transfer begins with the next received clock. In accordance with the SPI protocol, data is shifted MSB first. When all eight bits of the currently received data have been shifted into **SSPSR**, the data is moved to **SSPBUF** and the buffer full flag (bit **BF** of register **SSPSTAT**) and the SSP interrupt flag (bit **SSPIF** of **PIR1**) are set. This buffer allows a new transaction to begin before the previously received byte is read by the application. The received byte must be read from **SSPBUF** before this new transfer is completed, otherwise it will be overwritten by the new byte. If **SSPBUF** is not read by the application before the next byte to be transmitted is written to **SSPBUF**, the received byte will be lost. The buffer full flag **BF** indicates that a newly received byte has been placed in **SSPBUF**. When the **SSPBUF** is read, the **BF** flag is cleared.

Generally the SSP interrupt is used to signal the application that the transfer has been completed, but polling the **bf** flag may be used as an alternate to an interrupt. Any attempt to write to **SSPBUF** during the transfer will be ignored but the write collision detect flag (bit **WCOL** of register **SSPCON**) will be set. See the Module SPIPOLL.TXT for an example of **BF** flag polling.

In addition to the SSP data register **SSPBUF**, there are 7 special registers associated with the SPI. The special registers implement the control, status and data and clock timing required by the application.

SPI Control Registers (Figure 9-31)

Port C pins PC3, PC4 and PC5 are the SSP SPI lines SCK, MISO and MOSI respectively. The port C direction register **TRISC** must configure these lines as shown in Figure 9-31. PC3 (SCK) is configured as an output for master applications and as an input for slave applications. PC4 (MISO) is configured as an input and PC5 (MOSI) as an output. If the SS pin (PA5) is to be functional, PA5 must be configured as an input via **TRISA**. In our applications, SS is not functional (the PICmicro is always master) and PA5 may be used as a general port pin.

400

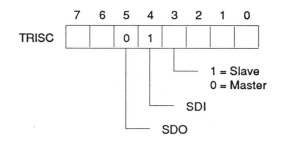

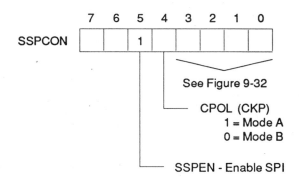

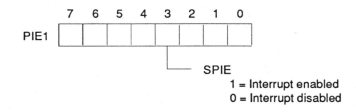

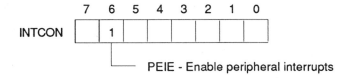

Figure 9-31   SSP Control Registers - SPI Mode

The SSP control register **SSPCON** must have bits 0 through 5 configured as in Figures 9-31 and 9-32. The SSP is enabled by setting the **SSPEN** bit of **SSPCON**. The clock polarity (CPOL) is determined by the state of the **CPOL** bit of **SSPCON**. Note that the SSP SPI clock phase (CPHA) is fixed at logic 1. The SSP SPI supports only SPI Mode A and Mode B. The SSP mode select bits **SSPM3** through **SSPM0** determine the SPI clock rates and SS functionality as shown in Figure 9-32.

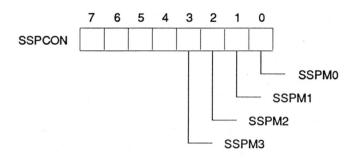

```
------------------------------------------------------
SSPM3 - SSPM0    Mode              Clock
------------------------------------------------------
      0000       Master    fosc/4
      0001       Master    fosc/16
      0010       Master    fosc/64
      0011       Master    TMR2/2
      0100       Slave     SCK Pin (SS Enabled)
      0101       Slave     SCK Pin (SS Disabled)
```

Figure 9-32   SSPCON - SSP Mode Select Bits

If the application is to respond to SPI interrupts, the peripheral interrupt enable bit **PEIE** of the **INTCON** register and the SSP interrupt enable bit **SSPIE** of the **PIE1** register must be set as shown in Figure 9-31. For these interrupt enables to be effective the global interrupt bit **GIE** of the **INTCON** register must be set.

SPI Status Registers (Figure 9-33)

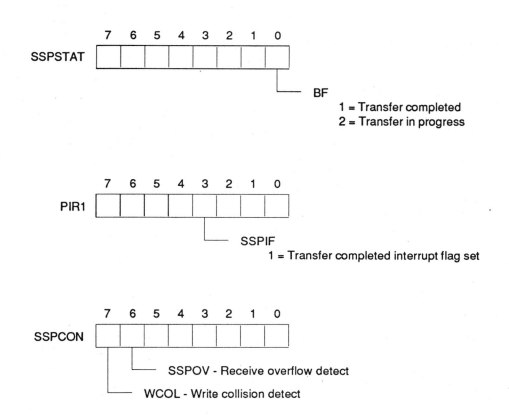

Figure 9-33   SSP Status Registers - SPI Mode

As described above, the buffer full flag **bf** of the SSP status register **SSPSTAT** is set when the SSP buffer **SSPBUF** is full. This flag is primarily used as an indication of a byte having been received. Flag **BF** is cleared when the buffer is read.

When an SPI transfer is completed the SSP interrupt flag **SSPIF** of the peripheral interrupts register **PIR1** is set. This flag must be cleared by the user prior to exiting the interrupt service.

If a write to **SSPBUF** is attempted during a transfer it will be ignored and the write collision detect flag **WCOL** of register **SSPCON** will be set. This flag must be cleared by the user.

If a new byte is received before the previously received byte has been read from **SSPBUF**, the receive overflow detect flag **SSPOV** of register **SSPCON** is set. This flag functions only in slave mode. This flag must be cleared by the user.

9.9.2 SSP Hardware SPI Serial EEPROM Communications

The bit-bang EEPROM communications services modules (EE25C.GRP) described in Section 9.5.1 may be adapted to the SSP SPI. These modules initiate transfer by writing a byte to a register and calling the bit-bang service SPIMD. The EE25C.GRP modules may be modified for implementation with the SSP SPI. The SSP SPI version is SSP25C.GRP.

The bit-bang write and call sequence is replaced with an SSP write and call sequence: write to **SSPBUF** and call SPIDONE. The write to **SSPBUF** initiates the SPI transfer and the module SPIDONE waits for the transfer to be completed.

The 25Cxxx EEPROMS are SPI Mode D devices, but the SSP SPI will only support Modes A and B. We can work around this limitation. The EEPROM may be successfully read via Mode A, but will not successfully complete a write operation using Mode A communications. To initiate a write, the clock must be low prior to de-select (see Figures 9-34 and 9-35). For all of the write functions in SSP25C.GRP, the clock is forced to be low before the device is de-selected. This is implemented with the module FIXER. FIXER re-configures the SSP SPI as Mode B to take the clock low (Mode B clock idles low). Note that FIXER is called only for write operations.

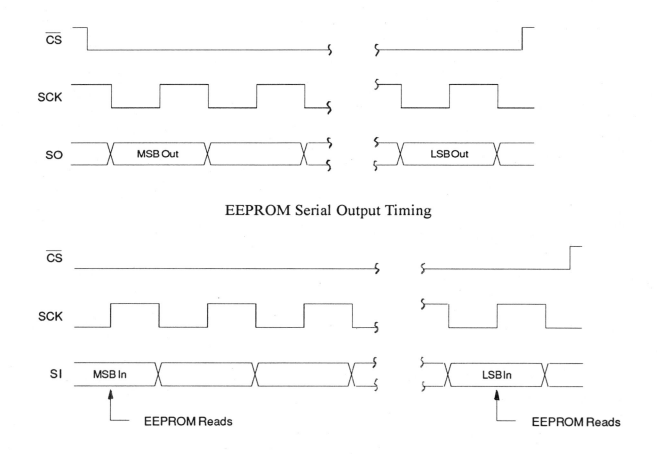

EEPROM Serial Output Timing

EEPROM Serial Intput Timing

Figure 9-34   25Cxxx EEPROM Clock And Data Timing

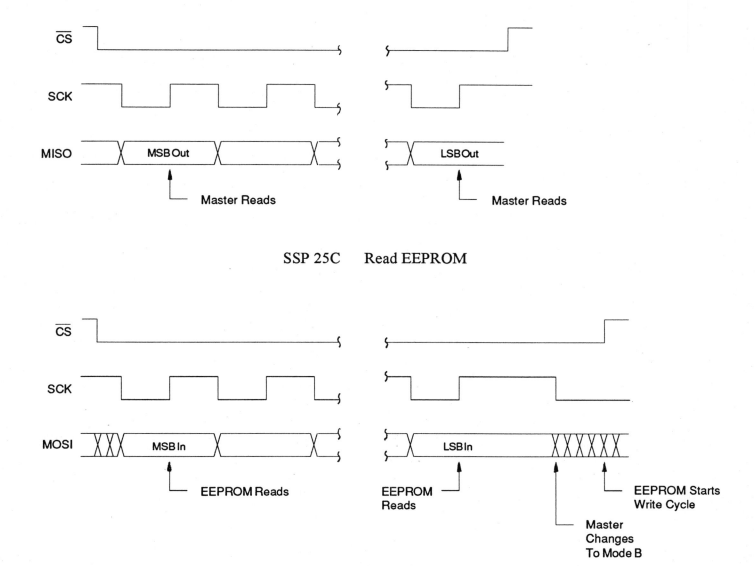

SSP 25C   Read EEPROM

SSP 25C   Write EEPROM

Figure 9-35   SSP 25C   Clock And Data Timing

```
;===============================================================================
;
;          Module: SPIDONE.TXT     (Receive Byte)
;
;-------------------------------------------------------------------------------
;
;          Tests for SSP SPI transmission/reception completed and
;          fetches received byte.
;          When completed, exits with received data byte in W register
;          See Section 9.9.1
;-------------------------------------------------------------------------------
spidone bsf     status,rp0      ;switch to bank 1
spidon1 btfss   sspstat,bf      ;completed ? if yes, skip next
        goto    spidon1         ;no. go try again
        bcf     status,rp0      ;yes. switch back to bank 0
        movf    sspbuf,w        ;get received data
        return                  ;& exit
;===============================================================================



;====== SSP25C.GRP =============================================================
;
;          COMMUNICATIONS WITH 25XXX SPI EEPROM  Using SSP Hardware SPI
;
;-------------------------------------------------------------------------------
;
;          Required workspace:
;
;                  datctr          data byte counter
;                  data0           data byte
;                  addr1           EEPROM address high byte
;                  addr0           EEPROM address low byte
;                  sspbuf          special register: SSP buffer
;                  sspstat         special register: SSP status
;                  bufstrt         begining of buffer (must be start of
;                                  contiguous memory. Buffer must be as deep
;                                  as required by application
;
;          Required equates:
;
;                  WREN    equ     06      write enable instruction
;                  WRDI    equ     04      write disable instruction
;                  RDSR    equ     05      read status register instruction
;                  WRSR    equ     01      write status register instruction
;                  READ    equ     03      read data from memory instruction
;                  WRITE   equ     02      write data to memory instruction
;                  cs      equ     nn      port B bit for eeprom chip select
;                  wip     equ     00      write in progress bit of EEPROM status
;
;      The EEPROM is an SPI Mode D device, but the BSSP ONLY supports
;      SPI Modes A and B. Reads from the EEPROM may be via Mode A, but
;      writes require Mode D. For write operations, the write is
;      initiated by a low-going select line when the clock line is LOW.
```

```
;        Mode A idles the clock high, so the clock must be taken low before
;        the device is de-selected. The sub-module FIXER implements this by
;        re-configuring the SSP for Mode B before de-selecting.
;
;        See Sections 9.9.1 and 9.9.2
;-------------------------------------------------------------------------
;        Module: WRITESR
;        Write to EEPROM status register
;
;        On entry: data to write to status register is in data0
;        Note: To disable all array protection: data0 = 0x00
;
;-------------------------------------------------------------------------
writesr call    modea           ;make sure Mode A
        bcf     portb,cs        ;select eeprom
        movlw   WREN            ;write enable instruction
        movwf   sspbuf          ;send it
        call    spidone         ;wait until spi finished
        call    fixer           ;make clock low before de-selecting
        nop
        bsf     portb,cs        ;de-select eeprom
        call    modea           ;return to Mode A
        bcf     portb,cs        ;select eeprom
        movlw   WRSR            ;write-to-status-register instruction
        movwf   sspbuf          ;send it
        call    spidone         ;wait until SPI done
        movf    data0,w         ;data for status register
        movwf   sspbuf          ;send it
        call    spidone         ;wait until SPI done
        call    fixer           ;config clock for write
        bsf     portb,cs        ;de-select eeprom
        call    poll            ;wait while eeprom busy
        retlw   0               ;exit
;-------------------------------------------------------------------------
;        Module: READSR
;        Read EEPROM status register
;
;        On exit: Status register contents in data0
;
;-------------------------------------------------------------------------
readsr  call    modea           ;make sure in Mode a
        bcf     portb,cs        ;select eeprom
        movlw   RDSR            ;read-status-register instruction
        movwf   sspbuf          ;send it
        call    spidone         ;wait until spi done
        movwf   sspbuf          ;send dummy to read register
        call    spidone         ;receive status byte
        movwf   data0           ;status byte to data0
        bsf     portb,cs        ;de-select eeprom
        retlw   0               ;exit
;-------------------------------------------------------------------------
;        Module: CLOSE
;        Disable all write operations
;
```

```
;-----------------------------------------------------------------------
close   call    modea           ;make sure in Mode A
        bcf     portb,cs        ;select eeprom
        movlw   WRDI            ;write-disable instruction
        movwf   sspbuf          ;send it
        call    spidone
        call    fixer           ;config clock for write
        bsf     portb,cs        ;de-select eeprom
        call    poll            ;wait until write cycle done
        retlw   0               ;exit
;-----------------------------------------------------------------------
;       Module: POLL
;       Poll EEPROM for busy
;
;-----------------------------------------------------------------------
poll    call    modea           ;make sure in Mode a
        bcf     portb,cs        ;select eeprom
        movlw   RDSR            ;read-status-register instruction
        movwf   sspbuf          ;send it
        call    spidone         ;wait until spi done
        movwf   sspbuf          ;send dummy to read status
        call    spidone         ;receive status byte
        movwf   data0           ;status byte to data0
        bsf     portb,cs        ;de-select eeprom
        btfsc   data0,wip       ;still busy ? if no, skip next
        goto    poll            ;yes. go try again
        retlw   0               ;no. exit
;-----------------------------------------------------------------------
;       Module: PREWRT
;       Send preamble for data write
;
;       On entry: EEPROM address in (addr1, addr0)
;
;       On exit: EEPROM selected and SCK high
;-----------------------------------------------------------------------
prewrt  call    modea           ;make sure Mode a
        bcf     portb,cs        ;select eeprom
        movlw   WREN            ;write-enable instruction
        movwf   sspbuf          ;send it
        call    spidone
        call    fixer           ;config clock for write
        bsf     portb,cs        ;de-select eeprom
        call    modea           ;return to Mode A
        bcf     portb,cs        ;select eeprom
        movlw   WRITE           ;write instruction
        movwf   sspbuf          ;send it
        call    spidone
        movf    addr1,w         ;eeprom address high byte
        movwf   sspbuf          ;send it
        call    spidone
        movf    addr0,w         ;eeprom address low byte
        movwf   sspbuf          ;send it
        call    spidone
        retlw   0               ;exit
```

```
;--------------------------------------------------------------------
;          Module: ONEOUT
;          One byte data write
;
;          On entry: EEPROM address in (addr1, addr0)
;                     Data byte in data0
;
;--------------------------------------------------------------------
oneout    call    prewrt          ;send write preamble
          movf    data0,w         ;data to write
          movwf   sspbuf          ;send it
          call    spidone
          call    fixer           ;config clock for write
          bsf     portb,cs        ;de-select eeprom
          call    poll            ;wait while eeprom busy
          retlw   0               ;exit
;--------------------------------------------------------------------
;          Module: MLTOUT
;          Multiple byte (page write) write
;
;          On entry: EEPROM start address in (addr1, addr0)
;                     Data bytes in buffer beginning at bufstrt
;                     Number of bytes to write in datctr
;
;          NOTE: Page is MAXIMUM of 16 bytes. Pages begin at EEPROM addresses
;                having lowest 4 bits = 0. Page writes may begin at any location
;                within the page, but CROSSING PAGE BOUNDRIES IS DANGEROUS.
;                See Section 9.5.1.
;--------------------------------------------------------------------
mltout    call    prewrt          ;send write preamble
          movlw   bufstrt         ;pointer to start of buffer
          movwf   fsr
mltout1   movf    indf,w          ;data byte from buffer
          movwf   sspbuf          ;send it
          call    spidone
          incf    fsr,f           ;point to next data
          decfsz  datctr,f        ;all bytes done ? if yes, skip next
          goto    mltout1         ;no. go send next byte
          call    fixer           ;config clock for write
          bsf     portb,cs        ;de-select eeprom
          call    poll            ;wait while eeprom busy
          retlw   0               ;exit
;--------------------------------------------------------------------
;          Module:PRERD
;          Send preamble for data read
;
;          On entry: EEPROM address in (addr1, addr0)
;
;          On exit: EEPROM selected and SCK high
;--------------------------------------------------------------------
prerd     call    modea
          bcf     portb,cs        ;select eeprom
          movlw   READ            ;read instruction
          movwf   sspbuf          ;send it
```

409

```
        call    spidone
        movf    addr1,w         ;eeprom address high byte
        movwf   sspbuf          ;send it
        call    spidone
        movf    addr0,w         ;eeprom address low byte
        movwf   sspbuf          ;send it
        call    spidone
        retlw   0               ;exit
;------------------------------------------------------------------
;       Module: ONEIN
;       One byte data read
;
;       On entry: EEPROM address in (addr1, addr0)
;
;       On exit: Read data byte in data0
;------------------------------------------------------------------
onein   call    prerd           ;send read preamble
        movwf   sspbuf          ;send dummy to read byte from eeprom
        call    spidone         ;receive eeprom byte
        movwf   data0           ;received byte to data0
        bsf     portb,cs        ;de-select eeprom
        retlw   0               ;exit
;------------------------------------------------------------------
;       Module: MLTIN
;       Multiple byte read
;
;       On entry: EEPROM start address in (addr1,addr0)
;                 Number of bytes to read in datctr
;
;       On exit; Bytes read in buffer beginning at bufstrt
;
;------------------------------------------------------------------
mltin   call    prerd           ;send read preamble
        movlw   bufstrt         ;pointer to start of buffer
        movwf   fsr
mltin1  movwf   sspbuf          ;send dummy to read byte
        call    spidone         ;receive byte (to w)
        movwf   indf            ;move it to buffer
        incf    fsr,f           ;point to next buffer location
        decfsz  datctr,f        ;all bytes done ? if yes, skip next
        goto    mltin1          ;no. go read next byte
        bsf     portb,cs        ;de-select eeprom
        retlw   0               ;exit
;------------------------------------------------------------------
;       FIXER
;       Takes clock low. For any write operations SPI EEPROM expects
;       clock to be low when de-select occurs. Fixer configures SSP
;       as SPI Mode B.
;       See Section 9.9.3
;------------------------------------------------------------------
fixer   bcf     sspcon,sspen    ;disable ssp
        bcf     sspcon,cpol     ;idle clock low (as in Mode B)
        bsf     sspcon,sspen    ;re-enable ssp
        return
```

```
;-------------------------------------------------------------------------------
;         MODEA    Configure SSP for Mode A
;-------------------------------------------------------------------------------
modea   bcf     sspcon,sspen    ;disable ssp
        bsf     sspcon,cpol     ;return to Mode A
        bsf     sspcon,sspen    ;re-enable ssp
        return
;===============================================================================
```

9.9.3 WHITE1.ASM: SSP Hardware SPI A/D and Display Application

The demonstration application WHITE1 is an SSP hardware SPI version of the bit-bang SPI application YELLOW1 in Section 9.4.1. They are functionally identical. WHITE1 displays an SPI A/D measured voltage to an SPI multi-digit LED display.

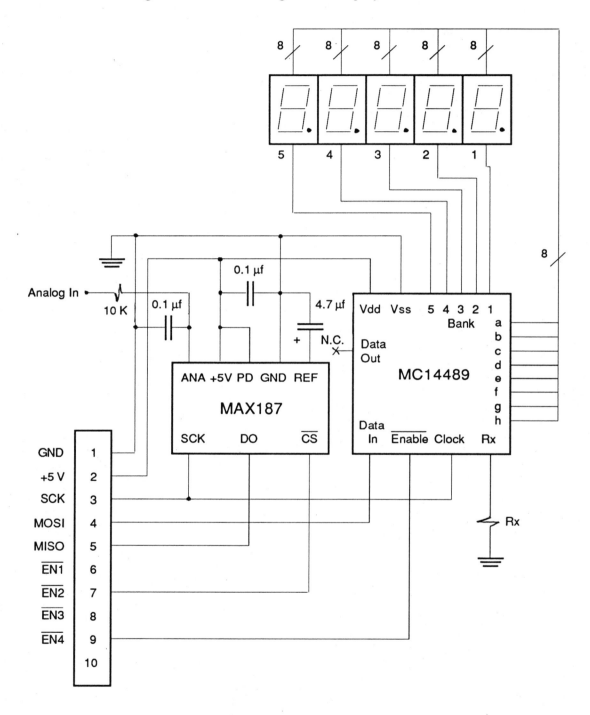

Figure 9-36   Slave Schematic; YELLOW1 And WHITE1 Applications

The module SSPATOD.TXT used in WHITE1.ASM is the SSP SPI service corresponding to the SPIATOD.TXT bit-bang service used in YELLOW1 (Sections 9.3 and 9.4). The MAX187 is a Mode D device and SPIATOD communicates with it using the bit-bang Mode D service SPIMD. Since the two-mode SSP SPI on the 16C63 does not implement Mode D transactions, some alternate method must be used to communicate with the MAX187. Carefull study of the MAX187 timing specification and the SPI mode timing diagrams in Figure 9-3 shows that it may be operated as a Mode A device. As a Mode A device, the leading high byte is not read because the first clock high-to-low transition shifts the MS bit of the conversion on to the data line to be read at the clock low-to-high transition. Thus two 8 bit SPI transfers will read the conversion result with four trailing zeros in the four least significant bits of the least significant byte. A simple normalization of the result, similar to that in SPIATOD, converts the result to a 12 bit value.

The Motorola MC14489 Display Driver is an SPI Mode D device. Since the two-mode SSP SPI on the 16C63 does not implement Mode D transactions, some alternate method must be used to communicate with the display driver. Using Mode A or changing modes during a transaction, as with the SSP SPI EEPROM services in Section 9.2.2, will not be successful because the MC14489 does not tolerate transitions on the enable (EN) line while the clock is high and the clock *must* idle low. Any attempt to change the mode prior to writing the data to the SSP register will be interpreted by the MC14489 as a clock transition and will introduce an extra leading data bit to the transaction. The easiest way to solve this problem is to bit-bang the MC14489 interface. The module PRINT89.GRP in WHITE1.ASM implements this 16C63 bit-bang display service. The sub-module MODED in PRINT89 is the 16C63 version of the bit-bang Mode D service SPIMD introduced in Section 9.2.1. If a PICmicro having the four-mode SSP SPI is used for this application, the display communications may be implemented with the SSP SPI operating in Mode D. When necessary, mixing hardware and bit-bang communications in a given application is an acceptable solution to any limitations imposed by the devices used in the application. WHITE1 serves as a demonstration of this technique.

The SPI specific A/D modules for the YELLOW1 bit-bang version of this application (modules SPIATOD and SPIMD) total 44 lines of code. The SPI specific modules for the WHITE1 SSP hardware version (modules SSPATOD and SPIDONE) total 28 lines of code. The reduction in code size for the SSP version is due primarily to the elimination of the bit-bang SPI service module SPIMD. The SSP version also requires three fewer registers because the SPIMD work area is no longer necessary. In essence, the SPIMD module has been replaced by the hardware SSP. In many cases this savings in program memory is less significant than the corresponding increase in dollar cost for a device having the SSP on-chip. If an application uses SPI devices requiring more than one SPI timing mode then each additional bit-bang SPI service module will increase the program code by about 20 lines. Most SPI devices are Mode A or Mode D devices, so at worst, an additional 40 lines of code must be weighed against an additional device cost of several dollars.

In some cases a significant advantage of the SSP hardware SPI over the bit-bang SPI may be in terms of speed: The hardware SPI can complete a transaction far faster than can the bit-bang SPI services. If an application cannot tolerate the delays imposed by the bit-bang services, the SSP hardware SPI is indispensable, but where speed and program memory space are not of major concern, bit-banging the SPI bus is a viable alternative to using the on-chip hardware SPI.

```
;======= WHITE1.ASM ============================================================
;
;       SPI Analog to Digital Converter to SPI 4 Digit LED Display
;       SSP Hareware SPI
;       Maxim MAX 187 SPI A/D
;       Motorola MC14489 SPI 5 Digit LED Display Decoder-Driver
;
;       PIC SSC Hardware SPI Communications  (SPI is NOT interrupt driven)
;
;       14 Bit PIC
;-------------------------------------------------------------------------------
        radix   hex         ;RADIX is HEX
;
        list p=16c63
;
;       STATUS REGISTER BIT DEFINITIONS:
c       equ     0           ;carry bit of status register (bit 0)
z       equ     2           ;zero flag bit of status register (bit 2)
dc      equ     1           ;digit carry
pd      equ     3           ;power down bit
to      equ     4           ;time out bit
rp0     equ     5           ;program page preselect, low bit
rp1     equ     6           ;program page preselect, high bit
;
;       DESTINATION BIT DEFINITIONS:
w       equ     0           ;destination working
f       equ     1           ;destination file
;
;-------------------------------------------------------------------------------
;     CPU EQUATES   (special function register memory map)
;
;   BANK 0:
indf    equ     00          ;indirect file register
tmr0    equ     01          ;timer
pcl     equ     02          ;program counter (low byte)
status  equ     03          ;status register
fsr     equ     04          ;indirect data pointer
porta   equ     05          ;port a
portb   equ     06          ;port b
portc   equ     07          ;port c
pclath  equ     0a          ;write buffer for program counter (high byte)
intcon  equ     0b          ;interrupt control register
pir1    equ     0c          ;peripheral interrupt flags
pir2    equ     0d          ;
tmr1l   equ     0e          ;TMR1 register low byte
tmr1h   equ     0f          ;                 high byte
t1con   equ     10          ;timer 1 control register
tmr2    equ     11          ;timer 2
t2con   equ     12          ;timer 2 control register
sspbuf  equ     13          ;SSP receive/xmit register
sspcon  equ     14          ;SSP control register
ccpr1l  equ     15          ;CCP 1 low byte
ccpr1h  equ     16          ;      high byte
ccp1con equ     17          ;CCP 1 control register
```

```
rcsta    equ    18         ;UART receive status & control register
txreg    equ    19         ;UART xmit data register
rcreg    equ    1a         ;UART receive register
ccpr2l   equ    1b         ;CCP 2 low byte
ccpr2h   equ    1c         ;       high byte
ccp2con  equ    1d         ;CCP 2 control register
;
;   BANK 1:
optreg   equ    01         ;option register              bank 1 (0x81)
trisa    equ    05         ;data direction register port a   bank 1 (0x85)
trisb    equ    06         ;data direction register port b   bank 1 (0x86)
trisc    equ    07         ;data direction register port c   bank 1 (0x87)
pie1     equ    0c         ;peripheral interrupt enable      bank 1 (0x8c)
pie2     equ    0d         ;                                 bank 1 (0x8d)
pcon     equ    0e         ;power control register           bank 1 (0x8e)
pr2      equ    12         ;timer 2 period register          bank 1 (0x92)
sspadd   equ    13         ;SSP address register             bank 1 (0x93)
sspstat  equ    14         ;SSP status register              bank 1 (0x94)
txsta    equ    18         ;UART xmit status & control       bank 1 (0x98)
spbrg    equ    19         ;UART baud rate generater         bank 1 (0x99)
;
;-------------------------------------------------------------------------
;       WORK AREA   (memory map)   Starts at 0020
;
systat   equ    0020       ;system status
counter  equ    0021       ;general counter
disdat0  equ    0022       ;display data
disdat1  equ    0023
disdat2  equ    0024
discon   equ    0025       ;display configuration
bitctr   equ    0026       ;bit counter for MODED service
datout   equ    0027       ;data out for MODED
datin    equ    0028       ;data in for MODED
;
data1    equ    002b       ;high data byte
data0    equ    002c       ;low data byte
;
;        for vert:
bcd4     equ    002d
bcd3     equ    002e
bcd2     equ    002f
bcd1     equ    0030
bcd0     equ    0031
pten1    equ    0032
pten0    equ    0033
index    equ    0034
;
;-------------------------------------------------------------------------
;        SYSTEM EQUATES
;
dispen   equ    04         ;port B4 is Display select
adcen    equ    06         ;port B6 is A/D select
mosi     equ    05         ;port C5 is SPI MOSI
miso     equ    04         ;port C4 is SPI MISO
```

415

```
sck      equ     03          ;port C3 is SPI SCK
;
ovrfl    equ     07          ;flag for asvert (bit 7 of systat)
;
bf       equ     0           ;sspstat buffer full flag
cpol     equ     4           ;sspcon clock polarity bit
sspen    equ     5           ;sspcon ssp enable bit
spiport  equ     portc
;----------------------------------------------------------------
         org     0x00        ;start of program memory
         goto    start       ;jump over tables
;
;----------------------------------------------------------------
tbl1     addwf   pcl,f       ;tables for asvert
         retlw   027
         retlw   003
         retlw   000
         retlw   000
;
tbl0     addwf   pcl,f
         retlw   010
         retlw   0e8
         retlw   064
         retlw   00a
;----------------------------------------------------------------
;
start    movlw   0ff
         movwf   porta
         movwf   portb       ;de-select all SPI devices
         bsf     status,rp0  ;switch to bank 1
         movlw   0000        ;all port A as outputs
         movwf   trisa
         movwf   trisb       ;all port B as outputs
;
;        Here we configure SPI:
         movlw   0017
         movwf   trisc       ;MOSI (SDO) & SCK as output, MISO (SDI)
;                             as input
         bcf     status,rp0  ;switch to bank 0
         movlw   012         ;SSP Not enabled, CPOL=1...
         movwf   sspcon      ;... SPI SPI Master Mode & clock=osc/64
;
;        Because SPI is not interrupt driven, intcon & pie1 are as at reset.
;
         movlw   00e1        ;configure display
         movwf   discon
         call    confg89
;
;
;        MAIN PROGRAM LOOP:
mloop    call    sspatod     ;measure voltage
         call    vert        ;convert 12 bit binary to packed bcd
         bcf     sspcon,sspen ;disable SSP (for bit-bang display service)
         call    print89     ;display measured voltage
```

```
        goto    mloop               ;go loop
;=================================================================
;       Module SSPATOD.TXT
;
;       SPI Communications with SPI A/D via SSP in SPI mode
;       SPI Clock Mode A (CPHA=1, CPOL=1)
;       SPI analog to digital converter MAX 187
;       A/D select line is port B bit adcen
;
;       On Entry: Expects SPI to be ready to transmit (does not test
;                 for ready and does not test for overwrite or collision).
;       On Exit: A/D count in (data1,data0)
;
;-----------------------------------------------------------------
sspatod bsf     portb,adcen         ;make sure A to D not enabled
        bcf     sspcon,sspen        ;disable SSP
        bsf     sspcon,cpol         ;Make sure SPI Mode A (CPOL=1)
        bsf     sspcon,sspen        ;re-enable SSP
        bcf     portb,adcen         ;select A/D (starts conversion)
        nop
sspad1  btfss   portb,miso          ;end of conversion ? if yes, skip next
        goto    sspad1              ;no. go try again
        movwf   sspbuf              ;yes. send dummy (do not care what dummy is)
        call    spidone             ;wait until SPI finished
        movwf   data1               ;received byte to data1
        movwf   sspbuf              ;send dummy byte
        movwf   data0               ;received byte to data0
        bsf     portb,adcen         ;deselect A/D
;
;       Here we arrange the 12 bits in the 12 lower bit positions of
;           data1, data0
        movlw   0f0
        swapf   data0,f             ;lowest data nibble to low nibble of data0
        swapf   data1,f             ;highest data nibble to low nibble of data1
        andwf   data1,w             ;keep middle data nibble
        iorwf   data0,f             ;data0 now has low 8 bits of A/D data
        movlw   0f                  ;clear high 4 bits of data1
        andwf   data1,f             ;data1 has high 4 bits of A/D data
;
        retlw   0                   ;exit
;=================================================================
;       Module: SPIDONE.TXT     (Receive Byte)
;
;       Tests for SSP SPI transmission/reception completed and
;       fetches received byte.
;       When completed, exits with received data byte in W register
;       See Section 9.9.1
;
;-----------------------------------------------------------------
spidone bsf     status,rp0          ;switch to bank 1
spidon1 btfss   sspstat,bf          ;completed ? if yes, skip next
        goto    spidon1             ;no. go try again
        bcf     status,rp0          ;yes. switch back to bank 0
        movf    sspbuf,w            ;get received data
```

```
            return                  ;& exit
;=============================================================================
;           Module: VERT89.TXT
;
;           For Use with Bit-Bang SPI
;           Convert 12 BIT A/D result to 4 digit packed BCD
;           (data1, data0) => (bcd3,bcd2,bcd1,bcd0)
;           (bcd3,bcd2,bcd1,bcd0) => (disdat1,disdat0)
;
;           Display Block:
;                   discon              Configuration word
;                   disdat0             Low Byte   (bank2, bank1)
;                   disdat1             Mid Byte   (bank4, bank3)
;                   disdat2             High Byte (dp, bank5)
;
;           NOTE: This Module PLACES CALLS TWO LEVELS DEEP
;                 The called routines vert4 and vert5 are part of this module
;
;-----------------------------------------------------------------------------
vert    clrf    index                   ;convert to bcd
vert1   clrf    counter
vert2   movf    index,w
        call    vert4
        call    vert5
        btfss   status,c
        goto    vert3
        incf    counter,f
        goto    vert2
vert3   movf    index,w
        call    vert4
        call    vert6
        movlw   bcd4
        movwf   fsr
        movf    index,w
        addwf   fsr,f
        movf    counter,w
        movwf   indf
        incf    index,f
        btfss   index,2
        goto    vert1
        movf    data0,w
        movwf   bcd0
;
;       Here we pack the BCD data into the display block
;
        movf    bcd3,w              ;MS digit to Mid Byte..
        movwf   disdat1
        swapf   disdat1,f           ;& to high nibble of Mid Byte
        movf    bcd2,w              ;next digit to low nibble of Mid Byte
        iorwf   disdat1,f
        movf    bcd1,w              ;next digit to Low Byte..
        movwf   disdat0
        swapf   disdat0,f           ;& to high nibble of Low Byte
        movf    bcd0,w              ;LS digit to low nibble of Low Byte
```

418

```
        iorwf   disdat0,f
        movlw   00c0                    ;decimal point and digit 5 (0) to high byte
        movwf   disdat2
        retlw   0                       ;exit
;-----------------------------------------------------------------------
vert4   call    tbl1                    ;read table
        movwf   pten1
        movf    index,w
        call    tbl0
        movwf   pten0
        return
;-----------------------------------------------------------------------
vert5   comf    pten1,f
        comf    pten0,f
        movf    pten0,w
        addlw   01
        movwf   pten0
        btfsc   status,c
        incf    pten1,f
vert6   movf    pten0,w
        addwf   data0,f
        bcf     systat,ovrfl
        btfsc   status,c
        bsf     systat,ovrfl
        movf    pten1,w
        addwf   data1,f
        btfss   systat,ovrfl
        goto    vertx
        btfsc   status,c
        goto    vert7
        movlw   01
        addwf   data1,f
        goto    vertx
vert7   incf    data1,f
vertx   return
;
;=========== PRINT89.GRP ================================================
;
;       Module PRINT89.GRP
;       Writes to MC14489 LED Display Driver
;       16C63 Bit-Bang SPI MODE D
;
;-----------------------------------------------------------------------
;
;       Display Driver select line is Port B, Bit dispen
;       MOSI is Port C, Bit mosi
;       MISO is Port C, Bit miso
;       Display Driver requires SPI Clock Mode D (CPHA=0, CPOL=0)
;
;       Requires the following equates:
;
;               dispen  equ  nn  (nn is port B bit for MC14489 Select
;               mosi    equ  05      MOSI is Port C5
;               miso    equ  04      MISO is Port C4
;               sck     equ  03      SCK is Port C3
```

419

```
;          Requires the following work space:
;
;          Display Block:
;                  discon          Configuration word
;                  disdat0         Low Byte   (bank2, bank1)
;                  disdat1         Mid Byte   (bank4, bank3)
;                  disdat2         High Byte  (dp, bank5)
;
;          This Module consists of three called subroutines. PRINT89 and CONFG89
;          are called by the application and MODED is called by PRINT89
;          or CONFG89
;
;          Subroutine PRINT89 sends digit data (5 digits) and decimal point
;          information to the device. On entry it expects the data to be in
;          disdat0, disdat1 and disdat2.
;
;          Subroutine CONFG89 sends the configuration word to the device. On
;          entry it expects the configuration word to be in discon.
;
;          Subroutine MODED is 16C63 Bit-Bang SPI Mode D service. (16C63 version
;          of SPIMD)
;-------------------------------------------------------------------------
print89 bcf     portc,sck       ;make sure clock idles low (Mode D)
        bcf     portb,dispen    ;select display
        movf    disdat2,w       ;high display byte
        movwf   datout          ;to SPI out register
        call    moded           ;send it (Mode D)
        movf    disdat1,w       ;mid display byte
        movwf   datout
        call    moded           ;send it
        movf    disdat0,w       ;low display byte
        movwf   datout
        call    moded           ;send it
        bsf     portb,dispen    ;de-select display
        return                  ;exit
;
confg89 bcf     portc,sck       ;make sure clock idles low (Mode D)
        bcf     portb,dispen    ;select display
        movf    discon,w        ;configuration word
        movwf   datout          ;to SPI out register
        call    moded           ;send it (Mode D)
        bsf     portb,dispen    ;de-select display
        return                  ;exit
;
;-------------------------------------------------------------------------
;          16C63 Bit-Bang SPI Mode D Service
;          Transfers 1 byte over the SPI bus
;          (Clock Mode D: CPHA = 0, CPOL = 0)
;
;          On Entry:  SCK line must be low
;                     Data to be sent is in datout
;
;          On Exit:   SCK line is low
;                     Data received is in datin
```

```
;--------------------------------------------------------------------
moded    movlw   d'8'               ;8 data bytes
         movwf   bitctr
moded0   rlf     datout,f           ;data out bit to MOSI
         btfss   status,c           ;bit = 1 ? if yes, skip next
         goto    moded1             ;no. go
         bsf     spiport,mosi       ;yes. set MOSI
         goto    moded2             ;& go
moded1   bcf     spiport,mosi       ;clear MOSI
moded2   nop
         nop
         bsf     spiport,sck        ;take SCK high
         bcf     status,c           ;clear carry
         btfsc   spiport,miso       ;MISO set ? if no, skip next
         bsf     status,c           ;set carry
         rlf     datin,f            ;MISO level to datin
         nop
         nop
         bcf     spiport,sck        ;take SCK low
         decfsz  bitctr,f           ;all bits done ? if yes, skip next
         goto    moded0             ;no. go do next bit
         return                     ;yes. exit
;--------------------------------------------------------------------
         end                        ;END OF PROGRAM
;====================================================================
```

9.9.4 IVORY1.ASM: SSP Hardware SPI Slave Application

The interrupt driven SSP SPI slave application IVORY1.ASM is an SPI version of the I²C slave LOWERER application FAWN1 (Section 8.6.1). IVORY1 is functionally identical to FAWN1. IVORY1 receives an ASCII upper case character and returns it as lower case while receiving the next upper case character from the master. See figure 9-37 for the IVORY1 schematic.

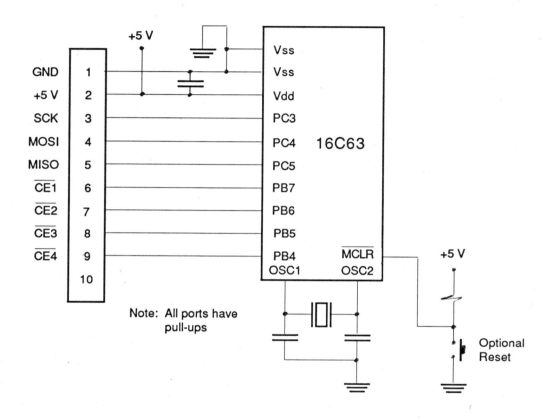

Figure 9-37   Schematic; SSP SPI Slave Applications

IVORY1 waits in a short loop to be selected. When selected it exits the loop, enables the SPI interrupt and waits in another short loop to be interrupted or de-selected. If interrupted, control is passed to the interrupt service. If de-selected it starts over with the first short loop.

The interrupt service receives the character, converts it to lower case and places it in the buffer to be clocked out by the next character from the master. This simple application serves primarily as an example of interrupt driven SSP SPI communications.

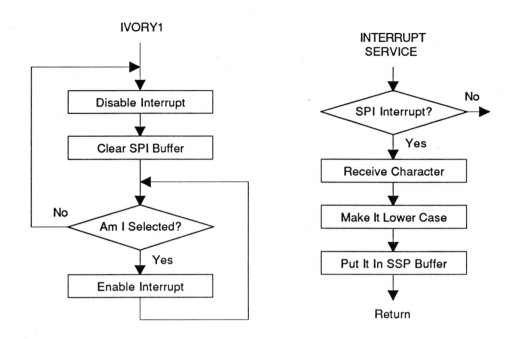

Figure 9-38   IVORY1

```
;======= IVORY1.ASM ============================================================
;
;       SPI Slave Application
;
;       PIC SSC SPI interrupt driven slave
;
;       Receives ASCII upper case character and returns lower case
;       After slave has been selected, it sends ascii NULL while receiving
;       first upper case character, then sends lower case while receiving
;       next upper case character. After sending the last upper case
;       character, the master must send a dummy character to receive the last
;       lower case.
;
;-------------------------------------------------------------------------------
        radix   hex         ;RADIX is HEX
;
        list p=16c63
;
;       STATUS REGISTER BIT DEFINITIONS:
c       equ     0           ;carry bit of status register (bit 0)
z       equ     2           ;zero flag bit of status register (bit 2)
dc      equ     1           ;digit carry
pd      equ     3           ;power down bit
to      equ     4           ;time out bit
rp0     equ     5           ;program page preselect, low bit
rp1     equ     6           ;program page preselect, high bit
;
```

```
;           DESTINATION BIT DEFINITIONS:
w        equ    0        ;destination working
f        equ    1        ;destination file
;
;-------------------------------------------------------------------
;      CPU EQUATES   (special function register memory map)
;
;  BANK 0:
indf     equ    00       ;indirect file register
tmr0     equ    01       ;timer
pcl      equ    02       ;program counter (low byte)
status   equ    03       ;status register
fsr      equ    04       ;indirect data pointer
porta    equ    05       ;port a
portb    equ    06       ;port b
portc    equ    07       ;port c
pclath   equ    0a       ;write buffer for program counter (high byte)
intcon   equ    0b       ;interrupt control register
pir1     equ    0c       ;peripheral interrupt flags
pir2     equ    0d
tmr1l    equ    0e       ;TMR1 register low byte
tmr1h    equ    0f       ;             high byte
t1con    equ    10       ;timer 1 control register
tmr2     equ    11       ;timer 2
t2con    equ    12       ;timer 2 control register
sspbuf   equ    13       ;SSP receive/xmit register
sspcon   equ    14       ;SSP control register
ccpr1l   equ    15       ;CCP 1 low byte
ccpr1h   equ    16       ;     high byte
ccp1con  equ    17       ;CCP 1 control register
rcsta    equ    18       ;UART receive status & control register
txreg    equ    19       ;UART xmit data register
rcreg    equ    1a       ;UART receive register
ccpr2l   equ    1b       ;CCP 2 low byte
ccpr2h   equ    1c       ;     high byte
ccp2con  equ    1d       ;CCP 2 control register
;
;  BANK 1:
optreg   equ    01     . ;option register              bank 1 (0x81)
trisa    equ    05       ;data direction register port a   bank 1 (0x85)
trisb    equ    06       ;data direction register port b   bank 1 (0x86)
trisc    equ    07       ;data direction register port c   bank 1 (0x87)
pie1     equ    0c       ;peripheral interrupt enable   bank 1 (0x8c)
pie2     equ    0d       ;                              bank 1 (0x8d)
pcon     equ    0e       ;power control register        bank 1 (0x8e)
pr2      equ    12       ;timer 2 period register       bank 1 (0x92)
sspadd   equ    13       ;SSP address register          bank 1 (0x93)
sspstat  equ    14       ;SSP status register           bank 1 (0x94)
txsta    equ    18       ;UART xmit status & control    bank 1 (0x98)
spbrg    equ    19       ;UART baud rate generater      bank 1 (0x99)
;
;-------------------------------------------------------------------
;      WORK AREA  (memory map)   Starts at 0020
;
;-------------------------------------------------------------------
```

```
;           SYSTEM EQUATES
;
slvsel   equ       07         ;port B7 is Slave select
miso     equ       05         ;port C5 (SDO) is SPI MISO
mosi     equ       04         ;port C4 (SDI) is SPI MOSI
sck      equ       03         ;port C3 is SPI SCK
;
ovrfl    equ       07         ;flag for asvert (bit 7 of systat)
;
bf       equ       0          ;sspstat buffer full flag
cpol     equ       4          ;sspcon clock polarity bit
gie      equ       7          ;intcon global interrupt enable bit
sspif    equ       3          ;pir1 SSP interrupt flag bit
peie     equ       6          ;intcon peripheral interrupt enable
;---------------------------------------------------------------------
         org       0x00       ;start of program memory
         goto      start      ;jump over version and int vector
         dw        0072       ;version code
         dw        006c
         dw        0073
         goto      intsrv     ;interrupt service vector
;
start    movlw     0ff
         movwf     porta
         movwf     portb      ;de-select all SPI devices
         bsf       status,rp0 ;switch to bank 1
         movlw     00ff       ;all port A as inputs
         movwf     trisa
         movwf     trisb      ;all port B as inputs
;
;         Here we configure SPI:
         movlw     001f
         movwf     trisc      ;MISO (SDO) as output, MOSI (SDI) & SCK
;                              as input
         bcf       status,rp0 ;switch to bank 0
         movlw     034
         movwf     sspcon     ;SPI enabled as slave, CPOL=1,
;                              SPI clock=osc/64
                             ;and NOT SS control is disabled
         bsf       intcon,peie ;enable perpherial interrupts
;
;         At this point global interrupts are disabled, so slave IVORY1 will
;         not respond to data on the SPI bus. Interrupts are enabled when slave
;         IVORY1 is selected.
;
;
;         MAIN PROGRAM LOOP:
;
mloop    bcf       intcon,gie ;disable interrupts
         bcf       pir1,sspif ;clear interrupt flag
         clrf      sspbuf     ;NULL to SPI buffer
mloop1   btfsc     portb,slvsel ;is slave selected ? if yes, skip next
         goto      mloop      ;no, go
         bsf       intcon,gie ;yes. enable interrupts
```

```
        goto    mloop1              ;go loop until SPI data is received or...
                                    ;until slave is de-selected
;
;-----------------------------------------------------------------------
;       INTERRUPT SERVICE
;
;       Adds 0x20 to received character and returns it via SPI bus.
;       NOTE: IVORY1 is so simple that it is not necessary to save
;             context when servicing interrupt
;-----------------------------------------------------------------------
intsrv  btfss   pir1,sspif          ;is it SPI interrupt ? if yes,skip next
        goto    intsrvx             ;no. go exit
        bcf     pir1,sspif          ;yes. clear interrupt flag
        movlw   020                 ;add 0x20 to received character
        addwf   sspbuf,f            ;and return it
intsrvx return                      ;exit
;-----------------------------------------------------------------------
        end                         ;END OF PROGRAM
;=======================================================================
```

9.9.5 Using the Section 9.9 Routines in Your Applications

Using the SSP SPI hardware is primarily a matter of configuring the hardware via the special registers and reading from or writing to the **SSPBUF** register along with paying attention to the special status registers. The two sample applications demonstrate polled and interrupt driven communications. That is about all you need to successfully apply the SSP SPI.

SSP and BSSP

The earlier version of the Synchronous Serial Port (Microchip designation used to be SSP, changed to BSSP; see Section 9.9.1) supports only SPI Modes A and B. The updated Synchronous Serial Port (current Microchip designation: SSP) supports all four SPI Modes. To avoid confusion, in the discussion below we shall refer to the updated version as the *four-mode* version and refer to the earlier version as the *two-mode* version.

The four-mode version implements the two highest bits of **SSPSTAT**. These bits are not implemented for the two-mode version. The new **SSPSTAT** bits, **SMP** and **CKE**, along with **SSPCON** bit **CKP** determine the SPI clock Mode as shown in Table 9-3. Note that bit **SMP** is cleared for all SPI Modes. For some Microwire applications **SMP** will be set.

Table 9-3

```
-----------------------------------------
       Four-Mode SSP SPI Master Clock
-----------------------------------------
               SSPCON   SSPSTAT   SSPSTAT
      Mode      CKP       SMP       CKE
-----------------------------------------
       A
  CPHA = 1       1         0         0
  CPOL = 1

       B
  CPHA = 1       0         0         0
  CPOL = 0

       C
  CPHA = 0       1         0         1
  CPOL = 1

       D
  CPHA = 0       0         0         1
  CPOL = 0
```

The EEPROM services SSP25C.GRP may be simplified when the four-mode SSP is used. Simply delete all calls to FIXER and configure all communications as Mode D. Be sure to change the mode selection at the start of the modules to Mode D. If all SPI communications in your application are Mode D, then the mode selection at the start of the modules may be deleted.

The application WHITE1 (Section 9.9.3) uses both hardware and bit-bang SPI communications. The SPI ports have the same SPI function for both the hardware and bit-bang implementations. When communications are to be bit-bang, the SSP SPI *must* be disabled to return the ports to the normal input/output configuration. For WHITE1 this is done in the main loop. For more complicated applications it would be safer to disable the SSP at the beginning of the bit-bang routine and re-enable it at the end of the routine.

The 16C63 bit-bang service MODED differs from SPIMD in only the port used for the SPI interface (port C for MODED and port B for SPIMD). If a literal is assigned as the SPI port (such as **spiport**) then SPIMD may be used with any PICmicro for applications requiring a mix of hardware and bit-bang SPI communications:

```
spiport equ     portc           ;16C63 port assignment
.
.
.
spimd   movlw   d'8'            ;8 data bytes
        movwf   bitctr
spimd0  rlf     datout,f        ;data out bit to MOSI
        btfss   status,c        ;bit = 1 ? if yes, skip next
        goto    spimd1          ;no. go
```

```
            bsf     spiport,mosi    ;yes. set MOSI
            goto    spimd2          ;& go
spimd1      bcf     spiport,mosi    ;clear MOSI
spimd2      nop
            nop
            bsf     spiport,sck     ;take SCK high
            bcf     status,c        ;clear carry
            btfsc   spiport,miso    ;MISO set ? if no, skip next
            bsf     status,c        ;set carry
            rlf     datin,f         ;MISO level to datin
            nop
            nop
            bcf     spiport,sck     ;take SCK low
            decfsz  bitctr,f        ;all bits done ? if yes, skip next
            goto    spimd0          ;no. go do next bit
            return                  ;yes. exit
```

All of the modules in SPICOMS.GRP (Section 9.2.1) may be changed in this manner.

9.10 Daisy Chaining SPI Devices

The nature of the SPI shift register architecture makes it possible for some SPI devices to be daisy chained. The advantage of daisy chaining is a reduction in the number of required device enable lines (only one enable line per chain). In general, a device that has both MOSI and MISO ports and that does not change its outputs or read its inputs until after the CE line returns high, is a candidate for daisy chaining. The MC14489 Display Driver described in Section 9.4 is an example of a device that would certainly be daisy chained for displays requiring more than 5 digits. Shift registers that have both data out and data in capability may also be daisy chained. EEPROMS may not be daisy chained because a downstream device would treat upstream outgoing data as an instruction or incoming data.

Chapter 10
The Microwire Serial Interface

The Microwire Serial Interface

The Microwire Interface serially transfers data between a microcontroller and a peripheral device. Each device may act simultaneously as a transmitter and a receiver. The microcontroller and each peripheral device has an output pin, an input pin and a clock pin.

The Microwire Interface was originally devised by National Semiconductor to allow their COPS microcontrollers to effectively communicate with peripheral devices. It was not defined as a bus but as an interface. As an interface the lines are not defined (as is done with the SPI lines), but the device serial communications pins are defined. Devices communicating via the Microwire Interface are designated as microcontrollers and peripherals. The microcontroller initiates the information transfer across the interface and generates the clock and control signals. The peripheral is controlled by the microcontroller. Each peripheral device in an application is controlled by a chip select line. Only one peripheral may be active at a time and a dedicated select is required for each peripheral. The Microwire transfer employs a simple shift register data transfer scheme (Figure 10-1).

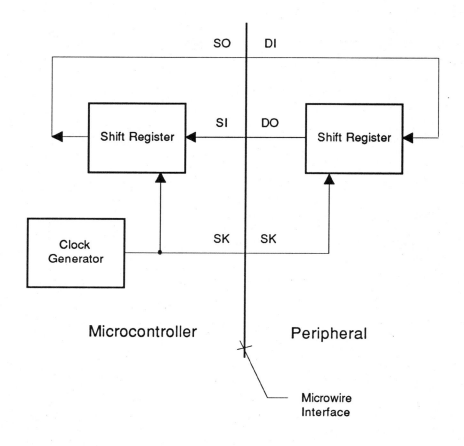

Figure 10-1   Microwire Interface

To preserve continuity with previous chapters, throughout this chapter we shall use the term master to designate the microcontroller and slave or peripheral to designate the peripheral device. Any reference to a master will be taken to mean a bit-bang master.

10.1 The Microwire Interface Specification (As a PICmicro Bit-Bang Master)

The master output and input pins are designated SO (serial out) and SI (serial in) respectively and the peripheral output and input pins as DO (data out) and DI (data in) respectively. The clock pin for both devices is designated as SK (serial clock). The master select output pin is designated as PX (peripheral exchange) and the peripheral select input pin as CS (chip select). These pins constitute the Microwire Interface.

Each peripheral device is selected by the master via individual PX pins (see Figure 10-2). A Microwire peripheral device is selected by a high (logic 1) on the CS input. Information can be transferred across the Microwire Interface at a rate of near zero bits/second to 250 Kbits/second and up to 1 Mbits/second for specific devices. Data is generally transferred in 8 bit blocks, most significant bit (MSB) first.

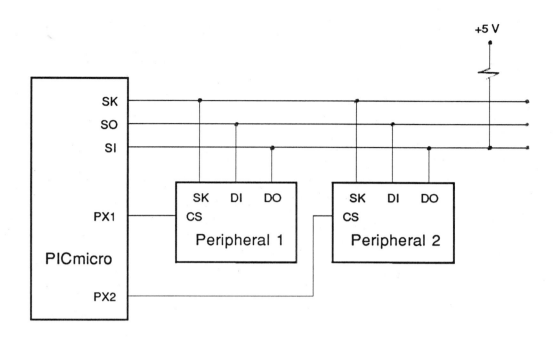

Figure 10-2   Typical Microwire Application

All data transfer is synchronized by the serial clock (SK). One bit of data is transferred for each clock cycle (Figure 10-3). In general, the Microwire Interface requires that *all* data *must* be valid around the rising clock. The *only* active edge of the clock is the *rising* edge. Data on the DI pin is clocked *into* the DI pin (read) on the *rising* edge and data out the DO pin is clocked *out of* the DO pin on the rising edge, but with some delay. This delay allows a bit-bang master to read the slave DO data on the *falling* edge of the clock or *just before* the *rising* edge (Figure 10-3). Some devices clock the data out the DO pin on the *falling* edge of the clock. In this case the bit-bang master should read the slave DO data *just before* the *rising* edge of the clock.

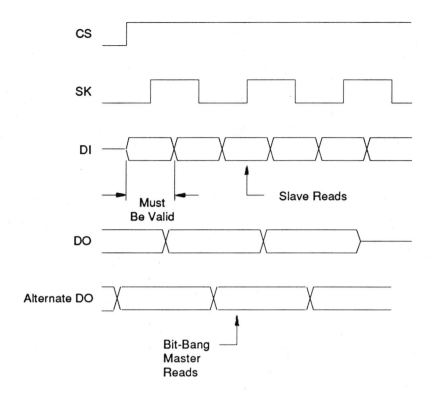

Figure 10-3   Microwire Timing

10.2 Microwire Bit-Bang Master and Slave Interface Services

Two pins of port B are used for Microwire bit-bang master SO and SI and a third pin is used for SK (see Figure 10-4). These pins should have pull-ups, but are not wired AND as with the I^2C bus because separate pins are used for SO and SI. SO and SK are configured as an output and SI as an input. The setup and clock high and low periods must not be less than 1 microsecond and the clock rate no more than 250 KHz. Some slave devices are capable of operating at higher rates, but the bit-bang clock rates are much lower than 250 kHz because all operations are done in software.

432

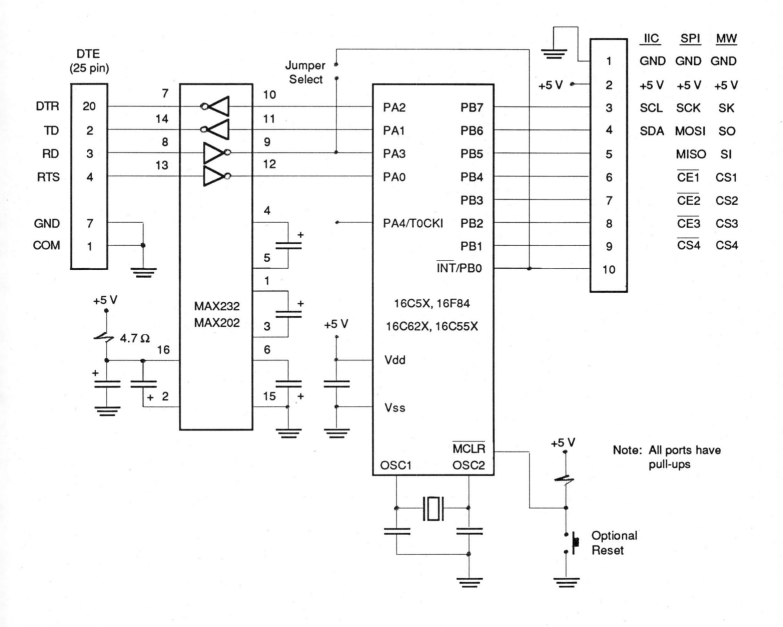

Figure 10-4   Schematic; Bit-Bang Master Applications

Bit-bang slave applications tend to be even slower than the bit-bang master services; requiring even slower master services. The master services may be slowed by adding time delay loops to each clock phase. These stretched clock services are described at the end of Section 10.2.1.

10.2.1 Microwire Bit-Bang Master Interface Services

The two modules in WIRECOMS.GRP are all that are necessary to model a MICROWIRE MASTER with the PICmicro. These are the Microwire *interface* services. They are all *called* functions. The modules are:

STBT   Send a start or dummy bit
MWIRE   Send and receive an eight bit byte

The Microwire specification places no restriction on the clock idle level (it even allows the clock to function continuously). The bit-bang master services idle the clock low and generate the clock only when it is required to transfer data across the Microwire Interface. On entry the Microwire modules in WIRECOMS expect the clock to be low and on exit it is low. As with the SPI services in chapter 9, the shift register is modeled with two eight bit bytes. Data to be transmitted by the master is found in **datout** and the data received in **datin**.

Send a Start or Dummy Bit (Module STBT.TXT and Figure 10-5)

STBT has two entry points: **stbt** to send a start (logic 1) bit and **dumbt** to send a dummy (logic 0) bit. On entry STBT takes SO high for a start bit or takes SO low for a dummy bit. A short time later SK is made high for two instruction cycles and then returned low. Two cycles after SK returns low, SO returns low and STBT exits. In summary: STBT places a 1 or 0 on SO, clocks it out and exits with SK low.

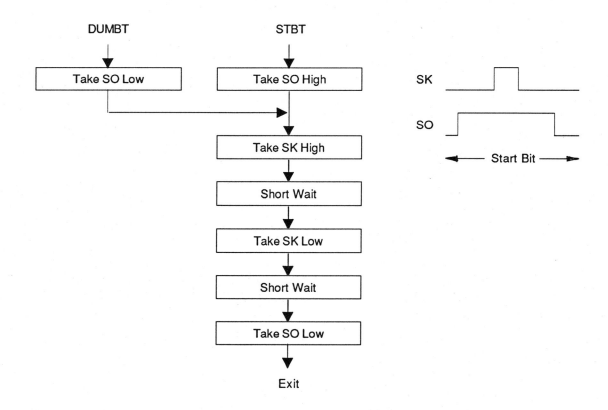

Figure 10-5   STBT - Send Microwire Start Bit

434

Send and Receive an Eight Bit Byte (Module MWIRE.TXT and Figure 10-6)

On entry, MWIRE initializes the bit counter and shifts a data bit from the buffer **datout** onto the SO pin. A short time later SI is read and SK is then made high for two instruction cycles and returned low. The read SI bit is shifted into the buffer **datin.** This process is continued until all eight bits have been transferred. The bits are counted by **bitctr**. On exit **datout** is corrupted, the received byte is in **datin** and SK is low. In summary: SO is updated while SK is low and DI is read just before SK goes high. Prior to exit, SK is returned low.

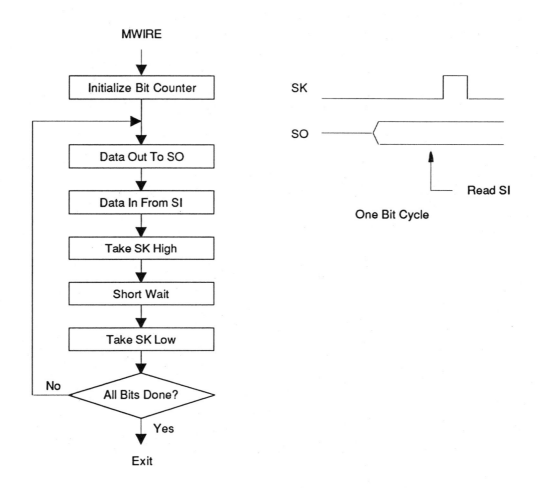

Figure 10-6   MWIRE - Send And Receive Microwire Byte

Note that both of the modules *require* SK to be low on entry and both exit with SK low. It is the responsibility of the application to make sure that SK is low before the modules are called.

```
;====== WIRECOMS.GRP =============================================================
;
;        WIRECOMS.GRP
;
;        Bit-Bang Microwire communications
;        PIC is master
;
;--------------------------------------------------------------------------------
;
;        Required work area:
;              datout  data to be sent by master
;              datin   data received by master
;
;        Required equates:
;              so      equ      nn      port b bit for SO line
;              si      equ      nn      port b bit for SI line
;              sck     equ      nn      port b bit for SCK line
;
;--------------------------------------------------------------------------------
;        Module: STBT
;        Sends Start bit or Dummy bit
;        Entry stbt: sends a HIGH bit (start)
;        Entry dumbt: sends a LOW bit (dummy)
;
;        On Entry: expects clock (sck) to be low
;
;        On exit: sck low and so low
;
;--------------------------------------------------------------------------------
stbt    bsf     portb,so        ;take SO high
        goto    stbt1
dumbt   bcf     portb,so        ;DUMMY bit entrance. make sure SO is low
        nop
stbt1   bsf     portb,sck       ;take SCK high
        nop
        bcf     portb,sck       ;take SCK low
        nop
        bcf     portb,so        ;take SO low
        return                  ;exit
;--------------------------------------------------------------------------------
;        Module: MWIRE
;        Send and Receive 8 bit byte
;
;        On entry: expects sck to be low
;                  data to be sent in datout
;                  data received in datin
;
;        On exit: sck is low
;                 data in datout is corrupted
;--------------------------------------------------------------------------------
mwire   movlw   d'8'            ;initialize bit counter
        movwf   bitctr
mwire1  rlf     datout,f        ;data out bit to SO
        btfss   status,c
```

```
        goto    mwire2
        bsf     portb,so
        goto    mwire3
mwire2  bcf     portb,so
mwire3  bcf     status,c        ;read data in
        btfsc   portb,si        ;SI line high ? if no, skip next
        bsf     status,c        ;yes. set carry
        rlf     datin,f         ;bit to data in
        bsf     portb,sck       ;take SCK high
        nop
        bcf     portb,sck       ;take SCK low
        decfsz  bitctr,f        ;all bits done ? if yes, skip next
        goto    mwire1          ;no. go do next bit
        return                  ;yes. exit
;========================================================================
```

Stretched Clock Services

The master services in WIRESLOW.GRP are stretched clock versions of the WIRECOMS services. These services are required when communicating with a bit-bang slave application. The clock rate is slowed by adding a time delay loop to each clock phase. This delay is generated by the subroutine FILLER. When called, FILLER adds approximately $(3*n)+7$ instruction cycles (where n is the literal **mwrate**). Filler is called at both the high and low clock phases, adding a total of approximately $(6*n)+14$ cycles to the clock period.

```
;====== WIRESLOW.GRP ====================================================
;
;       WIRESLOW.GRP
;
;       Bit-Bang Microwire Communications
;       PIC is master
;       NOTE: This is a slow (stretched clock period) version of WIRECOMS.TXT
;             Required when communicating with slow bit-bang slave.
;
;------------------------------------------------------------------------
;
;       Required work area:
;           datout      data to be sent by master
;           datin       data received by master
;           fillctr     time filler counter
;
;       Required equates:
;           so      equ     nn      port b bit for SO line
;           si      equ     nn      port b bit for SI line
;           sck     equ     nn      port b bit for SCK line
;
;------------------------------------------------------------------------
;       Module: STBT
;       Sends Start bit or Dummy bit
;       Entry stbt: sends a HIGH bit (start)
;       Entry dumbt: sends a LOW bit (dummy)
;
```

```
;         On Entry: expects clock (sck) to be low
;
;         On exit: sck low and so low
;
;--------------------------------------------------------------------
stbt    bsf     portb,so        ;take SO high
        goto    stbt1
dumbt   bcf     portb,so        ;DUMMY bit entrance. make sure SO is low
        nop
stbt1   call    filler          ;stretch it
        bsf     portb,sck       ;take SCK high
        call    filler
        bcf     portb,sck       ;take SCK low
        call    filler
        bcf     portb,so        ;take SO low
        return                  ;exit
;--------------------------------------------------------------------
;         Module: MWIRE
;         Send and Receive 8 bit byte
;
;         On entry: expects sck to be low
;                   data to be sent in datout
;                   data received in datin
;
;         On exit: sck is low
;--------------------------------------------------------------------
mwire   movlw   d'8'            ;initialize bit counter
        movwf   bitctr
mwire1  rlf     datout,f        ;data out bit to SO
        btfss   status,c
        goto    mwire2
        bsf     portb,so
        goto    mwire3
mwire2  bcf     portb,so
mwire3  call    filler          ;stretch it
        bcf     status,c        ;read data in:
        btfsc   portb,si        ;SI line high ? if no, skip next
        bsf     status,c        ;yes. set carry
        rlf     datin,f         ;bit to data in
        bsf     portb,sck       ;take SCK high
        call    filler          ;stretch it
        bcf     portb,sck       ;take SCK low
        call    filler          ;stretch it
        decfsz  bitctr,f        ;all bits done ? if yes, skip next
        goto    mwire1          ;no. go do next bit
        return                  ;yes. exit
;--------------------------------------------------------------------
;         Module: FILLER
;
;         Used to stretch clock period
;         When called, adds approx (3*n)+7 cycles where n is literal mwrate
;         in first line below.
;--------------------------------------------------------------------
filler  movlw   mwrate
```

```
        movwf    fillctr
filler1 decfsz   fillctr,f
        goto     filler1
        return
;================================================================================
```

10.2.2 Microwire Bit-Bang Slave Interface Services

Three lines of port A are used for slave DI, DO and SK (Figure 10-18). These lines should have pull-ups, but are not wired AND as with the I²C bus because the Microwire Interface uses separate lines for data out and data in. When configured as a bit-bang slave, the output DO must be configured as an output *only* when the slave is selected. When not selected, DO *must* be an input. The input DI and clock SK are configured as inputs.

The bit-bang setup and clock high and low periods are significantly longer than the minimum specified for the Microwire interface; so much so that successful communications requires clock stretching of the bit-bang master routines as in WIRESLOW.GRP described at the end of Section 10.2. The maximum clock rate for the slave routines in WIRESLAV.GRP (with 4 MHz crystal) is approximately 40 KHz.

The modules in WIRESLAV.GRP model a MICROWIRE SLAVE. The modules are the Microwire *slave interface* services and are all *called* functions. The modules are:

SLSTBT   Waits to be selected and waits for start bit
SLDMBT   Sends dummy bit
SLVXFR   Receives and sends a byte

Throughout these modules the data to be transmitted is found in the parameter **datout** and the data received in the parameter **datin**. The data bits for each byte are counted by **bitctr**.

Slave Waits to be Selected, then Waits for Start Bit (Module SLSTBT.TXT and Figure 10-7)

SLSTBT monitors the CS pin, waiting for the pin to go high. When the CS pin goes high, SLSTBT then monitors the SK pin, waiting for it to be high. When SK becomes high, DI is monitored. When DI becomes high, SLSTBT exits. In summary: SLSTBT waits to be selected then waits for DI high (start bit) at SK high. SLSTBT exits only after recognizing the start bit.

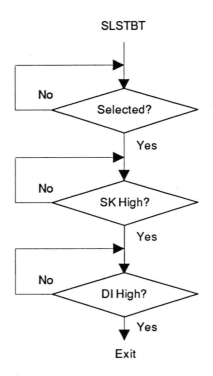

SLSTBT

Figure 10-7   SLSTBT - Microwire Slave Start bit Test

Slave Sends Dummy Byte (Module SLDMBT and Figure 10-8)

SLDMBT monitors SK, waiting for it to go low. When SK goes low, SLDMBT takes DO low and again monitors SK. When the SK goes high, SLDMBT exits. In summary: SLDMBT places a dummy bit (logic 0) on SO when the clock goes low and exits when the clock returns high.

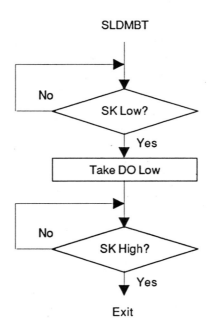

SLDMBT

Figure 10-8   SLDMBT - Microwire Slave Send Dummy Bit

Slave Receive and Send a Byte (Module SLVXFR and Figure 10-9)

On entry SLVXFR initializes the bit counter and monitors SK for low. When SK goes low, SLVXFR again monitors SK, but for high. When SK goes high, SLVXFR reads the DI pin, shifts the bit into **datin,** then shifts a bit from **datout** onto the DO pin. This sequence is repeated until all eight bits have been transferred. The bits are counted by **bitctr**. On exit **datout** is corrupted, the received byte is in **datin.** In summary: SLVXFR waits for the clock to cycle from low to high, reads the DI pin just after the clock goes high and writes to the DO pin. It repeats this sequence until all bits have been transferred.

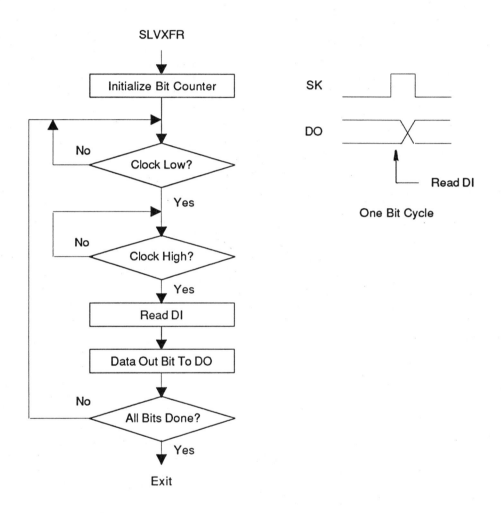

Figure 10-9   SLVXFR - Microwire Slave Data Transfer

```
;====== WIRESLAV.GRP ==========================================================
;
;          Bit Bang MICROWIRE slave communications
;          PIC is slave
;
;------------------------------------------------------------------------------
;
;          Required work area
;                  datout   data to be sent to master
;                  datin    data received from master
;                  bitctr   bit counter
;
;          Required equates
;                  do       equ     nn      port A bit for DO line
;                  di       equ     nn      port A bit for DI line
;                  sck      equ     nn      port A bit for SCK line
;                  select   equ     nn      port A bit for chip enable line
;
;          NOTE: Clock period should be approximately 25 uSec or longer.
;
;------------------------------------------------------------------------------
;          Module: SLSTBT
;          Waits for selected AND start bit
;
;------------------------------------------------------------------------------
slstbt  btfsc   porta,select    ;selected ? if yes, skip next
        goto    slstbt          ;no. go try again
        btfss   porta,sck       ;clock high ? if yes, skip next
        goto    slstbt          ;no. go try again
        btfss   porta,di        ;yes. DI high ? if yes, skip next
        goto    slstbt          ;no. go try again
        retlw   0               ;yes. exit
;------------------------------------------------------------------------------
;          Module: SLDMBT
;          Sends dummy (DO low) bit
;
;------------------------------------------------------------------------------
sldmbt  btfsc   porta,sck       ;clock low ? if yes, skip next
        goto    sldmbt          ;no. go try again
        bcf     portb,do        ;yes. take DO low
sldmbt1 btfss   porta,sck       ;clock high ? If yes, skip next
        goto    sldmbt1         ;no. go try again
        retlw   0               ;yes. exit
;------------------------------------------------------------------------------
;          Module: SLVXFR
;          Receive and send 8 bit byte
;
;------------------------------------------------------------------------------
slvxfr  movlw   d'8'            ;8 bit byte
        movwf   bitctr
slvxfr1 btfsc   porta,sck       ;clock low ? if yes, skip next
        goto    slvxfr1         ;no. go try again
slvxfr2 btfss   porta,sck       ;clock high ? if yes, skip next
        goto    slvxfr2         ;no. go try again
```

```
         bcf      status,c          ;yes. read DI line:
         btfsc    porta,di          ;DI line high ? if no, skip next
         bsf      status,c          ;yes. set carry
         rlf      datin,f           ;bit to data in
         rlf      datout,f          ;data out bit to DO
         btfss    status,c
         goto     slvxfr3
         bsf      porta,do
         goto     slvxfr4
slvxfr3  bcf      porta,do
slvxfr4  decfsz   bitctr,f          ;all bits done ? if yes, skip next
         goto     slvxfr1           ;no. go do next bit
         retlw    0                 ;yes. exit
;============================================================================
```

10.2.3 Using the Section 10.2 Routines in your Applications

Generally all of the routines can be used in your applications as written or with minor changes. For all routines, the entry and exit conditions, variables, port definitions and flag definitions are described in the xx.GRP and xx.TXT listings. All port assignments are arbitrary and may be changed to suit your application. See Sections 10.3, 10.4 and 10.5 for sample applications using the routines. The sample applications use the PIC16F84 but the routines may be used with other PICmicros with little or no change. The DO line should have a pull-up to eliminate the possibility of a floating input when all bit-bang slave devices are de-selected.

The routines introduced in Section 10.2 are:

WIRECOMS.GRP   Microwire Master Bit-Bang Communications Services
WIRESLV.GRP   Microwire Slave Bit-Bang Communications Services
WIRESLOW.GRP   Microwire Master Communications Service with Stretched Clock

The routines in these groups are all *called* functions. A bit-bang Microwire application using these functions is little more than a sequence of calls to these functions interspersed with specific application services.

Master Services

Most of your applications will generally use the Microwire bit-bang master services to communicate with standard Microwire hardware slave devices. These devices are capable of operating at the maximum clock rate of 250 KHz to 1 MHz. The Microwire bit-bang services generate the clock timing with software routines and are thus sensitive to crystal frequency. The modules in WIRECOMS clock at less than 70 KHz when a 4 MHz crystal is used. This presents no problem because the hardware devices generally can tolerate clock rates approaching zero bits per second. The clock period for the WIRECOMS modules is a function of crystal frequency only. The Modules in WIRESLOW.GRP illustrates the use of an added time delay to stretch the clock period if even slower clock rates are required by an application.

When using the Microwire bit-bang master bus services to communicate with a device using the Microwire bit-bang slave bus services, pay close attention to the clock rates because the bit-bang slave routines are generally slower than the master routines.

Carefully study the timing diagrams for any Microwire peripheral. Generally the peripheral devices will conform to the requirement that data-in (DI) be valid at the rising clock edge, but will place data on the DO line at times that are unique to the device. The routines in WIRE-COMS should work correctly with most Microwire devices, but it is prudent to check the timing.

The Microwire bit-bang master interface services are very easy to apply: Simply place the data byte to be sent in **datout**, select the device, call the service, then read the received data byte at **datin**. If you are communicating with a receive-only slave then ignore the received byte. Repeat the call to the service until all bytes are transferred then deselect the device. If you are communicating with a transmit-only slave then the contents of **datout** have no significance. Some devices require multiple select de-select cycles within a transaction. The Microwire Interface does not specify a transfer protocol, so pay careful attention to the specific device protocol.

Slave Services

When writing an application for a bit-bang slave your most important concern should be the state of the DO pin. When the slave is *not* selected, the DO pin *must* be configured as an input. Only configure the port as an output when you are anticipating sending a data byte. A slave application that only receives should *never* configure DO as an output. It is the responsibility of your application to monitor the CS pin and ensure that the DO pin is configured correctly.

Bit-bang slave applications are relatively slow. To ensure successful communications, slow the master clock rate down to a little below the maximum rate of the slave application. The maximum clock rate for the WIRESLV routines (with a 4 MHz crystal) is approximately 25 KHz. Also leave ample response time between selecting the slave and sending a byte of data to it. This response time and the necessary delay between bytes sent to the slave is primarily a function of the application. The services in SLOWCOMS are specifically for applications communicating with a bit-bang peripheral.

National Semiconductor specifies the Microwire master timing to be as follows: Data to be transmitted from the SO pin is shifted out on the *falling* edge of the SK clock and data in on the SI pin is latched in (read) on the *rising* edge of the SK clock (data *must* be valid at *rising* clock). If your bit-bang slave application is to communicate with a hardware master, make sure that it is compatible with the hardware timing.

10.3 Communicating with Microwire Serial EEPROMS

The 93C46 serial EEPROM is typical of most Microwire serial EEPROMS. It is a 1024 bit device configured as 64 registers of 16 bits each (16 bit memory bytes). The 93C46 serial interface conforms to the Microwire standard. Some 93xxx series EEPROMS may be configured with eight bit registers or sixteen bit registers. This configuration is determined by the level on an ORG pin. For example, the 93C86 may be configured as 2048 eight-bit registers or as 1024 sixteen-bit registers. The 93Cxx series devices do not support page write (with the exception of write-all and erase-all) or sequential read (with the exception of the National Semiconductor NM93CSxxL series). Some devices support a pin selectable write disable to provide hardware controlled write protect for the entire memory array.

The 93C46 has a fixed configuration of 64 sixteen bit registers and no hardware write protect. Data is clocked in on the DI pin for write operations and clocked out on the DO pin for read operations. All data transfers are 16 bit, preceded by an 8 bit instruction byte. The data transfer transactions are implemented as three 8 bit Microwire transactions and are preceded by a start bit (Figure 10-10). The transactions that do not involve data transfer are all eight bit instructions and are preceded by a start bit. Note that the CS pin must remain high for the duration of the entire transaction but must go low between consecutive transactions.

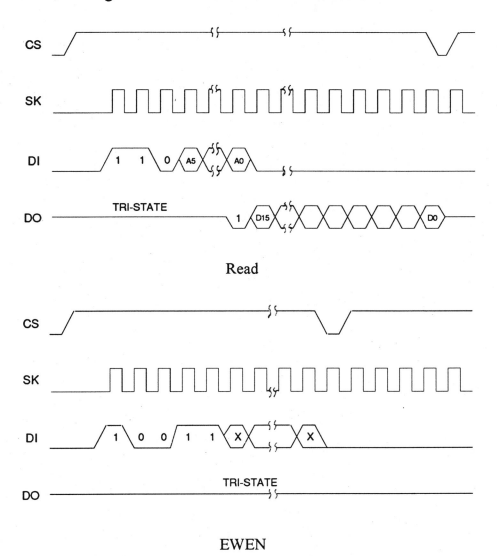

Read

EWEN

Figure 10-10   93C46 EEPROM Transactions

Note: TRI-STATE is a registered trademark of National Semiconductor

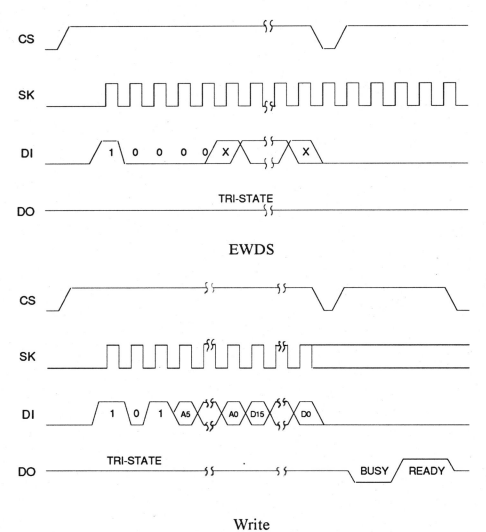

EWDS

Write

Figure 10-10 continued   93C46 EEPROM Transactions

446

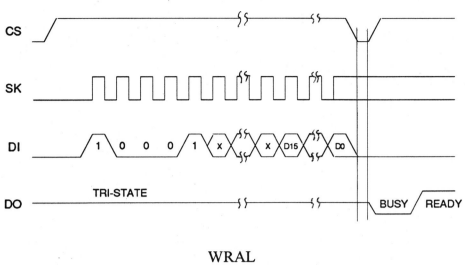

WRAL

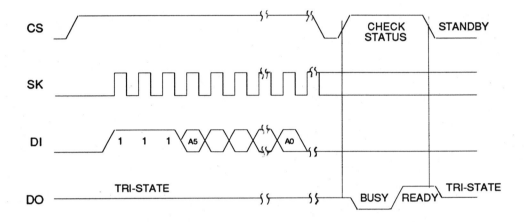

Erase

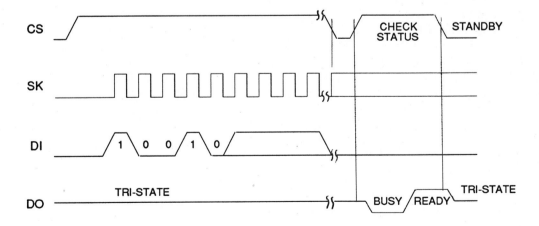

ERAL

Figure 10-10 continued   93C46 EEPROM Transactions

The 93C46 powers up in the Write disabled state. To enable erase or write, the Erase/Write Enable instruction (EWEN) must be implemented prior to attempting an erase or write operation. The device will remain Write enabled until powered down or until the Erase/Write Disable instruction (EWDS) is implemented. EWEN is not necessary for read operations. See Table 10-1 for the 93C46 instruction set.

Table 10-1   Instruction Set For 93C06 And 93C46

Instruction	Start Bit	Op Code	Address	Function
READ	1	10	A5 - A0	Read data
WRITE	1	01	A5 - A0	Write data
ERASE	1	11	A5 - A0	Erase data
EWDS	1	00	00 xxxx	Disable erase & write
WRAL	1	00	01 xxxx	Write all registers
ERAL	1	00	10 xxxx	Erase all registers
EWEN	1	00	11 xxxx	Enable erase & write

Instruction Format:

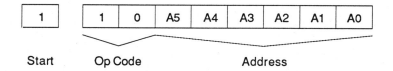

Start   Op Code   Address

The write or erase cycle begins immediately after the last data bit is received by the EEPROM and is self timed. The write and erase cycle times vary with manufacturer. The EEPROM may be polled to determine if it is busy with the write cycle. If CS pin is brought low after the last data bit of the write transaction and then returned high, the DO pin may be used for busy polling. The device holds DO low while it is busy with the write cycle and releases DO when not busy. The DO must have a pull-up for polling because DO is *released*, not driven high. Polling may be implemented by simply monitoring DO or by clocking a dummy byte to the EEPROM and testing the returned byte until it is 0xFF.

10.3.1 Microwire EEPROM Bit-Bang Communications Services

The modules in MW93C46.GRP, along with the two modules in WIRECOMS.GRP, are all that are needed to communicate with a 93C46 series EEPROM. The MW93C46.GRP modules each perform specific EEPROM operations:

EEOPEN   Enable erase and write
EECLOSE   Disable erase and write
EEPOLL   Poll DO pin for not-busy
EEWRITE   Write 16 bit data to a register
EEREAD   Read 16 bit data from a register
EERASE   Erase all registers

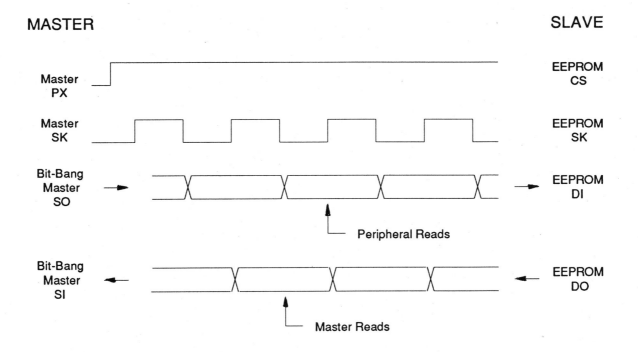

Figure 10-11   93xxx EEPROM Microwire Timing

Module Descriptions

See MW93C46.GRP and Figure 10-10. The function and implementation the modules EEOPEN, EECLOSE, EEPOLL and EERASE are described by the headers and comments for each individual module. See Section 10.2.1 for the Microwire services called by the MW93C46 modules.

EEOPEN enables the device for writes. If the device is in the write disabled state and EEOPEN is not called to enable it, the EEPROM will ignore any subsequent write transactions. The write disabled state prevents accidental writes to the EEPROM. To prevent accidental writes after a write session, the EEPROM should be placed in the write disable state with a call to EECLOSE.

449

EEPOLL tests the DO pin after a write and waits for a high (logic 1) on the pin to signal the completion of the write cycle. DO must have a pull-up because DO signals completion by going tri-state.

Write 16 Bit Data To Addressed Register (Module EEWRITE)

The write data and register address are passed to EEWRITE in **data1, data0** and **eeaddr**. Some early versions of the 93C46 do not feature the automatic erase-before-write cycle found in most current versions of this device. To accommodate these older devices, EEWRITE erases the addressed register immediately upon entry. After the erase cycle is finished, EEWRITE re-selects the device, sends the start bit followed by the addressed write instruction, followed by two data bytes (16 bit data). It then de-selects the device and polls for the completed write cycle. EEWRITE exits only after the write cycle has been completed.

Read 16 Bit Data From Addressed Register (Module EEREAD)

The register address is passed to EEREAD in **eeaddr**. On entry, EEREAD selects the EEPROM, sends the start bit followed by the addressed read instruction. It then sends a dummy *bit* followed by two dummy *bytes*. The dummy bytes serve to clock the read data out of the EEPROM. Prior to exiting, EEREAD de-selects the EEPROM. The received data bytes are passed from EEREAD in **data1** and **data0.**

```
;====== MW93C46.GRP =========================================================
;
;        MICROWIRE Bit-Bang communications with
;        Microwire EEPROM type 93C46 or similar.
;
;----------------------------------------------------------------------------
;
;        Requires following workspace:
;                Workspace required by WIRECOMS.TXT and:
;                eeaddr   eeprom address
;                data1    data high byte write to or read from eeprom
;                data0    data low byte
;
;        Requires following equates:
;                equates required by WIRECOMS.TXT  and:
;                ee       equ     nn      (Port B Bit for EEPROM Chip Enable)
;
;----------------------------------------------------------------------------
;        Module: EEOPEN
;        Enable EEPROM Erase and Write
;
;        Note: Polling for 'write completed ?' is included in this module.
;
;----------------------------------------------------------------------------
eeopen  bcf     portb,ee        ;de-select eeprom
        bcf     portb,sck       ;make sure SCK is low
        bsf     portb,ee        ;select eeprom
        call    stbt            ;send start bit
```

```
        movlw   30              ;enable erase & write instruction
        movwf   datout
        call    mwire           ;send it
        bcf     portb,ee        ;de-select
        call    eepoll          ;wait for eeprom to finish
        retlw   0               ;exit
;-------------------------------------------------------------------------
;       Module: EECLOSE
;       Disable EEPROM Erase and Write, then De-select EEPROM
;
;-------------------------------------------------------------------------
eeclose bsf     portb,ee        ;select eeprom
        call    stbt            ;send start bit
        clrf    datout          ;disable instruction
        call    mwire           ;send it
        bcf     portb,ee        ;de-select eeprom
        retlw   0               ;exit
;-------------------------------------------------------------------------
;       Module: eepoll
;       Poll eeprom DO pin for ready level
;
;-------------------------------------------------------------------------
eepoll  bsf     portb,ee        ;select eeprom
eepoll1 btfss   portb,si        ;EEPROM DO high ?
        goto    eepoll1         ;no. go try again
        bcf     portb,ee        ;yes. de-select EEPROM
        retlw   0               ;exit
;-------------------------------------------------------------------------
;       Module: EEWRITE
;       Write 16 bits to EEPROM
;
;       Note: Erase is included because some 93C46 EEPROMS do not feature
;             automatic erase before write. If not required, delete from
;             race1 to race2
;
;       Note: Polling for 'write completed ?' is included in this module.
;       Note: Each memory location is 16 bits with the most significant
;             bit in bit position 15. The 16 bit memory word is made up of
;             two 8 bit bytes (data1, data0) with the most siginificant
;             bit of data1 placed in bit position 15 and the least
;             significant bit of data0 placed in bit position 0.
;
;-------------------------------------------------------------------------
eewrite bsf     portb,ee        ;select eeprom
;
;race1   Here we send the erase instruction:(if not required, delete
;          from here)
        call    stbt            ;send start bit
        movlw   0c0             ;erase instruction              |
        iorwf   eeaddr,w        ;or with address                |
        movwf   datout          ;                               |
        call    mwire           ;send it                        |
        bcf     portb,ee        ;de-select eeprom               |
        call    eepoll          ;wait for ready                 V
```

451

```
;race2     At this point the erase has been completed      (to here)
;
          bsf     portb,ee          ;select eeprom
          call    stbt              ;send dtart bit
          movlw   40                ;write instruction
          iorwf   eeaddr,w          ;or with address
          movwf   datout
          call    mwire             ;send it
          movf    data1,w           ;data high byte
          movwf   datout
          call    mwire             ;send it
          movf    data0,w           ;data low byte
          movwf   datout
          call    mwire             ;send it
          bcf     portb,ee          ;de-select
          call    eepoll            ;wait for ready
          retlw   0                 ;exit
;-----------------------------------------------------------------------
;         Module: EEREAD
;         Read 16 bits from EEPROM
;
;         Reads 16 bit memory word as (data1, data0)
;-----------------------------------------------------------------------
eeread    bsf     portb,ee          ;select eeprom
          call    stbt
          movlw   80                ;read instruction
          iorwf   eeaddr,w          ;or with address
          movwf   datout
          call    mwire             ;send it
          call    dumbt             ;send dummy bit to clock out EEPROM leading 0
          clrf    datout            ;dummy byte to clock out read bytes
          call    mwire             ;send dummy byte
          movf    datin,w
          movwf   data1             ;high byte to data1
          clrf    datout            ;dummy byte to clock out read bytes
          call    mwire             ;send dummy byte
          movf    datin,w
          movwf   data0             ;low byte to data0
          bcf     portb,ee          ;de-select eeprom
          retlw   0                 ;exit
;-----------------------------------------------------------------------
;         Module: EERASE
;         Erase all registers
;
;         Note: Polling for 'write completed ?' is included in this module.
;-----------------------------------------------------------------------
eerase    bsf     portb,ee          ;select eeprom
          call    stbt              ;send start bit
          movlw   20                ;erase all instruction
          movwf   datout
          call    mwire             ;send it
          bcf     portb,ee          ;de-select eeprom
          call    eepoll            ;wait for ready
          retlw   0                 ;exit
;=======================================================================
```

10.3.2 Using the Section 10.2 Routines in Your Applications

Generally all of the routines can be used in your applications as written or with minor changes. For all routines, the entry and exit conditions, variables, port definitions and flag definitions are described in the xx.GRP and xx.TXT listings. All port assignments are arbitrary and may be changed to suit your application. The sample applications use the PIC16F84 but the routines may be used with other PICmicros with little or no change.

The routines introduced in Section 10.2 are in:

MW93C46.GRP   Microwire Bit-Bang Communications Services

The routines in this group are all *called* functions. They call the Microwire services in WIRE-COMS.GRP (Section 10.2.1).

The routines in MW93C46.GRP are adequate for 93C06 and 93C46 communications, but the larger 93Cxx EEPROMS require an instruction word of greater than eight bits. The 93C56 through 93C86 devices require up to 13 instruction bits. The MW93C46 modules may be modified to communicate with these larger EEPROMS by using two bytes for the instruction. Microwire transactions ignore any low (logic 0) bits clocked in prior to the start bit, so any instruction requiring more than 8 bits may be sent as a 16 bit instruction with the leading bits of the high byte set low as place fillers. But, you *must* include the start bit in the instruction high byte. The start bit must be the bit immediately preceding the highest significant instruction bit. For example, the instruction for reading a 93C86 (organized as a 1024 byte by 16 bit register device) is:

    0 0 0 1 1 0 a9 a8   a7 a6 a5 a4 a3 a2 a1 a0

where the left most high (1) bit of the high byte is the *start* bit. When modifying the modules be sure to delete the call to STBT for these two byte instructions.

If an EEPROM with pin selectable register size is required for your application and you select the 8 bit register size, you will have to modify the modules to transfer only one data byte (8 bits) per transaction.

For all EEPROM applications be sure to call EECLOSE when terminating an EEPROM communications session to ensure against any unintended writes. Your application should include a pull-up on DO to ensure a high DO for the write-completed polling. The modules that write to the EEPROM do not exit until the write operation has been completed. For an application where this wait cannot be tolerated, the modules may be modified to test for completed write cycle at entry and not write until the cycle is completed. Time may be saved because the write cycle may have been completed while your application was off doing something else.

10.4 Microwire Analog to Digital Converters

A great many Analog-to-Digital converters compatible with three wire serial communications schemes are available. Generally these serial converters may be used with both the SPI Bus and the Microwire Interface. For example: in Section 9.3 we applied the Maxim MAX187 A/D to the SPI bus with the SPI A/D service SPIATOD.TXT. This device may be used with the Microwire Interface by simply replacing the call to SPIMD in SPIATOD with a call to the Microwire send and receive service MWIRE. See Figure 10-12 and MW187AD.TXT. Note that MW187AD differs from the SPI version only in the designation of the serial data line (SI in place of MISO) and the call to MWIRE. The Microwire service MWIRE reads the leading high bit as the first bit received and reads the trailing low bits as the last 3 bits received; thus the two byte normalization is identical to that of the SPI and I^2C applications of this device.

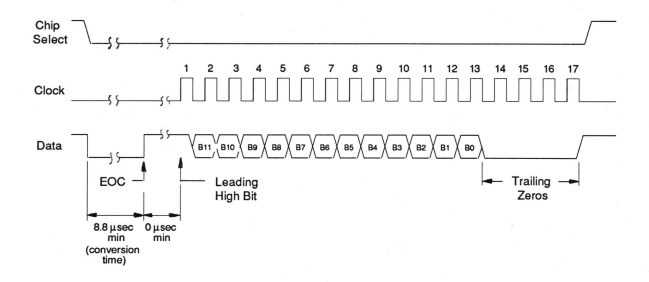

Figure 10-12   MAX187 A/D Microwire Timing

```
;====== MW187AD.TXT =============================================
;
;        Module MW187AD.TXT
;        Microwire analog to digital converter MAX 187
;        Bit-Bang Microwire
;
;----------------------------------------------------------------
;
;        A/D select line is    port B bit adcen
;        Serial in line is     port B bit si
;        Serial clock line is  port B bit sck
;
;        On Exit: A/D count in (data1,data0)
;----------------------------------------------------------------
spiatod bsf     portb,adcen    ;make sure A to D not enabled
        bcf     portb,sck      ;make sure clock line down
```

```
                bcf     portb,adcen      ;select A/D (starts conversion)
                nop
spiad1          btfss   portb,si         ;end of conversion ? if yes, skip next
                goto    spiad1           ;no. go try again
                call    mwire            ;yes. transfer data byte
                movf    datin,w          ;received byte to...
                movwf   data1            ;data1
                clrf    data0
                call    mwire            ;read low byte
                movf    datin,w          ;received byte to...
                movwf   data0            ;data0
                bsf     portb,adcen      ;deselect A/D
;
;       Here we arrange the 12 bits in the 12 lower bit positions of
;       data1, data0
                rrf     data1,f          ;DB5 to c
                rrf     data0,f          ;DB5 to data0
                rrf     data1,f          ;DB6 to c
                rrf     data0,f          ;DB6 to data0
                rrf     data1,f          ;DB7 to c
                rrf     data0,f          ;DB7 to data0. data0 has low byte of A/D data
                movlw   0f               ;clear high 4 bits of data1
                andwf   data1,f          ;data1 has high 4 bits of A/D data
;
                retlw   0                ;exit
;================================================================================
```

The ADC0832 is typical of Microwire analog to digital converters. It is described in the following section and is used to demonstrate the techniques necessary to communicate with a typical Microwire device.

10.4.1 Communicating with a Microwire A/D Converter

The National Semiconductor ADC0832 is a two channel, eight bit A/D converter configured to comply with the Microwire Interface. It may be configured to have two single ended input channels or a single differential input. The configuration is determined by the instruction byte sent to the device prior to receiving the conversion results (Figures 10-13 and 10-14).

The ADC0832 outputs the conversion data MSB-first followed by the same conversion data LSB-first as in Figure 10-13. Note that the low bit shares the same clock time slot for both the MSB-first and LSB-first data. The Microwire bit-bang services expect the serial data to conform to the Microwire MSB-first requirement, so we will ignore the LSB-first data. The easiest way to do this is to de-select the A/D after the low bit of the MSB-first data is clocked out.

455

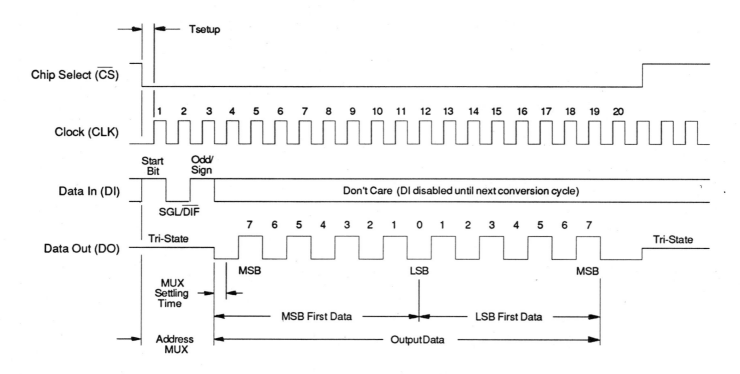

Figure 10-13   ADC0832 Transaction

The ADC0832 conversion data is clocked out as it is generated; necessitating a one-clock-cycle time-filler for the multiplexer to settle prior to conversion. This time-filler results in a leading low bit as part of the conversion result. This leading low bit may be ignored by treating the leading bit time slot as the last bit of the instruction byte because DI ignores any data clocked in after the ODD/SIGN bit of the instruction. After the instruction is clocked in, the conversion result is clocked out beginning with the MS bit. The leading four bits of the instruction must be low; the fifth bit is the start bit, the sixth and seventh bits configure the multiplexer and the eighth bit occupies the leading low bit time slot. See Figures 10-13 and 10-14.

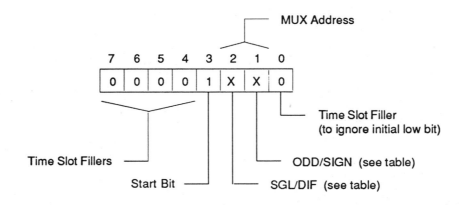

Single Ended MUX Mode				Differential MUX Mode			
MUX Address		Channel No.		MUX Address		Channel No.	
SGL/DIF	ODD/SIGN	0	1	SGL/DIF	ODD/SIGN	0	1
1	0	+		0	0	+	-
1	1		+	0	1	-	+

Figure 10-14   ADC0832 Instruction Byte

MW0832AD.TXT is the Microwire communications service for the ADC0832 configured as a two channel analog to digital converter. The ADC0832 may be configured as a differential converter by changing bits 1 and 2 of the instruction byte as per the table in Figure 10-14.

```
;====== MW0832AD.TXT ================================================
;
;       Module: MW0832AD.TXT
;       Microwire Analog to Digital Converter Service
;       National Semiconductor ADC0832 A/D
;
;--------------------------------------------------------------------
;
;       Requires following workspace:
;
;               Workspace required by WIRECOMS and:
;
;                   data0    channel 0 conversion result
;                   data1    channel 1 conversion result
;
```

```
;          Requires following equates:
;
;               ch0inst equ     0x0c    ;A/D instruction for channel 0
;               ch1inst equ     0x0e    :A/D instruction for channel 1
;
;
;          On exit, the conversion results are in data0 and data1.
;
;-----------------------------------------------------------------------
mwatod  bcf     portb,adsel     ;select A/D
        movlw   ch0inst         ;channel 0 instruction
        movwf   datout          ;send it
        call    mwire
        call    mwire           ;send dummy to receive conversion result
        movf    datin,w         ;channel 0 conversion result to data0
        movwf   data0
        bsf     portb,adsel     ;de-select
        nop
        bcf     portb,adsel     ;select
        movlw   ch1inst         ;channel 1 instruction
        movwf   datout          ;send it
        call    mwire
        call    mwire           ;send dummy to receive conversion result
        movf    datin,w
        movwf   data1           ;channel 1 conversion result to data1
        bsf     portb,adsel     ;de-select A/D
        return                  ;exit
;=======================================================================
```

10.4.2 PINK1.ASM: A Microwire A/D, Microwire EEPROM and Microwire to SPI Slave Application

PINK1 demonstrates the application of the Microwire Analog to Digital converter and EEPROM services described in Sections 10.4 and 10.3. PINK1 measures two A/D channels and stores the result to EEPROM. The measurements are repeated at 1 second intervals until 50 measurements have been completed. The stored measurements are then written to the SPI slave LCD display at 1 second intervals. The measurements are displayed as hexadecimal values.

The 93C46 EEPROM used in PINK1 stores data in 16 bit registers so the conversion data (eight bits) for each of the two A/D channels is stored in a single register. The channel 0 data is placed in the low eight bits and the channel 1 data in the high eight bits of the register. A block of 50 registers, beginning with register 1 and ending with register 50 (0x32), in the EEPROM are reserved for the A/D data. Register 0 is reserved for any configuration data or long-term flags required by an application. The first measurement is stored in register 50 and subsequent measurements in contiguous descending registers, ending with the last measurement in register 1.

458

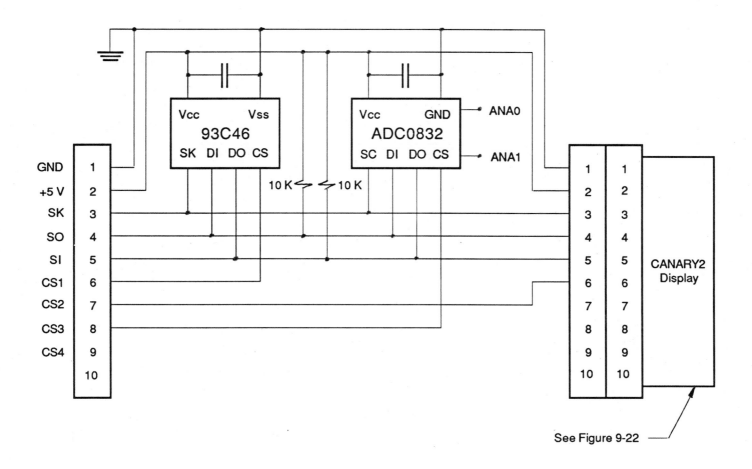

Figure 10-15   Slave Schematic; PINK1 Application

After 50 measurements have been completed, they are retrieved from the EEPROM and displayed to the SPI slave display application CANARY2. Figure 10-16 illustrates the relationship between the CANARY2 SPI timing and the WIRECOMS bit-bang Microwire timing. From Figure 10-16 it is apparent that the WIRECOMS services can be used unchanged to communicate with the SPI slave. Most SPI slave devices are compatible with the bit-bang Microwire services. Because the bit-bang SPI slave services in CANARY2 are relatively slow, the stretched clock version (WIRESLOW) of the WIRECOMS services are used in the PINK1 application.

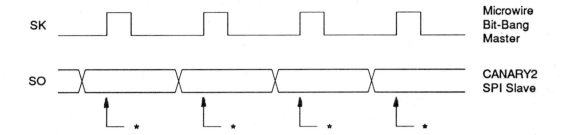

* CANARY2 Reads SO (MOSI)

Figure 10-16   CANARY2 SPI Slave On Microwire Interface

```
;====== PINK1.ASM =============================================================
;
;       Demonstrates application of Microwire A/D and EEPROM services.
;       Logs 50 two-channel A/D conversions to EEPROM then
;       retrieves them from EEPROM and writes them to SPI slave
;       LCD display
;
;------------------------------------------------------------------------------
        radix   hex             ;RADIX is HEX
;
        list p=16f84
;
;       STATUS REGISTER BIT DEFINITIONS:
c       equ     0               ;carry bit of status register (bit 0)
z       equ     2               ;zero flag bit of status register (bit 2)
dc      equ     1               ;digit carry
pd      equ     3               ;power down bit
to      equ     4               ;time out bit
rp0     equ     5               ;program page preselect, low bit
rp1     equ     6               ;program page preselect, high bit
;
;       DESTINATION BIT DEFINITIONS:
w       equ     0               ;destination working
f       equ     1               ;destination file
;
;------------------------------------------------------------------------------
;    CPU EQUATES   (special function register memory map)
;
;  BANK 0:
indf    equ     00              ;indirect file register
tmr0    equ     01              ;timer
pcl     equ     02              ;program counter (low byte)
status  equ     03              ;status register
fsr     equ     04              ;indirect data pointer
```

```
porta    equ    05           ;port a
portb    equ    06           ;port b
eedata   equ    08           ;eeprom data
eeadr    equ    09           ;eeprom address
pclath   equ    0a           ;write buffer for program counter (high byte)
intcon   equ    0b           ;interrupt control register
;
;   BANK 1:
optreg   equ    01           ;option register                    bank 1 (0x81)
trisa    equ    05           ;data direction register port a     bank 1 (0x85)
trisb    equ    06           ;data direction register port b     bank 1 (0x86)
eecon1   equ    08           ;eeprom control register            bank 1 (0x88)
;
;-----------------------------------------------------------------------
;       WORK AREA  (memory map)  Starts at 000c
;
;       For MICROWIRE applications:
datout   equ    000c         ;data byte to write to MWIRE bus
datin    equ    000d         ;data byte to read from MWIRE bus
bitctr   equ    000e         ;bit counter
fillctr  equ    000f         ;time delay counter
data1    equ    0010         ;high data byte
data0    equ    0011         ;low data byte
eeaddr   equ    0012         ;EEPROM address

;       For Display services:
ashex1   equ    0016         ;high byte ascii hex
ashex0   equ    0017         ;low byte ascii hex
dispdat  equ    0018         ;character to be displayed
;
;       For Delay Counters:
counter  equ    0019
cntra    equ    001a
cntrb    equ    001b
;-----------------------------------------------------------------------
;       SYSTEM EQUATES
;
dispen   equ    03           ;port B3 is SPI CANARY2 display select (EN2)
adsel    equ    02           ;port B2 is A/D select (EN3)
ee       equ    04           ;port B4 is EEPROM slave select (EN1)
si       equ    05           ;port B5 is SI
so       equ    06           ;port B6 is SO
sck      equ    07           ;port B7 is SK
mwrate   equ    04           ;determines clock rate
ch0inst  equ    0c           ;A/D channel 0 instruction
ch1inst  equ    0e           ;A/D channel 1 instruction
;
busy     equ    00           ;display busy flag bit (see CANARY2.ASM)
OH       equ    04f          ;ascii O
KAY      equ    04b          ;ascii K
SOH      equ    01           ;ascii SOH (clears display)
LF       equ    00a          ;ascii line feed
CR       equ    00d          ;ascii carriage return
SP       equ    020          ;ascii SPACE
```

461

```
;-------------------------------------------------------------------
        org     0x00            ;start of program memory
start   movlw   0c              ;SK and SO low, all selects high except
        movwf   portb           ;EEPROM which must be low for de-select
        clrf    porta
        bsf     status,rp0      ;switch to bank 1
        movlw   00e9            ;a0 & a3 inputs, a1, a2, a4 as outputs
        movwf   trisa
        movlw   0021            ;b5, b0 as input, others output
        movwf   trisb
        bcf     status,rp0      ;switch to bank 0
        call    dly
        movlw   SOH             ;initialize slave display
        movwf   dispdat
        call    mwdisp
        movlw   OH              ;OK followed by CR & LF to terminal
        movwf   dispdat
        call    mwdisp
        movlw   KAY
        movwf   dispdat
        call    mwdisp
        movlw   CR
        movwf   dispdat
        call    mwdisp
        movlw   LF
        movwf   dispdat
        call    mwdisp
;
        movlw   0x32            ;start of EEPROM memory block
        movwf   eeaddr
loop1   call    mwatod          ;make 2 channel measurements
        call    eeopen          ;enable EEPROM write
        call    eewrite         ;measurements to EEPROM
        call    eeclose         ;disable EEPROM write
        call    second          ;wait approx 1 second
        decfsz  eeaddr,f        ;all measurements done ?
        goto    loop1           ;no. go do next
        movlw   0x32            ;start of EEPROM block
        movwf   eeaddr
loop2   movlw   SOH             ;clear display
        movwf   dispdat
        call    mwdisp
        call    eeread          ;get 2 channel measurments
        call    hexasc          ;convert chan 0 data to ascii hex
        call    mwsplay         ;format and display chan 0 data
        movf    data1,w         ;get chan 1 data
        movwf   data0
        call    hexasc          ;convert it to ascii hex
        call    mwsplay         ;format and display chan 1 data
        call    second
        decfsz  eeaddr,f        ;all measuremunts displayed
        goto    loop2           ;no. go do next
dead    goto    dead            ;yes. done. dead loop
;-------------------------------------------------------------------
```

```
;         INCLUDES:
;         MW0832AD.TXT  ADC0832 A/D service  (Section 10.4.2)
;         WIRESLOW.GRP  Stretched Clock Microwire Services (Section 10.2.1)
;         MW93C46.GRP   EEPROM Communications  (Section 10.3.1)
;
;-----------------------------------------------------------------------
          include mw0832ad.txt
          include wireslow.grp
          include mw93c46.grp
;
;=======================================================================
;         Module: HEXASC
;         Converts 1 byte hex number to two ascii characters representing
;         hex number.
;         On entry: hex number in data0
;
;         On exit: ascii hex in ashex1 & ashex0
;-----------------------------------------------------------------------
hexasc   movf    data0,w        ;hex data
         andlw   0f             ;mask high nible
         call    hex2asc        ;convert it
         movwf   ashex0
         swapf   data0,w        ;swap nibbles
         andlw   0f             ;mask nibble
         call    hex2asc
         movwf   ashex1
         retlw   0
;-----------------------------
hex2asc  addlw   0x36           ;convert nibble to ascii
         btfss   status,dc      ;greater than 0x3f ? if yes, skip next
         addlw   0xf9           ;no. subtract 7
         addlw   0x01           ;yes. correction
         return                 ;exit
;-----------------------------------------------------------------------
;         Module: MWSPLAY
;         Format conversion for display
;
;-----------------------------------------------------------------------
mwsplay  movf    ashex1,w
         movwf   dispdat
         call    mwdisp
         movf    ashex0,w
         movwf   dispdat
         call    mwdisp
         movlw   SP
         movwf   dispdat
         call    mwdisp
         return
;-----------------------------------------------------------------------
;         Module: MWDISP
;         Send a character to the display CANARY2
;         Character to send is in dispdat
;         Exits only after slave accepts character
;-----------------------------------------------------------------------
```

463

```
mwdisp  movf    dispdat,w       ;character to send
        movwf   datout
        bcf     portb,dispen    ;select display
        call    mwire           ;send it
        bsf     portb,dispen    ;de-select display
        btfsc   datin,busy      ;was it accepted ?
        goto    mwdisp          ;no. go try again
        return                  ;yes. exit
;------------------------------------------------------------------
;       Module: SECOND.TXT      Wait approx. 1 second
;------------------------------------------------------------------
second  movlw   05
        movwf   counter
second1 call    dly
        decfsz  counter,f
        goto    second1
        return
;
dly     clrf    cntrb
dly0    clrf    cntra
dly1    decfsz  cntra,f
        goto    dly1
        decfsz  cntrb,f
        goto    dly0
        return
;------------------------------------------------------------------
        end                     ;END OF PROGRAM
;==================================================================
```

10.4.3 Using the Section 10.4 Routines in Your Applications

Generally all of the routines may be used in your applications as written or with minor changes. For all routines, the entry and exit conditions, variables, port definitions and flag definitions are described in the xx.GRP and xx.TXT listings. All port assignments are arbitrary and may be changed to suit your application. The sample applications use the PIC16F84 but the routines may be used with other PICmicros with little or no change.

The routines introduced in Section 10.2 are:

MW187AD.TXT   Microwire Bit-Bang MAX187 A/D Service
MW0832AD.TXT   Microwire Bit-Bang ADC0832 A/D Service
PINK1.ASM   Microwire Bit-Bang A/D, EEPROM and Display Application

The ADC0832 uses the serial clock (SK) as the internal conversion clock. This externally generated conversion clock technique places both minimum and maximum limits on the serial clock frequency of 10 KHz and 400 KHz respectively.

PINK1 uses the stretched clock version (WIRESLOW) of the WIRECOMS services because the bit-bang SPI slave display CANARY2 requires a slow clock. A clock cycle for the stretched clock version of MWIRE is approximately 23 + 6(n) instruction cycles, where n is the parameter **mwrate.** For PINK1, **mwrate** is 4, resulting in a clock rate of approximately 15 KHz (with 4 MHz crystal). If your application does not require a low serial clock rate, use the WIRECOMS services, but do not exceed 400 KHz.

The ADC0832 is a relatively simple device to apply to the Microwire interface, but the methodology used in MW0832AD may be applied to devices having more complex communications protocols. The key to setting up your communications is that generally Microwire slave devices will ignore any bits clocked into the device prior to the start bit and the individual device protocols generally ignore any bits clocked in when they are not expected.

The CANARY2 SPI display slave will accept new display data only when it is not busy. It indicates the busy state by releasing the MISO line (in effect setting the busy bit of the status returned by CANARY2, see Section 9.6.2) which is tested by the master. The module MWDISP in PINK1 sends a character to CANARY2, receives the status from CANARY2 and attempts to test the status busy bit to determine if the character was accepted. Since CANARY2 is an SPI Mode A device, the returned status bit synchronization has slipped one bit time as shown in Figure 10-17. As a result of this one bit slippage, the Microwire master reads bit 1 as bit 0. If CANARY2 status bit 1 is clear for not busy (as is bit 0) and the MISO line is released for busy, both a Microwire master and a Mode A SPI master will correctly recognize the busy/not busy status. Because all bits are high for busy and status bit 1 is always low, this requirement is satisfied.

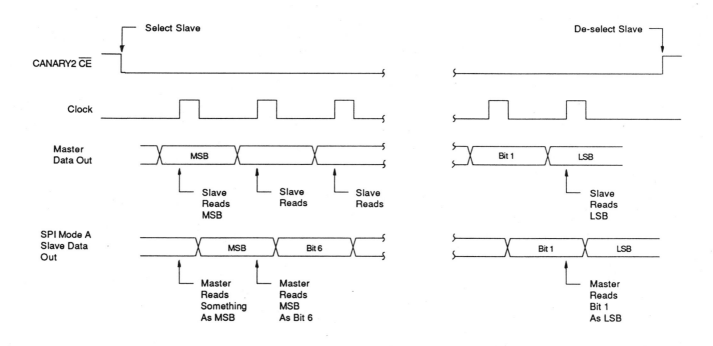

Figure 10-17   Microwire To SPI Mode A Slave Timing

When CANARY2 is busy and thus cannot receive a new character, it releases the MISO line which has the effect of making *all* returned bits high. In this case, the CANARY2 returned bits are not *individually* significant, and bit slippage presents no problem to the PINK1 application. If you have a bit-bang SPI slave application you wish to use with the bit-bang Microwire Interface, you can avoid the bit slippage problem by making the SPI slave a Mode D device. Mode D devices will directly interface with Microwire masters. Had the CANARY2 returned status been individually bit significant, the easiest way to have solved the bit slippage problem would have been to make it a Mode D device by replacing the calls to SPISMA with calls to SPISMD.

465

Hardware devices (and your bit-bang slave applications) may use a leading high bit (corresponding to the master start bit) along with extra bytes with filler (dummy) bits to avoid bit slippage. Extra bits with bit justification, as with the MAX187 in Section 10.4, may also be employed to make your slave device compatible with different bus schemes. However, the method of returning all high bits is certainly simpler to deal with and was specifically chosen for CANARY2 to make it compatible with both SPI Mode A and Microwire applications. Since the slave is normally required to release the data lines when it is not actively communicating, returning all high bits as a busy signal added no complexity to the CANARY2 application.

10.5 Microwire Bit-Bang Slave Applications

The parallel port slave application JADE1 is an eight bit input port to Microwire Interface device. The input data at the parallel port is transferred serially to the master. JADE1 is a simple demonstration of the Microwire slave services WIRESLAV.GRP. All of the WIRESLAV services are used in JADE1. See Figures 10-18 and 10-19 and JADE1.ASM.

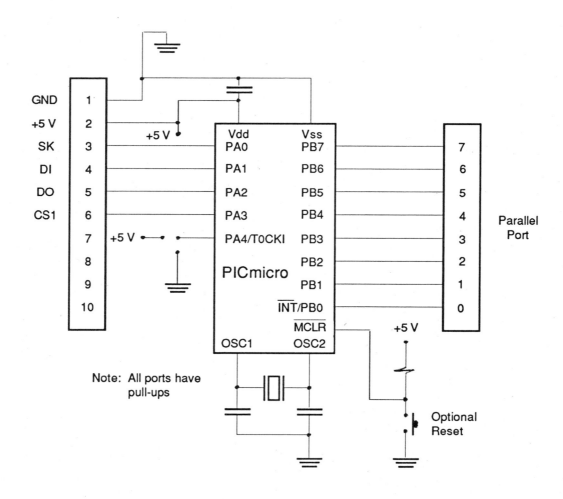

Figure 10-18   Schematic; Slave Application JADE1

466

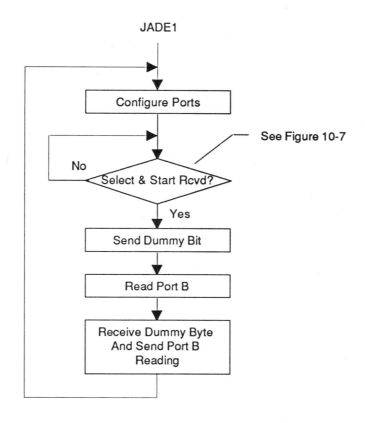

Figure 10-19   JADE1 Slave Parallel Port

10.5.1 JADE1.ASM: A Microwire Slave Parallel Port Application

JADE1 waits in a loop (WIRESLAV service SLSTBT) to be selected and started. If it is selected and has received a start bit, JADE1 sends a dummy bit (via SLDMBT), reads the input port (port B) and sends the port contents (via SLVXFR). After sending the port contents, JADE1 returns to the SLSTBT loop and again waits to be selected and started.

Master communication with JADE1 using the WIRECOMS services is quite simple:

```
bcf     portb,select    ;select slave JADE1
call    stbt            ;send start bit
call    dumbt           ;send dummy bit to clock out the
                        ;slave leading low bit
call    mwire           ;receive slave data (port contents)
bsf     portb,select    ;de-select slave JADE1
```

At this point the port input is in **datin**. The bit-bang WIRESLAV services are relatively slow, so the stretched clock version of the WIRECOMS services, the WIRESLOW services, must be used in the master application.

```
;====== JADE1.ASM ============================================================
;
;         Demonstrates application of WIRESLAV.GRP
;         When selected, reads port B and sends result to MICROWIRE master
;         on receipt of start bit. Data sent is preceeded by a 0 bit.
;         NOTE: Because bit-bang slave is slow, the master should have a
;         clock period of approximately 25 uSec or longer.
;
;----------------------------------------------------------------------------
          radix   hex        ;RADIX is HEX
;
          list p=16f84
;
;         STATUS REGISTER BIT DEFINITIONS:
c         equ     0          ;carry bit of status register (bit 0)
z         equ     2          ;zero flag bit of status register (bit 2)
dc        equ     1          ;digit carry
pd        equ     3          ;power down bit
to        equ     4          ;time out bit
rp0       equ     5          ;program page preselect, low bit
rp1       equ     6          ;program page preselect, high bit
;
;         DESTINATION BIT DEFINITIONS:
w         equ     0          ;destination working
f         equ     1          ;destination file
;
;----------------------------------------------------------------------------
;     CPU EQUATES  (special function register memory map)
;
;   BANK 0:
indf      equ     00         ;indirect file register
tmr0      equ     01         ;timer
pcl       equ     02         ;program counter (low byte)
status    equ     03         ;status register
fsr       equ     04         ;indirect data pointer
porta     equ     05         ;port a
portb     equ     06         ;port b
eedata    equ     08         ;eeprom data
eeadr     equ     09         ;eeprom address
pclath    equ     0a         ;write buffer for program counter (high byte)
intcon    equ     0b         ;interrupt control register
;
;   BANK 1:
optreg    equ     01         ;option register                  bank 1 (0x81)
trisa     equ     05         ;data direction register port a   bank 1 (0x85)
trisb     equ     06         ;data direction register port b   bank 1 (0x86)
eecon1    equ     08         ;eeprom control register          bank 1 (0x88)
;
;----------------------------------------------------------------------------
;     WORK AREA  (memory map)  Starts at 000c
;
datout    equ     000c       ;data sent to master
datin     equ     000d       ;data received from master
bitctr    equ     000e       ;bit counter
```

```
;
;-------------------------------------------------------------------
;       SYSTEM EQUATES
;
do      equ     02          ;port a2 is DO line
di      equ     01          ;port A1 is DI line
sck     equ     00          ;port A0 is SCK line
select  equ     03          ;port A3 is SELECT line

;-------------------------------------------------------------------
        org     0x00
start   movlw   0ff
        tris    portb               ;all port b input
        movwf   porta               ;port A2, A4 high
        movlw   00b
        tris    porta               ;PA0,1,3 as inputs, PA2,4 as output
;
slvloop call    slstbt              ;selected AND start bit ? returns if yes.
        call    sldmbt              ;yes. send dummy (0) bit
        movf    portb,w             ;read port b
        movwf   datout              ;send it
        call    slvxfr
        goto    start               ;& go loop
;============WIRESLAV.GRP=====================================================
;
;       Bit Bang MICROWIRE slave communications
;       PIC is slave
;
;       Required work area
;               datout  data to be sent to master
;               datin   data received from master
;               bitctr  bit counter
;
;       Required equates
;               do      equ     nn      port A bit for DO line
;               di      equ     nn      port A bit for DI line
;               sck     equ     nn      port A bit for SCK line
;               select  equ     nn      port A bit for chip enable line
;
;       NOTE: Clock period should be approximately 25 uSec or longer.
;-------------------------------------------------------------------
;       Module: SLSTBT
;       Waits for selected AND start bit
;
;-------------------------------------------------------------------
slstbt  btfsc   porta,select        ;selected ? if yes, skip next
        goto    slstbt              ;no. go try again
        btfss   porta,sck           ;clock high ? if yes, skip next
        goto    slstbt              ;no. go try again
        btfss   porta,di            ;yes. DI high ? if yes, skip next
        goto    slstbt              ;no. go try again
        retlw   0                   ;yes. exit
;-------------------------------------------------------------------
;       Module: SLDMBT
```

```
;           Sends dummy (DO low) bit
;
;-----------------------------------------------------------------
sldmbt   btfsc    porta,sck          ;clock low ? if yes, skip next
         goto     sldmbt             ;no. go try again
         bcf      portb,do           ;yes. take DO low
sldmbt1  btfss    porta,sck          ;clock high ? If yes, skip next
         goto     sldmbt1            ;no. go try again
         retlw    0                  ;yes. exit
;-----------------------------------------------------------------
;           Module: SLVXFR
;           Receive and send 8 bit byte
;
;-----------------------------------------------------------------
slvxfr   movlw    d'8'               ;8 bit byte
         movwf    bitctr
slvxfr1  btfsc    porta,sck          ;clock low ? if yes, skip next
         goto     slvxfr1            ;no. go try again
slvxfr2  btfss    porta,sck          ;clock high ? if yes, skip next
         goto     slvxfr2            ;no. go try again
         bcf      status,c           ;yes. read DI line:
         btfsc    porta,di           ;DI line high ? if no, skip next
         bsf      status,c           ;yes. set carry
         rlf      datin,f            ;bit to data in
         rlf      datout,f           ;data out bit to DO
         btfss    status,c
         goto     slvxfr3
         bsf      porta,do
         goto     slvxfr4
slvxfr3  bcf      porta,do
slvxfr4  decfsz   bitctr,f           ;all bits done ? if yes, skip next
         goto     slvxfr1            ;no. go do next bit
         retlw    0                  ;yes. exit
;-----------------------------------------------------------------
;
         end                         ;end of program
;=================================================================
```

Chapter 11
The Dallas 1-Wire Bus

The Dallas 1-Wire Serial Bus

The Dallas 1-Wire bus is a self clocking serial data transfer scheme requiring no clock signal. Because the data signals are self clocking, only one line is required. Each bit transmitted is associated with a time-slot, rather than a clock pulse. The bit value is determined by the wave form of the signal in the time-slot. A minimum and maximum period for a time-slot is defined. Within the limits imposed by the minimum and maximum time-slot period, the data transfer is fully asynchronous: bits may be transmitted at any time and no byte length is defined. The 1-Wire bus may be used for on board IC to IC communications or for twisted pair network communications. The Dallas MicroLAN network is based on the 1-Wire bus.

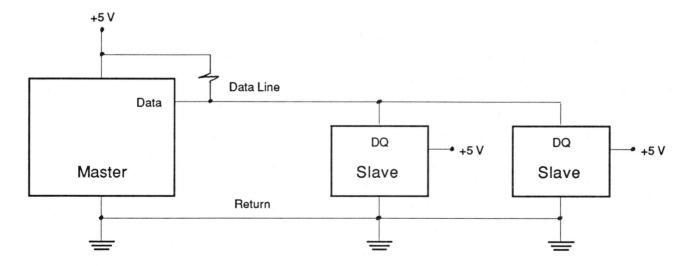

Figure 11-1   Dallas 1-wire Bus

11.1 Dallas 1-Wire Bus Specification

The serial data line is bi-directional, but data may flow only in one direction at a given time. Each device on the bus may operate as either a transmitter or receiver, but not simultaneously. Devices on the bus are defined as masters or slaves. A master is the device that initiates and controls the transfer of information over the data wire. All control signals and data are placed on the data wire. Both masters and slaves may operate as transmitters and receivers. Only one master may be on the bus. Each slave device on the bus has an unique address.

The 1-Wire data line is connected to a positive supply voltage via a pull-up resistor. When the bus is free, this wired-AND line is HIGH (released). The output stages of devices connected to the data line must be open drain or open collector to implement the wired-AND function.

11.1.1 Time-Slot Specifications

Only a master can initiate a time-slot. The master generates the start of a time-slot by pulling the data line LOW. Some time later, the master releases the line. If a slave is to send a data bit to the master, it then assumes control of the data line until the end of the time-slot. If the master is sending data it retains control of the data line throughout the time-slot.

Four master time-slot functions are defined: RESET, READ DATA, WRITE ONE and WRITE ZERO. The RESET function serves to initialize all slave devices. The READ DATA function reads a data bit placed on the data line by a slave device. The WRITE ONE and WRITE ZERO functions write a ONE or ZERO bit to the data line. These bits are read by one or more slave devices. Each function is implemented in one time-slot.

Three slave functions are defined: PRESENCE, WRITE ONE and WRITE ZERO. The PRESENCE function is a response to the RESET from the master. It signals the master that there is an active slave device on the bus. In response to a master READ DATA function, the slave places a data bit on the data line with the slave WRITE ONE or WRITE ZERO function. The slave may implement these functions *only* in response to the master RESET or READ DATA functions. Each function is implemented in one time-slot.

The various time-slot functions are characterized by the length (in time) of the time-slot and the wave form of the time-slot. Any device not holding the data line low is considered to have released the line. When the bus is idle all devices have released the line and the line idles high. The line *must* be high prior to any time-slot transaction. The master reads the data line only when it has released the line and the slave reads only when it has released the line. The minimum time that a device may hold the line low or released is 1 microsecond. The maximum time is determined by the function.

The RESET Time-Slot (Figure 11-2A)

The master generates the RESET function by taking the line low and holding it low for a minimum of 480 microseconds. The master then releases the line for an additional 480 microseconds. During this second 480 microsecond period the master reads the line. If one or more slaves are on the line, they take the line low, signaling their PRESENCE to the master. At the end of the RESET time-slot *all* devices have released the data line. The combined RESET and PRESENCE period may be any length greater than 480 microseconds, but the PRESENCE pulse must not exceed 240 microseconds (see Slave PRESENCE Pulse).

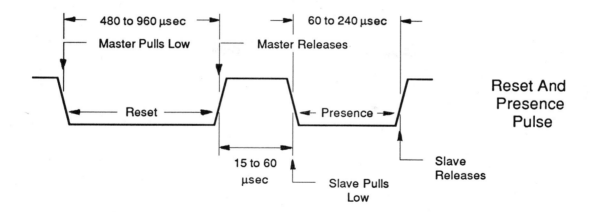

Figure 11-2A   Master Reset

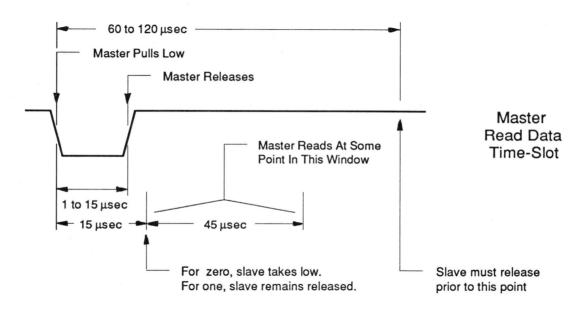

Figure 11-2B   Master Read Time-Slot

The Master READ DATA Time-Slot (Figure 11-2B)

The master initiates the READ DATA time-slot by pulling the data line low for a maximum of 15 microseconds, then releasing the data line for the remainder of the time-slot. In response the slave then places a data bit on the line (low for ZERO and released for ONE) and the master reads the data bit. The total time-slot length is 60 to 120 microseconds. The master reads the line at some point between 15 and 60 microseconds after the start of the time-slot. At the end of the READ DATA time-slot *all* devices have released the data line.

473

The Master WRITE ONE Time-Slot (Figure 11-3A)

The master initiates the WRITE ONE time-slot by pulling the data line low for a maximum of 15 microseconds, then releasing the data line for the remainder of the time-slot. The total time-slot length is 60 to 120 microseconds. The slave reads the line at some point between 15 and 60 microseconds after the start of the time-slot. At the end of the READ DATA time-slot *all* devices have released the data line.

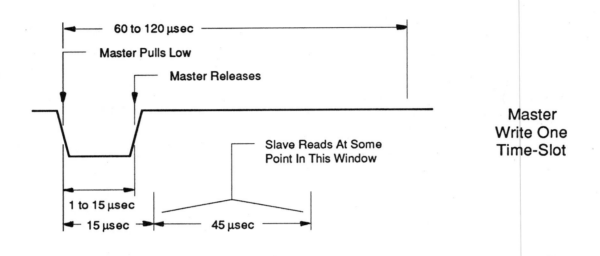

Figure 11-3A   Master Write One Time-Slot

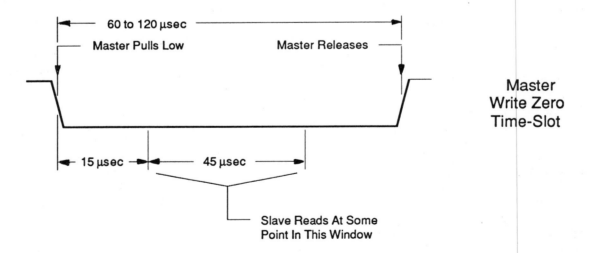

Figure 11-3B   Master Write Zero Time-Slot

474

The Master WRITE ZERO Time-Slot (Figure 11-3B)

The master generates the WRITE ZERO time-slot by pulling the data line low for the entire time-slot period. The total time-slot length is 60 to 120 microseconds. The slave reads the line at some point between 15 and 60 microseconds after the start of the time-slot. At the end of the READ DATA time-slot *all* devices have released the data line.

Slave PRESENCE Pulse (Figure 11-2A)

The PRESENCE pulse is generated by the slave in response to a RESET pulse from the master. The master generates the RESET pulse by holding the line low for at least 480 microseconds. The slave then takes the line low 15 to 60 microseconds after the master releases the line. The slave holds the line low for 60 to 240 microseconds then releases the line.

Slave WRITE ONE Time-Slot (Figure 11-2B)

The slave recognizes the master READ DATA time-slot as a maximum of 15 microseconds of line low. After the master releases the line the slave places a ONE on the line by doing nothing (remains released) for the remainder of the time-slot. The master reads the line shortly after releasing it.

Slave WRITE ZERO Time-Slot (Figure 11-2B)

The slave recognizes the master READ DATA time-slot as a maximum of 15 microseconds of line low. After the master releases the line the slave places a ZERO on the line by taking the line low. The master reads the line shortly after releasing it. The slave may hold the line low for the remainder of the time-slot but is not required to do so. Some slave devices hold the line low for only 15 microseconds beginning at the *start* of the time-slot. For this reason, master devices typically hold the line low for less than the maximum 15 microseconds and read immediately after releasing the line.

11.1.2 Communications Protocol

Because only one slave device at a time may be active on the bus, each slave device on the bus must have a unique address. A device becomes active only when it has been addressed by the master. This slave address is generally stored in ROM on the slave device. The Dallas devices typically have a 64 bit address stored in ROM. Each device manufactured has an unique address: an eight bit family code, a 48 bit serial number and an 8 bit Cyclical Redundancy Check (CRC) of the 56 bit concatenated family code and serial number. The CRC may be used as an error check. A slave device may have any number of address bits. The address of a device may be determined with a read ROM command. See the Dallas data book for details. When only one slave device is on the bus, addressing is not required.

The protocol for master to slave communications is primarily defined by the slave device function. Generally communications are initiated by the master with a RESET time-slot followed by several address bits. The device with the matching address becomes the only active slave on the bus. All devices on the bus are returned to inactive status with the RESET time-slot. After addressing the slave, the master is free to send commands or data or receive data. All communications are terminated with a RESET.

11.1.3 Hardware Specifications

The 1-Wire data line is connected to a +5 volt supply with a pull-up resistor or active pull-up. The maximum value for the pull-up resistor is 5000 ohms. If a large number of devices are on the bus, the drop across the pull-up resistor (primarily due to device input current) may be excessive. For a large number of devices, or a long cable, the pull-up resistor value must be reduced or the resistor replaced with some sort of active pull-up. The output stages of all devices on the 1-Wire bus must be open drain or open collector to implement this wired-AND configuration. Slave devices may draw operating power from the data line, but only if the load does not pull the line below the minimum data HIGH level. Dallas terms power derived from the data line as *parasite power*. Most of the Dallas slave devices are parasite powered. Parasite power is covered in greater detail in Section 11.3.1.

11.2 The PICmicro as a Bit-Bang 1-Wire Master and Slave

A convenient hardware configuration for bit-bang 1-Wire applications uses the PICmicro open drain output port to drive the data line and a second port to read the line. This two port connection to the 1-Wire bus simplifies both software and hardware.

All 1-Wire applications in this chapter drive the data line with port A4 (open drain output) and read the data line with port B1 (see Figure 11-4). Any port (except A4) may be used to read the line, but the open drain port *must* be used to drive the line to preserve the wired-AND character of the data line. This configuration applies to both master and slave implementations.

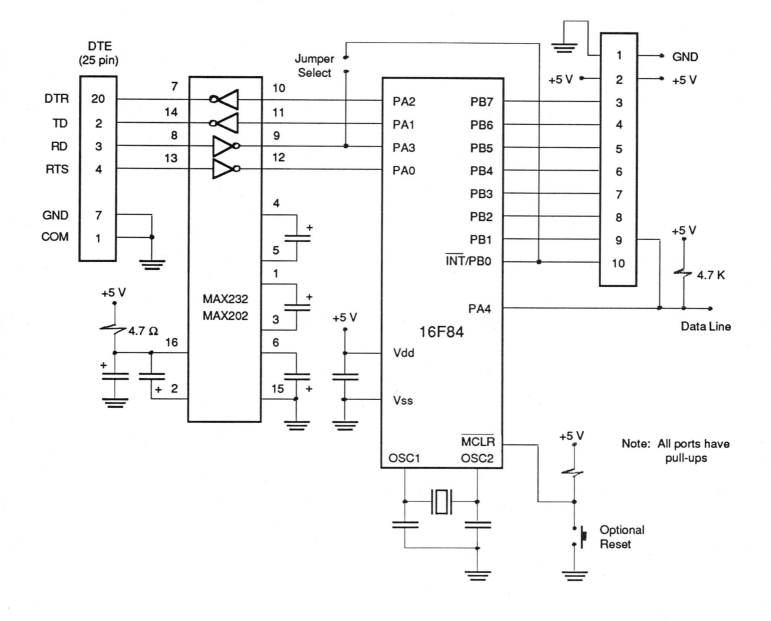

Figure 11-4   Schematic - Bit-Bang 1-Wire Master Applications

11.2.1 1-Wire Bit-Bang Master Bus Services

Three modules in DAL1WIRE.GRP are all that are necessary to implement the 1-Wire master bus functions. They are all *called* functions. These modules are:

DAL1WR   Generate a WRITE ONE or WRITE ZERO Time-Slot
DAL1RD   Read a Data Bit Time-Slot
DALRES   Send RESET and Receive PRESENCE

Two additional modules have been included in DAL1WIRE.GRP. These modules read and write 8 bit data bytes. They are also *called* functions. The modules are:

DALREC   Receive (read) an 8 Bit Byte
DALSND   Send (write) an 8 Bit Byte

On entry, the three 1-Wire bus function modules expect the data line to be released (HIGH) and they all release the line before exiting.

Module Descriptions:

Generate a WRITE ONE or WRITE ZERO Time-Slot
(Module DAL1WR and Figures 11-5 and 11-6)

The data bit to write is passed to the module via carry. On entry, DAL1WR takes the line low and holds it low for approximately 10 microseconds. If the data bit to write is zero, DAL1WR continues to hold the line low for approximately 60 microseconds then releases the line and exits. If the data bit to write is one, DAL1WR releases the line after the initial 10 microseconds then waits approximately 60 microseconds before exiting.

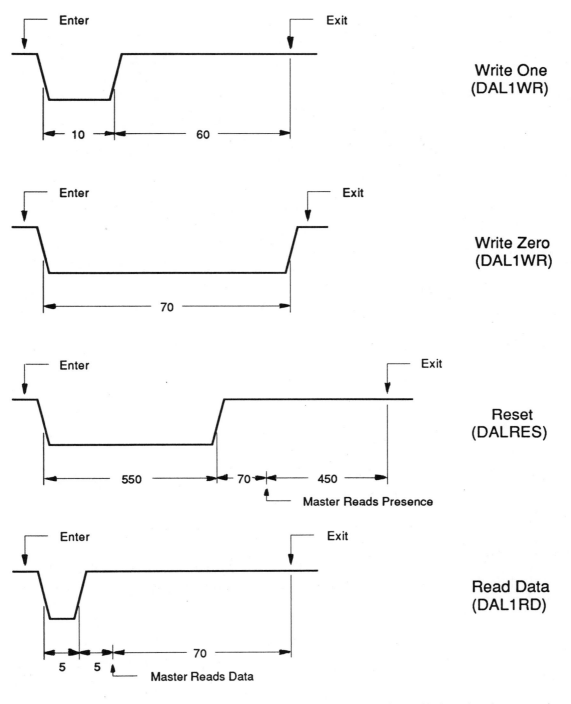

Enter | Exit
Write One (DAL1WR)
10 | 60

Enter | Exit
Write Zero (DAL1WR)
70

Enter | Exit
Reset (DALRES)
550 | 70 | 450
Master Reads Presence

Enter | Exit
Read Data (DAL1RD)
5 | 5 | 70
Master Reads Data

Note: All times in microseconds.

Figure 11-5   Master Bit-Bang Time-Slots

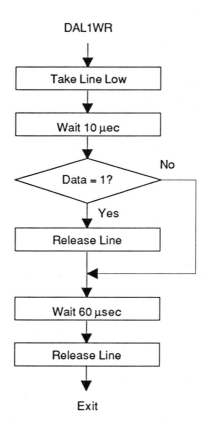

DAL1WR

Take Line Low

Wait 10 μec

Data = 1?   No

Yes

Release Line

Wait 60 μsec

Release Line

Exit

Figure 11-6   Master Bit-Bang Write Time-Slot (DAL1WR)

Read a Data Bit Time-Slot (Module DAL1RD and Figures 11-5 and 11-7)

On entry, DAL1RD takes the line low and holds it low for approximately 5 microseconds then releases it. Approximately 5 microseconds after releasing the line, DAL1RD reads the line. The state of the line (low or high) is transferred to the carry bit. Approximately 70 microseconds after reading the line DAL1RD exits. The read data bit is passed out via the carry.

480

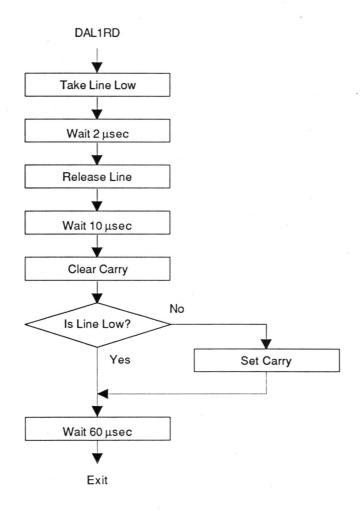

DAL1RD

Take Line Low

Wait 2 μsec

Release Line

Wait 10 μsec

Clear Carry

Is Line Low? — No → Set Carry

Yes

Wait 60 μsec

Exit

Figure 11-7   Master Bit-Bang read Time-Slot (DAL1RD)

Send RESET and Receive PRESENCE
(Module DALRES and Figures 11-5 and 11-8)

On entry, DALRES takes the data line low and holds it low for approximately 550 microseconds then releases it. Approximately 70 microseconds after releasing the line, DALRES reads the line and transfers the state of the line to the carry bit. If a PRESENCE is received, the carry is cleared (low). Approximately 450 microseconds after reading the line DALRES exits. The PRESENCE (or no presence) is passed out via the carry.

481

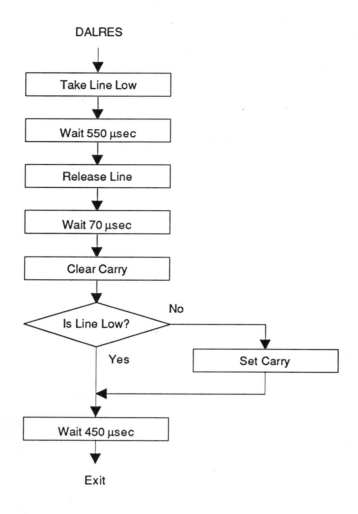

DALRES

Take Line Low

Wait 550 μsec

Release Line

Wait 70 μsec

Clear Carry

Is Line Low?

No

Yes

Set Carry

Wait 450 μsec

Exit

Figure 11-8   Bit-Bang Reset Pulse (DALRES)

Receive or Send an 8 Bit Byte

The modules DALREC and DALSND are not necessary for 1-Wire communications, but since the PICmicro is an 8 bit device, they are included as a convenience. They simply call the read or write modules eight times in sequence.

482

```
;====== DAL1WIRE.GRP ==========================================================
;
;         Dallas 1-wire Master serial bus services
;         Requires 4 MHz crystal
;
;         Includes following Modules:
;                 dal1wr  - write time slot
;                 dal1rd  - read time slot
;                 dal1res - send reset pulse and receive presence
;                 dalrec  - receive 8 bit data byte
;                 dalsnd  - send 8 bit data byte
;
;         Requires following work space:
;                 dlyctr  ;delay counter
;                 bitctr  ;bit counter
;                 indat   ;data byte received
;                 outdat  ;data byte to be sent
;
;         Requires following equates:
;                 wout    equ     04      ;port a4 is output
;                 win     equ     nn      ;port b bit for input
;
;------------------------------------------------------------------------------
;         DAL1WR
;         Bit Write  (generates write-1 or write-0 timeslot)
;         The bit to be sent is passed via the carry
;------------------------------------------------------------------------------
dal1wr  bcf     porta,wout      ;pull data line low
        movlw   0x03
        movwf   dlyctr          ;wait approx 10 u Sec
dal1wr1 decfsz  dlyctr,f
        goto    dal1wr1
        btfsc   status,c        ;release data line only if bit is 1
        bsf     porta,wout
        movlw   0x14            ;wait approx 60 u Sec
        movwf   dlyctr
dal1wr2 decfsz  dlyctr,f
        goto    dal1wr2
        bsf     porta,wout      ;release data line (bit = 0 release)
        return
;------------------------------------------------------------------------------
;         DAL1RD
;         Bit Read (read-data time slot)
;         The bit read is passed via the carry
;------------------------------------------------------------------------------
dal1rd  bcf     porta,wout      ;pull data line low
        movlw   0x01            ;wait approx 5 u Sec
        movwf   dlyctr
dal1rd0 decfsz  dlyctr,f
        goto    dal1rd0
        bsf     porta,wout      ;release data line
        movlw   0x01            ;wait approx 5 u Sec
        movwf   dlyctr
dal1rd1 decfsz  dlyctr,f
```

```
               goto     dal1rd1
               bcf      status,c        ;assume data is low
               btfsc    portb,win       ;is data low ? if yes, skip next
               bsf      status,c        ;no. set carry
               movlw    0x17            ;wait approx 70 u Sec
               movwf    dlyctr
dal1rd2        decfsz   dlyctr,f
               goto     dal1rd2
               return                   ;& exit
;------------------------------------------------------------------------
;       DALRES
;       Send Reset and Receive Presence (reset and presence pulse)
;       On exit, if presence received, carry is cleared
;------------------------------------------------------------------------
dalres  bcf      porta,wout      ;pull data line low
        movlw    0xb7            ;wait approx 550 u Sec
        movwf    dlyctr
dalres1 decfsz   dlyctr,f
        goto     dalres1
        bsf      porta,wout      ;release data line
        movlw    0x17            ;wait approx 70 uSec
        movwf    dlyctr
dalres2 decfsz   dlyctr,f
        goto     dalres2
        bsf      status,c        ;assume no presence
        btfss    portb,win       ;presence ? if no, skip next
        bcf      status,c        ;yes. clear carry
        movlw    0x95            ;wait approx 450 u Sec
        movwf    dlyctr
dalres3 decfsz   dlyctr,f
        goto     dalres3
        return                   ;exit
;------------------------------------------------------------------------
;       DALREC
;       Receive an 8 Bit Byte
;       On exit, received byte in INDAT
;------------------------------------------------------------------------
dalrec  movlw    0x08            ;8 bits
        movwf    bitctr
dalrec1 call     dal1rd          ;read a bit
        rrf      indat,f         ;bit to read register
        decfsz   bitctr,f        ;all 8 bits done ? If yes, skip next
        goto     dalrec1         ;no. go get next bit
        return                   ;yes. exit
;------------------------------------------------------------------------
;       DALSND
;       Send an 8 Bit Byte
;       On entry, byte to send is in OUTDAT.
;       On exit, OUTDAT is corrupted
;------------------------------------------------------------------------
dalsnd  movlw    0x08            ;8 bits
        movwf    bitctr
dalsnd1 rrf      outdat,f        ;get bit to send
        call     dal1wr          ;send it
```

484

```
        decfsz  bitctr,f          ;all 8 bits done ?
        goto    dalsnd1           ;no. go do next bit
        return                    ;yes. exit
;======================================================================
```

11.2.2 1-Wire Bit-Bang Slave Bus Services

Four modules in SLV1WIRE.GRP are all that are necessary to implement the 1-Wire slave bus functions. They are all *called* functions. These modules are:

DS1WAIT   Wait For a RESET Pulse
DS1IN   Read a Data Bit Time-Slot
DS1PRES   Send a PRESENCE Pulse
DS1WR   Generate a WRITE ONE or WRITE ZERO Time-Slot

Two additional modules have been included in SLV1WIRE.GRP. These modules read and write 8 bit data bytes. They are also *called* functions. The modules are:

DS1REC   Receive (read) an 8 Bit Byte
DS1SEN   Send (write) an 8 Bit Byte

The master may send a RESET pulse at any time, even during a read or write slot. The slave modules must be able to recognize this RESET and inform the slave application program of the RESET. In response to the RESET, the application program must return control to DS1WAIT. The slave modules pass the RESET out via the reset flag. The modules DS1IN and DS1WR recognize and flag this asynchronous RESET.

Module descriptions:

Wait For a RESET Pulse (Module DS1WAIT and Figure 11-9)

This is a *wait* and *see* module, similar to the I^{2}C module IIWAIT in Section 8.3.1. DS1WAIT monitors the data line until it recognizes a RESET pulse. If a reset pulse is received, it passes control to the slave application. If the data line is idle or any activity on the line is not a RESET pulse DS1WAIT continues to monitor the line. DS1WAIT exits *only* when a RESET is recognized. DS1WAIT exits via a jump (goto) to the slave application program. All applications *must* terminate with a jump back to DS1WAIT.

DS1WAIT polls the data line for a low state. If the line goes low and remains low for at least 400 microseconds DS1WAIT then waits for the line to be released, sends a PRESENCE pulse and exits to the application program. If the line does not remain low for 400 microseconds, DS1WAIT loops back and continues to poll the line.

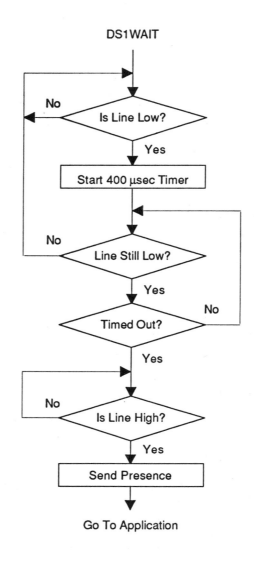

DS1WAIT

Is Line Low? — No

Yes

Start 400 μsec Timer

Line Still Low? — No

Yes

Timed Out? — No

Yes

Is Line High? — No

Yes

Send Presence

Go To Application

Figure 11-9   Slave Bit-Bang Wait And See (DS1WAIT)

Read a Data Bit Time-Slot (Module DS1IN and Figure 11-10)

DS1IN recognizes a WRITE ONE time-slot, WRITE ZERO time-slot or RESET pulse. The data bit read is passed out via the carry. If a RESET pulse is recognized, the reset-pulse-flag is set.

On entry, DS1IN polls the data line for a low state. When the line goes low, DS1IN waits 20 microseconds then re-tests the line. If the line has been released DS1IN sets the carry bit (data bit is one) and exits. If the line remains low after 20 microseconds, DS1IN continues to test the line for approximately 250 microseconds. If the line is released during this 250 microsecond period the carry bit is cleared (data bit is zero) and exits. If the line remains low after 250 microseconds the reset flag is set (RESET recognized) and DS1IN waits for the master to release the line. When the line is released DS1IN exits.

486

DS1IN

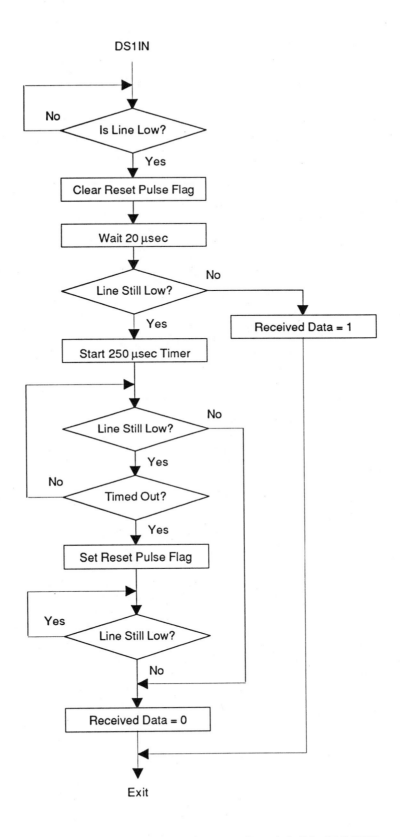

Figure 11-10   Slave Bit-Bang Read A Bit (DS1IN)

Send a PRESENCE Pulse (Module DS1PRES and Figure 11-11)

On entry, DS1PRES waits approximately 20 microseconds, takes the data line low and holds it low for approximately 160 microseconds. It then releases the line and exits.

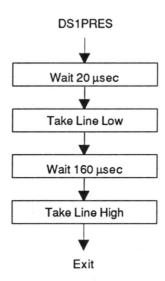

Figure 11-11   Slave Bit-Bang Send Presence (DS1PRES)

Generate a WRITE ONE or WRITE ZERO Time-Slot
(Module DS1WR and Figure 11-12)

The data bit to write is passed to the module via carry. If a RESET pulse is received during the write time-slot, DS1WR sets the reset flag and exits.

On entry, DS1WR waits for the line to be brought low by the master. Then, if the data bit is zero, DS1WR takes the line low and holds it low for approximately 20 microseconds, and releases it. If the data bit to write is one, DS1WR immediately releases the line, then waits 20 microseconds. After the initial 20 microsecond wait DS1WR immediately re-tests the line to make sure that is released (not held low by the master), and if released, exits. If the line is not released, DS1WR continues to test the line for 120 microseconds. If the line is released at some point prior to the completion of this 120 microsecond period, DS1WR exits. If the line remains low for more than 120 microseconds, DS1WR sets the reset flag. DS1WR does not exit until the line is released.

488

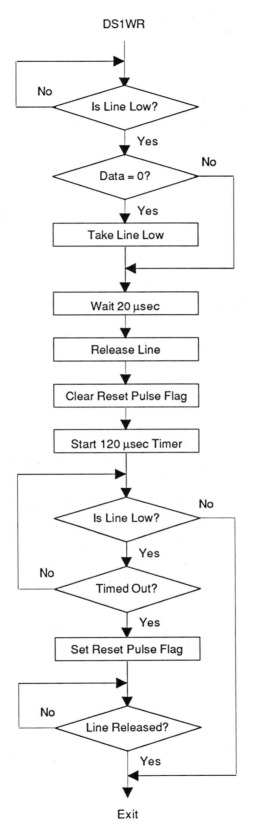

Figure 11-12 Slave Bit-Bang
Write A Bit (DS1WR)

489

Receive or Send an 8 Bit Byte

The modules DS1REC and DS1SEN are not necessary for 1-Wire communications, but since the PICmicro is an 8 bit device, they are included as a convenience. They simply call the read or write modules eight times in sequence. If the read or write module returns with the reset flag set, these 8 bit modules immediately return, passing the flag to the application (calling) program. It is the responsibility of the application program to return control to DS1WAIT.

```
;====== SLV1WIRE.GRP =======================================================
;
;        Dallas 1-Wire serial bus SLAVE services
;
;---------------------------------------------------------------------------
;
;        Includes Modules:
;                ds1wait - wait for reset pulse
;                ds1in   - read time-slot
;                ds1pres - presence pulse
;                ds1wr   - write time-slot
;                ds1rec  - receive 8 bit byte
;                ds1sen  - send 8 bit byte
;
;        Requires following workspace:
;                tmstmp  ;time stamp
;                dsstat  ;system status
;                bitctr  ;bit counter
;                indat   ;data byte received
;                outdat  ;data byte to be sent
;
;        Requires following equates:
;                dareset equ     nn        ;reset flag bit of dsstat
;                win     equ     nn        ;port a bit for input
;                wout    equ     04        ;port a4 is output
;
;        NOTE: Uses TMR0 and 4 MHz crystal. TMR0 must be configured for
;              internal clock  and 2:1 prescale.
;---------------------------------------------------------------------------
;        Module: ds1wait
;        Wait for a reset pulse.
;        On reception of reset pulse, sends presence then goes to
;        application.
;
;---------------------------------------------------------------------------
ds1wait btfsc    porta,win        ;data line low ? if yes, skip next
        goto     ds1wait          ;no. go try again
        bcf      dsstat,dareset   ;yes. clear reset flag
        movlw    0x37             ;start 400 u Sec timer (200 counts)
        movwf    tmr0
        bcf      intcon,toif
ds1wai1 btfsc    porta,win        ;data still low ? if yes, skip next
        goto     ds1wait          ;no. go wait for next data low
        movf     tmr0,w           ;get timer time stamp
```

```
          movwf    tmstmp
          btfsc    intcon,toif       ;timed out ? (long enough to be reset)
          goto     ds1wai2           ;yes. go
          goto     ds1wai1           ;no. go try again
ds1wai2   btfss    porta,win         ;line released ? if yes, skip next
          goto     ds1wai2           ;no. go try again until released
          call     ds1pres           ;yes. send presence
          goto     SLAVEAP           ;GO TO APPLICATION MODULE
                                     ;------------------------------------------
                                     ;The FIRST line of the APPLICATION Module
                                     ;MUST be labeled: SLAVEAP.
                                     ;
                                     ;The Application Module MUST terminate with
                                     ;ONLY a goto ds1wait.

;------------------------------------------------------------------------------
;         Module: ds1in
;         Slave input service (receives a bit). It recognizes the 1-wire write
;         one time slot, write zero time slot or reset pulse sent by the
;         master. The one and zero data bits are passed via the carry. If a
;         reset pulse is received, the reset pulse flag (dareset bit of dsstat)
;         is set. The application program MUST test for the reset pulse flag
;         and if the flag is set it must send the presence by calling the
;         presence service (ds1pres)
;
;------------------------------------------------------------------------------
ds1in     btfsc    porta,win         ;data line low ? if yes, skip next
          goto     ds1in             ;no. go try again
          bcf      dsstat,dareset    ;yes. clear reset flag
          movlw    0xf5              ;wait approx 20 u Sec
          movwf    tmr0
          bcf      intcon,toif
ds1in1    btfss    intcon,toif
          goto     ds1in1
          btfsc    porta,win         ;line still low ? if yes, skip next
          goto     ds1in5            ;no. go (data=1)
          movlw    0x80              ;yes. start approx 250 u Sec timer
          movwf    tmr0
          bcf      intcon,toif
ds1in2    btfsc    porta,win         ;line released ? if no, skip next
          goto     ds1in4            ;yes. go (data=0)
          btfss    intcon,toif       ;timed out ? if yes, skip next
          goto     ds1in2            ;no. go try again
          bsf      dsstat,dareset    ;yes. set reset flag
ds1in3    btfsc    porta,win         ;line released ? if yes, skip next
          goto     ds1in3            ;no. go try again until released
ds1in4    bcf      status,c          ;yes. pass data as 0
          goto     ds1inx            ;& go exit
;
ds1in5    bsf      status,c          ;pass data as 1
ds1inx    return                     ;exit
;------------------------------------------------------------------------------
;         Module: ds1pres
;         Sends the presence pulse.
```

491

```
;
;----------------------------------------------------------------
ds1pres movlw    0xf5            ;wait approx 20 u Sec
        movwf    tmr0
        bcf      intcon,toif
ds1pre1 btfss    intcon,toif    ;20 u Sec timed out ? if yes, skip next
        goto     ds1pre1        ;no. go try again
        bcf      porta,wout     ;yes. take data line low (presence)
        movlw    0xaf           ;& wait approx 160 u Sec
        movwf    tmr0
        bcf      intcon,toif
ds1pre2 btfss    intcon,toif    ;160 u Sec timed out ? if yes, skip next
        goto     ds1pre2        ;no. go try again
        bsf      porta,wout     ;yes. release data line
        return                  ;exit
;----------------------------------------------------------------
;       Module: ds1wr
;       Slave output service (Sends a bit).
;       On entry bit to be sent is passed via carry.
;       Assumes the master has sent a reset pulse if master does not
;       release line  within approx 140 u Sec. & sets reset flag.
;----------------------------------------------------------------
ds1wr   btfsc    porta,win      ;data line low ? if yes, skip next
        goto     ds1wr          ;no, go try again
        btfsc    status,c       ;yes. data bit = 0 ? if yes, skip next
        goto     ds1wr2         ;no. go
        bcf      porta,wout     ;yes. take line low
ds1wr2  movlw    0xf5           ;wait 20 u Sec
        movwf    tmr0
        bcf      intcon,toif    ;clear timer overflow
ds1wr3  btfss    intcon,toif    ;20 u Sec elapsed ? if yes, skip next
        goto     ds1wr3         ;no. go try again
        bsf      porta,wout     ;yes. release line
        bcf      dsstat,dareset ;clear reset flag
        movlw    0xc3           ;start 120 u Sec timer
        movwf    tmr0
        bcf      intcon,toif    ;clear timer overflow
ds1wr4  btfsc    porta,win      ;line released ? if no, skip next
        goto     ds1wrx         ;yes. go exit
        btfss    intcon,toif    ;120 u Sec elapsed ? if yes, skip next
        goto     ds1wr4         ;no. go test line again
        bsf      dsstat,dareset ;yes. set reset flag
ds1wr5  btfss    porta,win      ;line released ? if yes, skip next
        goto     ds1wr4         ;no. go try again until released
ds1wrx  return                  ;exit
;----------------------------------------------------------------
;       Module: ds1rec
;       Receive 8 bit byte
;       On exit, byte received is passed via indat
;----------------------------------------------------------------
ds1rec  movlw    0x08
        movwf    bitctr
ds1rec1 call     ds1in          ;receive bit
        btfsc    dsstat,dareset ;reset received ? if no, skip next
```

```
            goto    ds1recx             ;yes. go exit
            rrf     indat,f             ;bit to indat
            decfsz  bitctr,f            ;all 8 done ? if yes, skip next
            goto    ds1rec1             ;no. get next bit
ds1recx     return                      ;exit
;-------------------------------------------------------------------------
;           Module: ds1sen
;           Send 8 bit byte
;           On entry, byte to be sent is passed via outdat
;-------------------------------------------------------------------------
ds1sen      movlw   0x08
            movwf   bitctr
ds1sen1     rrf     outdat,f            ;get bit
            call    ds1wr               ;send it
            btfsc   dsstat,dareset      ;reset received ? if no, skip next
            goto    ds1senx             ;yes. go exit
            decfsz  bitctr,f
            goto    ds1sen1
ds1senx     return                      ;exit
;=========================================================================
```

11.2.3 Using the Section 11.2 Routines in Your Applications

Generally all of the routines can be used in your applications as written or with minor changes. For all routines, the entry and exit conditions, variables, port definitions and flag definitions are described in the xx.GRP listings. All port assignments (except port A4, the open drain data line driver) are arbitrary and may be changed to suit your application. See PURPLE1.ASM (Section 11.3.2) and PURPLE2.ASM (Section 11.4) for sample applications using the 1-Wire master routines and MAUVE1.ASM (Section 11.4) for a sample application using the 1-Wire slave routines. The sample applications use the PIC16F84 but the routines may be used with other PICmicros with little or no change.

The routines introduced in Section 11.2.1 are in:

DAL1WIRE.GRP   Dallas 1-Wire Bit-Bang Master Bus Services

The routines in this group are all *called* functions. A bit-bang 1-Wire application using the functions is little more than a sequence of calls to the functions interspersed with application specific services.

Most of your applications will generally use the 1-Wire bit-bang routines to communicate with standard hardware 1-Wire slave devices. The DAL1WIRE routines meet the Dallas specifications for the 1-Wire bus and will successfully communicate with standard 1-Wire hardware devices and with bit-bang slave devices implementing the SLV1WIRE routines.

All timing for the DAL1WIRE routines is handled in software and thus is sensitive to clock rate. The routines assume a crystal frequency of 4 MHz. If a different crystal frequency is to be used, the time delay loops must be modified to retain the same timing relationships as described in the module comments.

The routines introduced in Section 11.2.2 are:

SLV1WIRE.GRP   Dallas 1-Wire Bit-Bang Slave Bus Services

The routines in this group are all *called* functions except DS1WAIT. At power on or PICmicro MASTER CLEAR reset the slave program may do any necessary initialization and then must go to DS1WAIT. The balance of the application program may then be little more than a sequence of calls to the other SLV1WIRE functions interspersed with application specific services. But the application must always exit to DS1WAIT.

All timing for the SLV1WIRE routines is handled by Timer 0. The routines assume a crystal frequency of 4 MHz and Timer 0 uses the internal clock with a 2:1 pre-scale. If a different crystal frequency is used, the pre-scale or the Timer 0 presets must be changed to retain the correct timing.

When assigning slave addresses to your bit-bang slave applications be sure that all slaves on the bus have different addresses. No more than one device on the bus can have a given address.

11.3 Communicating with a 1-Wire Digital Thermometer

The Dallas DS1820 is an 1-Wire bus digital thermometer. The DS1820 features a temperature measurement range of -55 degrees to 125 degrees Celsius and non-volatile temperature alarm settings. It may be powered from a 5 volt supply or from the data line.

11.3.1 Parasite Power

The DS1820 may be powered from a 5 volt supply or from the data bus (parasite power). When powered from the data bus, the DS1820 requires only two connections: data line and return (Figure 11-13). This two connection capability makes it ideal for multi-drop distributed temperature sensing applications where any number of sensors may be placed on a twisted pair line.

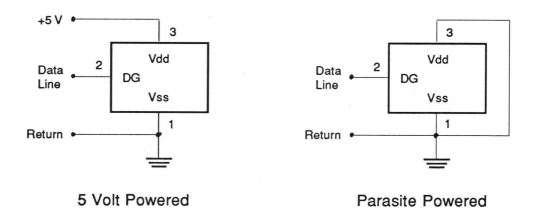

5 Volt Powered   Parasite Powered

Figure 11-13   DS1820 Configurations

494

Most Dallas 1-Wire bus devices are capable of parasite power operation. The device derives power from the bus by stealing current during the data line HIGH state. The current drawn from the data line charges a capacitor internal to the device (Figure 11-14). The capacitor stores enough charge to power the device during data line low states. If the data line remains low for an extended time, the device will loose power. All parasite powered devices will operate normally during the 480 to 960 microsecond RESET pulse period. The data line must be capable of supplying adequate current without dropping below the minimum HIGH level. When several devices are on the bus, the current demand can be large enough to require some sort of active pull-up on the data line.

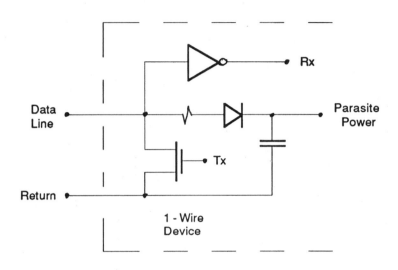

Figure 11-14   1-Wire Parasite Power

The DS1820 requires up to 1.5 ma for a period of 1/2 second to perform a temperature conversion. The accuracy of the conversion is guaranteed only if the supply voltage is close to 5 volts. A 5000 ohm pull-up will drop too much voltage during the conversion process. Reducing the pull-up resistance will solve this problem when only one DS1820 is on the bus. Adding several devices to the bus will require a stronger pull-up that is active only when the devices are performing the temperature conversion. Figure 11-15 illustrates a strong pull-up implementation. The strong pull-up may be active *only* during the temperature conversion period. At all other times the PNP transistor must be turned off. During the time that the strong pull-up is active, care must be taken to ensure that no device attempts to take the data line low because the sink current capability of the device will be exceeded. When a strong pull-up is employed and several DS1820 devices are on the bus they may all perform the temperature conversion at the same time. If communications with other devices on the bus must take place during the temperature conversion period, the DS1820 devices should be powered by a separate 5 volt supply and the strong pull-up deleted.

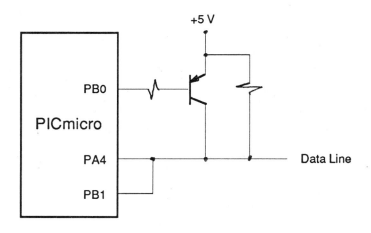

Figure 11-15   Strong Pull-Up

11.3.2 PURPLE1.ASM: A 1-Wire Bit-Bang DS1820 Thermometer Application

PURPLE1 demonstrates the application of the DAL1WIRE.GRP modules. At two second intervals it instructs the DS1820 to perform a temperature conversion and return the conversion result. PURPLE1 then converts the result to ASCII degrees Celsius and sends it to a terminal. The null modem cable in Figure 3-8 may be used for the terminal communications.

DS1820 Services (See PURPLE1.ASM and Figure 11-4)

The module DAS1820.GRP implements all of the DS1820 specific operations. Two modules, SIM1820.TXT and CEL1820.TXT are included in DAS1820.GRP. When called, SIM1820 returns the temperature with 1/2 degree precision as two bytes in the Dallas 16 bit, sign-extended two's-complement format. CEL1820 converts this sign-extended two's-complement value to a two byte binary temperature in degrees Celsius in 1/10 degree increments. For temperatures less than 0 degrees the negative flag is set.

SIM1820 assumes that the DS1820 is the only device on the bus. Normally any device on the 1-Wire bus must be addressed to initiate communications, but since the DS1820 is the only device on the bus addressing is not required. The DS1820 command set includes a command (*skip ROM*) that circumvents the need for addressing. Sending *skip ROM* to the DS1820 selects it just as would addressing it.

The SIM1820 command sequence to fetch a temperature reading is shown in Figure 11-16. If the DS1820 were not the only device on the bus, the *skip ROM* command would be replaced with the *match ROM* command followed by the 64 bit device address. If addressed correctly the DS1820 would be ready to receive the *convert temperature* command. If incorrectly addressed the device would ignore any following commands.

496

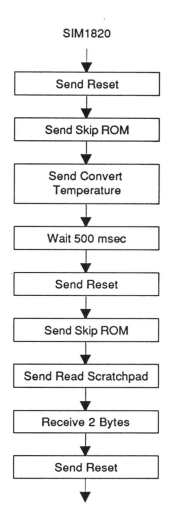

SIM1820

Send Reset

Send Skip ROM

Send Convert
Temperature

Wait 500 msec

Send Reset

Send Skip ROM

Send Read Scratchpad

Receive 2 Bytes

Send Reset

Figure 11-16   DS1820 Read Temperature

The *read scratchpad* command sets up the DS1820 to sequentially send the contents of the 8 byte scratchpad memory. The temperature data are found in the first two locations of the scratchpad, so SIM1820 receives only those two bytes. The final RESET pulse takes the device out of the read scratchpad mode and returns it to the idle state.

The 1/2 degree precision may be improved by receiving two additional bytes from the scratchpad and applying them to a correction procedure. See the Dallas Product Literature for more information on this increased resolution procedure.

CEL1820 converts the Dallas 16 bit, sign-extended two's-complement conversion result to a two byte binary temperature in degrees Celsius in 1/10 degree increments. If the conversion is negative CEL1820 generates the absolute value of the temperature by 2's complementing the low 8 bits of the conversion and sets the negative flag. The absolute value of the DS1820 conversion is in 1/2 degree increments (temperature multiplied by 2). To convert this into degrees Celsius in 1/10 degree increments, CEL1820 multiplies it by five.

Table 11-1   Dallas DS1820 Temperature To Data Relationships

```
-----------------------------------
        TEMPERATURE          DATA
-----------------------------------
        +125 C     00000000  11111010

        +25 C      00000000  00110010

        +0.5 C     00000000  00000001

        +0.0 C     00000000  00000000

        -0.5 C     11111111  11111111

        -25 C      11111111  11001110

        -55 C      11111111  10010010
```

```
;======= PURPLE1.ASM ==========================================================
;
;       Demonstrates application of Dallas 1-Wire Bit-Bang modules
;       DAL1WIRE.GRP. Communicates With Dallas DS1820 1-Wire Digital
;       Thermometer.  Converts Thermometer A/D 12 bit binary output
;       (degrees Celsius) to 4 digit ASCII and sends to terminal.
;       New temperature reading sent to terminal approx every 2 seconds.
;------------------------------------------------------------------------------
;
        radix   hex        ;RADIX is HEX
;
        list p=16f84
;
;       STATUS REGISTER BIT DEFINITIONS:
c       equ     0          ;carry bit of status register (bit 0)
z       equ     2          ;zero flag bit of status register (bit 2)
dc      equ     1          ;digit carry
pd      equ     3          ;power down bit
to      equ     4          ;time out bit
rp0     equ     5          ;program page preselect, low bit
rp1     equ     6          ;program page preselect, high bit
;
;       DESTINATION BIT DEFINITIONS:
w       equ     0          ;destination working
f       equ     1          ;destination file
;
;------------------------------------------------------------------------------
;       CPU EQUATES   (special function register memory map)
;
;   BANK 0:
indf    equ     00         ;indirect file register
tmr0    equ     01         ;timer
pcl     equ     02         ;program counter (low byte)
```

```
status    equ      03           ;status register
fsr       equ      04           ;indirect data pointer
porta     equ      05           ;port a
portb     equ      06           ;port b
eedata    equ      08           ;eeprom data
eeadr     equ      09           ;eeprom address
pclath    equ      0a           ;write buffer for program counter (high byte)
intcon    equ      0b           ;interrupt control register
;
;   BANK 1:
optreg    equ      01           ;option register                  bank 1 (0x81)
trisa     equ      05           ;data direction register port a   bank 1 (0x85)
trisb     equ      06           ;data direction register port b   bank 1 (0x86)
eecon1    equ      08           ;eeprom control register          bank 1 (0x88)
;
;----------------------------------------------------------------------
;       WORK AREA   (memory map)   Starts at 000c
;
dlyctr    equ      000d         ;delay counter
bitctr    equ      000e         ;bit counter
datctr    equ      000f         ;byte counter
counter   equ      0010         ;general counter
timctr    equ      0013         ;timeout counter
dsflags   equ      0014         ;system flags
temp      equ      0015         ;temporary storage
xmtreg    equ      0016         ;character xmitted to terminal
cntrb     equ      0017         ;delay counter parameters
cntra     equ      0018
;
data1     equ      0019         ;high data byte
data0     equ      001a         ;low data byte
indat     equ      001b
outdat    equ      001c
;
;       for asvert:
asc4      equ      0020
asc3      equ      0021
asc2      equ      0022
asc1      equ      0023
asc0      equ      0024
pten1     equ      0025
pten0     equ      0026
index     equ      0027
;----------------------------------------------------------------------
;       SYSTEM EQUATES
;
wout      equ      04           ;port a4 is master 1-wire data out
win       equ      01           ;port B1 is master 1-wire data in
xmit      equ      01           ;port A1 is async out
;
neg       equ      00           ;flag for negative temperature (bit 0 of dsflags)
ovrfl     equ      07           ;flag for davert (bit 7 of dsflags)
errflg    equ      01           ;error flag (bit 1 of dsflags)
;
```

```
OH        equ      04f        ;ascii O
KAY       equ      04b        ;ascii K
CEE       equ      043        ;ascii C
NEG       equ      02d        ;ascii dash
ee        equ      065        ;ascii e
LF        equ      00a        ;ascii line feed
CR        equ      00d        ;ascii carriage return
SP        equ      020        ;ascii space
DOT       equ      02e        ;ascii dot
;
;--------------------------------------------------------------------------
          org      0x00        ;start of program memory
          goto     start       ;jump over tables
;
;--------------------------------------------------------------------------
tbl1      addwf    pcl,f       ;tables for davert
          retlw    027
          retlw    003
          retlw    000
          retlw    000
;
tbl0      addwf    pcl,f
          retlw    010
          retlw    0e8
          retlw    064
          retlw    00a
;--------------------------------------------------------------------------
;
start     movlw    0ff
          movwf    portb        ;all ports high
          movwf    porta
          bsf      status,rp0   ;switch to bank 1
          movlw    00e9         ;a0 & a3 inputs, a1, a2, a4 as outputs
          movwf    trisa
          movlw    0002         ;initialize b1 as input, others outputs
          movwf    trisb
          bcf      status,rp0   ;switch to bank 0
          movlw    00c0
          movwf    portb
          movlw    OH           ;OK followed by CR & LF to terminal
          movwf    xmtreg
          call     asyxmt
          movlw    KAY
          movwf    xmtreg
          call     asyxmt
          call     nline
;
mloop     call     sim1820      ;measure temperature (Read DS1820)
          btfsc    dsflags,errflg ;error ? if no skip next
          call     diserr       ;yes. display error
          bcf      dsflags,errflg ;clear error flag
          call     cel1820      ;convert to 12 bit binary in 1/2 deg incre-
ments
          call     davert       ;convert 12 bit binary to bcd ascii
```

500

```
        movlw   SP                  ;display space
        movwf   xmtreg
        call    asyxmt
        call    disptmp             ;display temperature
        movlw   SP                  ;display space
        movwf   xmtreg
        call    asyxmt
        call    nline
        call    hlfsec              ;approx 1 1/2 second wait
        call    hlfsec
        call    hlfsec
        goto    mloop               ;go loop
;
;====== DAL1WIRE.GRP =======================================================
;
;       Dallas 1-wire Master serial bus services
;
;--------------------------------------------------------------------------
;       Requires 4 MHz crystal
;
;       Includes following Modules:
;               dal1wr  - write time slot
;               dal1rd  - read time slot
;               dal1res - send reset pulse and receive presence
;               dalrec  - receive 8 bit data byte
;               dalsnd  - send 8 bit data byte
;
;       Requires following work space:
;               dlyctr  ;delay counter
;               bitctr  ;bit counter
;               indat   ;data byte received
;               outdat  ;data byte to be sent
;
;       Requires following equates:
;               wout    equ     04      ;port a4 is output
;               win     equ     nn      ;port b bit for input
;
;--------------------------------------------------------------------------
;       DAL1WR
;       Bit Write  (generates write-1 or write-0 timeslot)
;       The bit to be sent is passed via the carry
;--------------------------------------------------------------------------
dal1wr  bcf     porta,wout          ;pull data line low
        movlw   0x03
        movwf   dlyctr              ;wait approx 10 u Sec
dal1wr1 decfsz  dlyctr,f
        goto    dal1wr1
        btfsc   status,c            ;release data line only if bit is 1
        bsf     porta,wout
        movlw   0x14                ;wait approx 60 u Sec
        movwf   dlyctr
dal1wr2 decfsz  dlyctr,f
        goto    dal1wr2
        bsf     porta,wout          ;release data line (bit = 0 release)
        return
```

501

```
;-------------------------------------------------------------------------
;       DAL1RD
;       Bit Read (read-data time slot)
;       The bit read is passed via the carry
;-------------------------------------------------------------------------
dal1rd  bcf     porta,wout      ;pull data line low
        movlw   0x01            ;wait approx 5 u Sec
        movwf   dlyctr
dal1rd0 decfsz  dlyctr,f
        goto    dal1rd0
        bsf     porta,wout      ;release data line
        movlw   0x01            ;wait approx 5 u Sec
        movwf   dlyctr
dal1rd1 decfsz  dlyctr,f
        goto    dal1rd1
        bcf     status,c        ;assume data is low
        btfsc   portb,win       ;is data low ? if yes, skip next
        bsf     status,c        ;no. set carry
        movlw   0x17            ;wait approx 70 u Sec
        movwf   dlyctr
dal1rd2 decfsz  dlyctr,f
        goto    dal1rd2
        return                  ;& exit
;-------------------------------------------------------------------------
;       DALRES
;       Send Reset and Receive Presence (reset and presence pulse)
;       On exit, if presence received, carry is cleared
;-------------------------------------------------------------------------
dalres  bcf     porta,wout      ;pull data line low
        movlw   0xb7            ;wait approx 550 u Sec
        movwf   dlyctr
dalres1 decfsz  dlyctr,f
        goto    dalres1
        bsf     porta,wout      ;release data line
        movlw   0x17            ;wait approx 70 uSec
        movwf   dlyctr
dalres2 decfsz  dlyctr,f
        goto    dalres2
        bsf     status,c        ;assume no presence
        btfss   portb,win       ;presence ? if no, skip next
        bcf     status,c        ;yes. clear carry
        movlw   0x95            ;wait approx 450 u Sec
        movwf   dlyctr
dalres3 decfsz  dlyctr,f
        goto    dalres3
        return                  ;exit
;-------------------------------------------------------------------------
;       DALREC
;       Receive an 8 Bit Byte
;       On exit, received byte in INDAT
;-------------------------------------------------------------------------
dalrec  movlw   0x08            ;8 bits
        movwf   bitctr
```

```
dalrec1 call    dal1rd          ;read a bit
        rrf     indat,f         ;bit to read register
        decfsz  bitctr,f        ;all 8 bits done ? If yes, skip next
        goto    dalrec1         ;no. go get next bit
        return                  ;yes. exit
;-------------------------------------------------------------------
;       DALSND
;       Send an 8 Bit Byte
;       On entry, byte to send is in OUTDAT.
;       On exit, OUTDAT is corrupted
;-------------------------------------------------------------------
dalsnd  movlw   0x08            ;8 bits
        movwf   bitctr
dalsnd1 rrf     outdat,f        ;get bit to send
        call    dal1wr          ;send it
        decfsz  bitctr,f        ;all 8 bits done ?
        goto    dalsnd1         ;no. go do next bit
        return                  ;yes. exit
;
;====== DAS1820.GRP =================================================
;
;       Dallas DA1820 services
;
;-------------------------------------------------------------------
;       Includes the following modules:
;               sim1820.txt
;               cel1820.txt
;-------------------------------------------------------------------
;       SIM1820.TXT
;       Get DS1820 temperature.
;       DS1820 is data line powered (parasite power) and is only device on
;       the 1-wire bus. Confirms presence. If not present, sets error flag
;       (bit 1 of dsflags).
;
;       Requires following modules:
;                       dalres          send reset
;                       dal1rd          read a byte from 1-wire bus
;                       dal1wr          write a byte to 1-wire bus
;                       dalsnd          send 8 bit byte
;                       dalrec          receive 8 bit byte
;                       hlfsec          500 mSec delay
;
;       Requires the following workspace:
;                       workspace required by dal1wire.grp
;                       workspace required by hlfsec.txt
;                       dsflags         ;system flags
;                       data1           ;data high byte
;                       data0           ;data low byte
;
;       Requires the following equates:
;               equates required by dal1wire.grp
;               neg     equ     nn      ;negative flag bit of dsflags
;
;-------------------------------------------------------------------
```

503

```
sim1820  call    dalres          ;send reset & receive presence
         bcf     dsflags,errflg  ;clear error flag
         btfsc   status,c        ;presence received ? if yes, skip next
         bsf     dsflags,errflg  ;no. set error flag
         movlw   0xcc            ;yes. skip-rom command
         movwf   outdat          ;send it
         call    dalsnd
         movlw   0x44            ;convert T command
         movwf   outdat          ;send it
         call    dalsnd
         call    hlfsec          ;wait 500 mSec for temperature reading.
         call    dalres          ;send reset
         movlw   0xcc            ;skip-rom command
         movwf   outdat          ;send it
         call    dalsnd
         movlw   0xbe            ;read-scratchpad command
         movwf   outdat          ;send it
         call    dalsnd
         call    dalrec          ;receive 1st byte
         movf    indat,w         ;& keep it
         movwf   data0
         call    dalrec          ;receive 2nd byte
         movf    indat,w         ;& keep it
         movwf   data1
         call    dalres          ;send reset & receive presence
         return                  ;exit
;------------------------------------------------------------------------
;        CEL1820.TXT
;        Convert DS1820 data to 16 bit Degrees Celsius
;        (in 1/10 degree increments)
;
;        On entry, DS1820 data in data1,data0
;        On exit, Temperature in Degrees Celsius in data1,data0
;------------------------------------------------------------------------
cel1820  bcf     dsflags,neg     ;clear negative flag
         btfss   data1,1         ;negative ? if yes, skip next
         goto    cel1            ;no go
         comf    data0,f         ;yes. 2's complement
         incf    data0,f
         bsf     dsflags,neg     ;set negative flag
cel1     clrf    data1           ;prepare to multiply by 5
         movf    data0,w         ;keep data0 for now (in w)
         bcf     status,c        ;multiply by 5 (4*data0 + data0)
         rlf     data0,f
         rlf     data1,f
         bcf     status,c
         rlf     data0,f
         rlf     data1,f
         addwf   data0,f
         btfsc   status,c
         incf    data1,f
celx     return                  ;& exit
;========================================================================
```

```
;          Module: DAVERT.TXT
;          Convert 12 BIT A/D result to 4 digit ascii
;          (data1, data0) => (asc3,asc2,asc1,asc0)
;
;          NOTE: This Module PLACES CALLS TWO LEVELS DEEP
;                The called routines davert4 and davert5 are part of this module
;
;          Requires following workspace:
;                  index    ;table index
;                  counter  ;general counter
;                  data1    ;data high byte
;                  data0    ;data low byte
;                  asc3     ;ascii high byte (1000's)
;                  asc2
;                  asc1
;                  asc0     ;ascii low byte (1's)
;
;          Requires tables:
;
;          tbl1     addwf   pcl,f            ;tables for davert
;                   retlw   027
;                   retlw   003
;                   retlw   000
;                   retlw   000
;
;          tbl0     addwf   pcl,f
;                   retlw   010
;                   retlw   0e8
;                   retlw   064
;                   retlw   00a
;
;-----------------------------------------------------------------------
davert  clrf    index           ;convert to bcd, then to ascii
davert1 clrf    counter
davert2 movf    index,w
        call    davert4
        call    davert5
        btfss   status,c
        goto    davert3
        incf    counter,f
        goto    davert2
davert3 movf    index,w
        call    davert4
        call    davert6
        movlw   asc4
        movwf   fsr
        movf    index,w
        addwf   fsr,f
        movlw   030             ;convert to ascii
        addwf   counter,w
        movwf   indf            ;and place in ascii block
        incf    index,f
        btfss   index,2
        goto    davert1
        movlw   30
```

505

```
        addwf   data0,w
        movwf   asc0
        return
;-----------------------------------------------------------------
davert4 call    tbl1                    ;read table
        movwf   pten1
        movf    index,w
        call    tbl0
        movwf   pten0
        return
;-----------------------------------------------------------------
davert5 comf    pten1,f                 ;convert to bcd
        comf    pten0,f
        movf    pten0,w
        addlw   01
        movwf   pten0
        btfsc   status,c
        incf    pten1,f
davert6 movf    pten0,w
        addwf   data0,f
        bcf     dsflags,ovrfl
        btfsc   status,c
        bsf     dsflags,ovrfl
        movf    pten1,w
        addwf   data1,f
        btfss   dsflags,ovrfl
        goto    davertx
        btfsc   status,c
        goto    davert7
        movlw   01
        addwf   data1,f
        goto    davertx
davert7 incf    data1,f
davertx return
;-----------------------------------------------------------------
;       Module DISPTMP
;       Displays temperature to terminal
;
;-----------------------------------------------------------------
disptmp movlw   SP                      ;display space
        movwf   xmtreg
        call    asyxmt
        btfss   dsflags,neg             ;negative ? if yes, skip next
        goto    distmp1                 ;no, go
        movlw   NEG                     ;yes. display negative
        movwf   xmtreg
        call    asyxmt
        goto    distmp2                 ;& go
distmp1 movlw   SP                      ;display space
        movwf   xmtreg
        call    asyxmt
distmp2 movf    asc3,w                  ;display ascii of temperature
        movwf   xmtreg                  ;100's
        call    asyxmt
```

```
        movf    asc2,w          ;10's
        movwf   xmtreg
        call    asyxmt
        movf    asc1,w          ;1's
        movwf   xmtreg
        call    asyxmt
        movlw   DOT             ;decimal point
        movwf   xmtreg
        call    asyxmt
        movf    asc0,w          ;1/10's
        movwf   xmtreg
        call    asyxmt
        movlw   SP              ;display space
        movwf   xmtreg
        call    asyxmt
        movlw   CEE             ;display C
        movwf   xmtreg
        call    asyxmt
        return
;-----------------------------------------------------------------------
;       Module NLINE
;       Start new line
;
;       Sends carriage return and line feed to terminal
;-----------------------------------------------------------------------
nline   movlw   CR
        movwf   xmtreg
        call    asyxmt
        movlw   LF
        movwf   xmtreg
        call    asyxmt
        return
;-----------------------------------------------------------------------
;       Module DISERR
;       Displays error message (inserts e in front of temperature
;       reading)
;
;-----------------------------------------------------------------------
diserr  movlw   ee        ;ASCII e
        movwf   xmtreg
        call    asyxmt
        return
;=======================================================================
;       Module: asyxmt.txt
;       Send a character     8 bits, 1 start, 1 stop, no parity
;       On entry: character to be sent is in xmtreg & port a1 must be high
;       On exit: transmit port is high (marking)
;
;       porta,xmit   is transmit port
;-----------------------------------------------------------------------
asyxmt  bcf     porta,xmit      ;start bit
        call    full            ;wait 1 bit time
        movlw   08              ;8 bit character length
        movwf   bitctr          ;to bit counter
```

507

```
asyxmt1  rrf     xmtreg,f       ;rotate bit out thru carry
         btfsc   status,c       ;carry = 0 ? IF YES, SKIP
         goto    asyxmt2        ;no. carry = 1. go set pa1
         bcf     porta,xmit     ;data bit = 0. clear pa1
         goto    asyxmt3        ;& go
asyxmt2  bsf     porta,xmit     ;data bit = 1. set pa1
;
asyxmt3  call    full           ;wait 1 bit time
         decfsz  bitctr,f       ;all 8 bits sent ? if yes, skip
         goto    asyxmt1        ;no, go do next bit
;
         bsf     porta,xmit     ;all bits done. do stop bit (marking)
         call    full           ;wait 1 bit time
         retlw   0              ;EXIT
;--------------------------------------------------------------------
full     movlw   d'3'           ;wait 1 bit time (2400 bits per second)
         movwf   cntrb
vdly0    movlw   d'43'
         movwf   cntra
vdly1    decfsz  cntra,f        ;dec counter a, skip if zero
         goto    vdly1          ;not zero. dec it again
         decfsz  cntrb,f        ;dec counter b, skip if zero
         goto    vdly0          ;not zero. do loop again
         retlw   0              ;exit
;--------------------------------------------------------------------
hlfsec   movlw   0x05           ;approx 1/2 second delay
         movwf   temp
hlfsec1  clrf    counter
hlfsec2  call    full           ;approx 0.416 mSec
         decfsz  counter,f
         goto    hlfsec2
         decfsz  temp,f
         goto    hlfsec1
         return
;--------------------------------------------------------------------
         end                    ;END OF PROGRAM
;====================================================================
```

11.4 A Dallas 1-Wire Bit-Bang Slave Application

The parallel port slave application MAUVE1 functions as an eight bit input port to 1-Wire bus device. The input data at the PICmicro port B is transferred serially to the master. MAUVE1 serves to demonstrate the application of the 1-Wire bit-bang slave services in SLV1WIRE.GRP. All of the SLV1WIRE services are used in MAUVE1. The master program PURPLE2 communicates with MAUVE1. MAUVE1 sends the port data to a terminal as ASCII binary. The null modem cable in Figure 3-8 may be used for the terminal communications. See Figure 11-17, MAUVE1.ASM and PURPLE2.ASM.

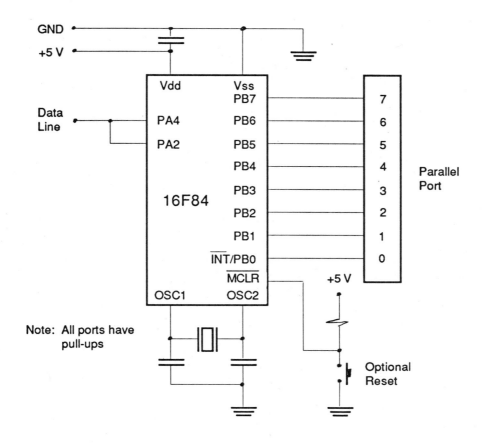

Figure 11-17   Schematic; Bit-Bang Slave Application MAUVE1

11.4.1 MAUVE1.ASM: A 1-Wire Slave Parallel Port Application

MAUVE1 waits in a loop (SLV1WIRE service DS1WAIT) for a RESET pulse. On receipt of the RESET pulse, MAUVE1 returns a PRESENCE then waits to be addressed. If the next byte received is not the MAUVE1 address it goes back to waiting for a RESET pulse. If the correct address is received MAUVE1 reads port B and sends the port B data to the master. It then returns to the wait loop DS1WAIT.

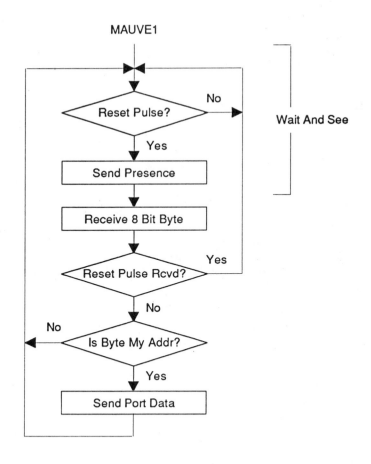

MAUVE1

```
          Reset Pulse?  ──No──►                    ┐
                │                                   │
                │Yes                                ├ Wait And See
                ▼                                   │
          Send Presence                             ┘
                │
                ▼
          Receive 8 Bit Byte
                │
                ▼
          Reset Pulse Rcvd? ──Yes──►
                │
                │No
                ▼
     ◄──No── Is Byte My Addr?
                │
                │Yes
                ▼
          Send Port Data
```

Figure 11-18   Slave Application MAUVE1

```
;====== MAUVE1.ASM =========================================================
;
;       Demonstrates application of Dallas 1-Wire Bit-Bang Slave modules
;       SLV1WIRE.GRP.
;
;---------------------------------------------------------------------------
        radix   hex       ;RADIX is HEX
;
        list p=16f84
;
;       STATUS REGISTER BIT DEFINITIONS:
c       equ     0         ;carry bit of status register (bit 0)
z       equ     2         ;zero flag bit of status register (bit 2)
dc      equ     1         ;digit carry
pd      equ     3         ;power down bit
to      equ     4         ;time out bit
rp0     equ     5         ;program page preselect, low bit
rp1     equ     6         ;program page preselect, high bit
;
;       DESTINATION BIT DEFINITIONS:
```

```
w         equ     0            ;destination working
f         equ     1            ;destination file
;
;--------------------------------------------------------------------
;        CPU EQUATES   (special function register memory map)
;
;   BANK 0:
indf      equ     00           ;indirect file register
tmr0      equ     01           ;timer
pcl       equ     02           ;program counter (low byte)
status    equ     03           ;status register
fsr       equ     04           ;indirect data pointer
porta     equ     05           ;port a
portb     equ     06           ;port b
eedata    equ     08           ;eeprom data
eeadr     equ     09           ;eeprom address
pclath    equ     0a           ;write buffer for program counter (high byte)
intcon    equ     0b           ;interrupt control register
;
;   BANK 1:
optreg    equ     01           ;option register                bank 1 (0x81)
trisa     equ     05           ;data direction register port a bank 1 (0x85)
trisb     equ     06           ;data direction register port b bank 1 (0x86)
eecon1    equ     08           ;eeprom control register        bank 1 (0x88)
;
toif      equ     02           ;timer overflow flag (bit 2 of intcon)
;--------------------------------------------------------------------
;        WORK AREA   (memory map)   Starts at 000c
;
bitctr    equ     000e         ;bit counter
dsstat    equ     000f         ;system status register
tmstmp    equ     0010         ;time stamp
indat     equ     0011         ;received data byte
outdat    equ     0012         ;sent data byte
temp0     equ     0013         ;temporary storage
;
;--------------------------------------------------------------------
;        SYSTEM EQUATES
;
wout      equ     04           ;port a4 is master 1-wire data out
win       equ     02           ;port a2 is master 1-wire data in
;
dareset   equ     07           ;reset flag (bit dareset of dsstat)
mycode    equ     80           ;device code for this application
;
;--------------------------------------------------------------------
          org     0x00              ;start of program memory
;
start     movlw   0xff
          movwf   portb             ;all ports high
          movwf   porta
          bsf     status,rp0        ;switch to bank 1
          movlw   0x0f              ;a0, a1, a2, a3 inputs, a4 as output
          movwf   trisa
```

511

```
            movlw    0xff                 ;all port b as inputs
            movwf    trisb
            movlw    0xd0                 ;TMR0 internal clock and 2:1 prescale
            movwf    optreg
            bcf      status,rp0           ;switch to bank 0
            movlw    00c0
            movwf    portb
;
main        goto     ds1wait              ;wait for reset pulse
;
SLAVEAP     call     ds1rec               ;receive data byte
            btfsc    dsstat,dareset       ;reset received ? if no, skip next
            goto     ds1wait              ;yes. exit this app and go wait for reset
pulse
            movlw    mycode               ;is byte received my code ?
            subwf    indat,f
            btfss    status,z             ;if yes, skip next
            goto     ds1wait              ;no. exit this app and go wait for reset
pulse
            movf     portb,w              ;yes. get port b
            movwf    outdat               ;and send it
            call     ds1sen
            goto     ds1wait              ;& exit this app and go wait for reset pulse.
;
;======= SLV1WIRE.GRP =========================================================
;
;       Dallas 1-Wire serial bus SLAVE services
;
;-----------------------------------------------------------------------------
;
;       Includes Modules:
;               ds1wait - wait for reset pulse
;               ds1in   - read time-slot
;               ds1pres - presence pulse
;               ds1wr   - write time-slot
;               ds1rec  - receive 8 bit byte
;               ds1sen  - send 8 bit byte
;
;       Requires following workspace:
;               tmstmp   ;time stamp
;               dsstat   ;system status
;               bitctr   ;bit counter
;               indat    ;data byte received
;               outdat   ;data byte to be sent
;
;       Requires following equates:
;               dareset equ     nn      ;reset flag bit of dsstat
;               win     equ     nn      ;port a bit for input
;               wout    equ     04      ;port a4 is output
;
;       NOTE: Uses TMR0 and 4 MHz crystal. TMR0 must be configured for
;             internal clock  and 2:1 prescale.
;-----------------------------------------------------------------------------
```

```
;       Module: ds1wait
;       Wait for a reset pulse.
;       On reception of reset pulse, sends presence then goes to
;       application.
;
;----------------------------------------------------------------------
ds1wait btfsc   porta,win       ;data line low ? if yes, skip next
        goto    ds1wait         ;no. go try again
        bcf     dsstat,dareset  ;yes. clear reset flag
        movlw   0x37            ;start 400 u Sec timer (200 counts)
        movwf   tmr0
        bcf     intcon,toif
ds1wai1 btfsc   porta,win       ;data still low ? if yes, skip next
        goto    ds1wait         ;no. go wait for next data low
        movf    tmr0,w          ;get timer time stamp
        movwf   tmstmp
        btfsc   intcon,toif     ;timed out ? (long enough to be reset)
        goto    ds1wai2         ;yes. go
        goto    ds1wai1         ;no. go try again
ds1wai2 btfss   porta,win       ;line released ? if yes, skip next
        goto    ds1wai2         ;no. go try again until released
        call    ds1pres         ;yes. send presence
        goto    SLAVEAP         ;GO TO APPLICATION MODULE xxxxxxxx
                                ;----------------------------------------
                                ;The FIRST line of the APPLICATION Module
                                ;MUST be labeled: SLAVEAP.
                                ;
                                ;The Application Module MUST terminate with
                                ;ONLY a goto ds1wait.

;----------------------------------------------------------------------
;       Module: ds1in
;       Slave input service (receives a bit). It recognizes the 1-wire write
;       one time slot, write zero time slot or reset pulse sent by the
;       master. The one and zero data bits are passed via the carry. If a
;       reset pulse is received, the reset pulse flag (dareset bit of dsstat)
;       is set. The application program MUST test for the reset pulse flag
;       and if the flag is set it must send the presence by calling the
;       presence service (ds1pres)
;
;----------------------------------------------------------------------
ds1in   btfsc   porta,win       ;data line low ? if yes, skip next
        goto    ds1in           ;no. go try again
        bcf     dsstat,dareset  ;yes. clear reset flag
        movlw   0xf5            ;wait approx 20 u Sec
        movwf   tmr0
        bcf     intcon,toif
ds1in1  btfss   intcon,toif
        goto    ds1in1
        btfsc   porta,win       ;line still low ? if yes, skip next
        goto    ds1in5          ;no. go (data=1)
        movlw   0x80            ;yes. start approx 250 u Sec timer
        movwf   tmr0
        bcf     intcon,toif
```

```
ds1in2   btfsc    porta,win          ;line released ? if no, skip next
         goto     ds1in4             ;yes. go (data=0)
         btfss    intcon,toif        ;timed out ? if yes, skip next
         goto     ds1in2             ;no. go try again
         bsf      dsstat,dareset     ;yes. set reset flag
ds1in3   btfsc    porta,win          ;line released ? if yes, skip next
         goto     ds1in3             ;no. go try again until released
ds1in4   bcf      status,c           ;yes. pass data as 0
         goto     ds1inx             ;& go exit
;
ds1in5   bsf      status,c           ;pass data as 1
ds1inx   return                      ;exit
;-----------------------------------------------------------------------
;        Module: ds1pres
;        Sends the presence pulse.
;
;-----------------------------------------------------------------------
ds1pres  movlw    0xf5               ;wait approx 20 u Sec
         movwf    tmr0
         bcf      intcon,toif
ds1pre1  btfss    intcon,toif        ;20 u Sec timed out ? if yes, skip next
         goto     ds1pre1            ;no. go try again
         bcf      porta,wout         ;yes. take data line low (presence)
         movlw    0xaf               ;& wait approx 160 u Sec
         movwf    tmr0
         bcf      intcon,toif
ds1pre2  btfss    intcon,toif        ;160 u Sec timed out ? if yes, skip next
         goto     ds1pre2            ;no. go try again
         bsf      porta,wout         ;yes. release data line
         return                      ;exit
;-----------------------------------------------------------------------
;        Module: ds1wr
;        Slave output service (Sends a bit).
;        On entry bit to be sent is passed via carry.
;        Assumes the master has sent a reset pulse if master does not
;        release line within approx 140 u Sec. & sets reset flag.
;
;-----------------------------------------------------------------------
ds1wr    btfsc    porta,win          ;data line low ? if yes, skip next
         goto     ds1wr              ;no, go try again
         btfsc    status,c           ;yes. data bit = 0 ? if yes, skip next
         goto     ds1wr2             ;no. go
         bcf      porta,wout         ;yes. take line low
ds1wr2   movlw    0xf5               ;wait 20 u Sec
         movwf    tmr0
         bcf      intcon,toif        ;clear timer overflow
ds1wr3   btfss    intcon,toif        ;20 u Sec elapsed ? if yes, skip next
         goto     ds1wr3             ;no. go try again
         bsf      porta,wout         ;yes. release line
         bcf      dsstat,dareset     ;clear reset flag
         movlw    0xc3               ;start 120 u Sec timer
         movwf    tmr0
         bcf      intcon,toif        ;clear timer overflow
```

```
ds1wr4  btfsc   porta,win        ;line released ? if no, skip next
        goto    ds1wrx           ;yes. go exit
        btfss   intcon,toif      ;120 u Sec elapsed ? if yes, skip next
        goto    ds1wr4           ;no. go test line again
        bsf     dsstat,dareset   ;yes. set reset flag
ds1wr5  btfss   porta,win        ;line released ? if yes, skip next
        goto    ds1wr4           ;no. go try again until released
ds1wrx  return                   ;exit
;----------------------------------------------------------------------
;       Module: ds1rec
;       Receive 8 bit byte
;       On exit, byte received is passed via indat
;----------------------------------------------------------------------
ds1rec  movlw   0x08
        movwf   bitctr
ds1rec1 call    ds1in            ;receive bit
        btfsc   dsstat,dareset   ;reset received ? if no, skip next
        goto    ds1recx          ;yes. go exit
        rrf     indat,f          ;bit to indat
        decfsz  bitctr,f         ;all 8 done ? if yes, skip next
        goto    ds1rec1          ;no. get next bit
ds1recx return                   ;exit
;----------------------------------------------------------------------
;       Module: ds1sen
;       Send 8 bit byte
;       On entry, byte to be sent is passed via outdat
;----------------------------------------------------------------------
ds1sen  movlw   0x08
        movwf   bitctr
ds1sen1 rrf     outdat,f         ;get bit
        call    ds1wr            ;send it
        btfsc   dsstat,dareset   ;reset received ? if no, skip next
        goto    ds1senx          ;yes. go exit
        decfsz  bitctr,f
        goto    ds1sen1
ds1senx return                   ;exit
;----------------------------------------------------------------------
        end                      ;END OF PROGRAM
;======================================================================


;====== PURPLE2.ASM ===================================================
;
;       Communicates with Dallas 1-Wire Bit-Bang Slave application MAUVE1.
;       Gets MAUVE1 port inputs and sends them to terminal in ASCII binary
;       form.
;
;----------------------------------------------------------------------
        radix   hex        ;RADIX is HEX
;
        list p=16f84
;
```

515

```
;            STATUS REGISTER BIT DEFINITIONS:
c         equ     0           ;carry bit of status register (bit 0)
z         equ     2           ;zero flag bit of status register (bit 2)
dc        equ     1           ;digit carry
pd        equ     3           ;power down bit
to        equ     4           ;time out bit
rp0       equ     5           ;program page preselect, low bit
rp1       equ     6           ;program page preselect, high bit
;
;            DESTINATION BIT DEFINITIONS:
w         equ     0           ;destination working
f         equ     1           ;destination file
;
;-------------------------------------------------------------------------
;       CPU EQUATES   (special function register memory map)
;
;   BANK 0:
indf      equ     00          ;indirect file register
tmr0      equ     01          ;timer
pcl       equ     02          ;program counter (low byte)
status    equ     03          ;status register
fsr       equ     04          ;indirect data pointer
porta     equ     05          ;port a
portb     equ     06          ;port b
eedata    equ     08          ;eeprom data
eeadr     equ     09          ;eeprom address
pclath    equ     0a          ;write buffer for program counter (high byte)
intcon    equ     0b          ;interrupt control register
;
;   BANK 1:
optreg    equ     01          ;option register                 bank 1 (0x81)
trisa     equ     05          ;data direction register port a   bank 1 (0x85)
trisb     equ     06          ;data direction register port b   bank 1 (0x86)
eecon1    equ     08          ;eeprom control register          bank 1 (0x88)
;
;-------------------------------------------------------------------------
;       WORK AREA   (memory map)   Starts at 000c
;
dlyctr    equ     000d        ;delay counter
bitctr    equ     000e        ;bit counter
datctr    equ     000f        ;byte counter
counter   equ     0010        ;general counter
timctr    equ     0013        ;timeout counter
dsflags   equ     0014        ;system flags
temp      equ     0015        ;temporary storage
xmtreg    equ     0016        ;character xmitted to terminal
cntrb     equ     0017        ;delay counter parameters
cntra     equ     0018
;
indat     equ     001b
outdat    equ     001c
;
```

```
;------------------------------------------------------------------------
;          SYSTEM EQUATES
;
wout      equ      04         ;port a4 is master 1-wire data out
win       equ      01         ;port B1 is master 1-wire data in
xmit      equ      01         ;port A1 is async out
;
ovrfl     equ      07         ;flag for davert (bit 7 of dsflags)
errflg    equ      01         ;error flag (bit 1 of dsflags)
mauvcod   equ      80         ;mauvel device code
;
OH        equ      04f        ;ascii O
KAY       equ      04b        ;ascii K
ONE       equ      031        ;ascii 1
ZERO      equ      030        ;ascii 0
ee        equ      065        ;ascii e
LF        equ      00a        ;ascii line feed
CR        equ      00d        ;ascii carriage return
;
;------------------------------------------------------------------------
          org      0x00                   ;start of program memory
;
start     movlw    0ff
          movwf    portb                  ;all ports high
          movwf    porta
          bsf      status,rp0             ;switch to bank 1
          movlw    00e9                   ;a0 & a3 inputs, a1, a2, a4 as outputs
          movwf    trisa
          movlw    0002                   ;initialize b1 as input, others outputs
          movwf    trisb
          bcf      status,rp0             ;switch to bank 0
          movlw    00c0
          movwf    portb
          movlw    OH                     ;OK followed by CR & LF to terminal
          movwf    xmtreg
          call     asyxmt
          movlw    KAY
          movwf    xmtreg
          call     asyxmt
          call     nline
;
mloop     call     getmauv                ;get mauvel port data
          btfsc    dsflags,errflg         ;error ? if no, skip next
          call     diserr                 ;yes. send error message
          movlw    08                     ;no. 8 data bits to send to terminal
          movwf    counter
mloop1    movlw    ONE                    ;assume port bit is one
          movwf    xmtreg
          rlf      indat,f                ;get bit
          btfsc    status,c               ;is bit zero ? if yes, skip next
          goto     mloop2                 ;no. go send ONE to terminal
          movlw    ZERO                   ;yes. send ZERO to terminal
          movwf    xmtreg
```

517

```
mloop2   call     asyxmt          ;send bit to terminal
         decfsz   counter,f       ;all eight bits sent ? if yes, skip next
         goto     mloop1          ;no. go do next bit
         call     nline           ;yes. start new line on terminal
         call     hlfsec          ;approx 2 second wait
         call     hlfsec
         call     hlfsec
         call     hlfsec
         goto     mloop           ;go loop
;
;====== GETMAUVE.TXT ========================================================
;
;        GETMAUVE.TXT
;        Communicate with bit-bang slave application MAUVE1.
;        On exit, mauve1 port data passed via indat
;
;----------------------------------------------------------------------------
;        Requires following modules:
;                        dalres            send reset
;                        dal1rd            read a byte from 1-wire bus
;                        dal1wr            write a byte to 1-wire bus
;                        dalsnd            send 8 bit byte
;                        dalrec            receive 8 bit byte
;                        full              416 uSec delay
;
;        Requires the following workspace:
;                        workspace required by dal1wire.grp
;                        workspace required by full.txt
;                        dsflags (system flags)
;
;        Requires the following equates:
;                        equates required by dal1wire.grp
;                        mauvcod equ     0x80    ;device code for mauve1 application
;----------------------------------------------------------------------------
getmauv  call     dalres          ;send reset & receive presence
         bcf      dsflags,errflg  ;clear error flag
         btfsc    status,c        ;presence received ? if yes, skip next
         bsf      dsflags,errflg  ;no. set error flag
         movlw    mauvcod         ;yes. mauve1 device code
         movwf    outdat          ;send it
         call     full            ;wait 416 uSec
         call     dalsnd
         call     full            ;wait 416 uSsec
         call     dalrec          ;receive port data from mauve1
         return                   ;exit
;
;----------------------------------------------------------------------------
;        INCLUDED FILES
;
;        DAL1WIRE.GRP    Dallas 1-Wire Master services
;----------------------------------------------------------------------------
         include  dal1wire.grp
;
```

```
;-----------------------------------------------------------------
;       Module NLINE
;       Start new line
;
;       Sends carriage return and line feed to terminal
;-----------------------------------------------------------------
nline   movlw   CR
        movwf   xmtreg
        call    asyxmt
        movlw   LF
        movwf   xmtreg
        call    asyxmt
        return
;-----------------------------------------------------------------
;       Module DISERR
;       Displays error message (inserts e in front of mauve1 port data)
;
;-----------------------------------------------------------------
diserr  movlw   ee          ;ASCII e
        movwf   xmtreg
        call    asyxmt
        return
;=================================================================
;       Module: asyxmt.txt
;       Send a character      8 bits, 1 start, 1 stop, no parity
;       On entry: character to be sent is in xmtreg & port a1 must be high
;       On exit: transmit port is high (marking)
;
;       porta,xmit  is transmit port
;-----------------------------------------------------------------
asyxmt  bcf     porta,xmit      ;start bit
        call    full            ;wait 1 bit time
        movlw   08              ;8 bit character length
        movwf   bitctr          ;to bit counter
asyxmt1 rrf     xmtreg,f        ;rotate bit out thru carry
        btfsc   status,c        ;carry = 0 ? IF YES, SKIP
        goto    asyxmt2         ;no. carry = 1. go set pa1
        bcf     porta,xmit      ;data bit = 0. clear pa1
        goto    asyxmt3         ;& go
asyxmt2 bsf     porta,xmit      ;data bit = 1. set pa1
;
asyxmt3 call    full            ;wait 1 bit time
        decfsz  bitctr,f        ;all 8 bits sent ? if yes, skip
        goto    asyxmt1         ;no, go do next bit
;
        bsf     porta,xmit      ;all bits done. do stop bit (marking)
        call    full            ;wait 1 bit time
        retlw   0               ;EXIT
;-----------------------------------------------------------------
full    movlw   d'3'            ;wait 1 bit time (2400 bits per second)
        movwf   cntrb
vdly0   movlw   d'43'
        movwf   cntra
vdly1   decfsz  cntra,f         ;dec counter a, skip if zero
```

519

```
        goto     vdly1                ;not zero. dec it again
        decfsz   cntrb,f              ;dec counter b, skip if zero
        goto     vdly0                ;not zero. do loop again
        retlw    0                    ;exit
;-----------------------------------------------------------------
hlfsec  movlw    0x05                 ;approx 1/2 second delay
        movwf    temp
hlfsec1 clrf     counter
hlfsec2 call     full                 ;approx 0.416 mSec
        decfsz   counter,f
        goto     hlfsec2
        decfsz   temp,f
        goto     hlfsec1
        return
;-----------------------------------------------------------------
        end                          ;END OF PROGRAM
;=================================================================
```

Appendix A
Using Terminal Programs with the Demonstration Applications

Several of the demonstration programs communicate with a computer terminal running a terminal emulation program. Before the personal computer was invented, *terminals* were used to communicate with large computers or data communications equipment. A terminal emulation program literally *emulates* these terminals. This emulation is necessary because the terminal standards have been carried over to current usage. Several different terminal standards were in use, thus the terminal emulator programs must be capable of emulating at least some of these standards. The most commonly emulated standards are TTY (teletype), two DEC terminal types: VT-52 and VT-100, and the ANSI standard. For most modern communications applications and for the demonstration applications in this book, the ANSI standard is used.

For the demonstration programs, you may use any terminal emulation program capable of implementing the ANSI standard. **Terminal** (tm) for Windows (tm) 3 and **HyperTerminal** (tm) for Windows 95 are examples of ANSI capable terminal emulation programs that you may use with the applications.

Your terminal emulator must be configured as follows:

1. Communicate via a Serial Port (not modem).

2. Data rate: 2400 bits per second.

3. Data format: 8 data bits, 1 stop bit and no parity bit.

4. Local Echo must be turned OFF (if you see rreeppeeaatteedd letters, the local echo is on).

5. Flow control: a. For most of the applications, flow control should be selected as OFF.
     b. For INDIGO1, INDIGO2, INDIGO3 and RED1 flow control should be selected as HARDWARE.
     c. For INDIGO5 flow control should be selected as XON/XOFF.

Appendix B
Demonstration Applications Hardware

The demonstration applications may be implemented on one or more of three circuit boards: two boards for PICmicro master applications (18 pin and 28 pin) and the third board for PICmicro bit-bang slave applications (18 pin). The SSP SPI slave applications may be implemented on the 28 pin master board. Figures A-1 through A-3 are the schematics for these three boards. To accommodate the slight hardware variations from application to application, jumper select circuitry is included for each board.

Where hardware slave devices are required, additional circuit boards can be designed using the slave application schematics found in chapters 8 through 11.

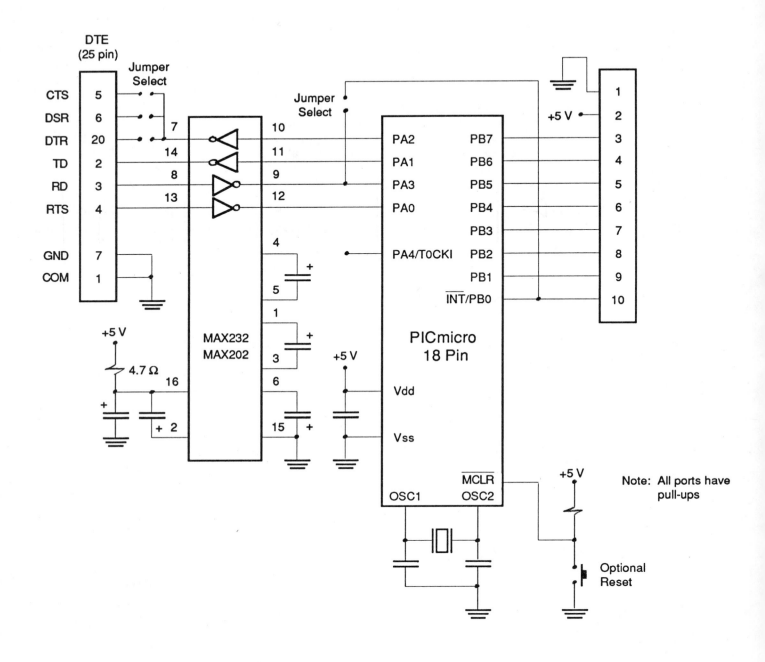

Figure A-1   18 Pin Master Applications Circuit Board

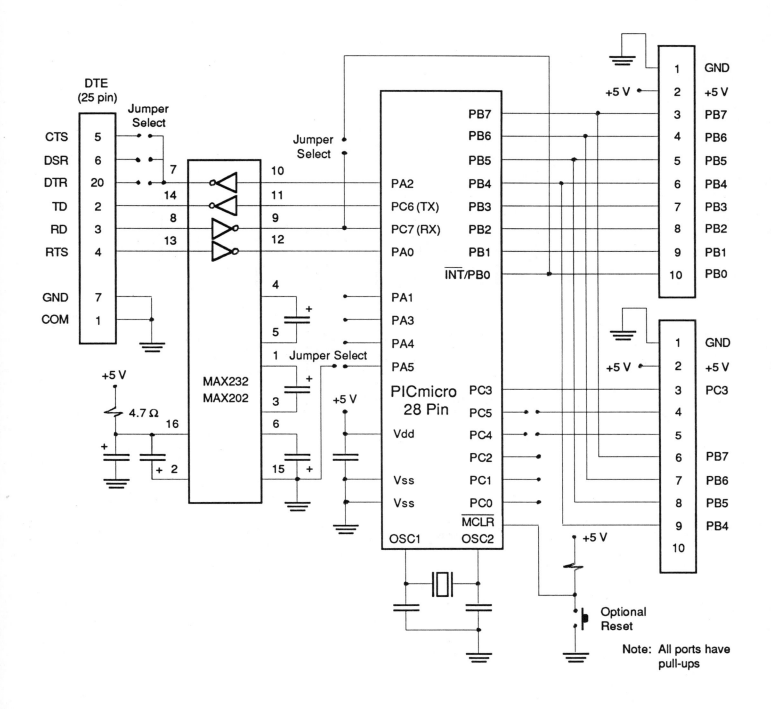

Figure A-2   28 Pin Master And Slave Applications Circuit Board

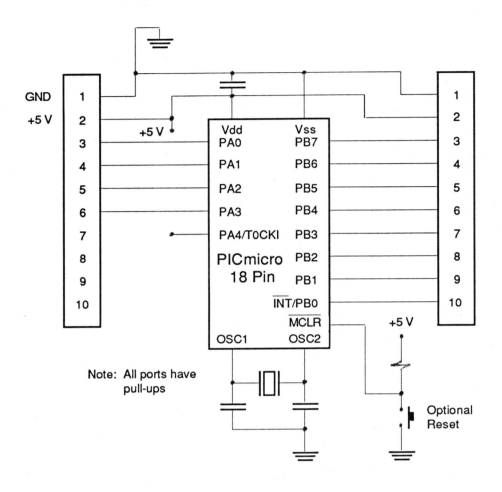

Figure A-3   18 Pin Slave Applications Circuit Board

526